MOBILE SUIT

GUNDAM

THE ORIGIN

—SOLOMON—

YOSHIKAZU YASUHIKO

ORIGINAL STORY BY:
YOSHIYUKI TOMINO • HAJIME YATATE

MECHANICAL DESIGN BY:
KUNIO OKAWARA

Mobile Suit Gundam
THE ORIGIN

X

—SOLOMON—

CONTENTS

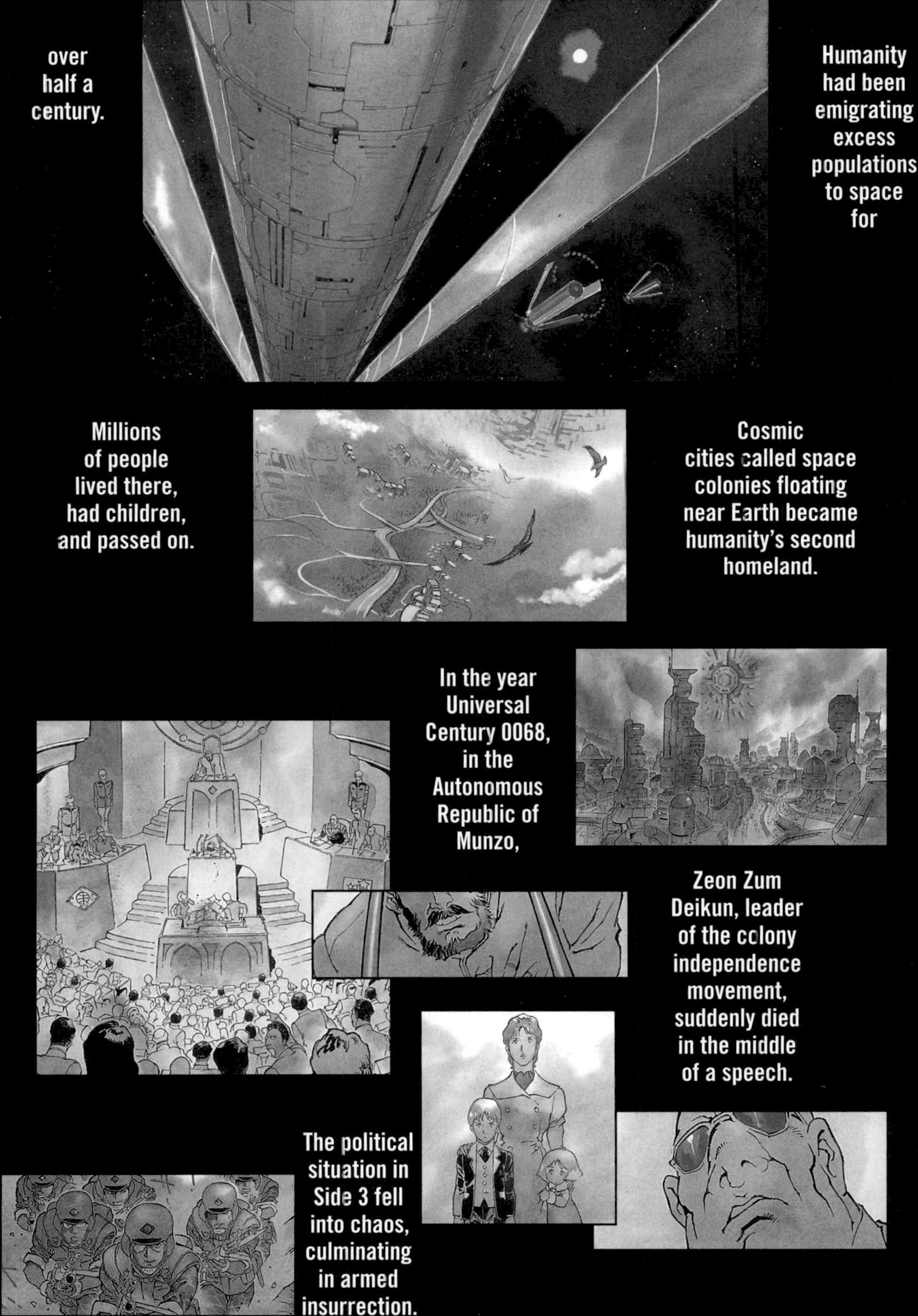

Humanity had been emigrating excess populations to space for
over half a century.
Cosmic cities called space colonies floating near Earth became humanity's second homeland.
Millions of people lived there, had children, and passed on.
In the year Universal Century 0068, in the Autonomous Republic of Munzo,
Zeon Zum Deikun, leader of the colony independence movement, suddenly died in the middle of a speech.
The political situation in Side 3 fell into chaos, culminating in armed insurrection.

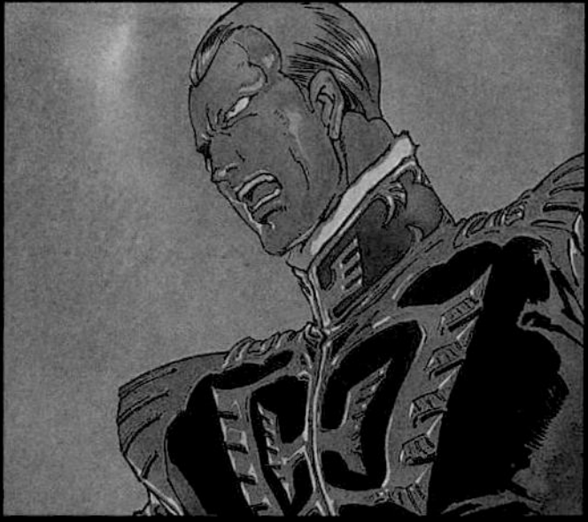

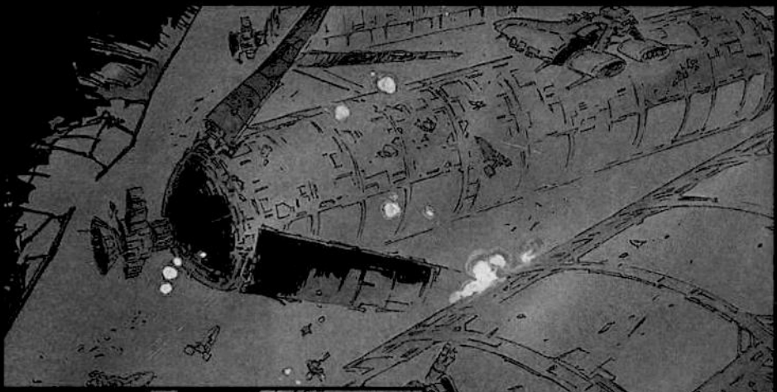

Led by the eldest Zabi sibling, Gihren, who saw fit to use even motherland colonies as weapons of destruction,

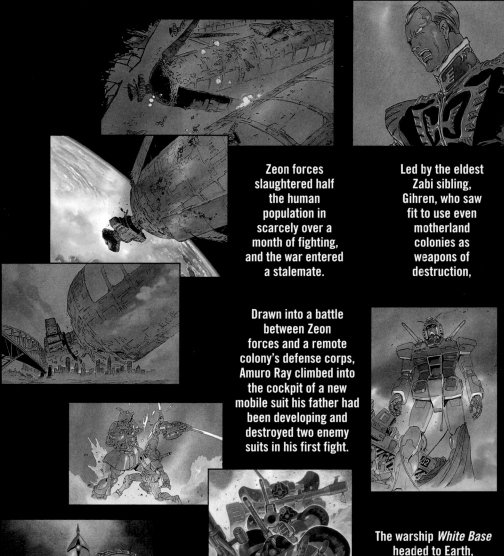

Zeon forces slaughtered half the human population in scarcely over a month of fighting, and the war entered a stalemate.

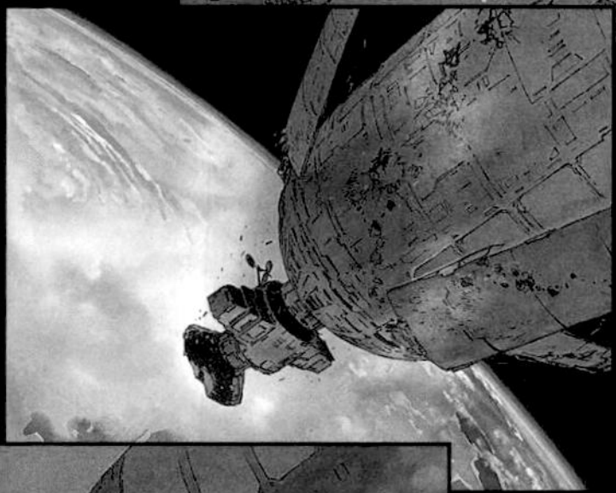

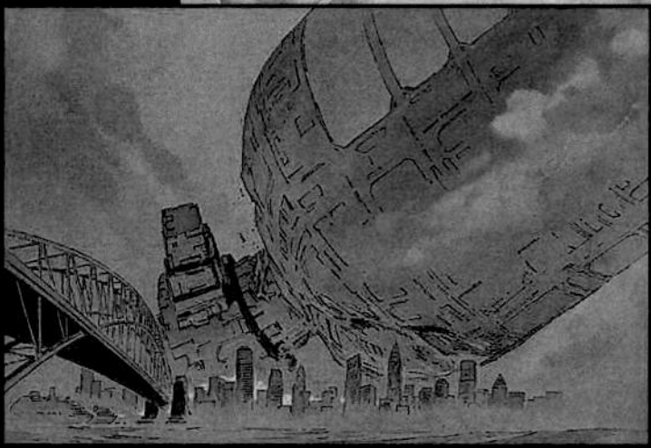

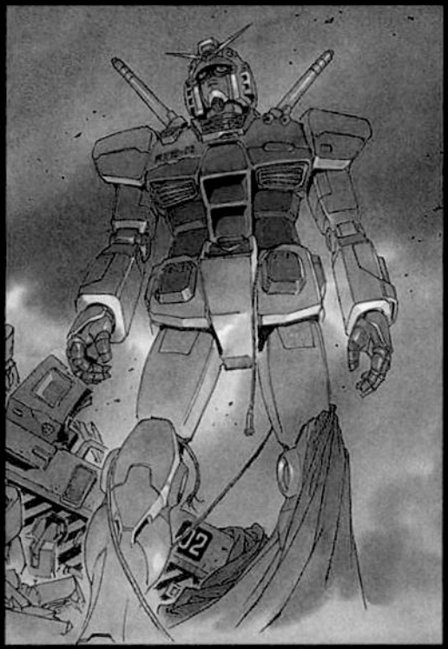

Drawn into a battle between Zeon forces and a remote colony's defense corps, Amuro Ray climbed into the cockpit of a new mobile suit his father had been developing and destroyed two enemy suits in his first fight.

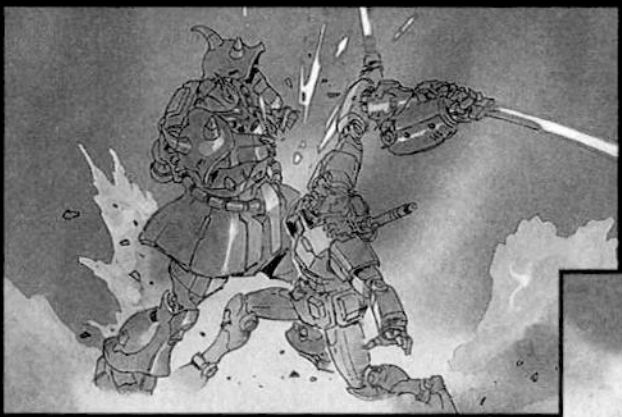

The warship *White Base* headed to Earth, where the crew excelled in battle after battle, catching the attention of military leadership. After repelling Zeon's fierce attack at Jaburo, the Earth Federation Forces launched a massive counter-offensive.

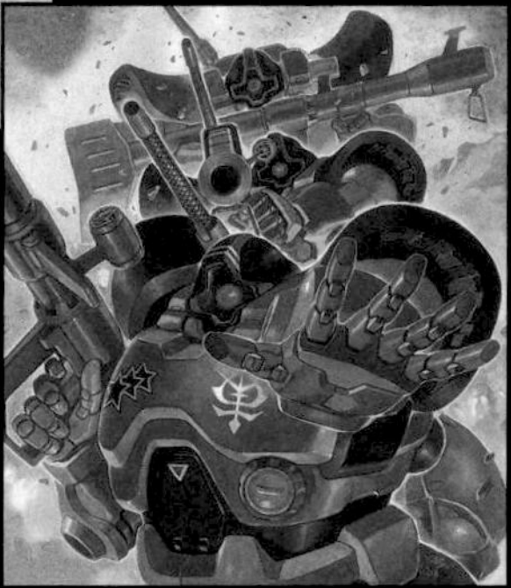

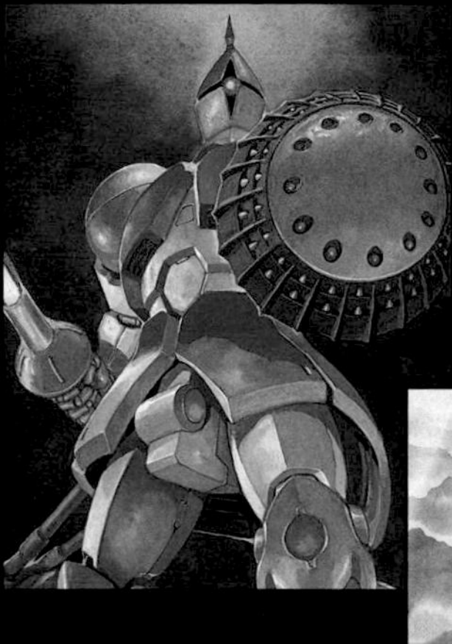

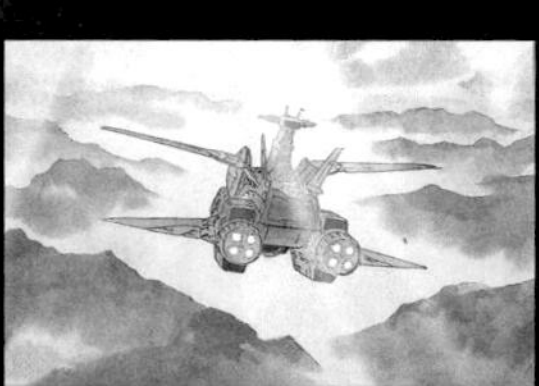

In space once again, Amuro found his missing father in the neutral colony of Side 6, but the brilliant mind behind the Gundam's development was no longer that.

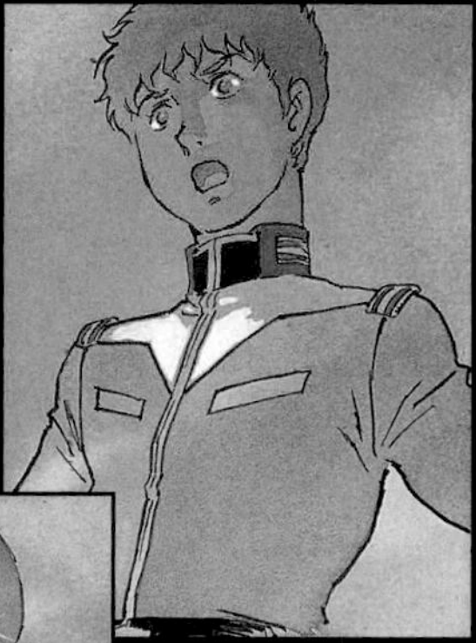

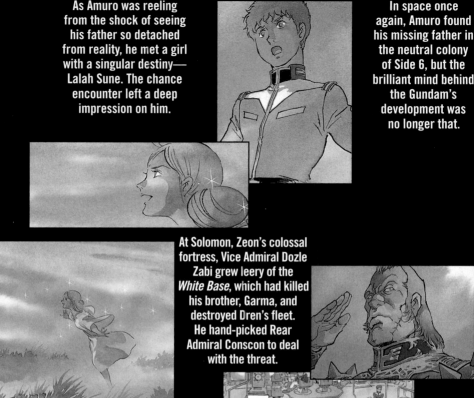

As Amuro was reeling from the shock of seeing his father so detached from reality, he met a girl with a singular destiny—Lalah Sune. The chance encounter left a deep impression on him.

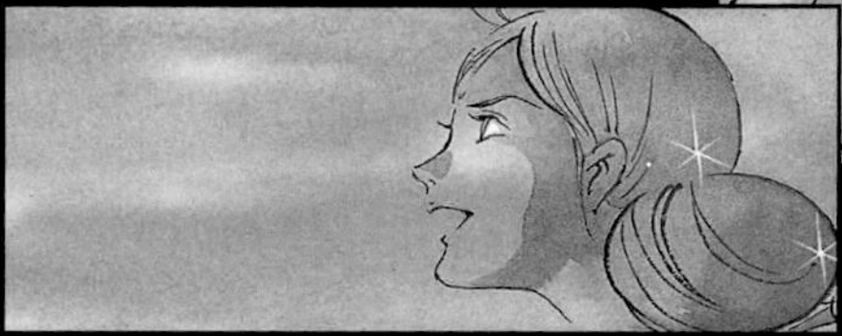

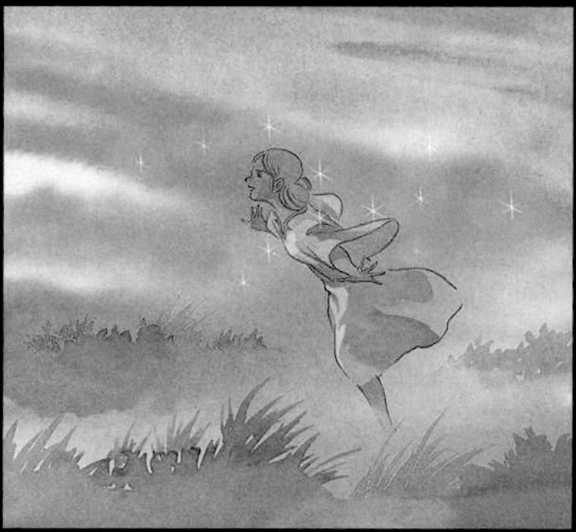

At Solomon, Zeon's colossal fortress, Vice Admiral Dozle Zabi grew leery of the *White Base*, which had killed his brother, Garma, and destroyed Dren's fleet. He hand-picked Rear Admiral Conscon to deal with the threat.

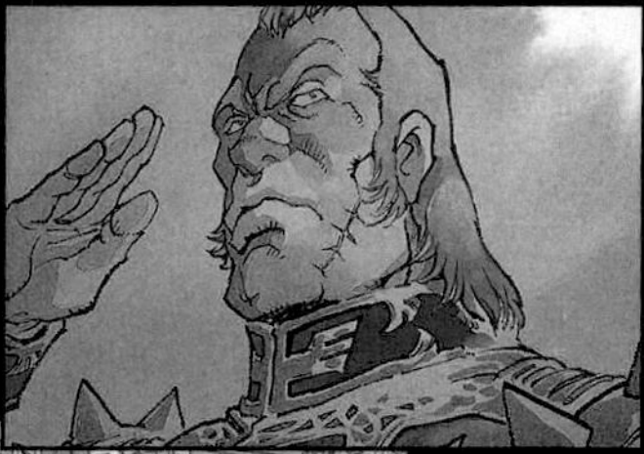

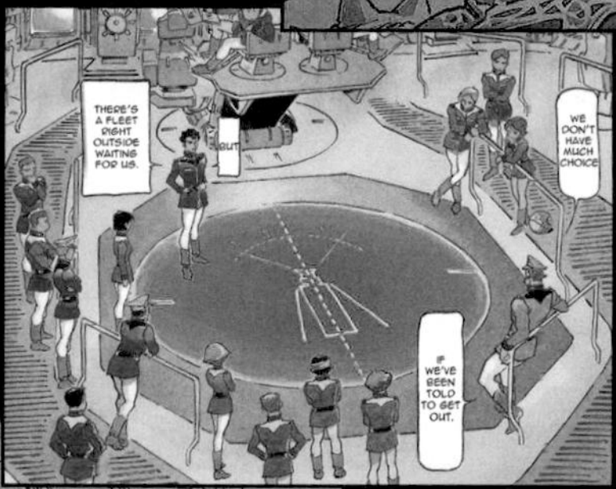
WE DON'T HAVE MUCH CHOICE
THERE'S A FLEET RIGHT OUTSIDE WAITING FOR US.
BUT
IF WE'VE BEEN TOLD TO GET OUT.

Conscon's fleet lay in wait in Side 6's neutral space but was annihilated by the *White Base* alone, losing a Musai-class cruiser, twelve Dom heavy mobile suits, and the flagship. Overcoming that peril, the *White Base* crew received orders to disrupt Zeon's secret operations on Texas Colony.

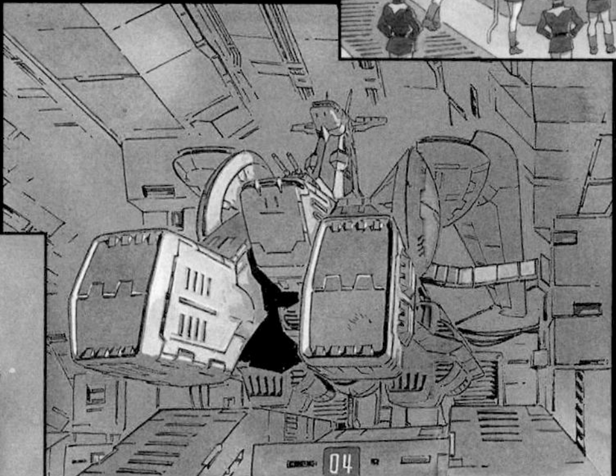
04

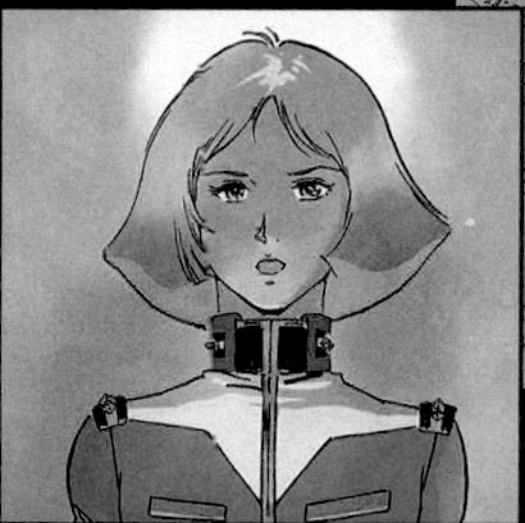

Amuro and the others in the *White Base* mobile suit team infiltrated the colony, and inside fell prey to the all-range attack of the Braw Bro, a mobile armor designed to be piloted by trained Newtypes. Even as he saw his comrades fall, Amuro defeated the Braw Bro, only to have the Gundam take heavy damage in a battle with archrival Char and his new state-of-the-art mobile suit, the Gelgoog.

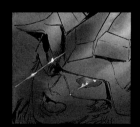

When Lalah ran onto the battlefield, Char had to leave the nearly-destroyed Gundam to protect her. He then ordered his men to evacuate Texas Colony and headed alone to his old home. In the place where he'd spent his youth, Char reunited with Artesia, his younger sister.

He spoke to her of "the renewal of man" and the future that would be opened up by the Newtypes' supremacy over Oldtypes. Knowing that she served on the *White Base* now as Sayla Mass, he left her with a message for Amuro.

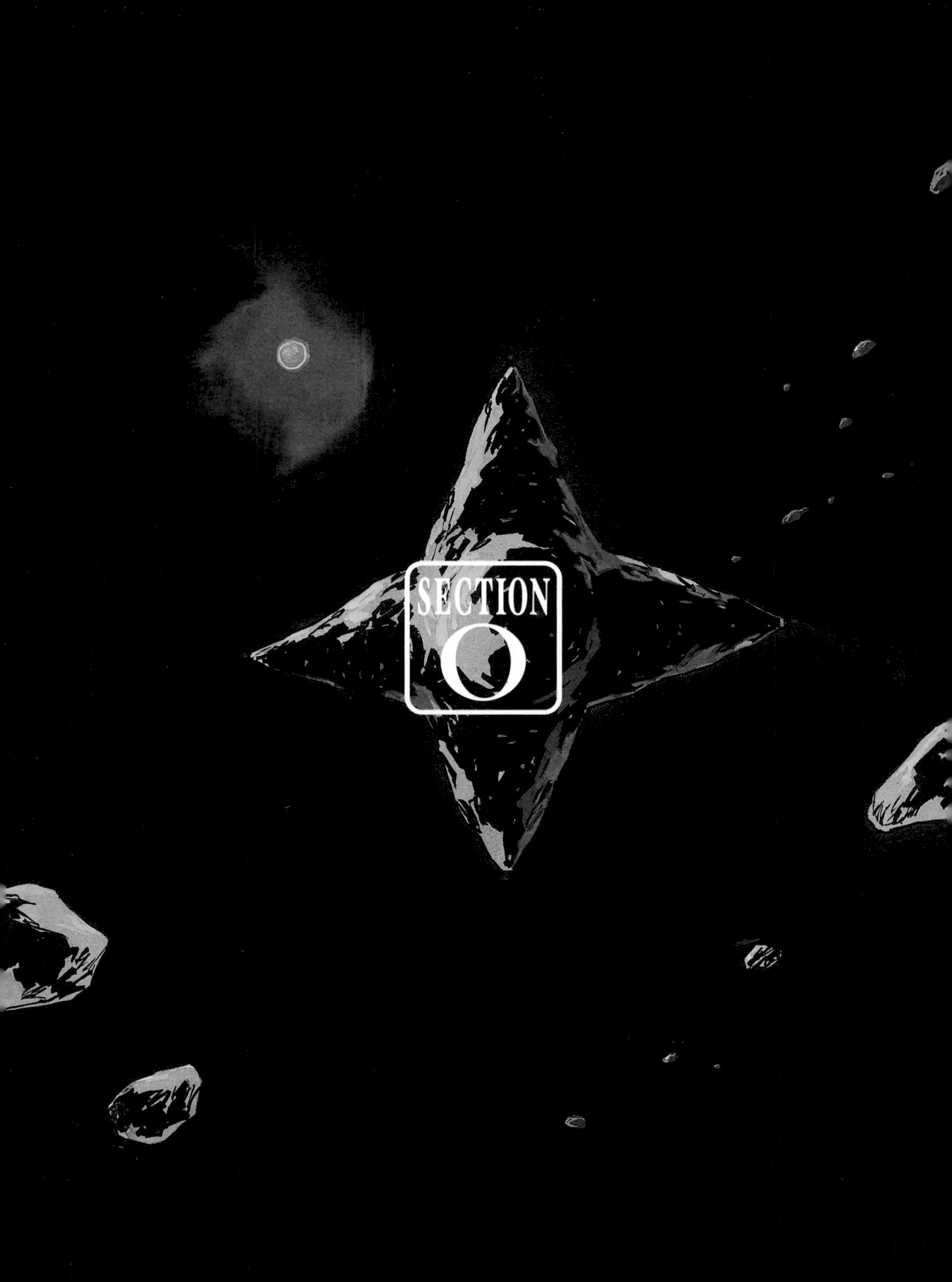
SECTION
O

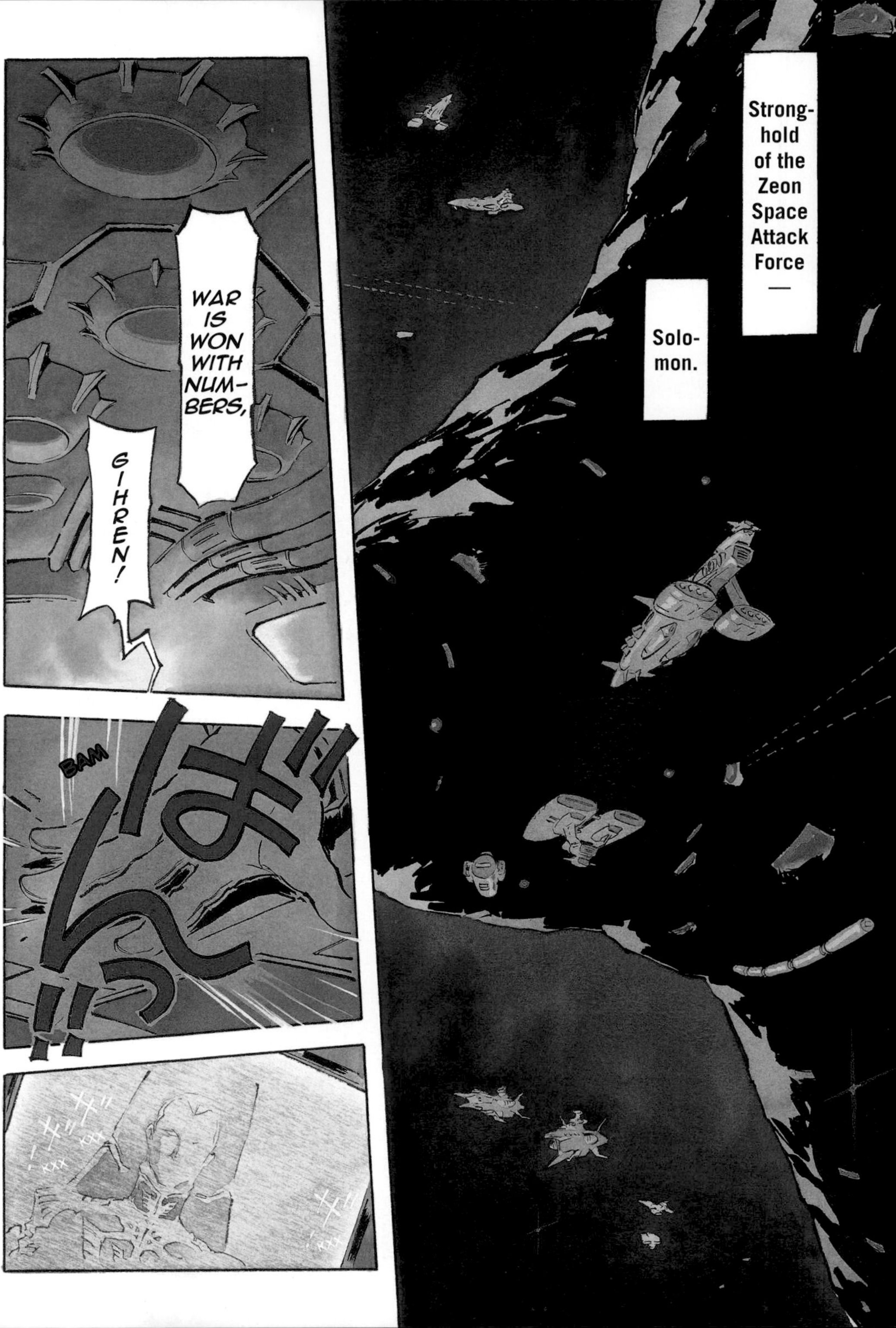
Strong-hold of the Zeon Space Attack Force —
Solo-mon.
WAR IS WON WITH NUM-BERS,
GIHREN!
BAM
ばんっ!!

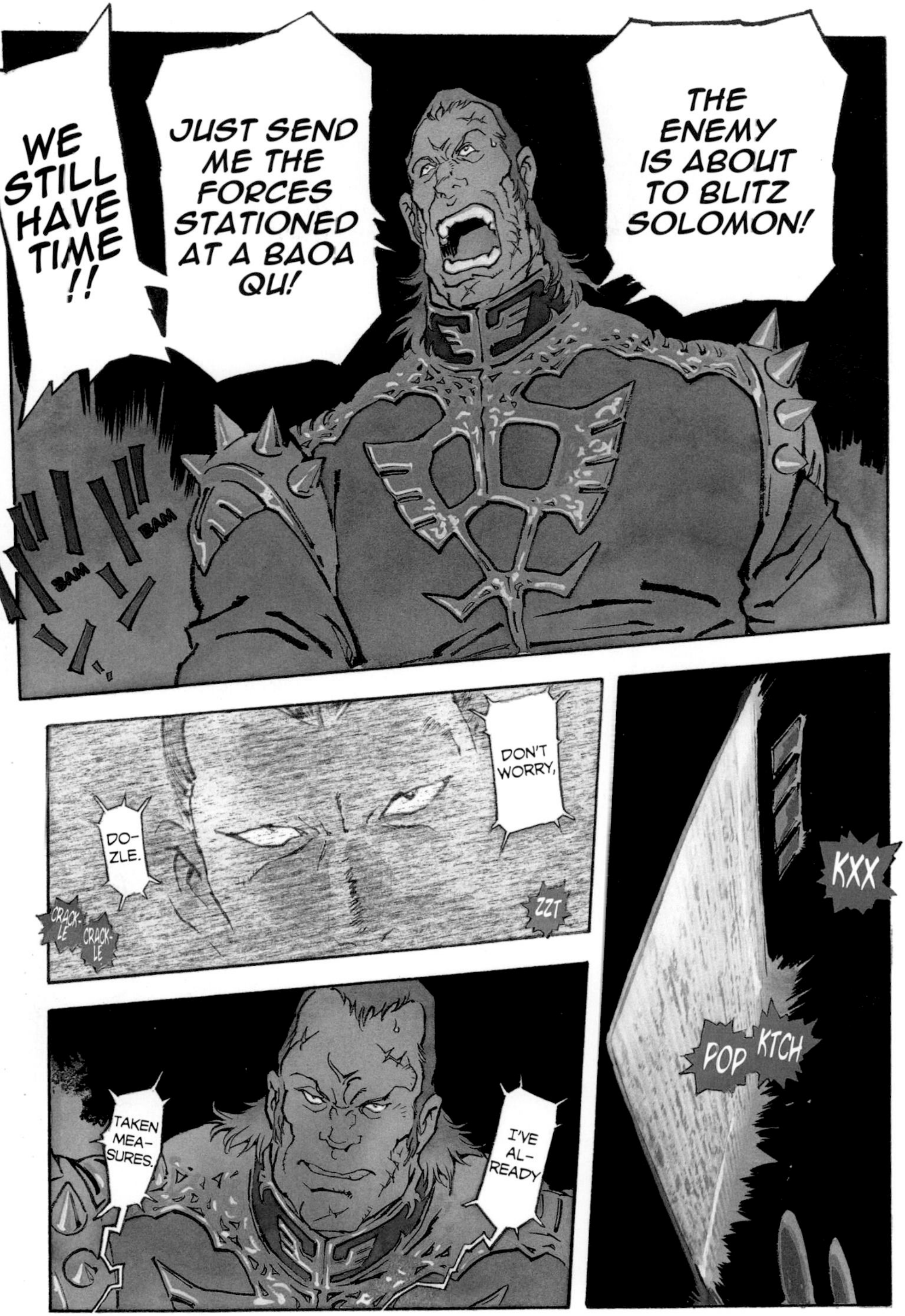
THE ENEMY IS ABOUT TO BLITZ SOLOMON!
JUST SEND ME THE FORCES STATIONED AT A BAOA QU!
WE STILL HAVE TIME!!
BAM
BAM
KXX
KTCH
POP
DON'T WORRY,
DO-ZLE.
ZZT
CRACK-LE
CRACK-LE
I'VE AL-READY
TAKEN MEA-SURES.

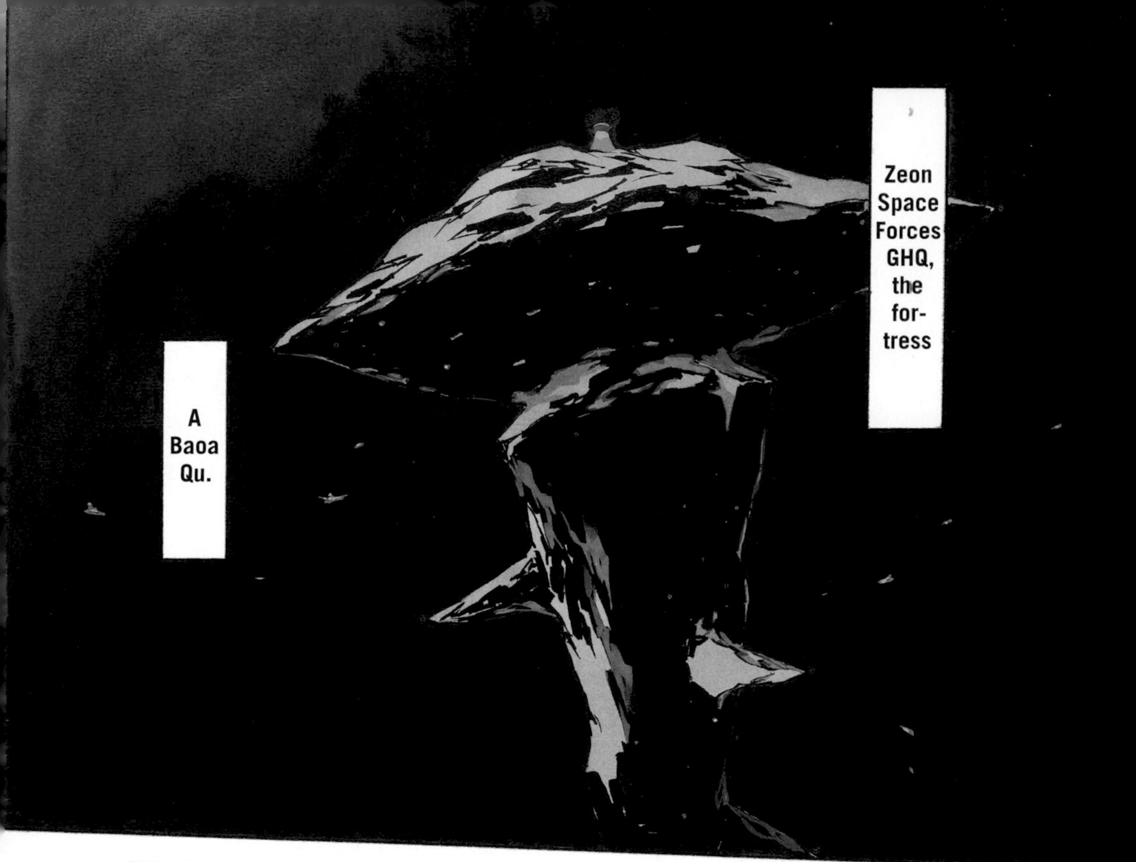
Zeon Space Forces GHQ, the fortress
A Baoa Qu.

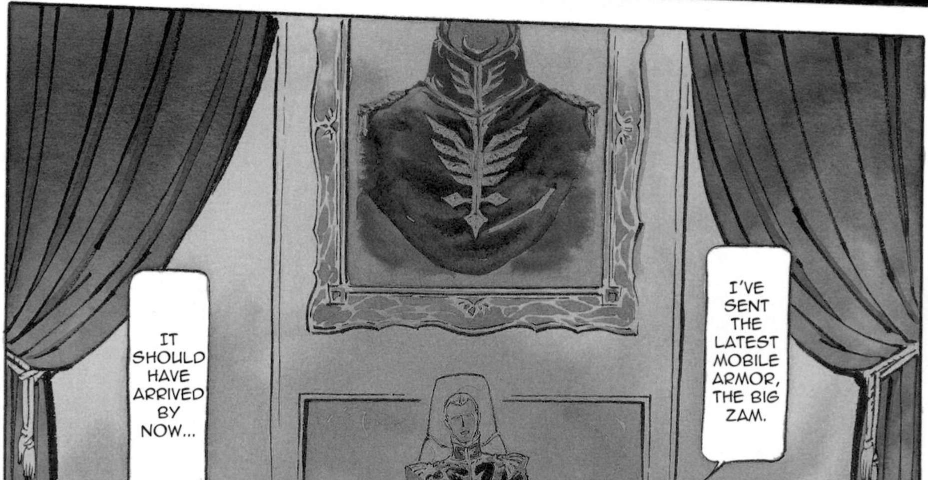
I'VE SENT THE LATEST MOBILE ARMOR, THE BIG ZAM.
IT SHOULD HAVE ARRIVED BY NOW...

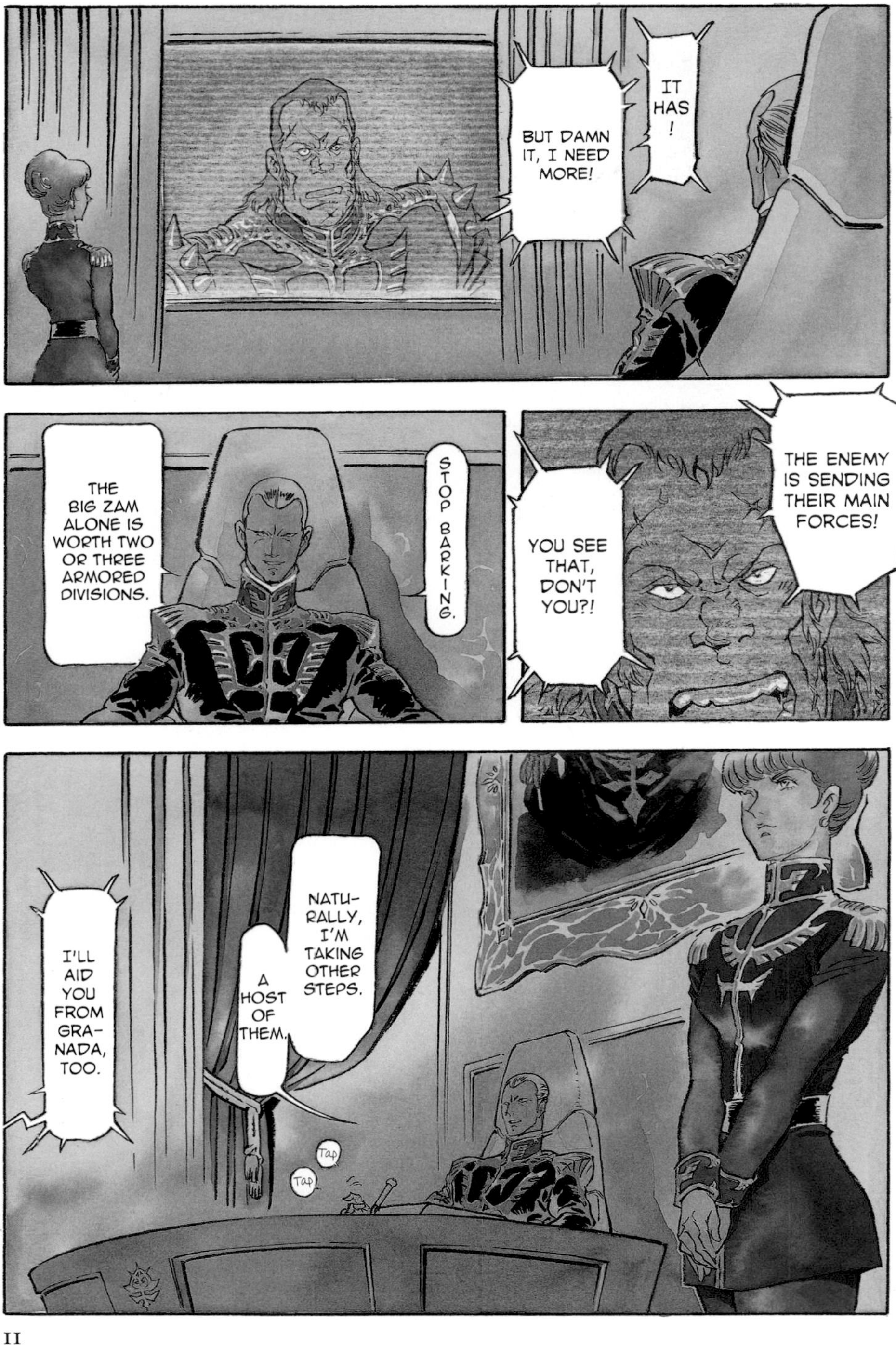
IT HAS!
BUT DAMN IT, I NEED MORE!
THE ENEMY IS SENDING THEIR MAIN FORCES!
YOU SEE THAT, DON'T YOU?!
STOP BARKING.
THE BIG ZAM ALONE IS WORTH TWO OR THREE ARMORED DIVISIONS.
NATU-RALLY, I'M TAKING OTHER STEPS.
A HOST OF THEM.
I'LL AID YOU FROM GRA-NADA, TOO.
Tap
Tap

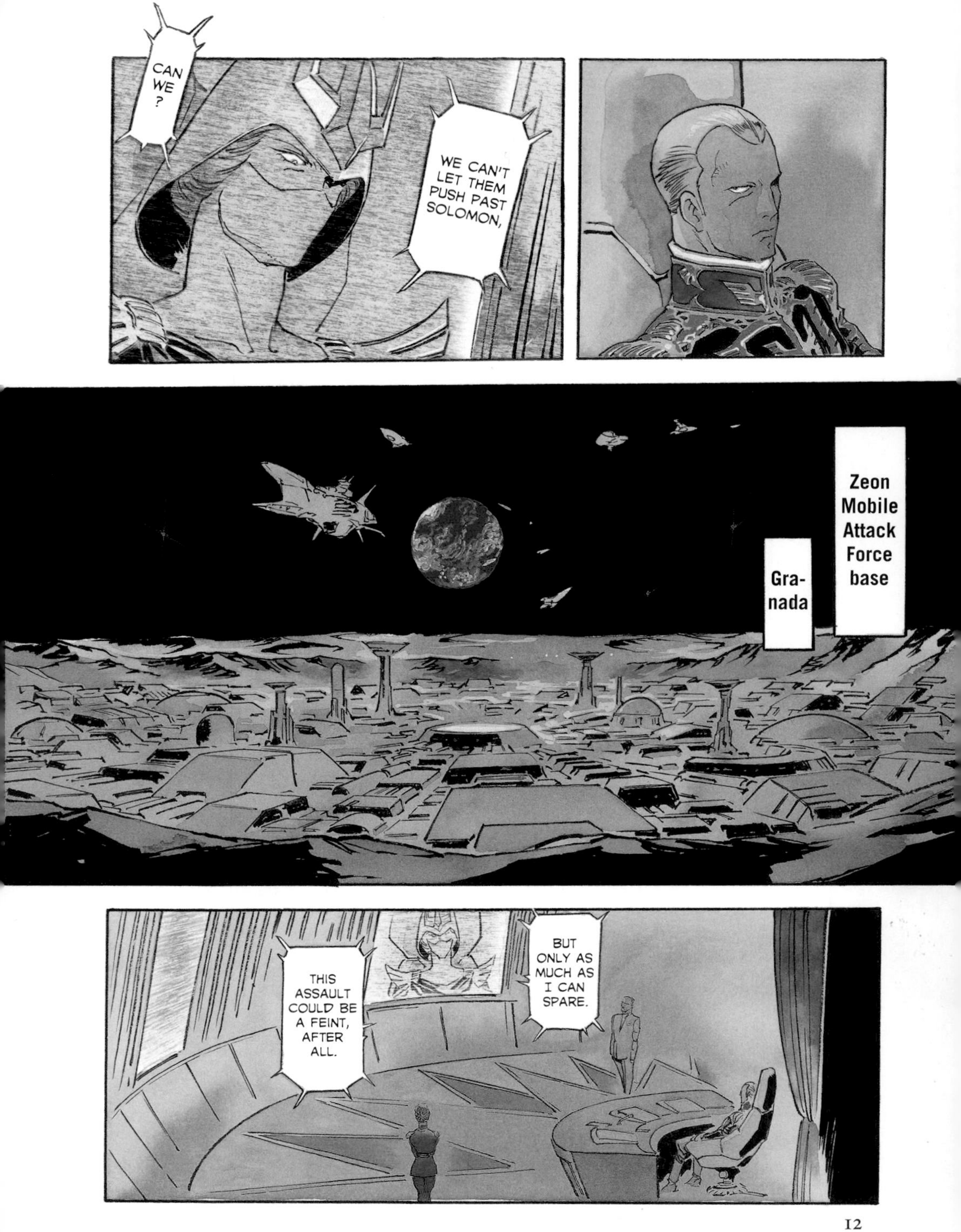
WE CAN'T LET THEM PUSH PAST SOLOMON,
CAN WE?
Zeon Mobile Attack Force base
Gra- nada
BUT ONLY AS MUCH AS I CAN SPARE.
THIS ASSAULT COULD BE A FEINT, AFTER ALL.

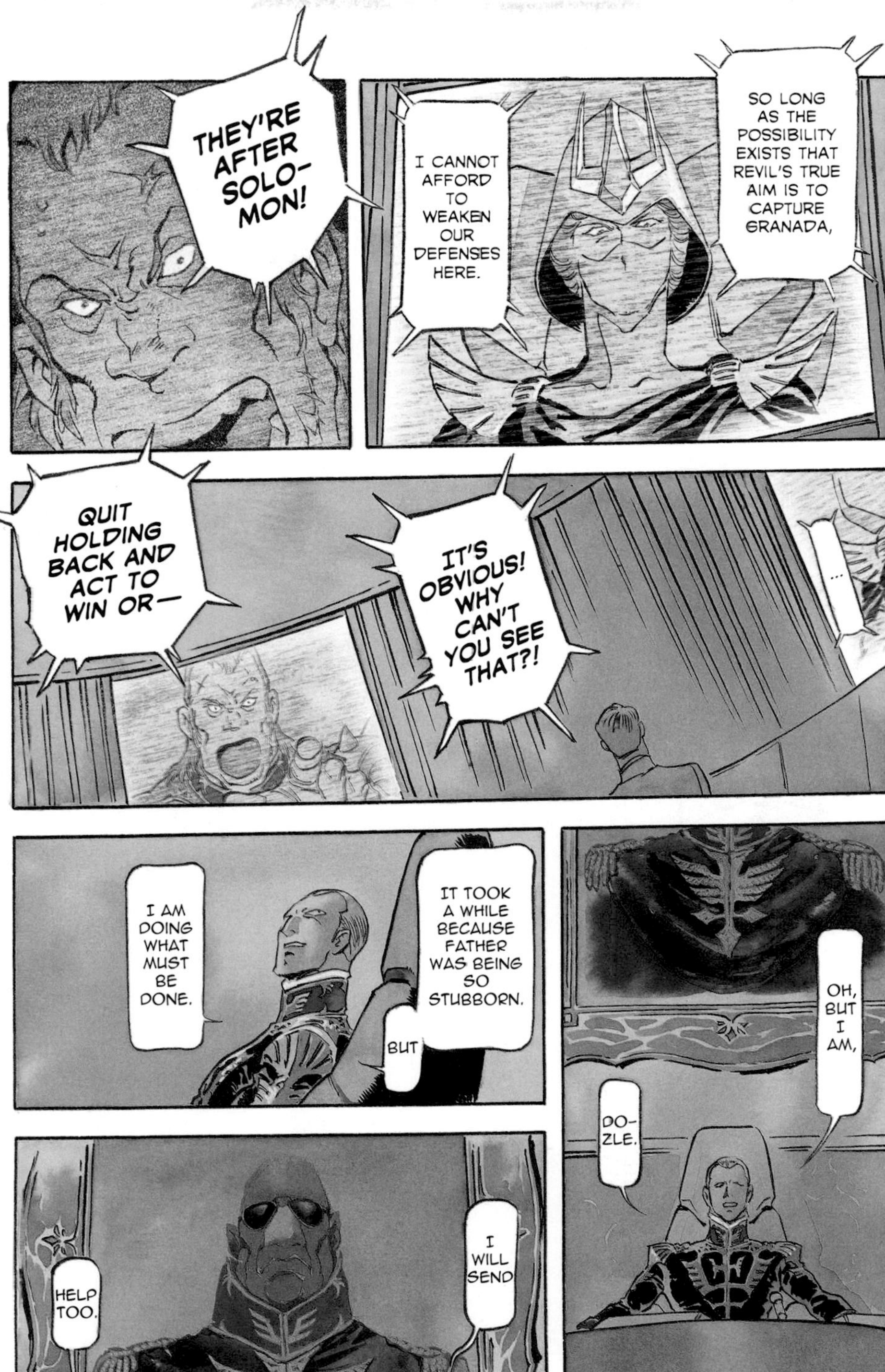
SO LONG AS THE POSSIBILITY EXISTS THAT REVIL'S TRUE AIM IS TO CAPTURE GRANADA,
I CANNOT AFFORD TO WEAKEN OUR DEFENSES HERE.
THEY'RE AFTER SOLO-MON!
...
IT'S OBVIOUS! WHY CAN'T YOU SEE THAT?!
QUIT HOLDING BACK AND ACT TO WIN OR—
OH, BUT I AM,
DOZ-LE.
IT TOOK A WHILE BECAUSE FATHER WAS BEING SO STUBBORN.
BUT
I AM DOING WHAT MUST BE DONE.
I WILL SEND
HELP TOO.

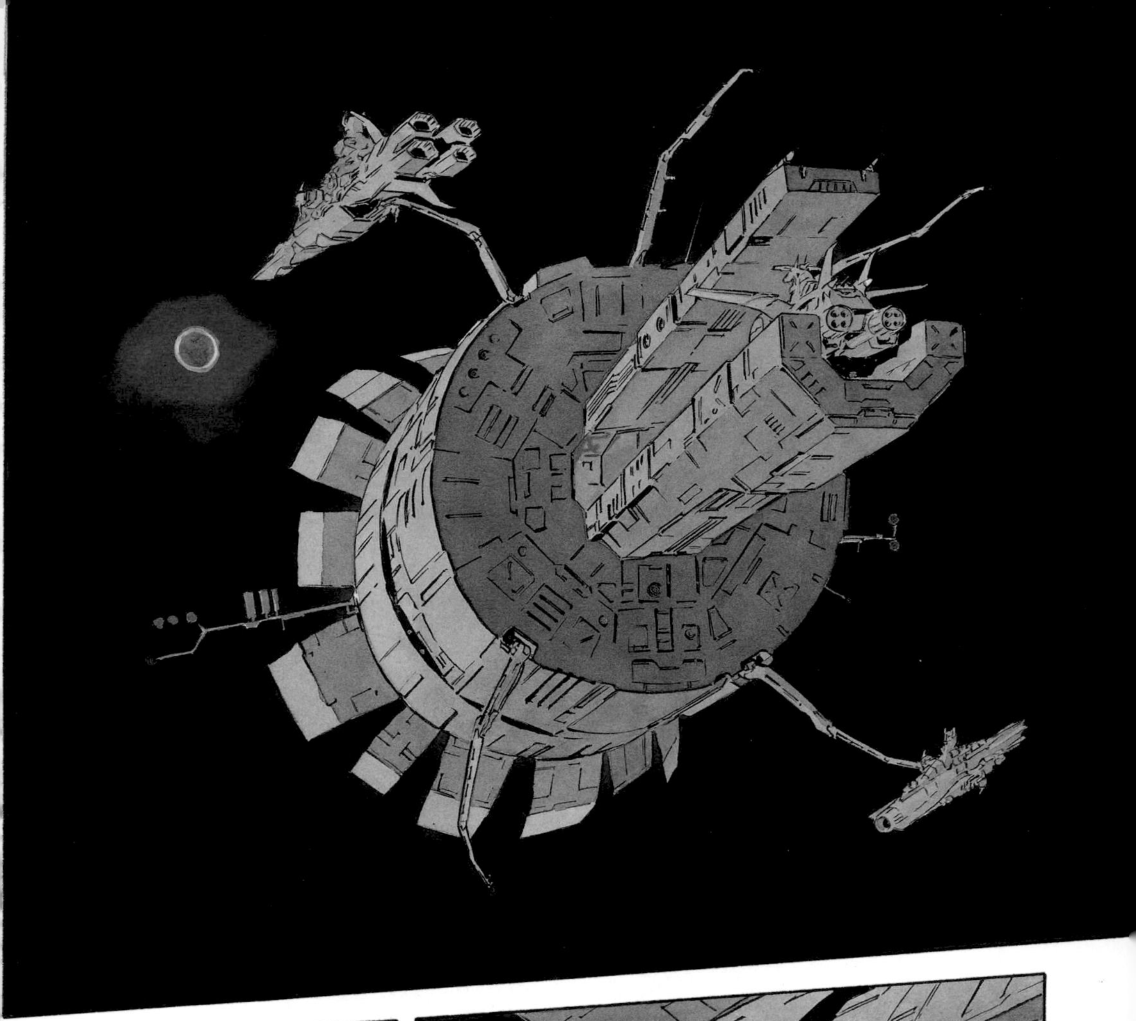

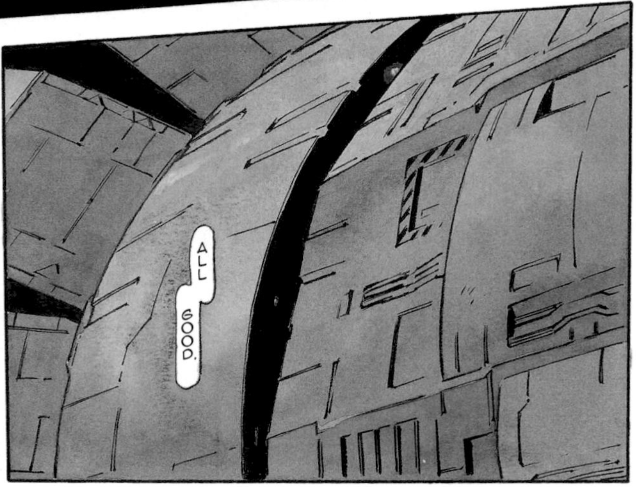
ALL GOOD.

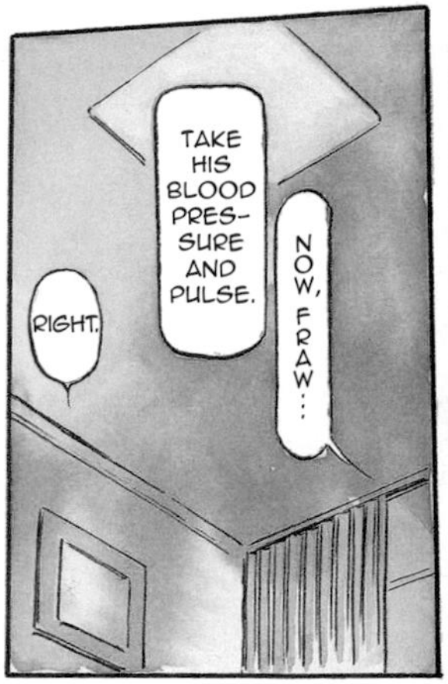
NOW, FRAW…
TAKE HIS BLOOD PRES-SURE AND PULSE.
RIGHT.

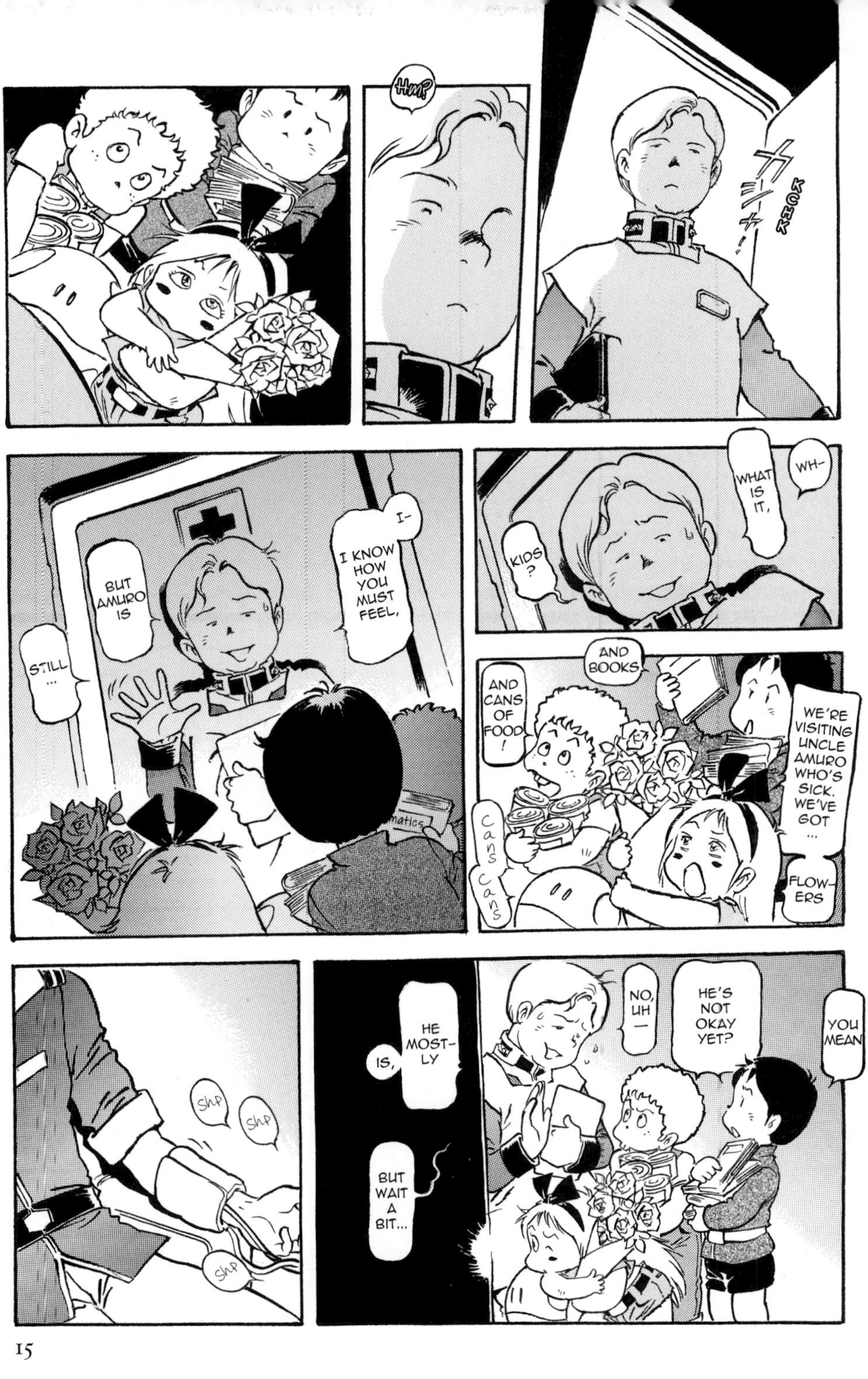
KCHK
HM?
WH-
WHAT IS IT,
KIDS?
WE'RE VISITING UNCLE AMURO WHO'S SICK. WE'VE GOT ...
FLOW-ERS
AND BOOKS
AND CANS OF FOOD!
Cans Cans
I-
I KNOW HOW YOU MUST FEEL,
BUT AMURO IS
STILL ...
YOU MEAN
HE'S NOT OKAY YET?
NO, UH —
HE MOST-LY
IS,
BUT WAIT A BIT...
Shp
Shp
Shp

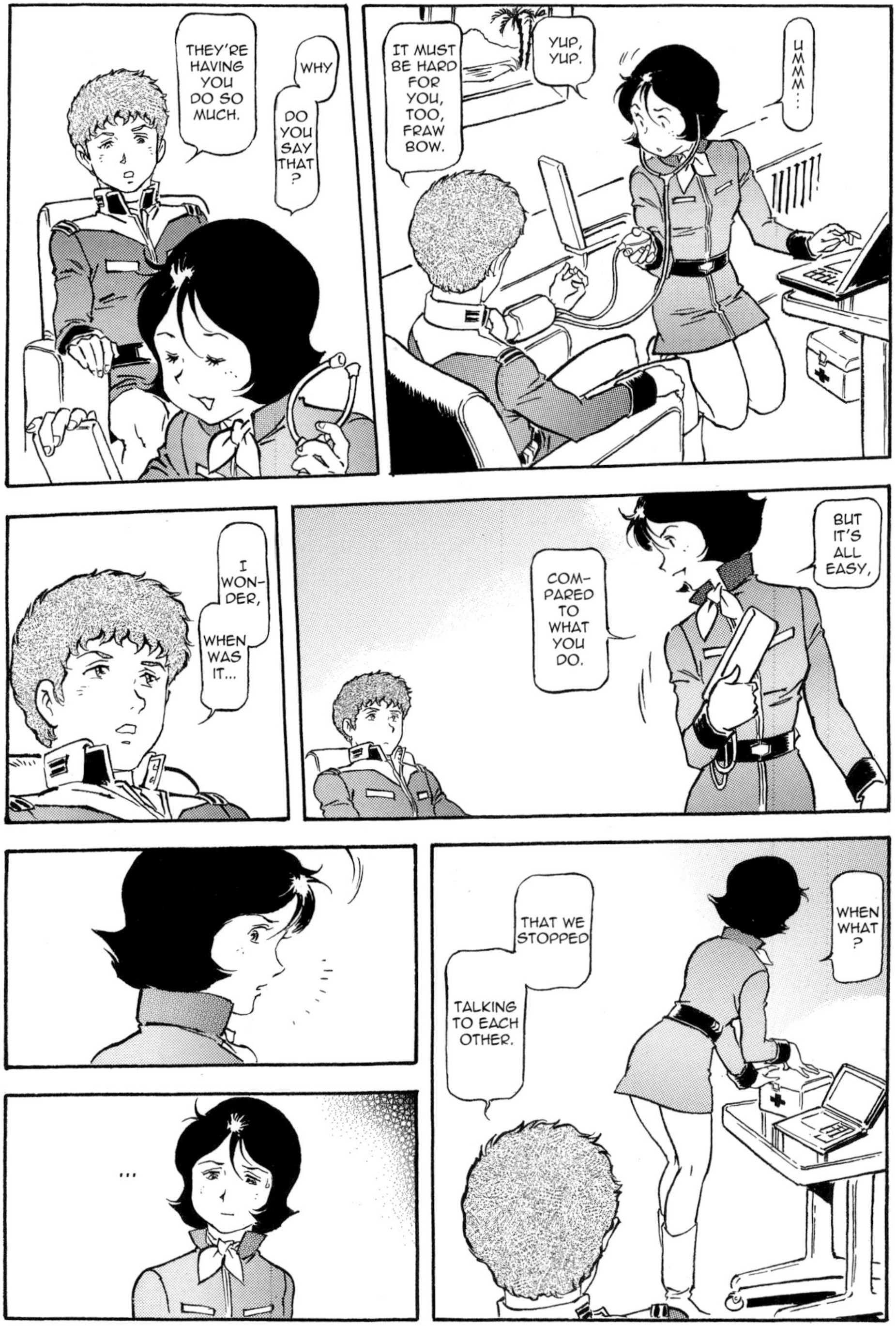
UMMM...
YUP, YUP.
IT MUST BE HARD FOR YOU, TOO, FRAW BOW.
WHY DO YOU SAY THAT?
THEY'RE HAVING YOU DO SO MUCH.
BUT IT'S ALL EASY,
COMPARED TO WHAT YOU DO.
I WONDER,
WHEN WAS IT...
WHEN WHAT?
THAT WE STOPPED
TALKING TO EACH OTHER.
...

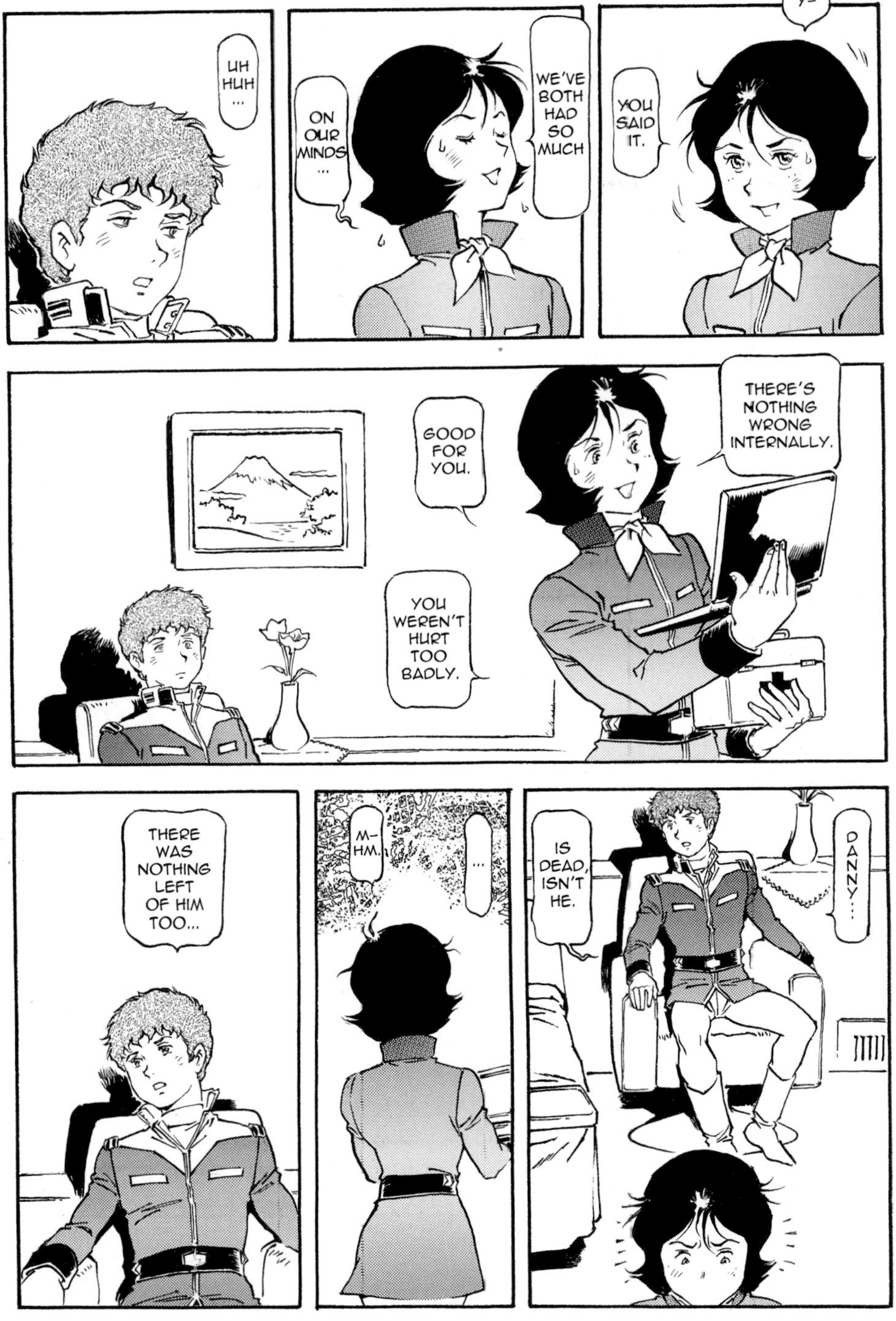
Y-
YOU SAID IT.
WE'VE BOTH HAD SO MUCH
ON OUR MINDS ...
UH HUH ...
THERE'S NOTHING WRONG INTERNALLY.
GOOD FOR YOU.
YOU WEREN'T HURT TOO BADLY.
DANNY...
IS DEAD, ISN'T HE.
...
M-HM.
THERE WAS NOTHING LEFT OF HIM TOO...

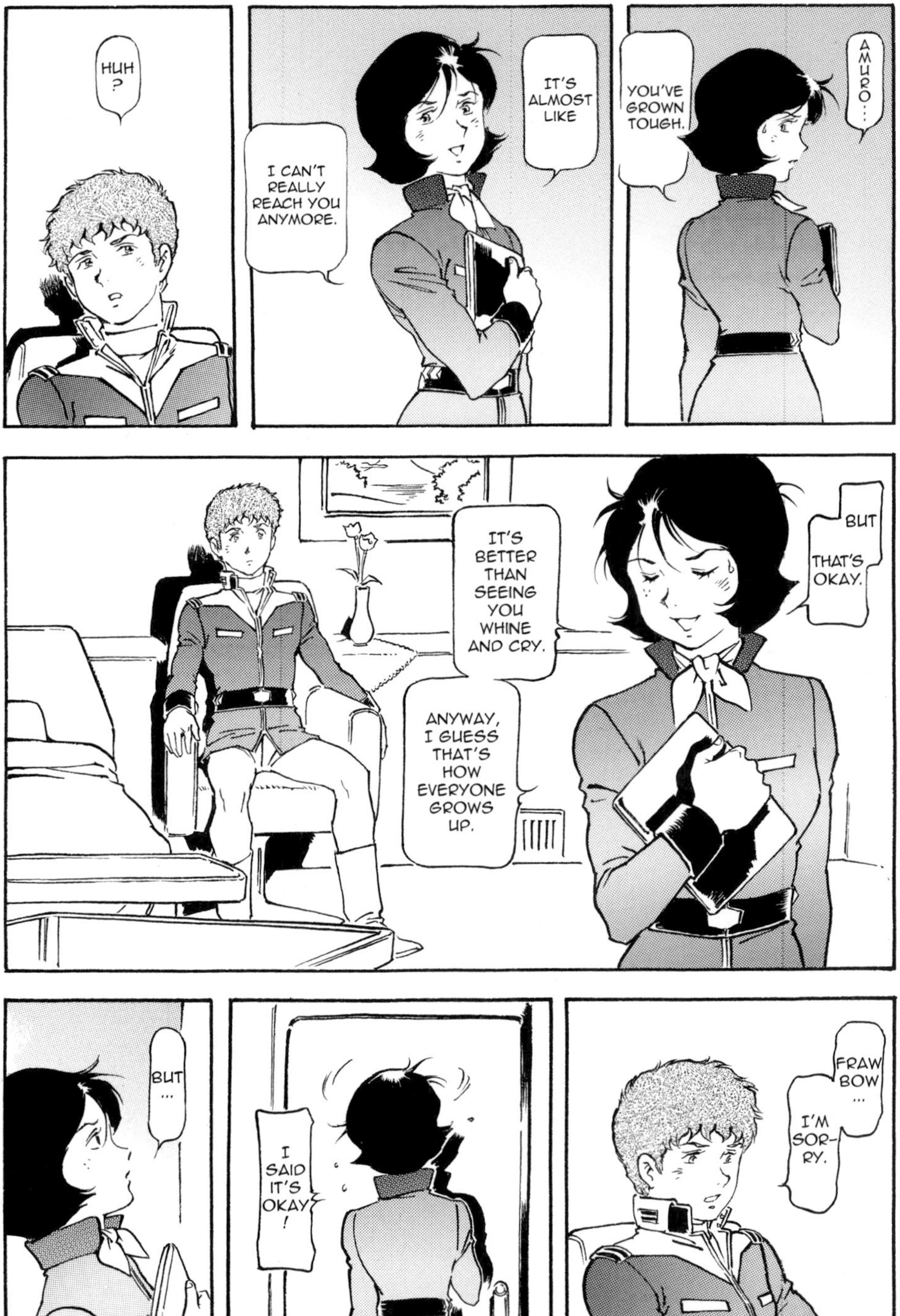
AMURO...
YOU'VE GROWN TOUGH.
IT'S ALMOST LIKE
I CAN'T REALLY REACH YOU ANYMORE.
HUH?
BUT THAT'S OKAY.
IT'S BETTER THAN SEEING YOU WHINE AND CRY.
ANYWAY, I GUESS THAT'S HOW EVERYONE GROWS UP.
FRAW BOW...
I'M SOR-RY.
I SAID IT'S OKAY!
BUT...

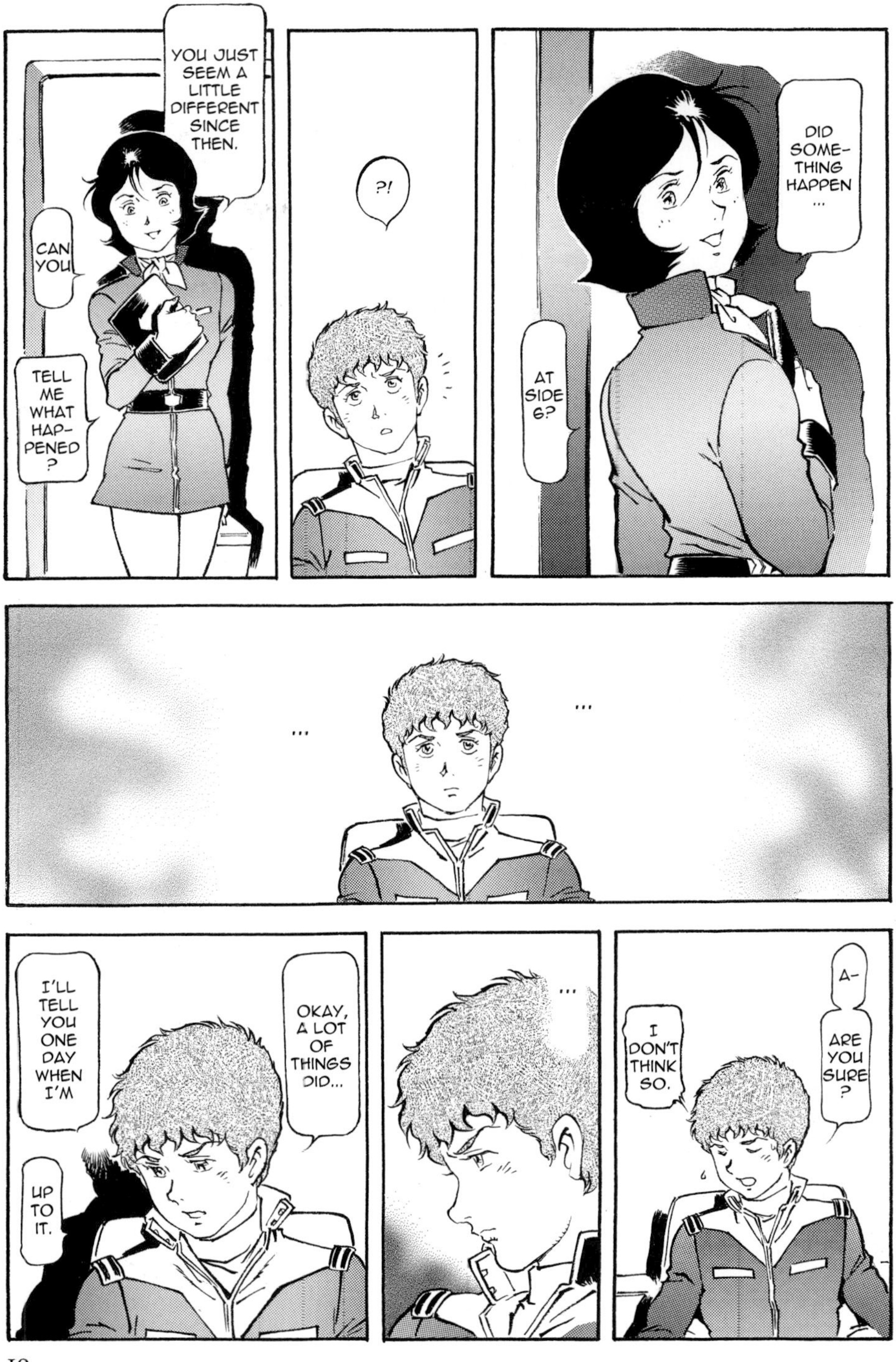
DID SOME-THING HAPPEN ...
AT SIDE 6?
?!
YOU JUST SEEM A LITTLE DIFFERENT SINCE THEN.
CAN YOU
TELL ME WHAT HAP-PENED ?
...
...
A-
ARE YOU SURE ?
I DON'T THINK SO.
...
OKAY, A LOT OF THINGS DID...
I'LL TELL YOU ONE DAY WHEN I'M
UP TO IT.

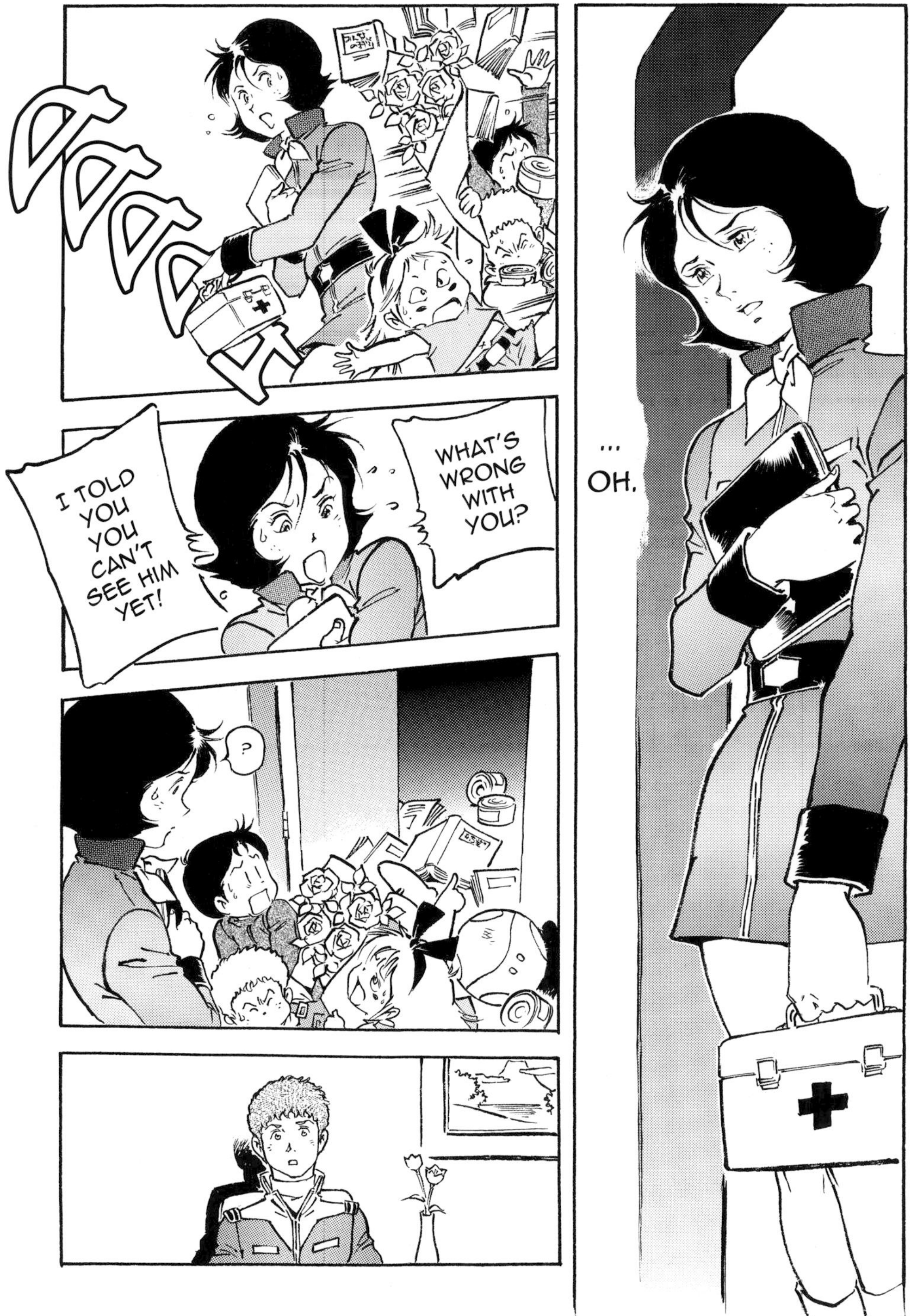
... OH.
WHAT'S WRONG WITH YOU?
I TOLD YOU YOU CAN'T SEE HIM YET!
?

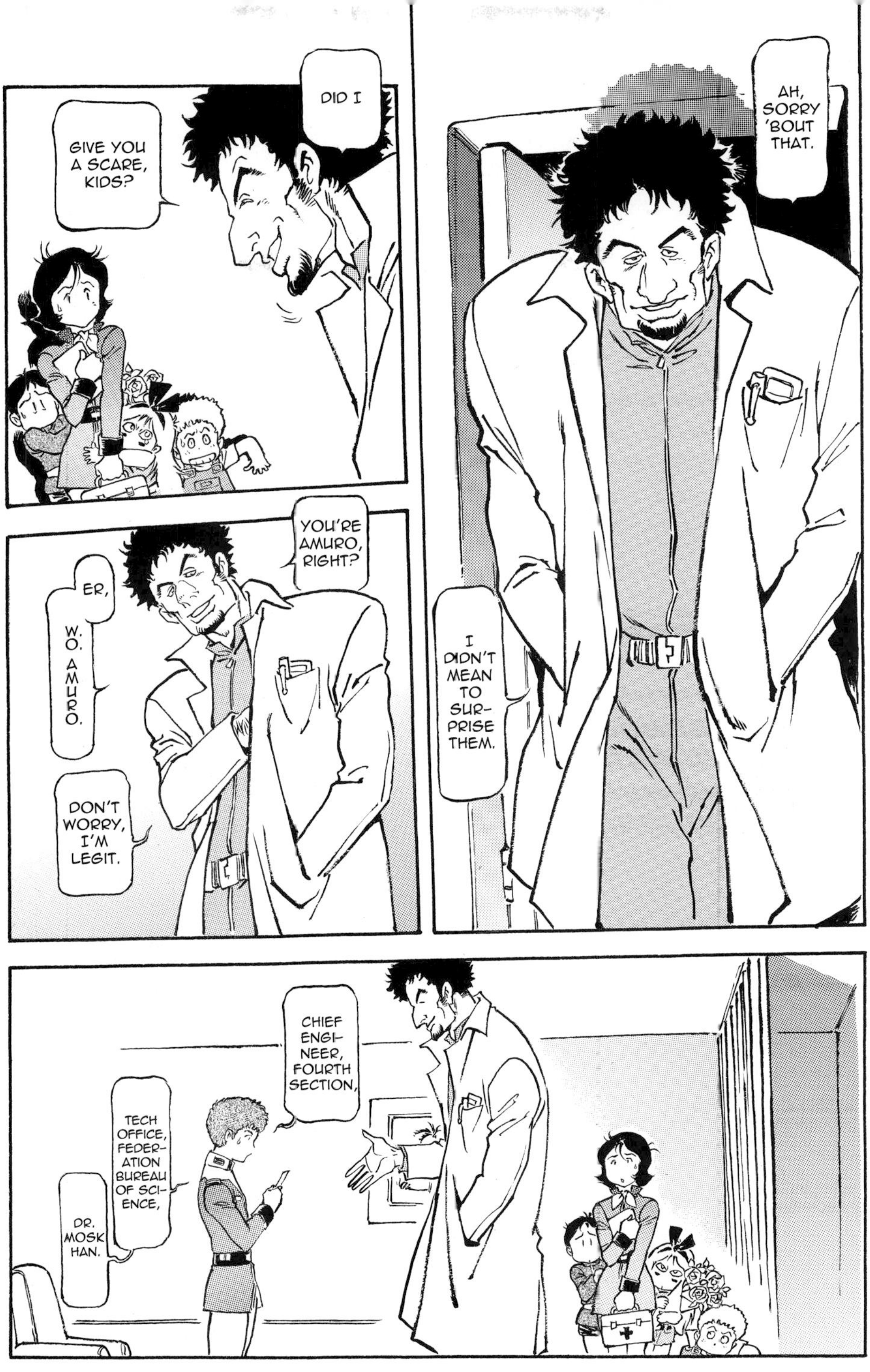
AH, SORRY 'BOUT THAT.
I DIDN'T MEAN TO SUR-PRISE THEM.
DID I
GIVE YOU A SCARE, KIDS?
YOU'RE AMURO, RIGHT?
ER, W.O. AMURO.
DON'T WORRY, I'M LEGIT.
CHIEF ENGI-NEER, FOURTH SECTION,
TECH OFFICE, FEDER-ATION BUREAU OF SCI-ENCE,
DR. MOSK HAN.

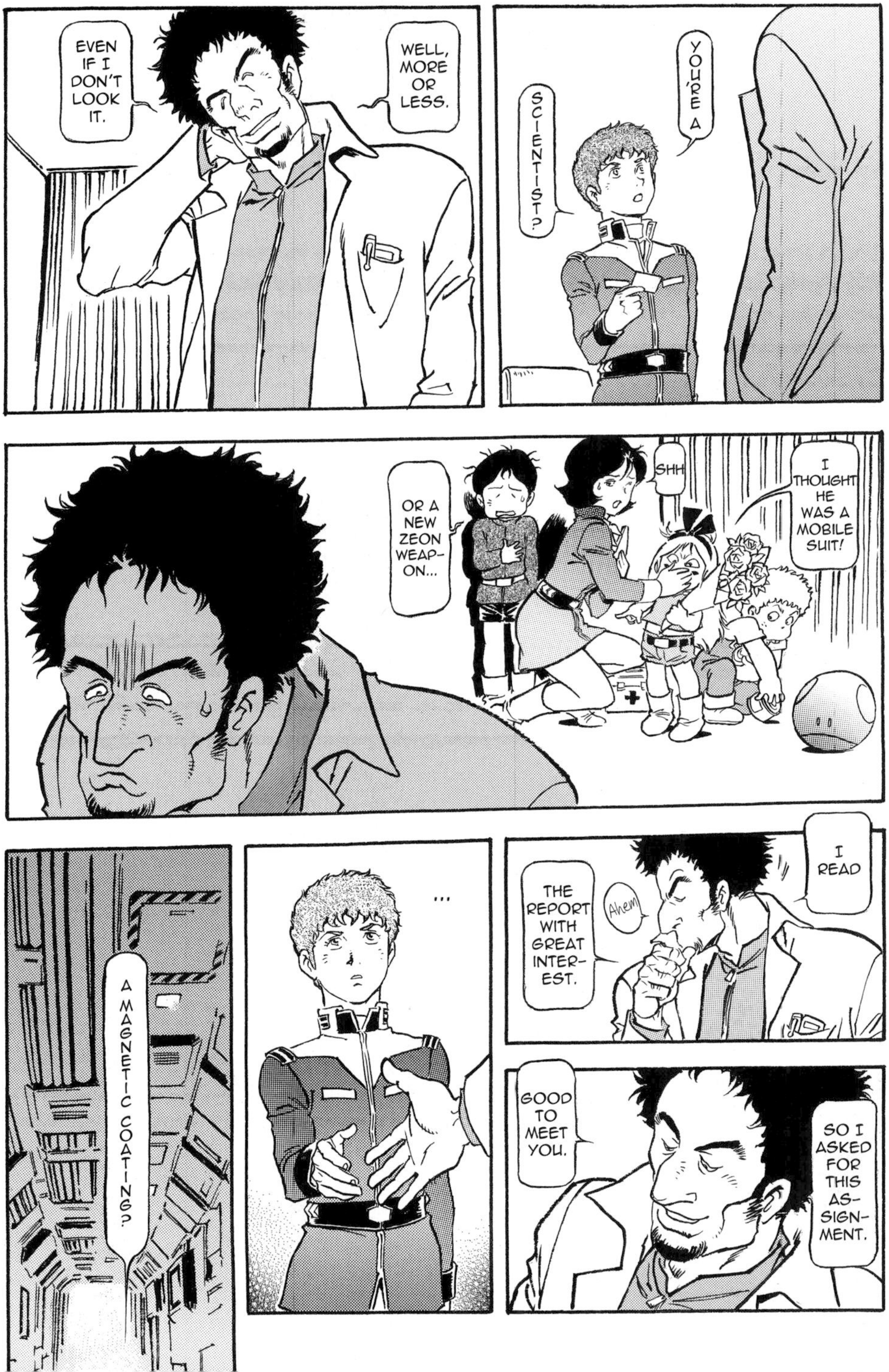
YOU'RE A
SCIENTIST?
WELL, MORE OR LESS.
EVEN IF I DON'T LOOK IT.
I THOUGHT HE WAS A MOBILE SUIT!
SHH
OR A NEW ZEON WEAP-ON...
I READ
Ahem
THE REPORT WITH GREAT INTER-EST.
SO I ASKED FOR THIS AS-SIGN-MENT.
GOOD TO MEET YOU.
...
A MAGNETIC COATING?

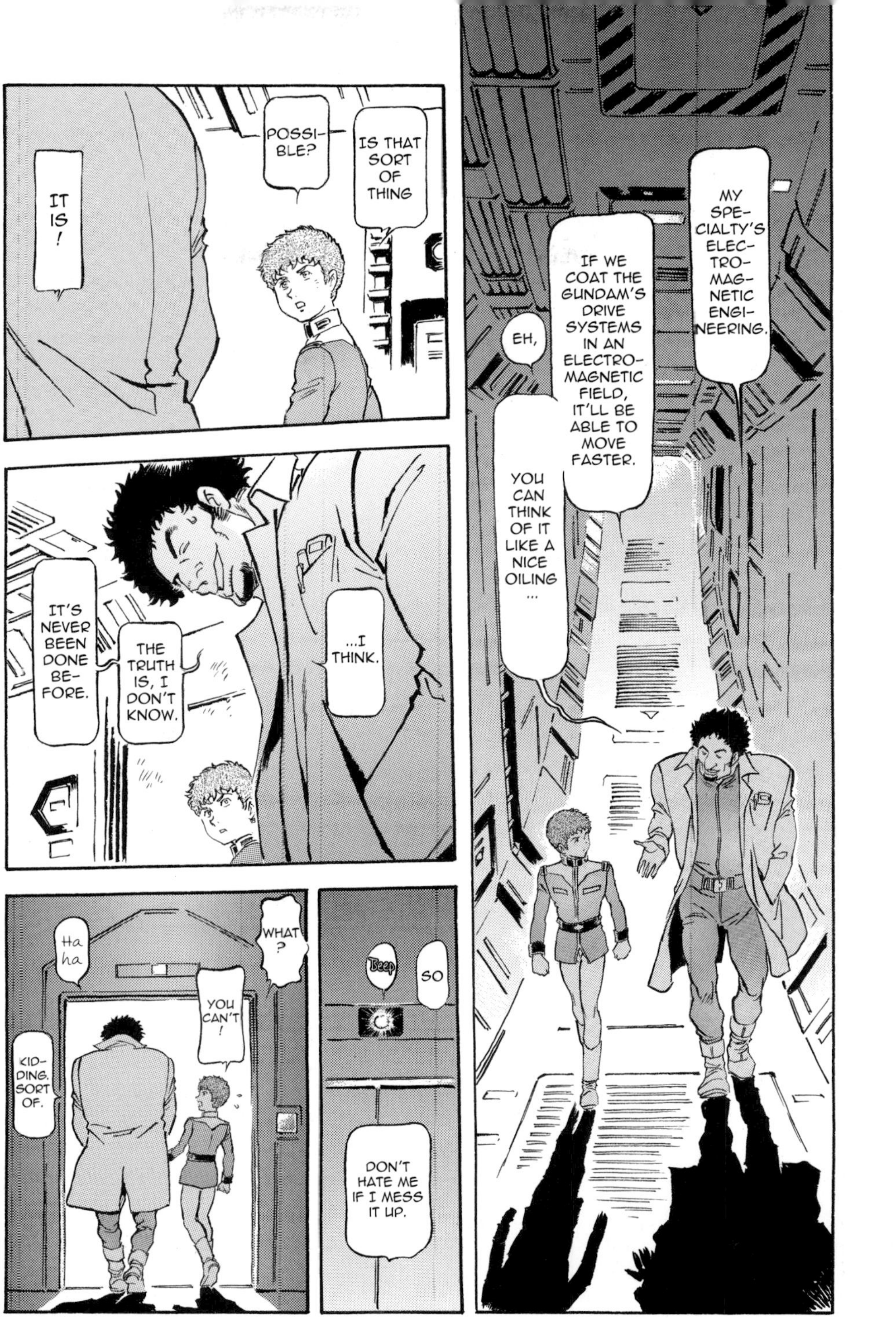
MY SPECIALTY'S ELECTROMAGNETIC ENGINEERING.
IF WE COAT THE GUNDAM'S DRIVE SYSTEMS IN AN ELECTROMAGNETIC FIELD, IT'LL BE ABLE TO MOVE FASTER.
EH,
YOU CAN THINK OF IT LIKE A NICE OILING ...
IS THAT SORT OF THING
POSSIBLE?
IT IS!
...I THINK.
THE TRUTH IS, I DON'T KNOW.
IT'S NEVER BEEN DONE BEFORE.
SO
Beep
DON'T HATE ME IF I MESS IT UP.
WHAT?
YOU CAN'T!
Ha ha
KIDDING, SORT OF.

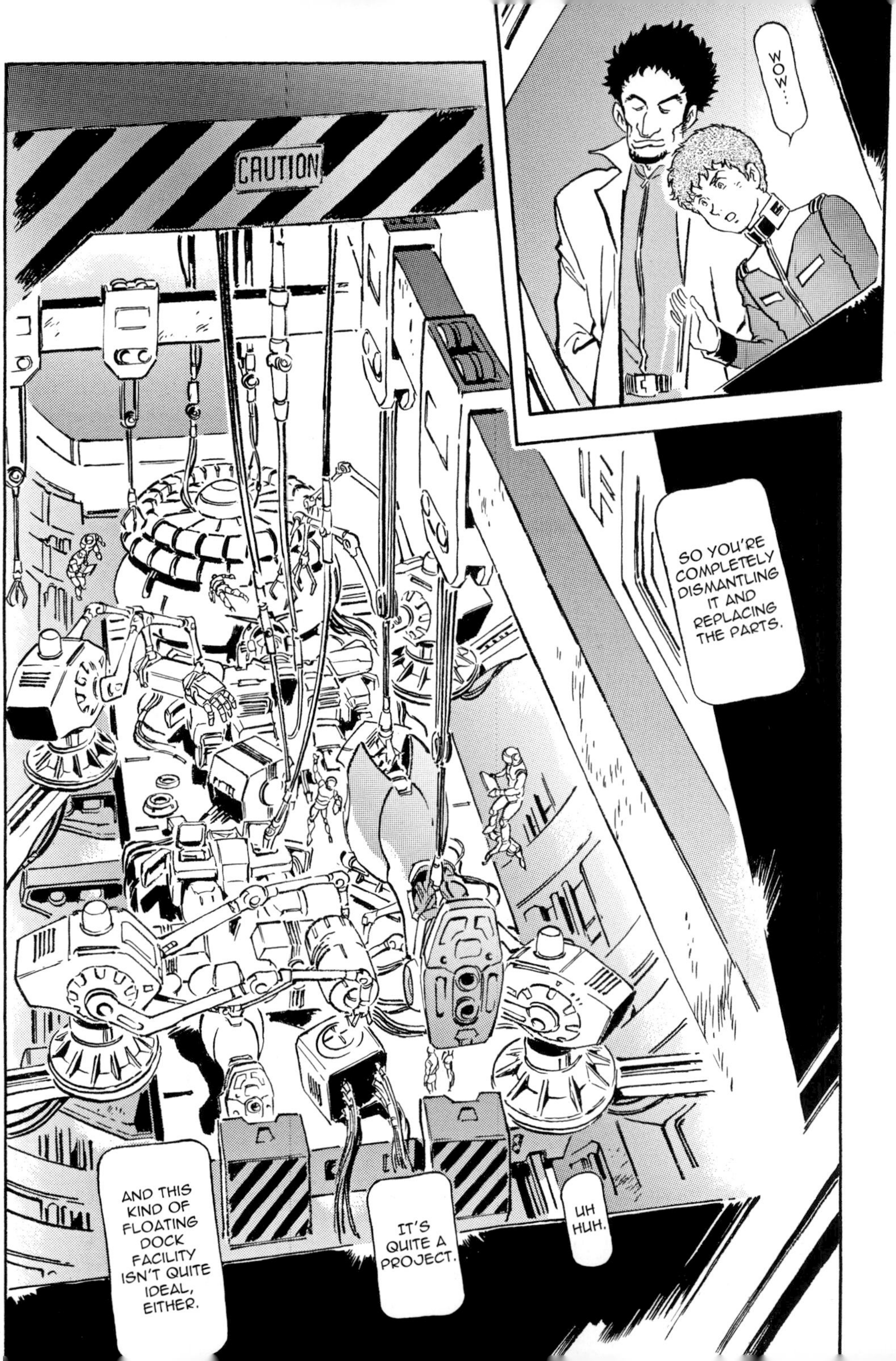
WOW...
CAUTION
SO YOU'RE COMPLETELY DISMANTLING IT AND REPLACING THE PARTS.
UH HUH.
IT'S QUITE A PROJECT.
AND THIS KIND OF FLOATING DOCK FACILITY ISN'T QUITE IDEAL, EITHER.

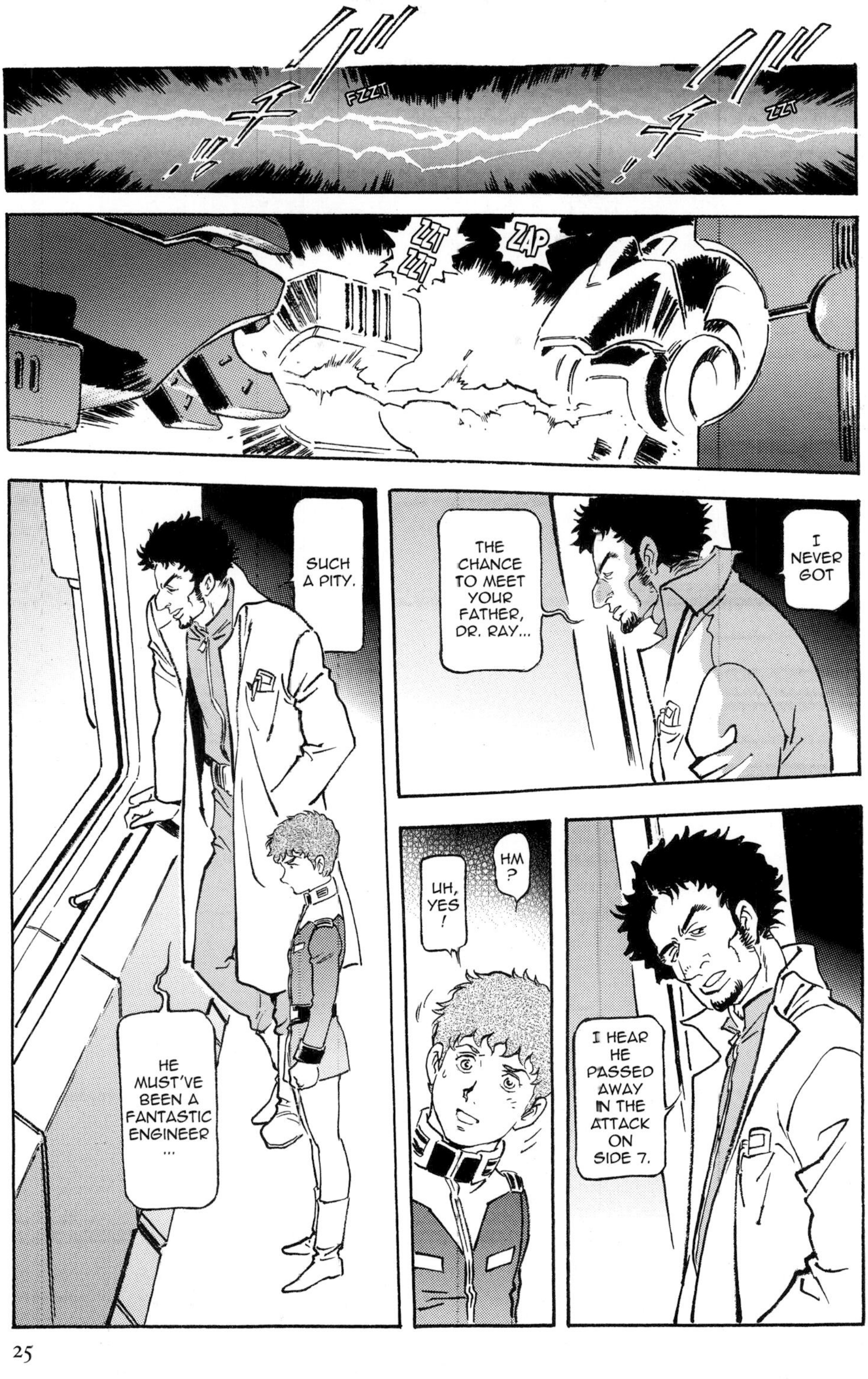
ZZT
FZZT
ZAP
ZZT ZZT
I NEVER GOT
THE CHANCE TO MEET YOUR FATHER, DR. RAY...
I HEAR HE PASSED AWAY IN THE ATTACK ON SIDE 7.
HM?
UH, YES!
SUCH A PITY.
HE MUST'VE BEEN A FANTASTIC ENGINEER...

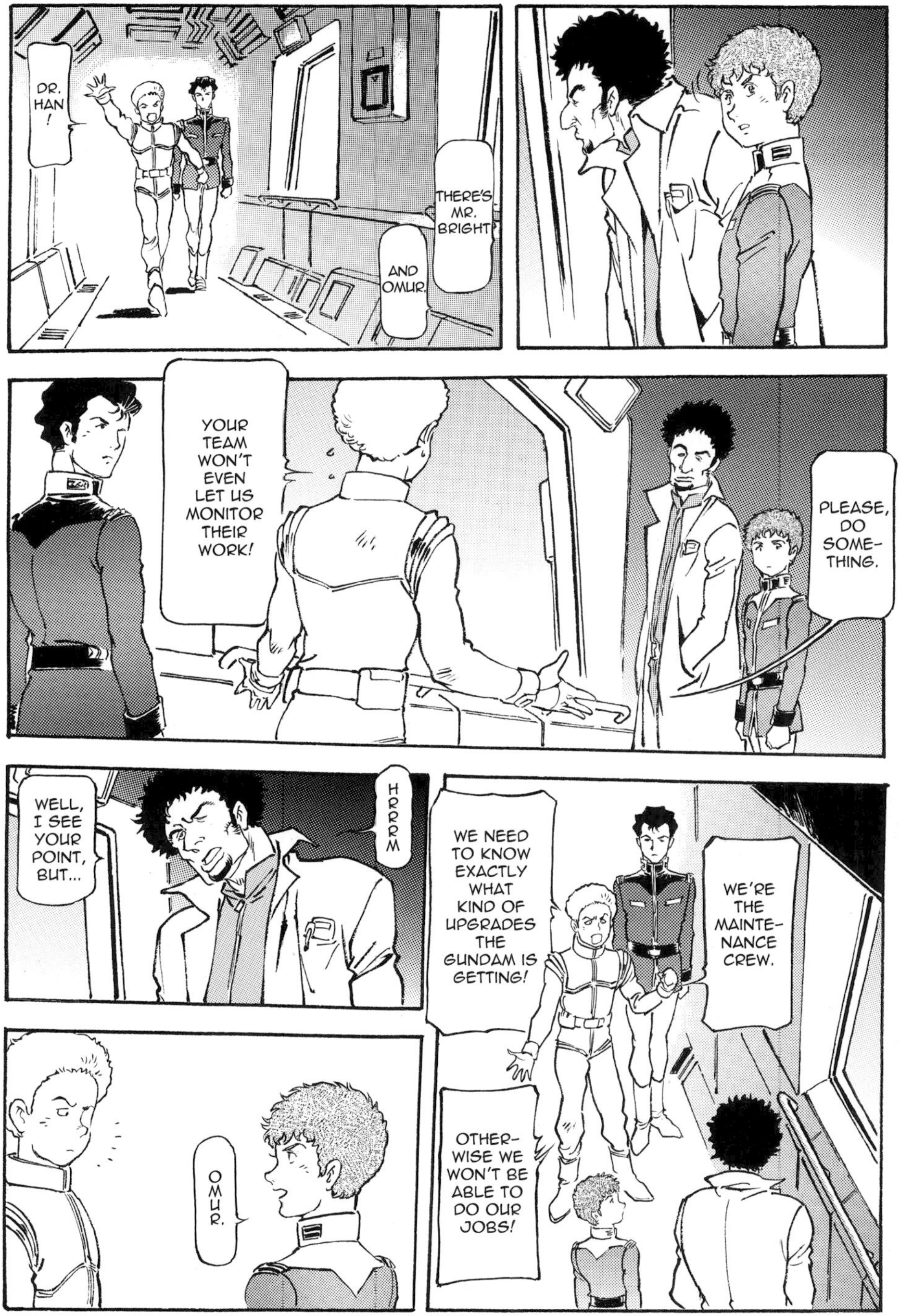
THERE'S MR. BRIGHT
AND OMUR.
DR. HAN!
PLEASE, DO SOME-THING.
YOUR TEAM WON'T EVEN LET US MONITOR THEIR WORK!
WE'RE THE MAINTE-NANCE CREW.
WE NEED TO KNOW EXACTLY WHAT KIND OF UPGRADES THE GUNDAM IS GETTING!
OTHER-WISE WE WON'T BE ABLE TO DO OUR JOBS!
HRRRM
WELL, I SEE YOUR POINT, BUT...
OMUR.

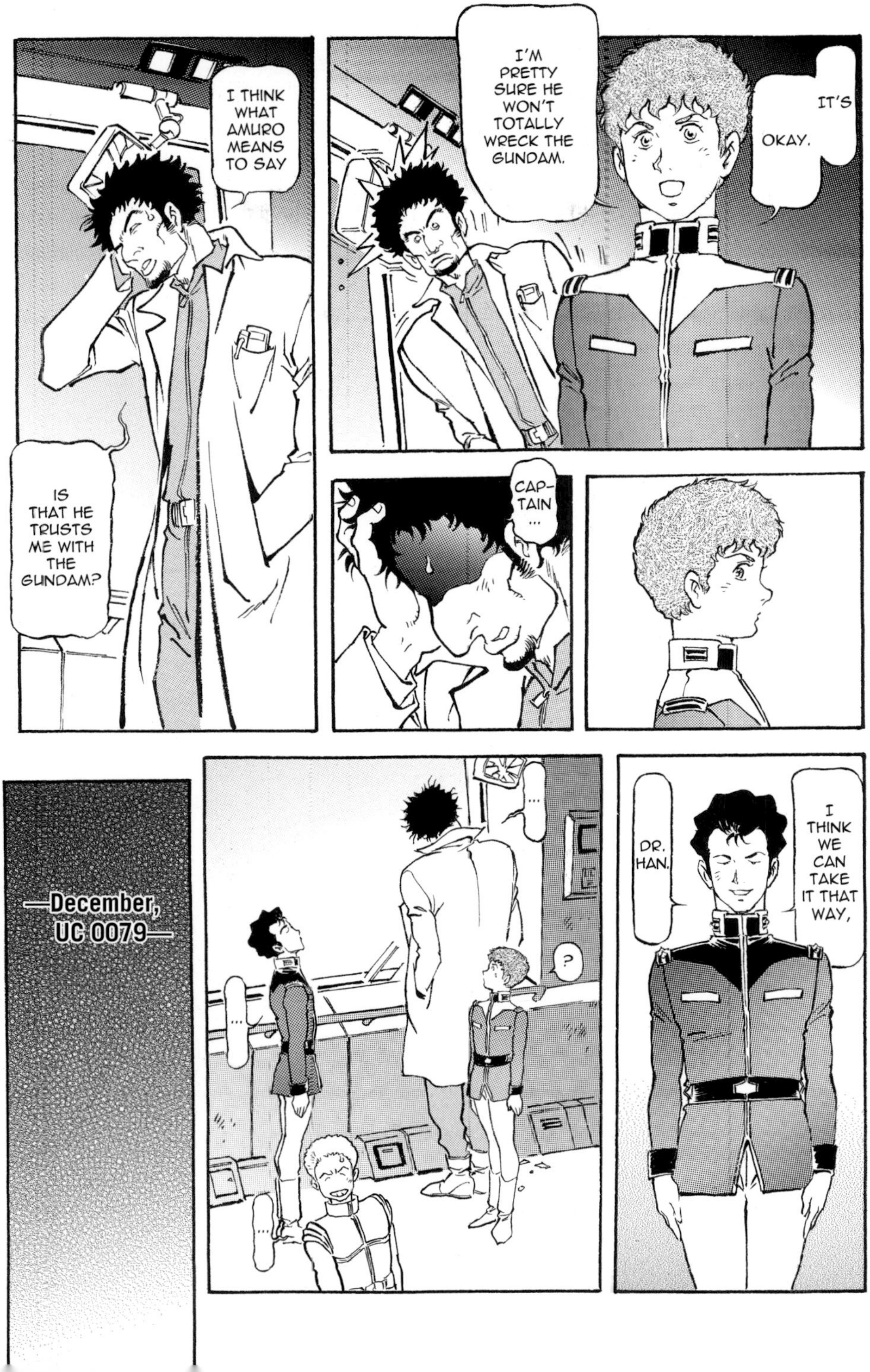
IT'S OKAY.
I'M PRETTY SURE HE WON'T TOTALLY WRECK THE GUNDAM.
I THINK WHAT AMURO MEANS TO SAY
IS THAT HE TRUSTS ME WITH THE GUNDAM?
CAP-TAIN ...
I THINK WE CAN TAKE IT THAT WAY,
DR. HAN.
...
?
...
...
—December, UC 0079—

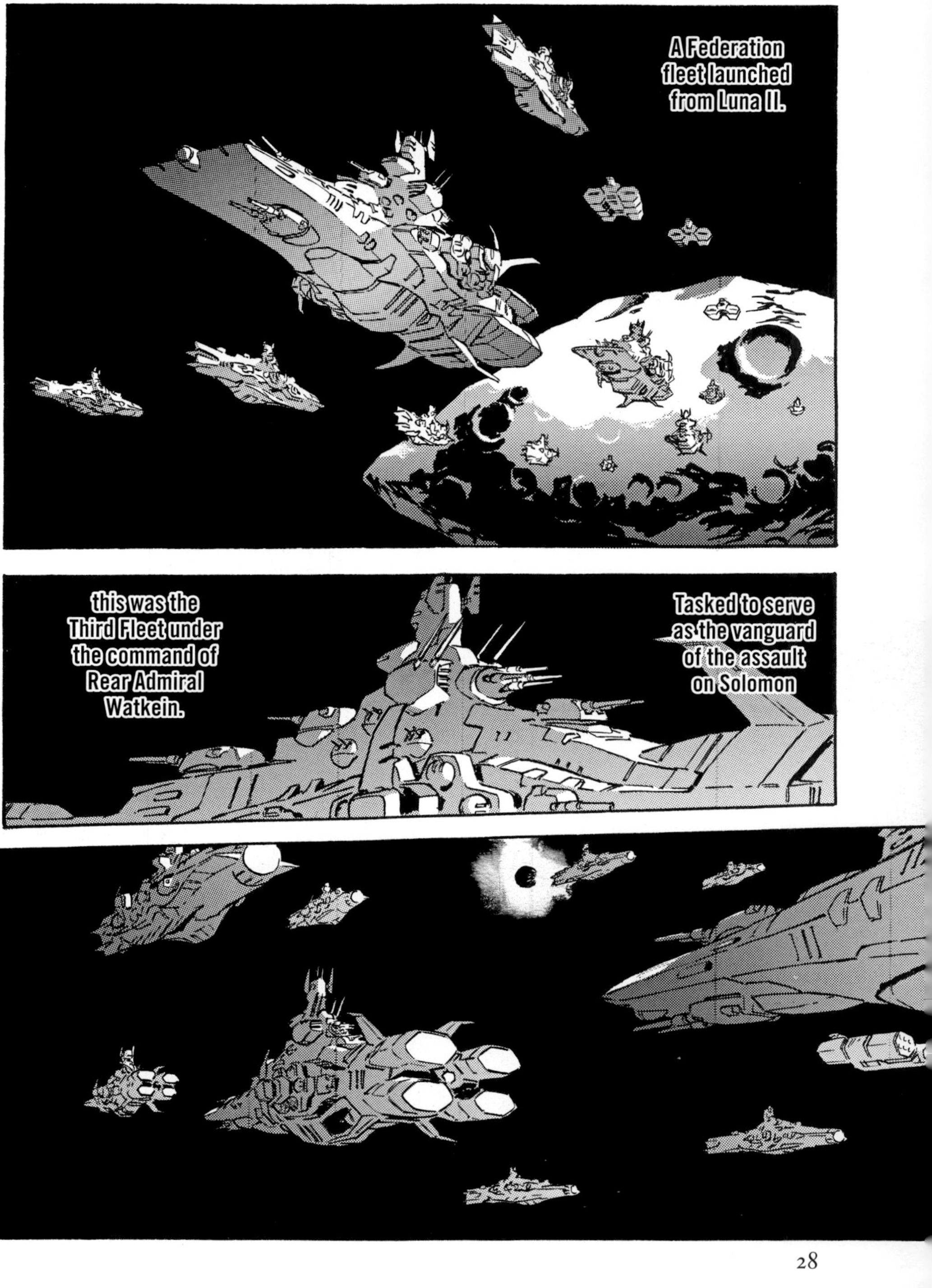
A Federation fleet launched from Luna II.
Tasked to serve as the vanguard of the assault on Solomon
this was the Third Fleet under the command of Rear Admiral Watkein.

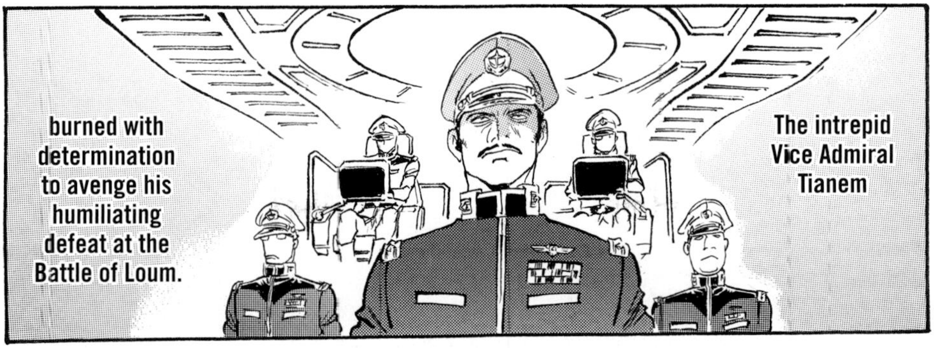
The intrepid Vice Admiral Tianem
burned with determination to avenge his humiliating defeat at the Battle of Loum.
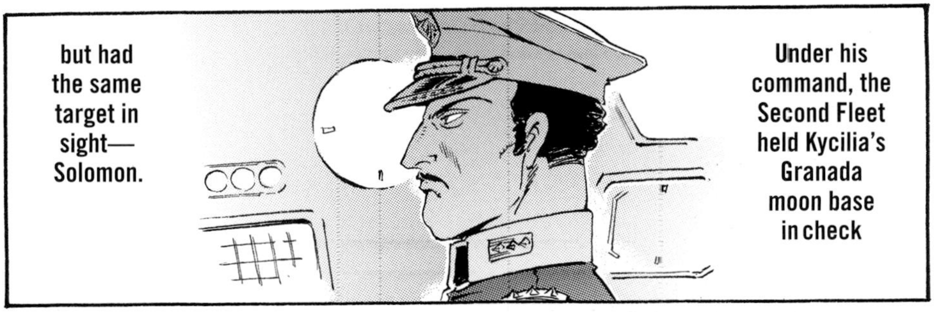
Under his command, the Second Fleet held Kycilia's Granada moon base in check
but had the same target in sight—Solomon.
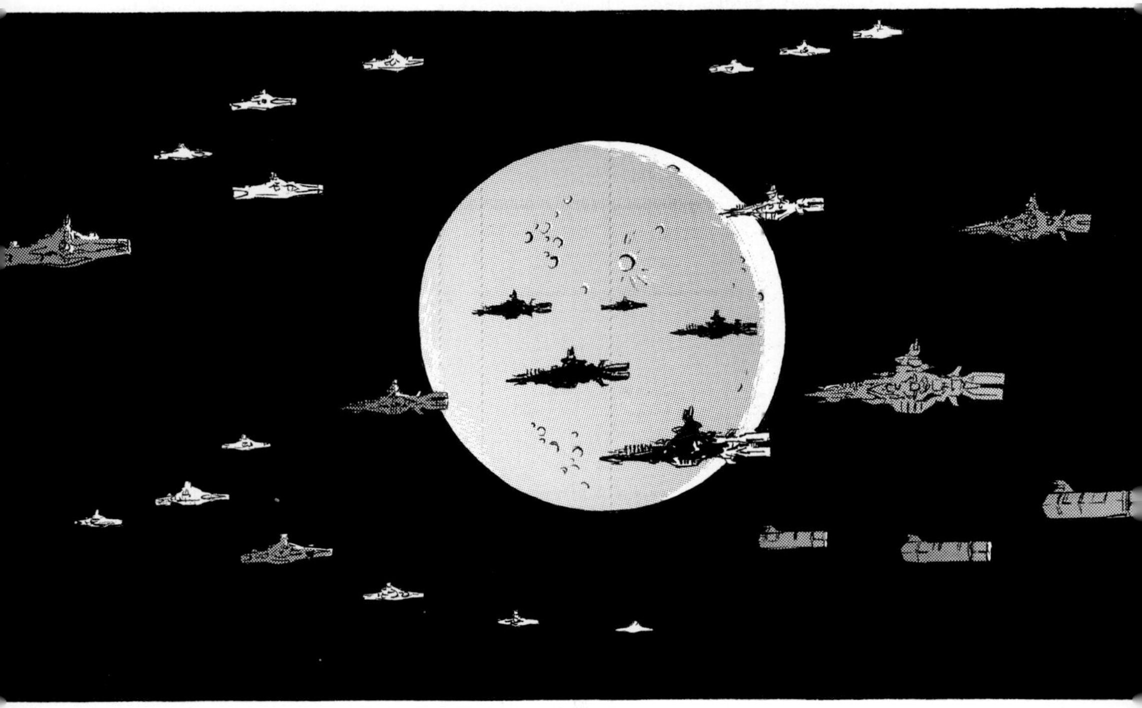

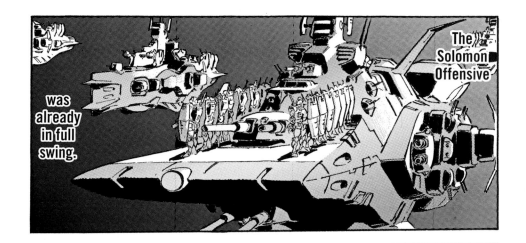

The
Solomon
Offensive

was
already
in full
swing.

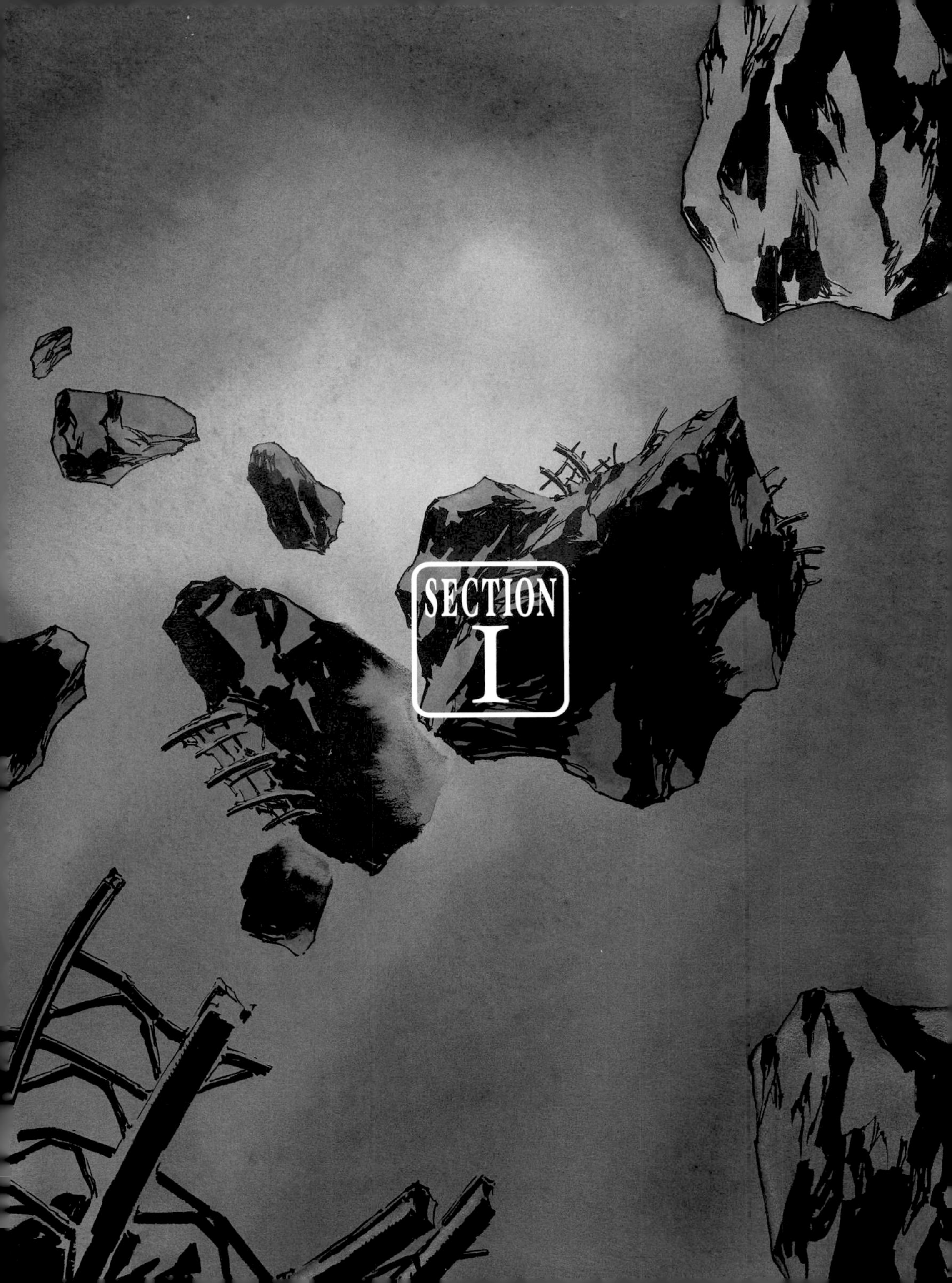
SECTION
I

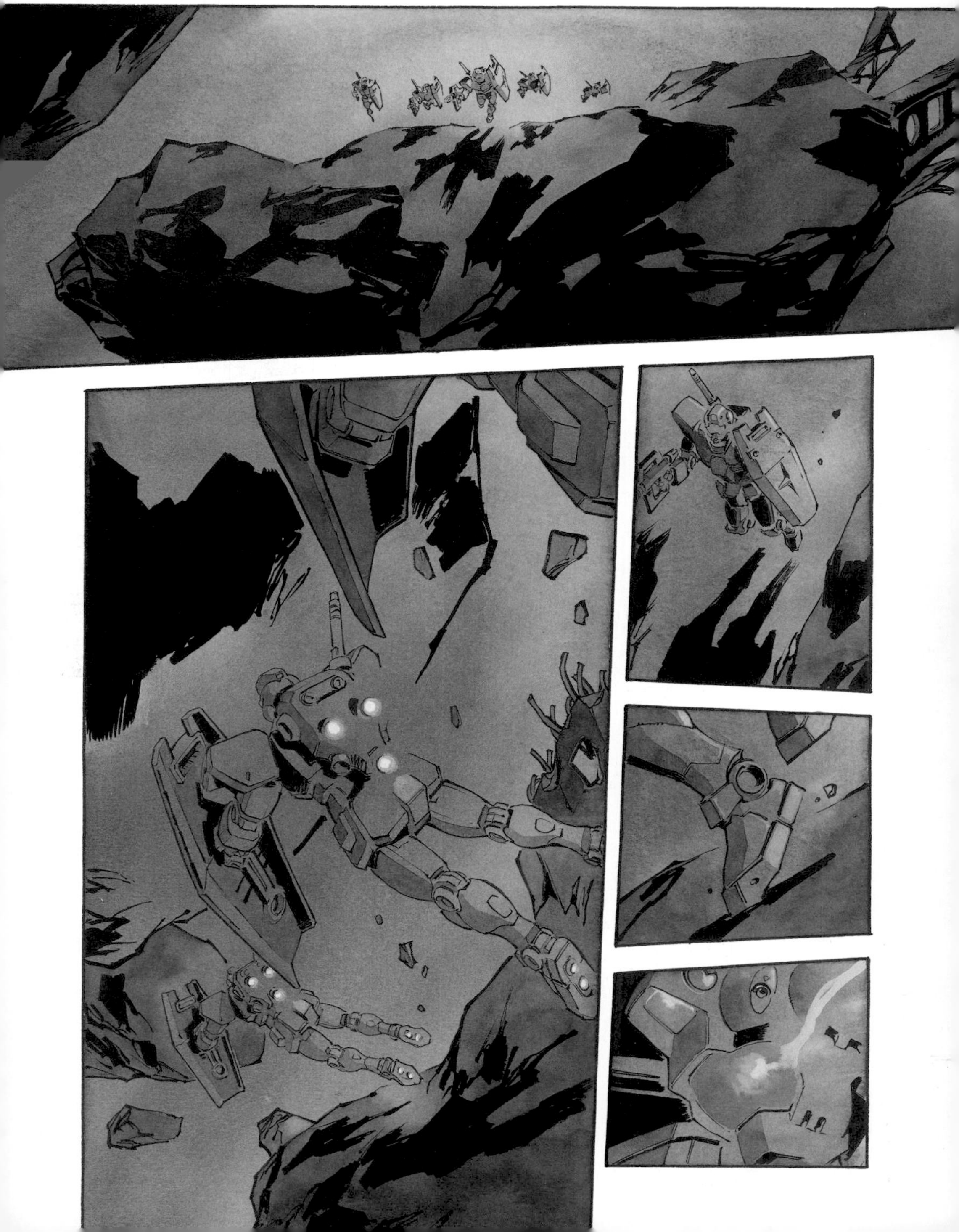

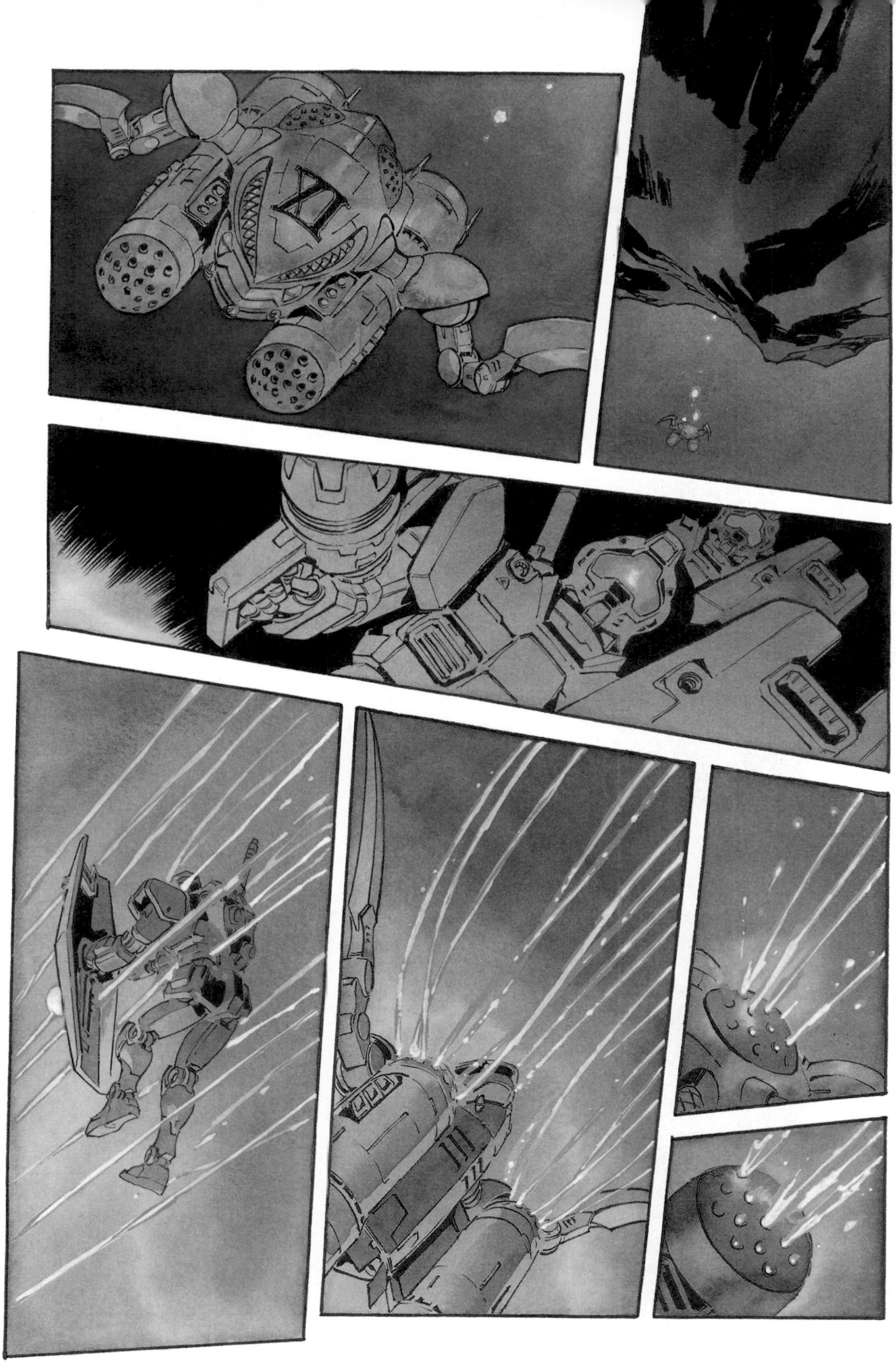

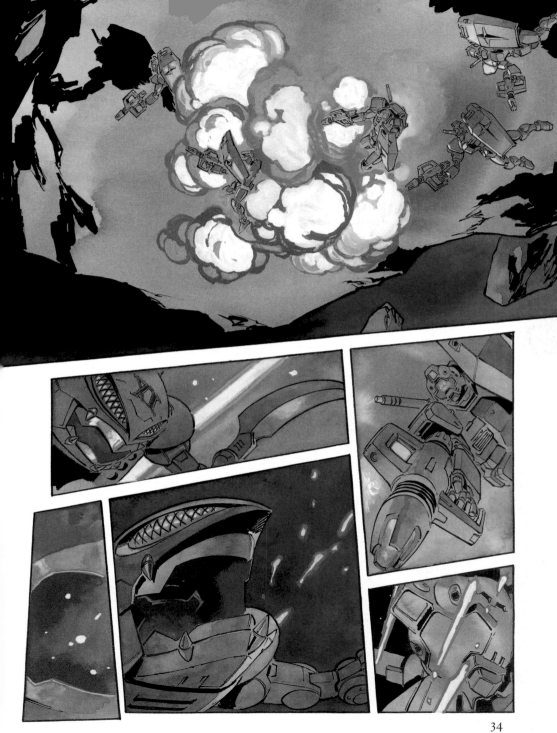

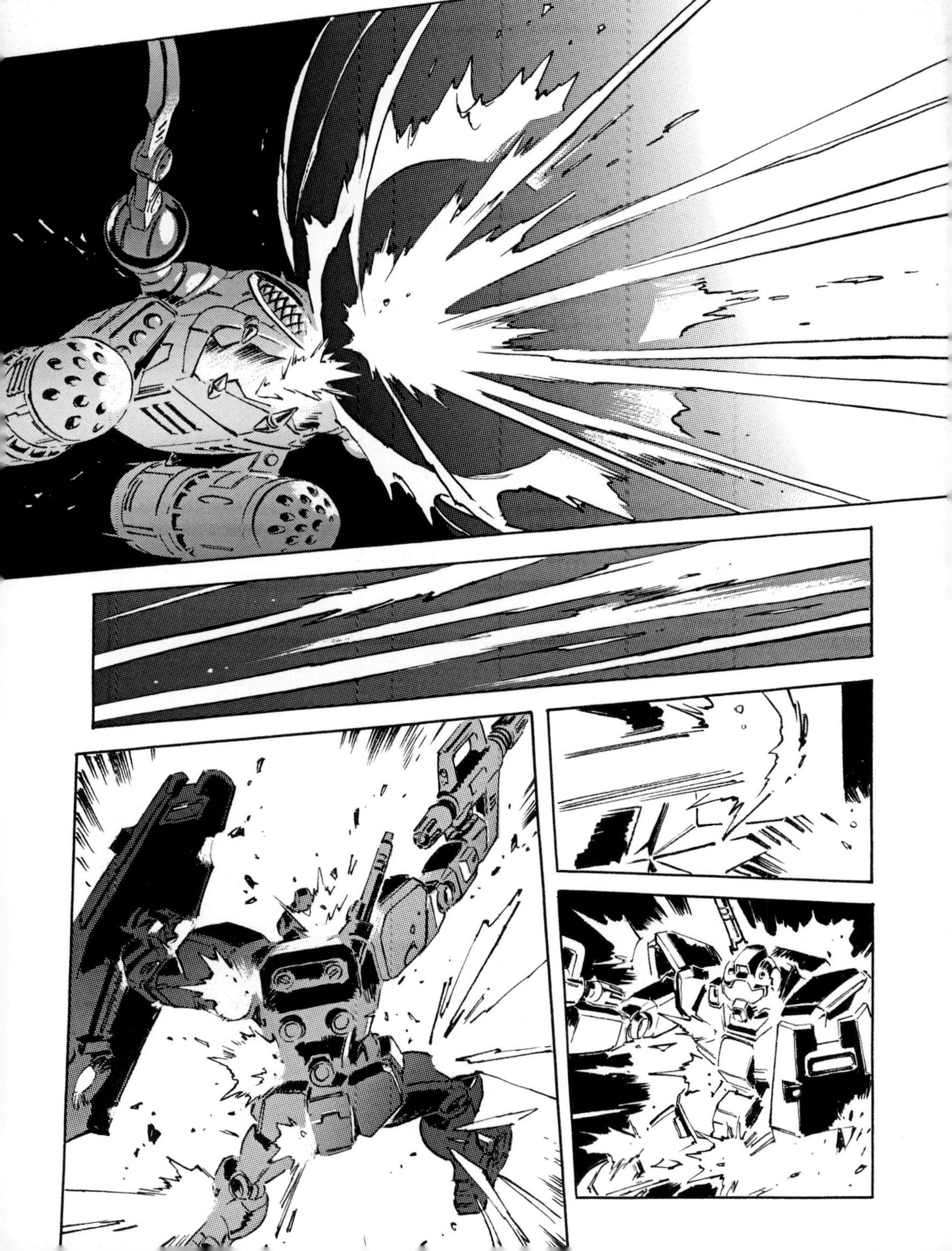

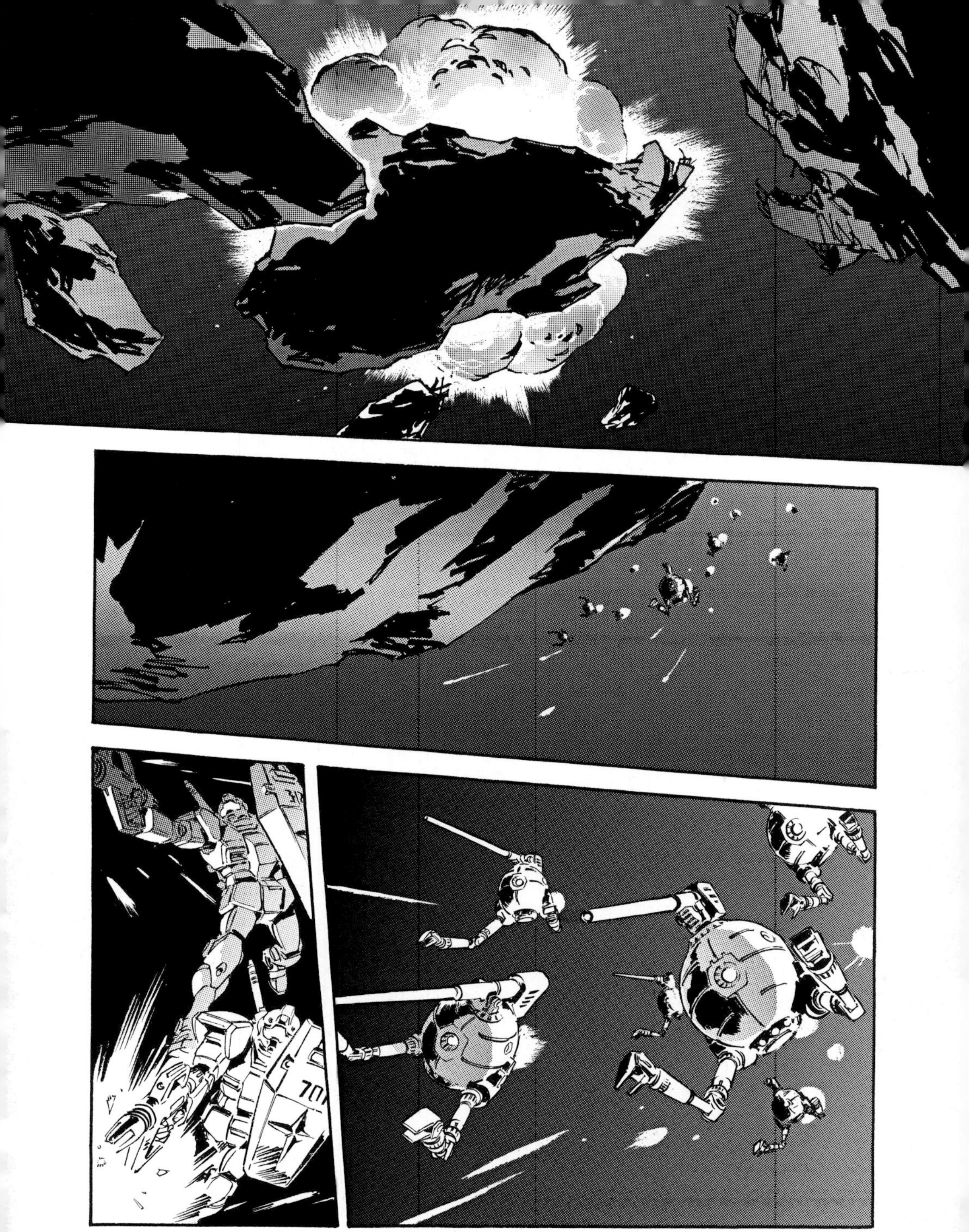
701

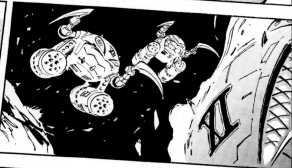

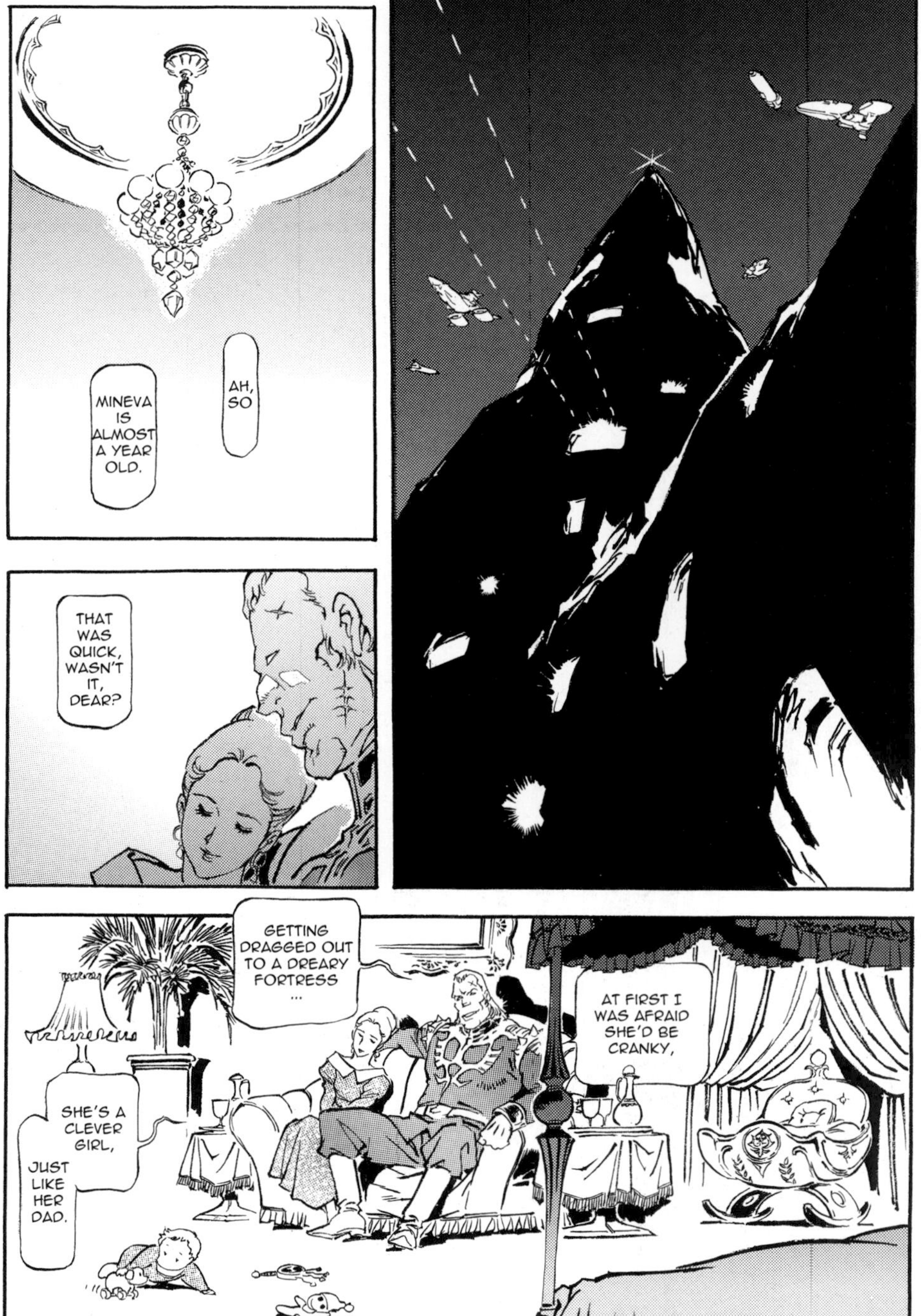
AH, SO
MINEVA IS ALMOST A YEAR OLD.
THAT WAS QUICK, WASN'T IT, DEAR?
AT FIRST I WAS AFRAID SHE'D BE CRANKY,
GETTING DRAGGED OUT TO A DREARY FORTRESS ...
SHE'S A CLEVER GIRL,
JUST LIKE HER DAD.

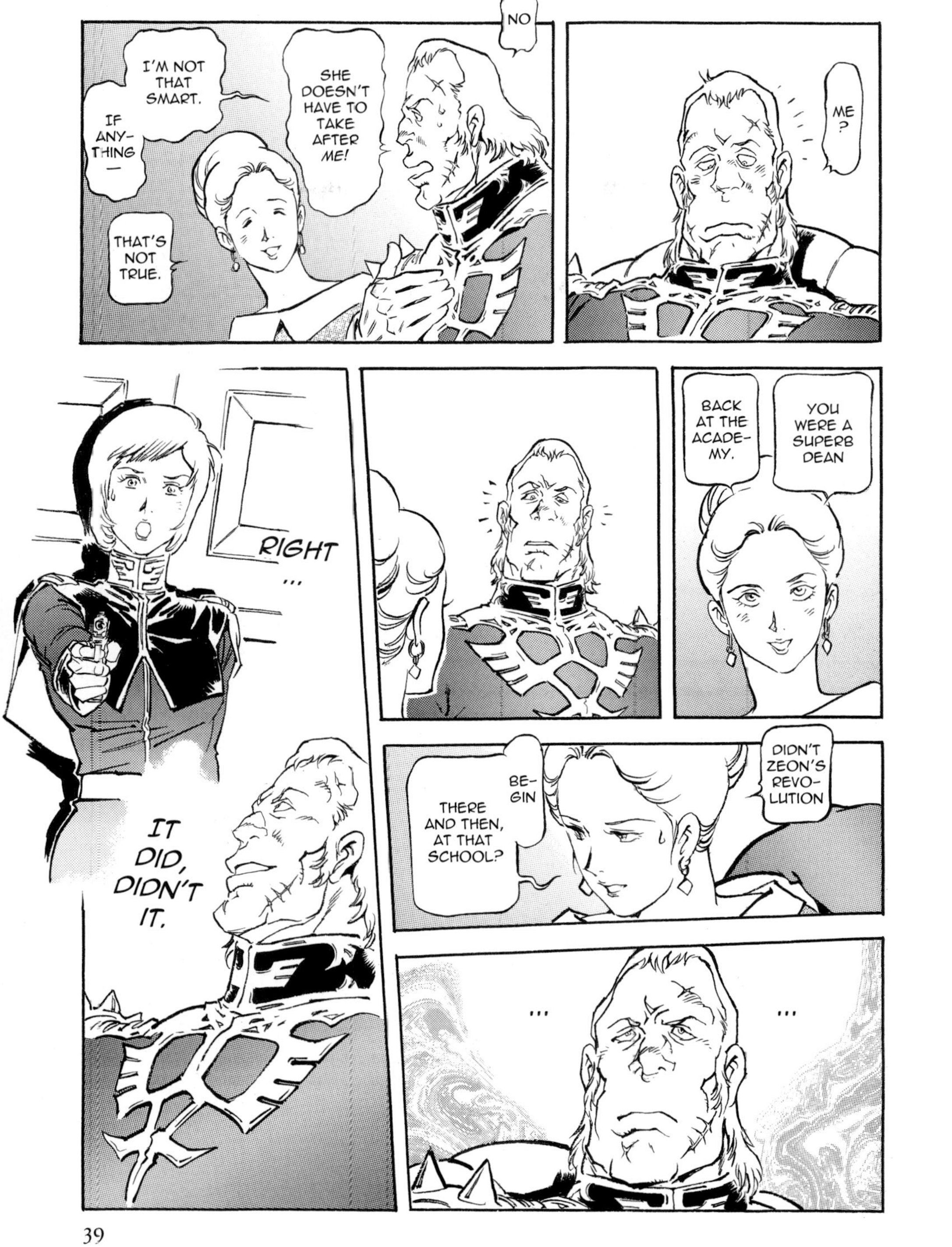
ME?
NO
SHE DOESN'T HAVE TO TAKE AFTER ME!
I'M NOT THAT SMART.
IF ANYTHING—
THAT'S NOT TRUE.
YOU WERE A SUPERB DEAN
BACK AT THE ACADEMY.
DIDN'T ZEON'S REVOLUTION
BEGIN
THERE AND THEN, AT THAT SCHOOL?
...
...
RIGHT ...
IT DID, DIDN'T IT.

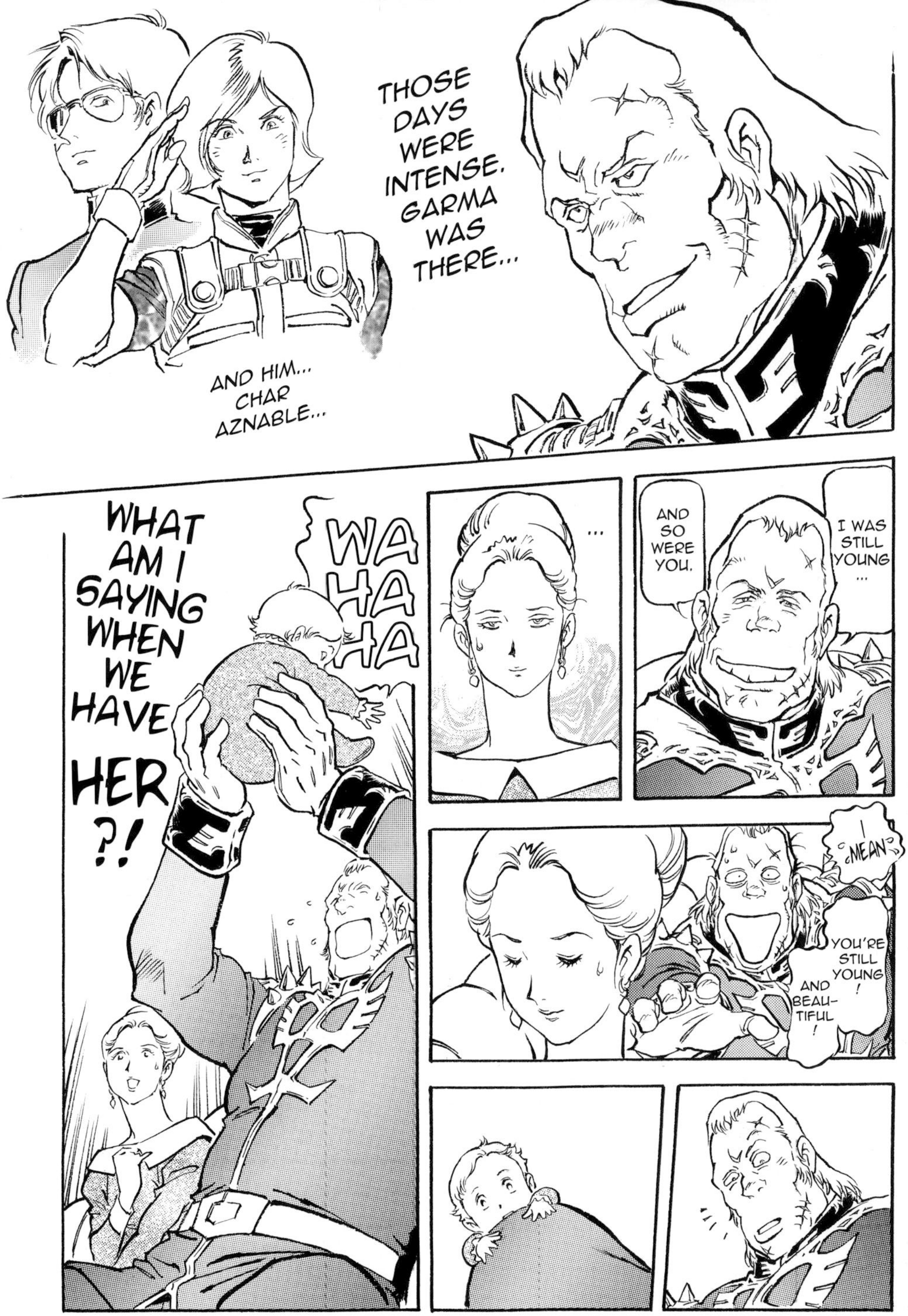
THOSE DAYS WERE INTENSE. GARMA WAS THERE...
AND HIM... CHAR AZNABLE...
I WAS STILL YOUNG...
AND SO WERE YOU.
...
I MEAN
YOU'RE STILL YOUNG!
AND BEAUTIFUL!
WA HA HA
WHAT AM I SAYING WHEN WE HAVE HER?!

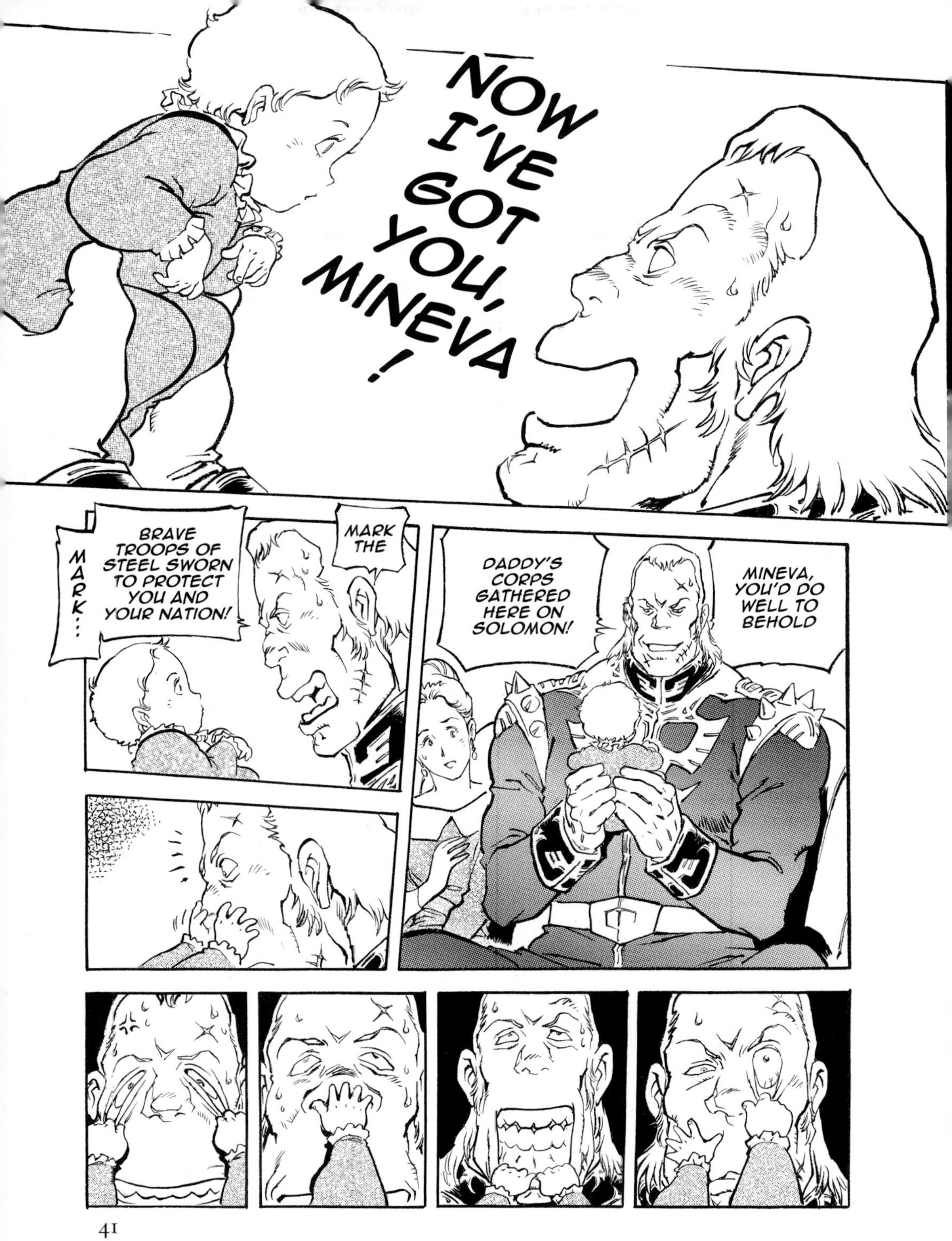
NOW I'VE GOT YOU, MINEVA!
MINEVA, YOU'D DO WELL TO BEHOLD
DADDY'S CORPS GATHERED HERE ON SOLOMON!
MARK THE
BRAVE TROOPS OF STEEL SWORN TO PROTECT YOU AND YOUR NATION!
MARK...

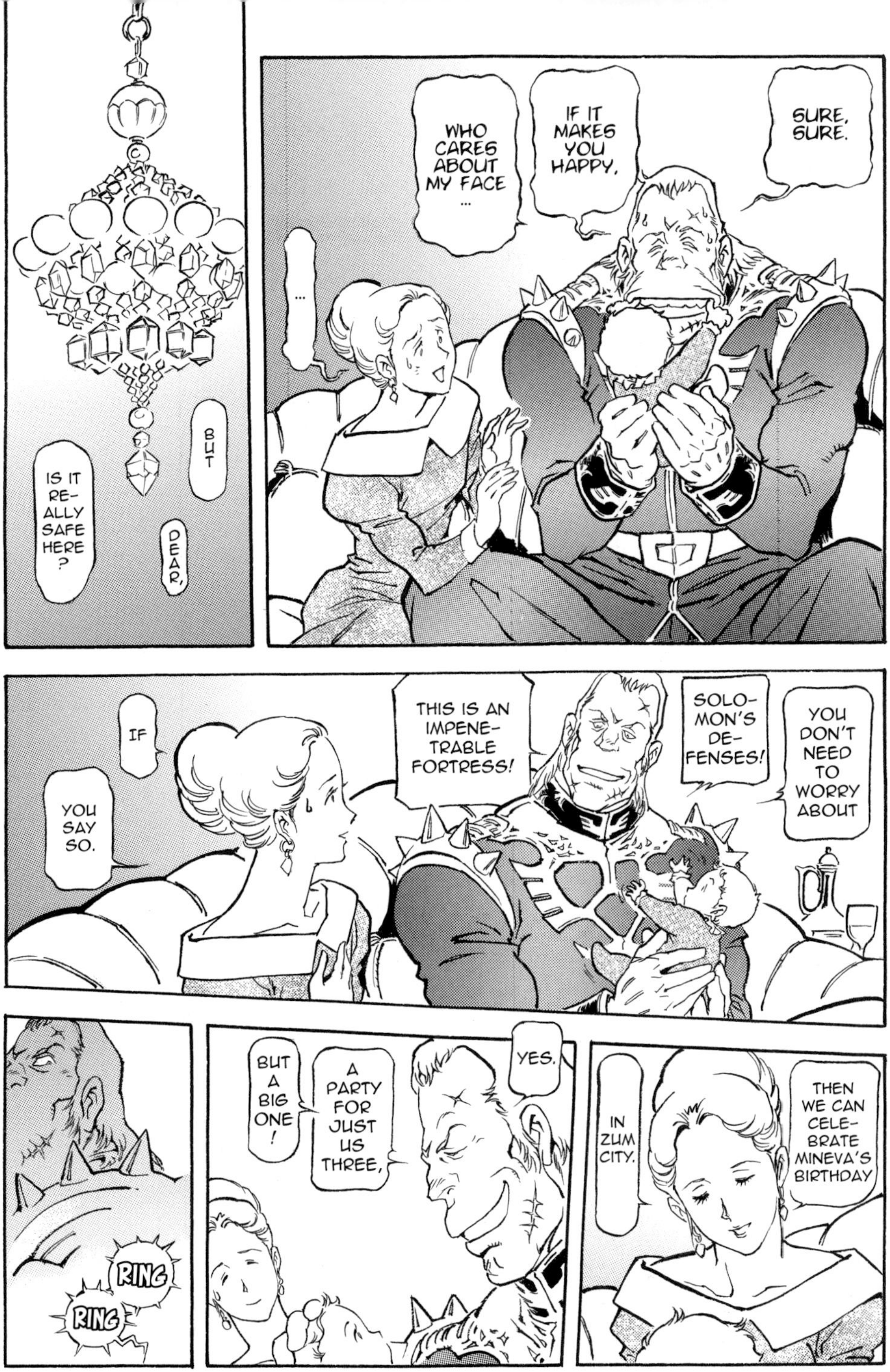
SURE, SURE.
IF IT MAKES YOU HAPPY,
WHO CARES ABOUT MY FACE ...
...
BUT
DEAR,
IS IT RE-ALLY SAFE HERE?
YOU DON'T NEED TO WORRY ABOUT
SOLO-MON'S DE-FENSES!
THIS IS AN IMPENE-TRABLE FORTRESS!
IF
YOU SAY SO.
THEN WE CAN CELE-BRATE MINEVA'S BIRTHDAY
IN ZUM CITY.
YES.
A PARTY FOR JUST US THREE,
BUT A BIG ONE!
RING
RING

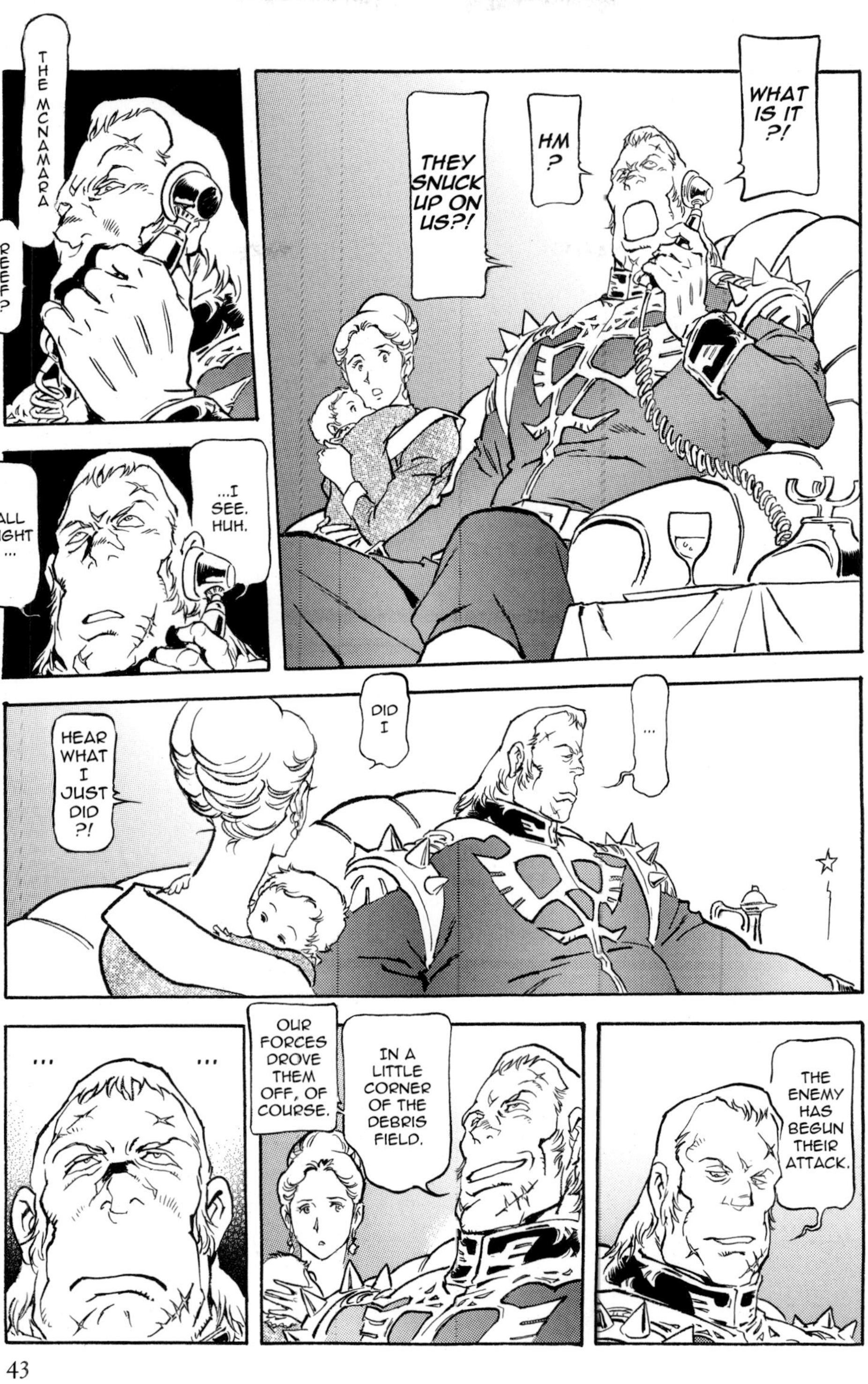
WHAT IS IT ?!
HM ?
THEY SNUCK UP ON US?!
THE MCNAMARA REEF?
...I SEE. HUH.
ALL RIGHT ...
...
DID I
HEAR WHAT I JUST DID ?!
THE ENEMY HAS BEGUN THEIR ATTACK.
IN A LITTLE CORNER OF THE DEBRIS FIELD.
OUR FORCES DROVE THEM OFF, OF COURSE.
... ...

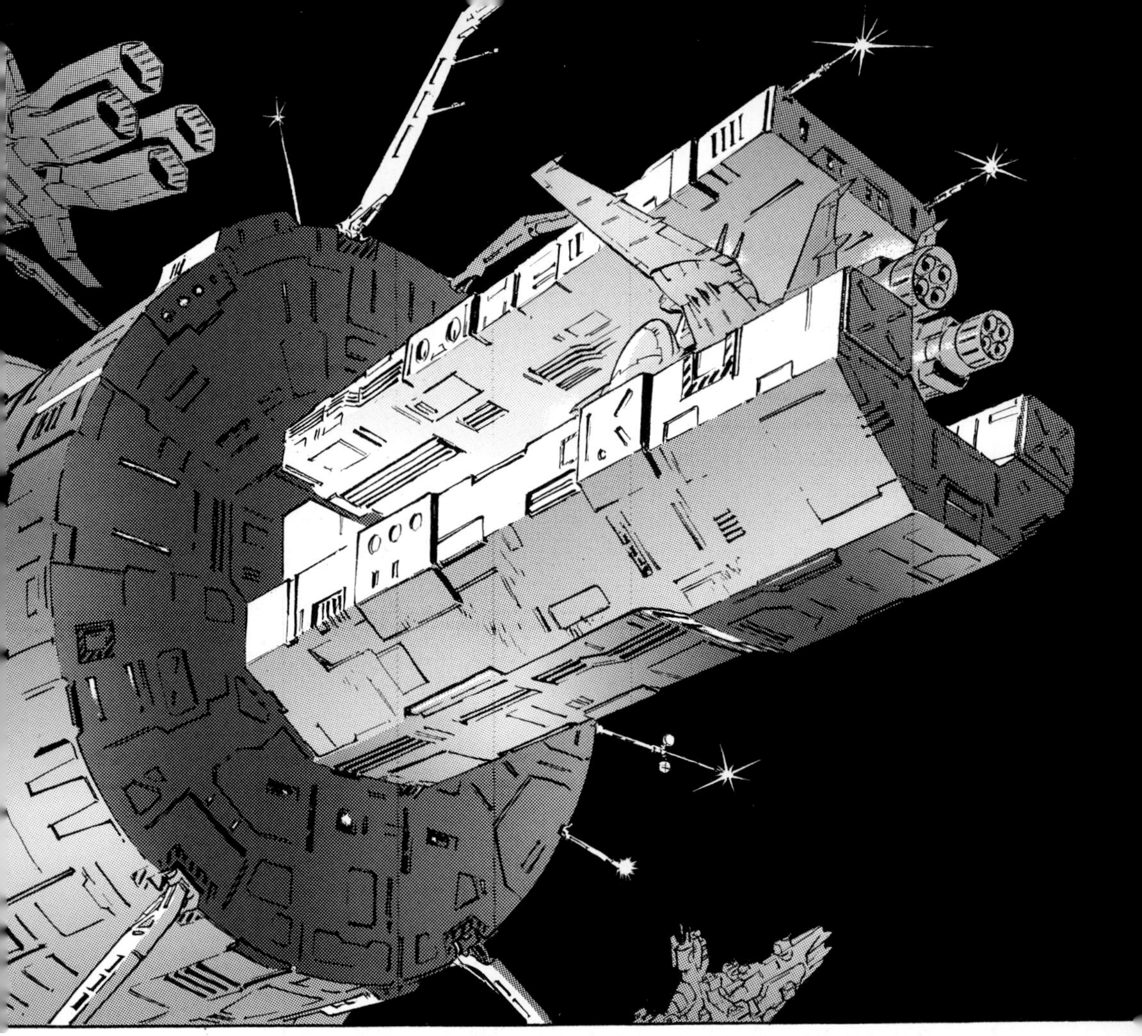

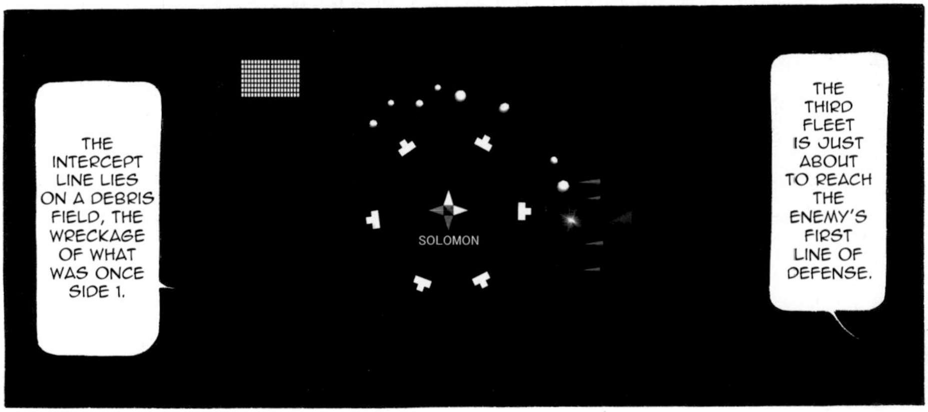
THE THIRD FLEET IS JUST ABOUT TO REACH THE ENEMY'S FIRST LINE OF DEFENSE.
SOLOMON
THE INTERCEPT LINE LIES ON A DEBRIS FIELD, THE WRECKAGE OF WHAT WAS ONCE SIDE 1.

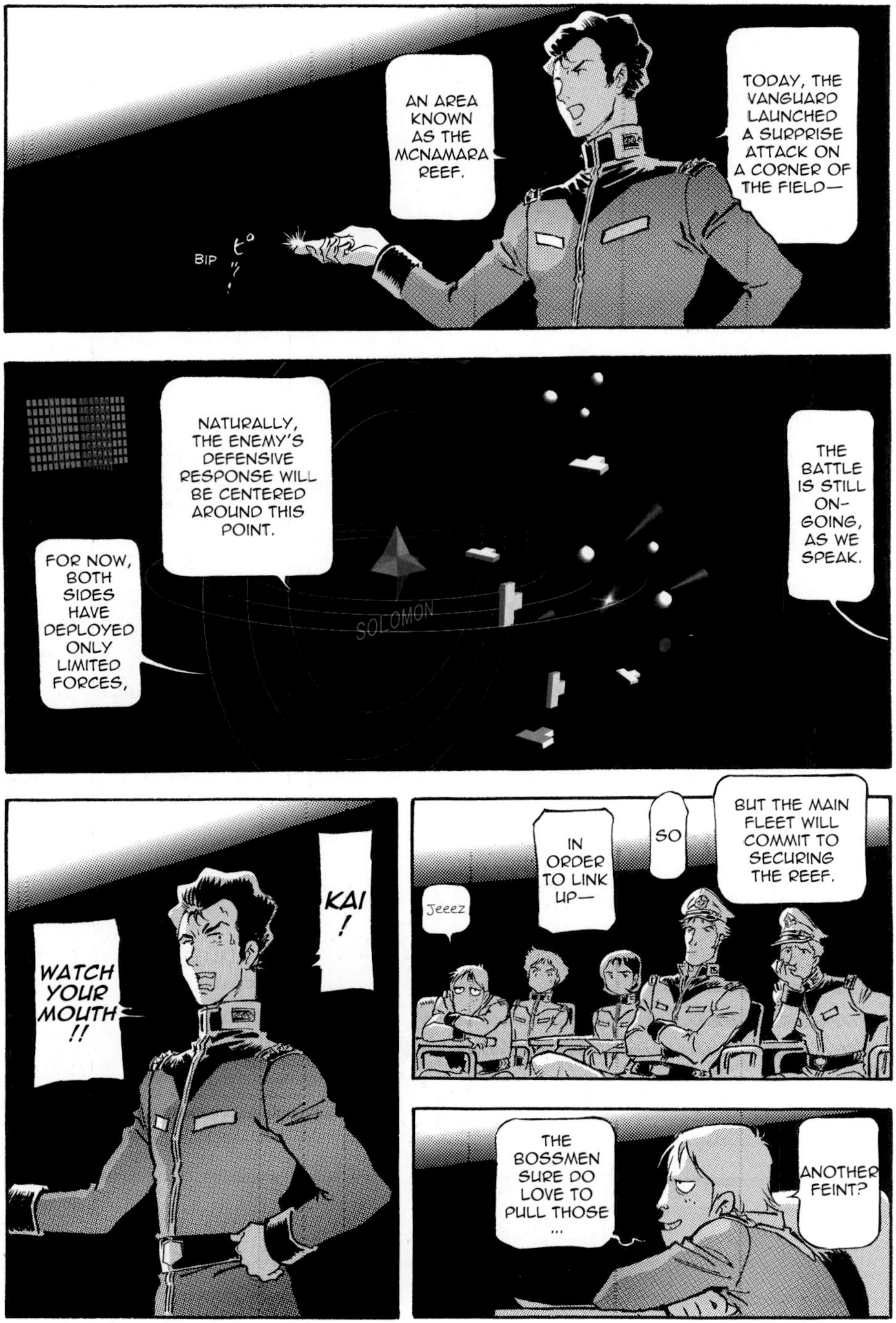
TODAY, THE VANGUARD LAUNCHED A SURPRISE ATTACK ON A CORNER OF THE FIELD—
AN AREA KNOWN AS THE MCNAMARA REEF.
BIP
THE BATTLE IS STILL ON-GOING, AS WE SPEAK.
NATURALLY, THE ENEMY'S DEFENSIVE RESPONSE WILL BE CENTERED AROUND THIS POINT.
SOLOMON
FOR NOW, BOTH SIDES HAVE DEPLOYED ONLY LIMITED FORCES,
BUT THE MAIN FLEET WILL COMMIT TO SECURING THE REEF.
SO
IN ORDER TO LINK UP—
Jeeez
ANOTHER FEINT?
THE BOSSMEN SURE DO LOVE TO PULL THOSE ...
KAI!
WATCH YOUR MOUTH!!

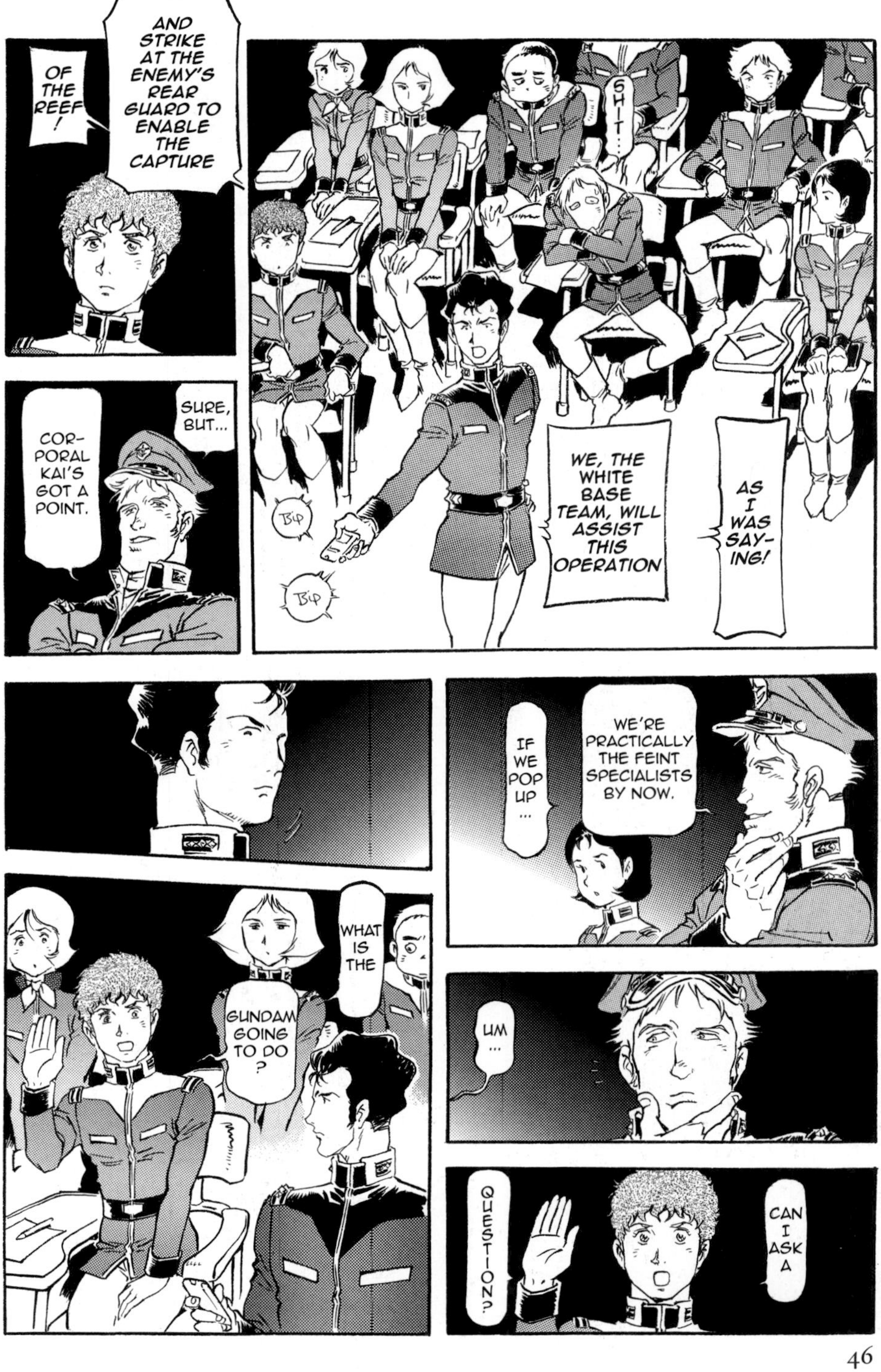
SHIT...
AS I WAS SAYING!
WE, THE WHITE BASE TEAM, WILL ASSIST THIS OPERATION
Bip
Bip
AND STRIKE AT THE ENEMY'S REAR GUARD TO ENABLE THE CAPTURE
OF THE REEF!
SURE, BUT...
CORPORAL KAI'S GOT A POINT.
WE'RE PRACTICALLY THE FEINT SPECIALISTS BY NOW.
IF WE POP UP ...
UM ...
CAN I ASK A QUESTION?
WHAT IS THE GUNDAM GOING TO DO?

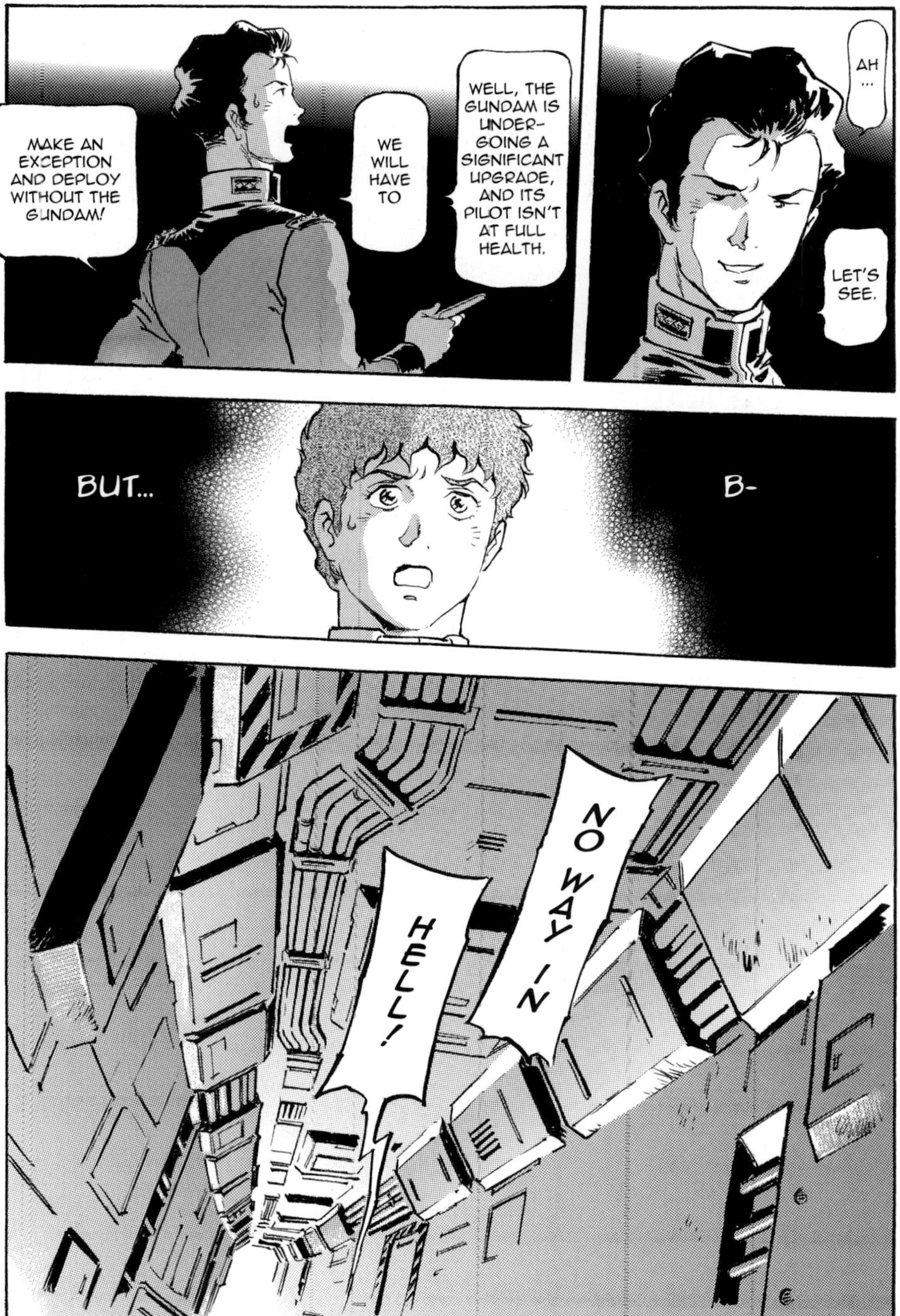
AH ...
LET'S SEE.
WELL, THE GUNDAM IS UNDERGOING A SIGNIFICANT UPGRADE, AND ITS PILOT ISN'T AT FULL HEALTH.
WE WILL HAVE TO
MAKE AN EXCEPTION AND DEPLOY WITHOUT THE GUNDAM!
B-
BUT...
NO WAY IN
HELL!

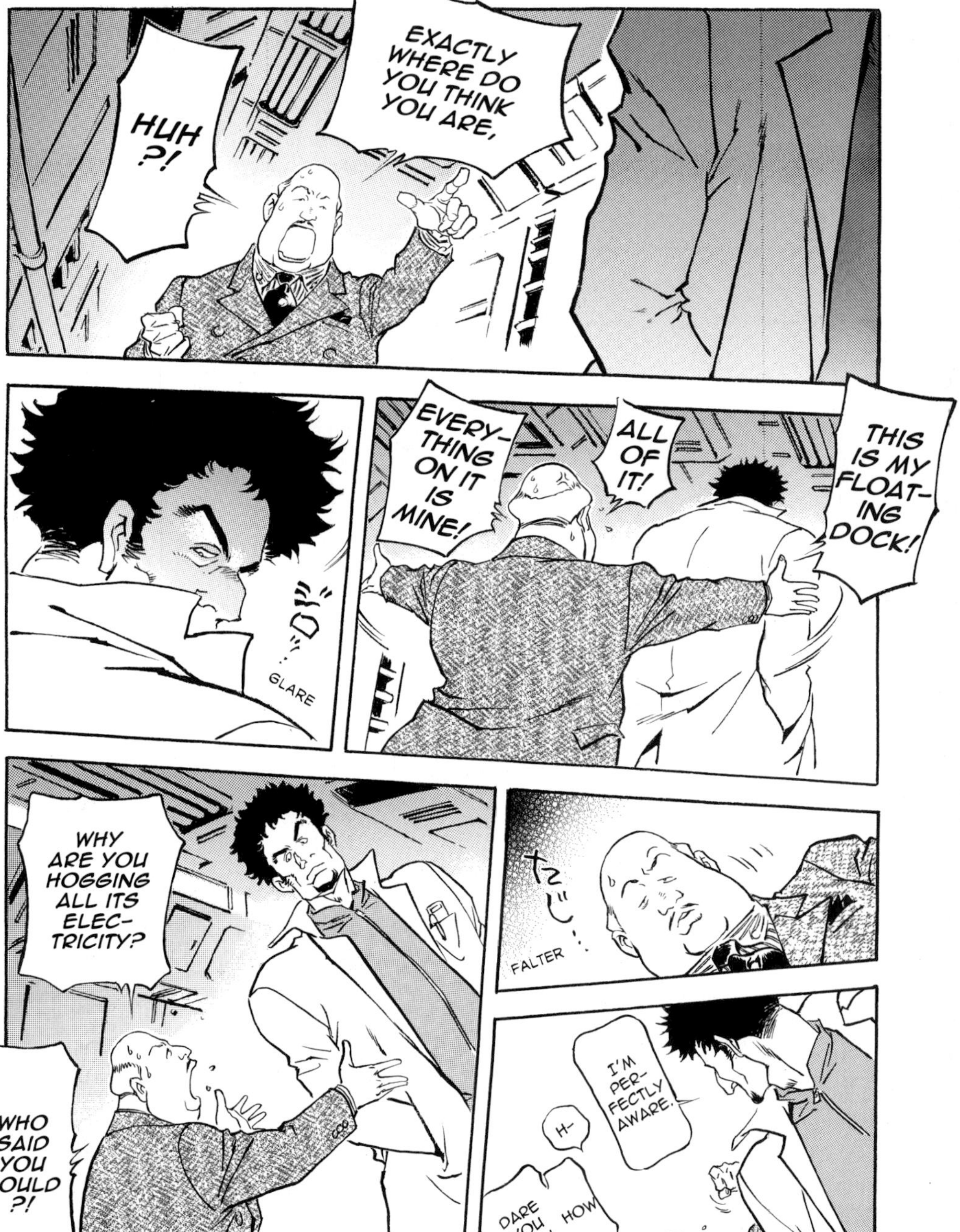
EXACTLY WHERE DO YOU THINK YOU ARE,
HUH ?!
THIS IS MY FLOAT-ING DOCK!
ALL OF IT!
EVERY-THING ON IT IS MINE!
GLARE
たじ…
FALTER
I'M PER-FECTLY AWARE.
H-
HOW DARE YOU THEN ?
WHY ARE YOU HOGGING ALL ITS ELEC-TRICITY?
WHO SAID YOU COULD ?!

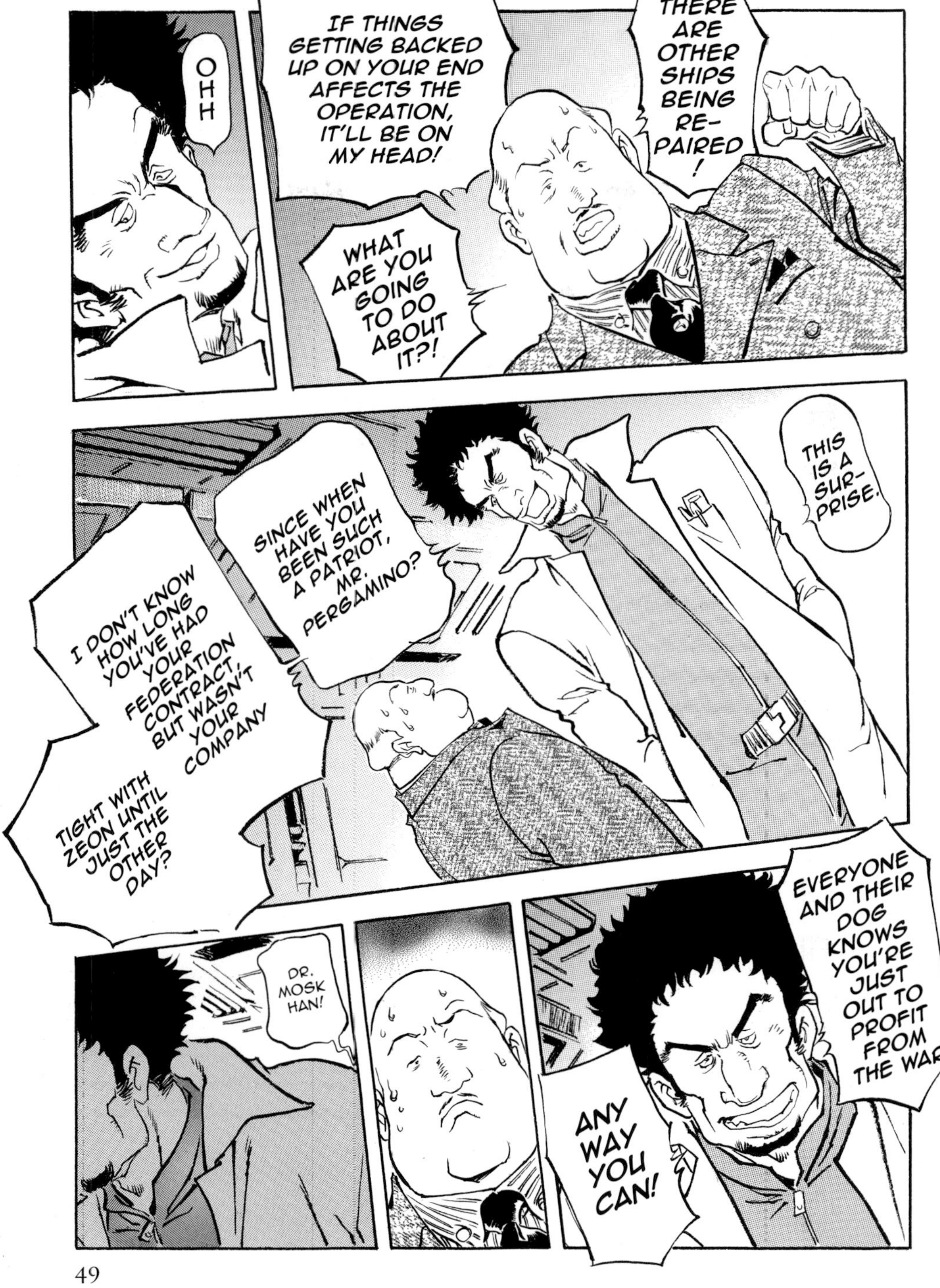
THERE ARE OTHER SHIPS BEING RE-PAIRED!
IF THINGS GETTING BACKED UP ON YOUR END AFFECTS THE OPERATION, IT'LL BE ON MY HEAD!
WHAT ARE YOU GOING TO DO ABOUT IT?!
OHH
THIS IS A SUR-PRISE.
SINCE WHEN HAVE YOU BEEN SUCH A PATRIOT, MR. PERGAMINO?
I DON'T KNOW HOW LONG YOU'VE HAD YOUR FEDERATION CONTRACT, BUT WASN'T YOUR COMPANY
TIGHT WITH ZEON UNTIL JUST THE OTHER DAY?
EVERYONE AND THEIR DOG KNOWS YOU'RE JUST OUT TO PROFIT FROM THE WAR
ANY WAY YOU CAN!
DR. MOSK HAN!

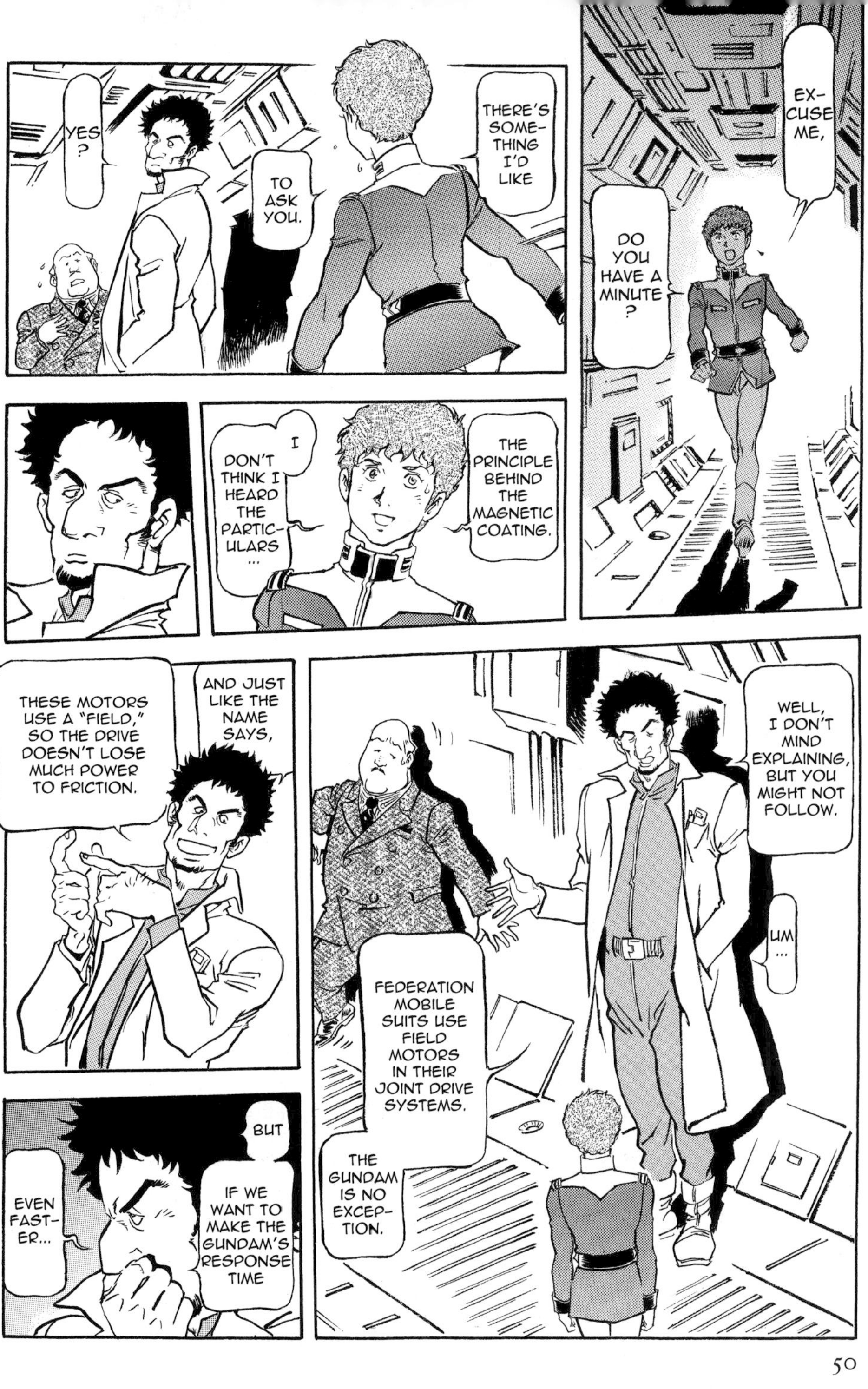
EXCUSE ME,
DO YOU HAVE A MINUTE?
THERE'S SOMETHING I'D LIKE
TO ASK YOU.
YES?
THE PRINCIPLE BEHIND THE MAGNETIC COATING.
I DON'T THINK I HEARD THE PARTICULARS...
WELL, I DON'T MIND EXPLAINING, BUT YOU MIGHT NOT FOLLOW.
UM...
FEDERATION MOBILE SUITS USE FIELD MOTORS IN THEIR JOINT DRIVE SYSTEMS.
THE GUNDAM IS NO EXCEPTION.
AND JUST LIKE THE NAME SAYS,
THESE MOTORS USE A "FIELD," SO THE DRIVE DOESN'T LOSE MUCH POWER TO FRICTION.
BUT
IF WE WANT TO MAKE THE GUNDAM'S RESPONSE TIME
EVEN FASTER...

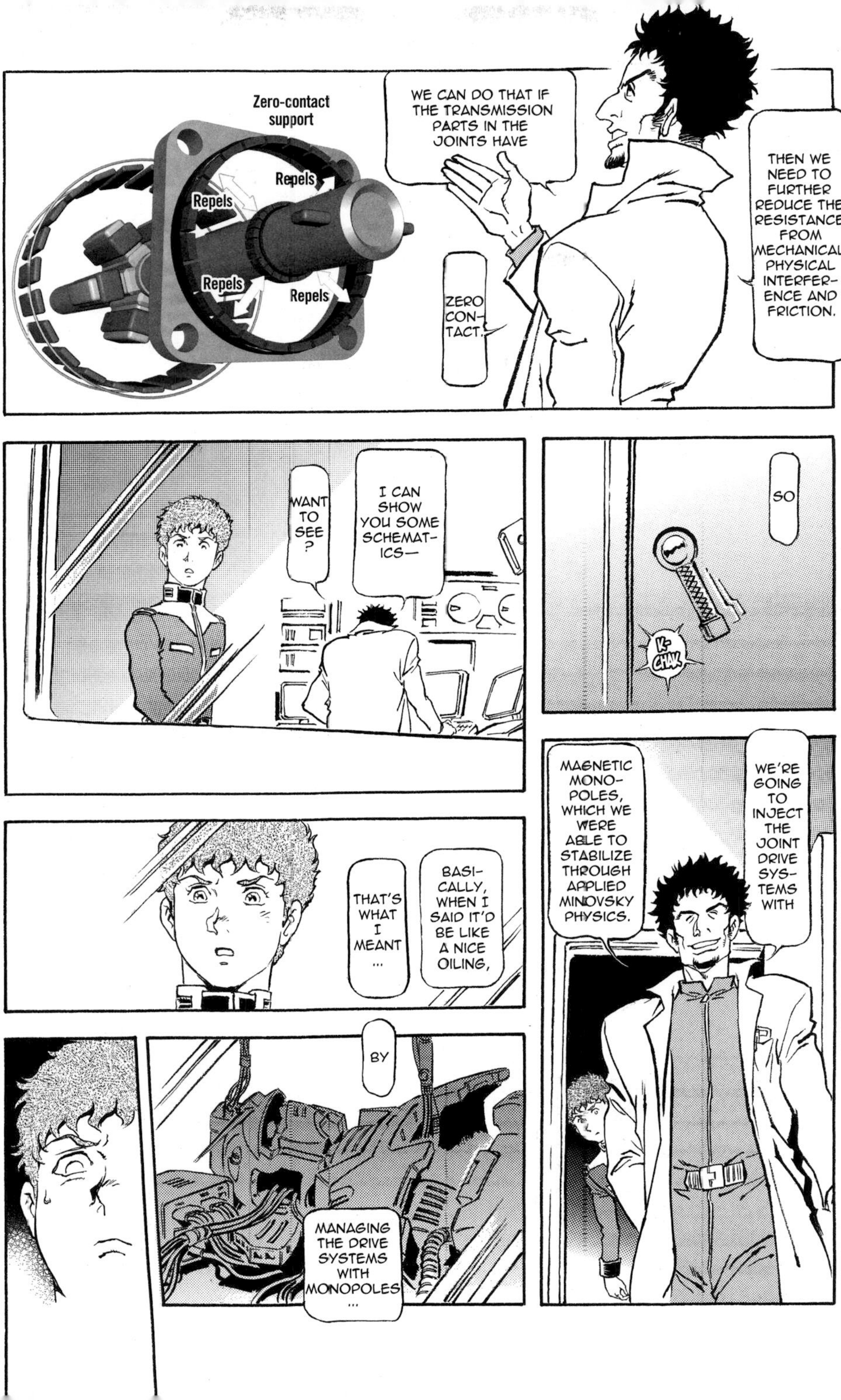

THEN WE NEED TO FURTHER REDUCE THE RESISTANCE FROM MECHANICAL, PHYSICAL INTERFERENCE AND FRICTION.
WE CAN DO THAT IF THE TRANSMISSION PARTS IN THE JOINTS HAVE
ZERO CONTACT.
Zero-contact support
Repels
Repels
Repels
Repels
I CAN SHOW YOU SOME SCHEMATICS—
WANT TO SEE?
SO
K-CHAK
WE'RE GOING TO INJECT THE JOINT DRIVE SYSTEMS WITH
MAGNETIC MONOPOLES, WHICH WE WERE ABLE TO STABILIZE THROUGH APPLIED MINOVSKY PHYSICS.
BASICALLY, WHEN I SAID IT'D BE LIKE A NICE OILING,
THAT'S WHAT I MEANT...
BY
MANAGING THE DRIVE SYSTEMS WITH MONOPOLES...

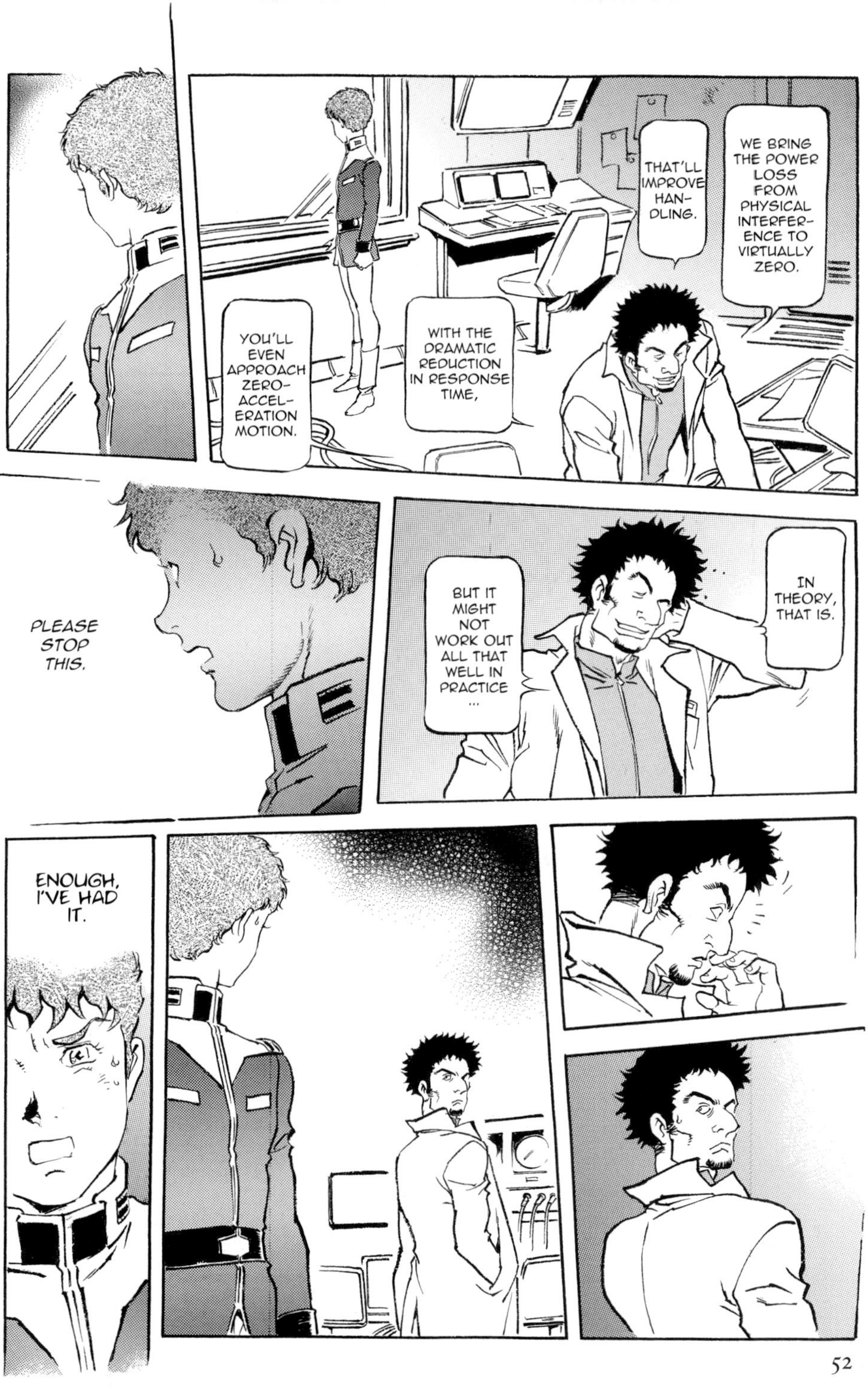
WE BRING THE POWER LOSS FROM PHYSICAL INTERFERENCE TO VIRTUALLY ZERO.
THAT'LL IMPROVE HAN-DLING.
WITH THE DRAMATIC REDUCTION IN RESPONSE TIME,
YOU'LL EVEN APPROACH ZERO-ACCEL-ERATION MOTION.
IN THEORY, THAT IS.
BUT IT MIGHT NOT WORK OUT ALL THAT WELL IN PRACTICE ...
PLEASE STOP THIS.
ENOUGH, I'VE HAD IT.

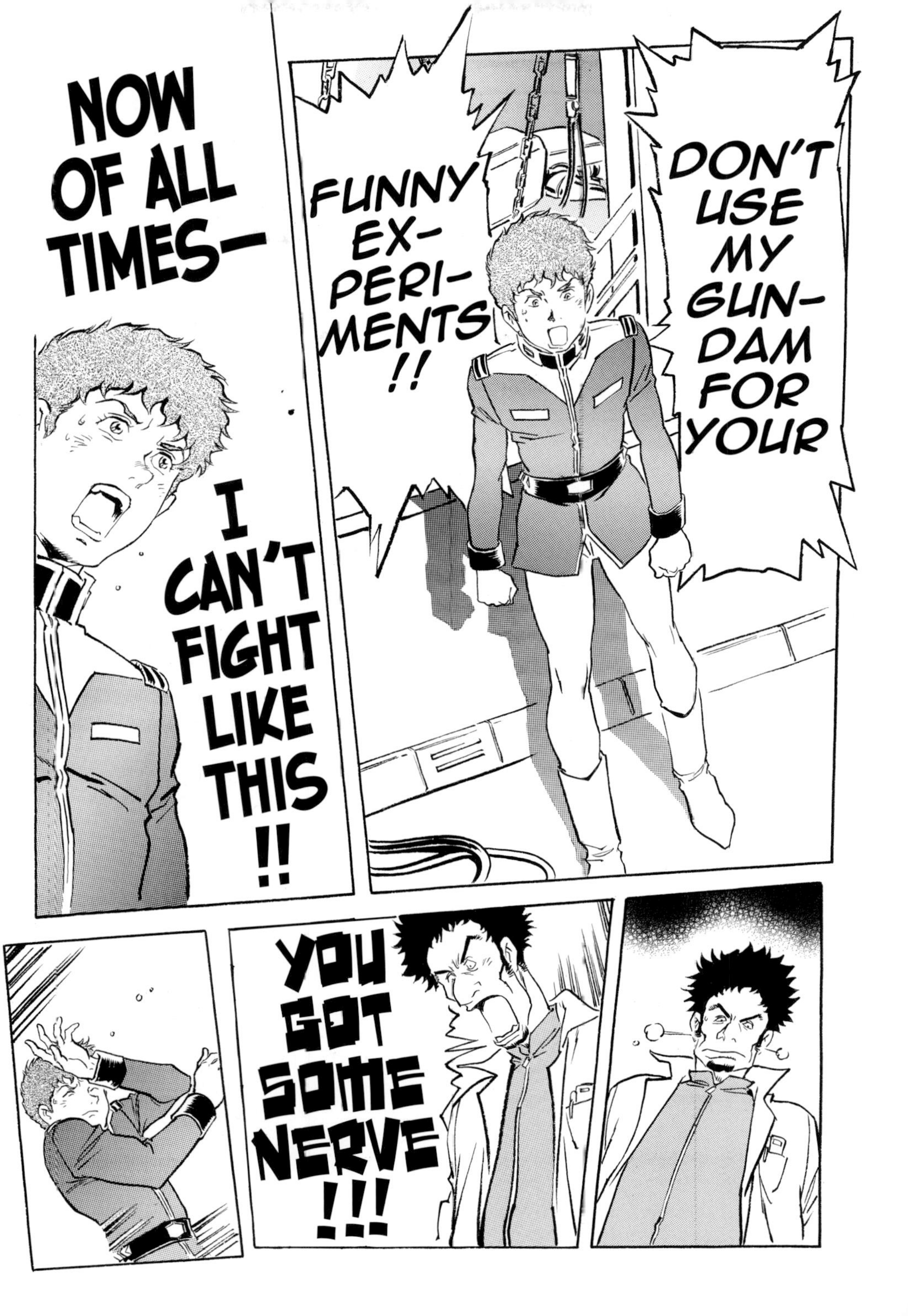
DON'T USE MY GUNDAM FOR YOUR
FUNNY EXPERIMENTS!!
NOW OF ALL TIMES—
I CAN'T FIGHT LIKE THIS!!
YOU GOT SOME NERVE!!!

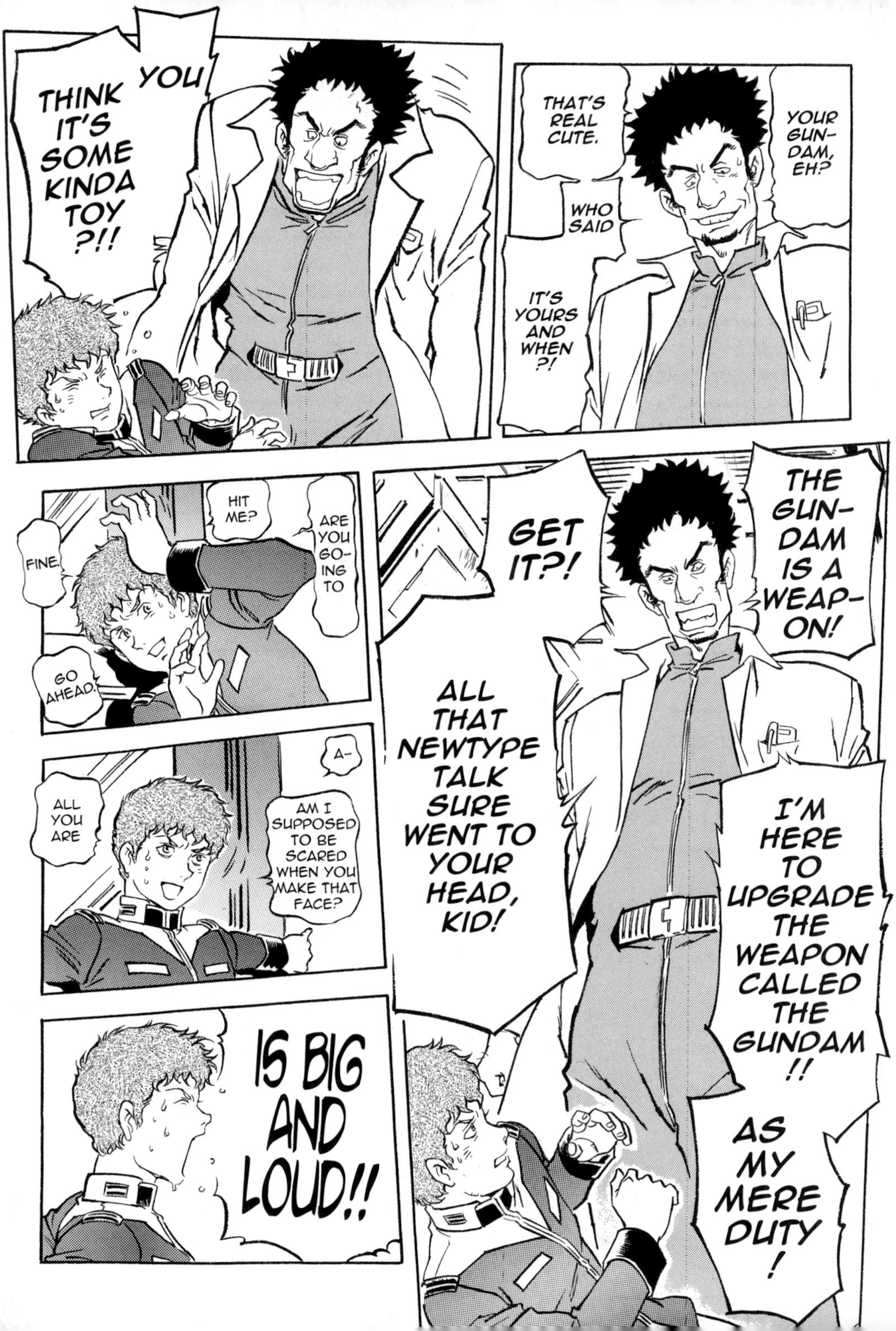

YOUR GUN-DAM, EH?
THAT'S REAL CUTE.
WHO SAID
IT'S YOURS AND WHEN ?!
YOU
THINK IT'S SOME KINDA TOY ?!!
THE GUN-DAM IS A WEAP-ON!
GET IT?!
ALL THAT NEWTYPE TALK SURE WENT TO YOUR HEAD, KID!
I'M HERE TO UPGRADE THE WEAPON CALLED THE GUNDAM !!
AS MY MERE DUTY !
ARE YOU GO-ING TO
HIT ME?
FINE.
GO AHEAD.
A-
AM I SUPPOSED TO BE SCARED WHEN YOU MAKE THAT FACE?
ALL YOU ARE
IS BIG AND LOUD!!

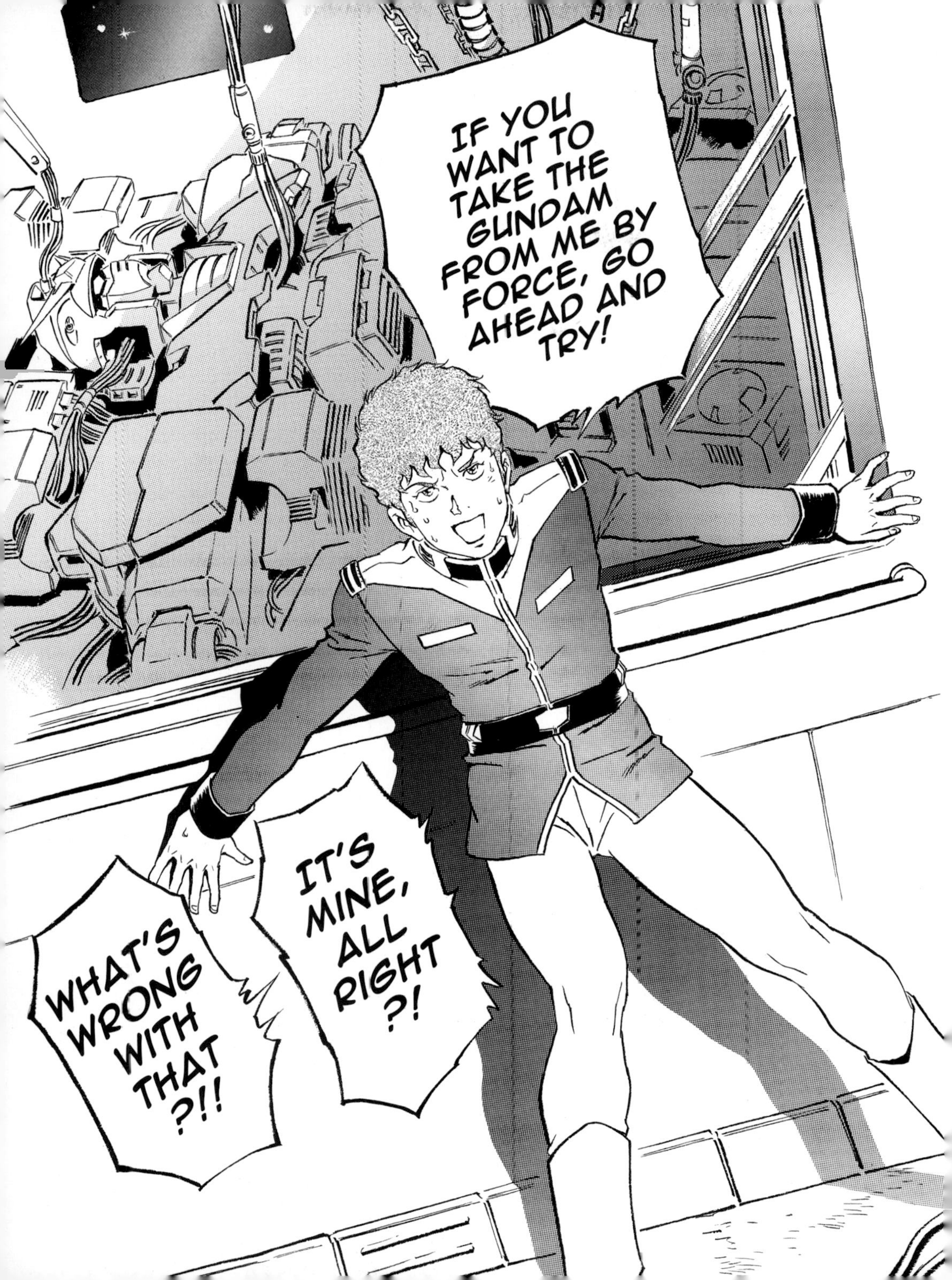
IF YOU WANT TO TAKE THE GUNDAM FROM ME BY FORCE, GO AHEAD AND TRY!
IT'S MINE, ALL RIGHT?!
WHAT'S WRONG WITH THAT?!!

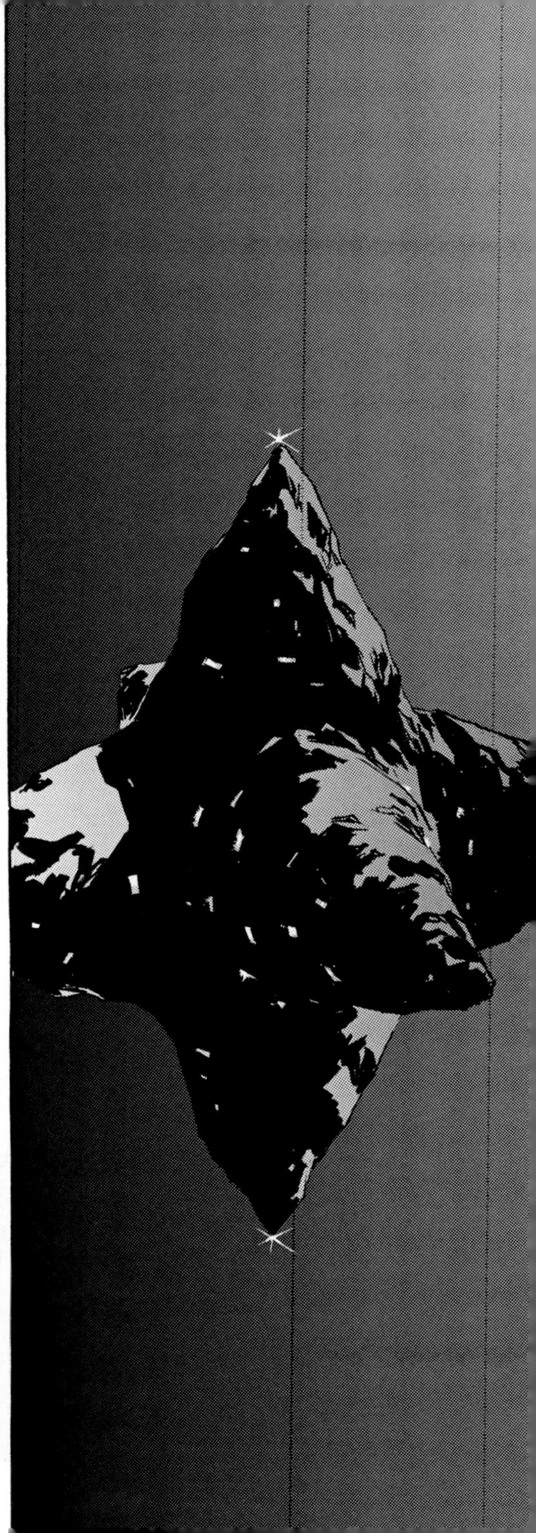

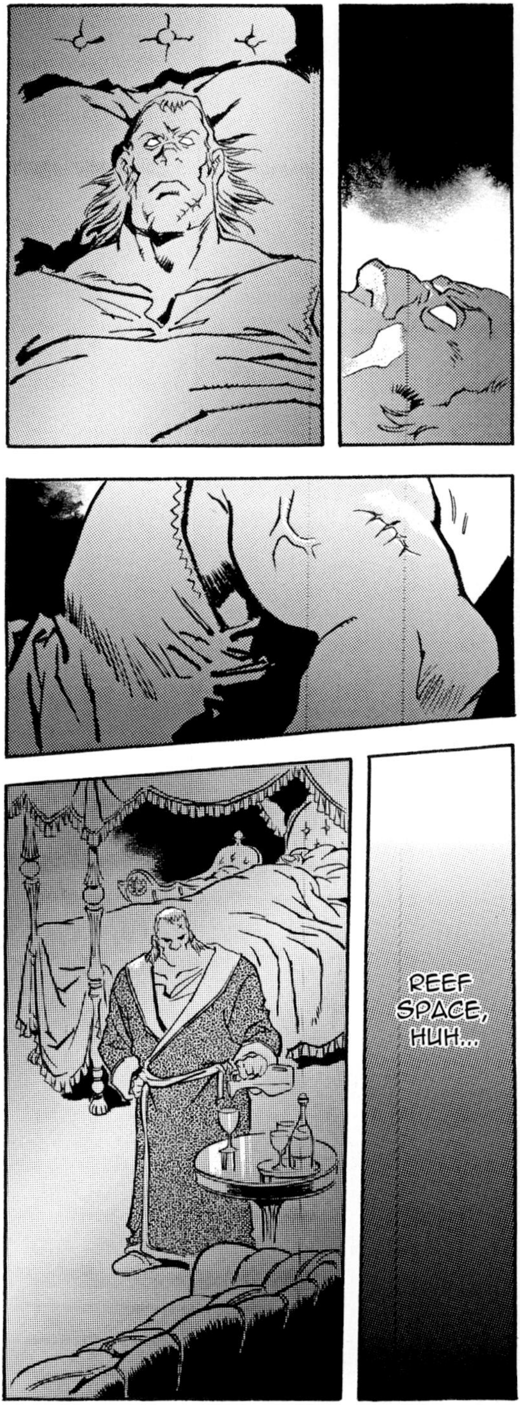
REEF SPACE, HUH...

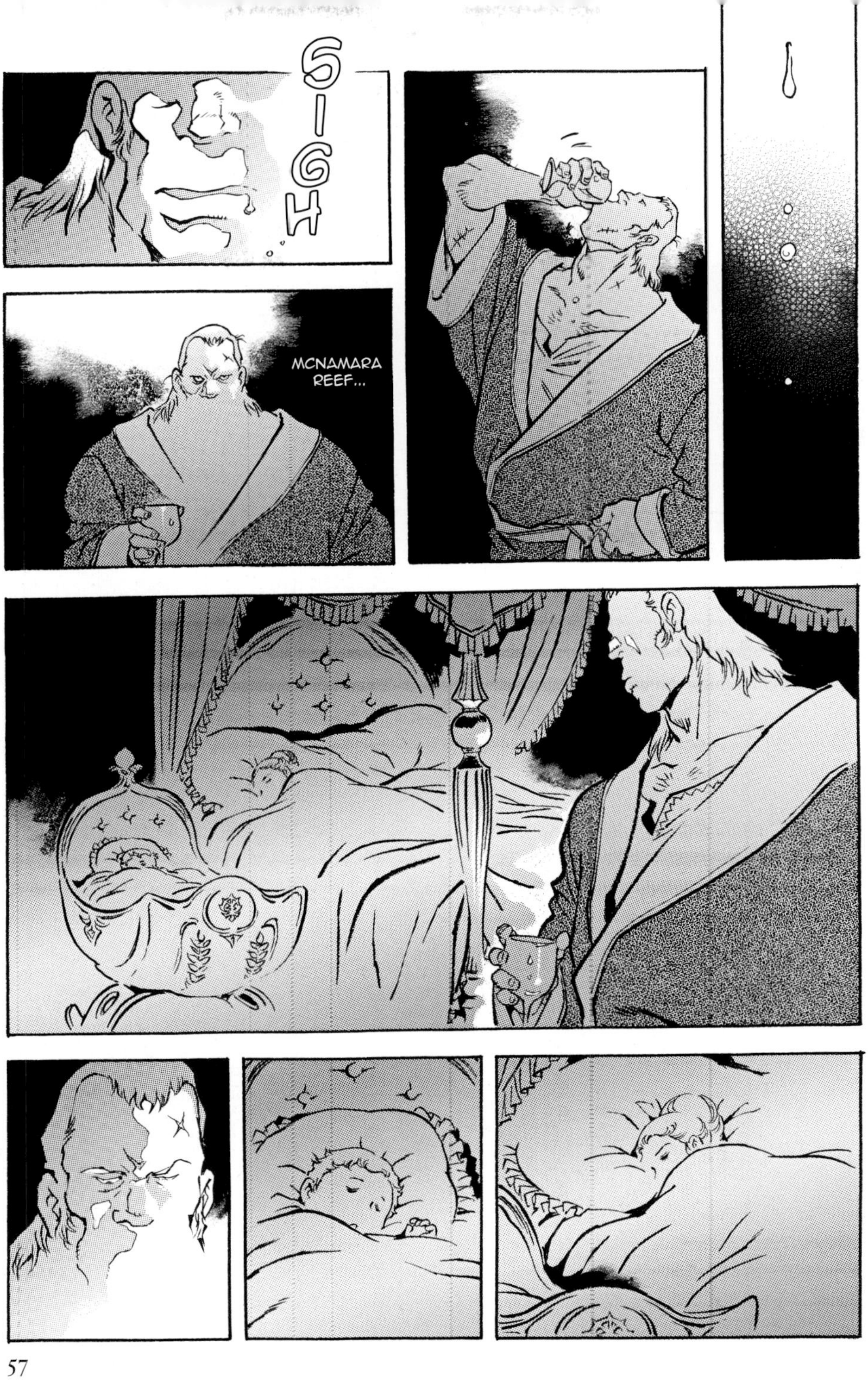
SIGH
MCNAMARA REEF...

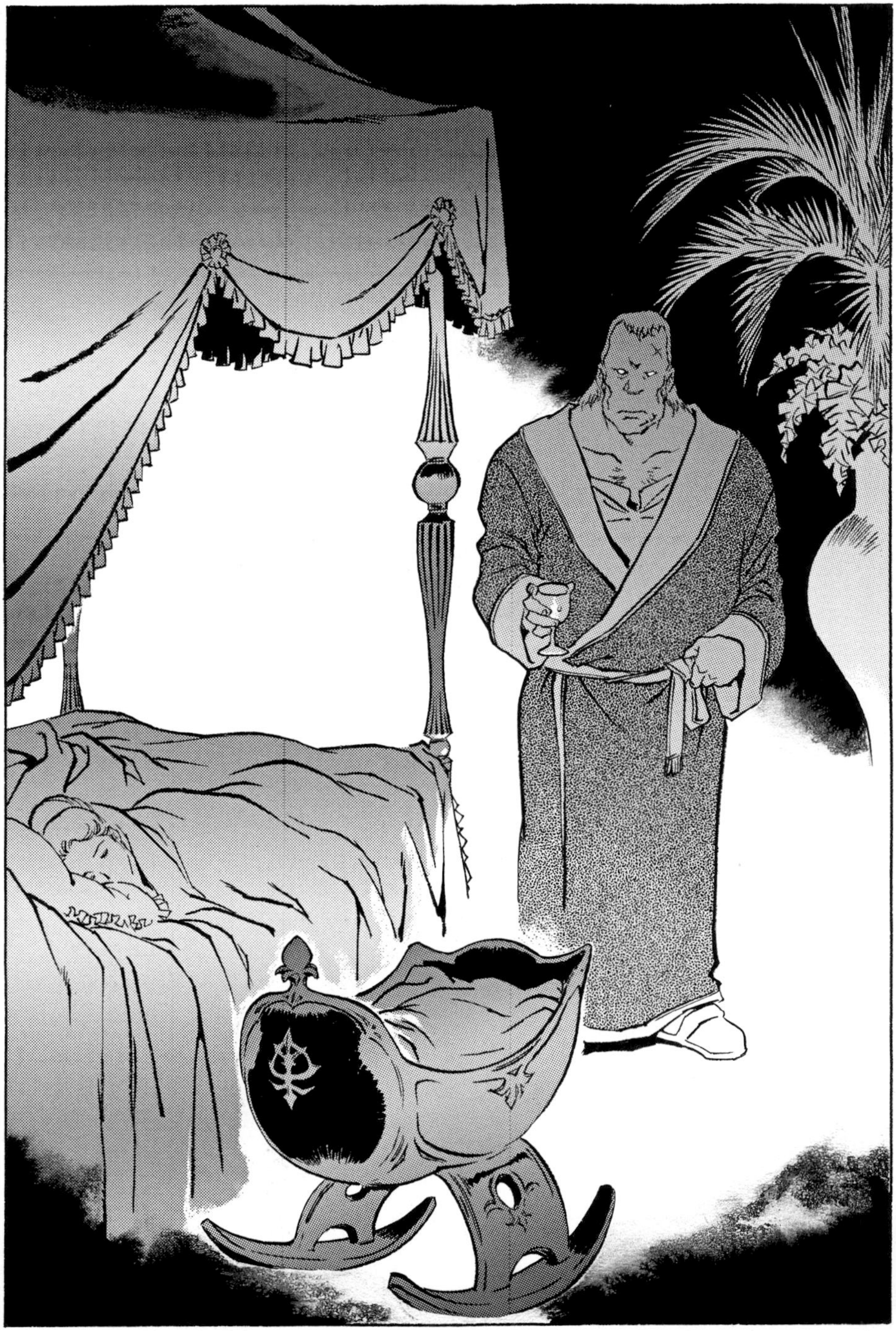

SECTION II

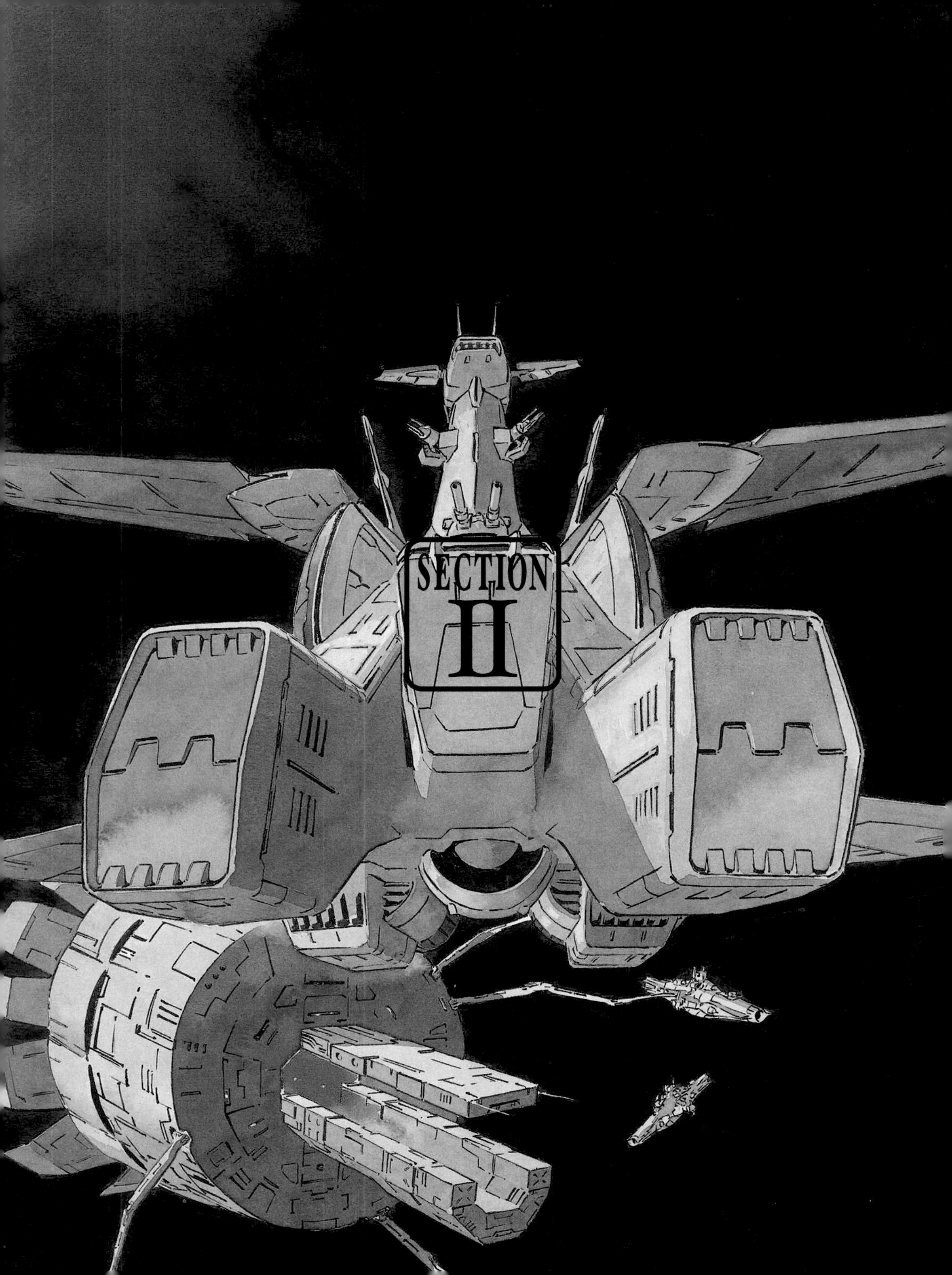

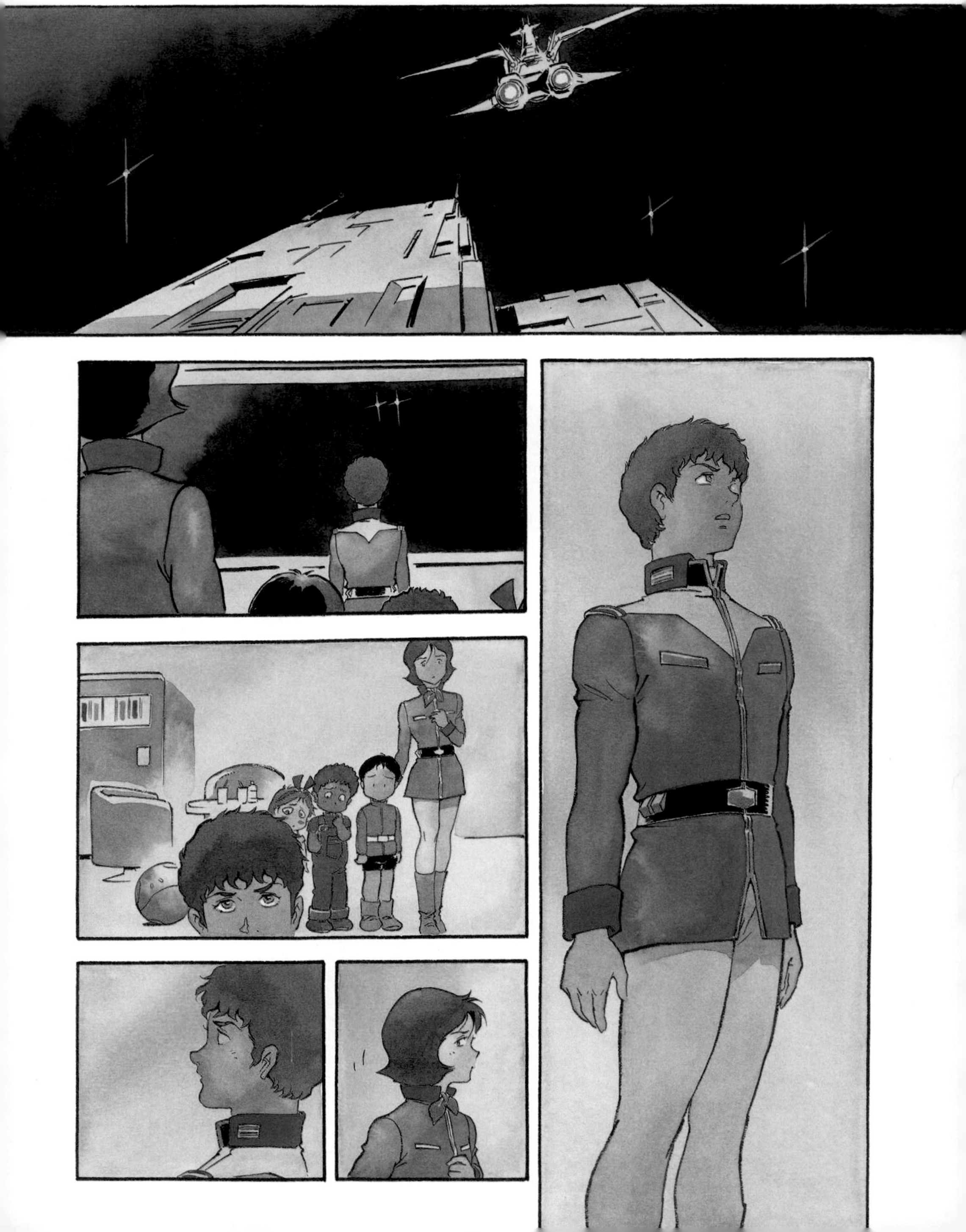

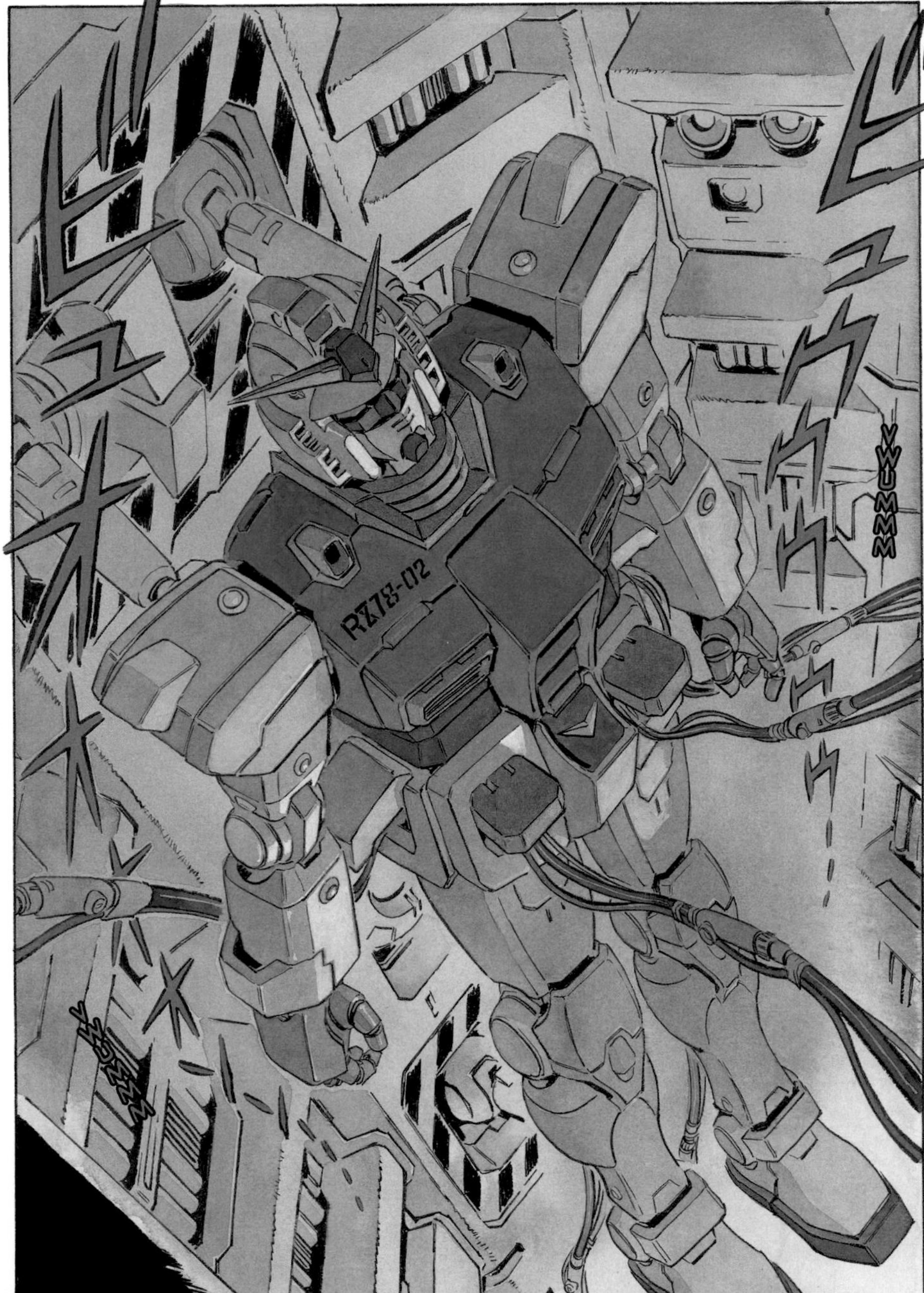
VWUMMM
RX78-02
VWUMMM

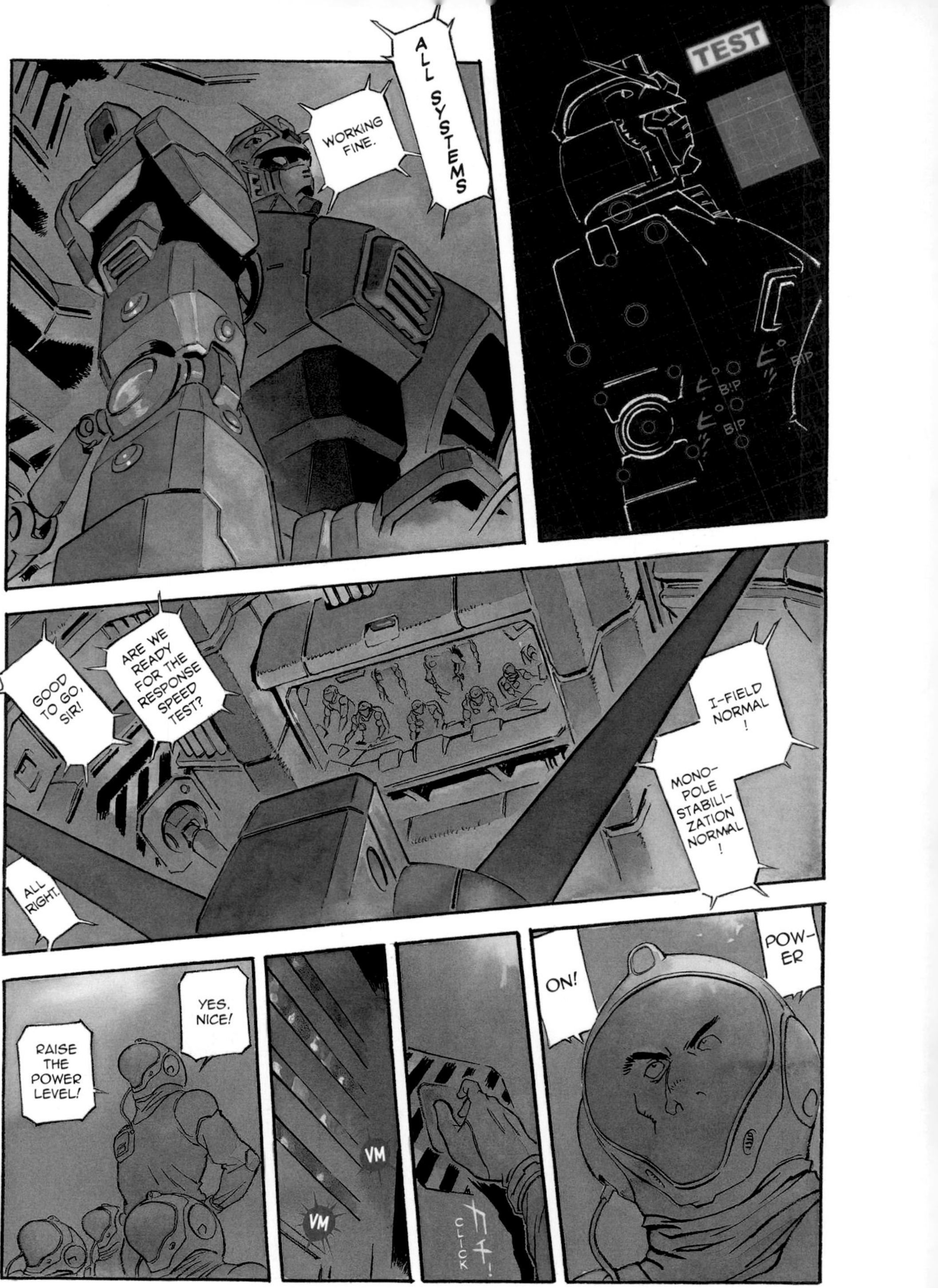
TEST
BIP
BIP
BIP
ALL SYSTEMS
WORKING FINE.
I-FIELD NORMAL!
MONO-POLE STABILI-ZATION NORMAL!
ARE WE READY FOR THE RESPONSE SPEED TEST?
GOOD TO GO, SIR!
ALL RIGHT.
POW-ER
ON!
CLICK
VM
VM
YES. NICE!
RAISE THE POWER LEVEL!

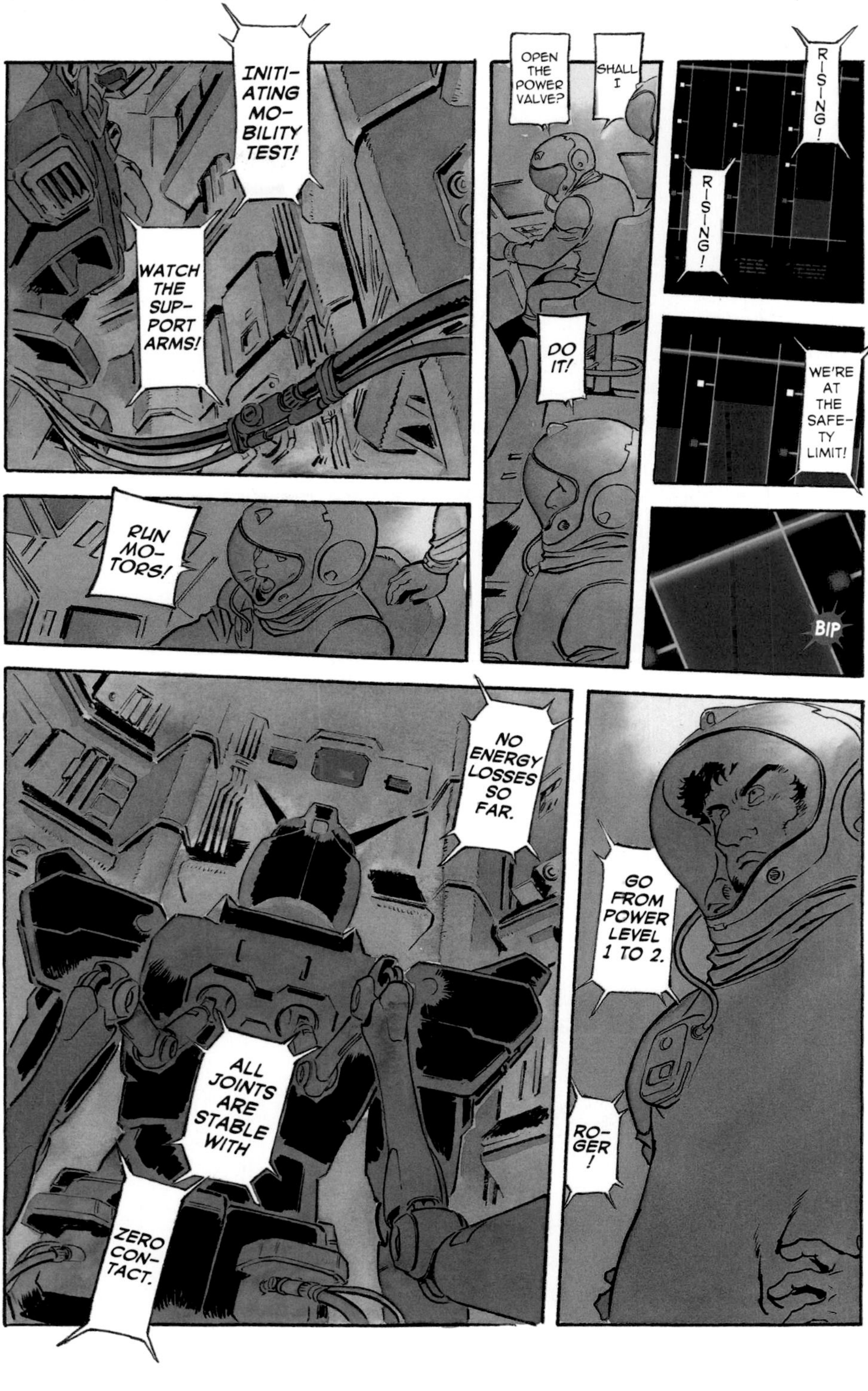
RISING!
RISING!
WE'RE AT THE SAFETY LIMIT!
BIP
SHALL I
OPEN THE POWER VALVE?
DO IT!
INITIATING MOBILITY TEST!
WATCH THE SUPPORT ARMS!
RUN MOTORS!
GO FROM POWER LEVEL 1 TO 2.
ROGER!
NO ENERGY LOSSES SO FAR.
ALL JOINTS ARE STABLE WITH
ZERO CONTACT.

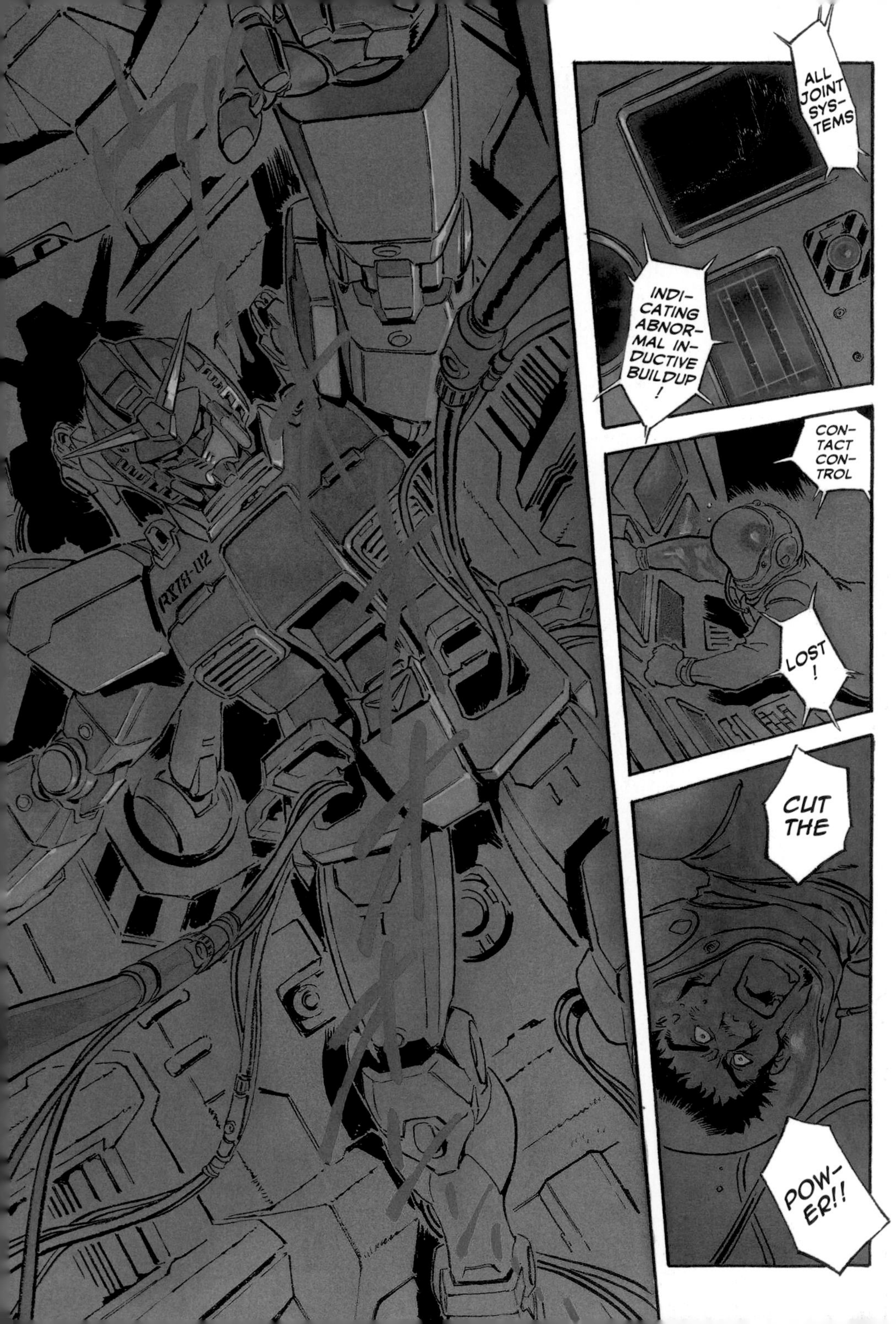
ALL JOINT SYS-TEMS
INDI-CATING ABNOR-MAL IN-DUCTIVE BUILDUP!
CON-TACT CON-TROL
LOST!
CUT THE
POW-ER!!

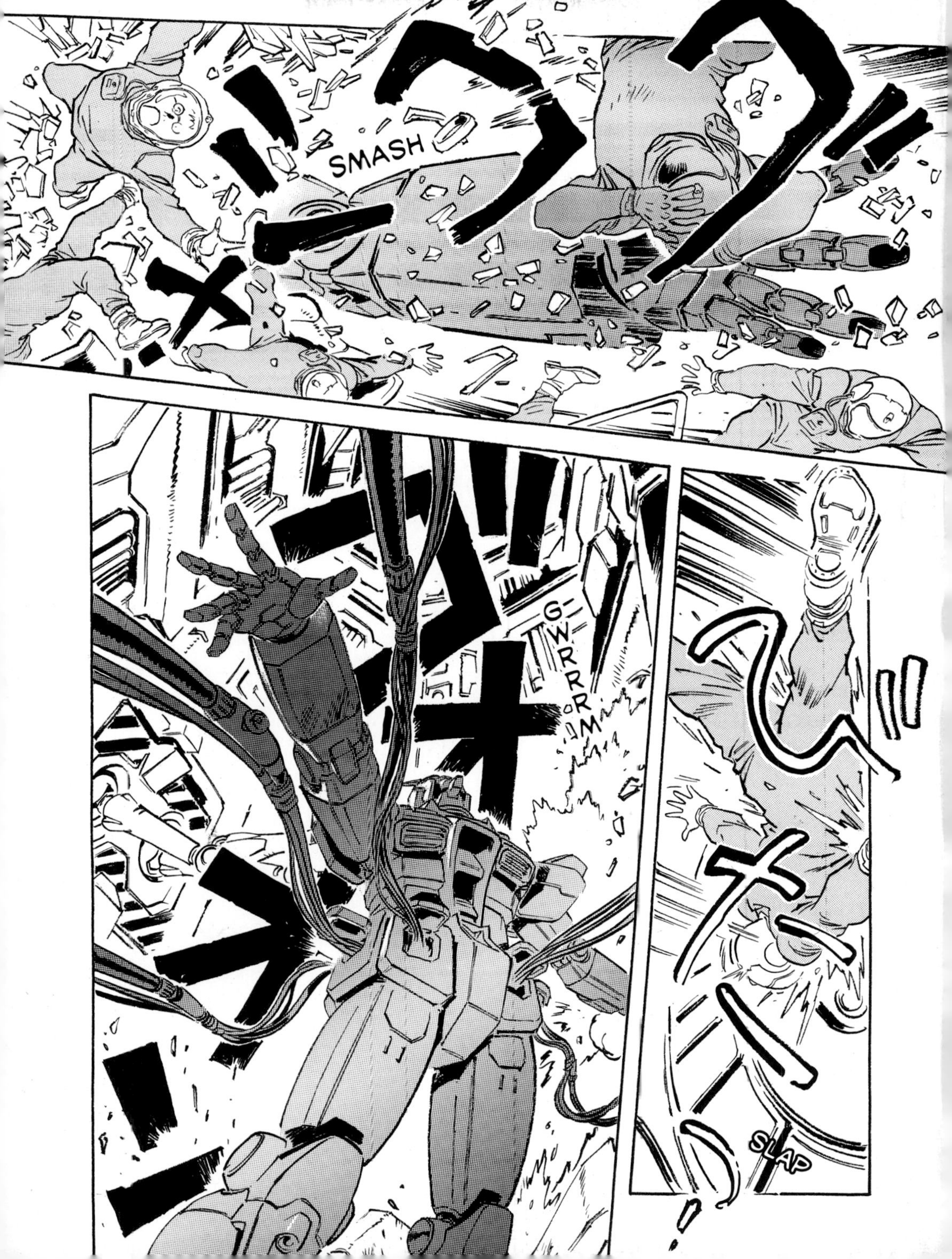
SMASH
SLAP
GWRRRM

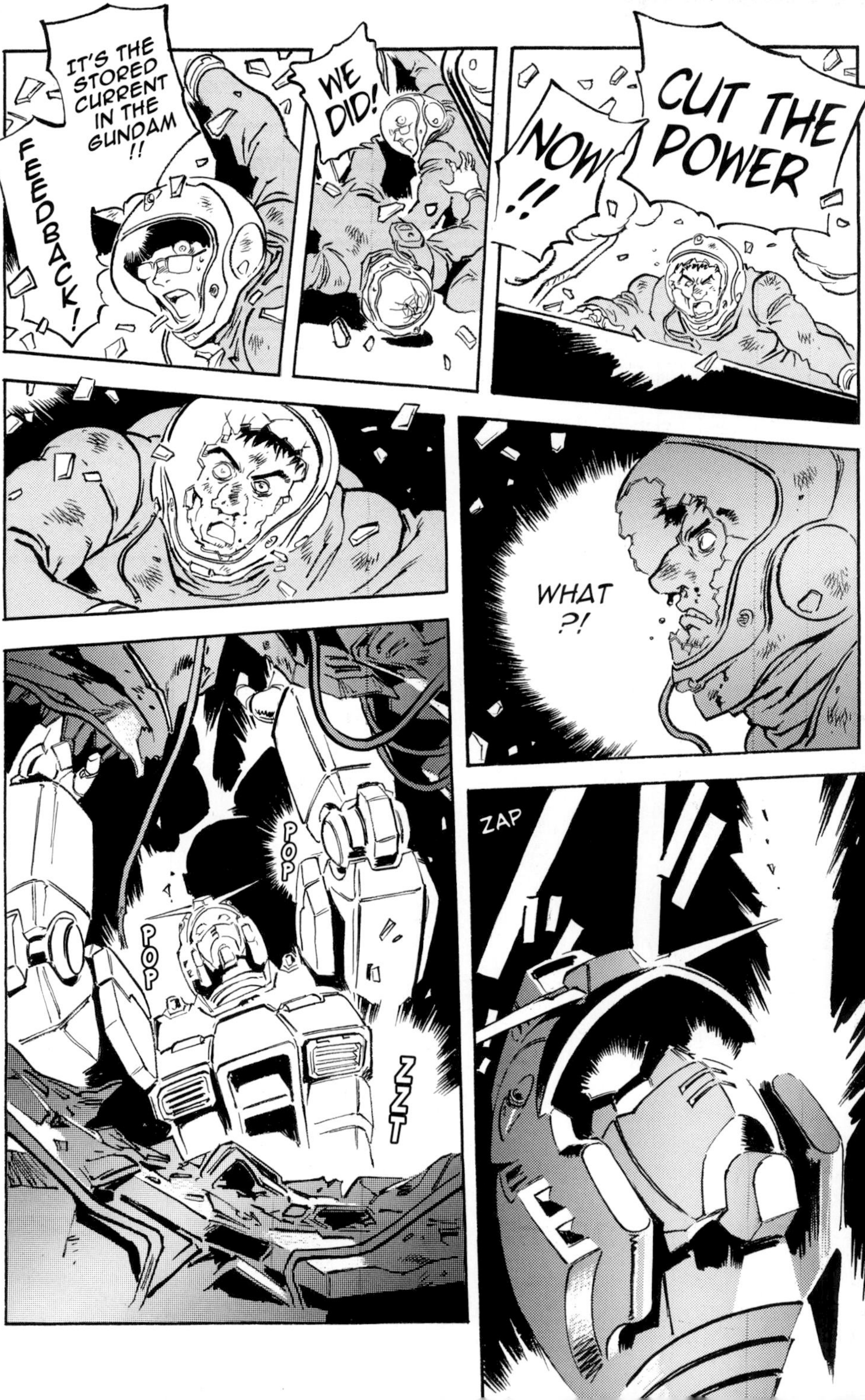
CUT THE POWER
NOW!!
WE DID!
IT'S THE STORED CURRENT IN THE GUNDAM!!
FEEDBACK!
WHAT?!
ZAP
POP POP
POP POP
ZZZT

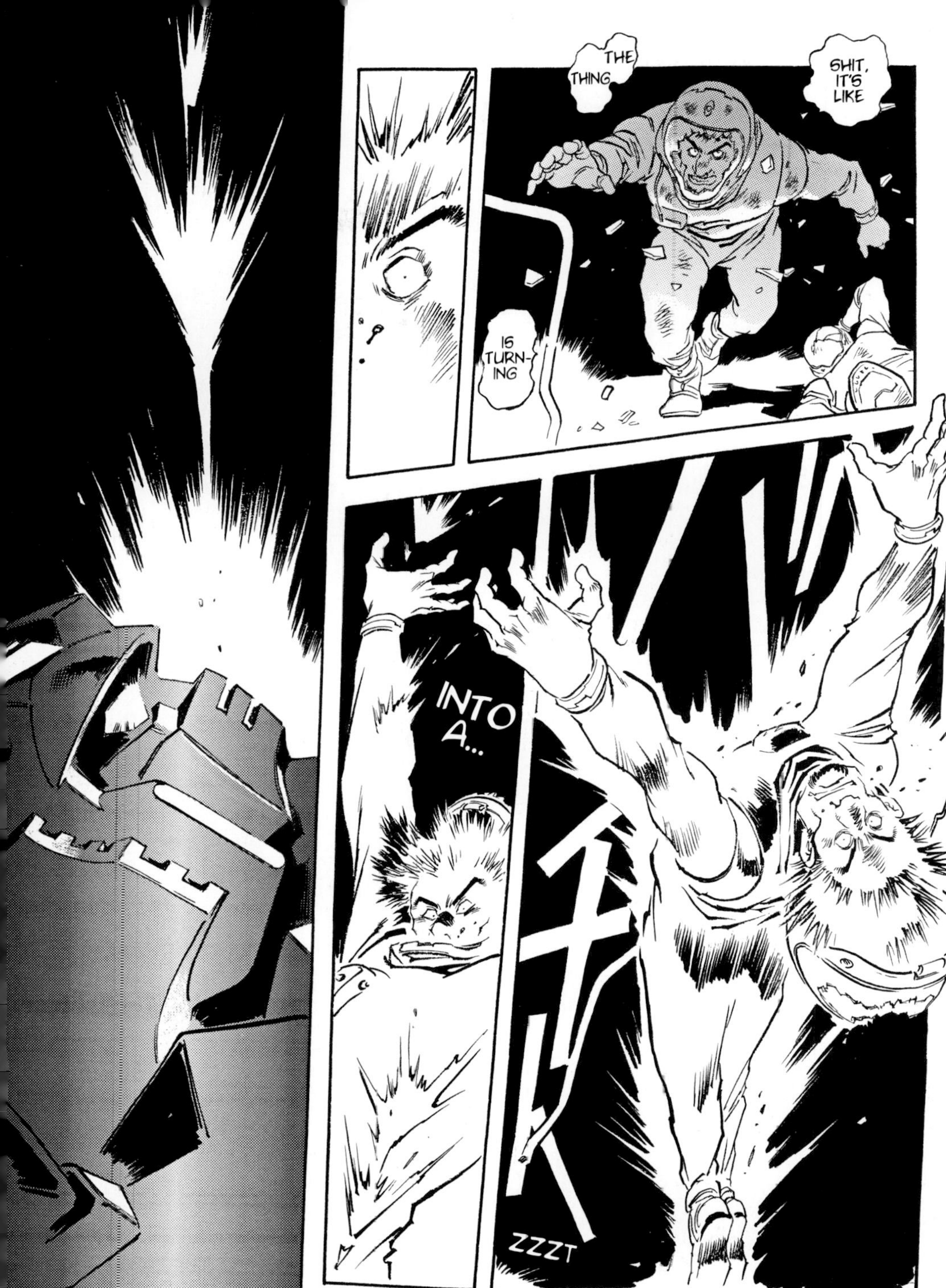
SHIT, IT'S LIKE
THE THING
IS TURNING
INTO A...
ZZZT

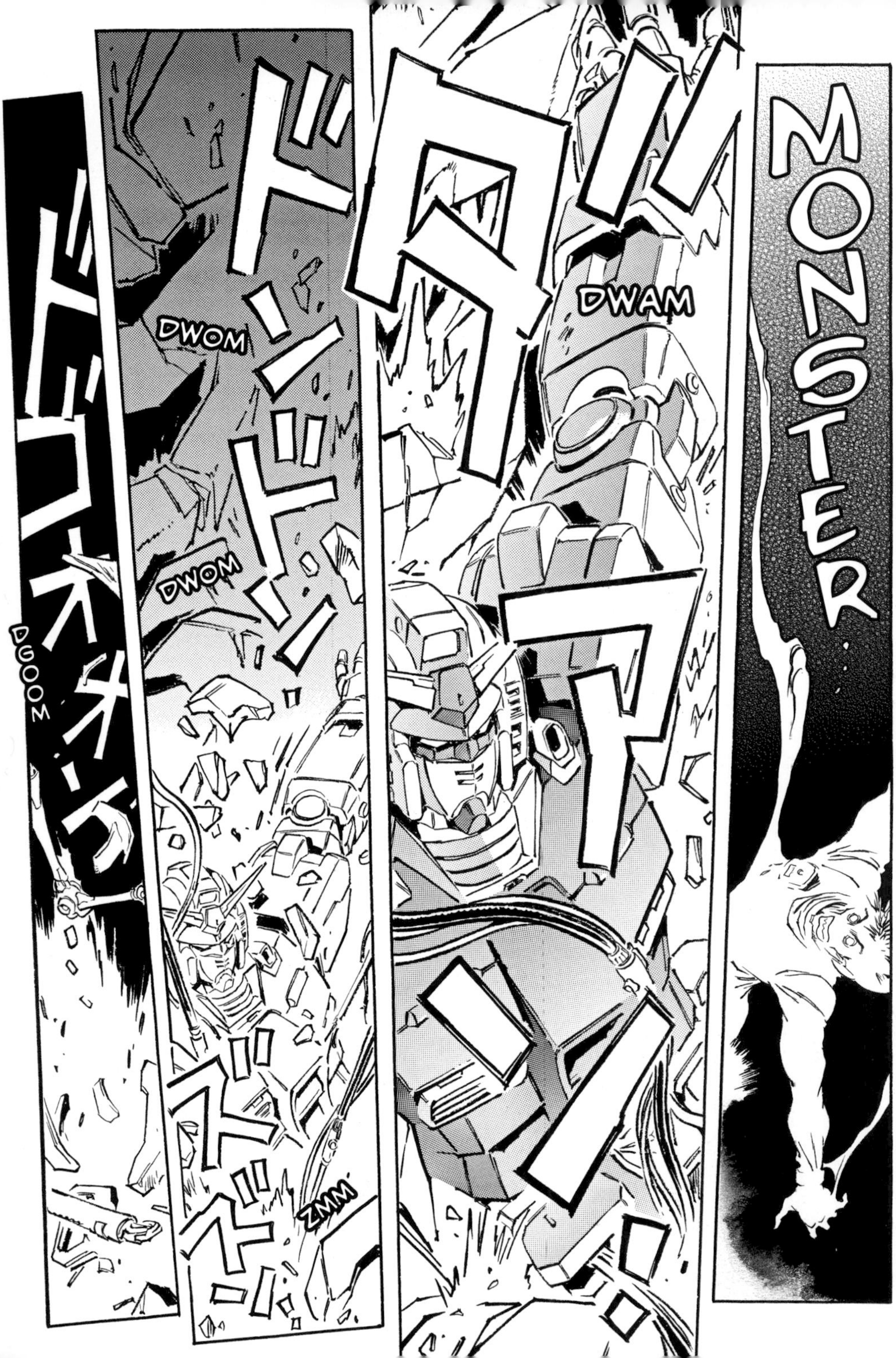
MONSTER...
DWAM
DWOM
DWOM
ZMM
DGOOM

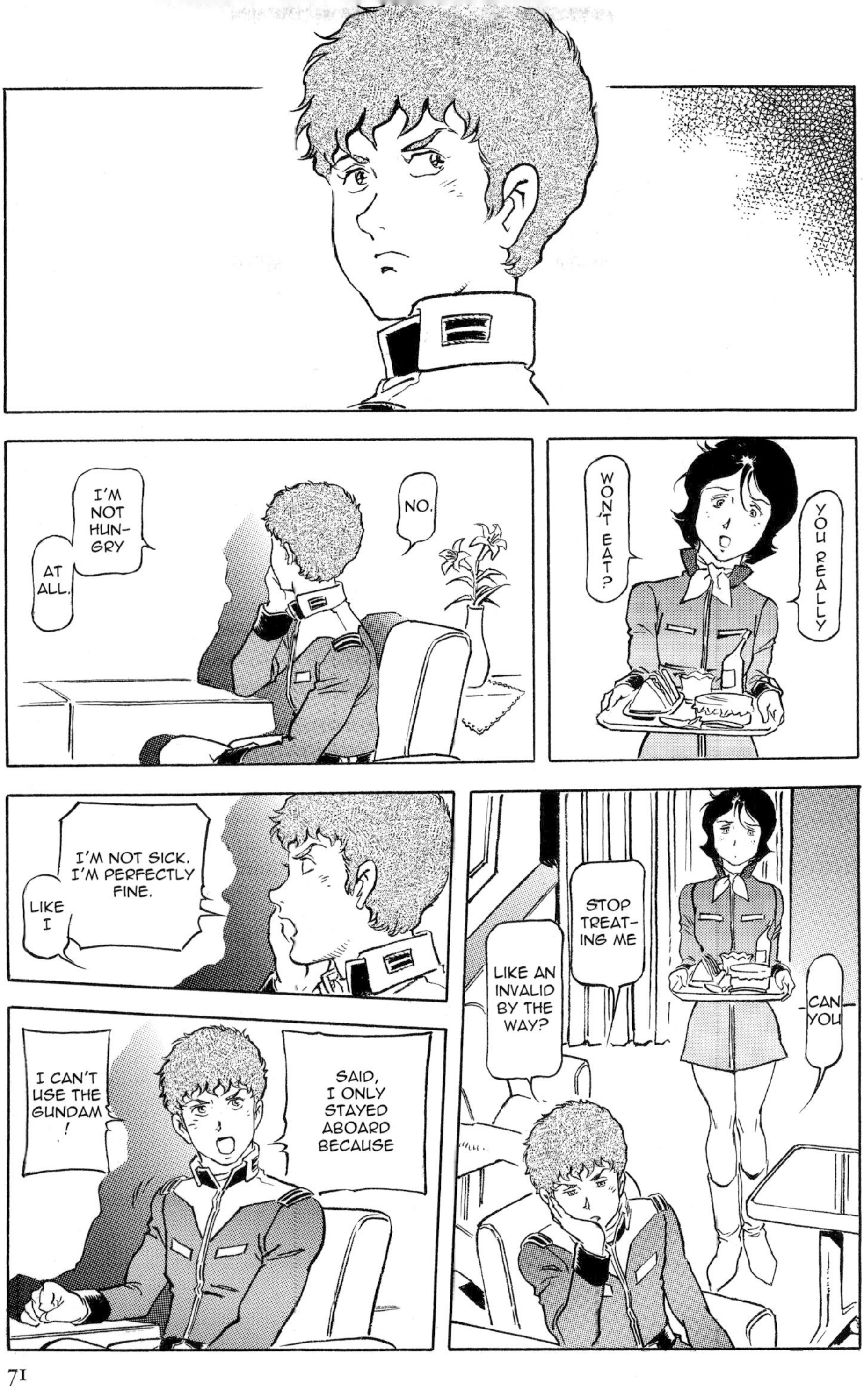
YOU REALLY
WON'T EAT?
NO.
I'M NOT HUNGRY
AT ALL.
CAN YOU
STOP TREATING ME
LIKE AN INVALID BY THE WAY?
I'M NOT SICK. I'M PERFECTLY FINE.
LIKE I
SAID, I ONLY STAYED ABOARD BECAUSE
I CAN'T USE THE GUNDAM!

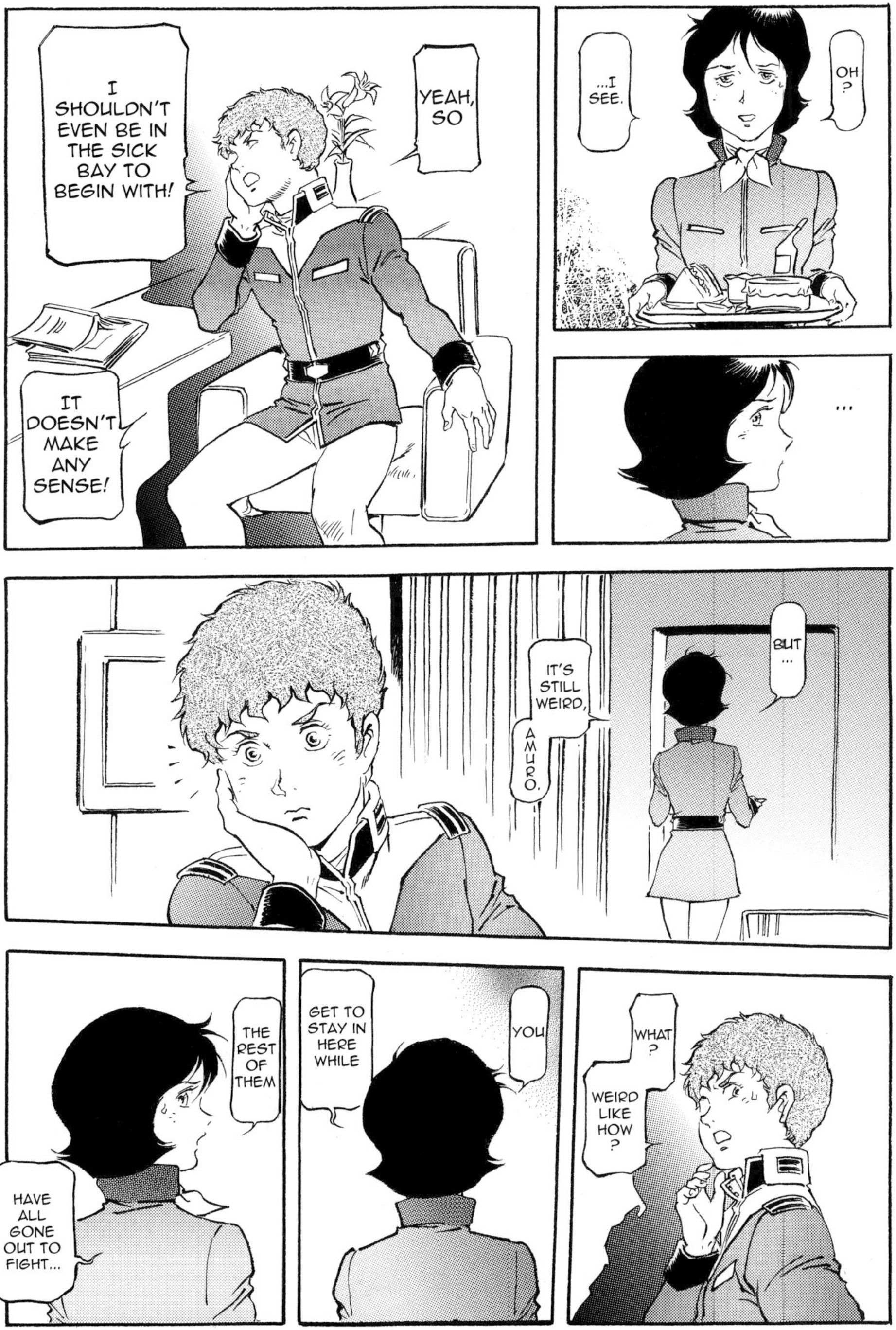
OH?
...I SEE.
...
YEAH, SO
I SHOULDN'T EVEN BE IN THE SICK BAY TO BEGIN WITH!
IT DOESN'T MAKE ANY SENSE!
BUT...
IT'S STILL WEIRD,
AMURO.
WHAT?
WEIRD LIKE HOW?
YOU
GET TO STAY IN HERE WHILE
THE REST OF THEM
HAVE ALL GONE OUT TO FIGHT...

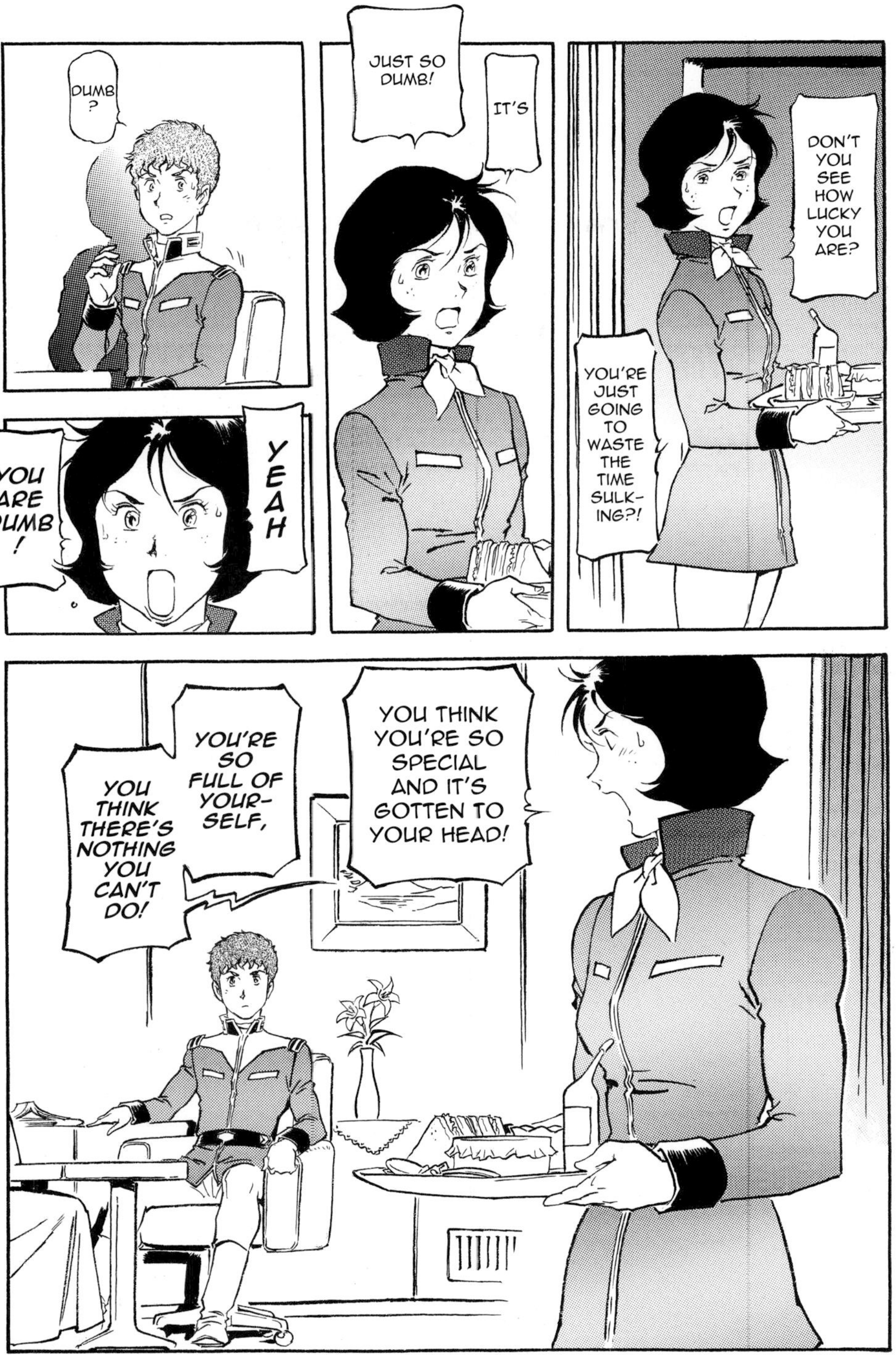
DON'T YOU SEE HOW LUCKY YOU ARE?
YOU'RE JUST GOING TO WASTE THE TIME SULK-ING?!
IT'S
JUST SO DUMB!
DUMB?
YEAH
YOU ARE DUMB!
YOU THINK YOU'RE SO SPECIAL AND IT'S GOTTEN TO YOUR HEAD!
YOU'RE SO FULL OF YOUR-SELF,
YOU THINK THERE'S NOTHING YOU CAN'T DO!

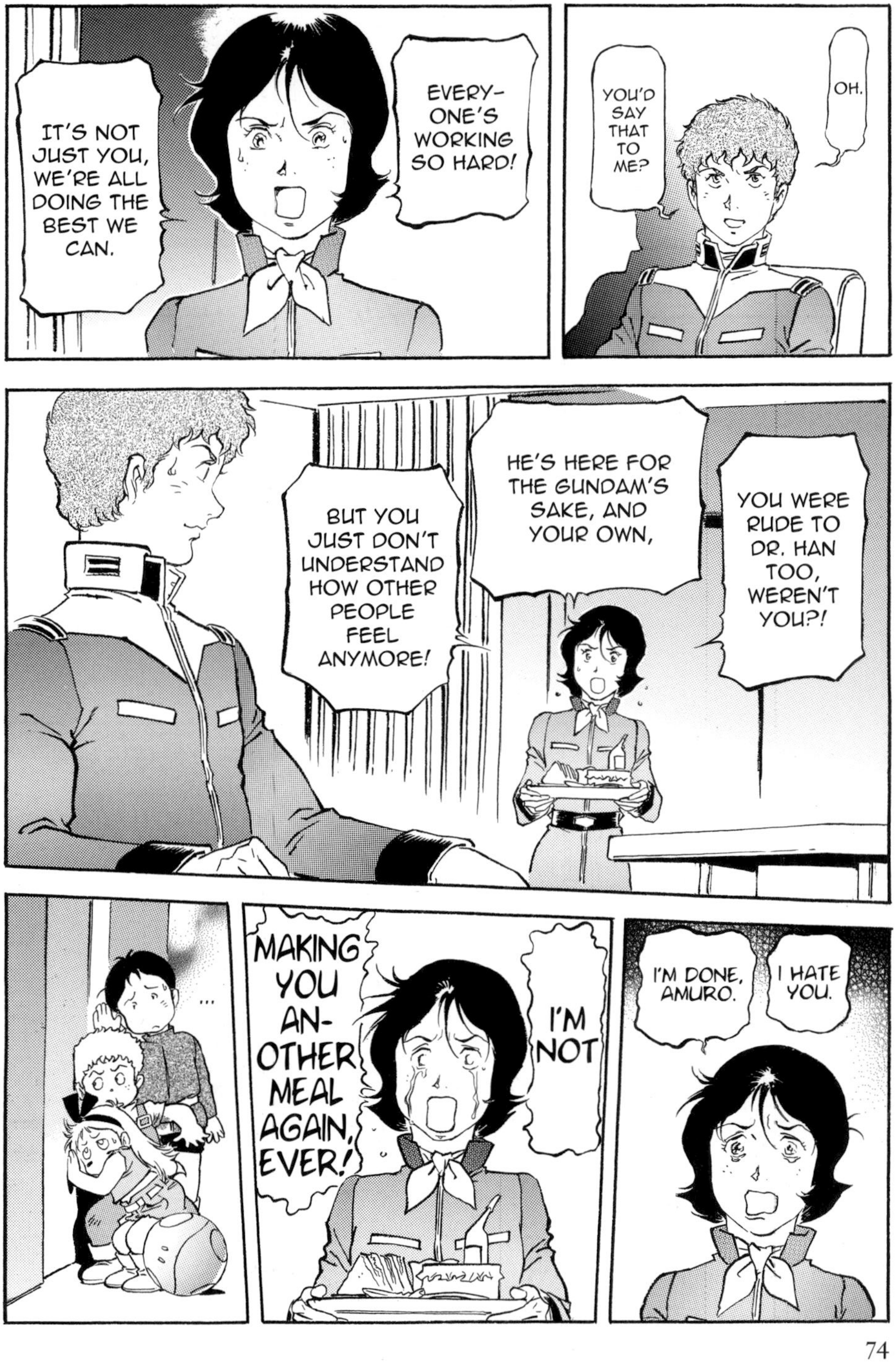
OH.
YOU'D SAY THAT TO ME?
EVERY-ONE'S WORKING SO HARD!
IT'S NOT JUST YOU, WE'RE ALL DOING THE BEST WE CAN.
YOU WERE RUDE TO DR. HAN TOO, WEREN'T YOU?!
HE'S HERE FOR THE GUNDAM'S SAKE, AND YOUR OWN,
BUT YOU JUST DON'T UNDERSTAND HOW OTHER PEOPLE FEEL ANYMORE!
I HATE YOU.
I'M DONE, AMURO.
I'M NOT
MAKING YOU AN-OTHER MEAL AGAIN, EVER!
...

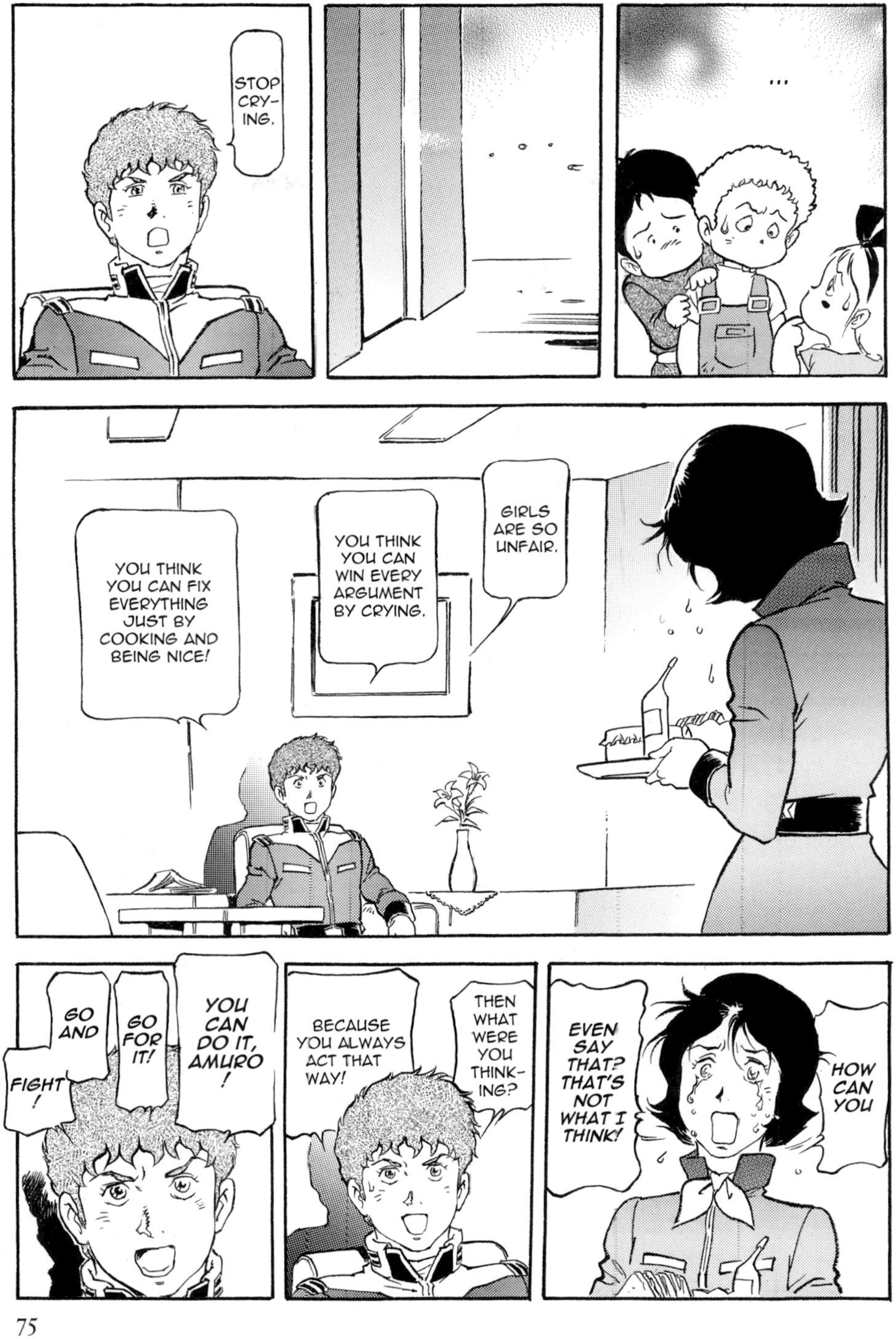
...
STOP CRY-ING.
GIRLS ARE SO UNFAIR.
YOU THINK YOU CAN WIN EVERY ARGUMENT BY CRYING.
YOU THINK YOU CAN FIX EVERYTHING JUST BY COOKING AND BEING NICE!
HOW CAN YOU
EVEN SAY THAT? THAT'S NOT WHAT I THINK!
THEN WHAT WERE YOU THINK-ING?
BECAUSE YOU ALWAYS ACT THAT WAY!
YOU CAN DO IT, AMURO!
GO FOR IT!
GO AND
FIGHT!

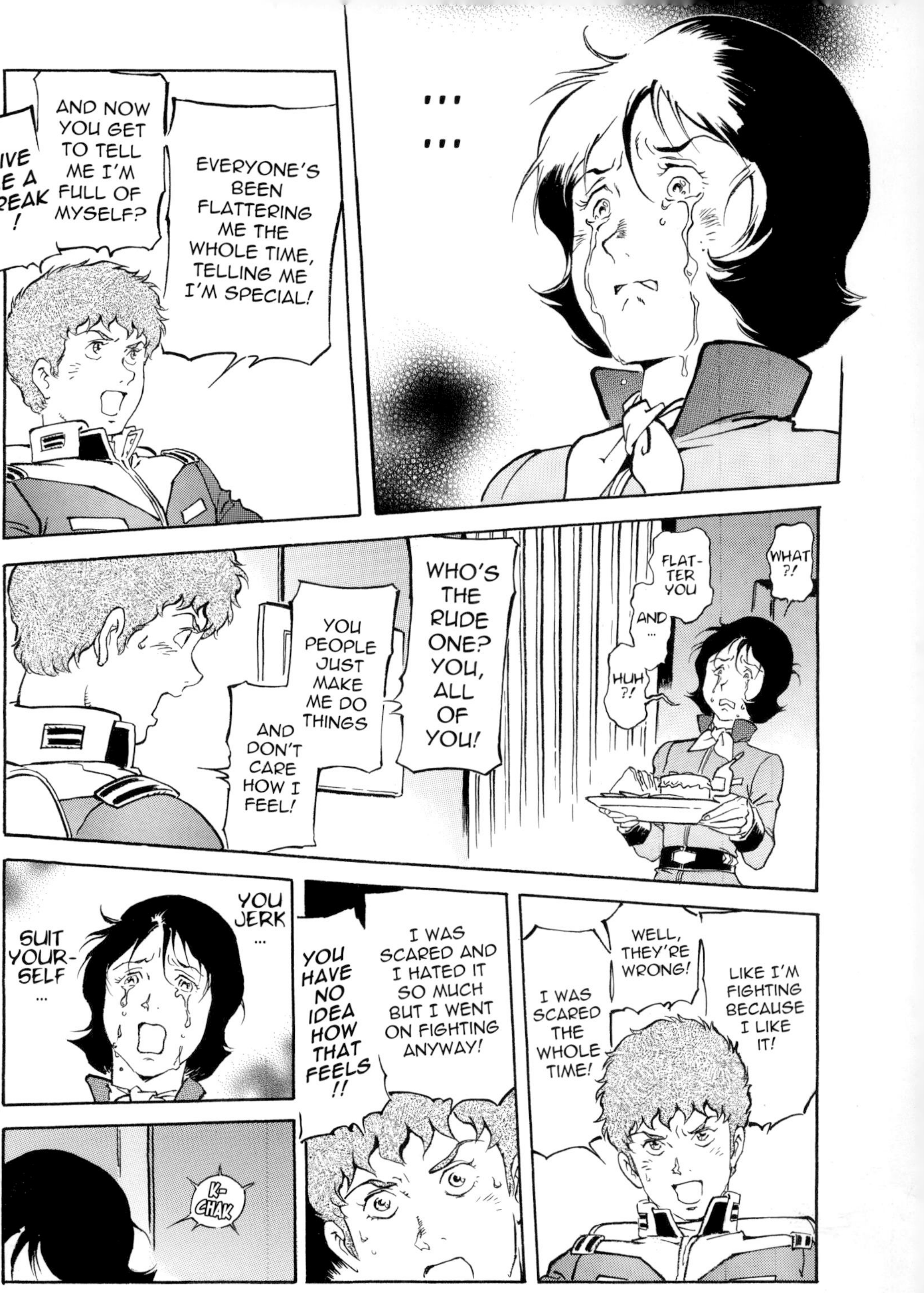
...
...
EVERYONE'S BEEN FLATTERING ME THE WHOLE TIME, TELLING ME I'M SPECIAL!
AND NOW YOU GET TO TELL ME I'M FULL OF MYSELF?
GIVE ME A BREAK!
WHAT?!
FLATTER YOU
AND...
HUH?!
WHO'S THE RUDE ONE? YOU, ALL OF YOU!
YOU PEOPLE JUST MAKE ME DO THINGS
AND DON'T CARE HOW I FEEL!
LIKE I'M FIGHTING BECAUSE I LIKE IT!
WELL, THEY'RE WRONG!
I WAS SCARED THE WHOLE TIME!
I WAS SCARED AND I HATED IT SO MUCH BUT I WENT ON FIGHTING ANYWAY!
YOU HAVE NO IDEA HOW THAT FEELS!!
YOU JERK...
SUIT YOURSELF...
K-CHAK

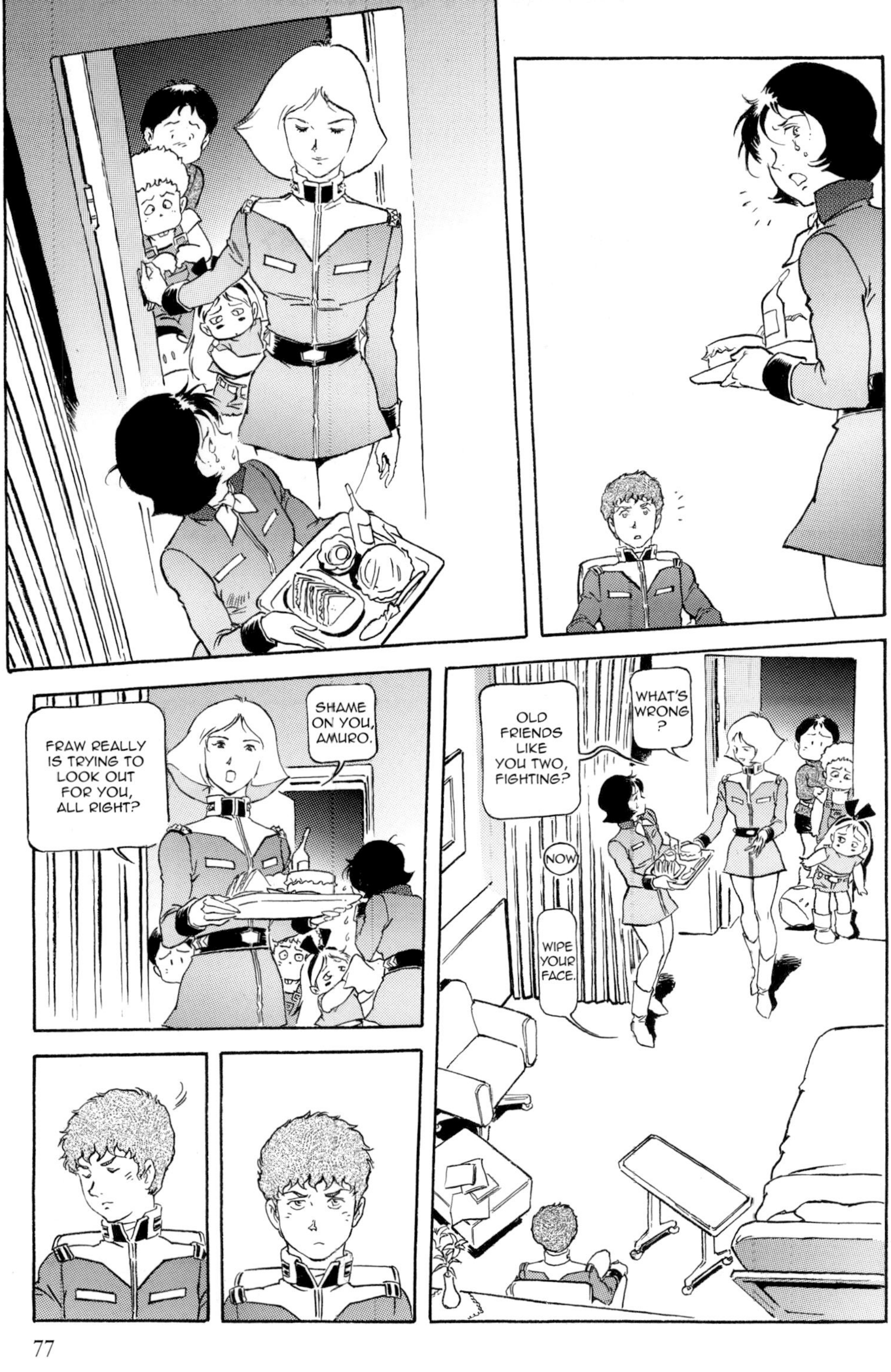
WHAT'S WRONG?
OLD FRIENDS LIKE YOU TWO, FIGHTING?
NOW
WIPE YOUR FACE.
SHAME ON YOU, AMURO.
FRAW REALLY IS TRYING TO LOOK OUT FOR YOU, ALL RIGHT?

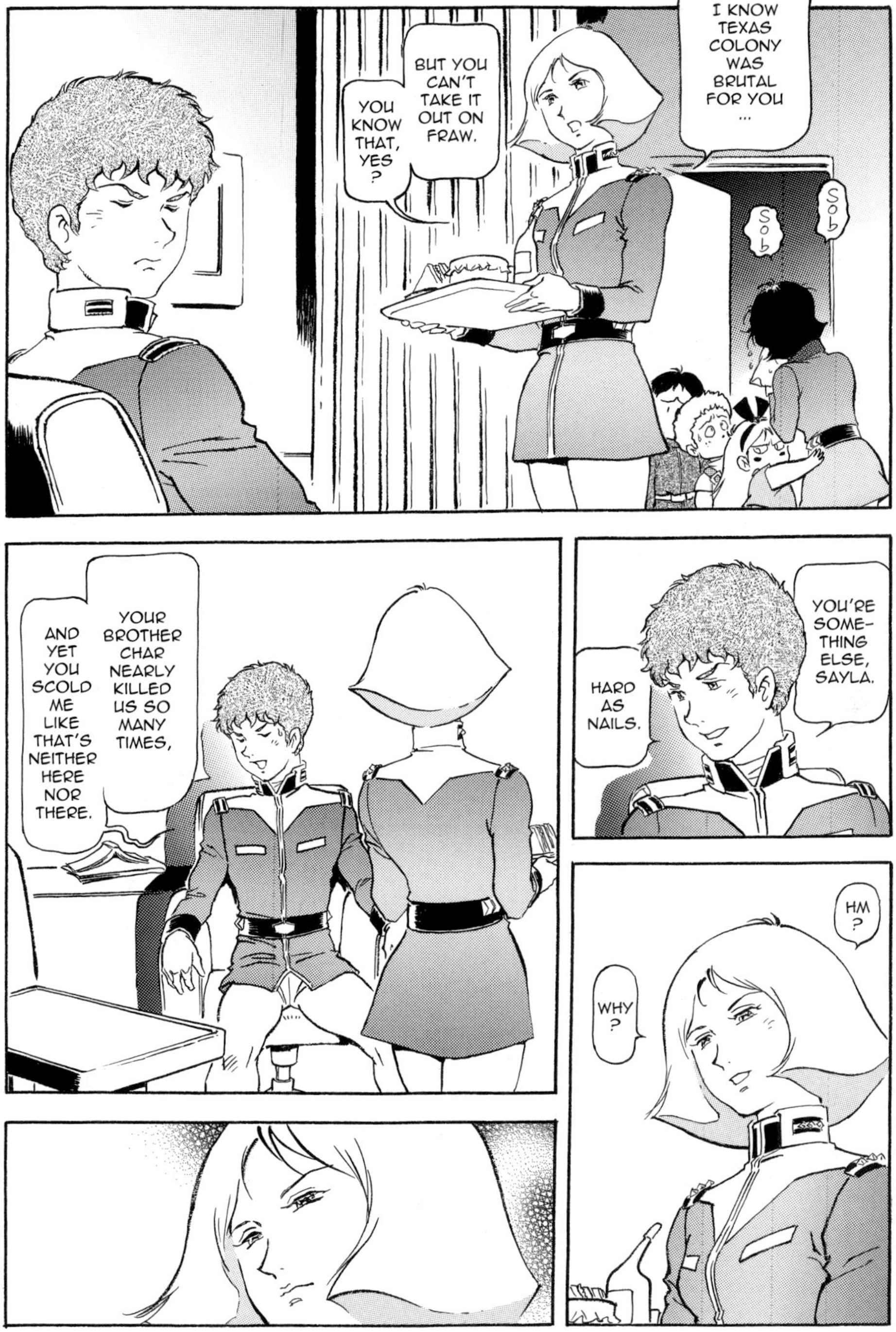
I KNOW TEXAS COLONY WAS BRUTAL FOR YOU ...
Sob
Sob
BUT YOU CAN'T TAKE IT OUT ON FRAW.
YOU KNOW THAT, YES?
YOU'RE SOMETHING ELSE, SAYLA.
HARD AS NAILS.
YOUR BROTHER CHAR NEARLY KILLED US SO MANY TIMES,
AND YET YOU SCOLD ME LIKE THAT'S NEITHER HERE NOR THERE.
HM?
WHY?

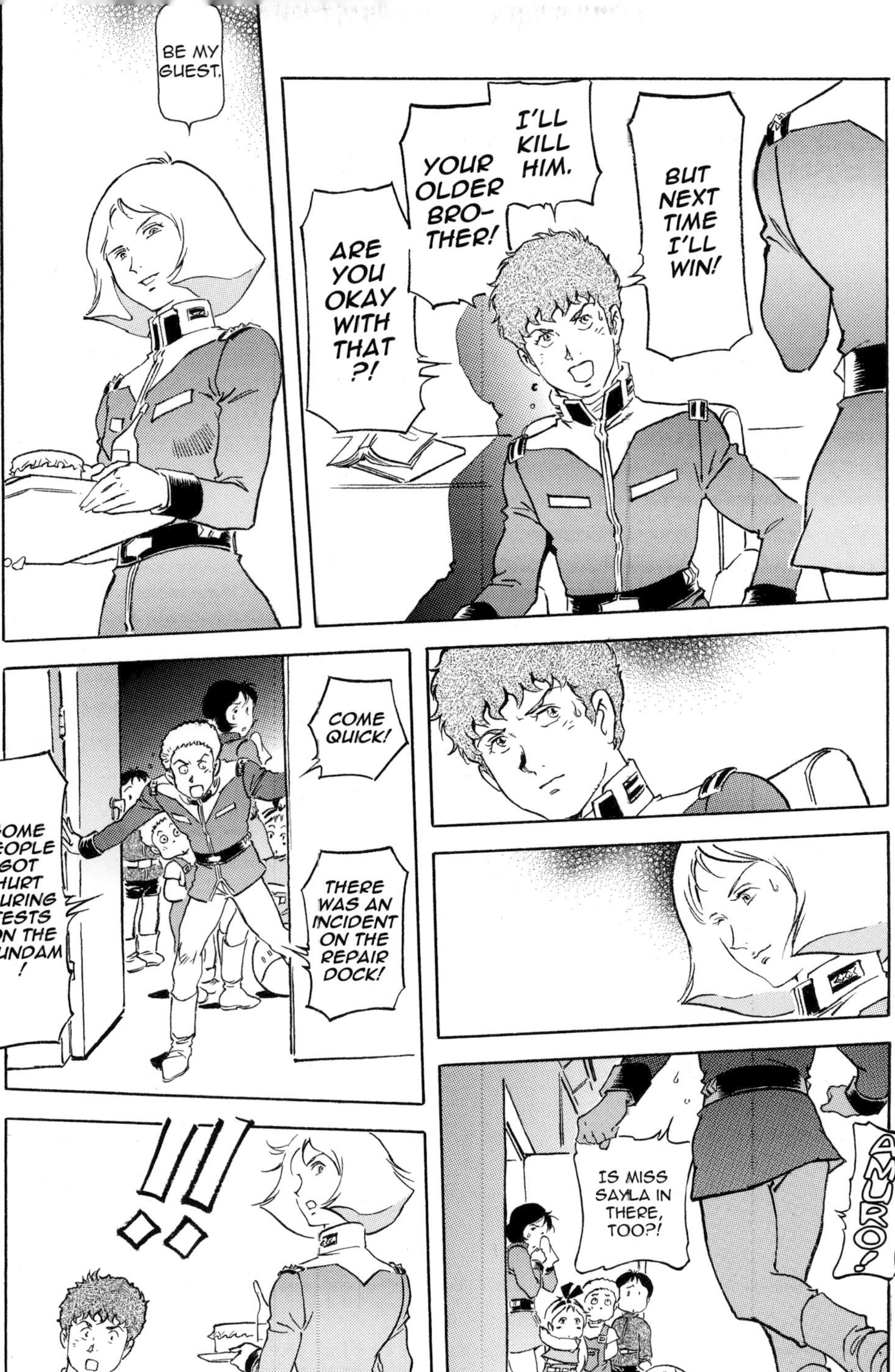
BUT NEXT TIME I'LL WIN!
I'LL KILL HIM.
YOUR OLDER BRO- THER!
ARE YOU OKAY WITH THAT ?!
BE MY GUEST.
COME QUICK!
THERE WAS AN INCIDENT ON THE REPAIR DOCK!
SOME PEOPLE GOT HURT DURING TESTS ON THE GUNDAM !
AMURO!
IS MISS SAYLA IN THERE, TOO?!
!!

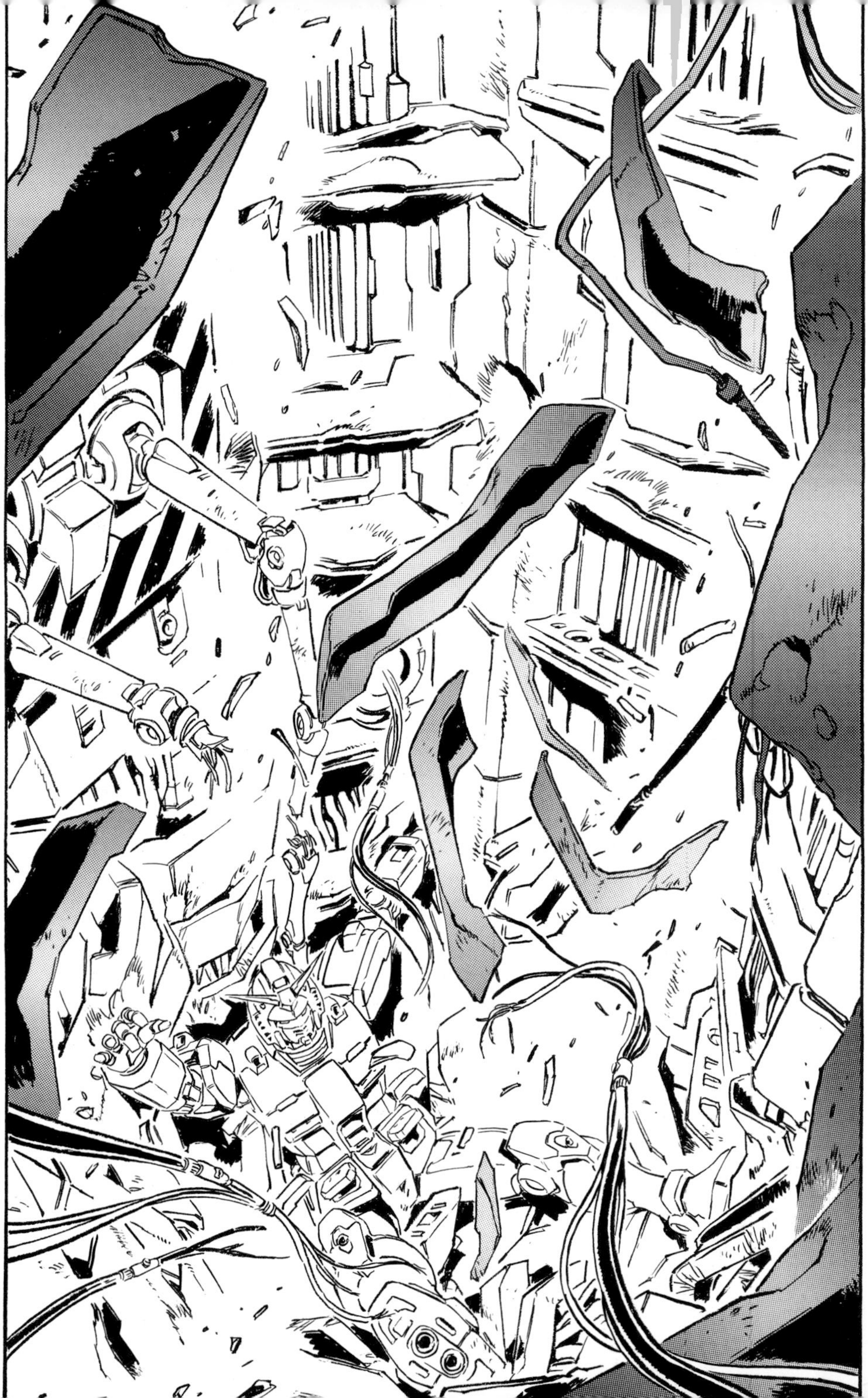

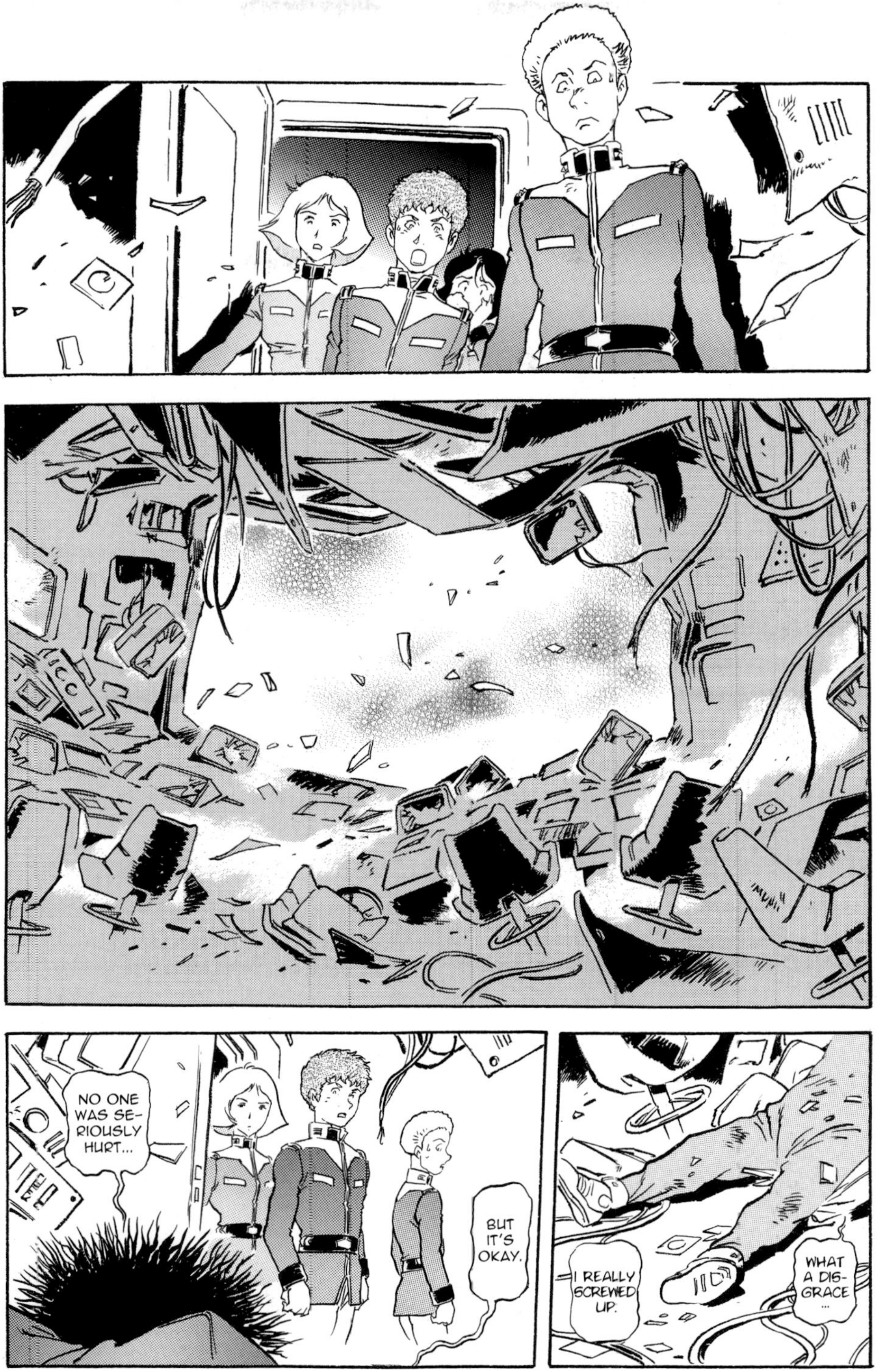
WHAT A DIS-GRACE...
I REALLY SCREWED UP.
BUT IT'S OKAY.
NO ONE WAS SE-RIOUSLY HURT...

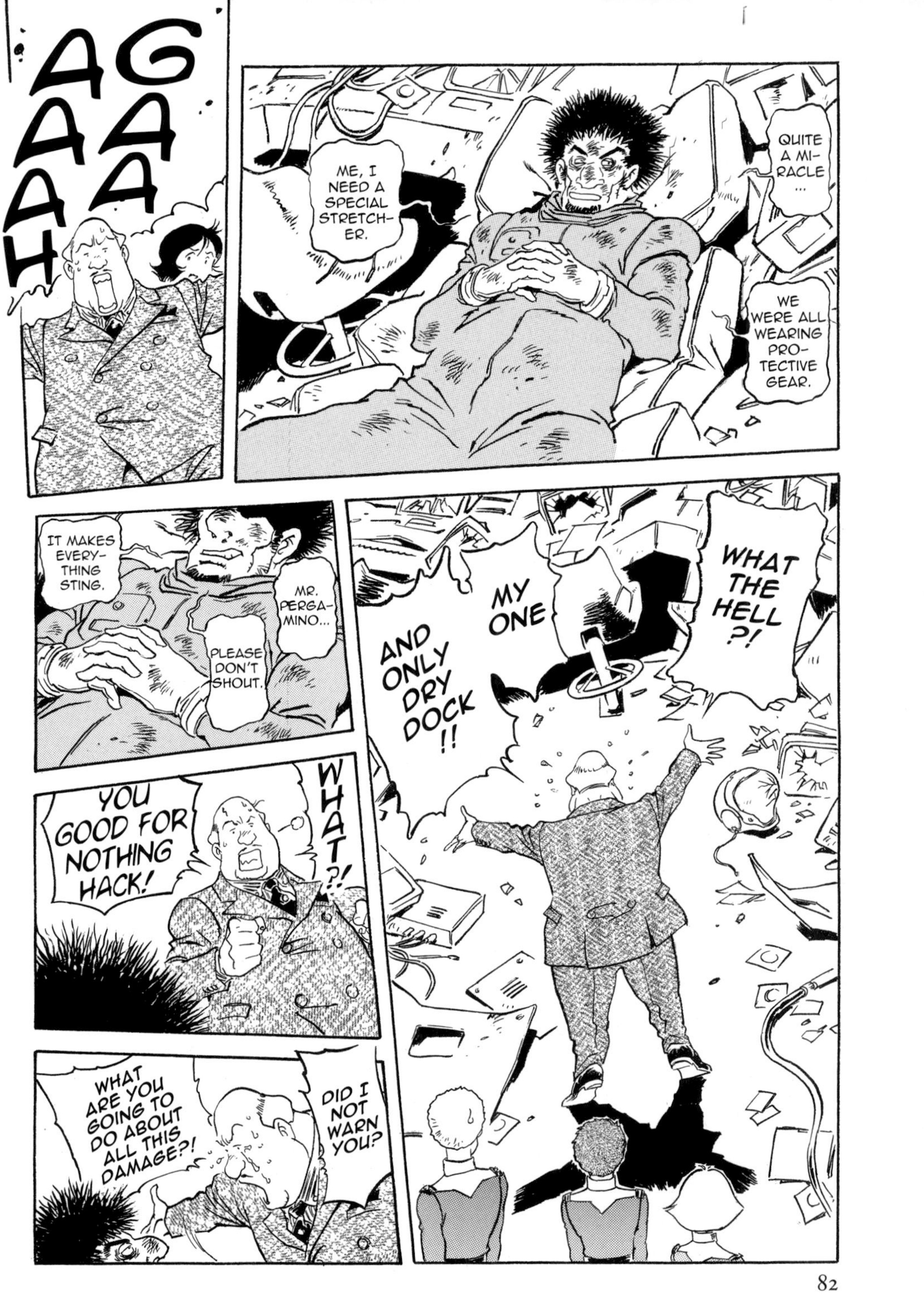
QUITE A MIRACLE...
WE WERE ALL WEARING PROTECTIVE GEAR.
ME, I NEED A SPECIAL STRETCHER.
AGAAAAAH
WHAT THE HELL?!
MY ONE AND ONLY DRY DOCK!!
MR. PERGAMINO...
PLEASE DON'T SHOUT.
IT MAKES EVERYTHING STING.
WHAT?!
YOU GOOD FOR NOTHING HACK!
DID I NOT WARN YOU?
WHAT ARE YOU GOING TO DO ABOUT ALL THIS DAMAGE?!

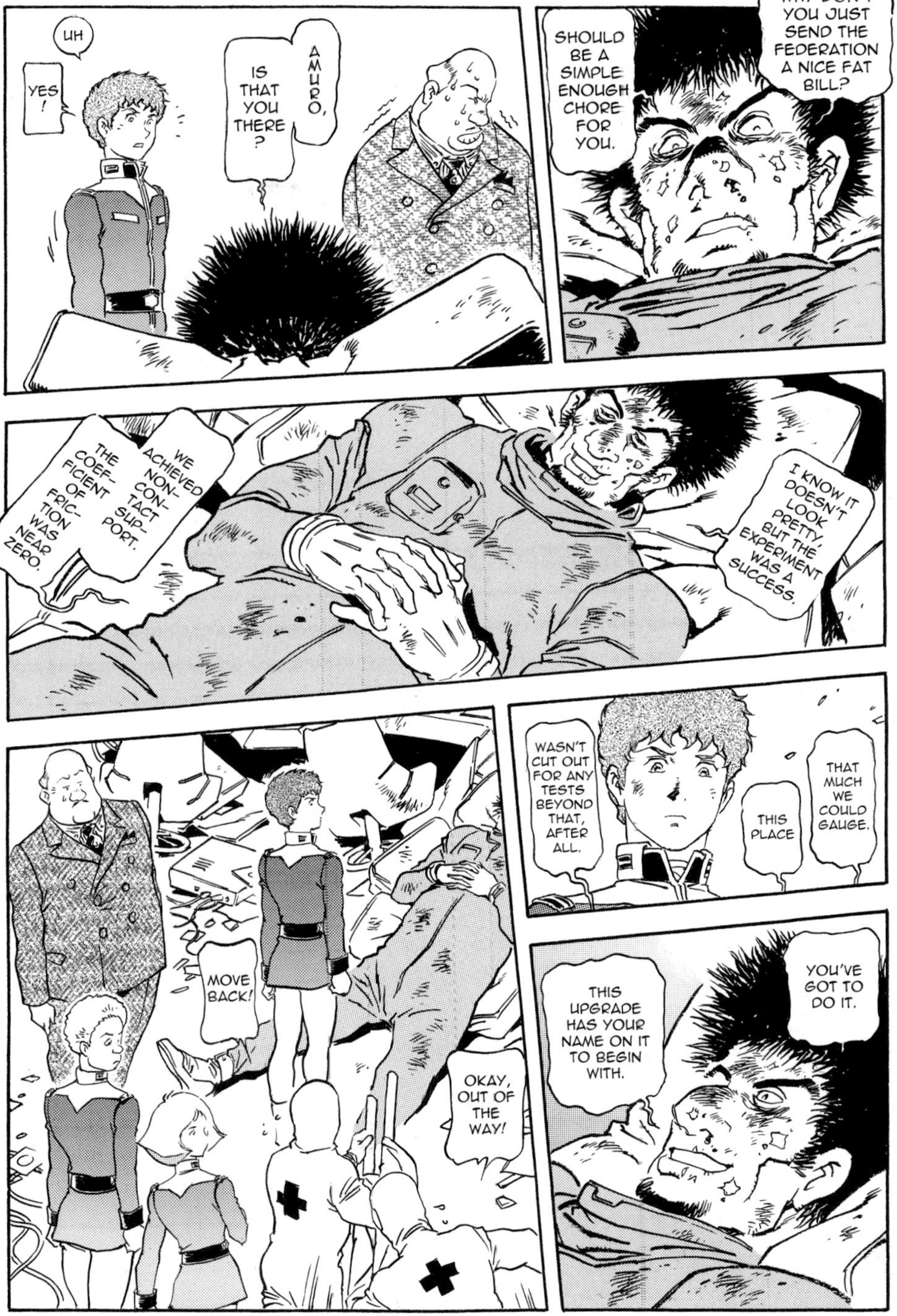

WHY DON'T YOU JUST SEND THE FEDERATION A NICE FAT BILL?
SHOULD BE A SIMPLE ENOUGH CHORE FOR YOU.
AMURO, IS THAT YOU THERE?
UH
YES!
I KNOW IT DOESN'T LOOK PRETTY, BUT THE EXPERIMENT WAS A SUCCESS.
WE ACHIEVED NON-CONTACT SUPPORT.
THE COEFFICIENT OF FRICTION WAS NEAR ZERO.
THAT MUCH WE COULD GAUGE.
THIS PLACE
WASN'T CUT OUT FOR ANY TESTS BEYOND THAT, AFTER ALL.
YOU'VE GOT TO DO IT.
THIS UPGRADE HAS YOUR NAME ON IT TO BEGIN WITH.
MOVE BACK!
OKAY, OUT OF THE WAY!

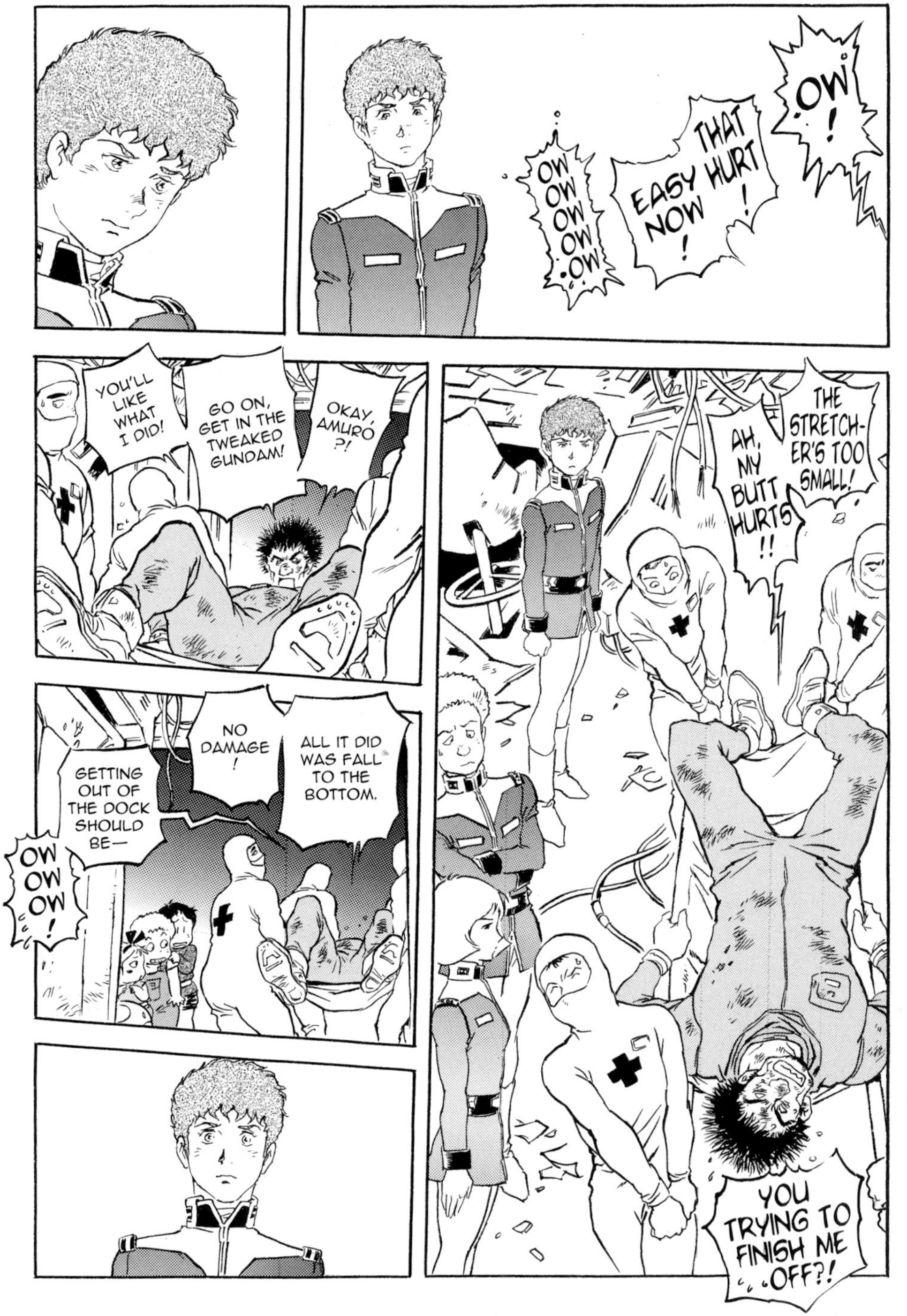
OW!
EASY NOW! THAT HURT!
OW OW OW OW OW
THE STRETCHER'S TOO SMALL!
AH, MY BUTT HURTS!!
YOU TRYING TO FINISH ME OFF?!
OKAY, AMURO?!
GO ON, GET IN THE TWEAKED GUNDAM!
YOU'LL LIKE WHAT I DID!
ALL IT DID WAS FALL TO THE BOTTOM.
NO DAMAGE!
GETTING OUT OF THE DOCK SHOULD BE—
OW OW OW!

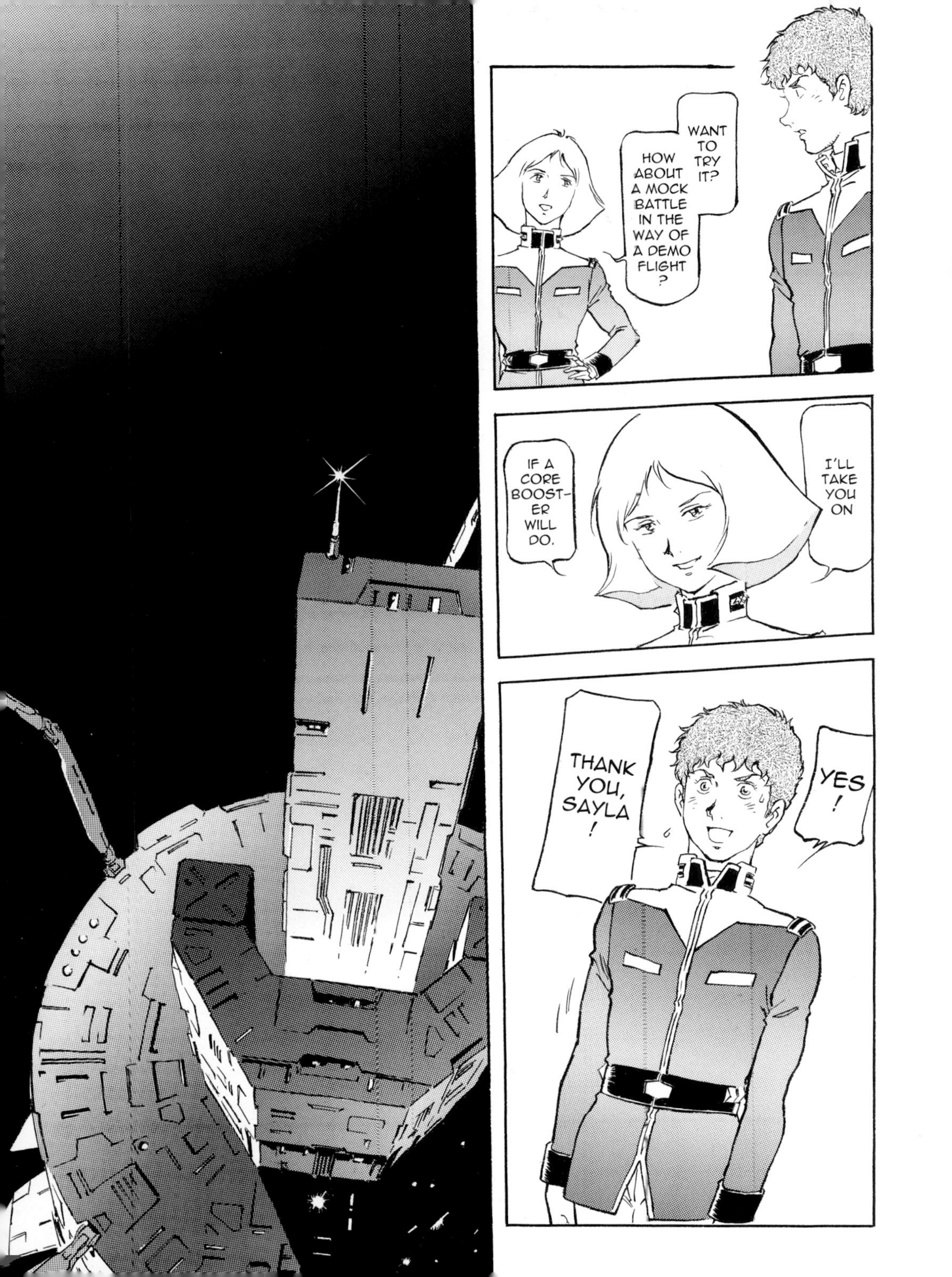
WANT TO TRY IT?
HOW ABOUT A MOCK BATTLE IN THE WAY OF A DEMO FLIGHT?
I'LL TAKE YOU ON
IF A CORE BOOST-ER WILL DO.
YES!
THANK YOU, SAYLA!

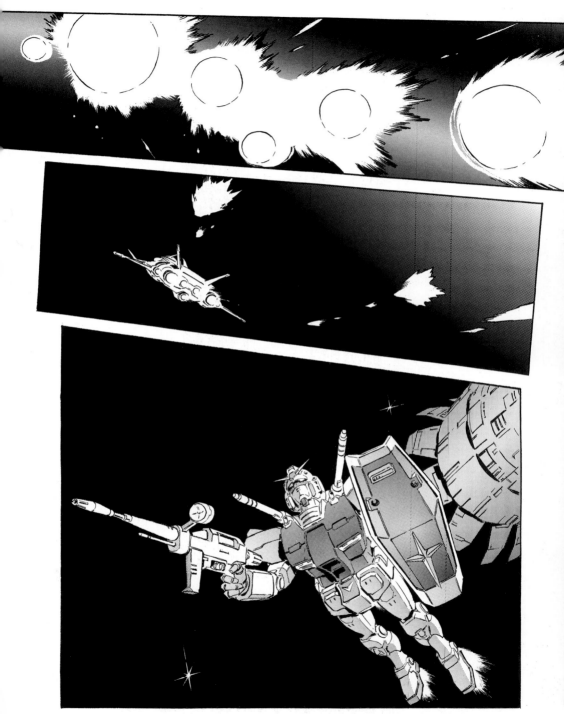

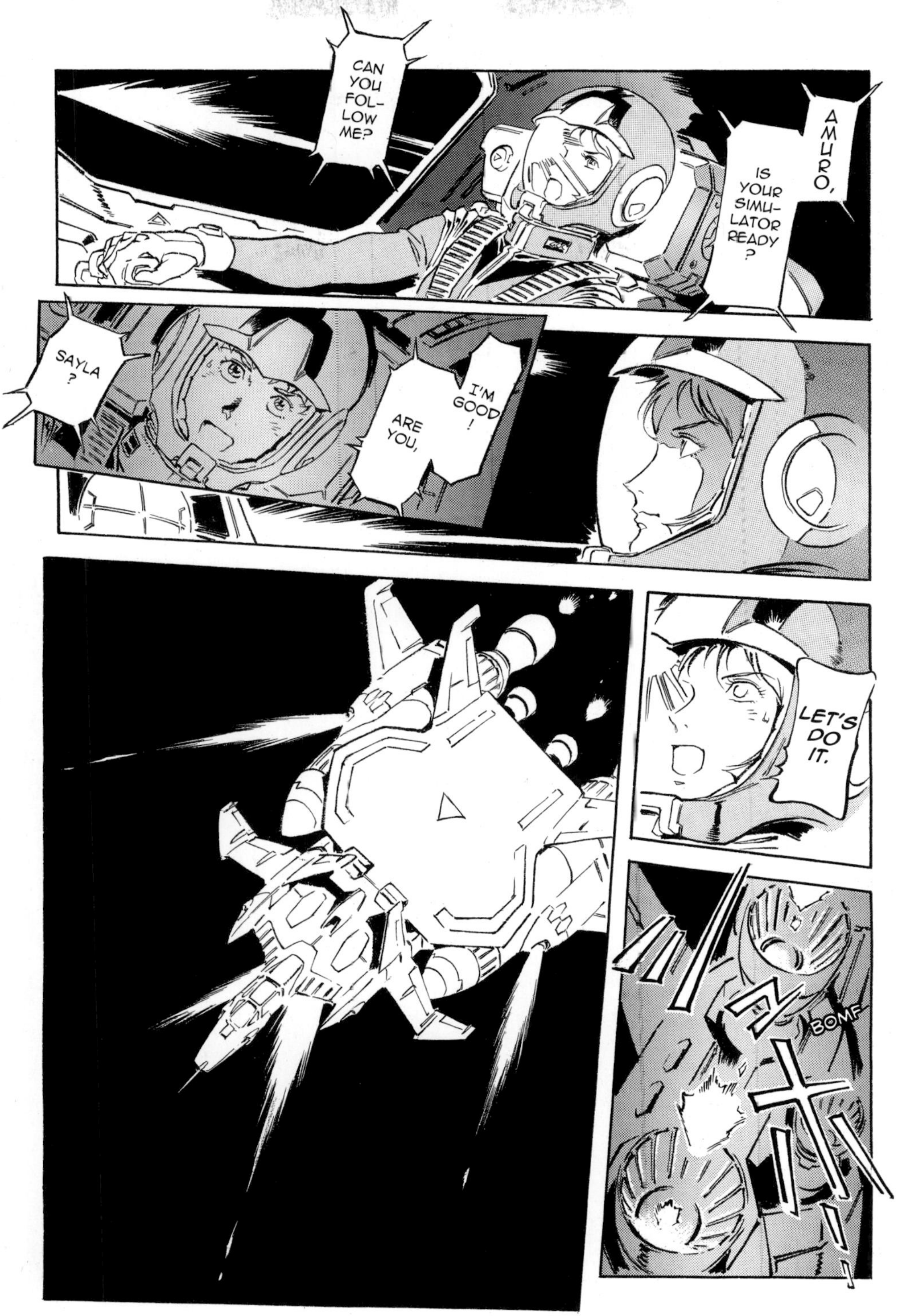
AMURO, IS YOUR SIMULATOR READY?
CAN YOU FOLLOW ME?
I'M GOOD!
ARE YOU,
SAYLA?
LET'S DO IT.
BOMF

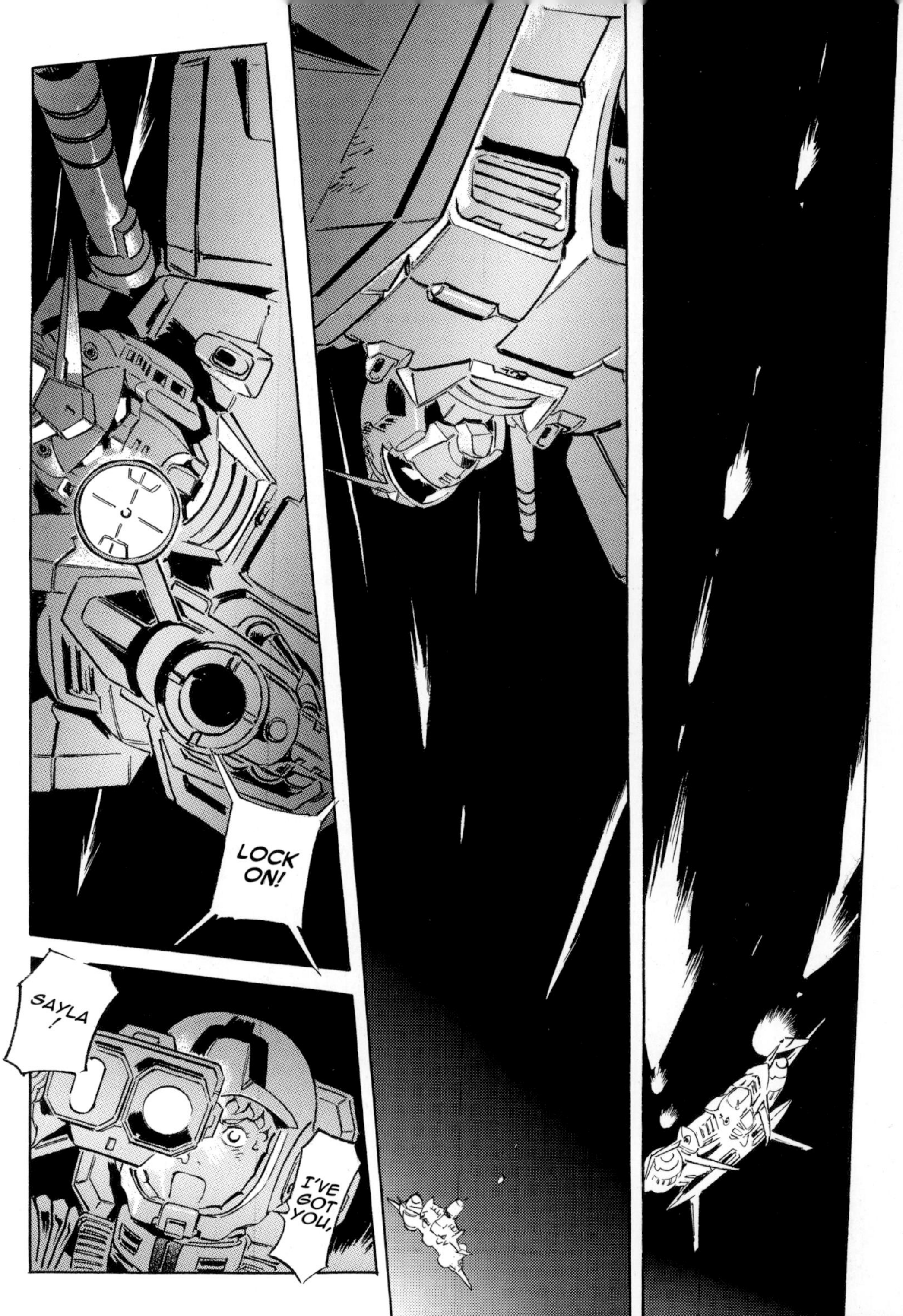
LOCK ON!
I'VE GOT YOU,
SAYLA!

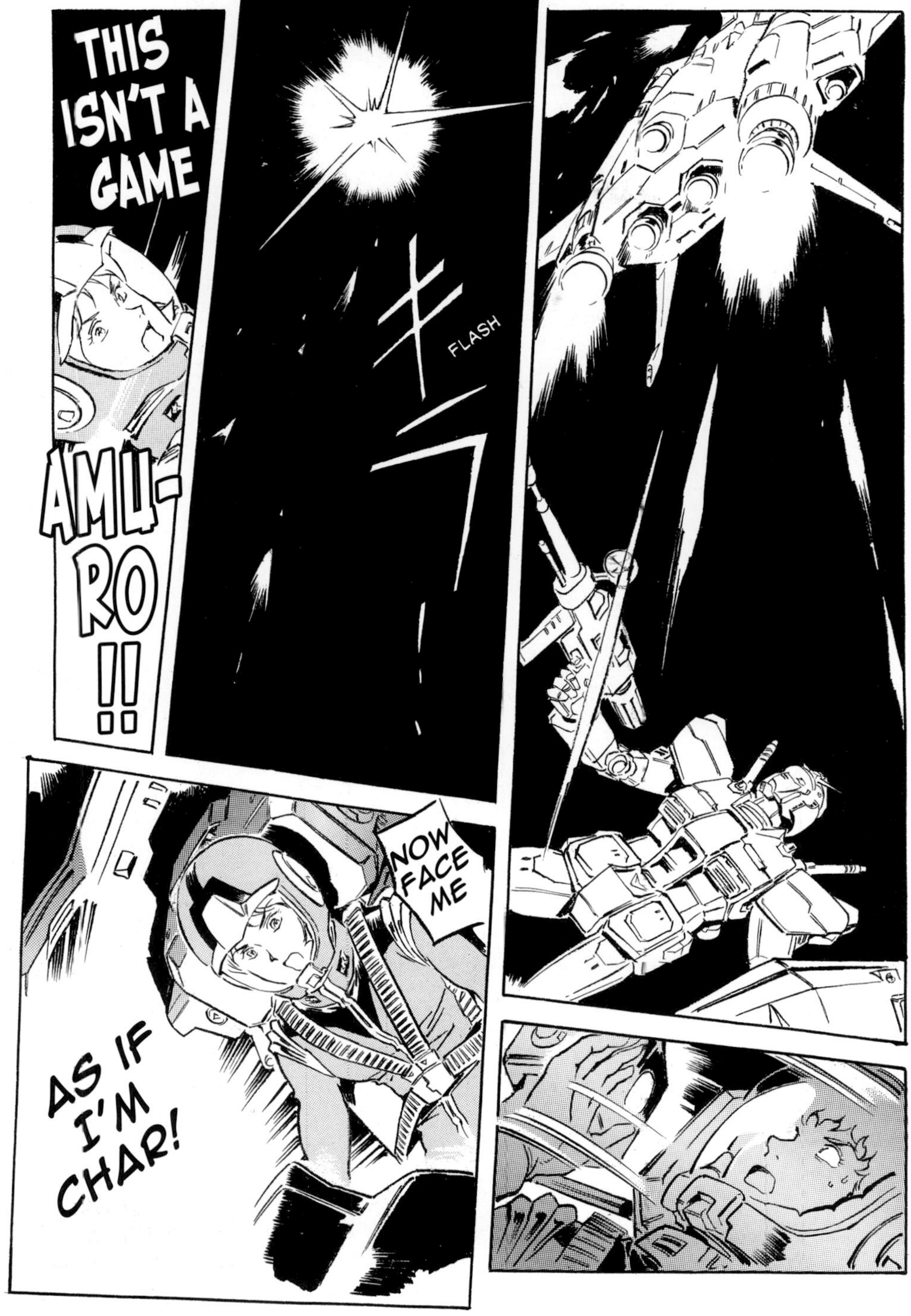
FLASH
THIS ISN'T A GAME
AMU-RO!!
NOW FACE ME
AS IF I'M CHAR!

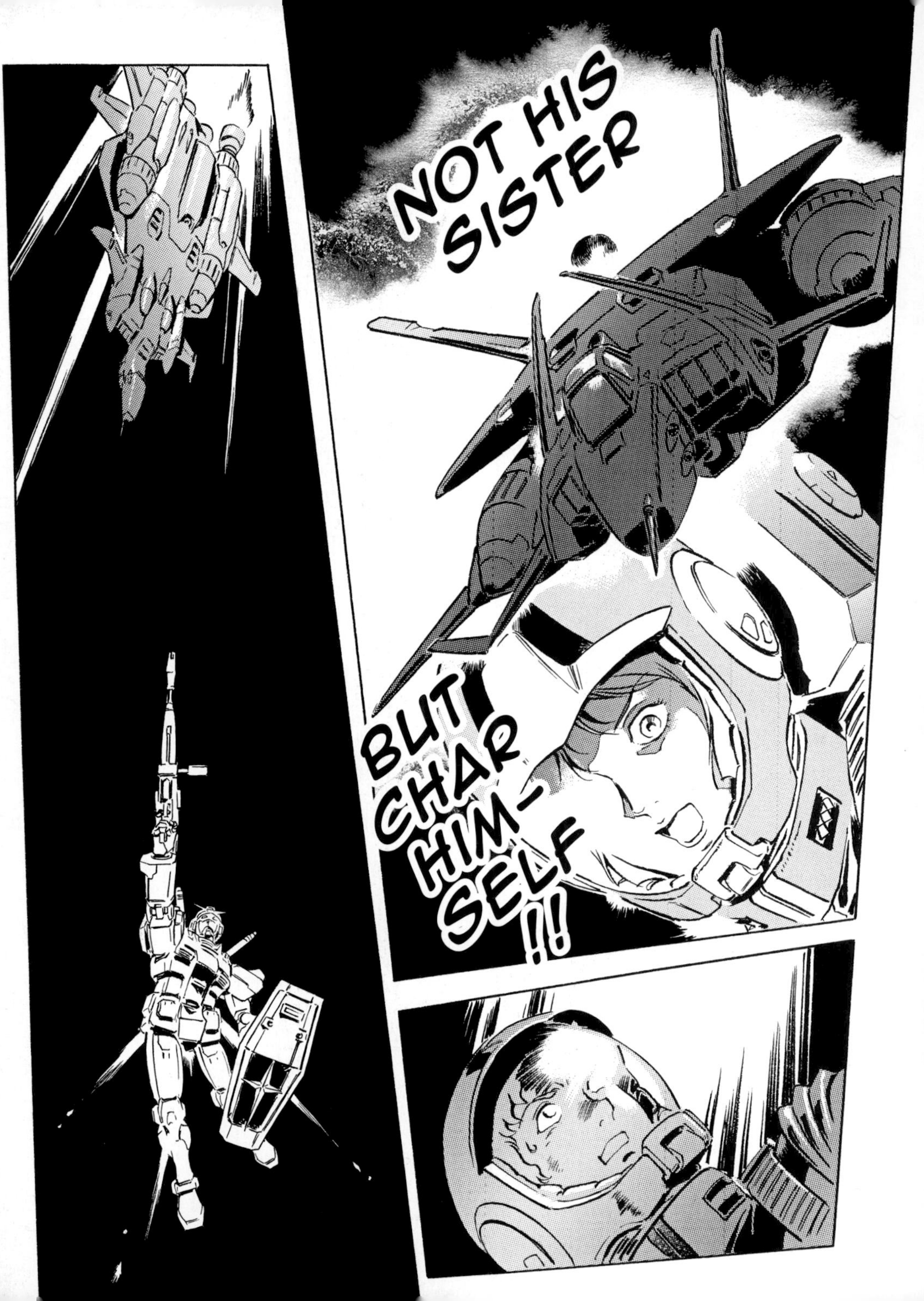
NOT HIS SISTER
BUT CHAR HIMSELF!!

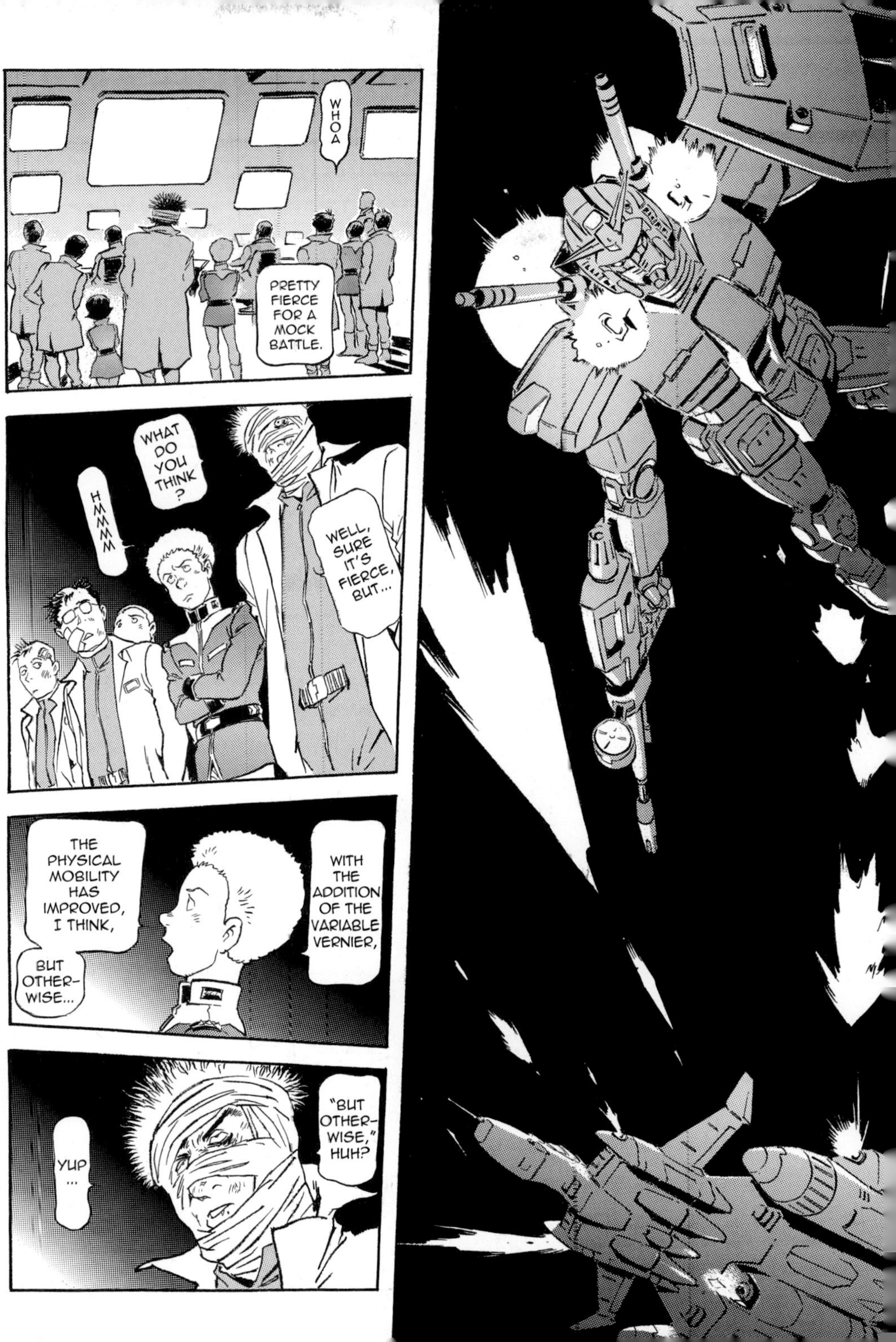
WHOA
PRETTY FIERCE FOR A MOCK BATTLE.
WHAT DO YOU THINK?
HMMMM
WELL, SURE IT'S FIERCE, BUT...
WITH THE ADDITION OF THE VARIABLE VERNIER,
THE PHYSICAL MOBILITY HAS IMPROVED, I THINK,
BUT OTHERWISE...
"BUT OTHERWISE," HUH?
YUP...

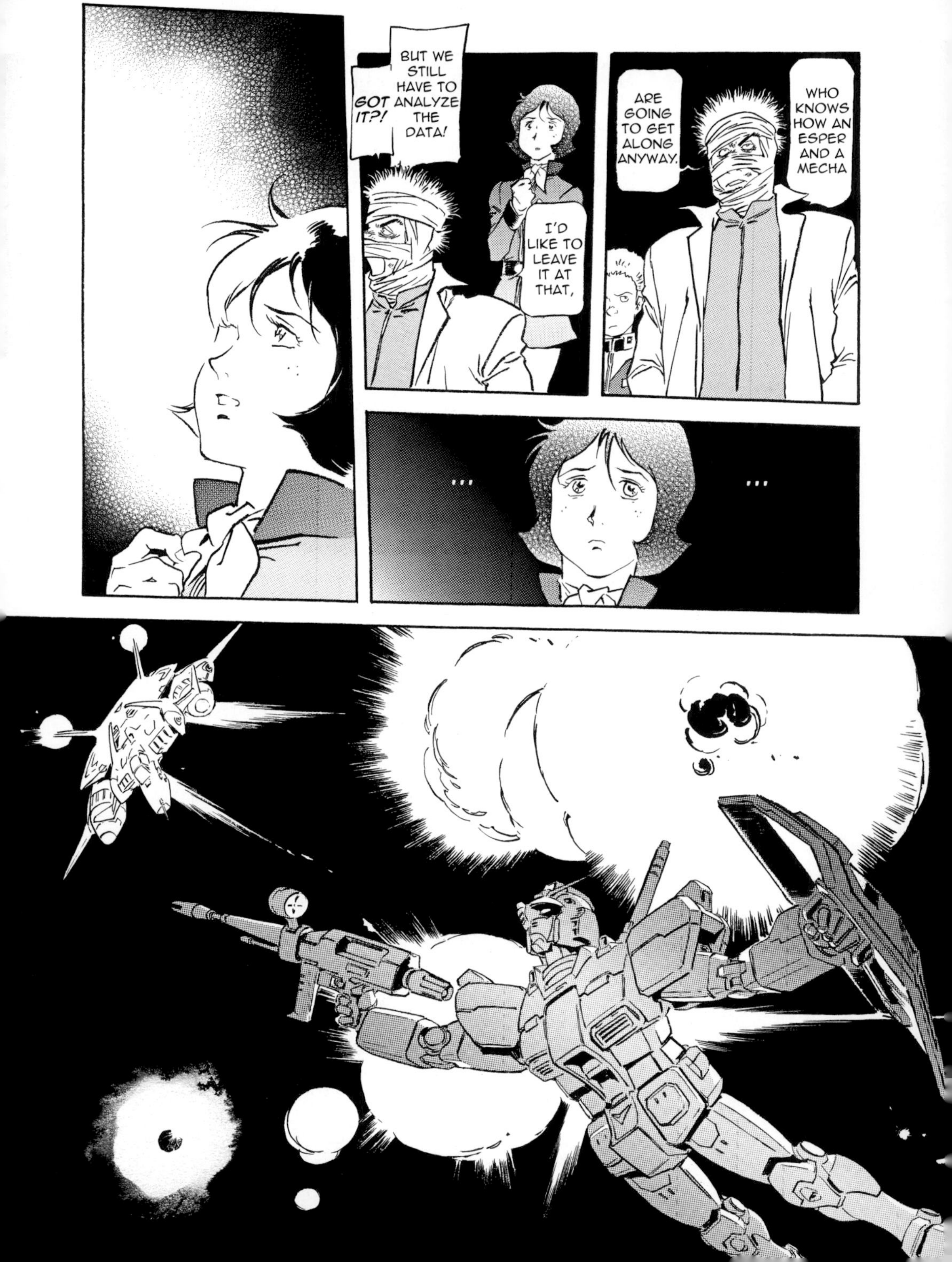

WHO KNOWS HOW AN ESPER AND A MECHA
ARE GOING TO GET ALONG ANYWAY.
I'D LIKE TO LEAVE IT AT THAT,
BUT WE STILL HAVE TO ANALYZE THE DATA!
GOT IT?!
...
...

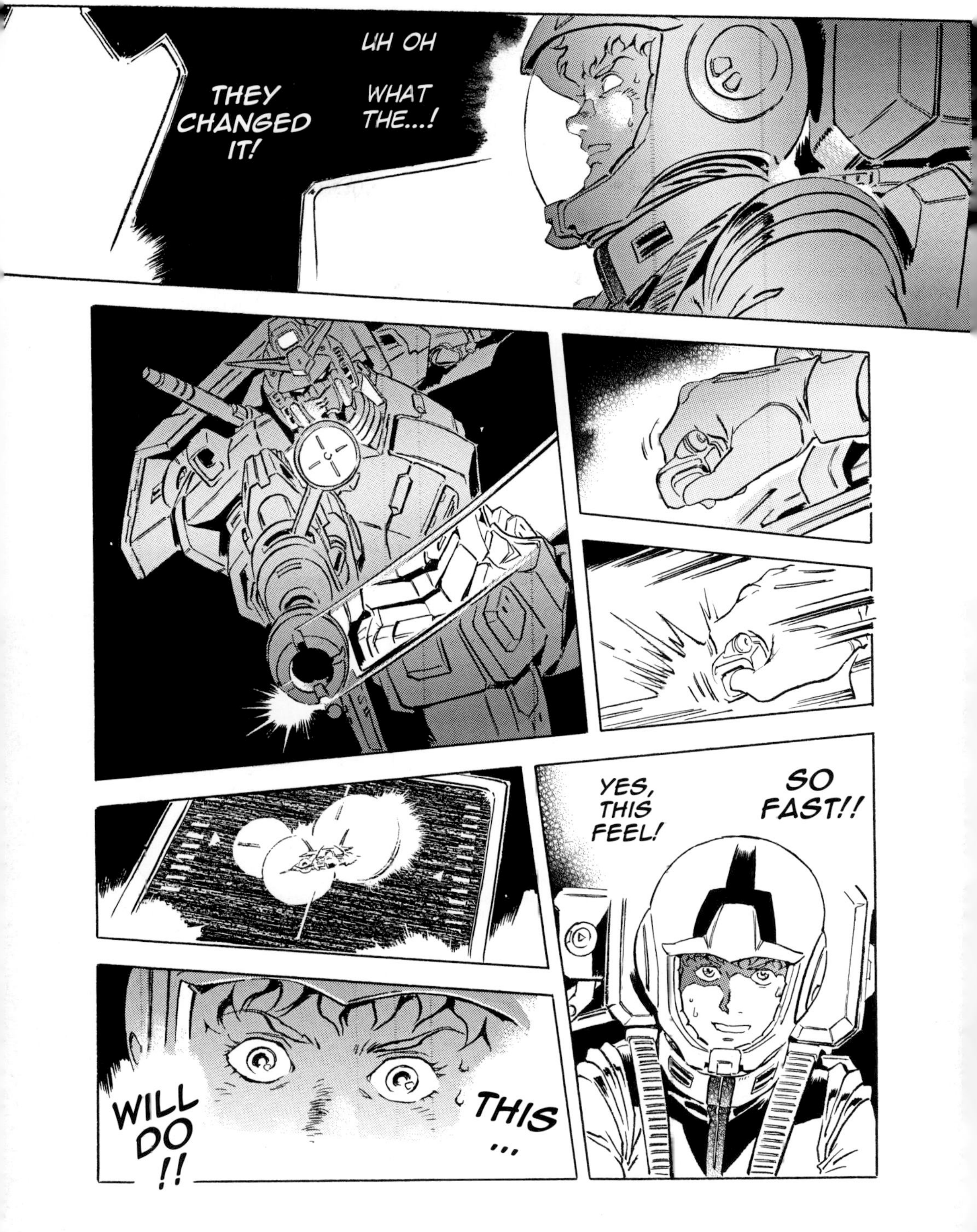
UH OH
WHAT THE...!
THEY CHANGED IT!
SO FAST!!
YES, THIS FEEL!
THIS...
WILL DO!!

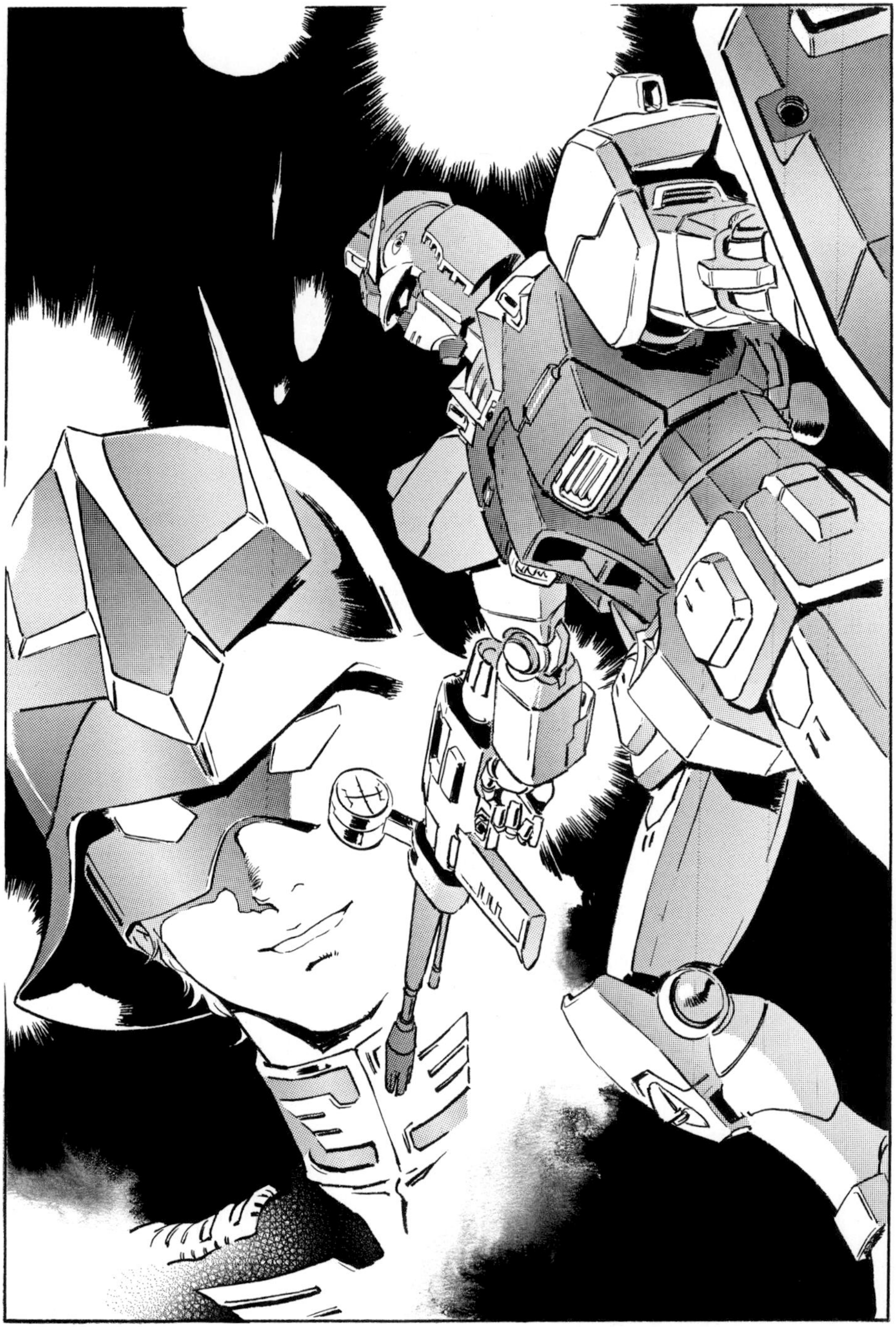

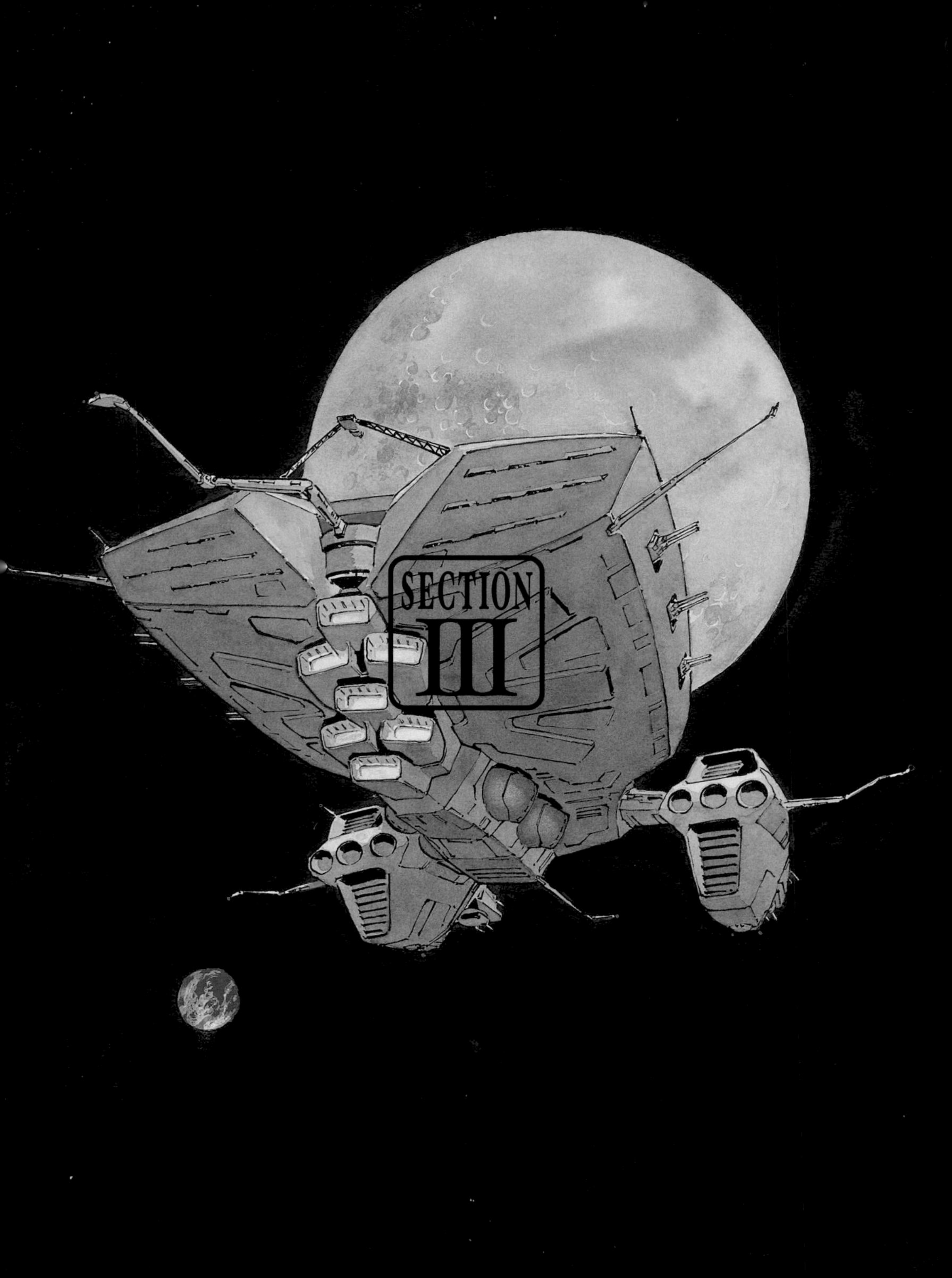
SECTION III

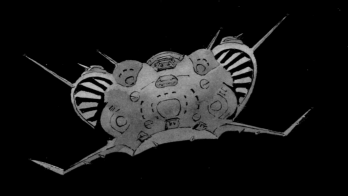

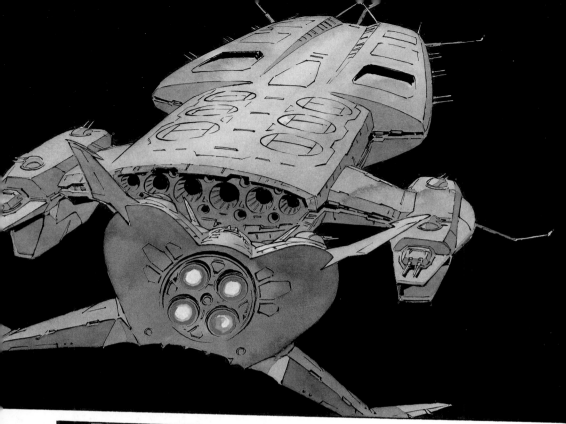

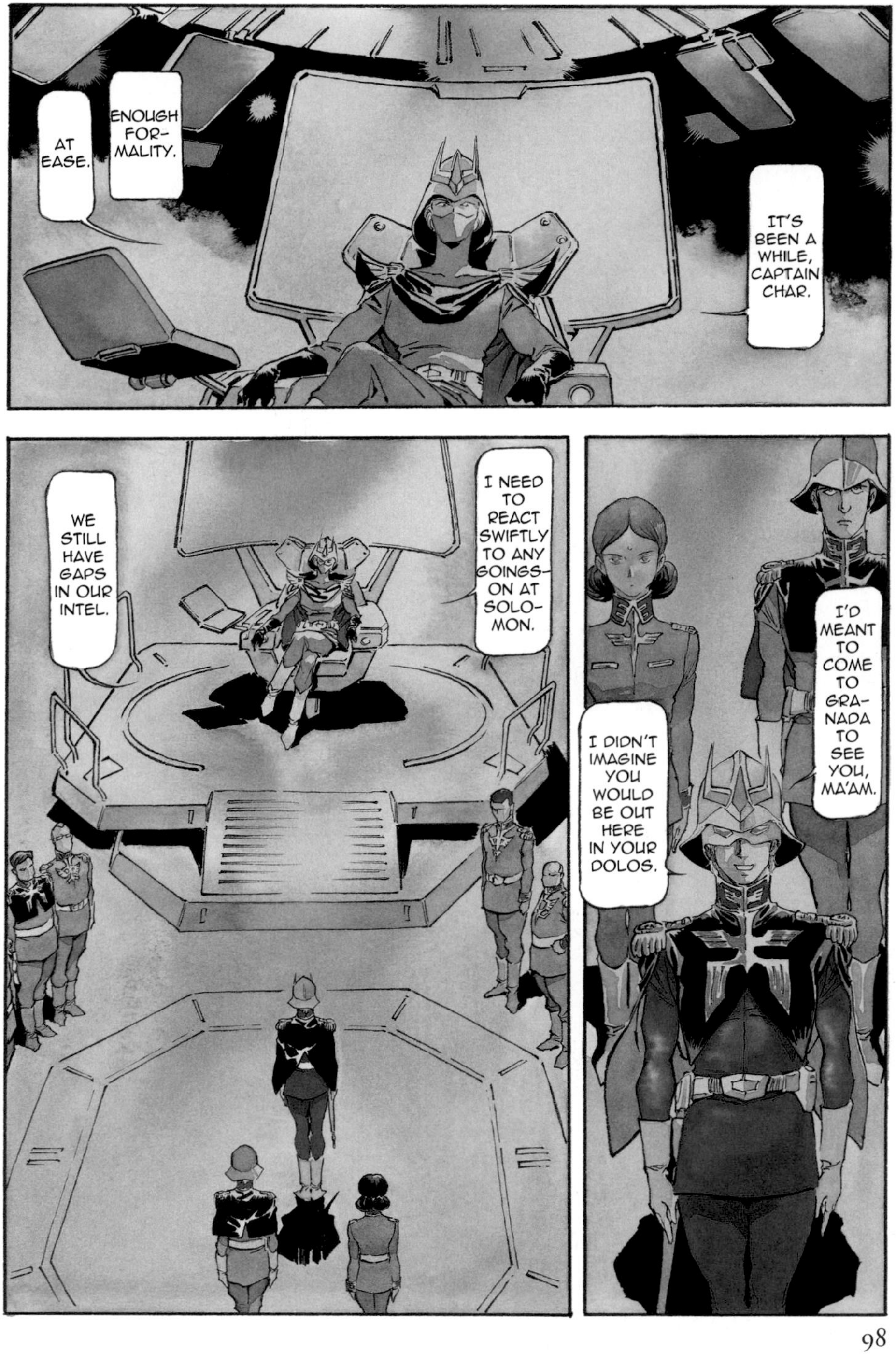
IT'S BEEN A WHILE, CAPTAIN CHAR.
ENOUGH FOR-MALITY.
AT EASE.
I'D MEANT TO COME TO GRA-NADA TO SEE YOU, MA'AM.
I DIDN'T IMAGINE YOU WOULD BE OUT HERE IN YOUR DOLOS.
I NEED TO REACT SWIFTLY TO ANY GOINGS-ON AT SOLO-MON.
WE STILL HAVE GAPS IN OUR INTEL.

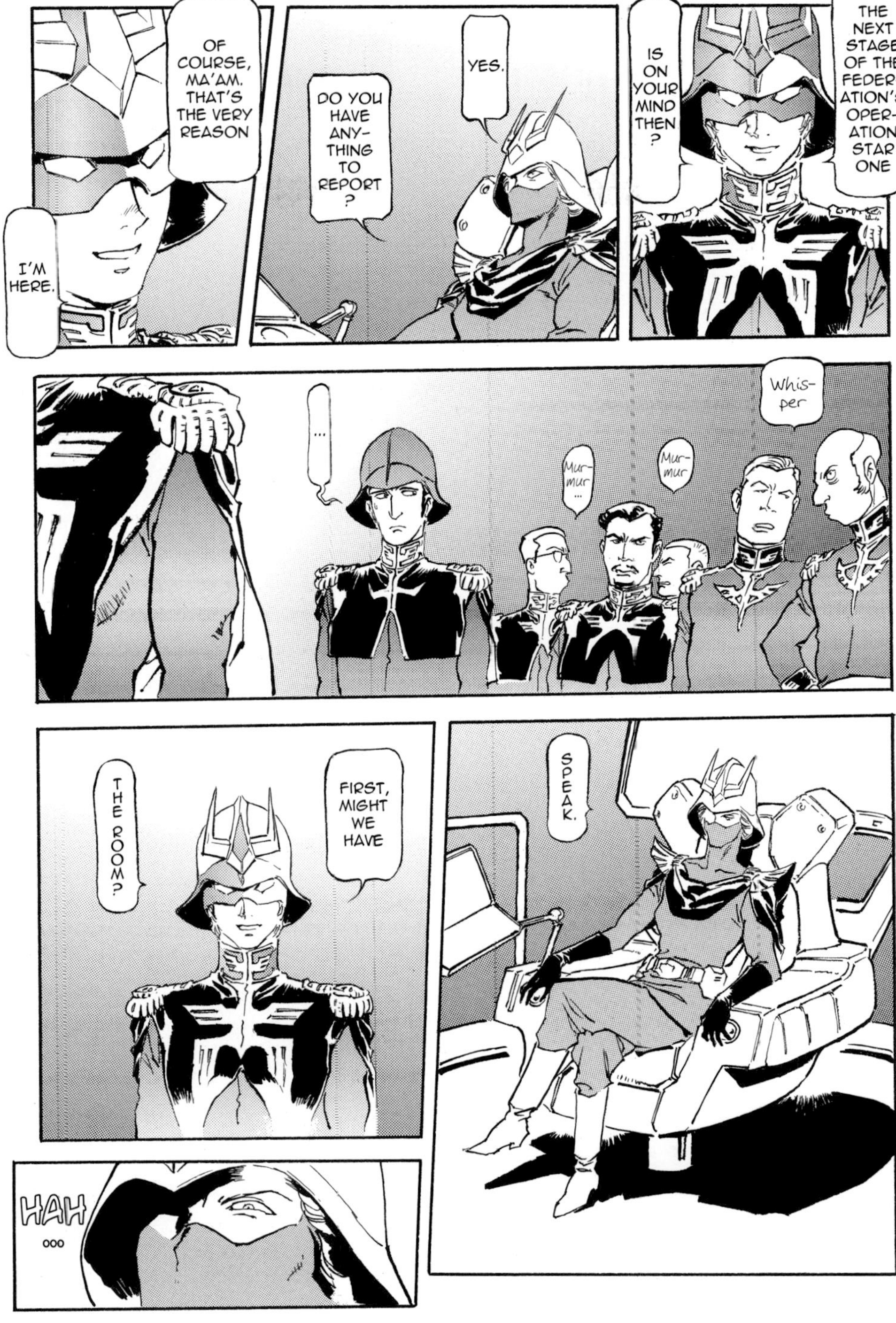
THE NEXT STAGE OF THE FEDERATION'S OPERATION STAR ONE
IS ON YOUR MIND THEN?
YES.
DO YOU HAVE ANYTHING TO REPORT?
OF COURSE, MA'AM. THAT'S THE VERY REASON
I'M HERE.
Whis-per
Mur-mur
Mur-mur...
...
SPEAK.
FIRST, MIGHT WE HAVE
THE ROOM?
HAH
ooo

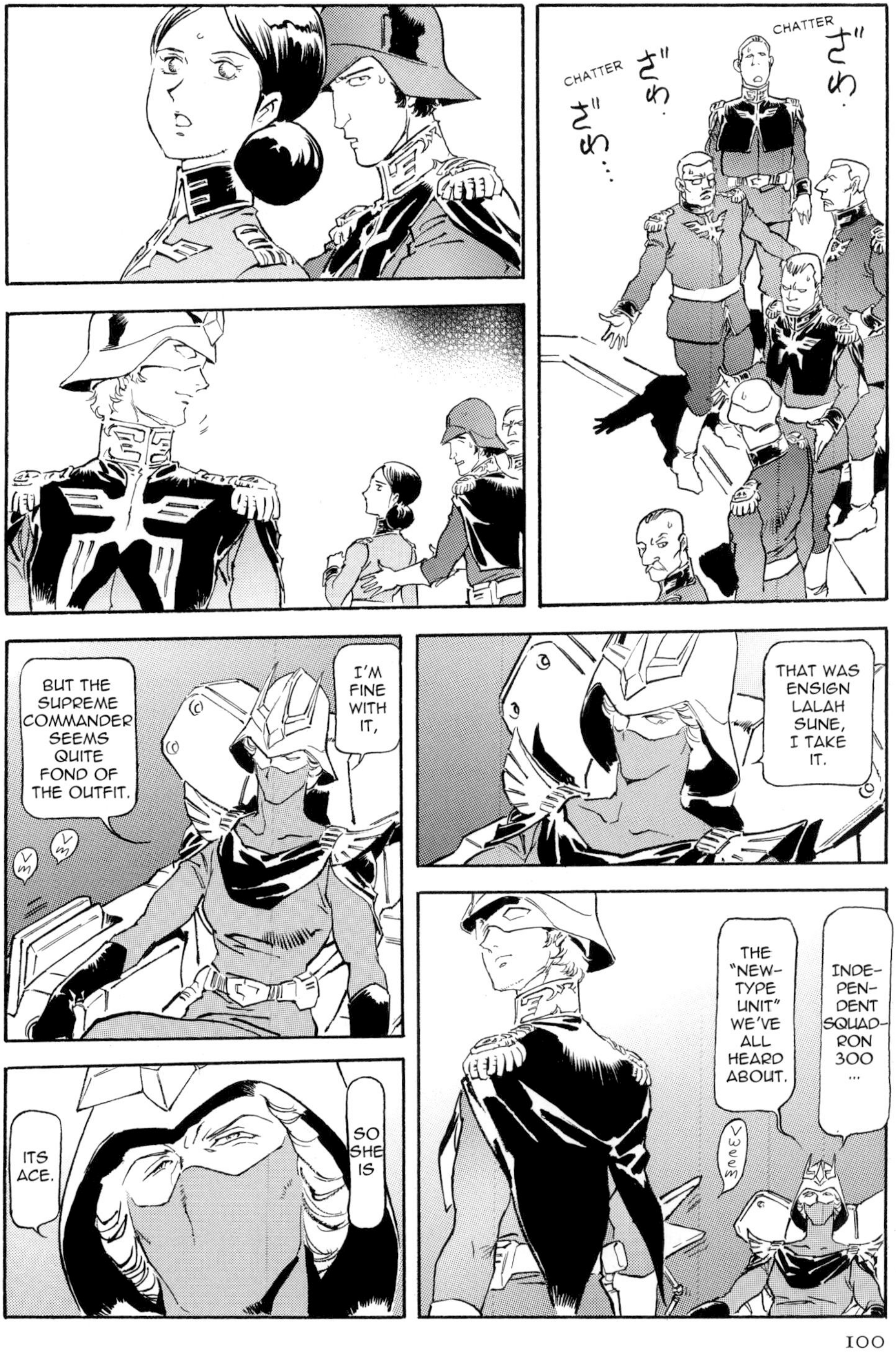
CHATTER
ざわ
CHATTER
ざわ
ざわ…
THAT WAS ENSIGN LALAH SUNE, I TAKE IT.
I'M FINE WITH IT,
BUT THE SUPREME COMMANDER SEEMS QUITE FOND OF THE OUTFIT.
Vm
Vm
INDEPENDENT SQUADRON 300 …
THE "NEWTYPE UNIT" WE'VE ALL HEARD ABOUT.
Vweem
SO SHE IS
ITS ACE.

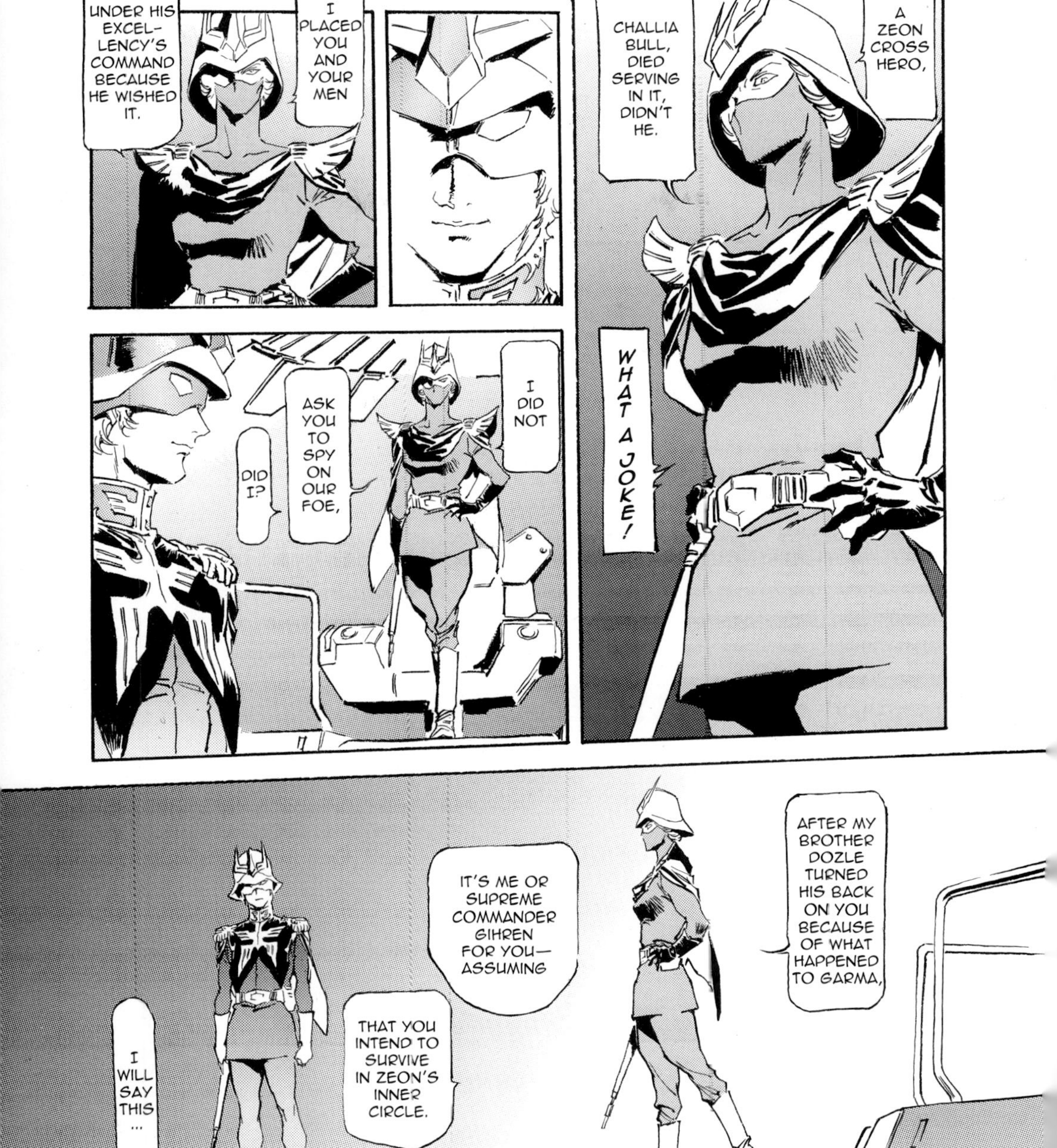
A ZEON CROSS HERO,
CHALLIA BULL, DIED SERVING IN IT, DIDN'T HE.
WHAT A JOKE!
I PLACED YOU AND YOUR MEN
UNDER HIS EXCEL-LENCY'S COMMAND BECAUSE HE WISHED IT.
I DID NOT
ASK YOU TO SPY ON OUR FOE,
DID I?
AFTER MY BROTHER DOZLE TURNED HIS BACK ON YOU BECAUSE OF WHAT HAPPENED TO GARMA,
IT'S ME OR SUPREME COMMANDER GIHREN FOR YOU— ASSUMING
THAT YOU INTEND TO SURVIVE IN ZEON'S INNER CIRCLE.
I WILL SAY THIS ...

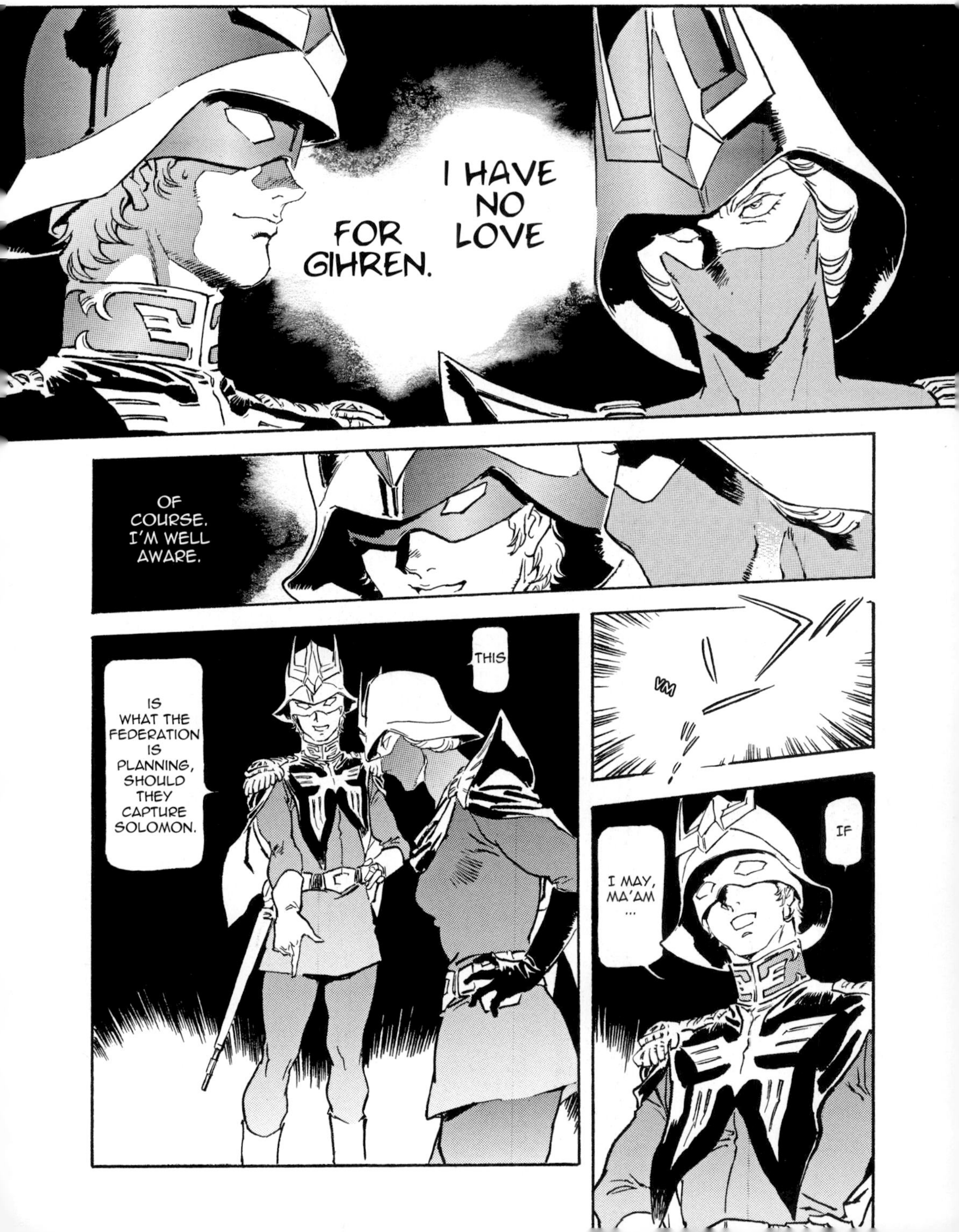
I HAVE NO LOVE FOR GIHREN.
OF COURSE. I'M WELL AWARE.
VM
IF
I MAY, MA'AM ...
THIS
IS WHAT THE FEDERATION IS PLANNING, SHOULD THEY CAPTURE SOLOMON.

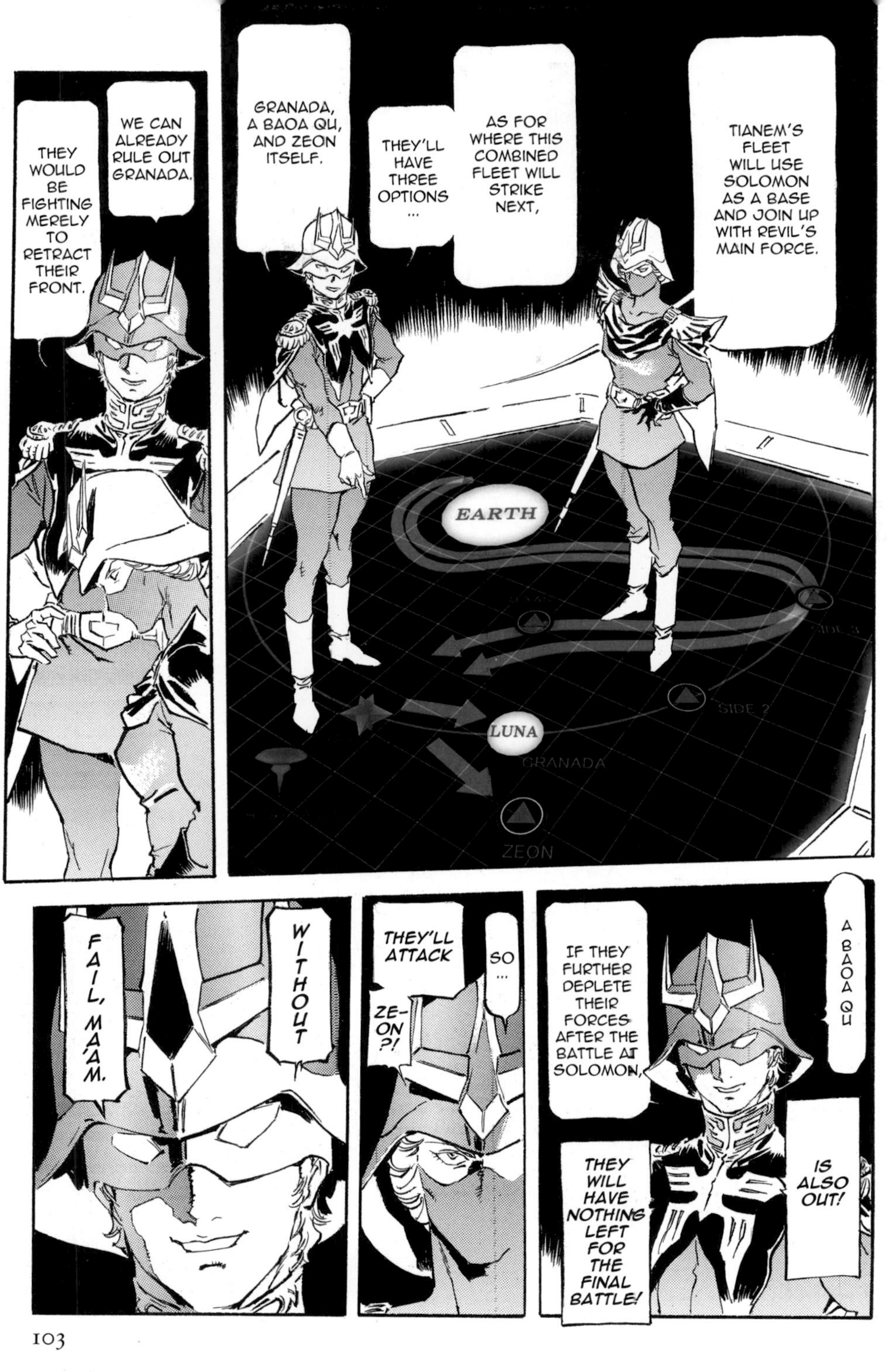
TIANEM'S FLEET WILL USE SOLOMON AS A BASE AND JOIN UP WITH REVIL'S MAIN FORCE.
AS FOR WHERE THIS COMBINED FLEET WILL STRIKE NEXT,
THEY'LL HAVE THREE OPTIONS ...
GRANADA, A BAOA QU, AND ZEON ITSELF.
EARTH
SIDE 3
SIDE 2
LUNA
GRANADA
ZEON
WE CAN ALREADY RULE OUT GRANADA.
THEY WOULD BE FIGHTING MERELY TO RETRACT THEIR FRONT.
A BAOA QU
IF THEY FURTHER DEPLETE THEIR FORCES AFTER THE BATTLE AT SOLOMON,
IS ALSO OUT!
THEY WILL HAVE NOTHING LEFT FOR THE FINAL BATTLE!
SO ...
THEY'LL ATTACK
ZE-ON?!
WITHOUT
FAIL, MA'AM.

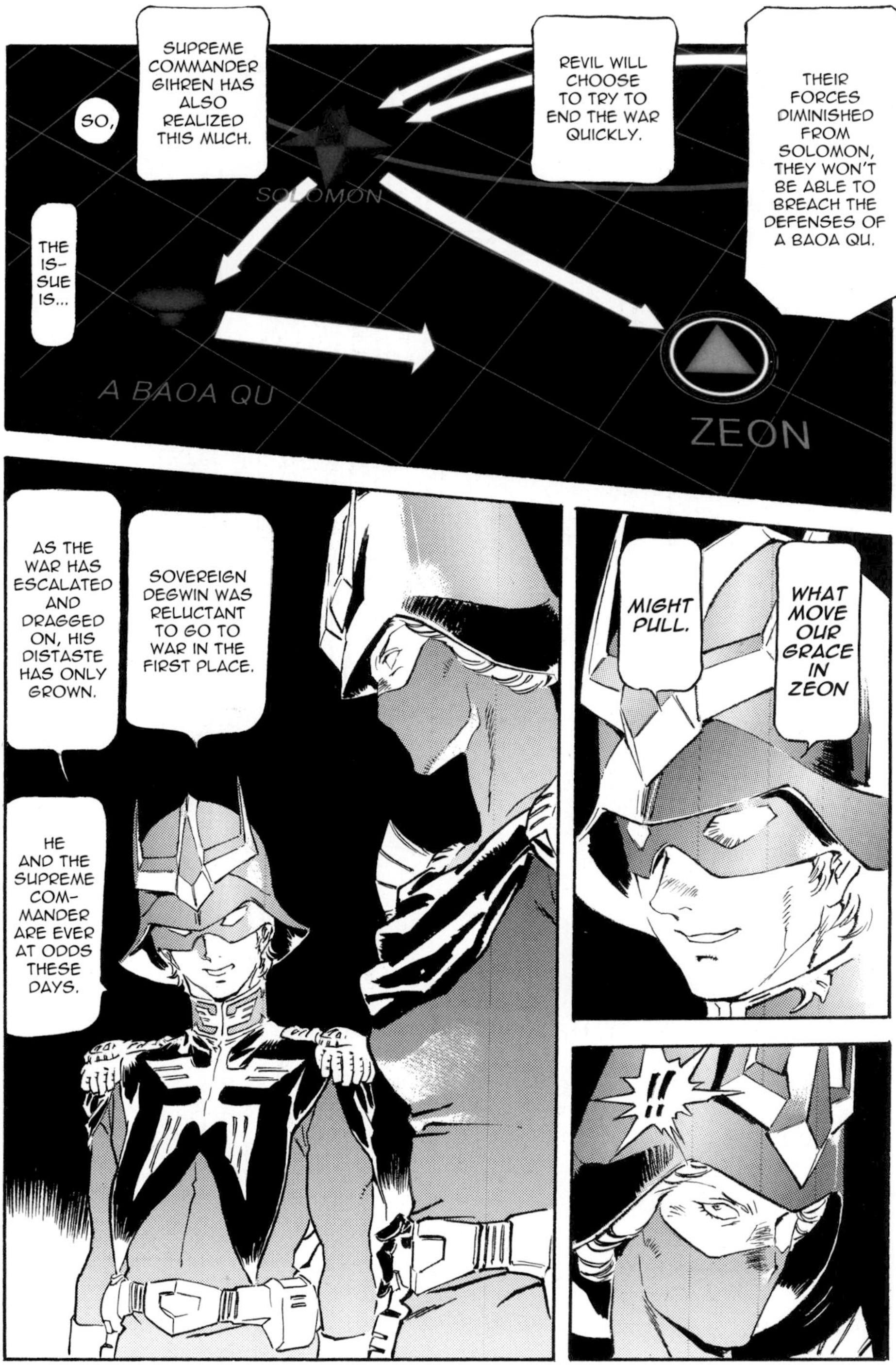
THEIR FORCES DIMINISHED FROM SOLOMON, THEY WON'T BE ABLE TO BREACH THE DEFENSES OF A BAOA QU.
REVIL WILL CHOOSE TO TRY TO END THE WAR QUICKLY.
SUPREME COMMANDER GIHREN HAS ALSO REALIZED THIS MUCH.
SO,
SOLOMON
THE IS-SUE IS...
ZEON
A BAOA QU
WHAT MOVE OUR GRACE IN ZEON
MIGHT PULL.
!!
SOVEREIGN DEGWIN WAS RELUCTANT TO GO TO WAR IN THE FIRST PLACE.
AS THE WAR HAS ESCALATED AND DRAGGED ON, HIS DISTASTE HAS ONLY GROWN.
HE AND THE SUPREME COM-MANDER ARE EVER AT ODDS THESE DAYS.

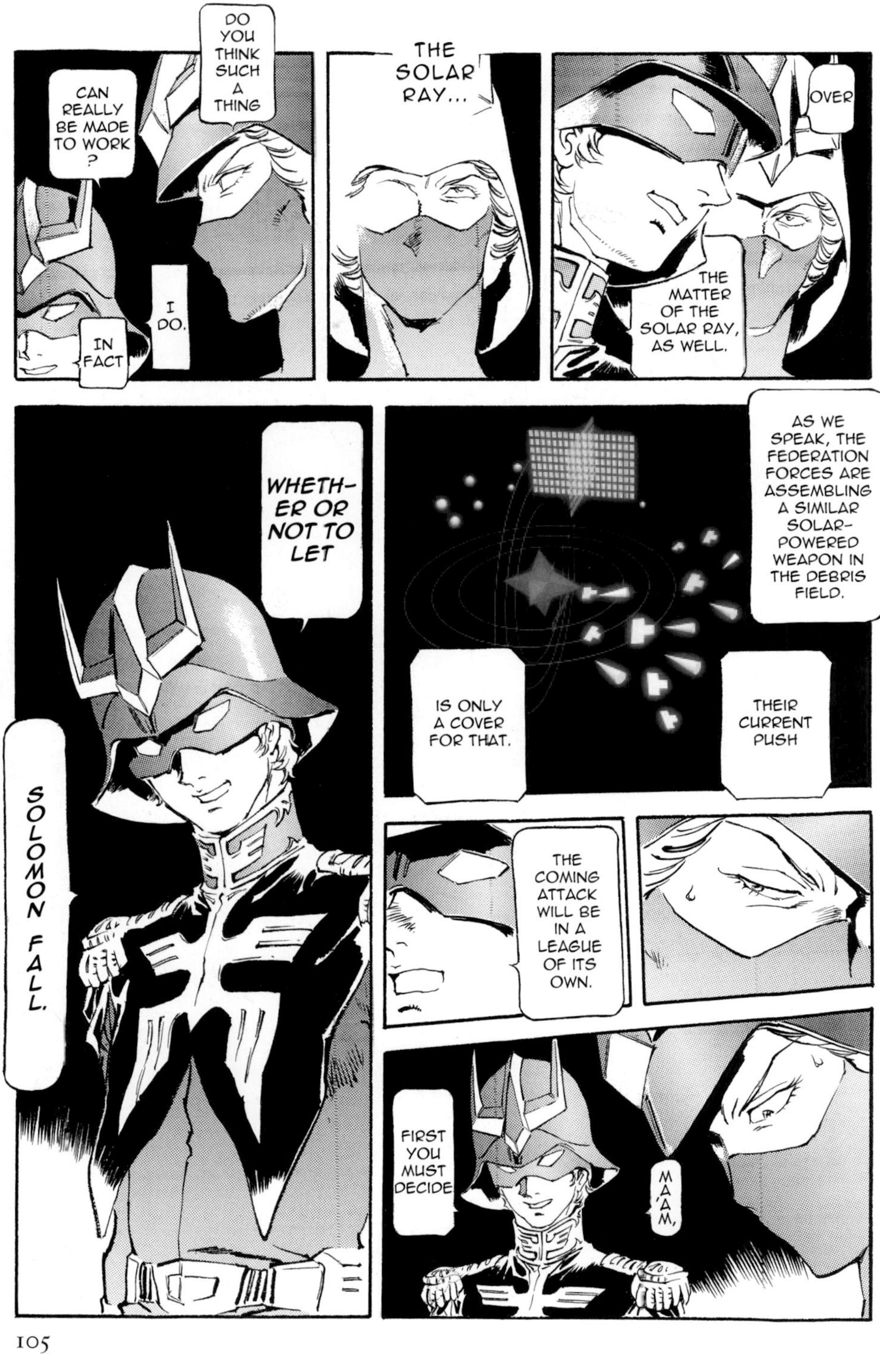
OVER
THE MATTER OF THE SOLAR RAY, AS WELL.
THE SOLAR RAY...
DO YOU THINK SUCH A THING
CAN REALLY BE MADE TO WORK?
I DO.
IN FACT
AS WE SPEAK, THE FEDERATION FORCES ARE ASSEMBLING A SIMILAR SOLAR-POWERED WEAPON IN THE DEBRIS FIELD.
THEIR CURRENT PUSH
IS ONLY A COVER FOR THAT.
THE COMING ATTACK WILL BE IN A LEAGUE OF ITS OWN.
MA'AM,
FIRST YOU MUST DECIDE
WHETH-ER OR NOT TO LET
SOLOMON FALL.

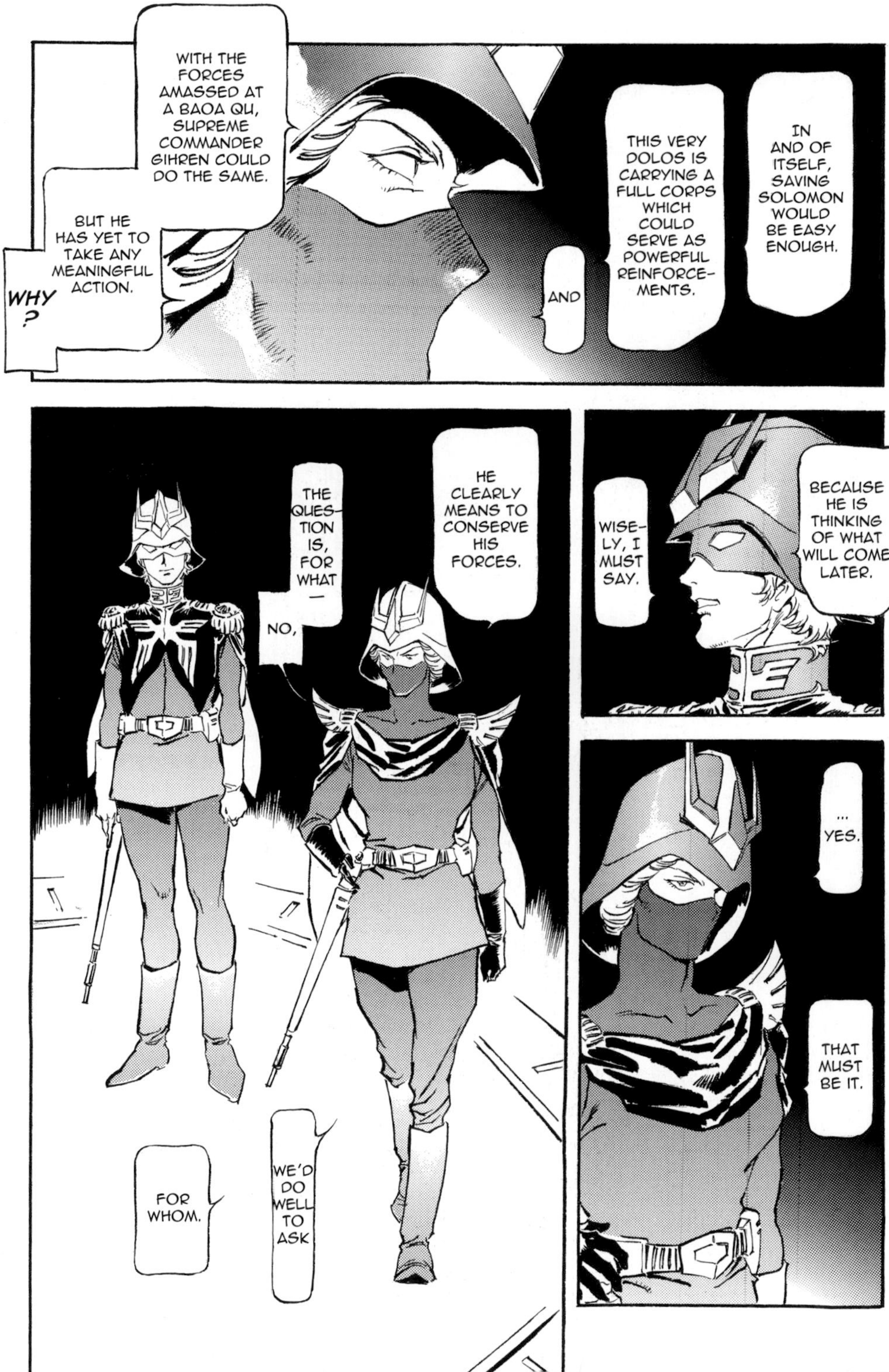

IN AND OF ITSELF, SAVING SOLOMON WOULD BE EASY ENOUGH.
THIS VERY DOLOS IS CARRYING A FULL CORPS WHICH COULD SERVE AS POWERFUL REINFORCEMENTS.
AND
WITH THE FORCES AMASSED AT A BAOA QU, SUPREME COMMANDER GIHREN COULD DO THE SAME.
BUT HE HAS YET TO TAKE ANY MEANINGFUL ACTION.
WHY?
BECAUSE HE IS THINKING OF WHAT WILL COME LATER.
WISELY, I MUST SAY.
... YES.
THAT MUST BE IT.
HE CLEARLY MEANS TO CONSERVE HIS FORCES.
THE QUESTION IS, FOR WHAT—
NO,
WE'D DO WELL TO ASK
FOR WHOM.

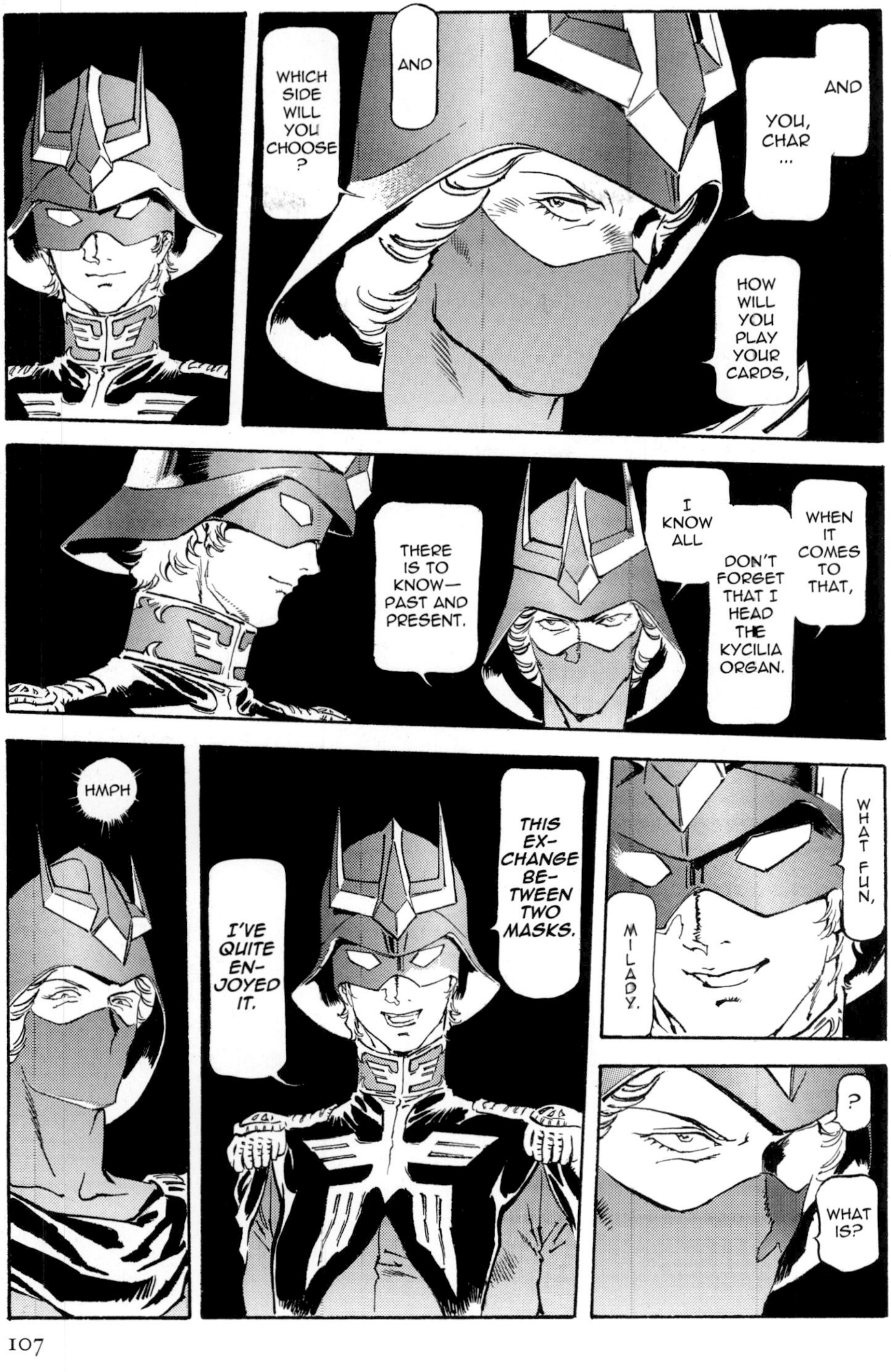
AND YOU, CHAR ...
HOW WILL YOU PLAY YOUR CARDS,
AND
WHICH SIDE WILL YOU CHOOSE ?
WHEN IT COMES TO THAT,
DON'T FORGET THAT I HEAD THE KYCILIA ORGAN.
I KNOW ALL
THERE IS TO KNOW— PAST AND PRESENT.
WHAT FUN,
MILADY.
?
WHAT IS?
THIS EX-CHANGE BE-TWEEN TWO MASKS.
I'VE QUITE EN-JOYED IT.
HMPH

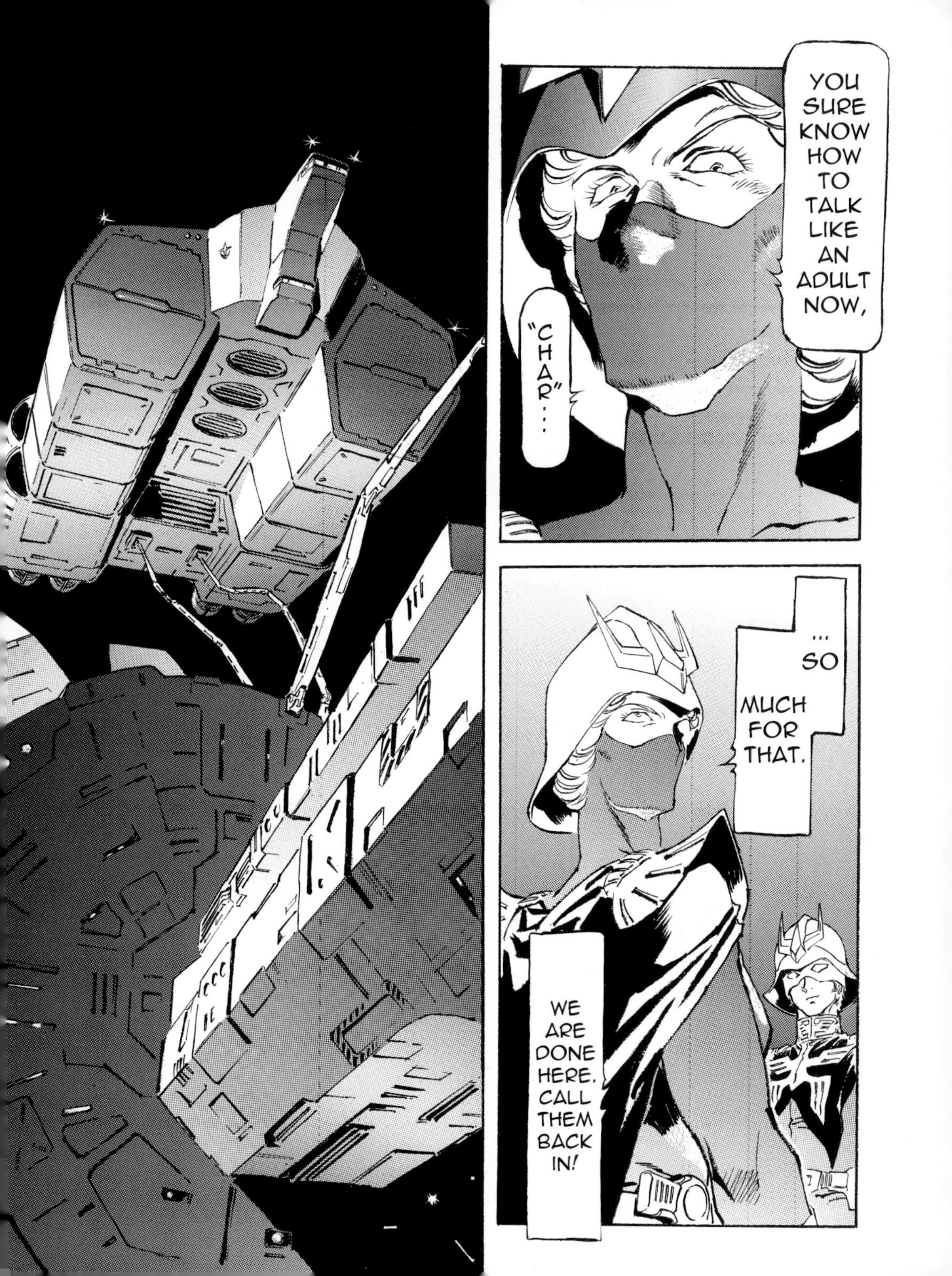
YOU SURE KNOW HOW TO TALK LIKE AN ADULT NOW,
"CHAR"...
... SO MUCH FOR THAT.
WE ARE DONE HERE. CALL THEM BACK IN!

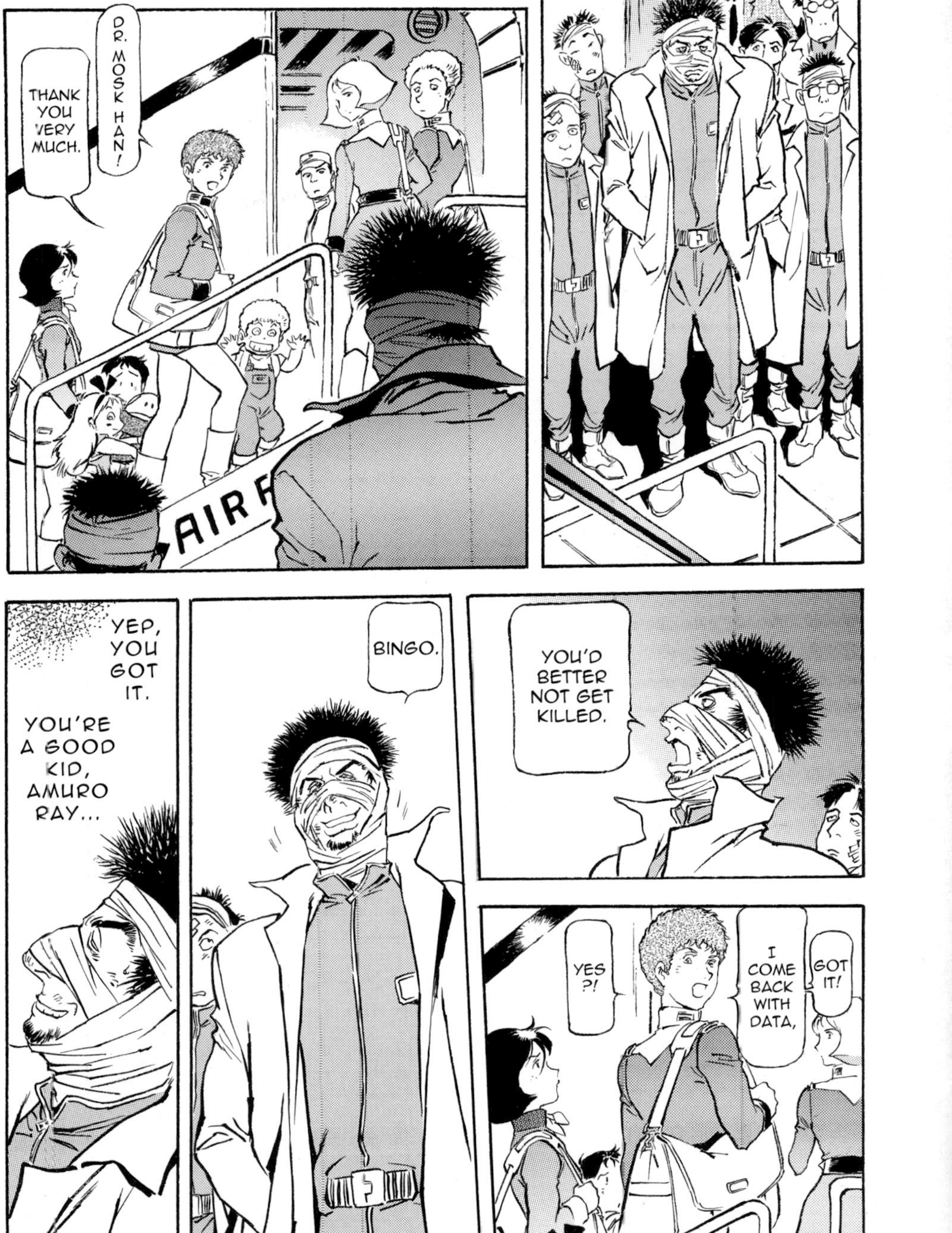
DR. MOSK HAN!
THANK YOU VERY MUCH.
YOU'D BETTER NOT GET KILLED.
GOT IT!
I COME BACK WITH DATA,
YES?!
BINGO.
YEP, YOU GOT IT.
YOU'RE A GOOD KID, AMURO RAY...

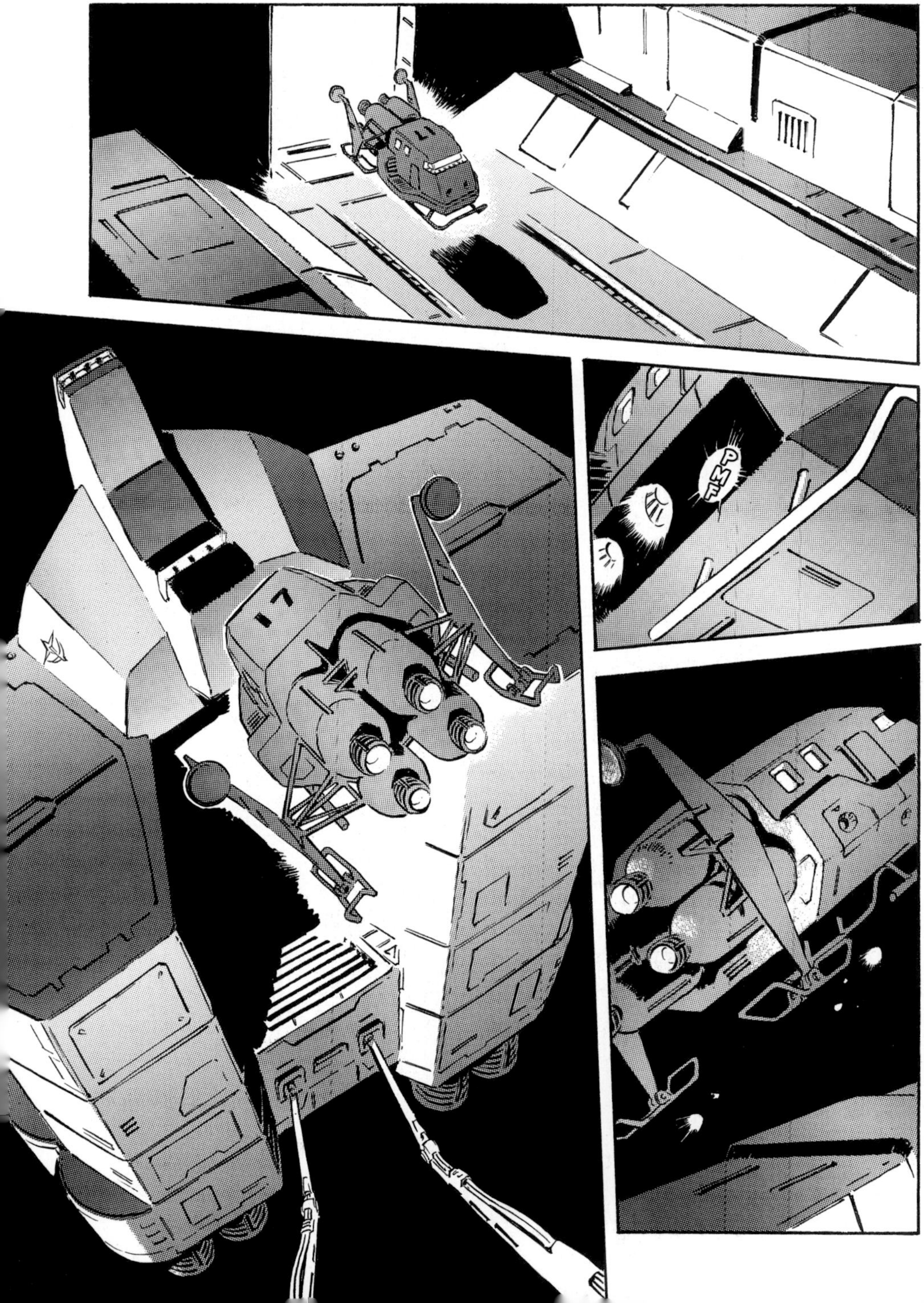
PMF

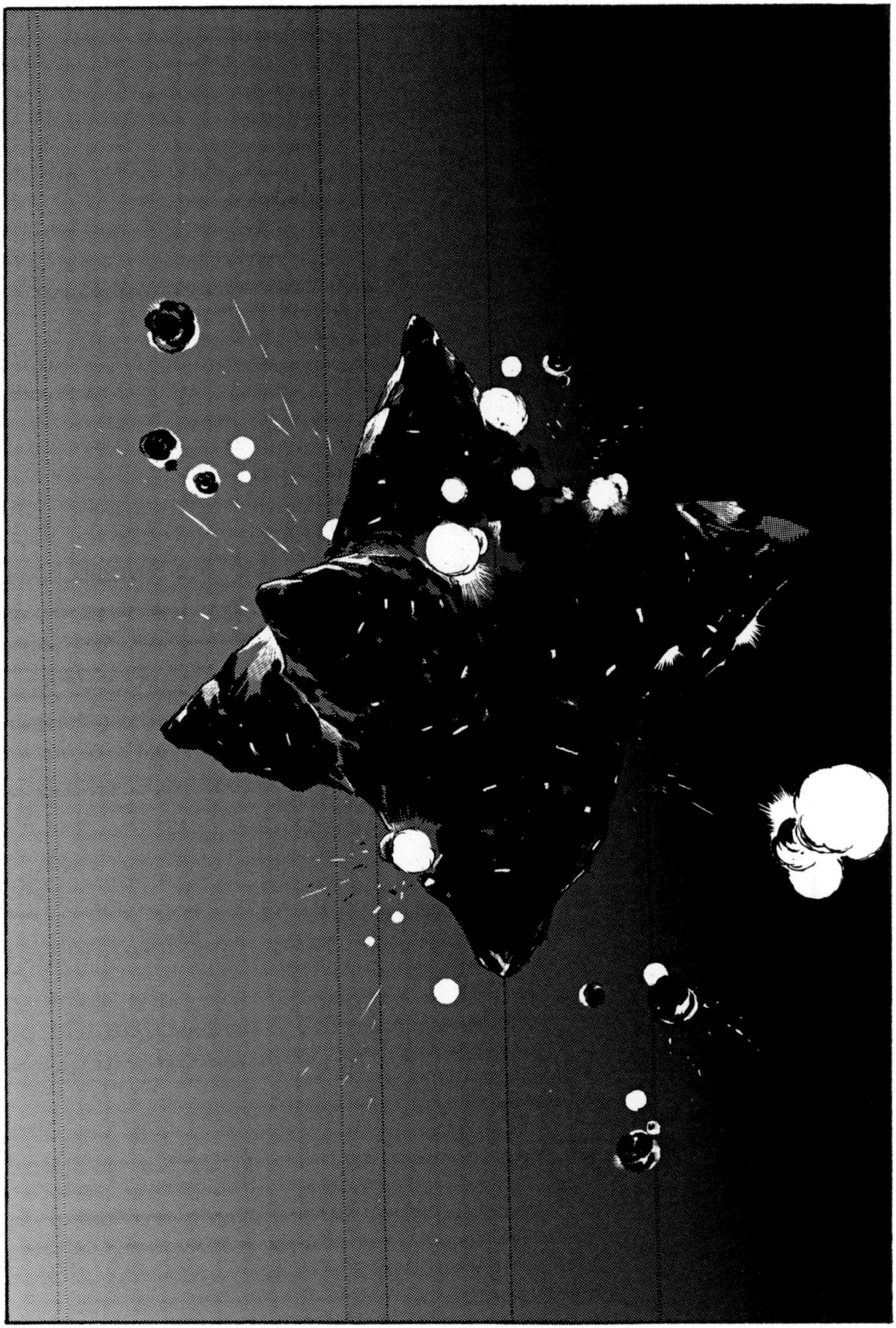

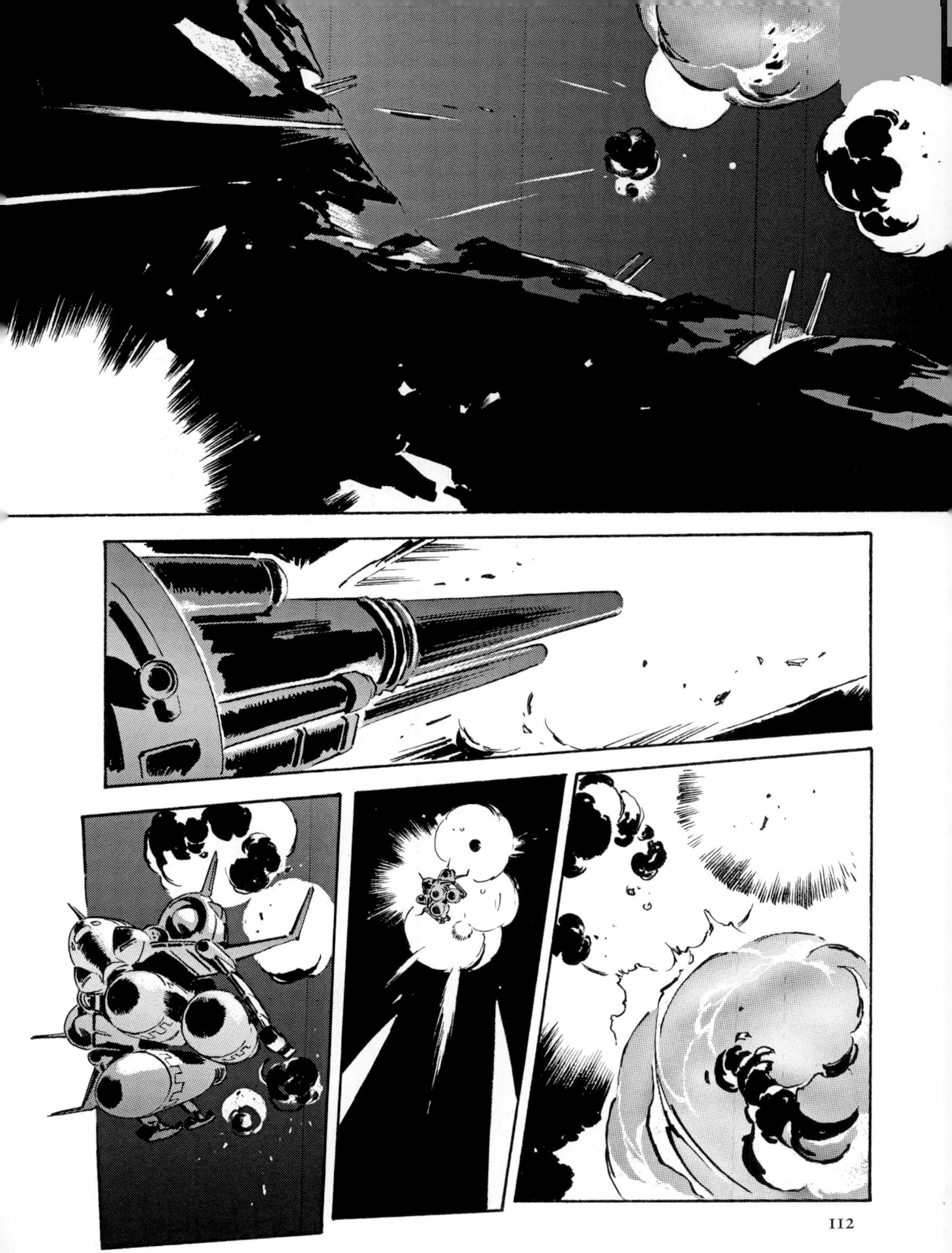

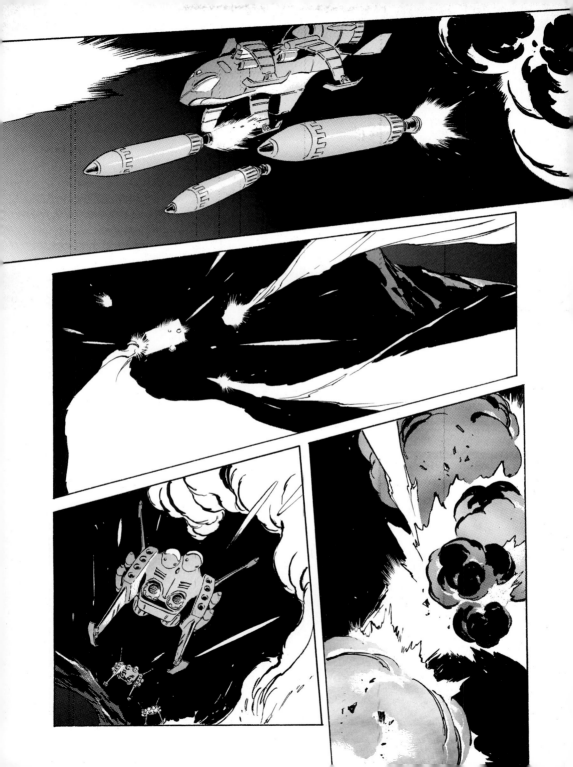

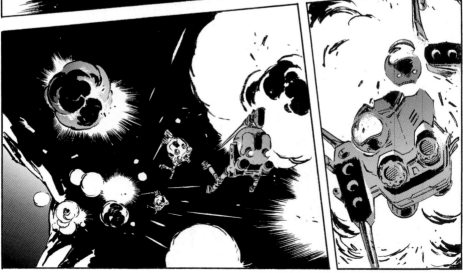

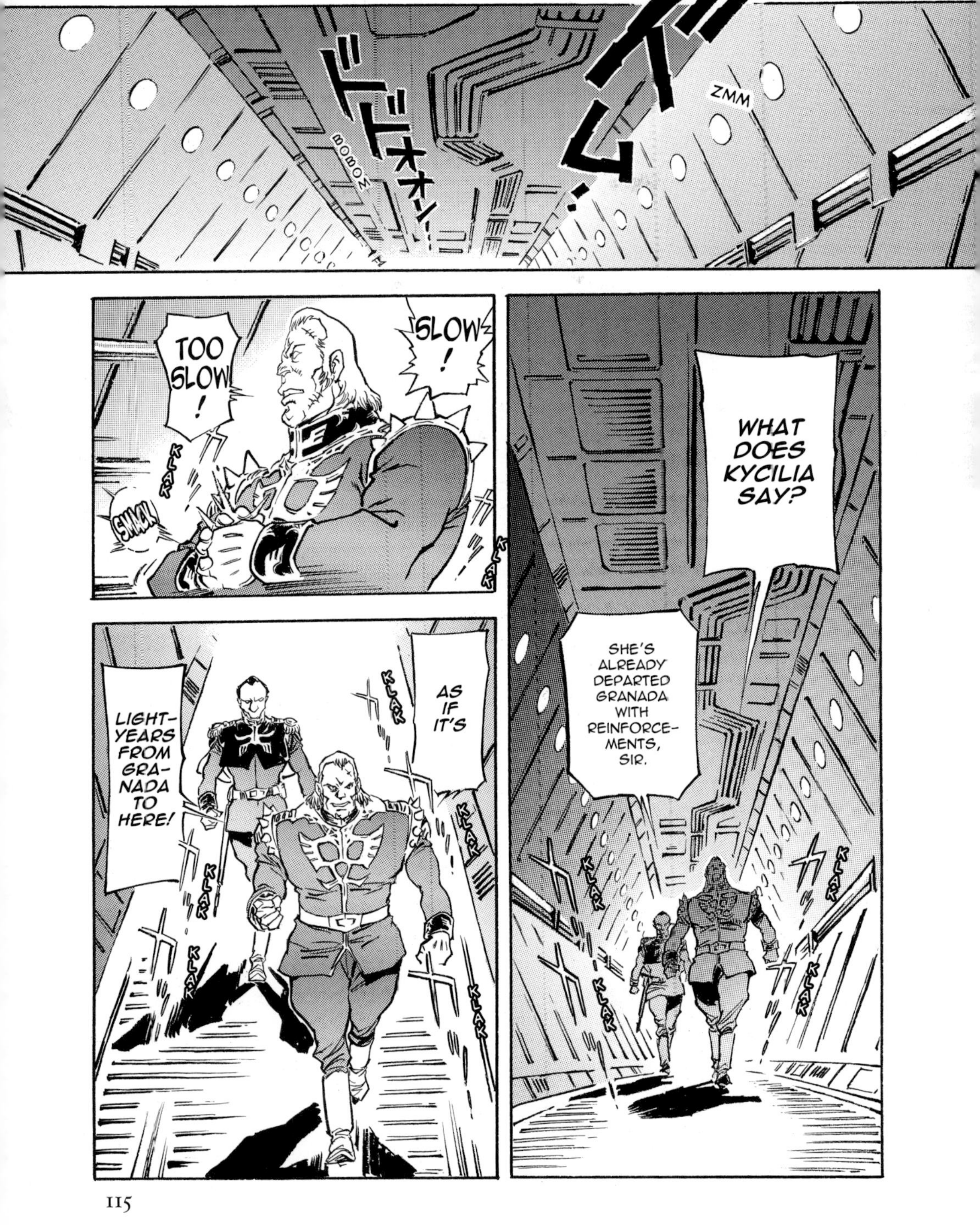
ZMM
BOBOOM
WHAT DOES KYCILIA SAY?
SHE'S ALREADY DEPARTED GRANADA WITH REINFORCEMENTS, SIR.
KLAK
KLAK
KLAK
KLAK
SLOW!
TOO SLOW!
KLAK
SMACK
KLAK
AS IF IT'S
LIGHT-YEARS FROM GRANADA TO HERE!
KLAK
KLAK
KLAK
KLAK
KLAK

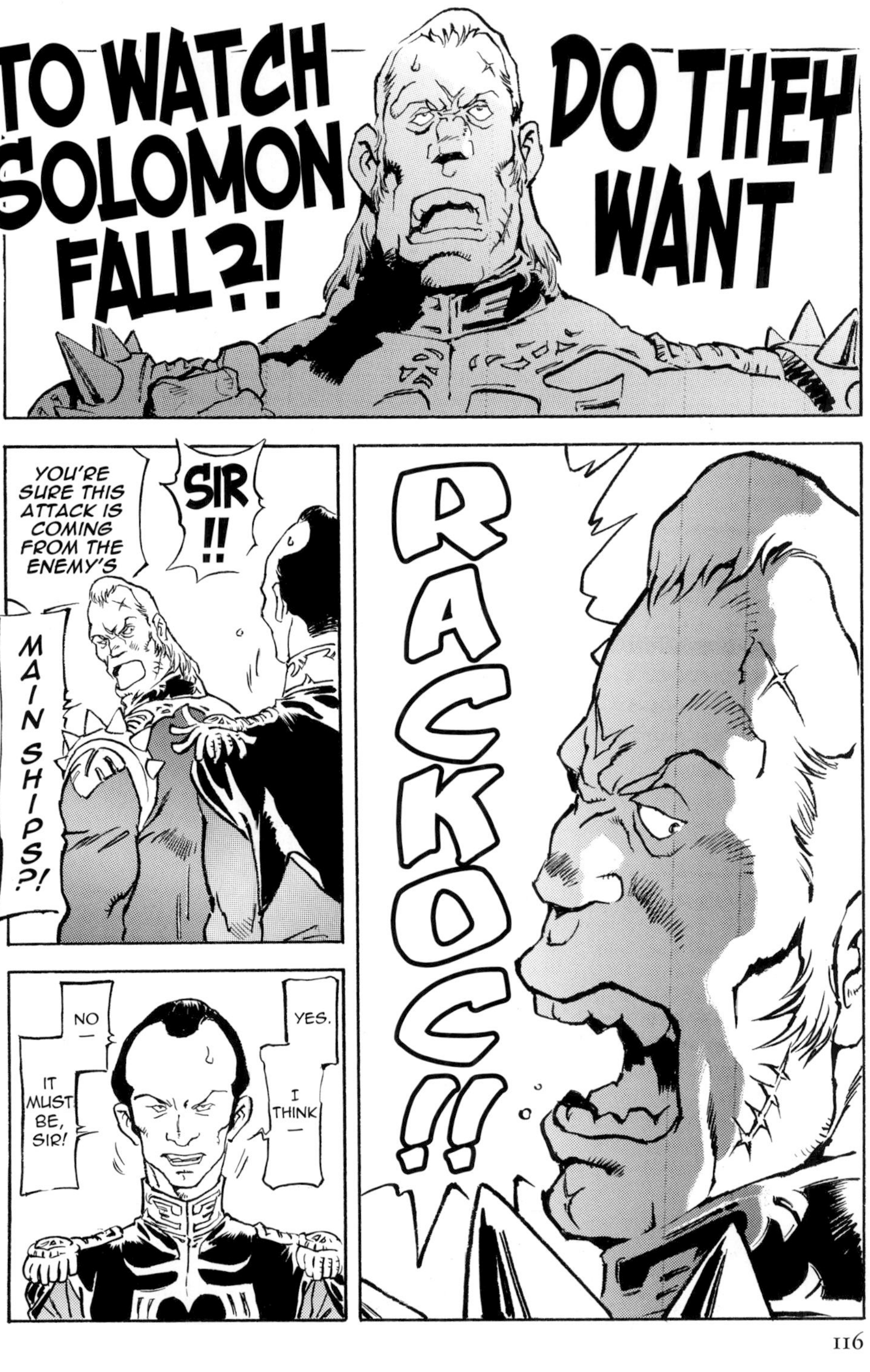
DO THEY WANT
TO WATCH SOLOMON FALL?!
RACKOC!!
SIR !!
YOU'RE SURE THIS ATTACK IS COMING FROM THE ENEMY'S
MAIN SHIPS?!
YES.
I THINK —
NO —
IT MUST BE, SIR!

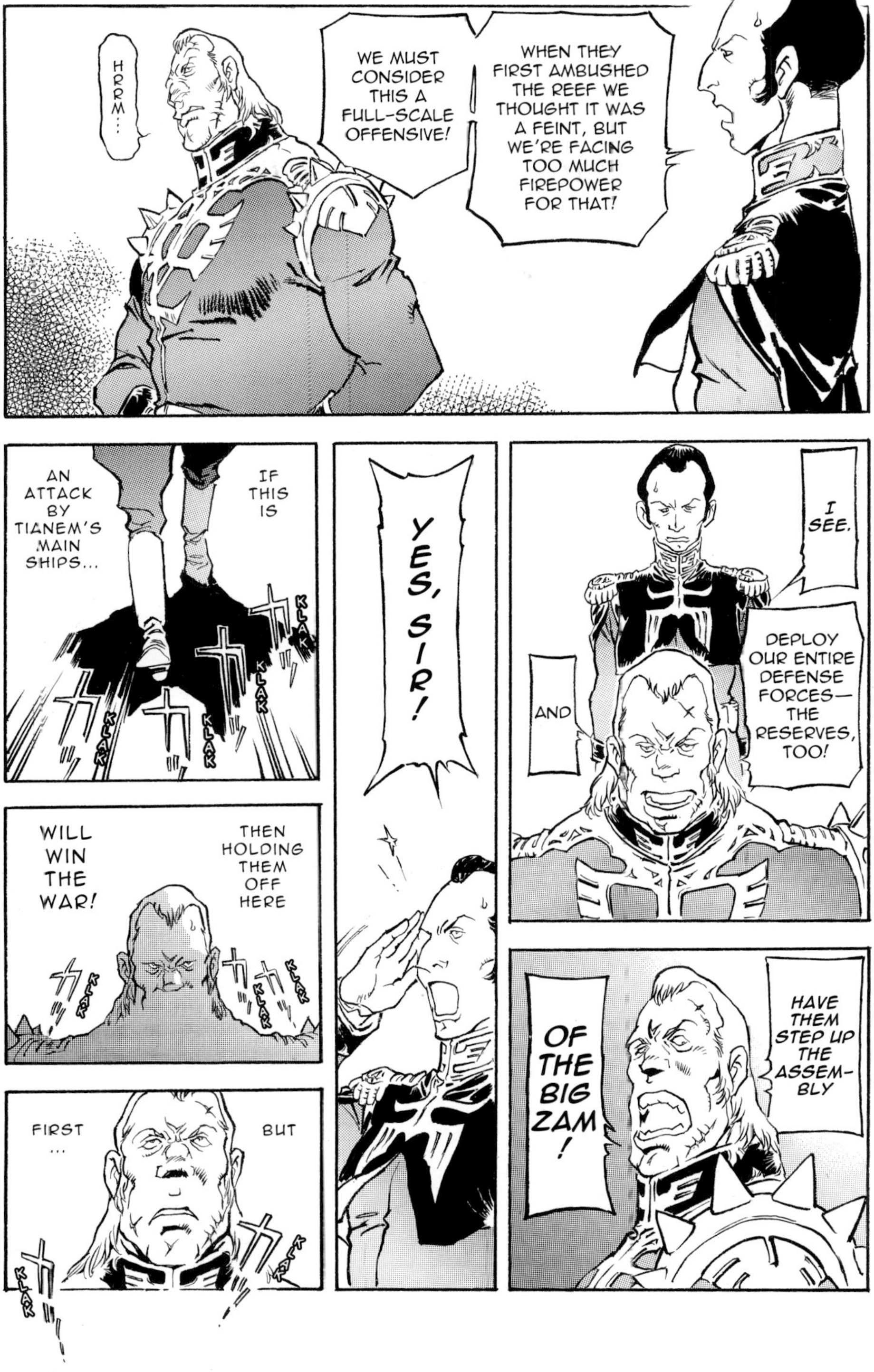
WHEN THEY FIRST AMBUSHED THE REEF WE THOUGHT IT WAS A FEINT, BUT WE'RE FACING TOO MUCH FIREPOWER FOR THAT!
WE MUST CONSIDER THIS A FULL-SCALE OFFENSIVE!
HRRM...
I SEE.
DEPLOY OUR ENTIRE DEFENSE FORCES—THE RESERVES, TOO!
AND
HAVE THEM STEP UP THE ASSEMBLY
OF THE BIG ZAM!
YES, SIR!
IF THIS IS
AN ATTACK BY TIANEM'S MAIN SHIPS...
KLAK KLAK KLAK KLAK
THEN HOLDING THEM OFF HERE
WILL WIN THE WAR!
KLAK KLAK KLAK
BUT
FIRST ...
KLAK KLAK

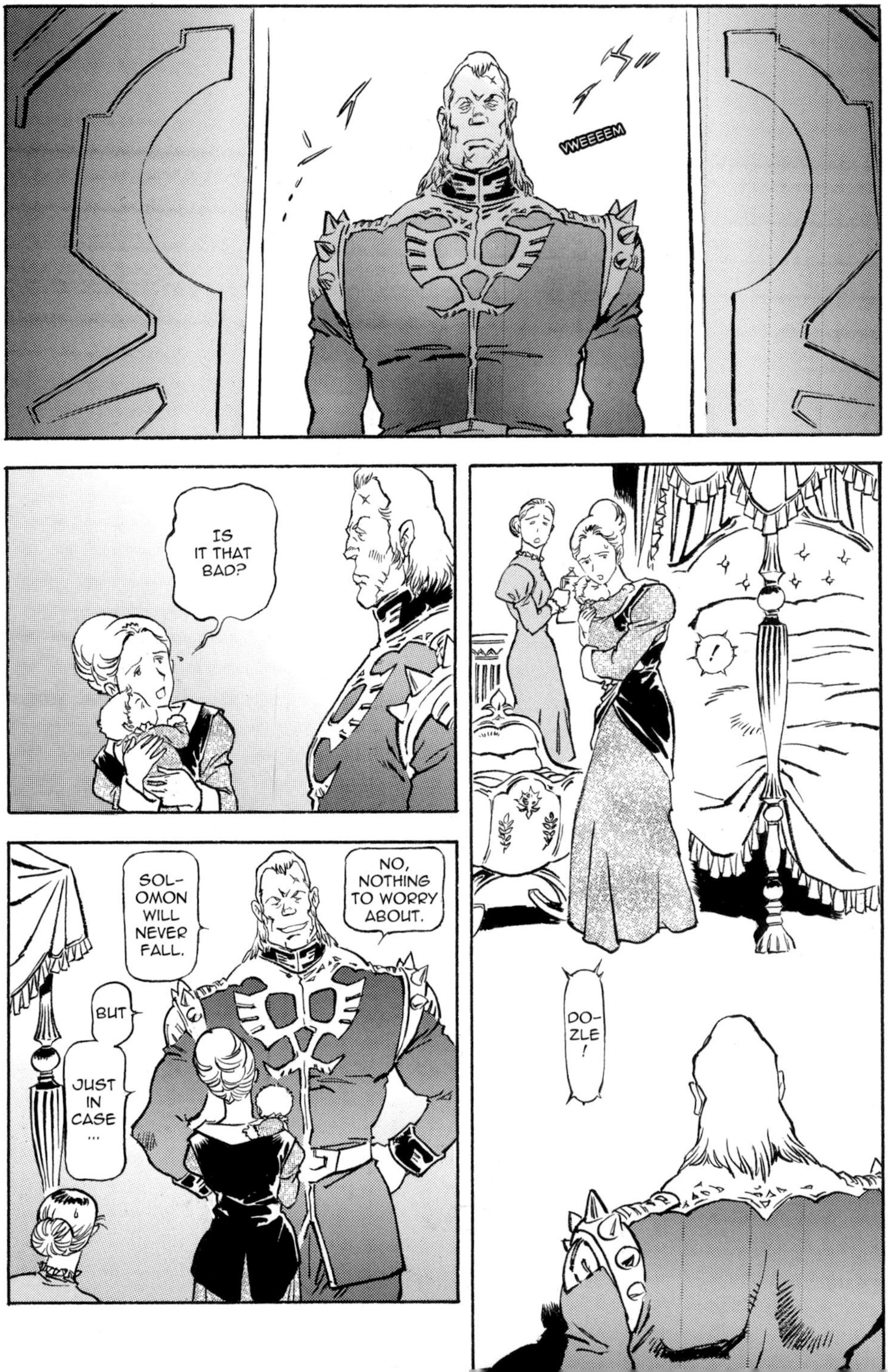
VWEEEEM
!
DO-ZLE!
IS IT THAT BAD?
NO, NOTHING TO WORRY ABOUT.
SOL-OMON WILL NEVER FALL.
BUT
JUST IN CASE ...

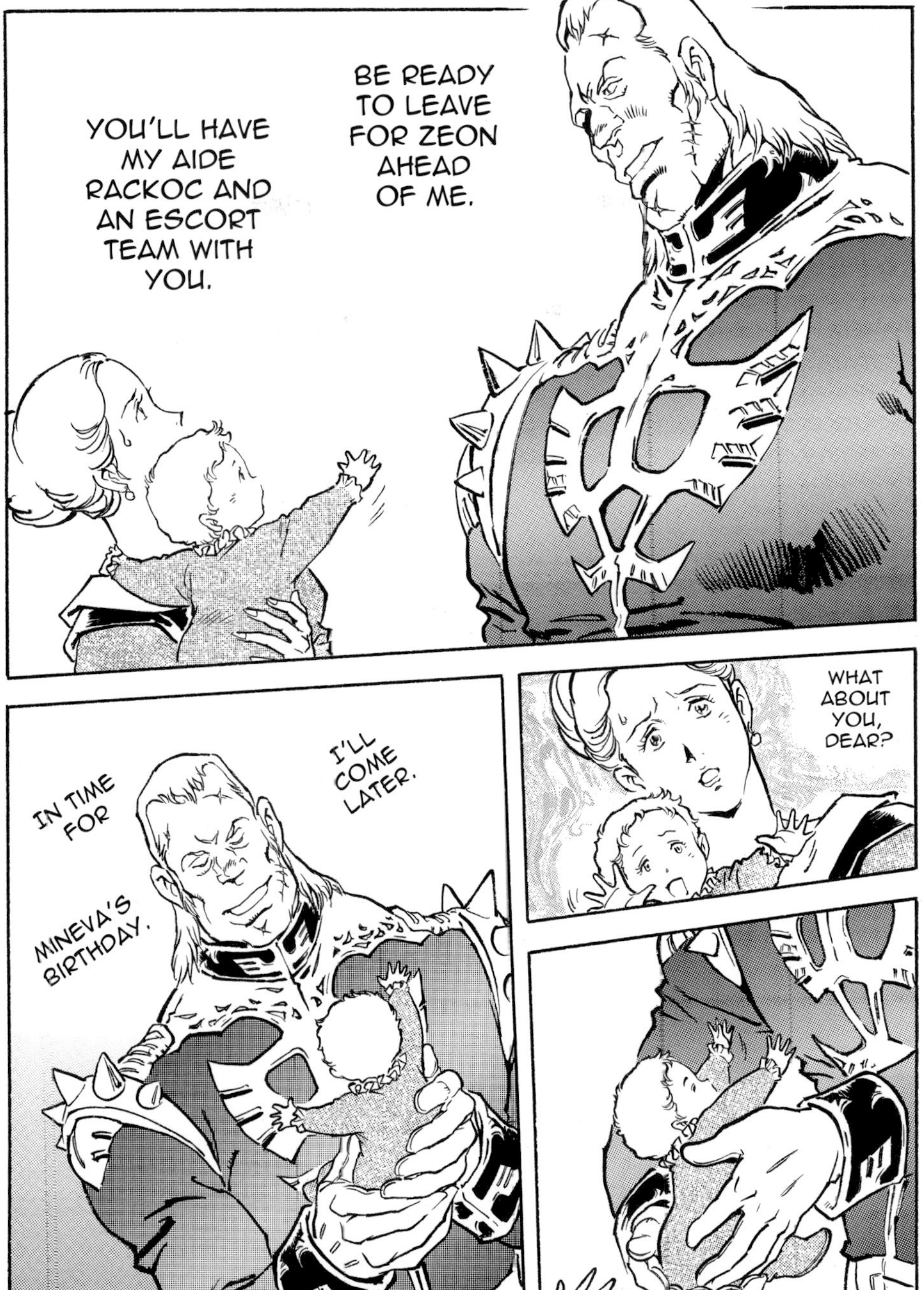

BE READY TO LEAVE FOR ZEON AHEAD OF ME.
YOU'LL HAVE MY AIDE RACKOC AND AN ESCORT TEAM WITH YOU.
WHAT ABOUT YOU, DEAR?
I'LL COME LATER.
IN TIME FOR
MINEVA'S BIRTHDAY.

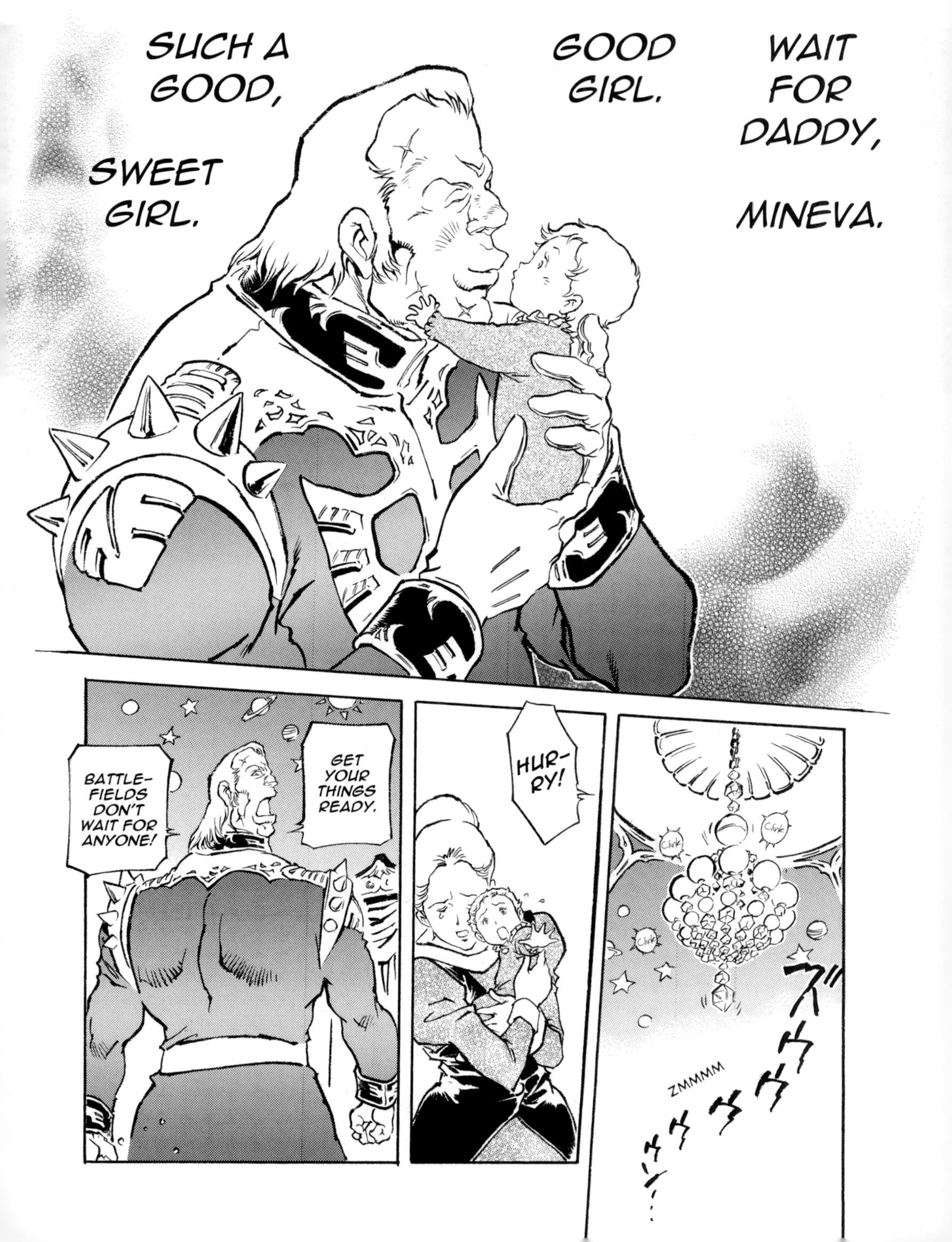
WAIT FOR DADDY, MINEVA.
GOOD GIRL.
SUCH A GOOD, SWEET GIRL.
Clink
Clink
Clink
ZMMMM
HURRY!
GET YOUR THINGS READY.
BATTLEFIELDS DON'T WAIT FOR ANYONE!

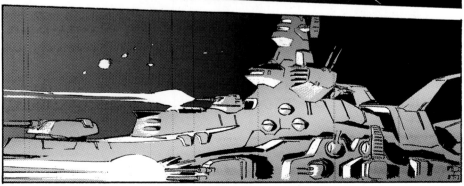

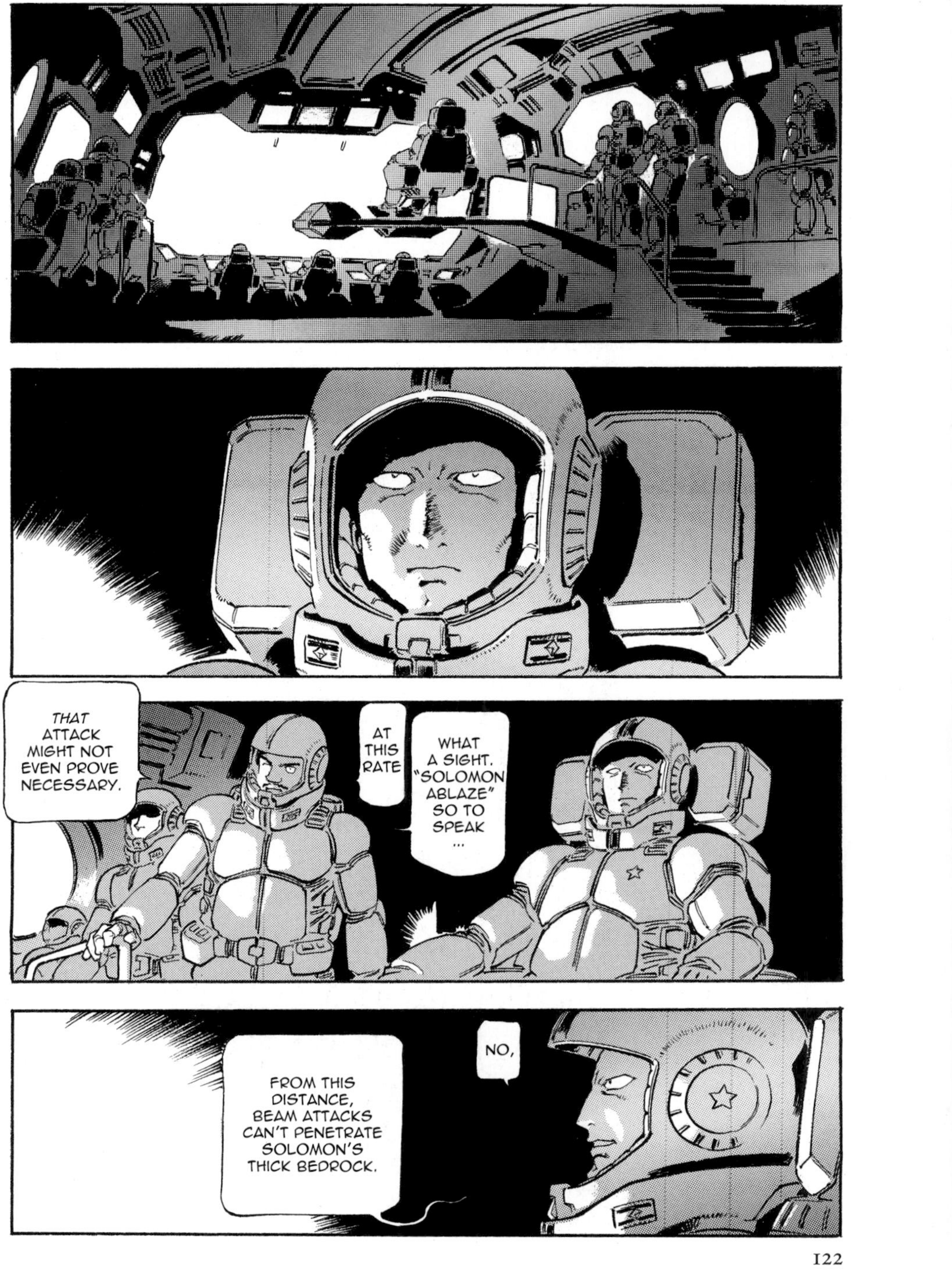
WHAT A SIGHT. "SOLOMON ABLAZE" SO TO SPEAK ...
AT THIS RATE
THAT ATTACK MIGHT NOT EVEN PROVE NECESSARY.
NO,
FROM THIS DISTANCE, BEAM ATTACKS CAN'T PENETRATE SOLOMON'S THICK BEDROCK.

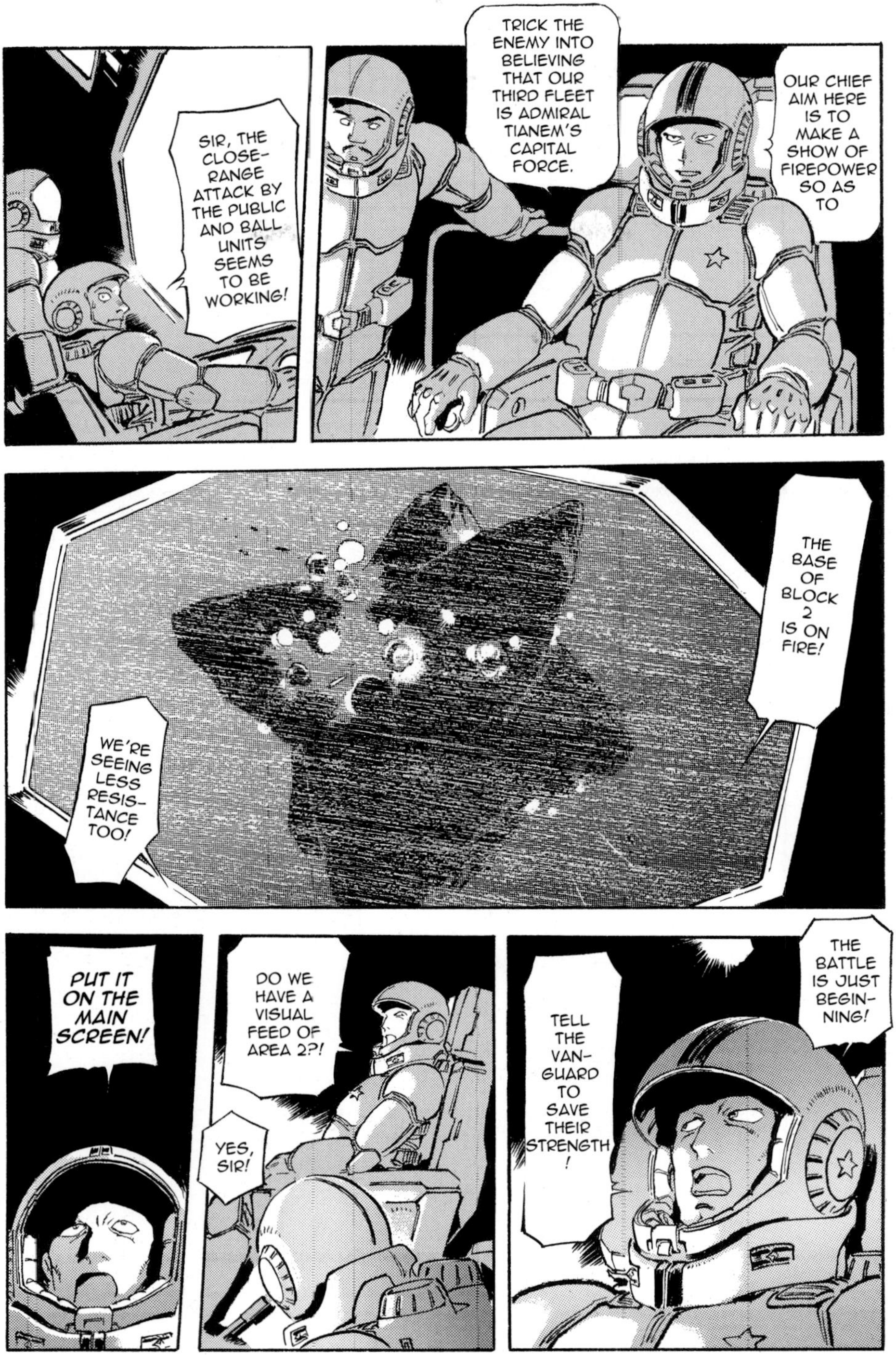

OUR CHIEF AIM HERE IS TO MAKE A SHOW OF FIREPOWER SO AS TO
TRICK THE ENEMY INTO BELIEVING THAT OUR THIRD FLEET IS ADMIRAL TIANEM'S CAPITAL FORCE.
SIR, THE CLOSE-RANGE ATTACK BY THE PUBLIC AND BALL UNITS SEEMS TO BE WORKING!
THE BASE OF BLOCK 2 IS ON FIRE!
WE'RE SEEING LESS RESISTANCE TOO!
THE BATTLE IS JUST BEGINNING!
TELL THE VANGUARD TO SAVE THEIR STRENGTH!
DO WE HAVE A VISUAL FEED OF AREA 2?!
YES, SIR!
PUT IT ON THE MAIN SCREEN!

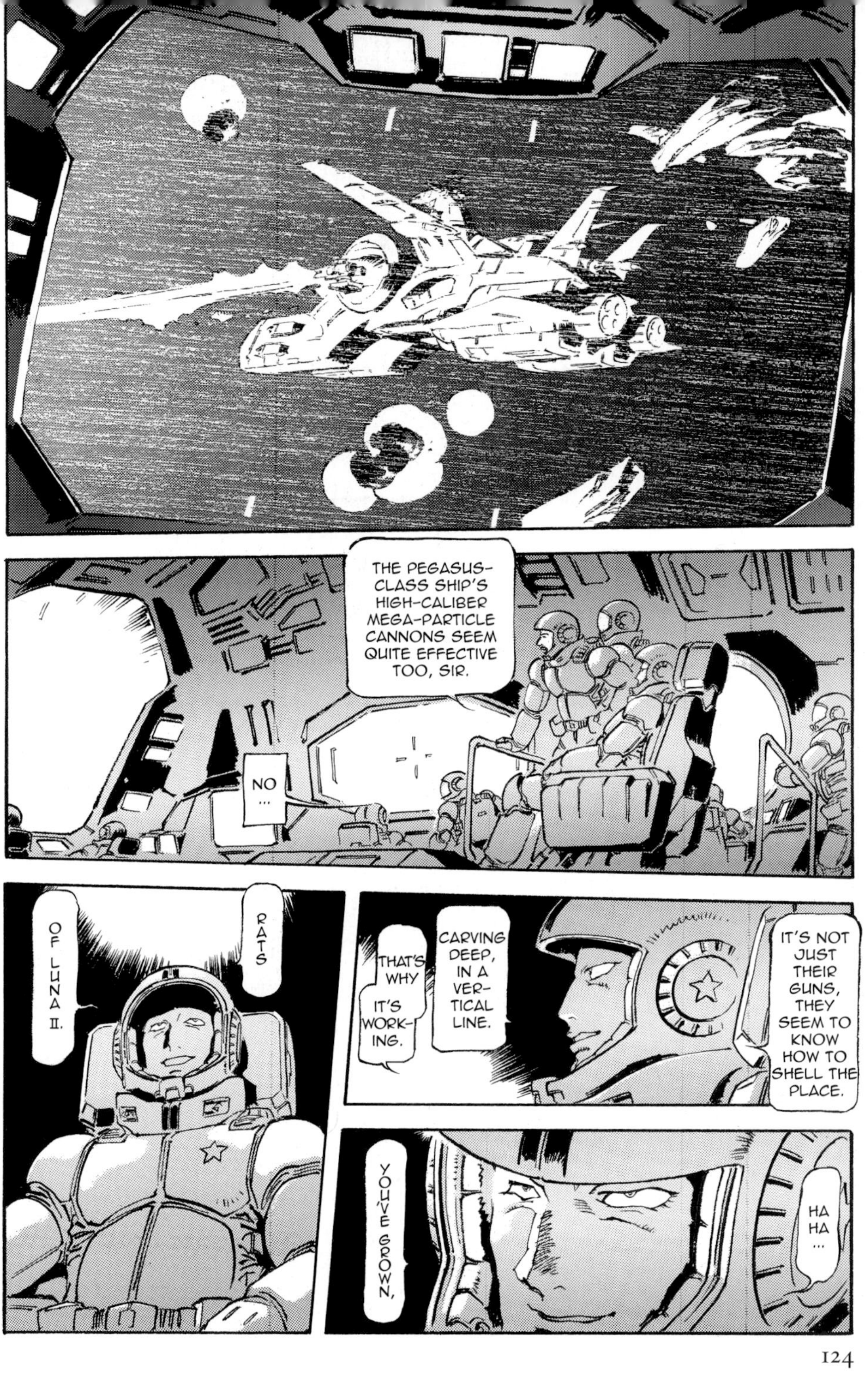
THE PEGASUS-CLASS SHIP'S HIGH-CALIBER MEGA-PARTICLE CANNONS SEEM QUITE EFFECTIVE TOO, SIR.
NO ...
IT'S NOT JUST THEIR GUNS, THEY SEEM TO KNOW HOW TO SHELL THE PLACE.
CARVING DEEP, IN A VERTICAL LINE.
THAT'S WHY IT'S WORKING.
HA HA ...
YOU'VE GROWN,
RATS
OF LUNA II.

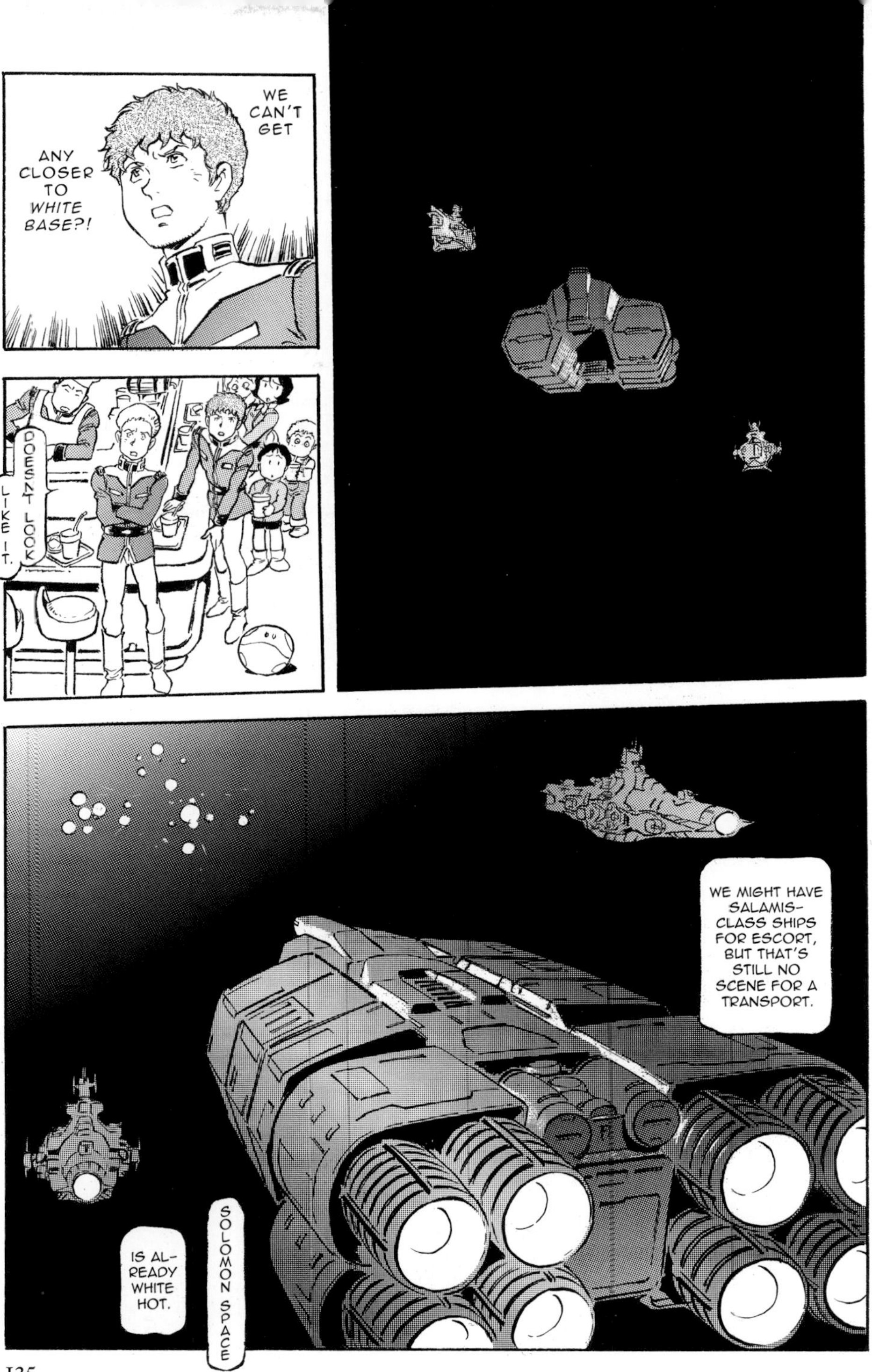
WE CAN'T GET ANY CLOSER TO WHITE BASE?!
DOESN'T LOOK LIKE IT.
WE MIGHT HAVE SALAMIS-CLASS SHIPS FOR ESCORT, BUT THAT'S STILL NO SCENE FOR A TRANSPORT.
SOLOMON SPACE
IS ALREADY WHITE HOT.

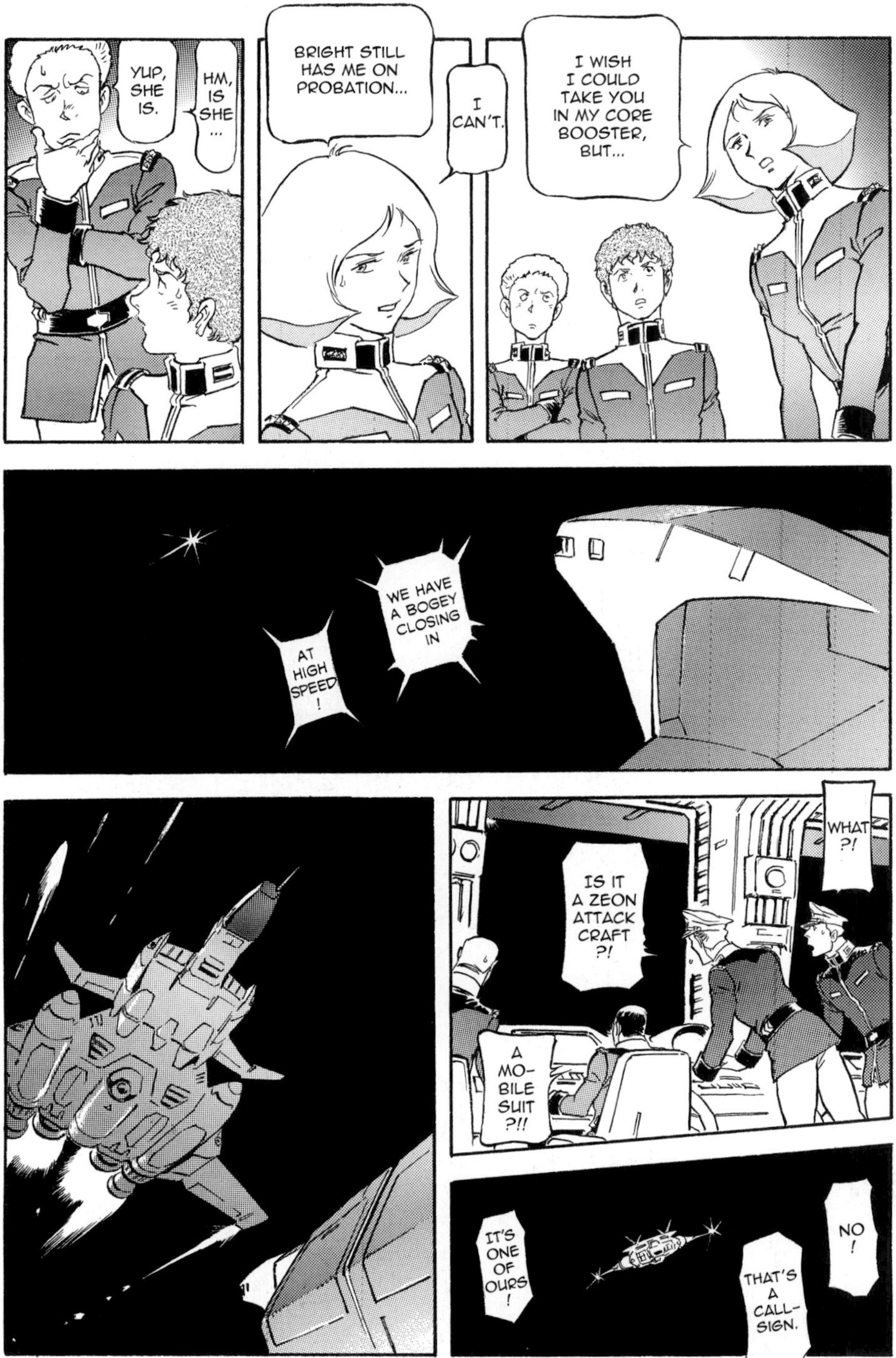
I WISH I COULD TAKE YOU IN MY CORE BOOSTER, BUT...
BRIGHT STILL HAS ME ON PROBATION...
I CAN'T.
HM, IS SHE ...
YUP, SHE IS.
WE HAVE A BOGEY CLOSING IN
AT HIGH SPEED!
WHAT?!
IS IT A ZEON ATTACK CRAFT?!
A MO-BILE SUIT?!!
NO!
THAT'S A CALL-SIGN.
IT'S ONE OF OURS!

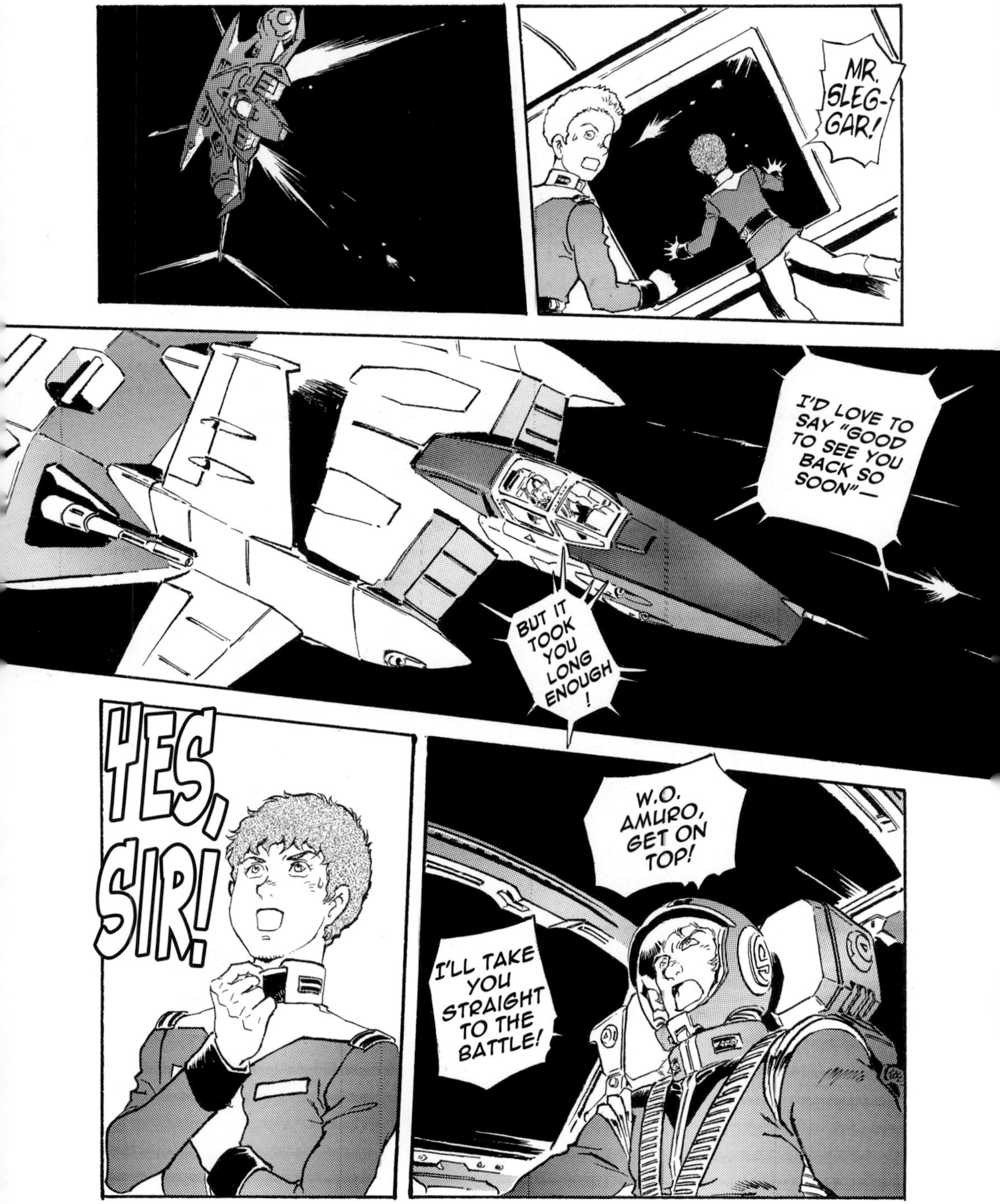

MR. SLEG-GAR!
I'D LOVE TO SAY "GOOD TO SEE YOU BACK SO SOON"—
BUT IT TOOK YOU LONG ENOUGH!
W.O. AMURO, GET ON TOP!
I'LL TAKE YOU STRAIGHT TO THE BATTLE!
YES, SIR!

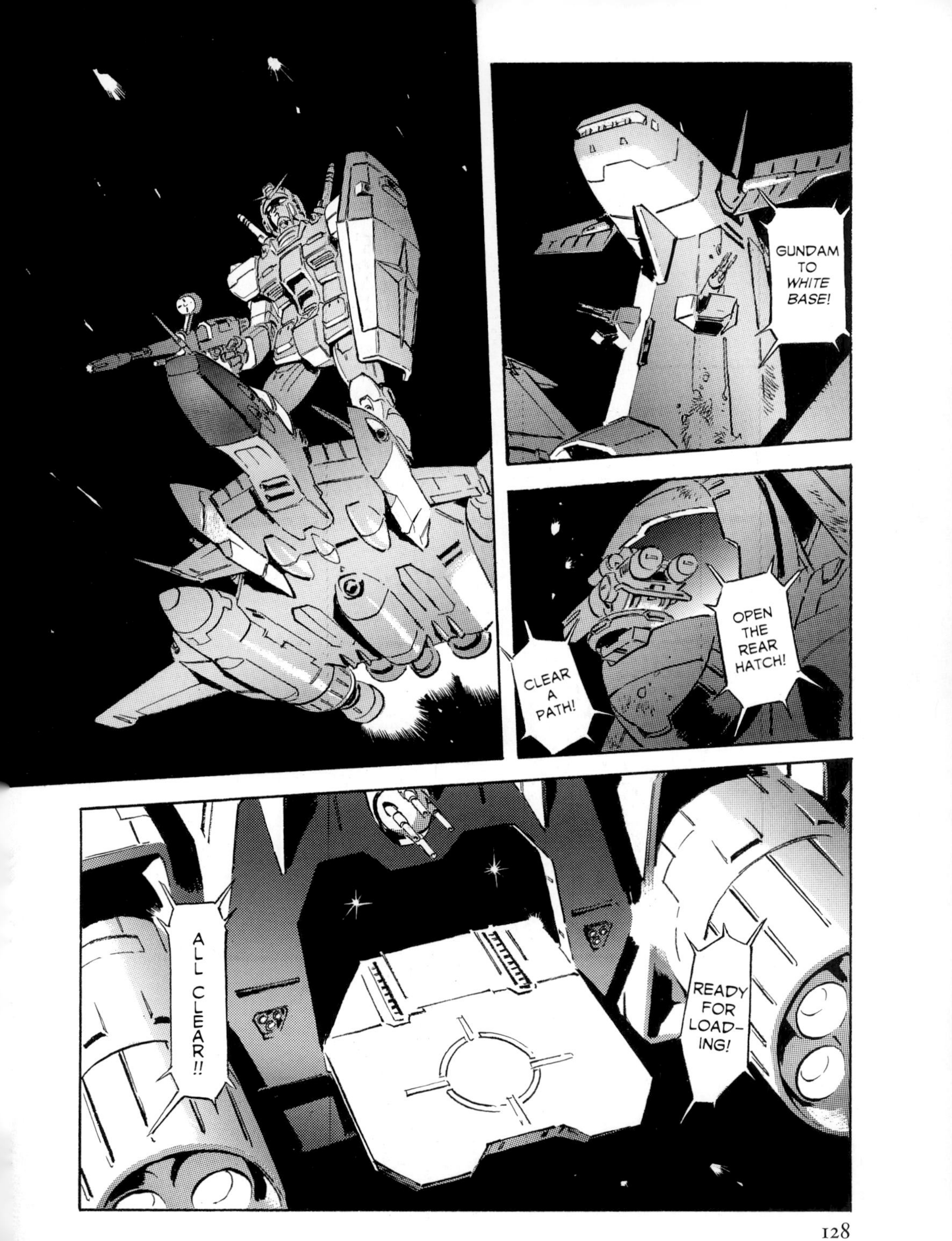
GUNDAM TO WHITE BASE!
OPEN THE REAR HATCH!
CLEAR A PATH!
READY FOR LOAD-ING!
ALL CLEAR!!

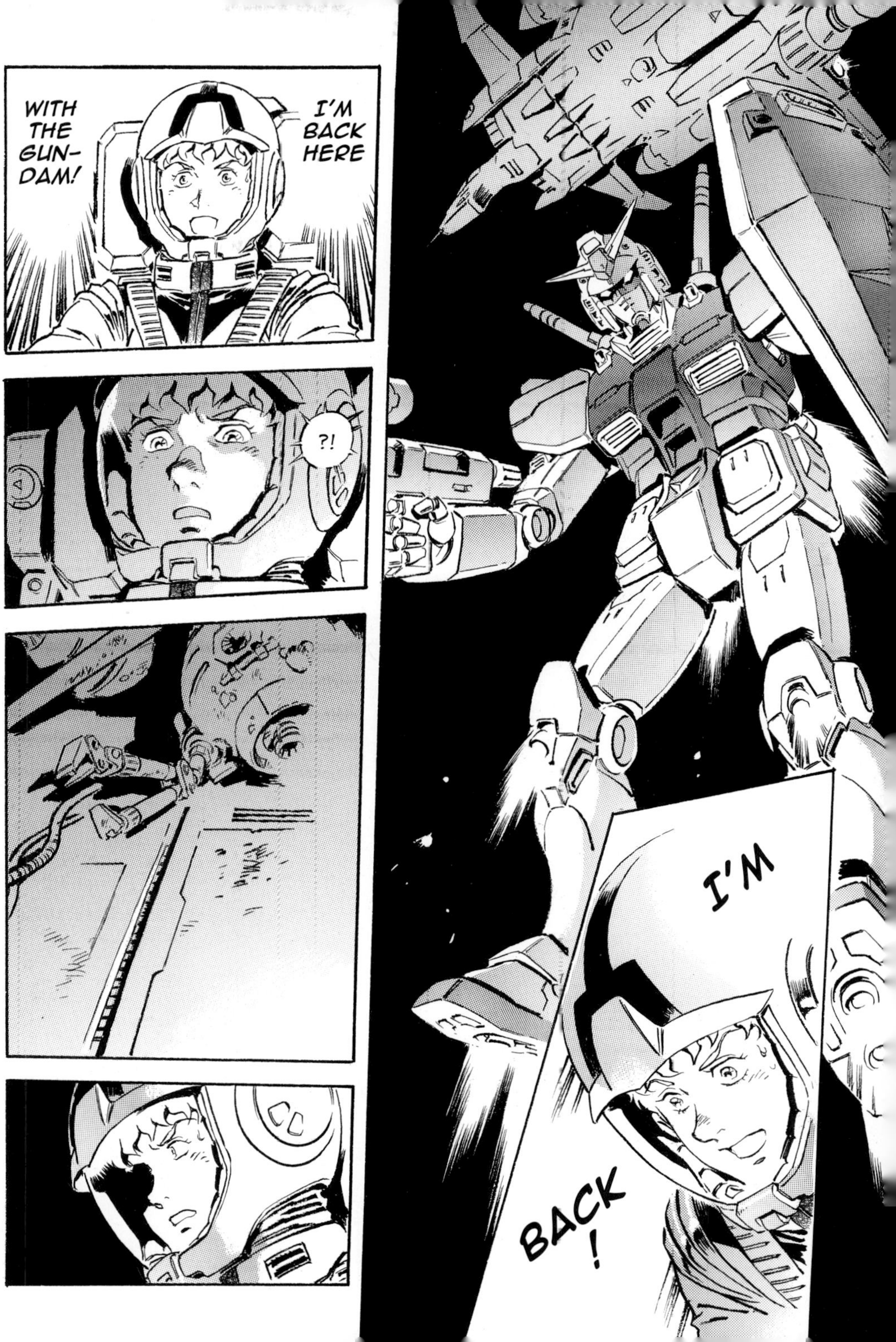
I'M
BACK
!
I'M BACK HERE
WITH THE GUN-DAM!
?!

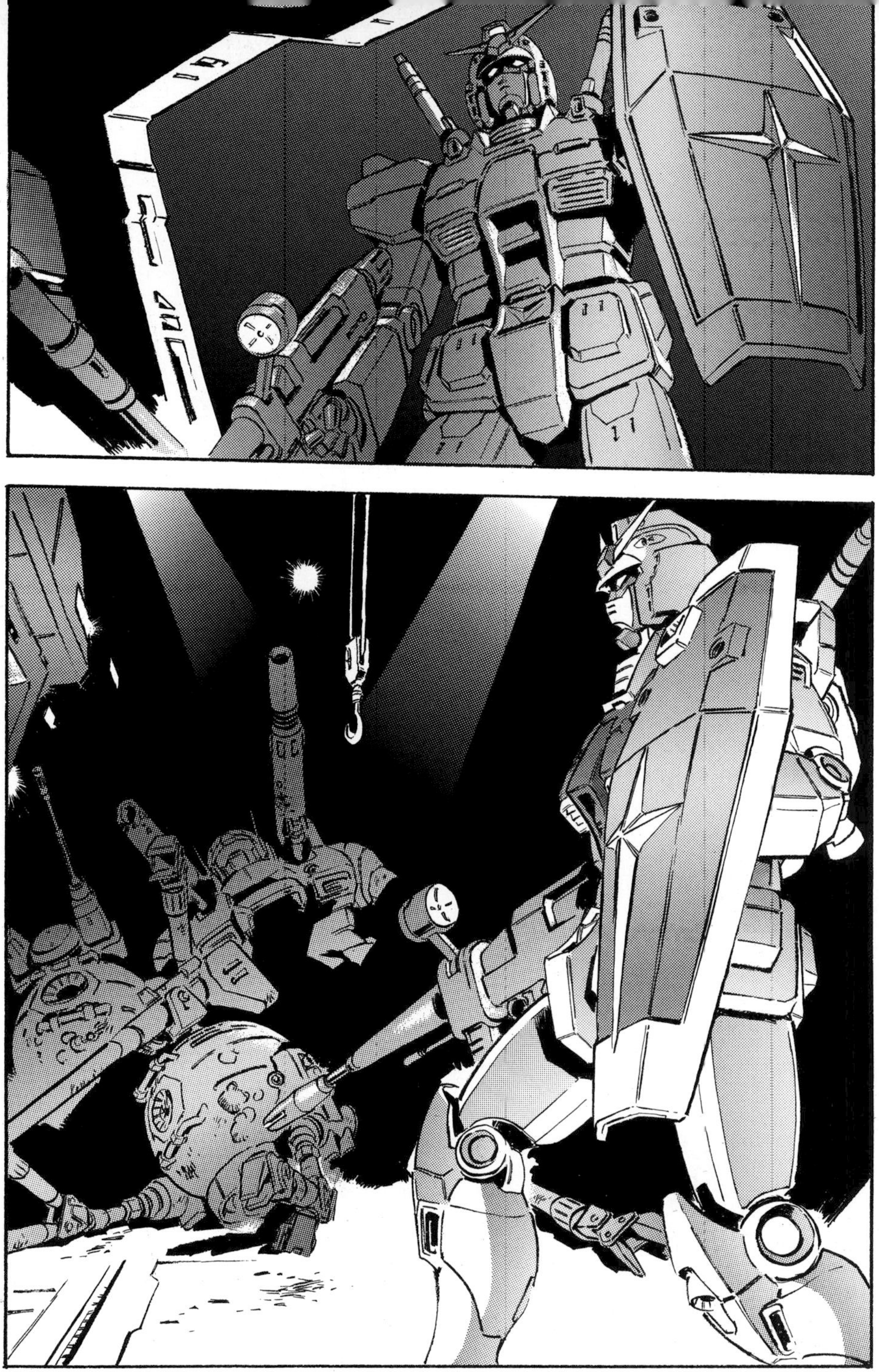

SECTION IV

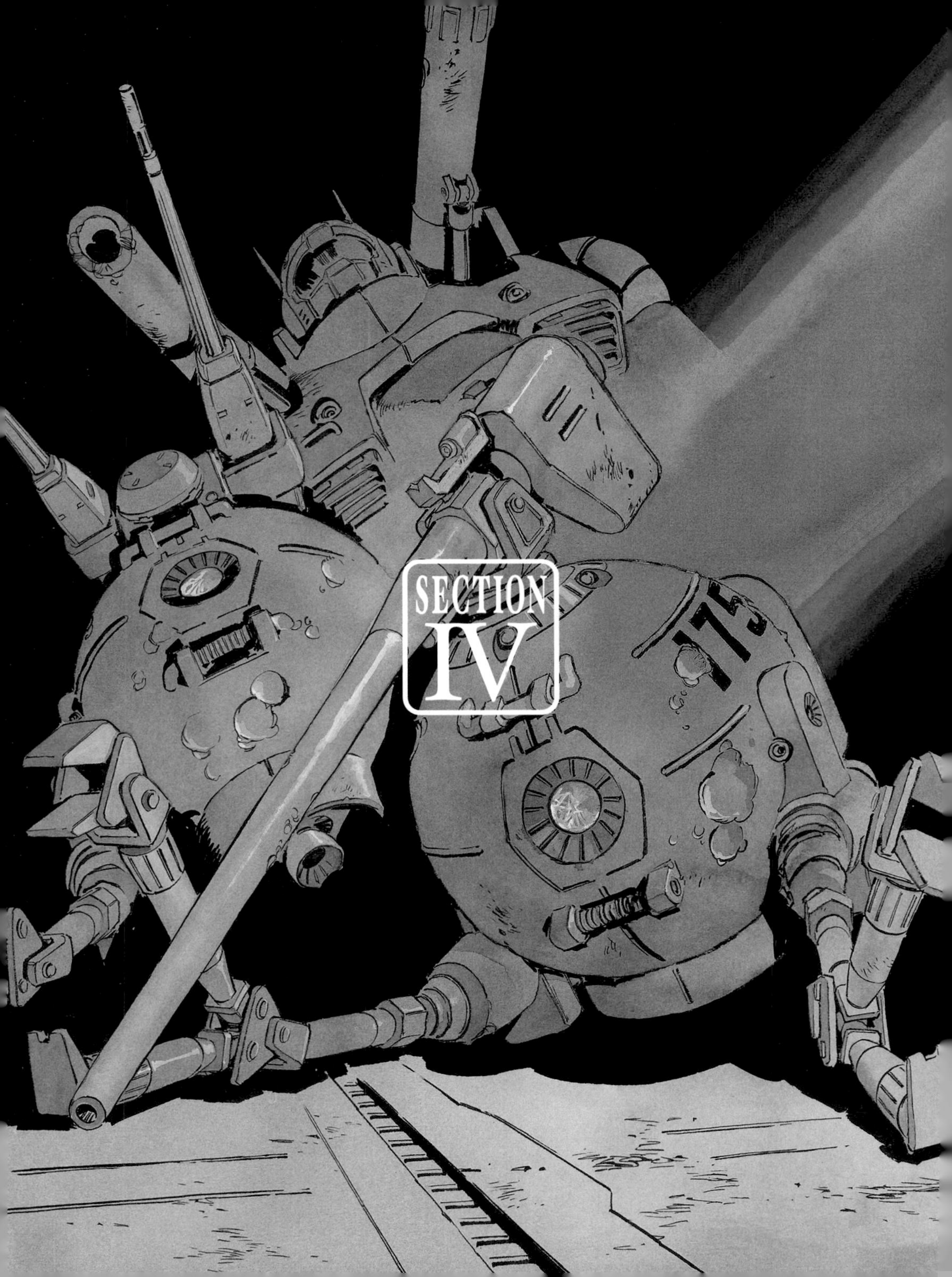
175

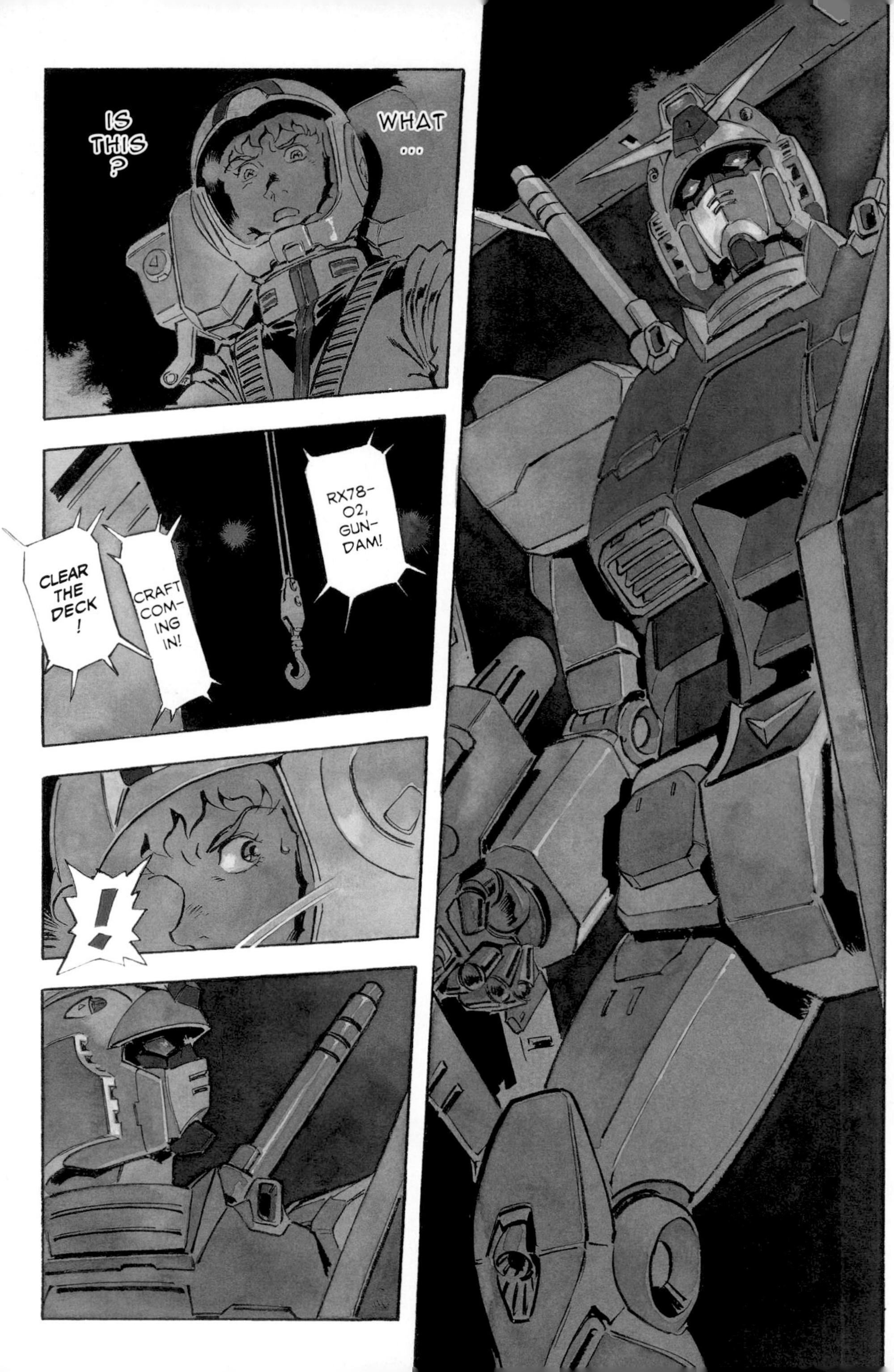
WHAT ...
IS THIS ?
RX78-02, GUNDAM!
CRAFT COMING IN!
CLEAR THE DECK!
!

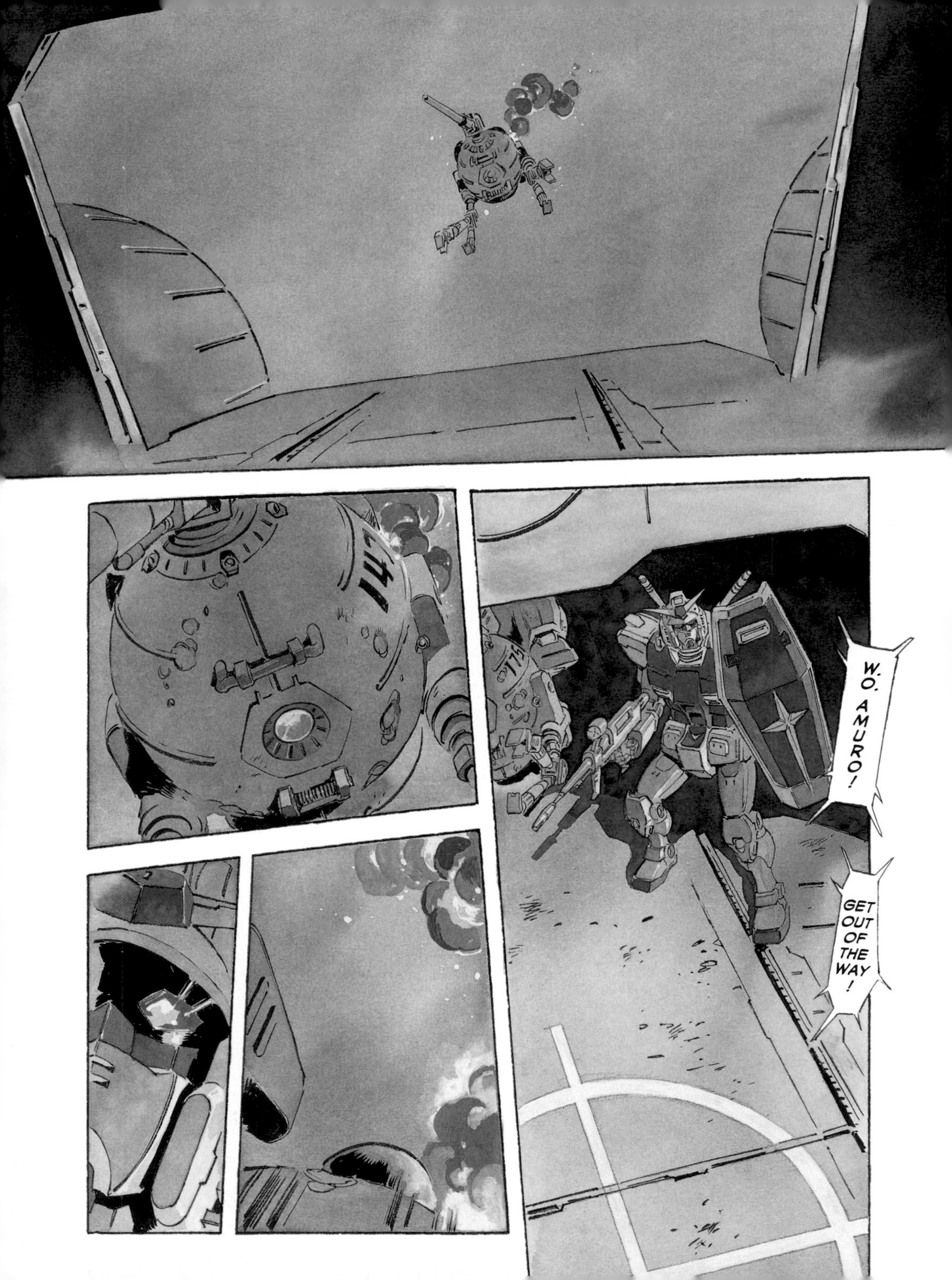
W.O. AMURO!
GET OUT OF THE WAY!

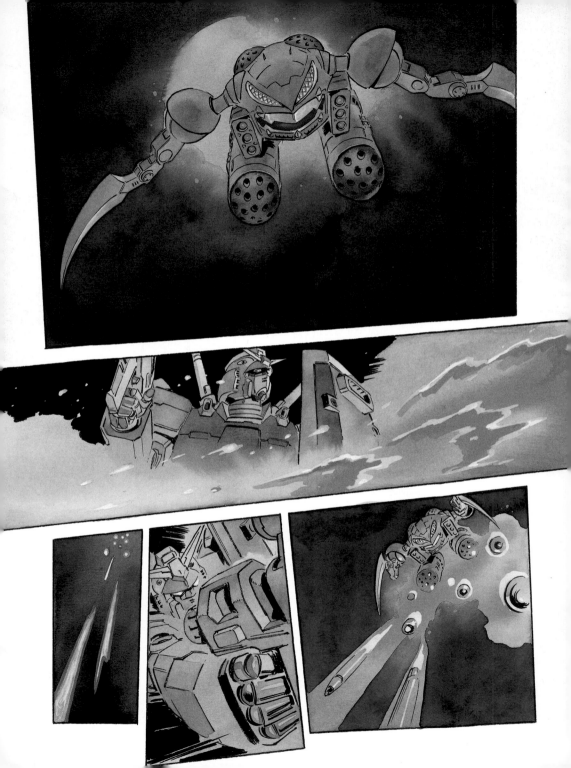

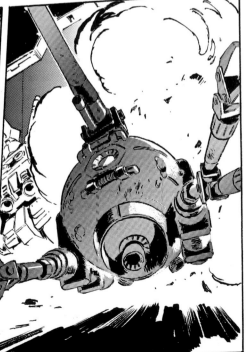

WHOA

THE WHITE ONE?!

NEXT KILL!

LOOKS LIKE YOU'LL BE SERGEANT DMITRI'S

FLASH

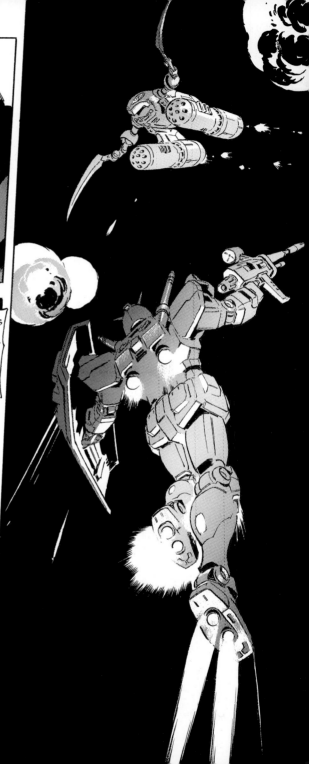

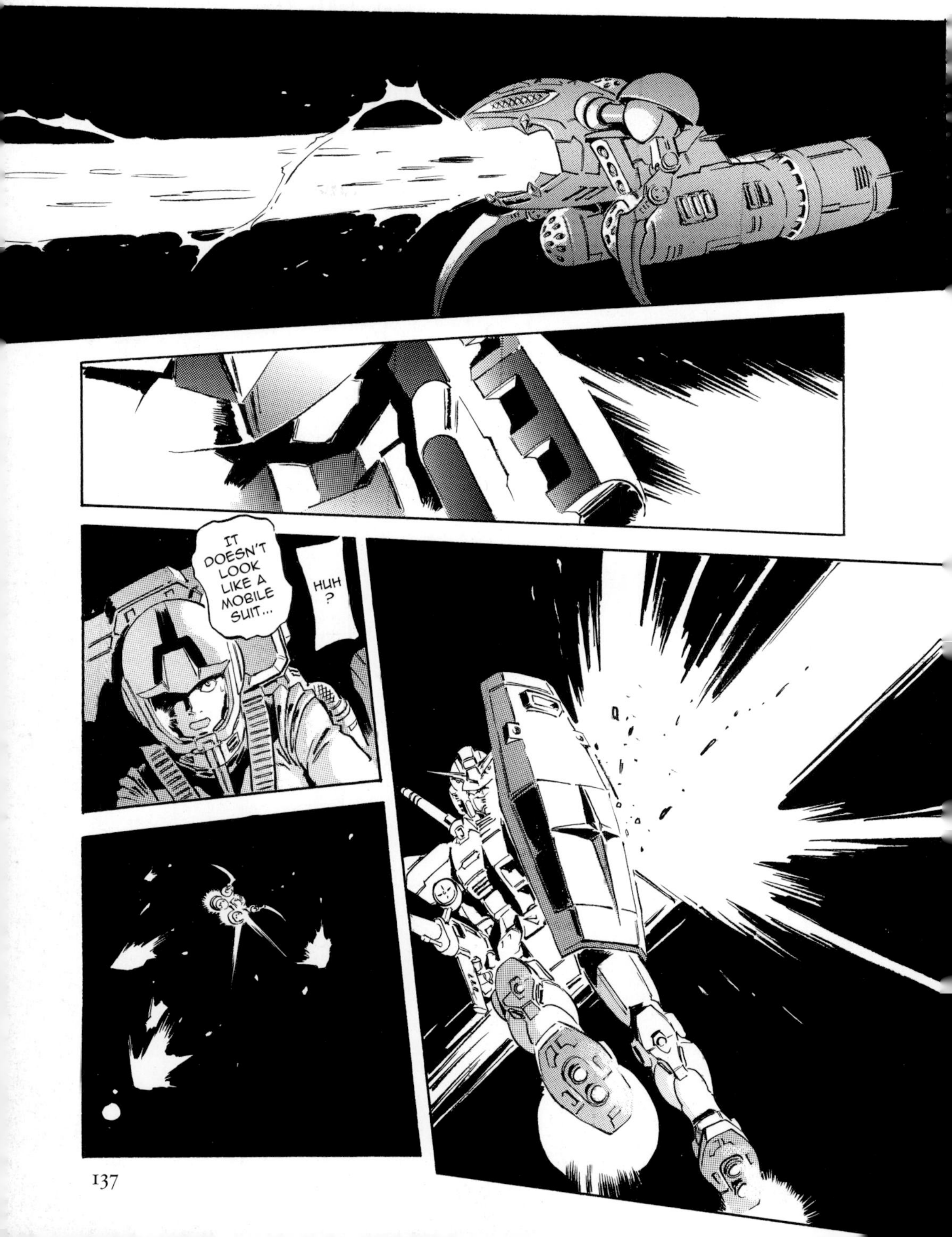
HUH ?
IT DOESN'T LOOK LIKE A MOBILE SUIT...

I BETTER WATCH OUT...

I MIGHT NOT HAVE BEEN ABLE TO DODGE THAT BEFORE THE UPGRADE.

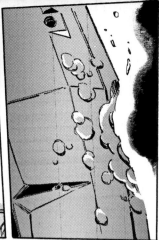

STAY BACK!

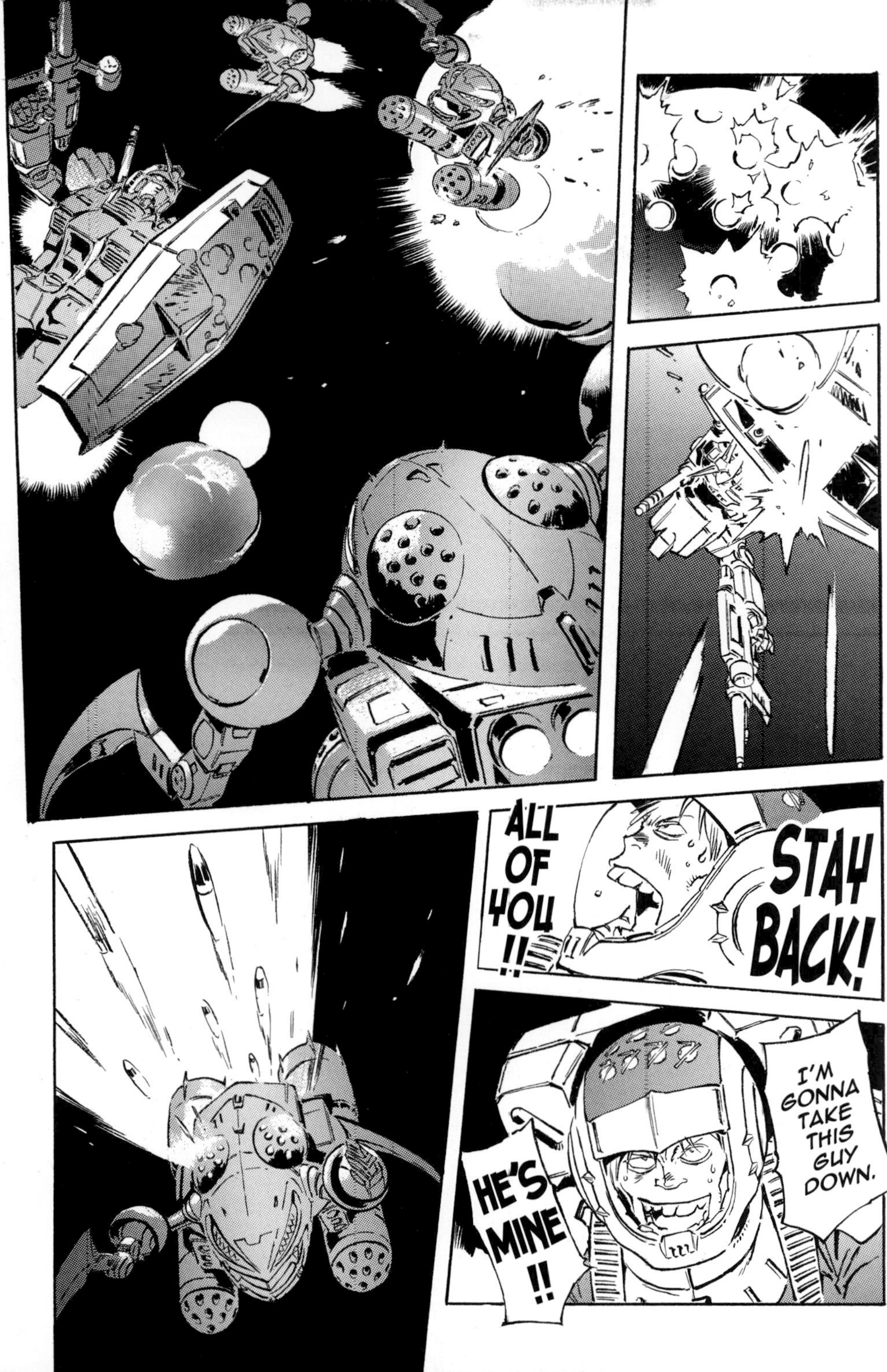
STAY BACK!
ALL OF YOU!!
I'M GONNA TAKE THIS GUY DOWN.
HE'S MINE!!

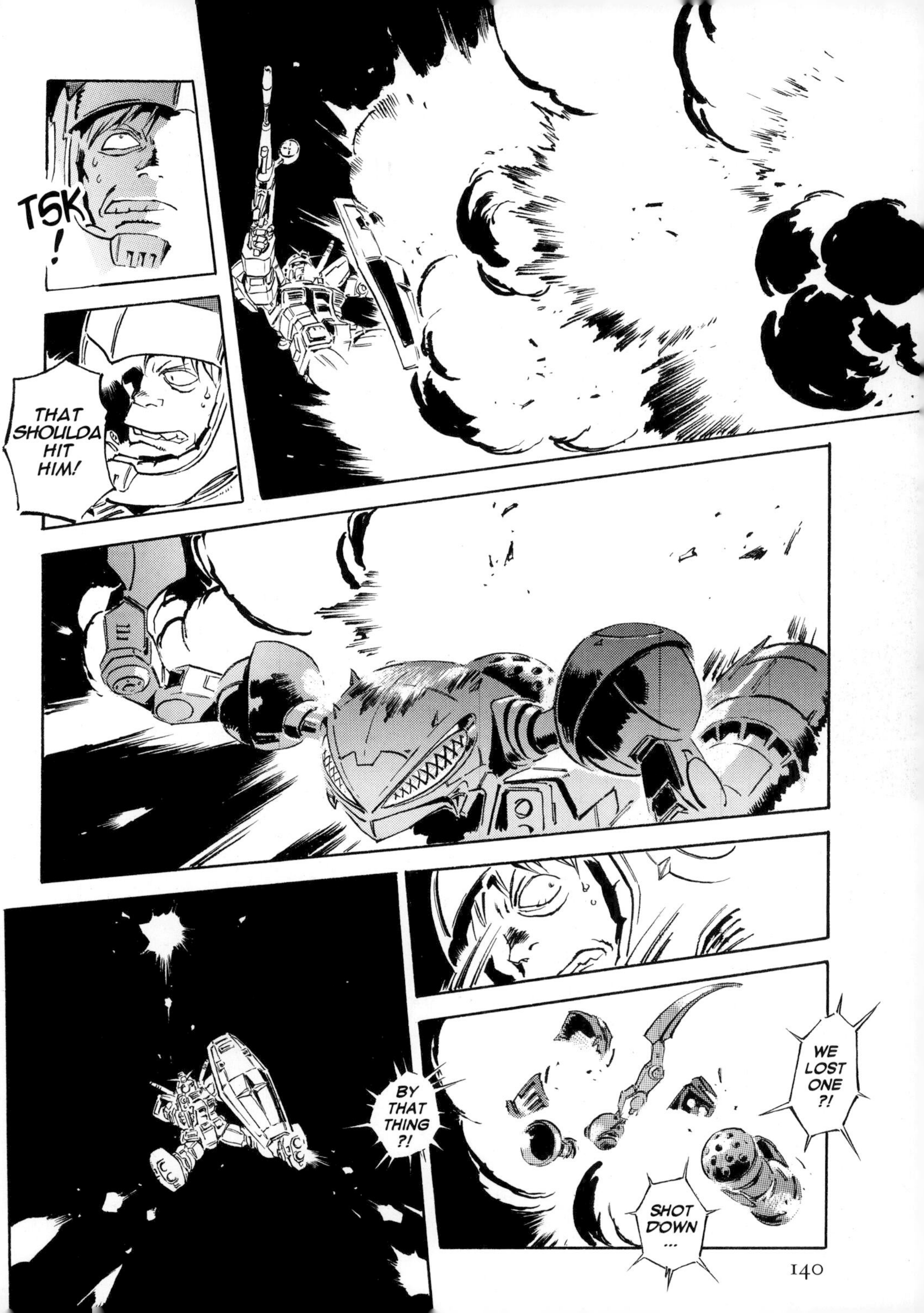
TSK!
THAT SHOULDA HIT HIM!
WE LOST ONE?!
SHOT DOWN...
BY THAT THING?!

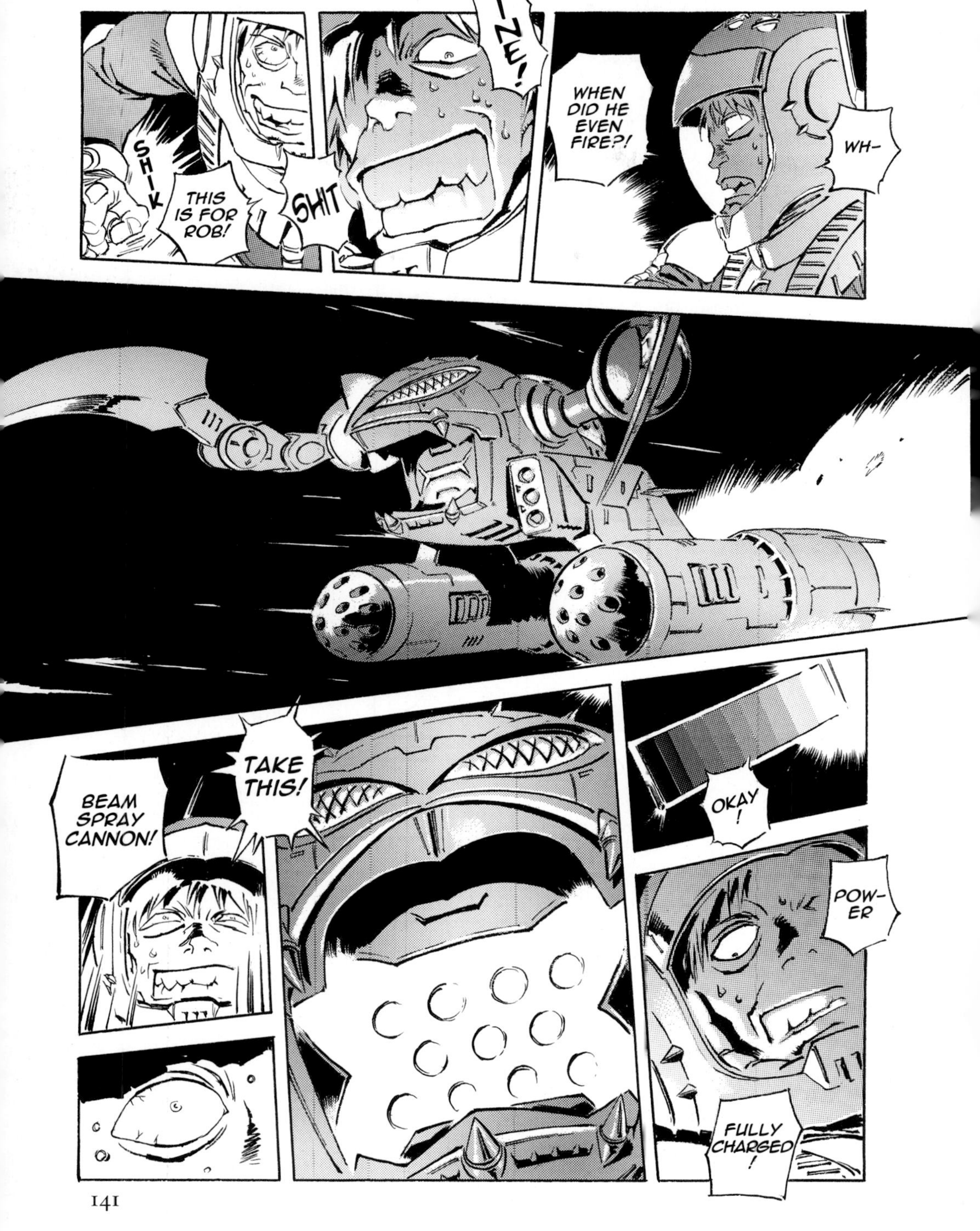
WH-
WHEN DID HE EVEN FIRE?!
FINE!
SHIT
SHIK
THIS IS FOR ROB!
OKAY!
POWER
FULLY CHARGED!
TAKE THIS!
BEAM SPRAY CANNON!

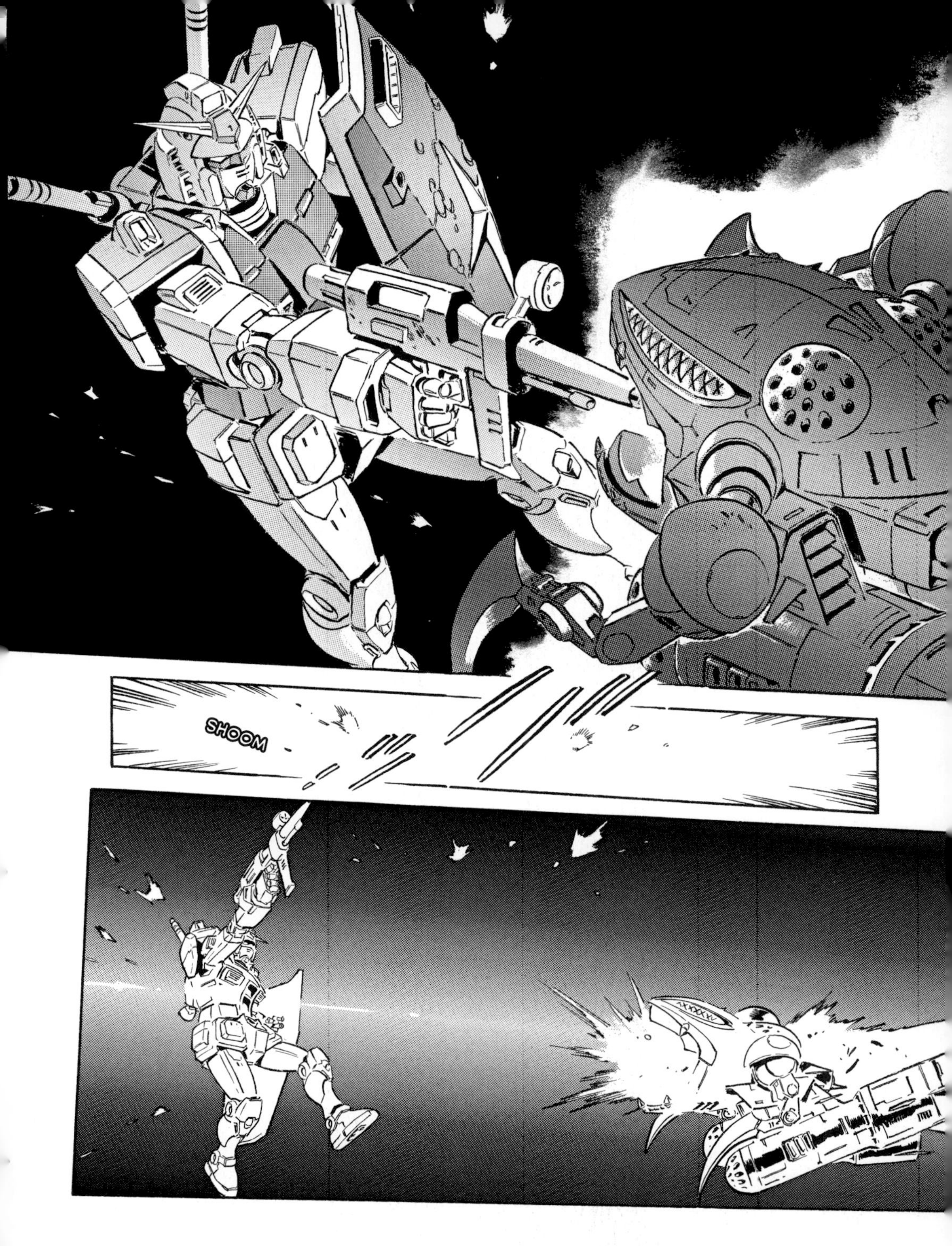
SHOOM

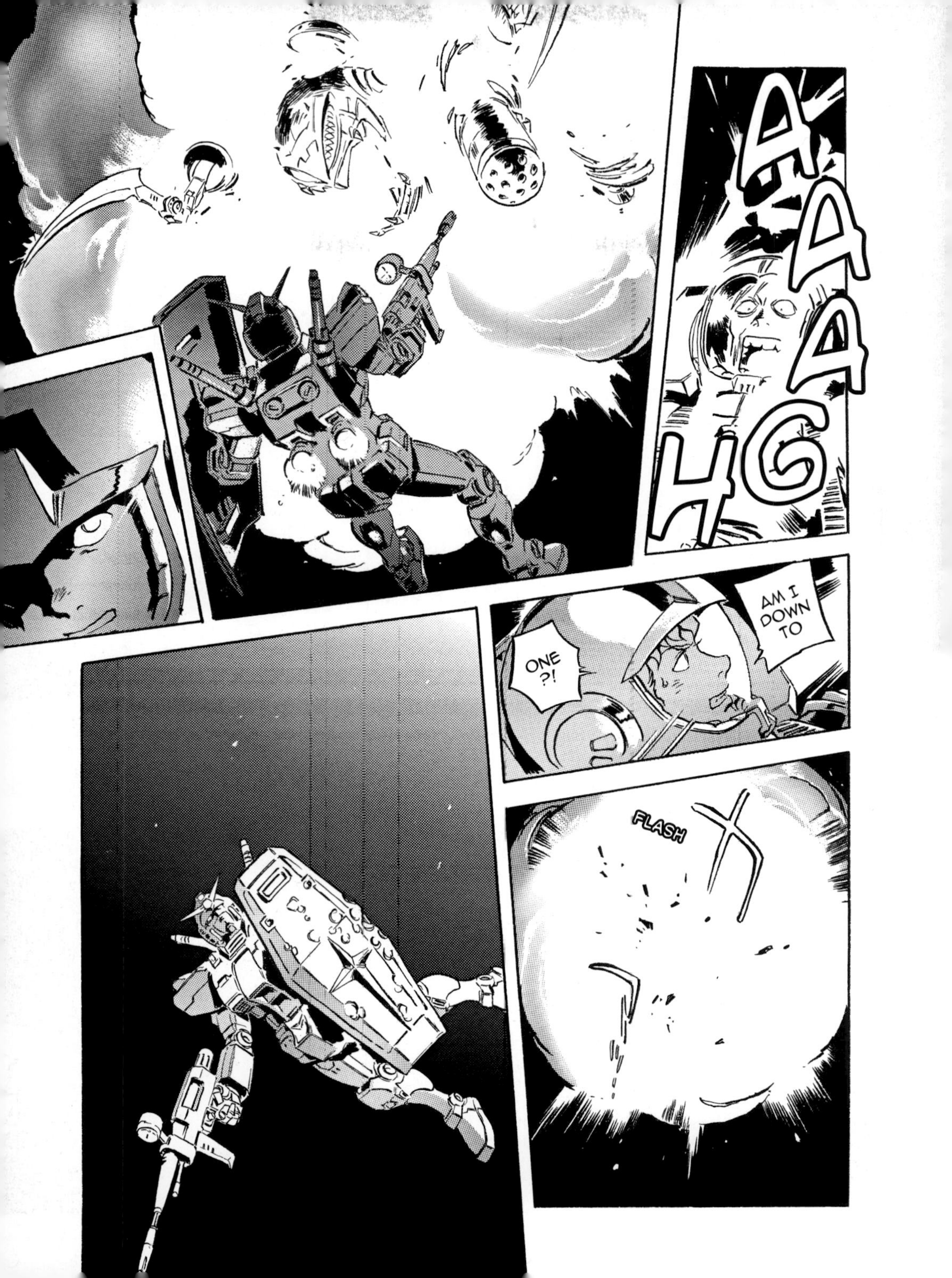
AAAAHG
AM I DOWN TO
ONE ?!
FLASH

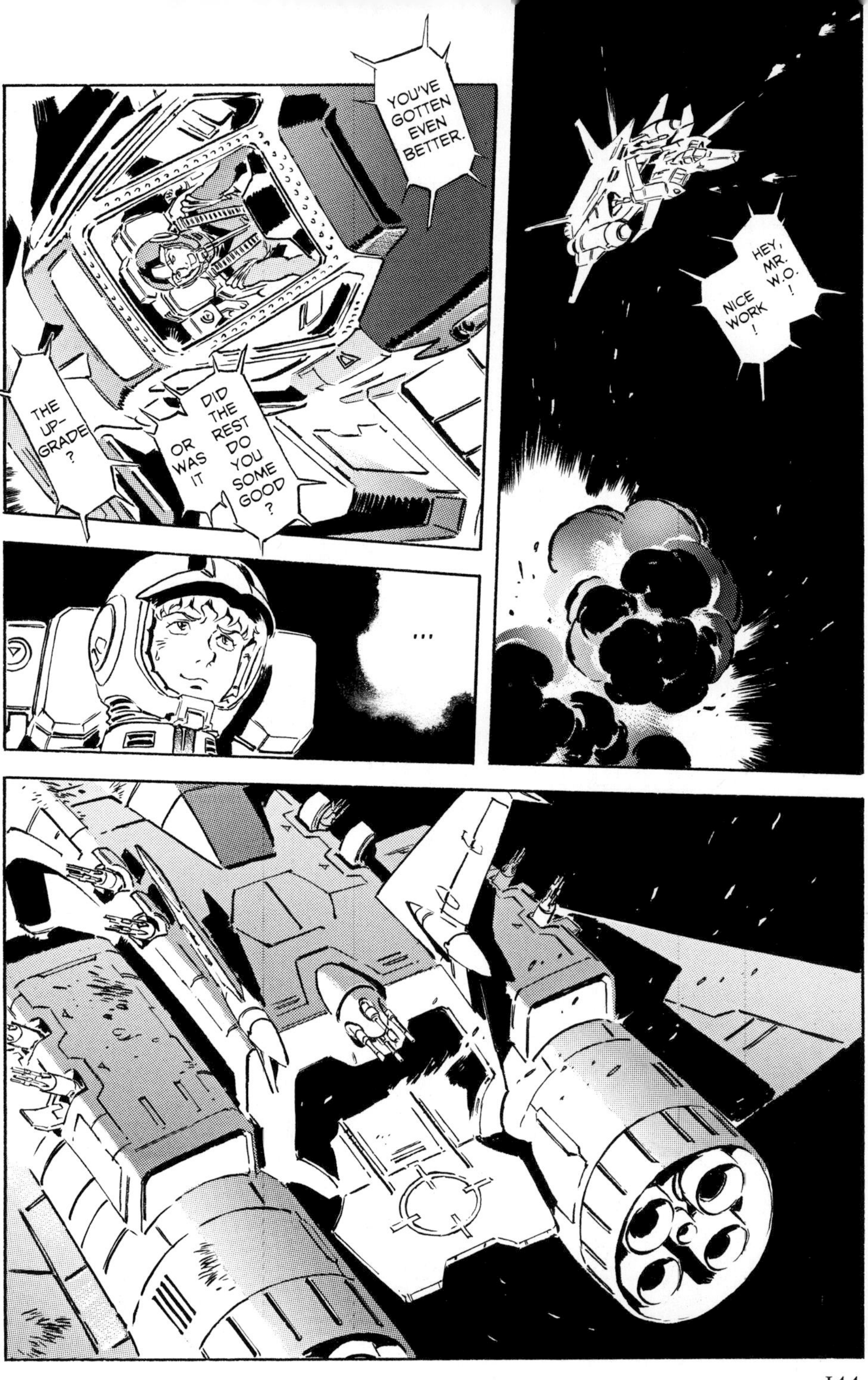
HEY, MR. W.O.! NICE WORK!
YOU'VE GOTTEN EVEN BETTER.
DID THE REST DO YOU SOME GOOD?
OR WAS IT
THE UP-GRADE?
...

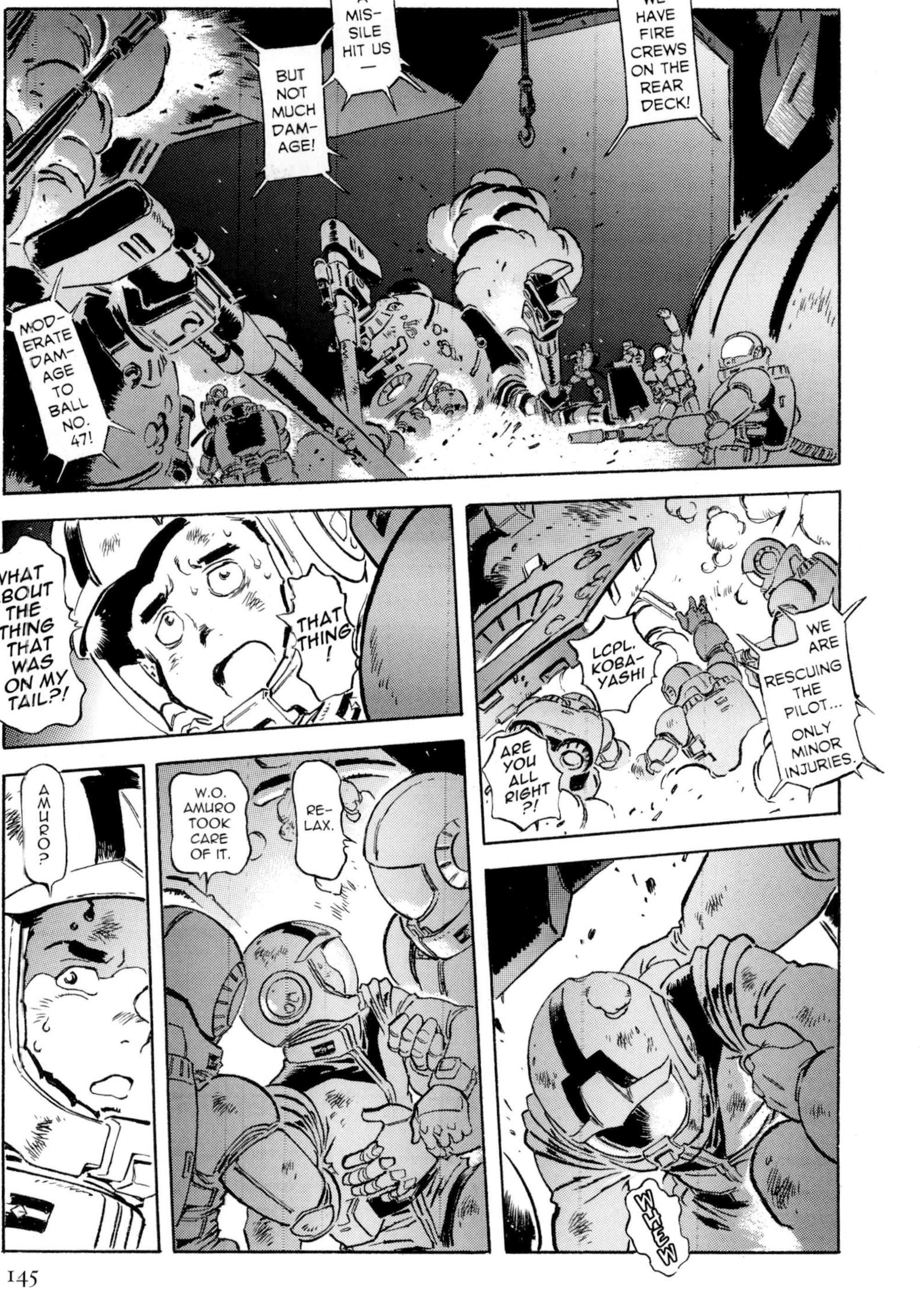
WE HAVE FIRE CREWS ON THE REAR DECK!
A MISSILE HIT US —
BUT NOT MUCH DAMAGE!
MODERATE DAMAGE TO BALL NO. 47!
WE ARE RESCUING THE PILOT... ONLY MINOR INJURIES.
LCPL. KOBAYASHI
ARE YOU ALL RIGHT?!
THAT THING!
WHAT ABOUT THE THING THAT WAS ON MY TAIL?!
WHEW
RELAX.
W.O. AMURO TOOK CARE OF IT.
AMURO?

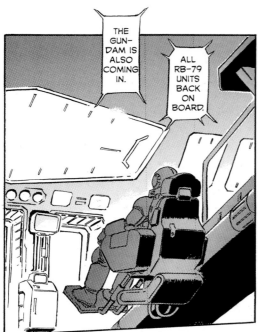

HE DID IT!
THAT'S ALL OF THEM.
MAN, HE'S GOOD ...
ALL RB-79 UNITS BACK ON BOARD.
THE GUN-DAM IS ALSO COMING IN.
SO HE'S BACK.
AMURO...
AND THAT WAS HIS FIRST OUTING
SINCE THEY FINISHED THE MAGNETIC COATING.
DID YOU
NOTICE THE DIF-FER-ENCE?

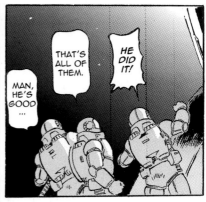

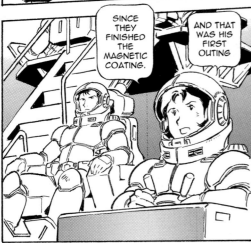

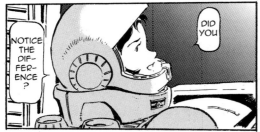

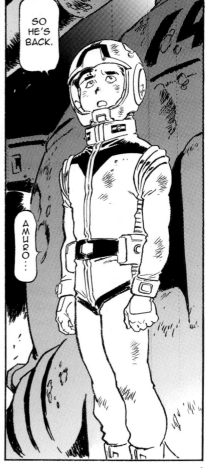

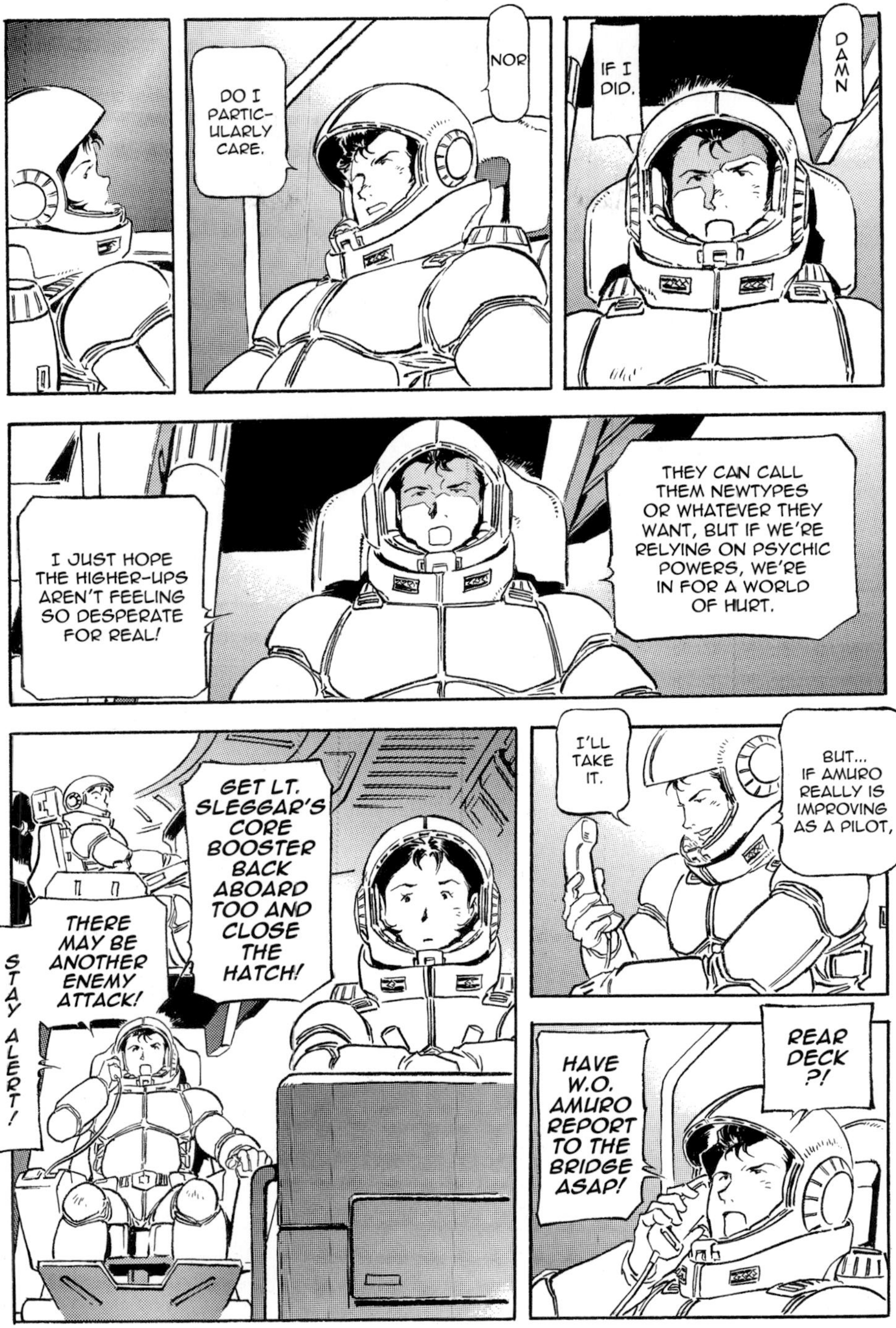
DAMN
IF I DID.
NOR
DO I PARTIC-ULARLY CARE.
THEY CAN CALL THEM NEWTYPES OR WHATEVER THEY WANT, BUT IF WE'RE RELYING ON PSYCHIC POWERS, WE'RE IN FOR A WORLD OF HURT.
I JUST HOPE THE HIGHER-UPS AREN'T FEELING SO DESPERATE FOR REAL!
BUT... IF AMURO REALLY IS IMPROVING AS A PILOT,
I'LL TAKE IT.
REAR DECK?!
HAVE W.O. AMURO REPORT TO THE BRIDGE ASAP!
GET LT. SLEGGAR'S CORE BOOSTER BACK ABOARD TOO AND CLOSE THE HATCH!
THERE MAY BE ANOTHER ENEMY ATTACK!
STAY ALERT!

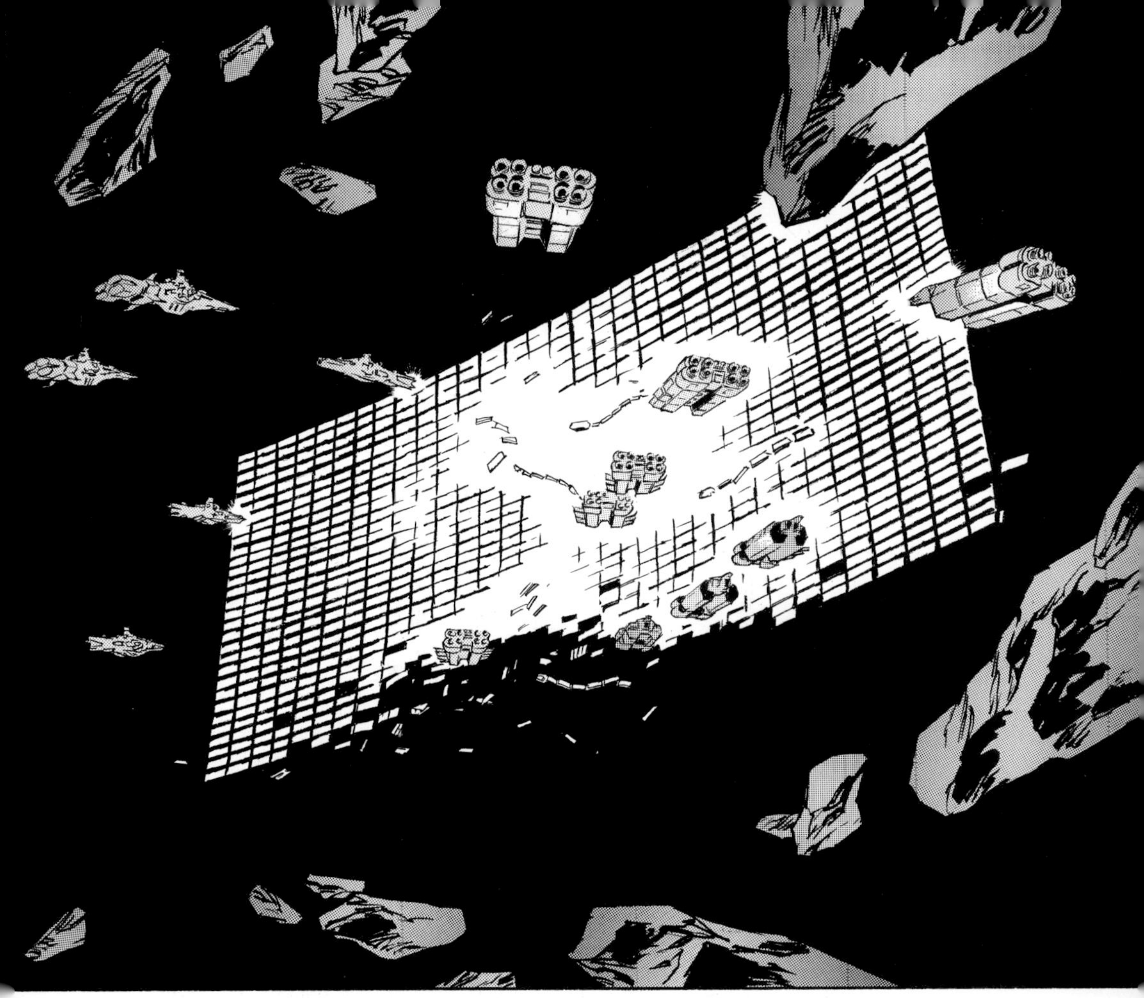

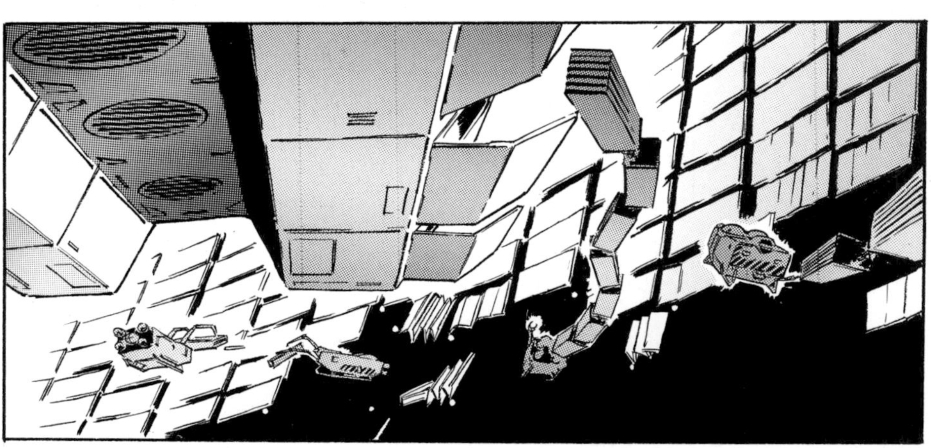

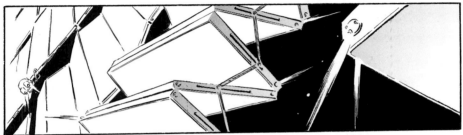

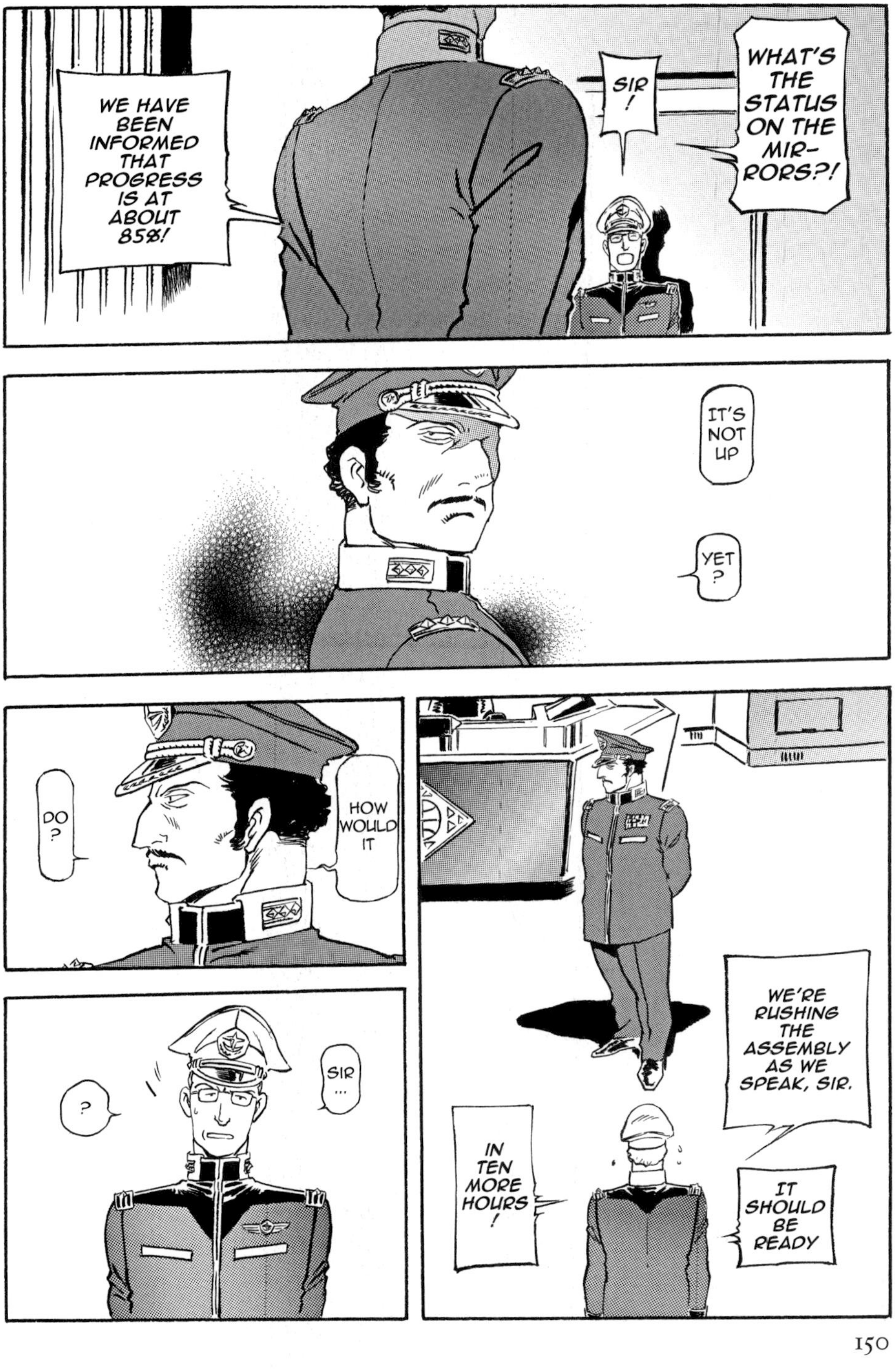
WHAT'S THE STATUS ON THE MIRRORS?!
SIR!
WE HAVE BEEN INFORMED THAT PROGRESS IS AT ABOUT 85%!
IT'S NOT UP
YET?
WE'RE RUSHING THE ASSEMBLY AS WE SPEAK, SIR.
IT SHOULD BE READY
IN TEN MORE HOURS!
HOW WOULD IT
DO?
SIR...
?

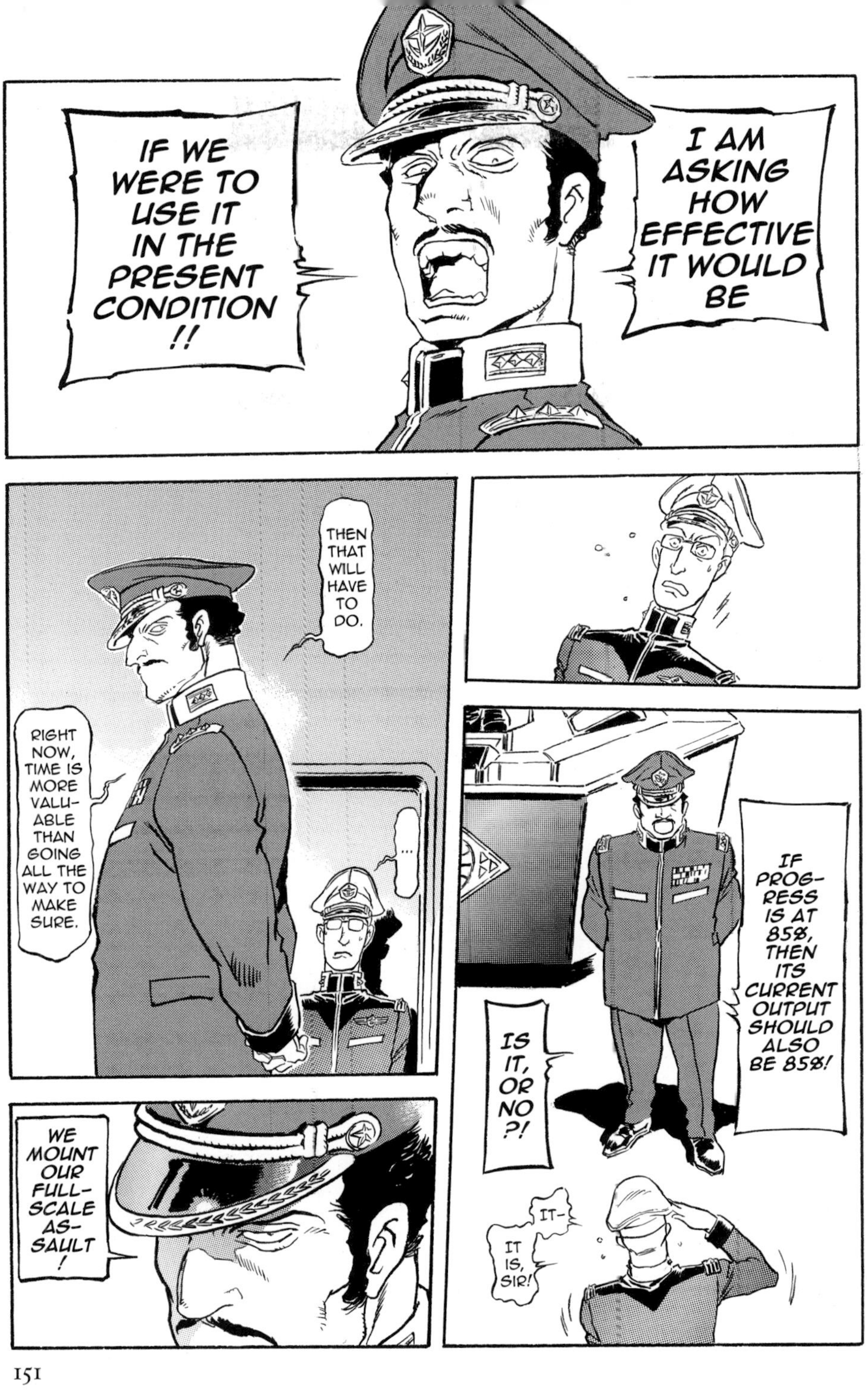
I AM ASKING HOW EFFECTIVE IT WOULD BE
IF WE WERE TO USE IT IN THE PRESENT CONDITION !!
IF PROGRESS IS AT 85%, THEN ITS CURRENT OUTPUT SHOULD ALSO BE 85%!
IS IT, OR NO?!
IT-
IT IS, SIR!
THEN THAT WILL HAVE TO DO.
RIGHT NOW, TIME IS MORE VALUABLE THAN GOING ALL THE WAY TO MAKE SURE.
...
WE MOUNT OUR FULL-SCALE ASSAULT!

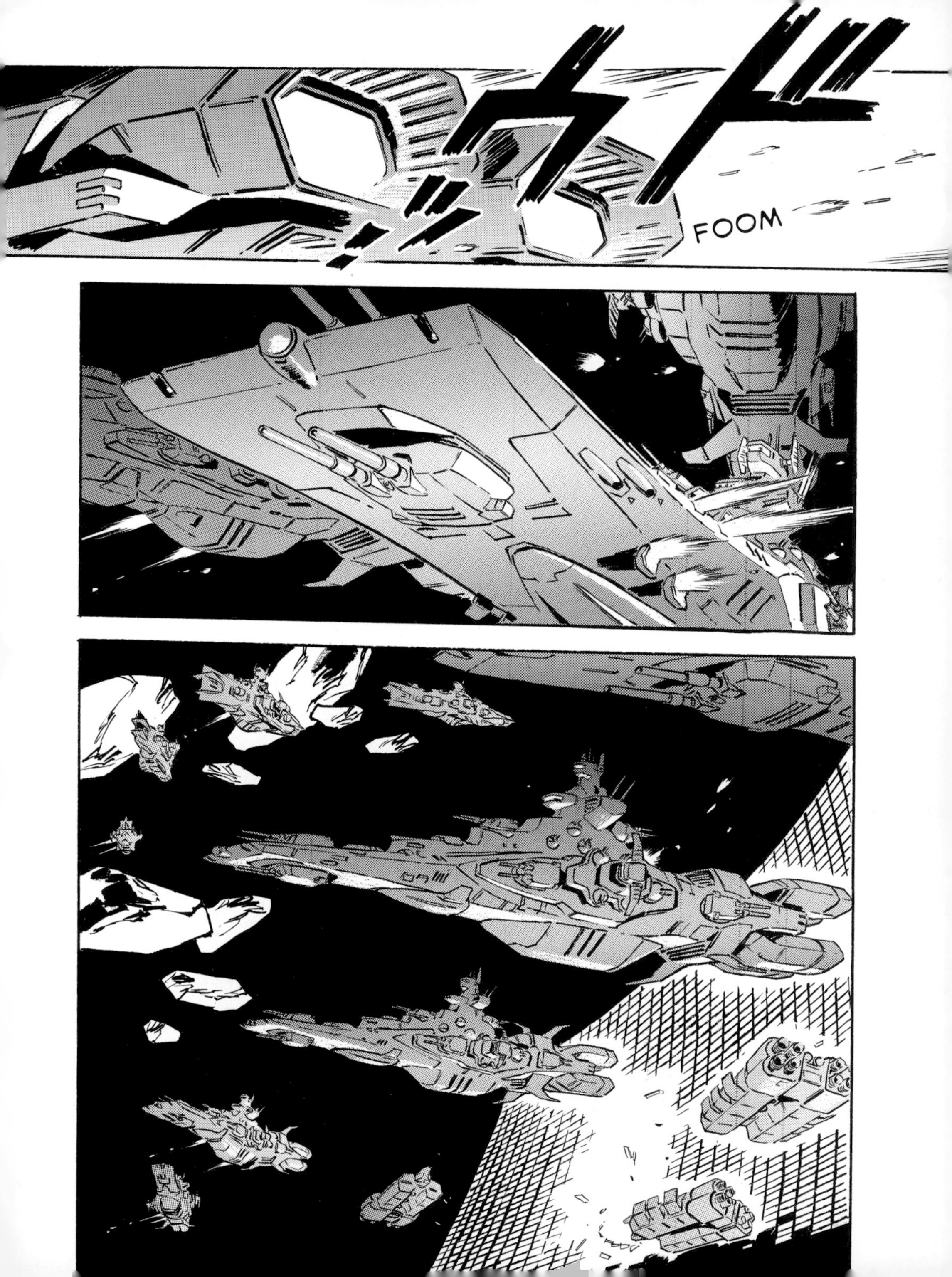
FOOM

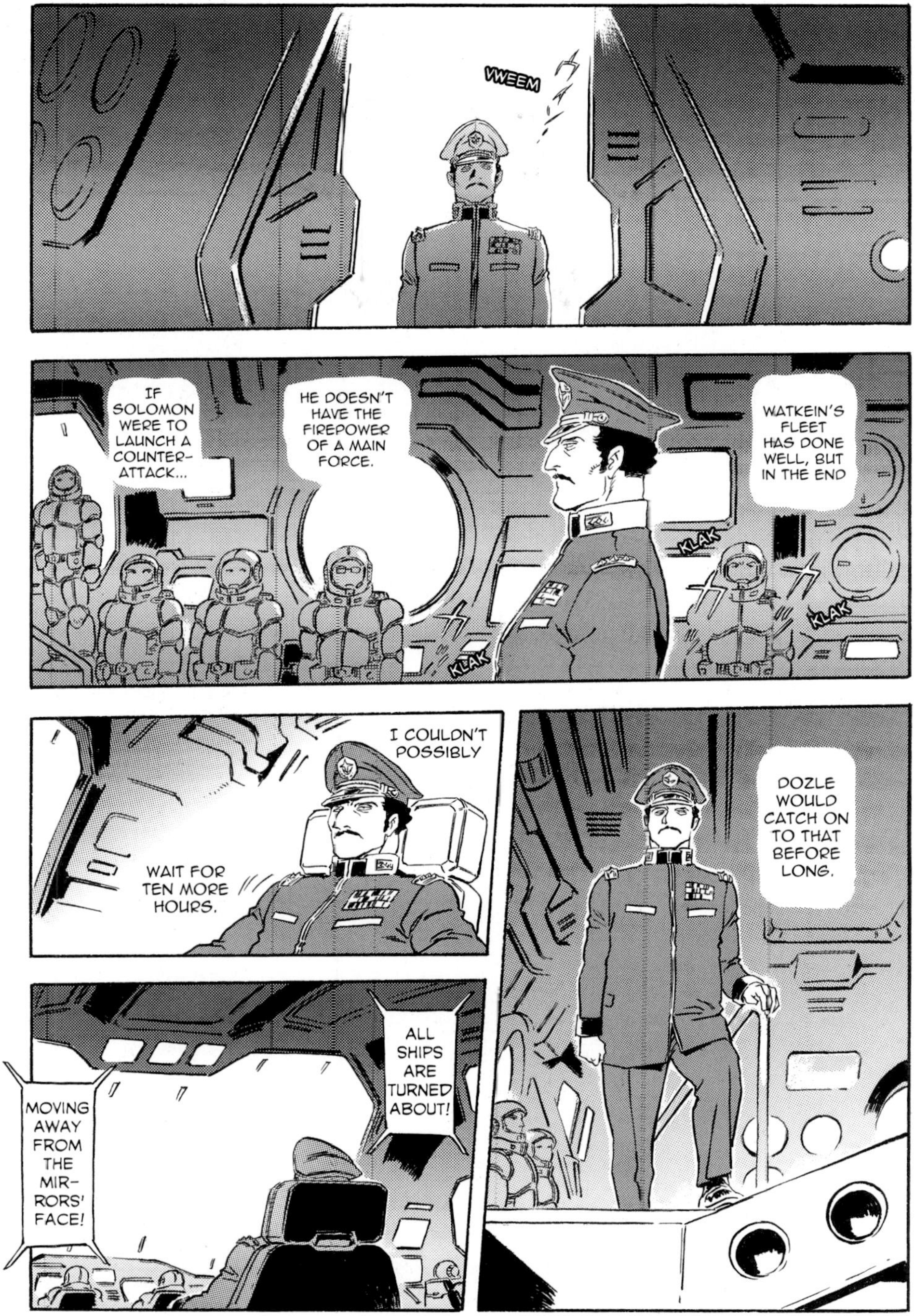
VWEEM
WATKEIN'S FLEET HAS DONE WELL, BUT IN THE END
HE DOESN'T HAVE THE FIREPOWER OF A MAIN FORCE.
IF SOLOMON WERE TO LAUNCH A COUNTER-ATTACK...
KLAK
KLAK
KLAK
DOZLE WOULD CATCH ON TO THAT BEFORE LONG.
I COULDN'T POSSIBLY
WAIT FOR TEN MORE HOURS.
ALL SHIPS ARE TURNED ABOUT!
MOVING AWAY FROM THE MIR-RORS' FACE!

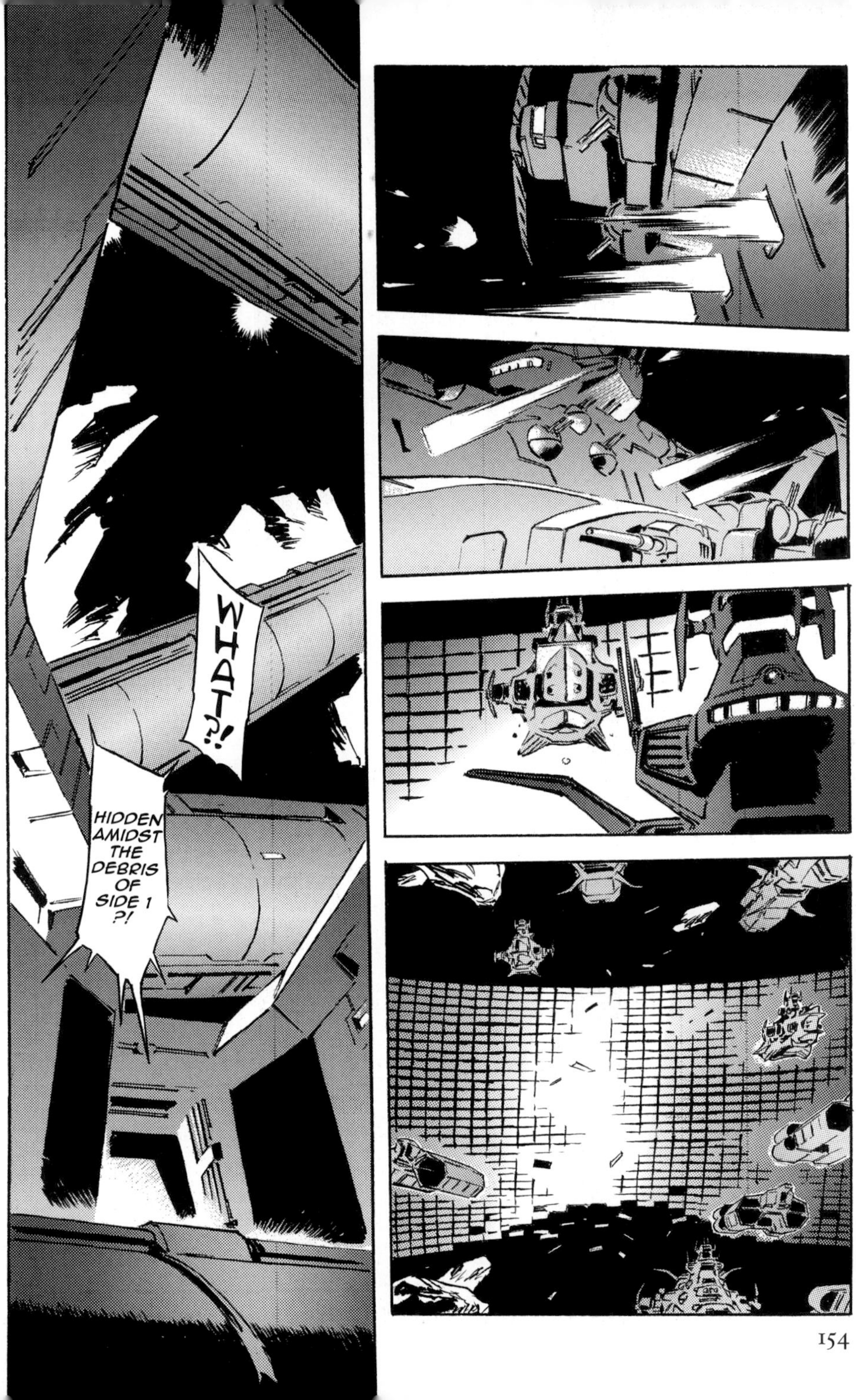
WHAT?!
HIDDEN AMIDST THE DEBRIS OF SIDE 1 ?!

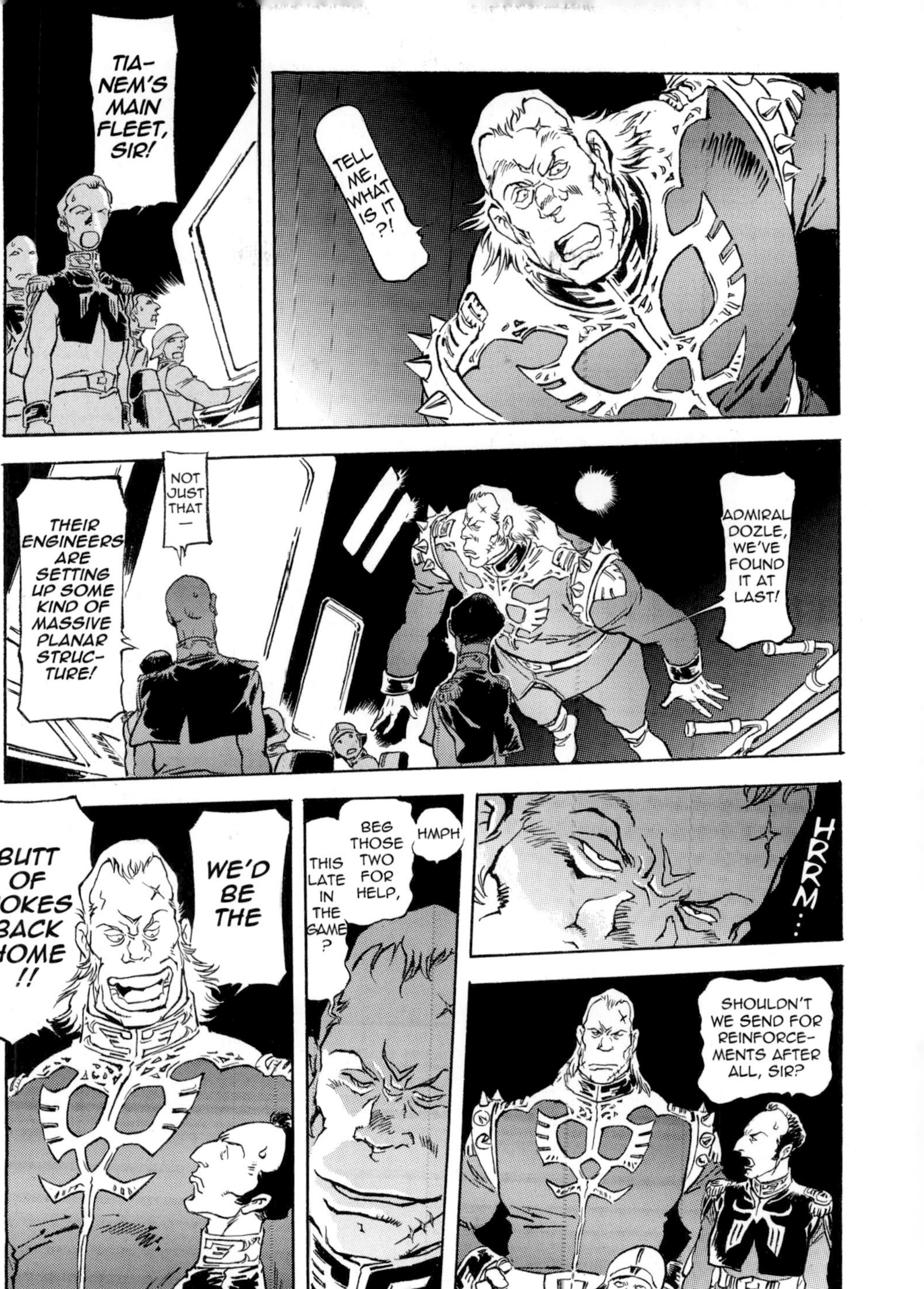
TELL ME, WHAT IS IT ?!
TIA-NEM'S MAIN FLEET, SIR!
ADMIRAL DOZLE, WE'VE FOUND IT AT LAST!
NOT JUST THAT —
THEIR ENGINEERS ARE SETTING UP SOME KIND OF MASSIVE PLANAR STRUCTURE!
HRRM...
SHOULDN'T WE SEND FOR REINFORCEMENTS AFTER ALL, SIR?
HMPH
BEG THOSE TWO FOR HELP,
THIS LATE IN THE GAME ?
WE'D BE THE
BUTT OF JOKES BACK HOME !!

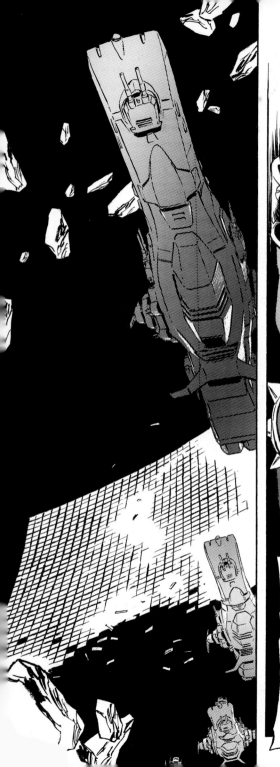
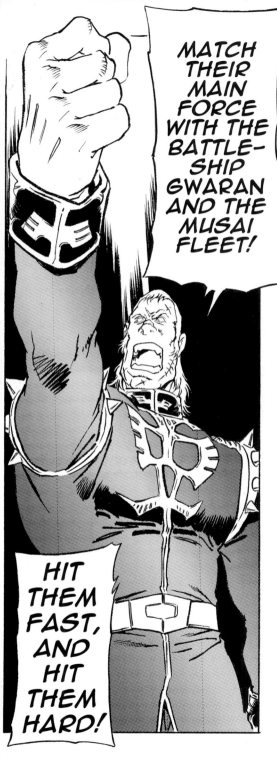

MATCH THEIR MAIN FORCE WITH THE BATTLE-SHIP GWARAN AND THE MUSAI FLEET!

HIT THEM FAST, AND HIT THEM HARD!

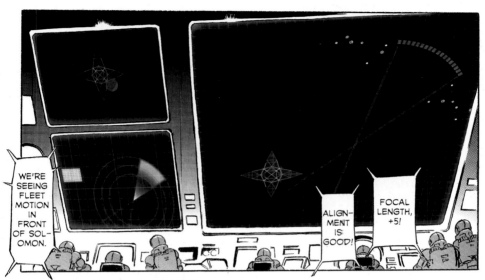

FOCAL LENGTH, +5!
ALIGNMENT IS GOOD!
WE'RE SEEING FLEET MOTION IN FRONT OF SOLOMON.
IGNORE THAT!
HURRY UP AND GET IT IN FOCUS!
TARGET!
SPACEGATE, BASE OF VERTEX ANGLE NO. 4!
GLEAM

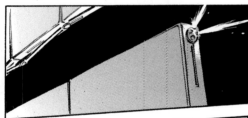

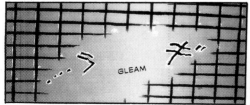

AIMING!
4!
3!
2!
1!
ALIGN-MENT GOOD!
TAR-GET
IN FO-CUS!
FIRE

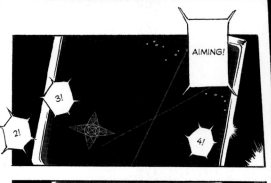

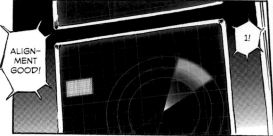

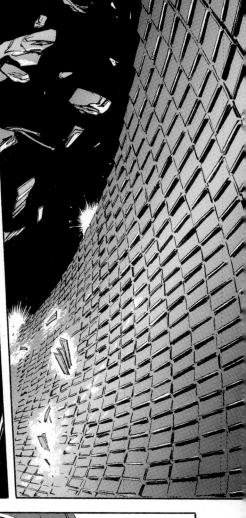

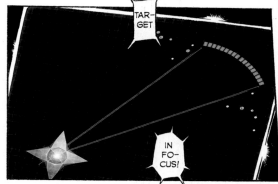

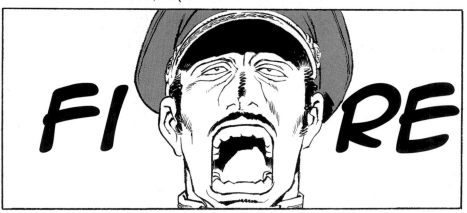

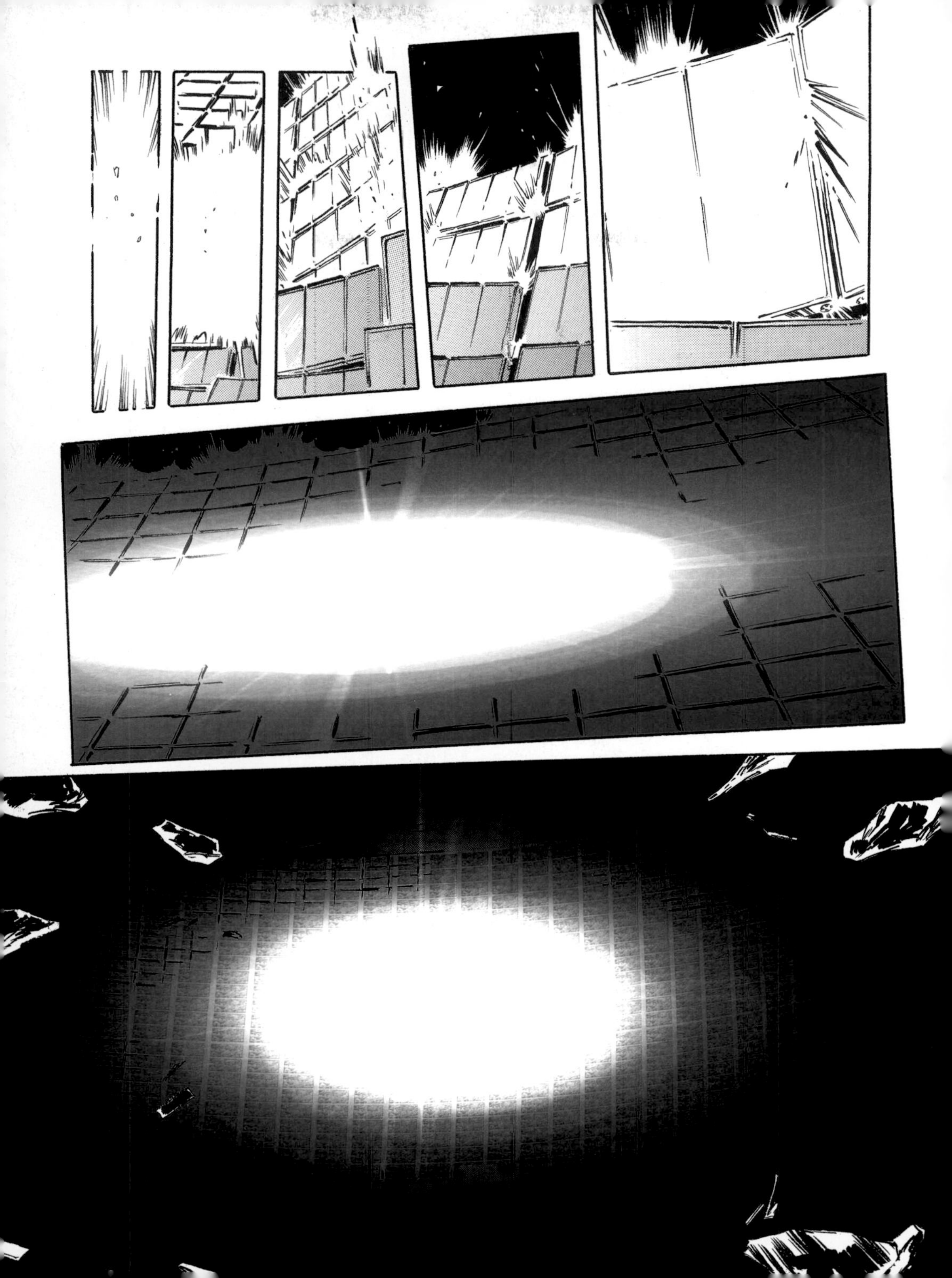

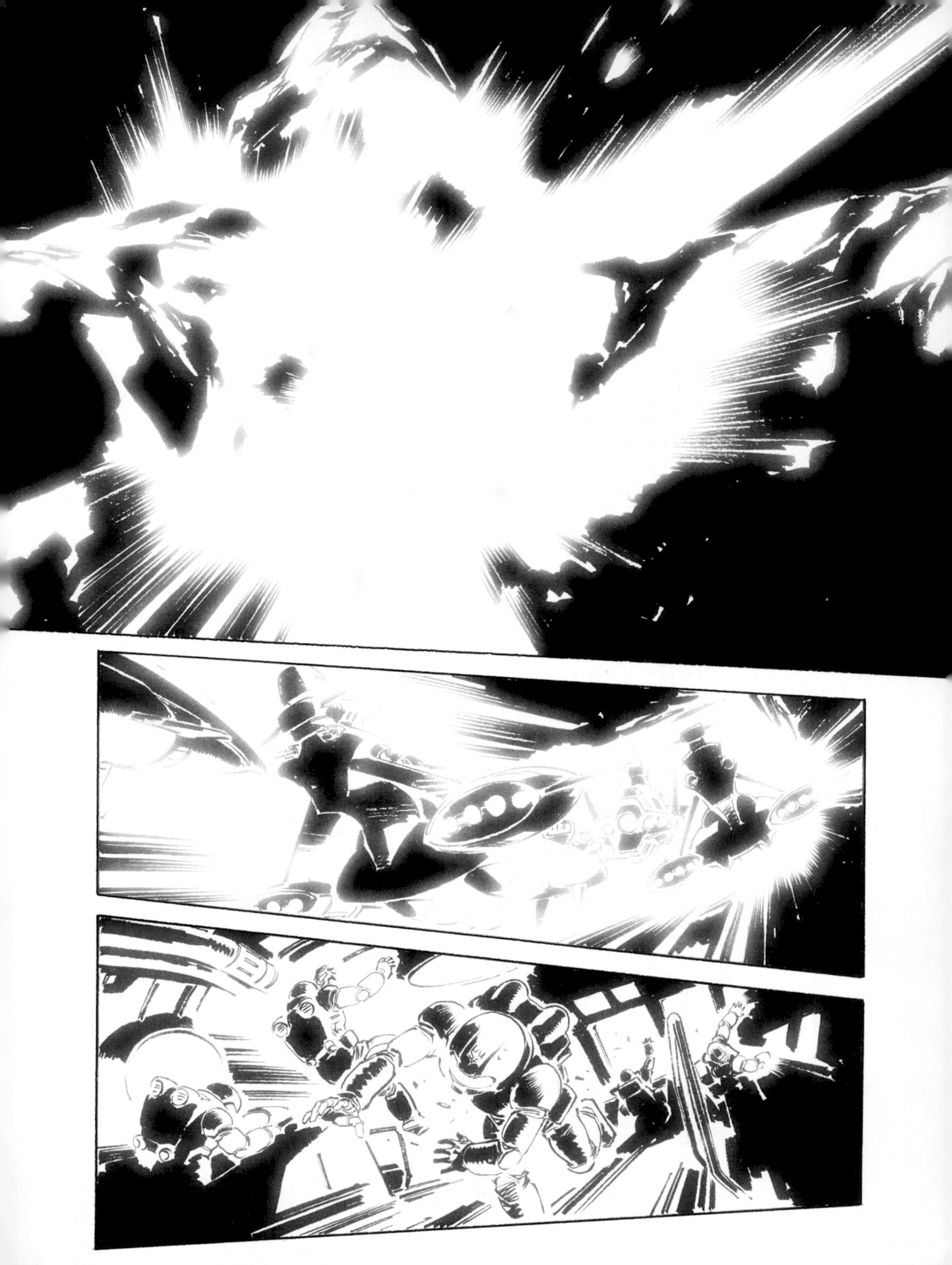

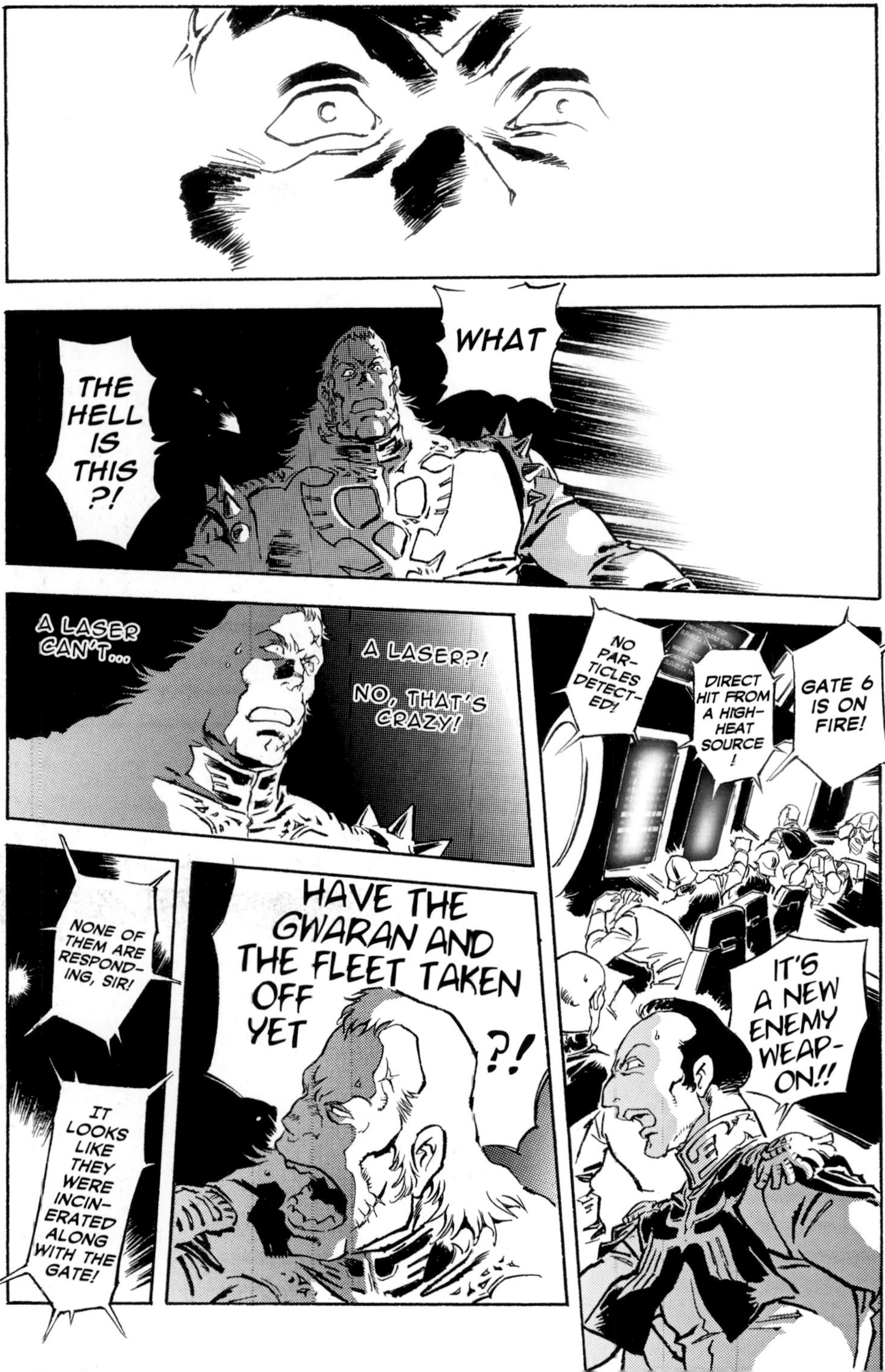
WHAT
THE HELL IS THIS ?!
GATE 6 IS ON FIRE!
DIRECT HIT FROM A HIGH-HEAT SOURCE!
NO PARTICLES DETECTED!
IT'S A NEW ENEMY WEAPON!!
A LASER?!
NO, THAT'S CRAZY!
A LASER CAN'T...
HAVE THE GWARAN AND THE FLEET TAKEN OFF YET ?!
NONE OF THEM ARE RESPONDING, SIR!
IT LOOKS LIKE THEY WERE INCINERATED ALONG WITH THE GATE!

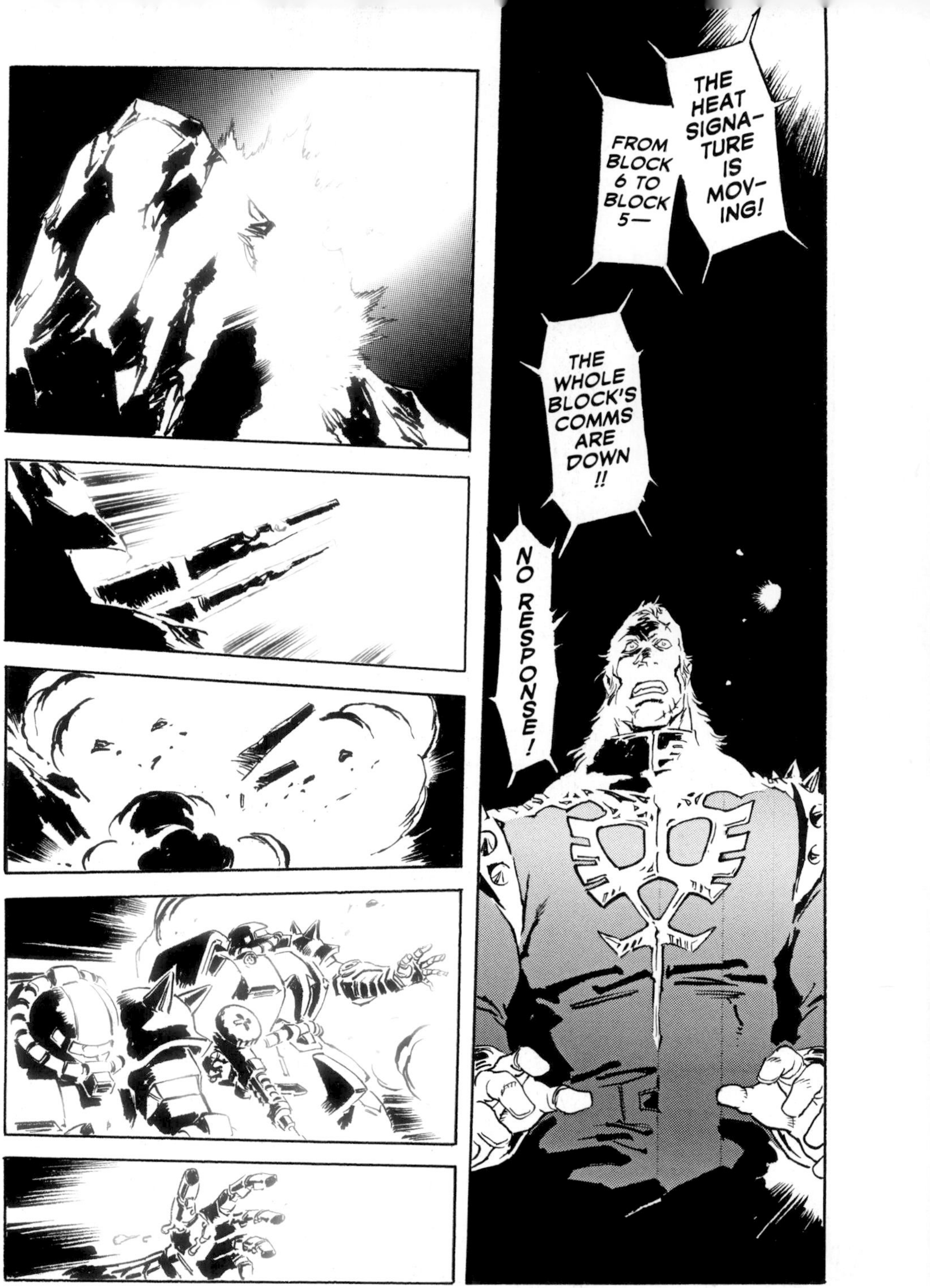
THE HEAT SIGNA-TURE IS MOV-ING!
FROM BLOCK 6 TO BLOCK 5—
THE WHOLE BLOCK'S COMMS ARE DOWN!!
NO RESPONSE!

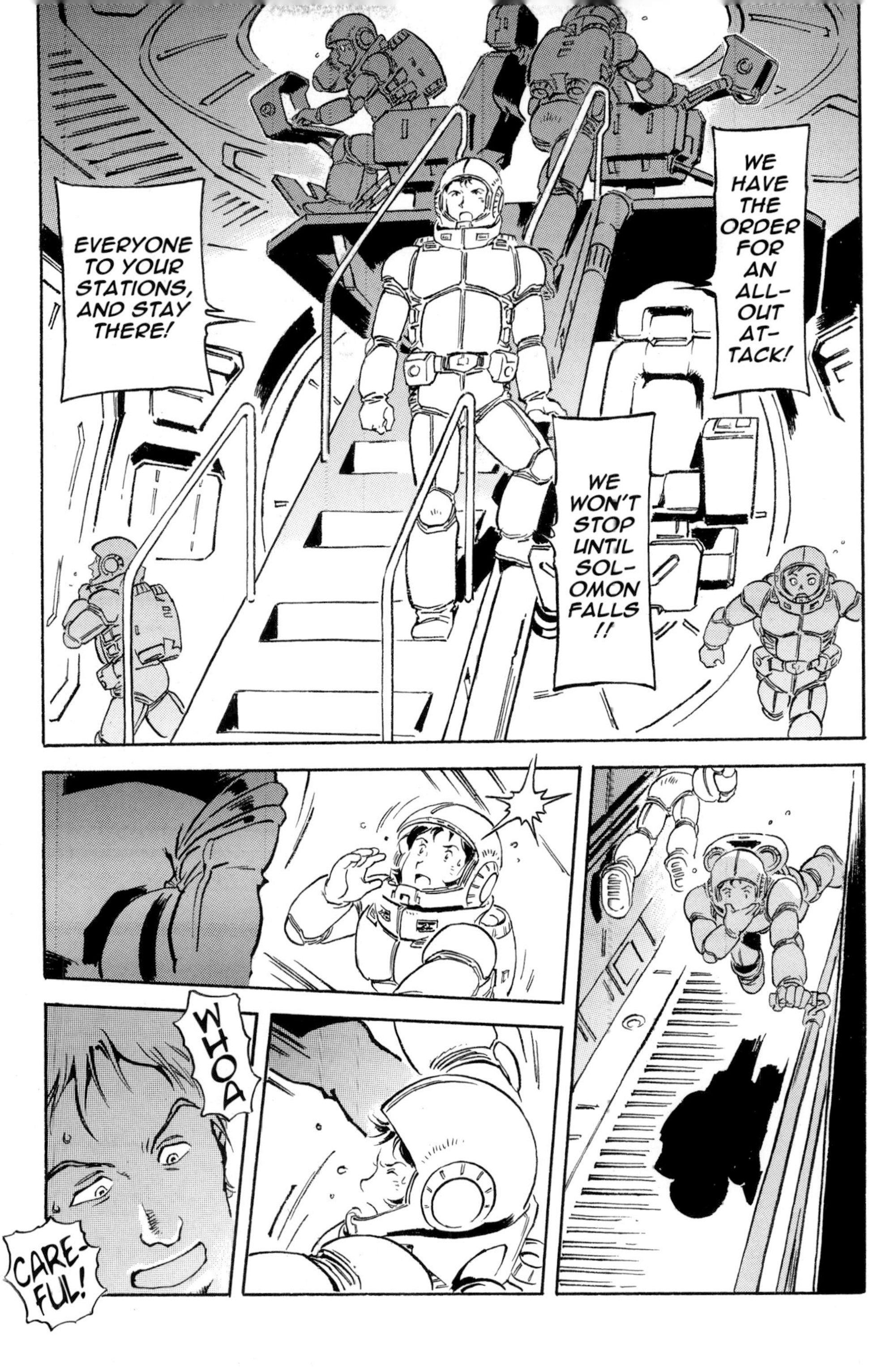
WE HAVE THE ORDER FOR AN ALL-OUT AT-TACK!
WE WON'T STOP UNTIL SOL-OMON FALLS!!
EVERYONE TO YOUR STATIONS, AND STAY THERE!
WHOA
CARE-FUL!

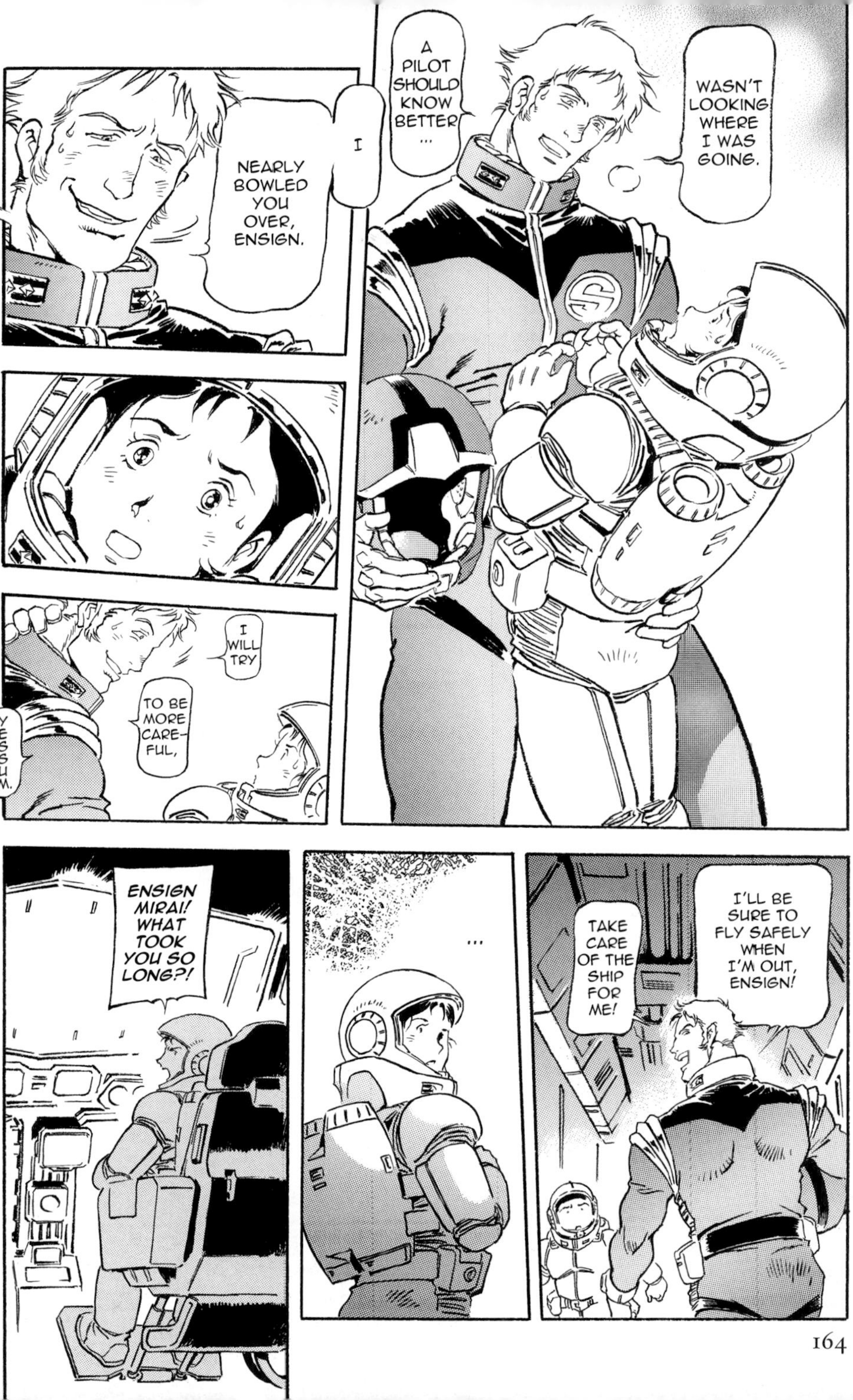
WASN'T LOOKING WHERE I WAS GOING.
A PILOT SHOULD KNOW BETTER...
I
NEARLY BOWLED YOU OVER, ENSIGN.
I WILL TRY
TO BE MORE CAREFUL,
YESSUM.
I'LL BE SURE TO FLY SAFELY WHEN I'M OUT, ENSIGN!
TAKE CARE OF THE SHIP FOR ME!
...
ENSIGN MIRAI! WHAT TOOK YOU SO LONG?!

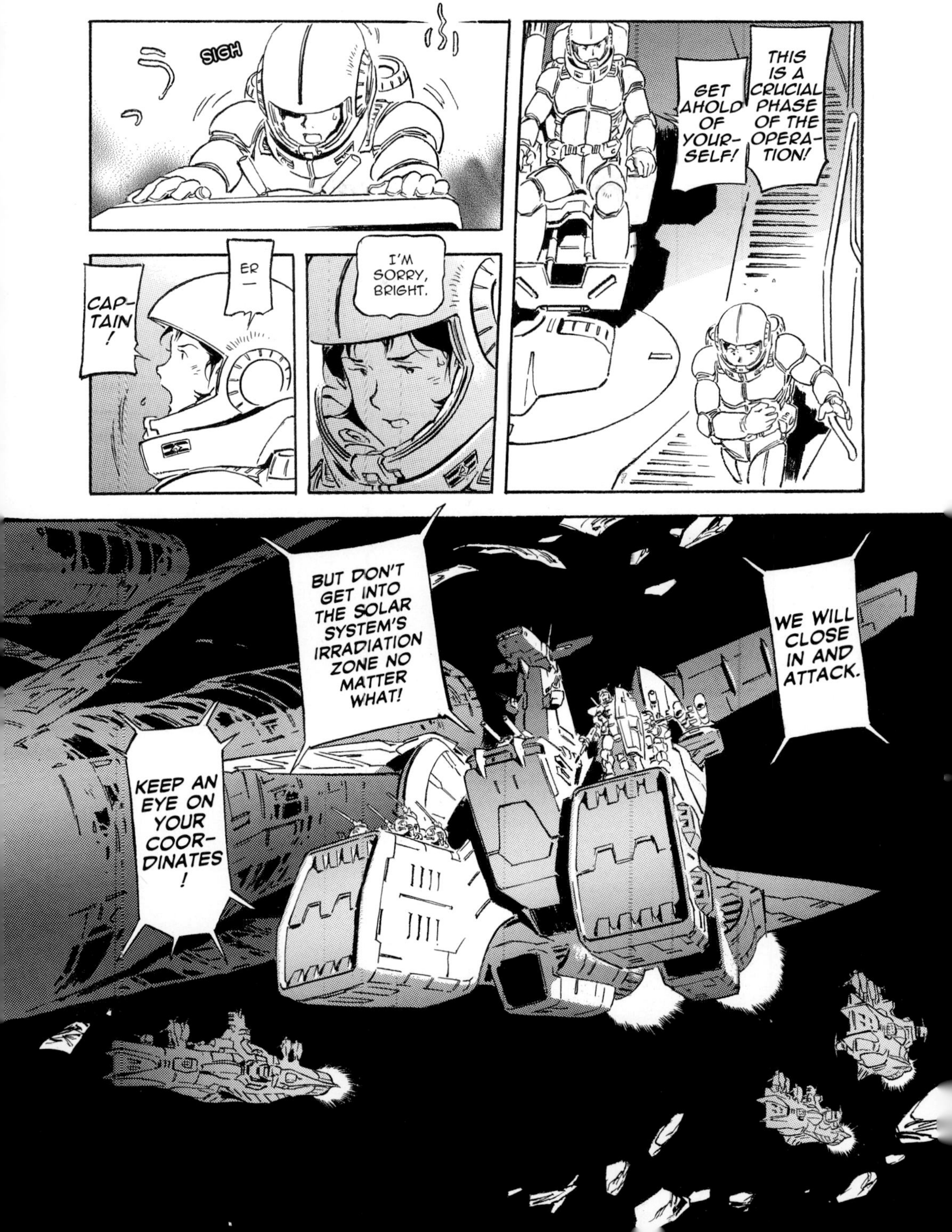
THIS IS A CRUCIAL PHASE OF THE OPERATION!
GET AHOLD OF YOURSELF!
SIGH
I'M SORRY, BRIGHT.
ER —
CAPTAIN!
WE WILL CLOSE IN AND ATTACK.
BUT DON'T GET INTO THE SOLAR SYSTEM'S IRRADIATION ZONE NO MATTER WHAT!
KEEP AN EYE ON YOUR COORDINATES!

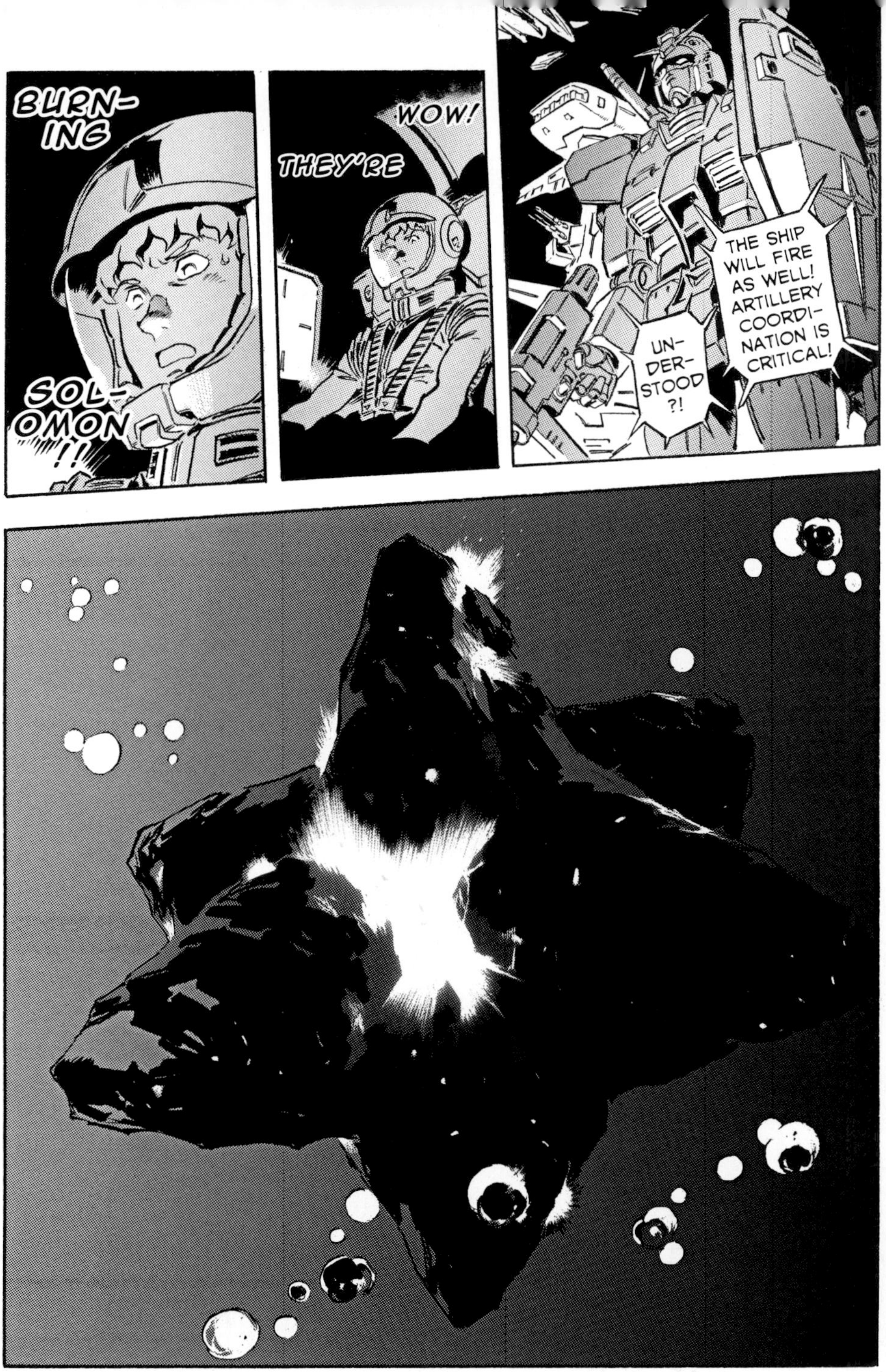
THE SHIP WILL FIRE AS WELL! ARTILLERY COORDI-NATION IS CRITICAL!
UN-DER-STOOD?!
WOW!
THEY'RE
BURN-ING
SOL-OMON!!

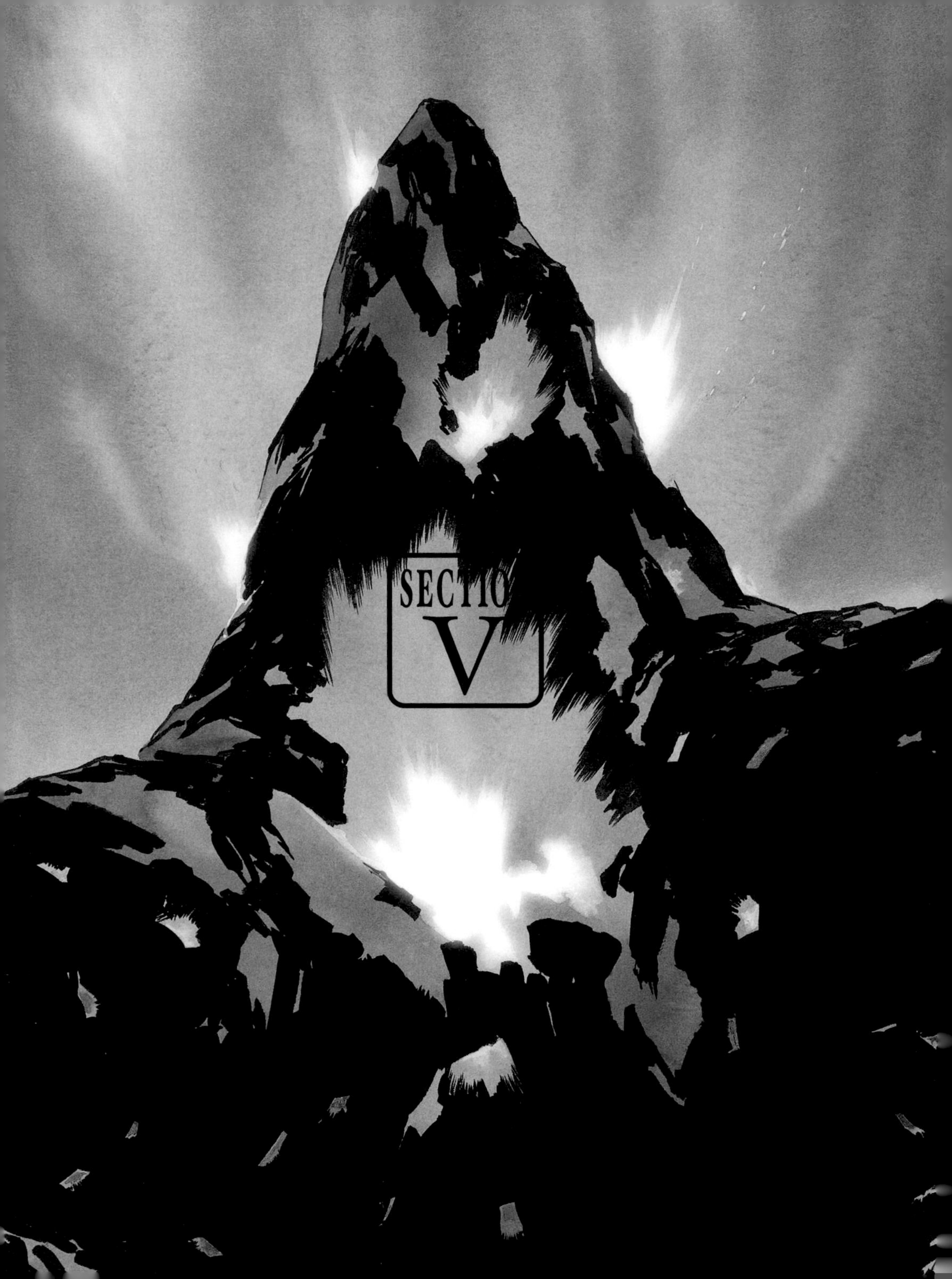
SECTIO
V

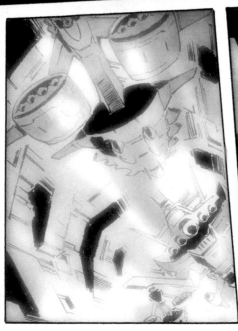

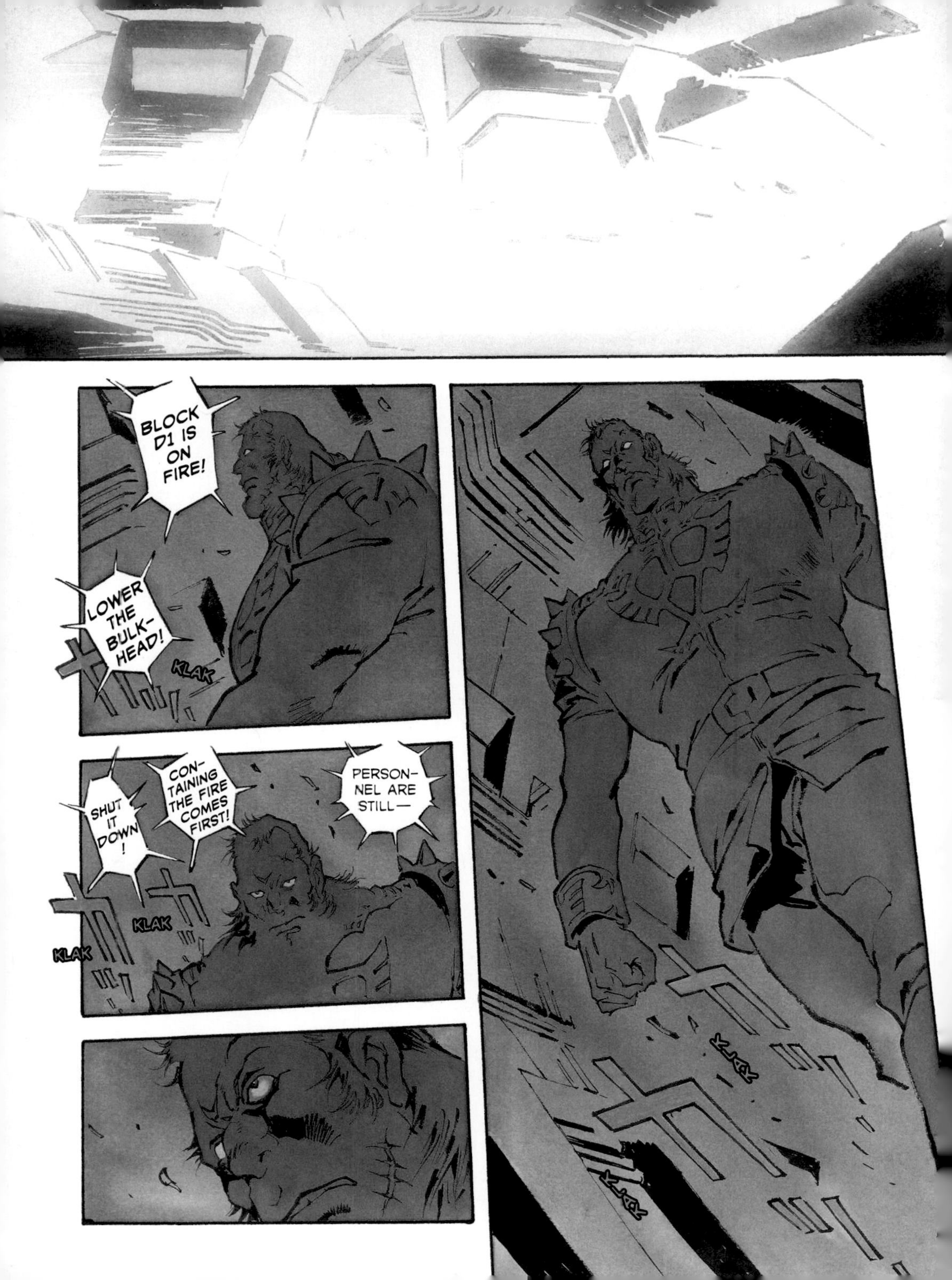
KLAK
KLAK
BLOCK D1 IS ON FIRE!
LOWER THE BULKHEAD!
KLAK
PERSONNEL ARE STILL—
CONTAINING THE FIRE COMES FIRST!
SHUT IT DOWN!
KLAK
KLAK

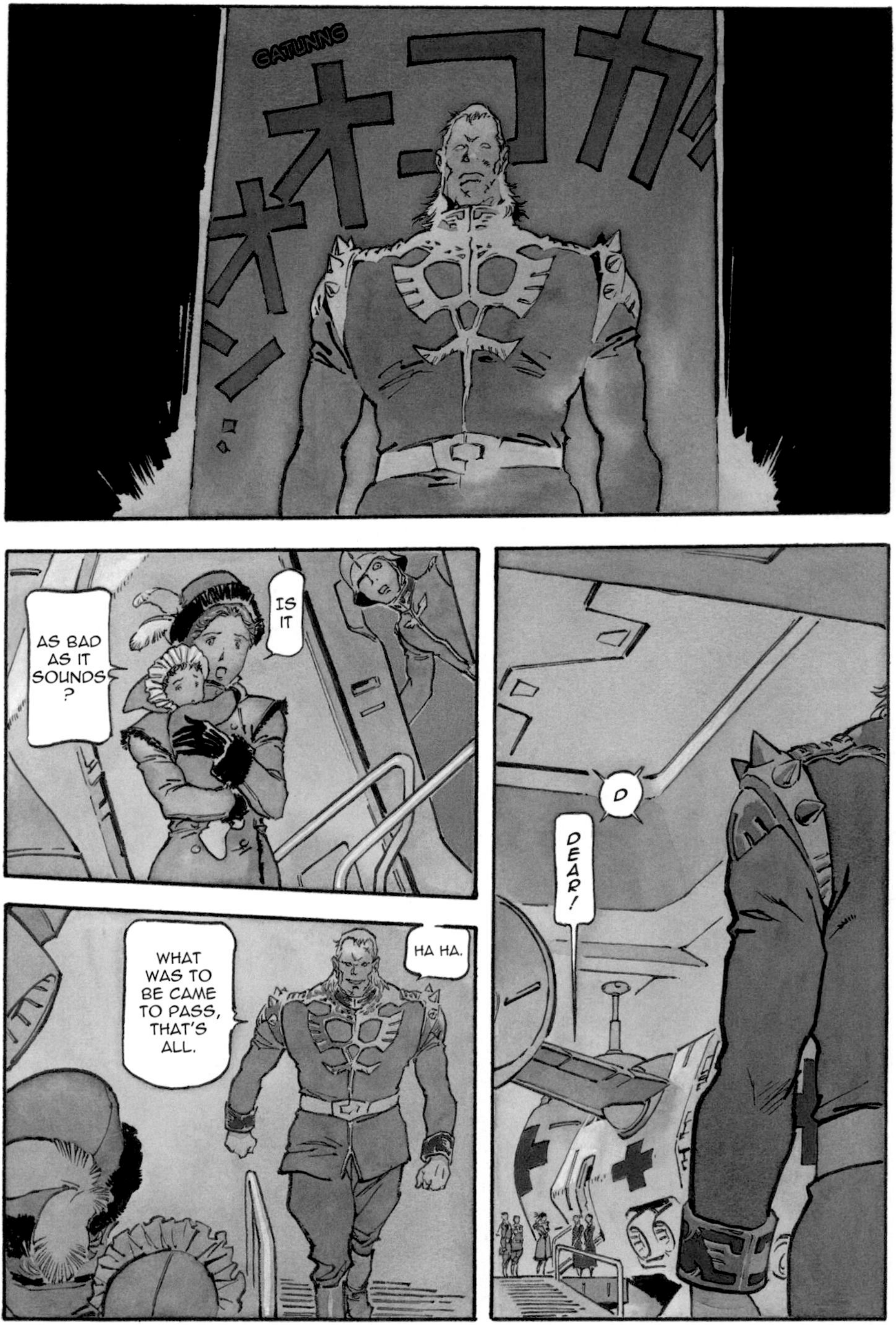
GATUNNG
D
DEAR!
IS IT
AS BAD AS IT SOUNDS?
HA HA.
WHAT WAS TO BE CAME TO PASS, THAT'S ALL.

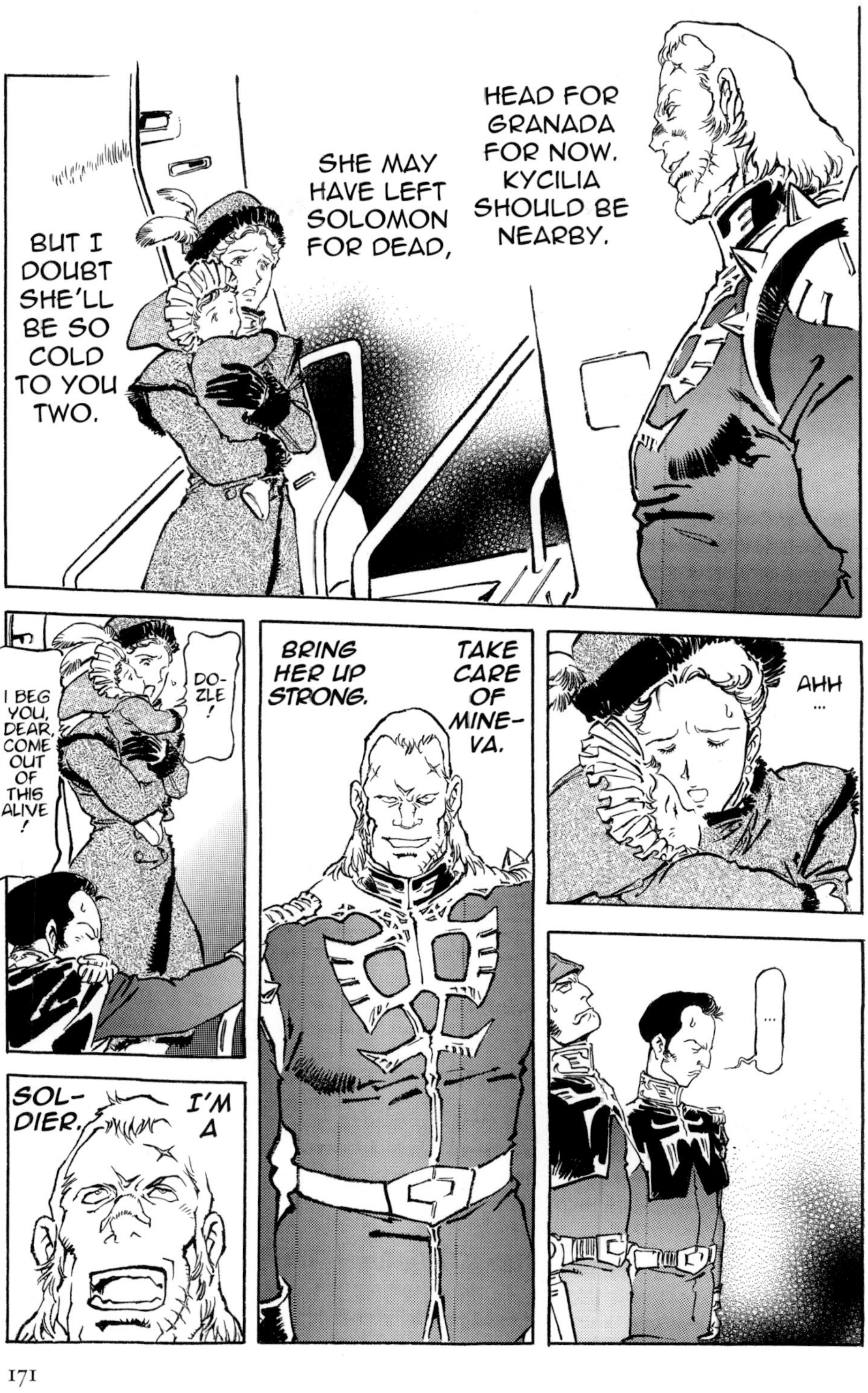
HEAD FOR GRANADA FOR NOW. KYCILIA SHOULD BE NEARBY.
SHE MAY HAVE LEFT SOLOMON FOR DEAD,
BUT I DOUBT SHE'LL BE SO COLD TO YOU TWO.
AHH ...
...
TAKE CARE OF MINE-VA.
BRING HER UP STRONG.
DO-ZLE!
I BEG YOU, DEAR, COME OUT OF THIS ALIVE!
I'M A SOL-DIER.

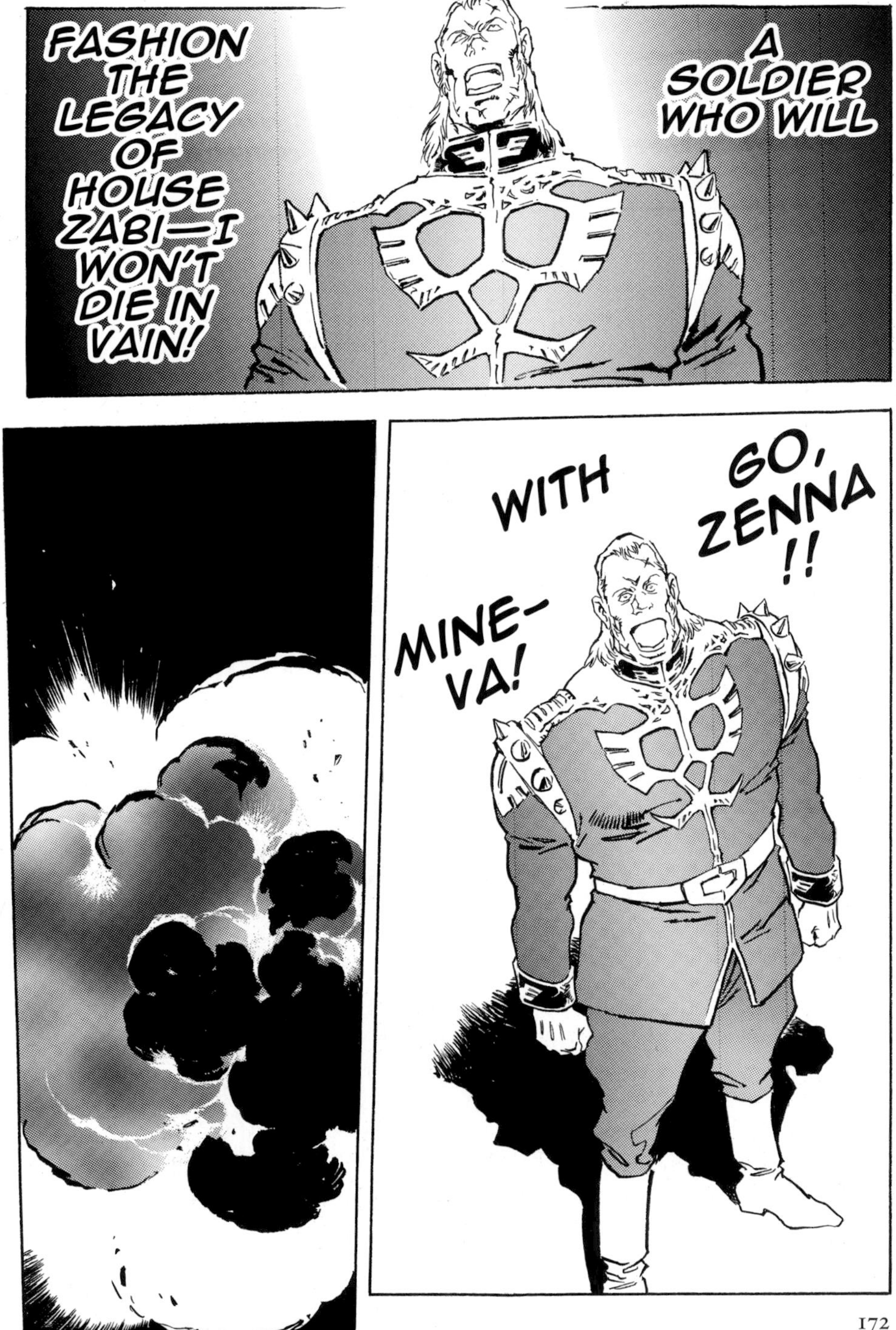
A SOLDIER WHO WILL
FASHION THE LEGACY OF HOUSE ZABI—I WON'T DIE IN VAIN!
GO, ZENNA!!
WITH MINE-VA!

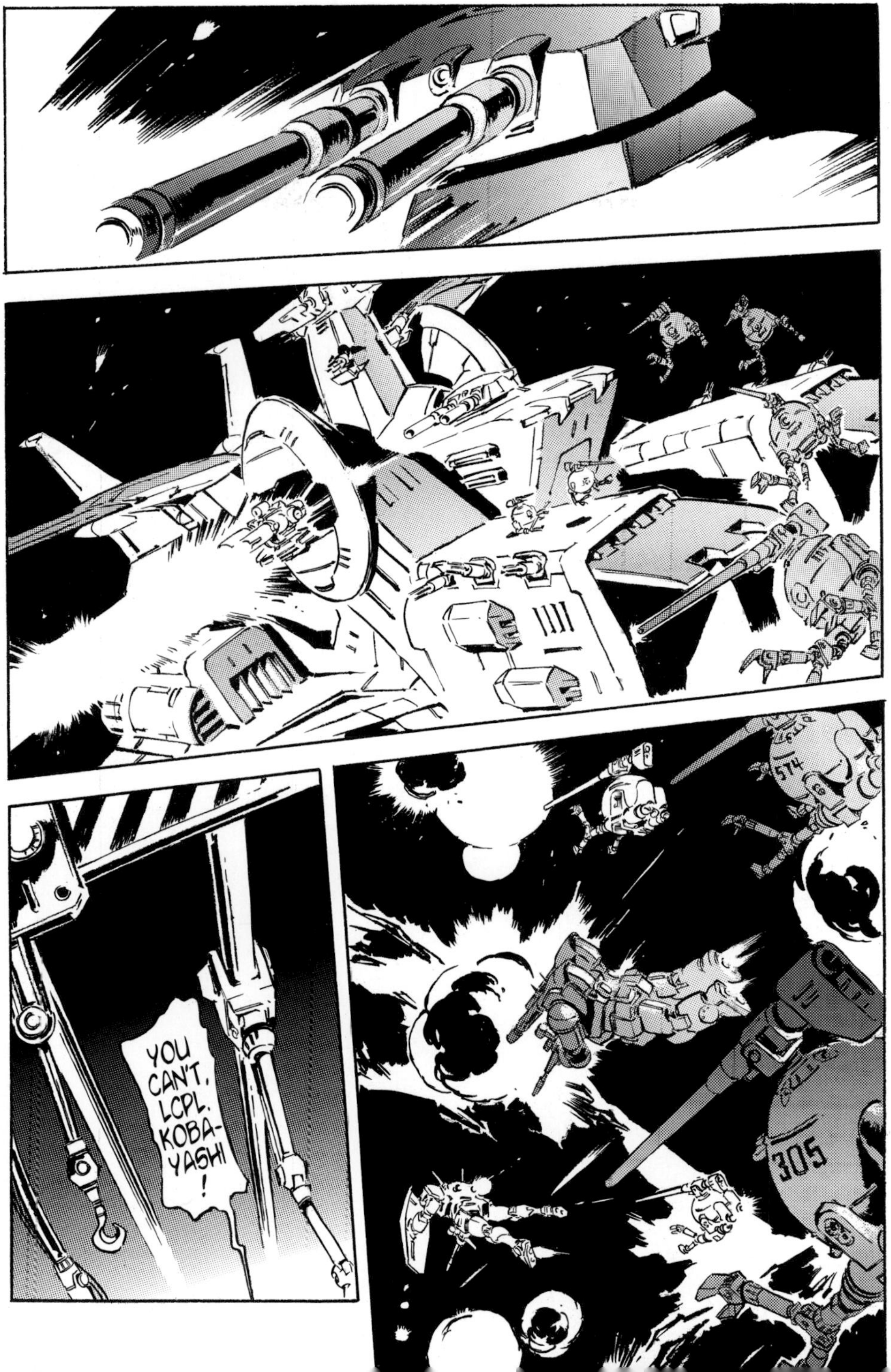
YOU CAN'T, LCPL. KOBA-YASHI!

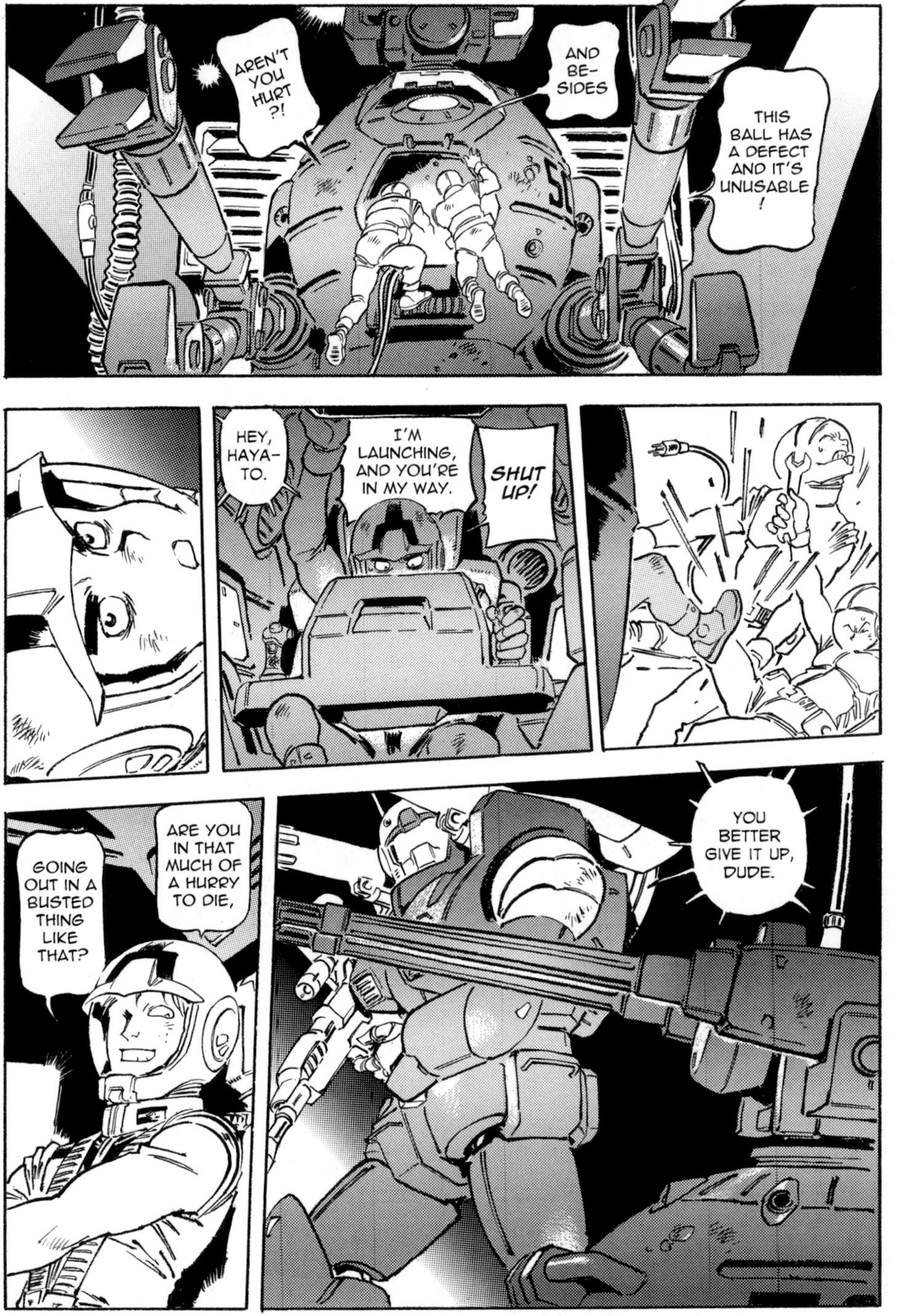
AREN'T YOU HURT?!
AND BE-SIDES
THIS BALL HAS A DEFECT AND IT'S UNUSABLE!
HEY, HAYA-TO.
I'M LAUNCHING, AND YOU'RE IN MY WAY.
SHUT UP!
YOU BETTER GIVE IT UP, DUDE.
ARE YOU IN THAT MUCH OF A HURRY TO DIE,
GOING OUT IN A BUSTED THING LIKE THAT?

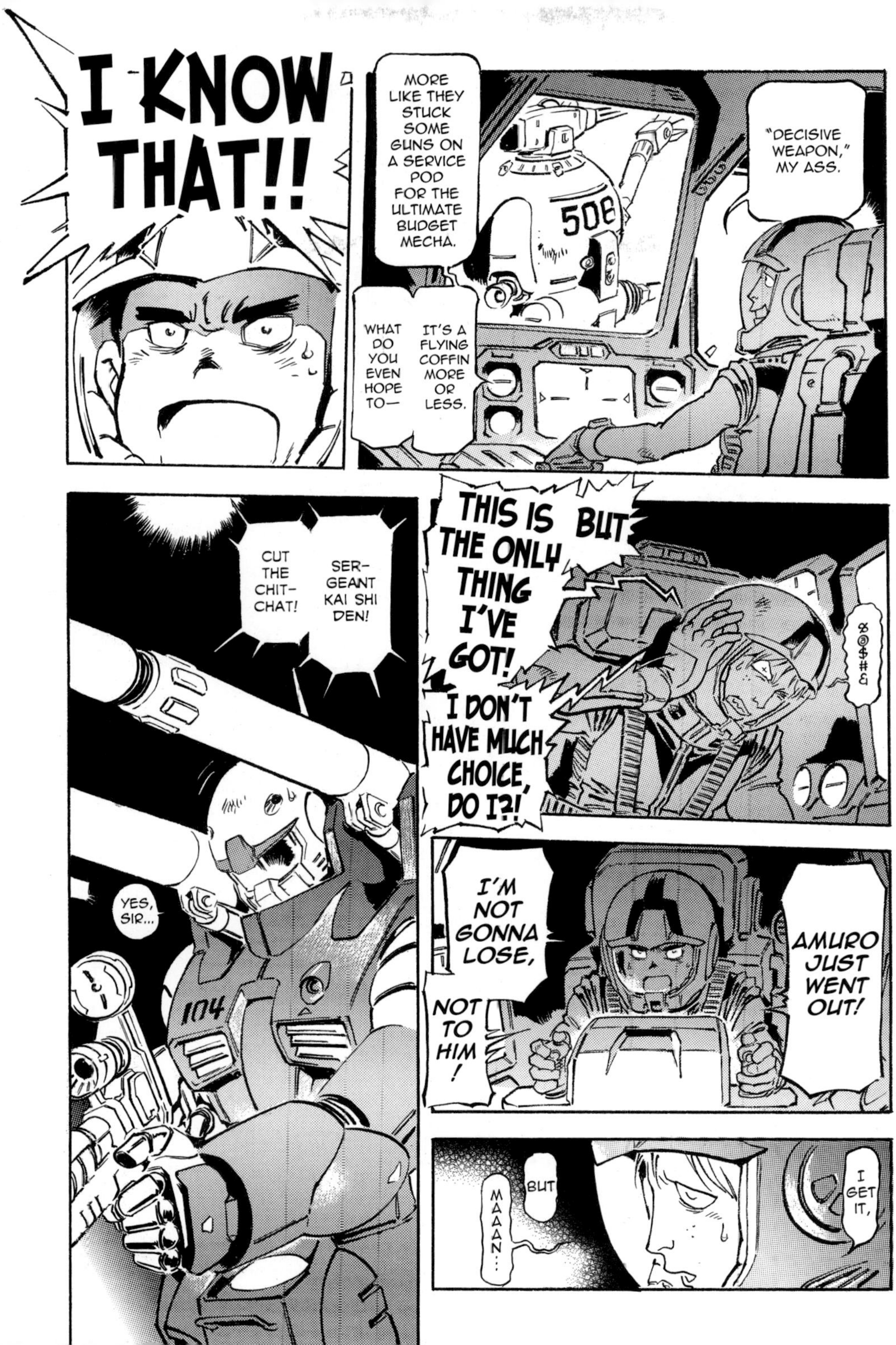
"DECISIVE WEAPON," MY ASS.
MORE LIKE THEY STUCK SOME GUNS ON A SERVICE POD FOR THE ULTIMATE BUDGET MECHA.
506
IT'S A FLYING COFFIN MORE OR LESS.
WHAT DO YOU EVEN HOPE TO—
I KNOW THAT!!
THIS IS THE ONLY THING I'VE GOT!
BUT I DON'T HAVE MUCH CHOICE, DO I?!
AMURO JUST WENT OUT!
I'M NOT GONNA LOSE,
NOT TO HIM!
I GET IT,
BUT
MAAAAN....
SER-GEANT KAI SHI DEN!
CUT THE CHIT-CHAT!
104
YES, SIR...

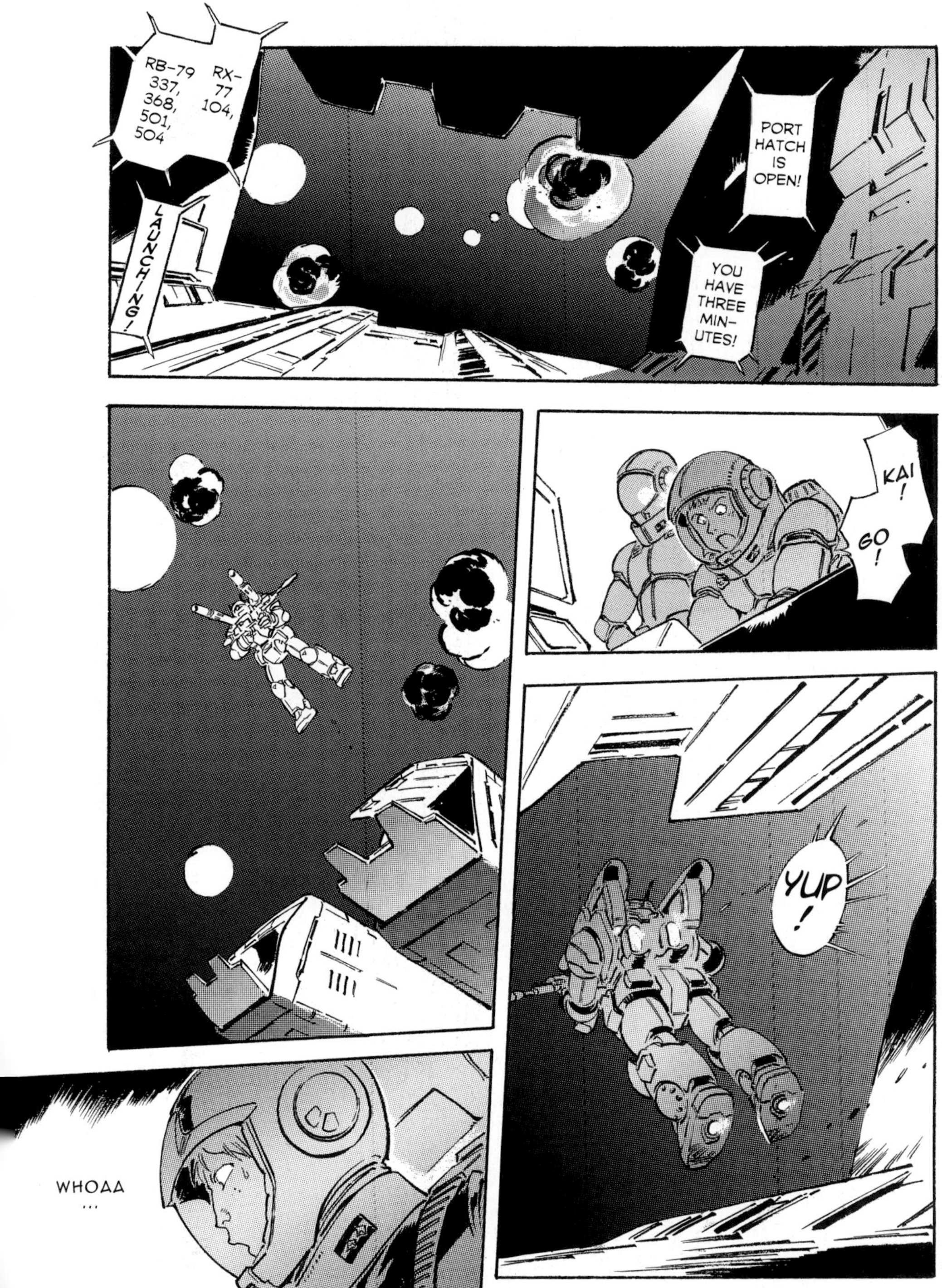
PORT HATCH IS OPEN!
YOU HAVE THREE MINUTES!
RX-77 104, RB-79 337, 368, 501, 504
LAUNCHING!
KAI!
GO!
YUP!
WHOAA ...

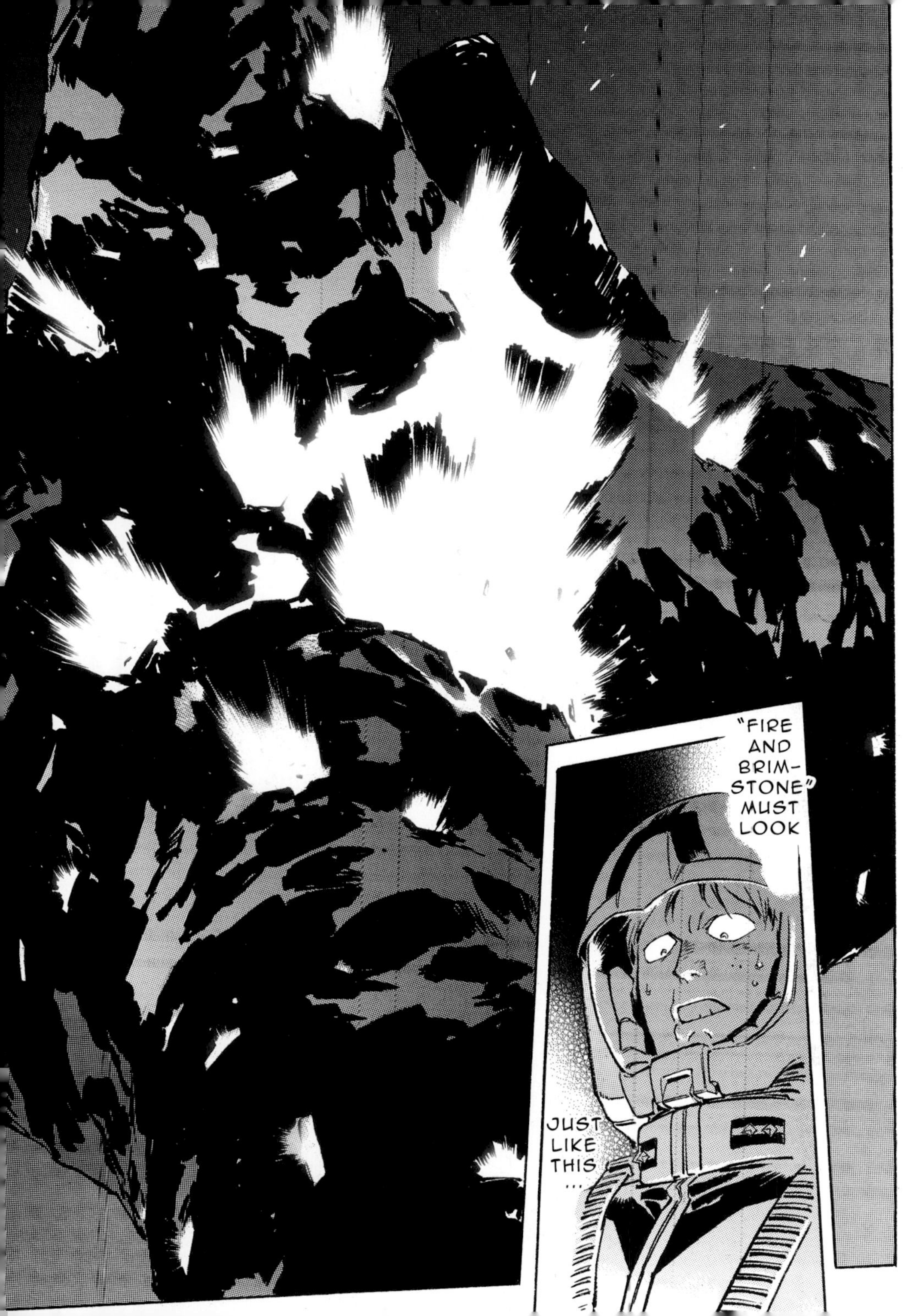
"FIRE AND BRIM- STONE" MUST LOOK
JUST LIKE THIS ...

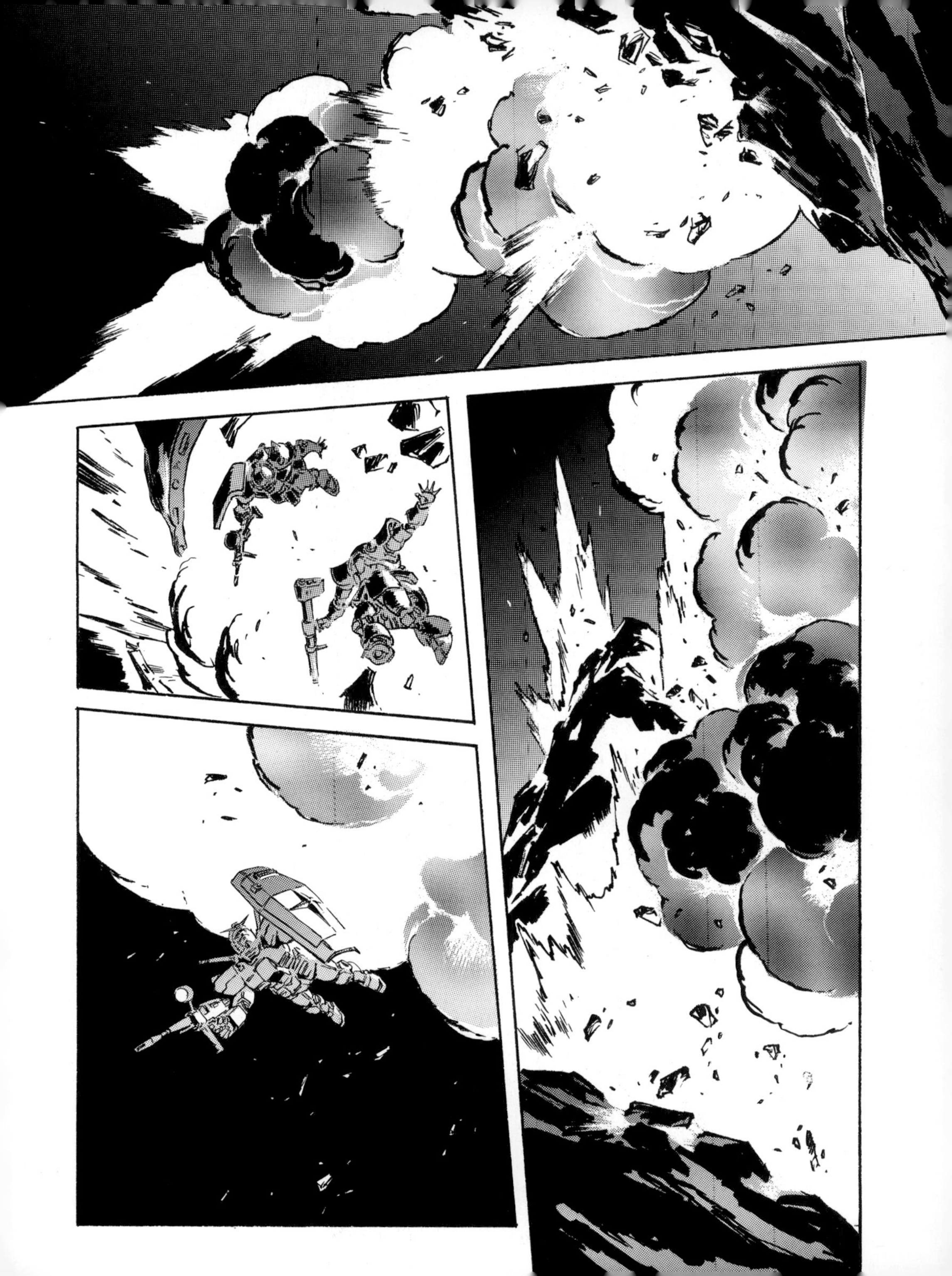

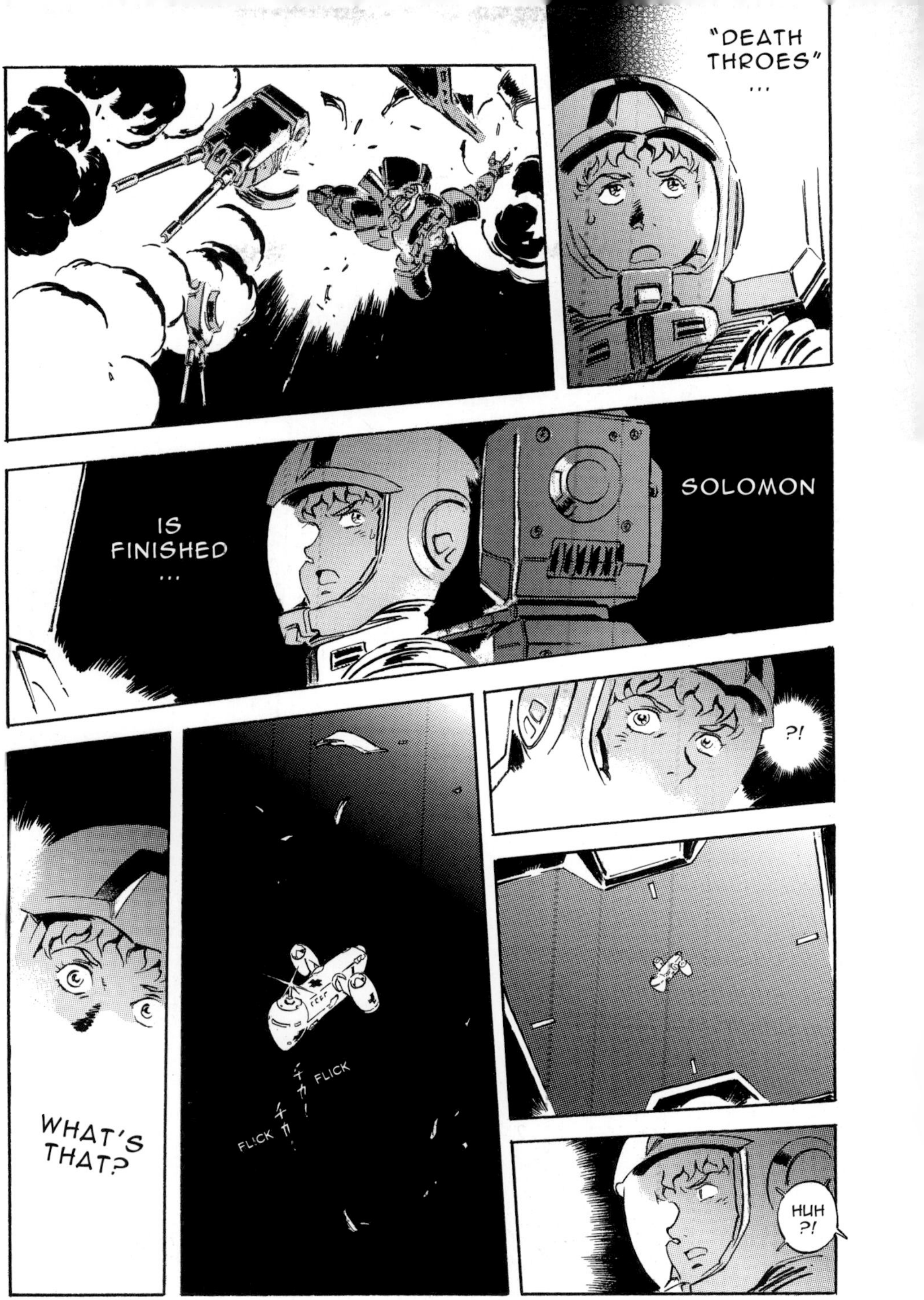
"DEATH THROES" ...
SOLOMON
IS FINISHED ...
?!
HUH ?!
チカ!
FLICK
チカ
FLICK
WHAT'S THAT?

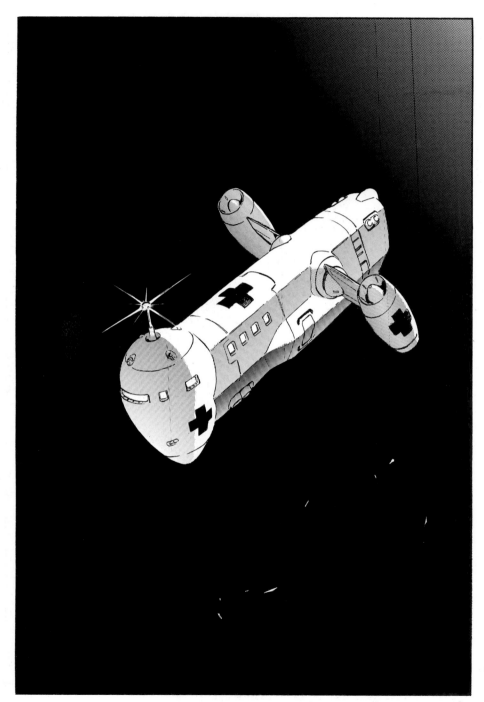

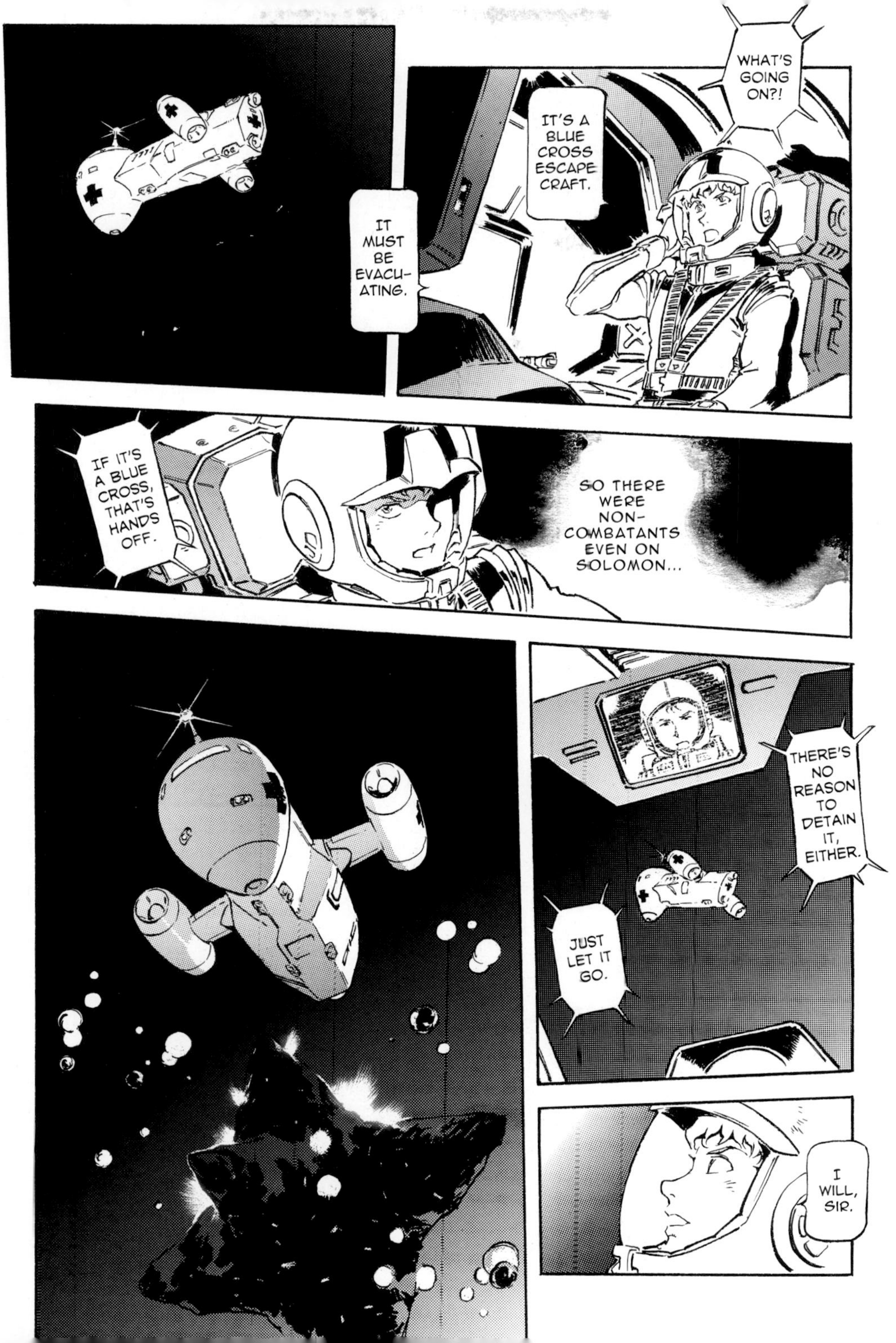
WHAT'S GOING ON?!
IT'S A BLUE CROSS ESCAPE CRAFT.
IT MUST BE EVACUATING.
SO THERE WERE NON-COMBATANTS EVEN ON SOLOMON...
IF IT'S A BLUE CROSS, THAT'S HANDS OFF.
THERE'S NO REASON TO DETAIN IT, EITHER.
JUST LET IT GO.
I WILL, SIR.

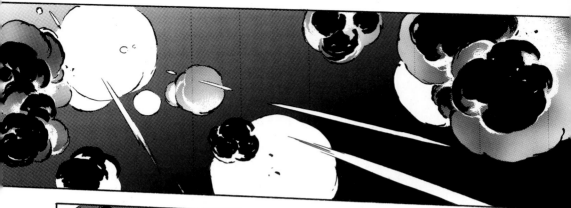

ME, OF ALL GUYS?

TSK

RE-TURN-ING!

SLEG-GAR IN 005 IS

WHAT A

STUPID BLUN-DER TOO!

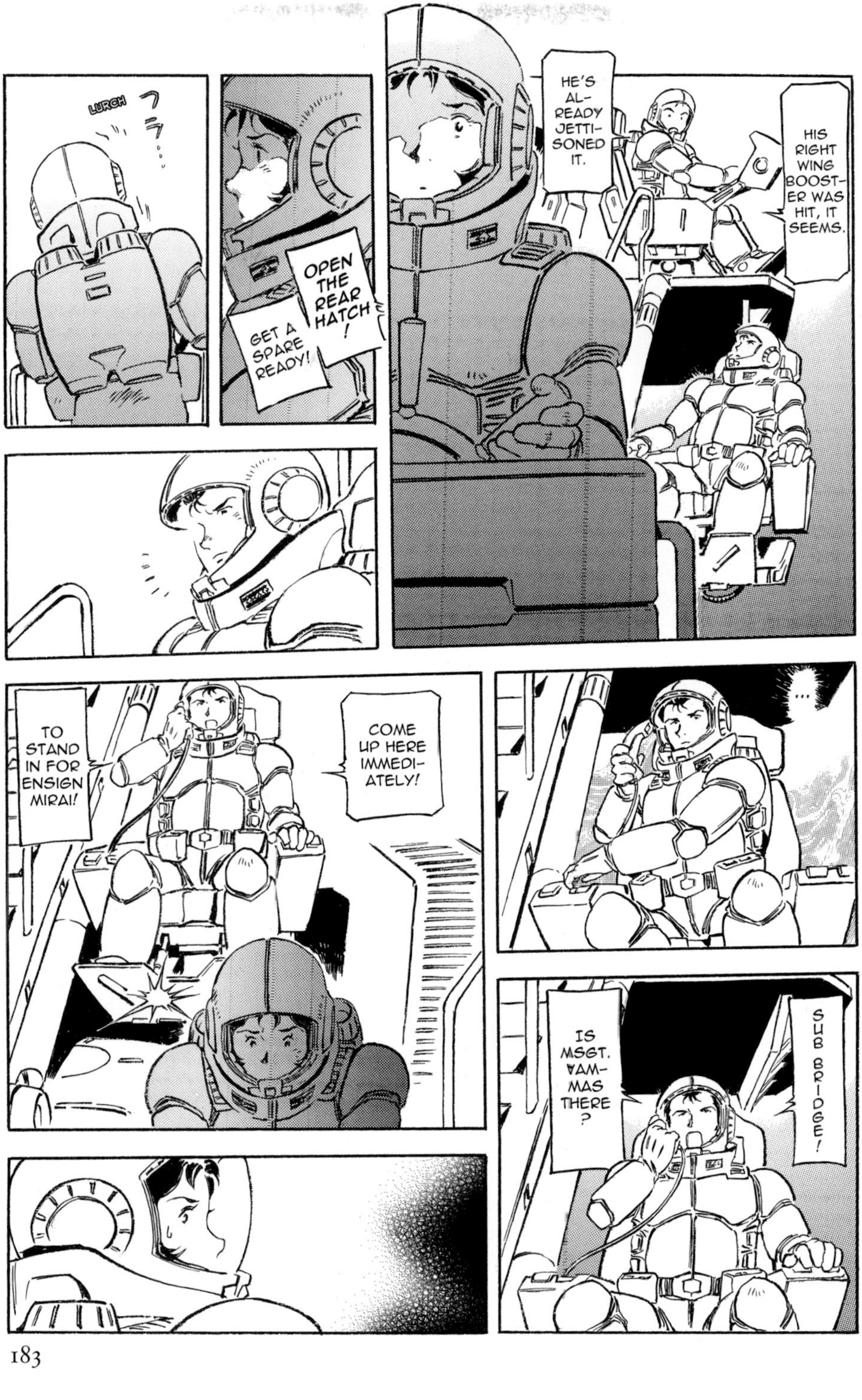
HIS RIGHT WING BOOSTER WAS HIT, IT SEEMS.
HE'S ALREADY JETTISONED IT.
OPEN THE REAR HATCH!
GET A SPARE READY!
LURCH
...
COME UP HERE IMMEDIATELY!
TO STAND IN FOR ENSIGN MIRAI!
SUB BRIDGE!
IS MSGT. YAMMAS THERE?

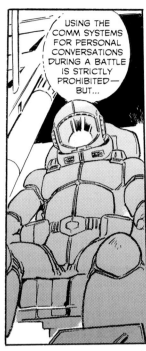

YOU LOOK PRETTY TIRED.
TAKE A BREAK.
...
USING THE COMM SYSTEMS FOR PERSONAL CONVERSATIONS DURING A BATTLE IS STRICTLY PROHIBITED— BUT...
COME ON, MIRAI.
DO YOU REALLY THINK IT'S BEYOND ME TO
SHOW YOU ANY CONSID-ERATION AT ALL?
I'LL WAIT FOR YOU, HOWEVER LONG IT TAKES.
SO DON'T WORRY.

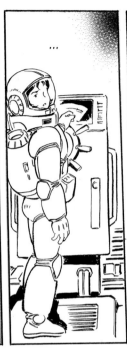

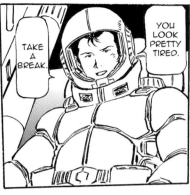

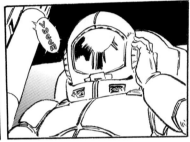

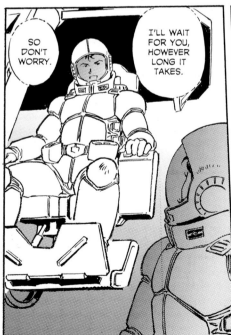

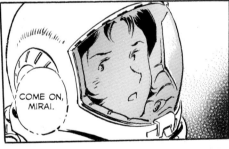

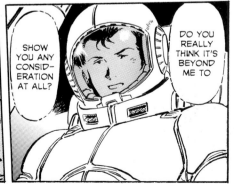

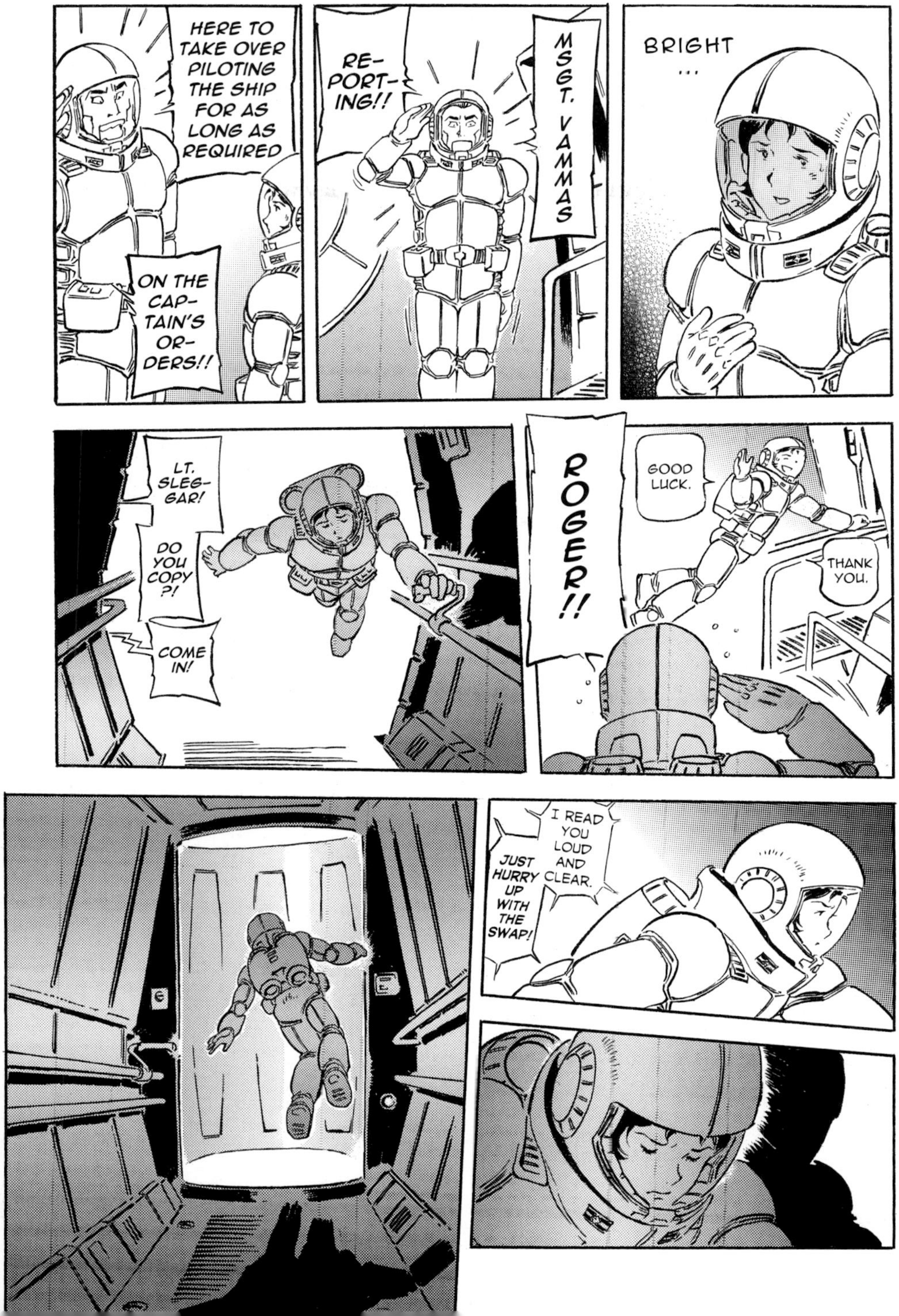
BRIGHT ...
MSGT. VAMMAS
RE-PORT-ING!!
HERE TO TAKE OVER PILOTING THE SHIP FOR AS LONG AS REQUIRED
ON THE CAP-TAIN'S OR-DERS!!
ROGER!!
GOOD LUCK.
THANK YOU.
LT. SLEG-GAR!
DO YOU COPY ?!
COME IN!
I READ YOU LOUD AND CLEAR.
JUST HURRY UP WITH THE SWAP!

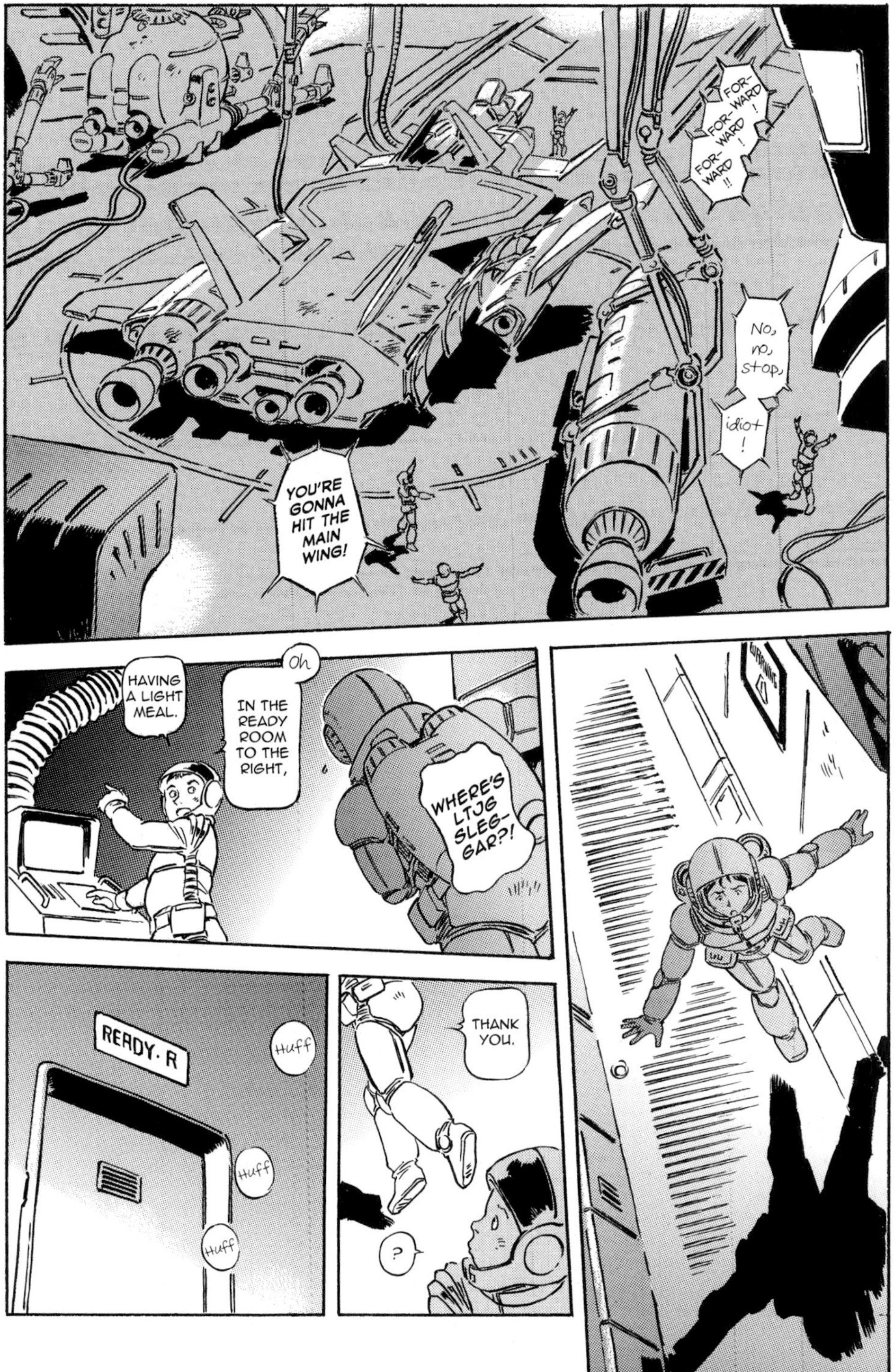
FOR-WARD! FOR-WARD! FOR-WARD!!
No, no, stop, idiot!
YOU'RE GONNA HIT THE MAIN WING!
WHERE'S LTJG SLEGGAR?!
Oh
IN THE READY ROOM TO THE RIGHT,
HAVING A LIGHT MEAL.
THANK YOU.
?
READY・R
Huff
Huff
Huff

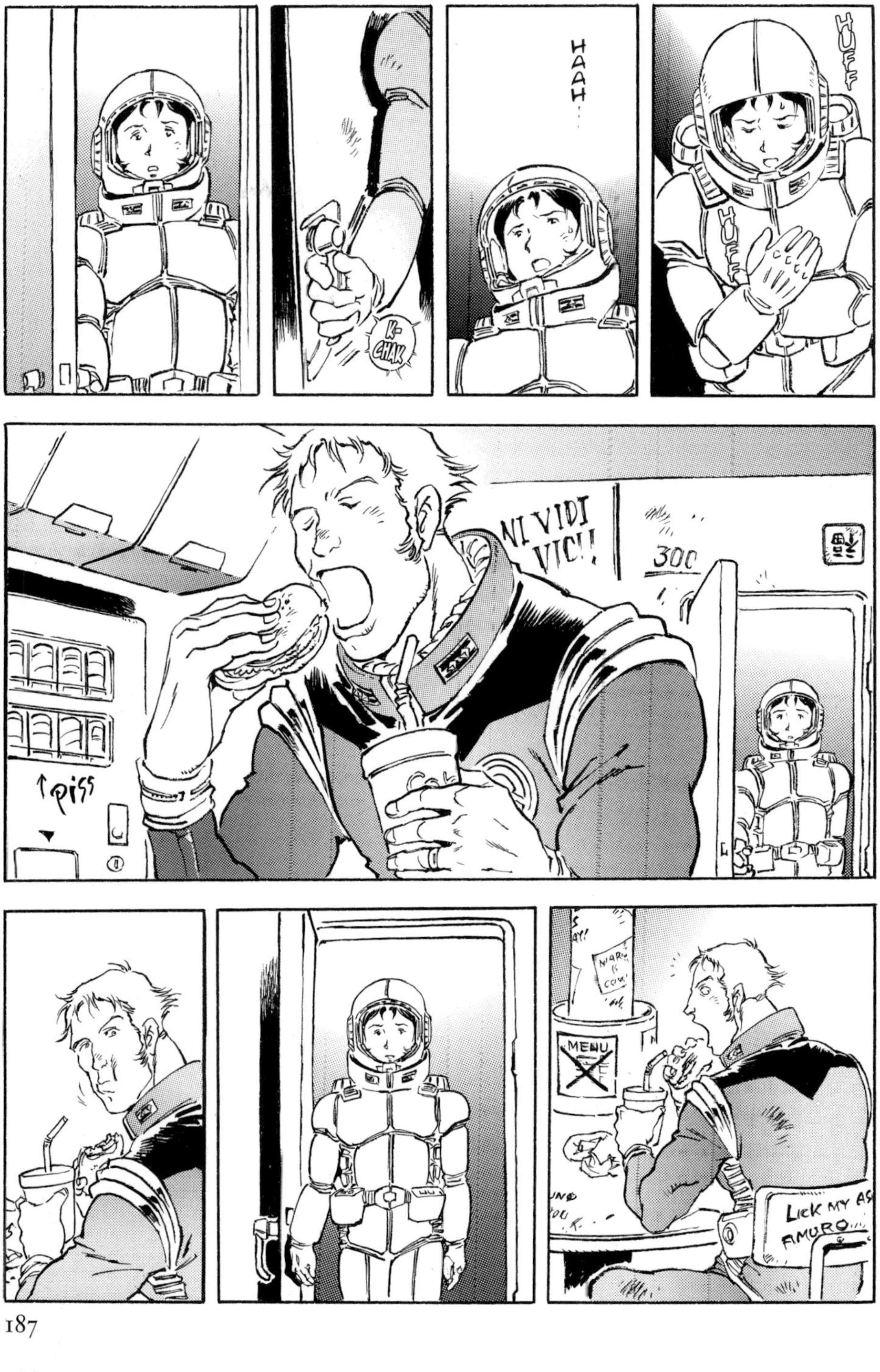
HUFF
HUFF
HAAAH...
K-CHAK
NI VIDI VICI!!
300
↑piss
MENU
LICK MY AS
AMURO

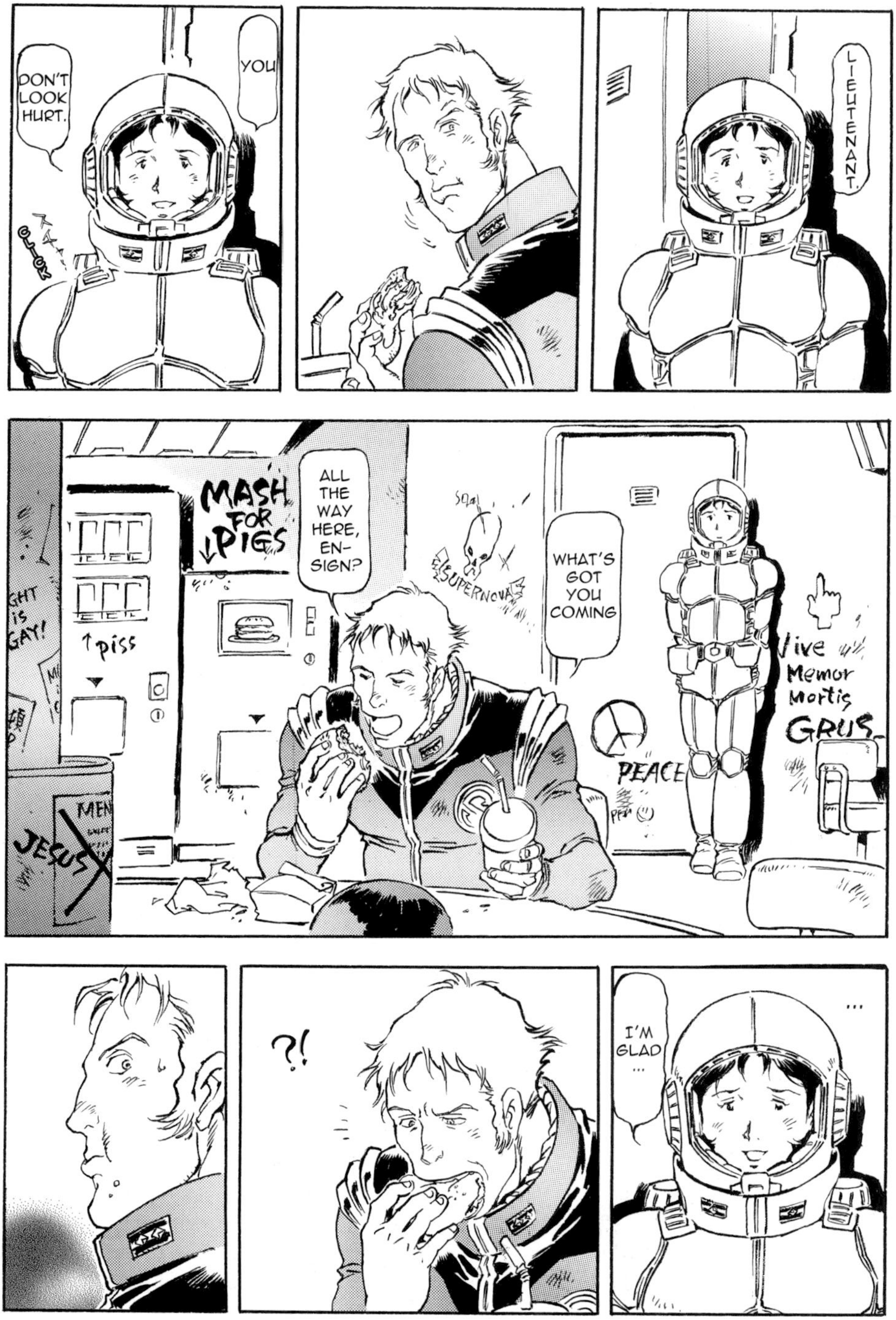
LIEUTENANT.
YOU
DON'T LOOK HURT.
CLICK
WHAT'S GOT YOU COMING
ALL THE WAY HERE, EN-SIGN?
Vive Memor Mortis GRUS
SUPERNOVA
PEACE
MASH FOR PIGS
↑piss
GHT is GAY!
MEN
JESUS
...
I'M GLAD ...
?!

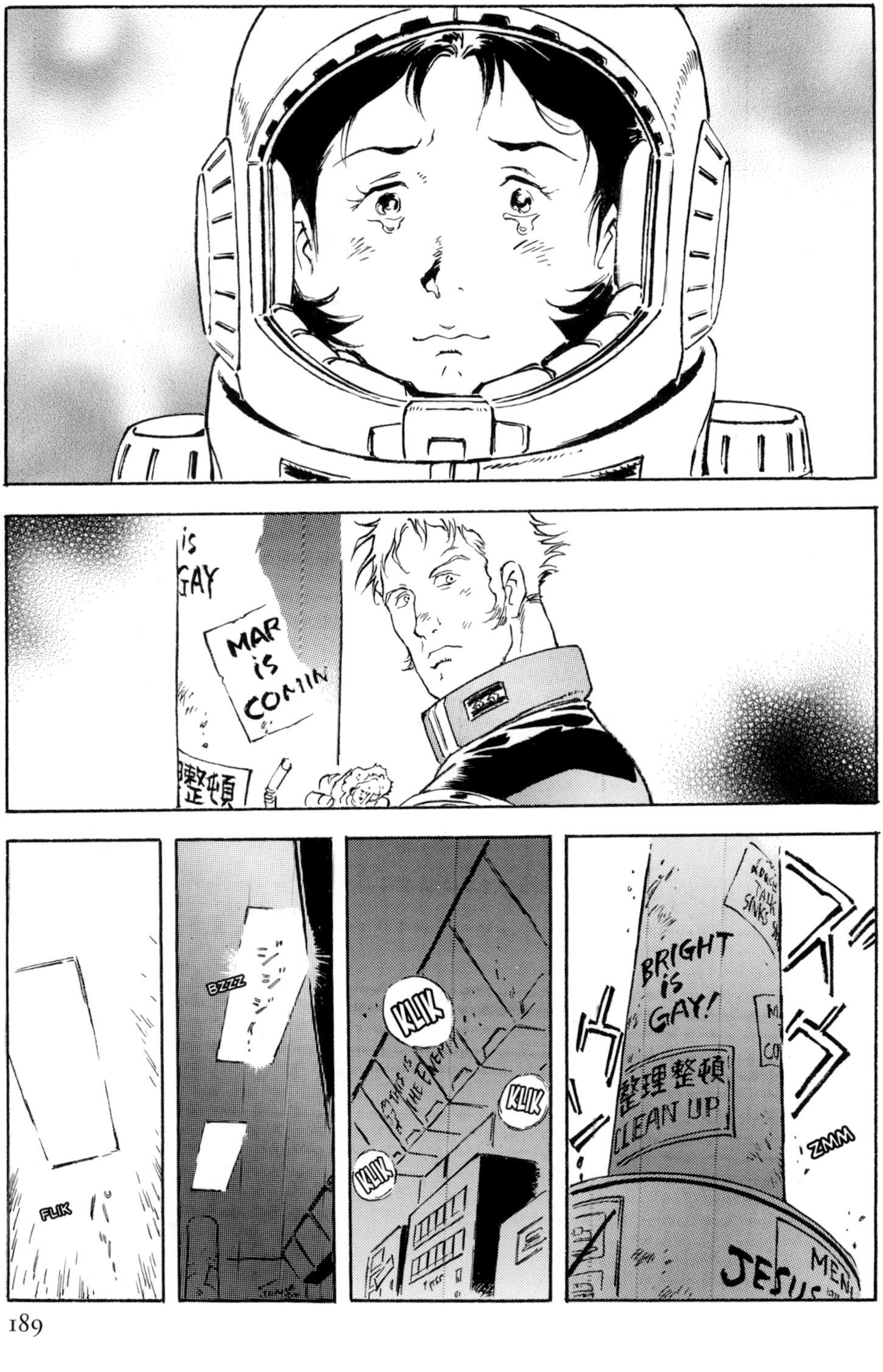
is
GAY
MAR
is
COMIN
BRIGHT is GAY!
整理整頓
CLEAN UP
ZMM
JESUS
KLIK
KLIK
KLIK
BZZZ
FLIK

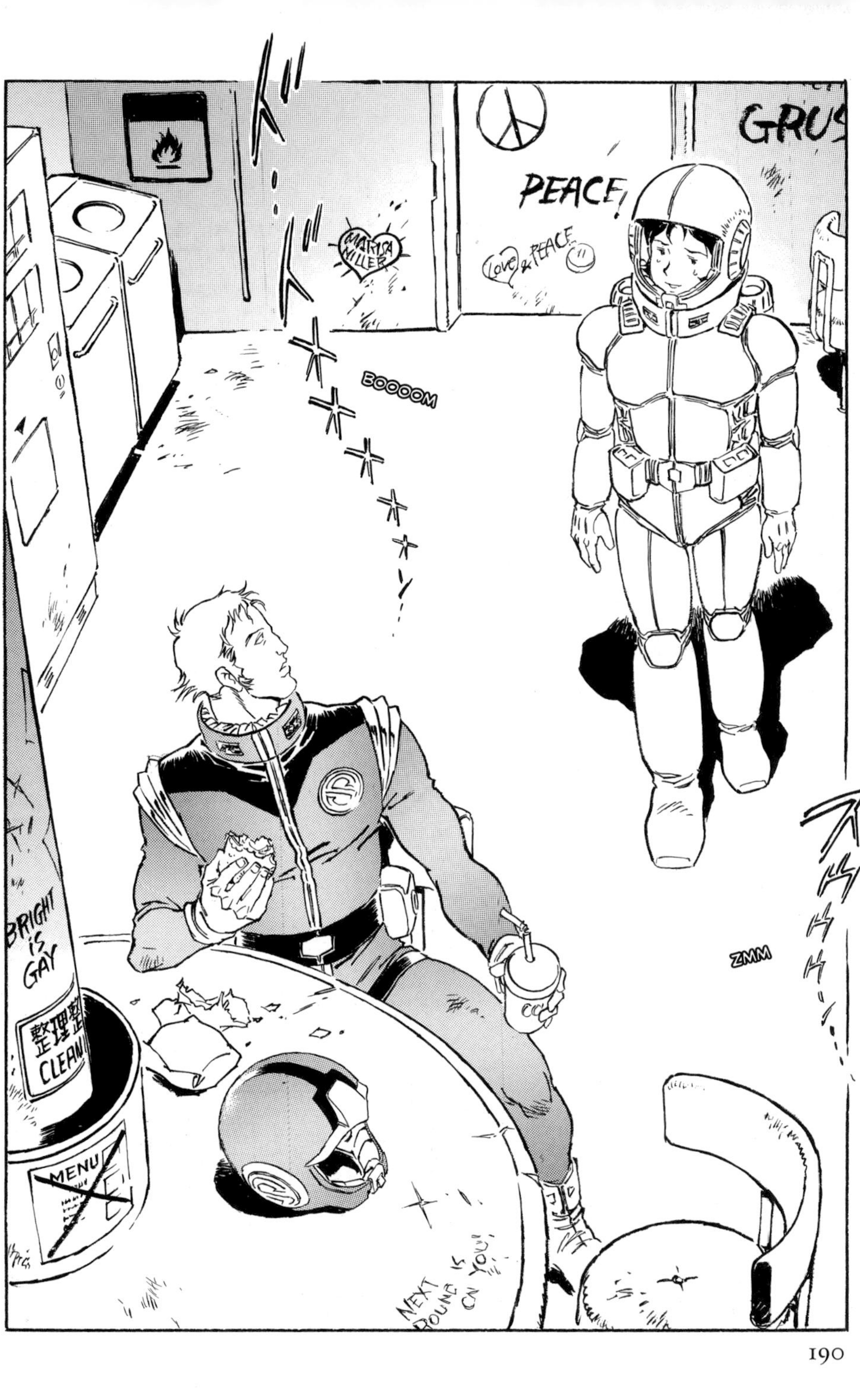
BOOOOM
PEACE!
MARISA MILLER
Love & PEACE
ZMM
BRIGHT IS GAY
CLEAN
MENU
NEXT ROUND IS ON YOU!

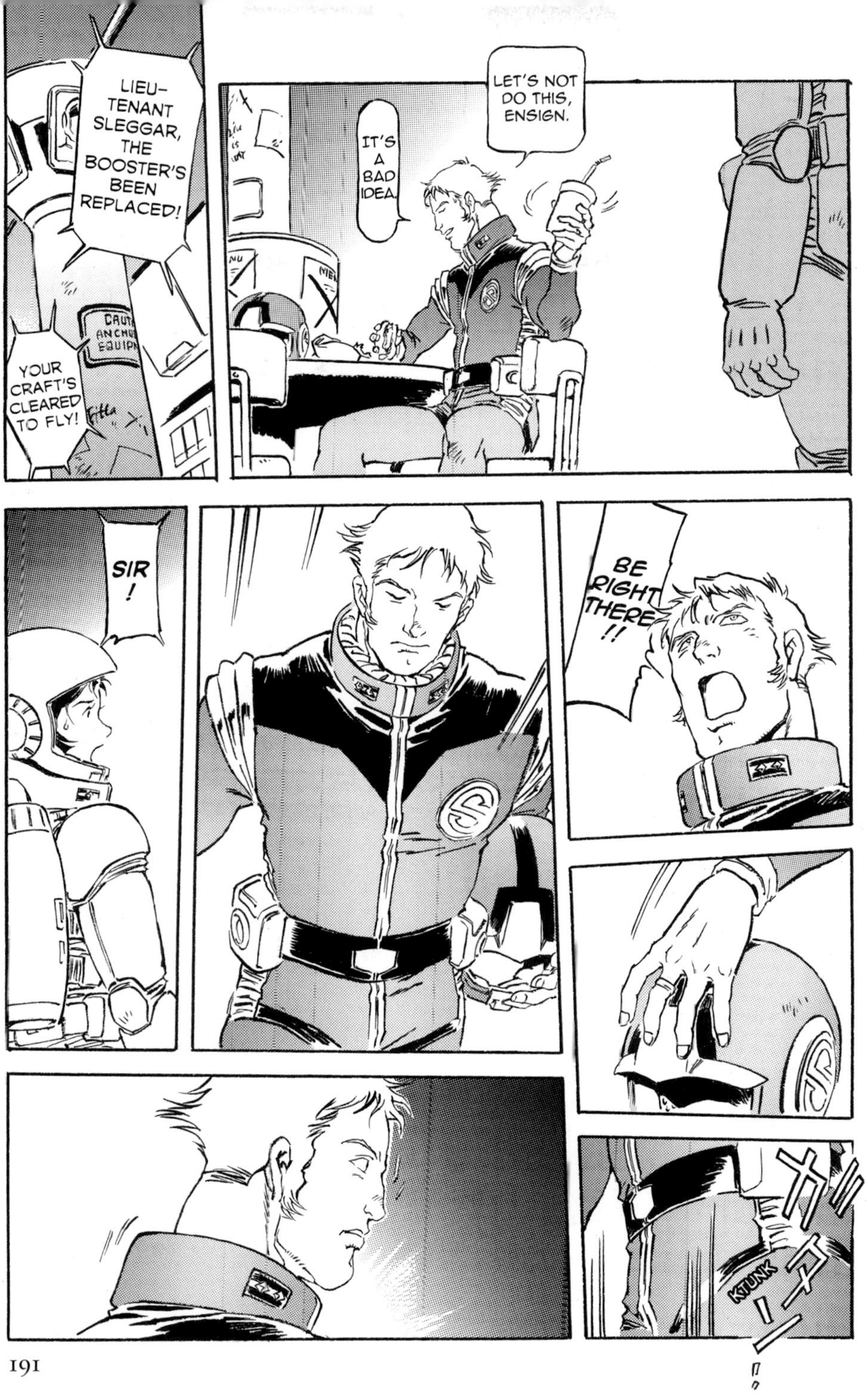
LET'S NOT DO THIS, ENSIGN.
IT'S A BAD IDEA.
LIEU-TENANT SLEGGAR, THE BOOSTER'S BEEN REPLACED!
YOUR CRAFT'S CLEARED TO FLY!
BE RIGHT THERE!!
KTUNK
SIR!

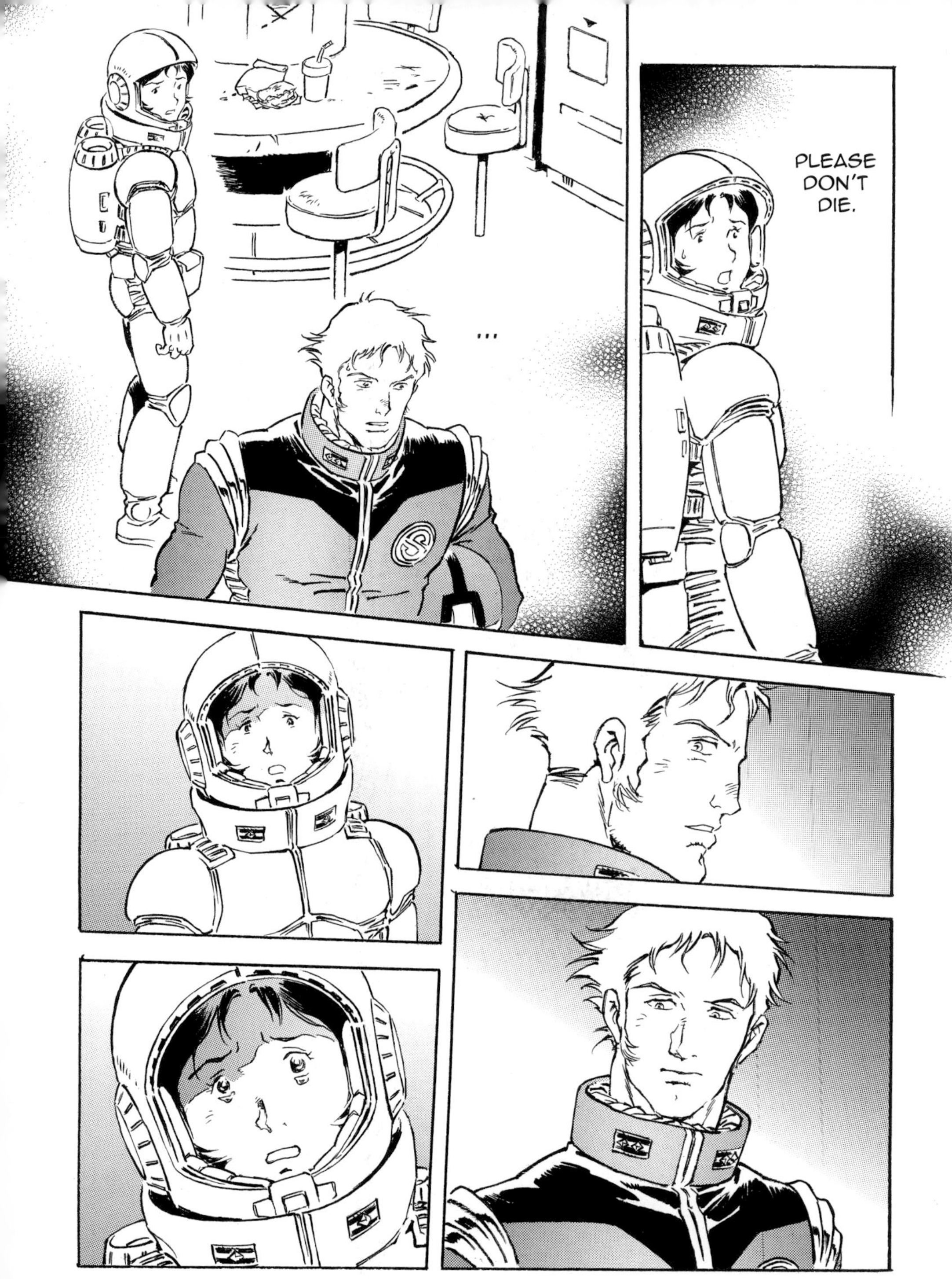
PLEASE DON'T DIE.
...

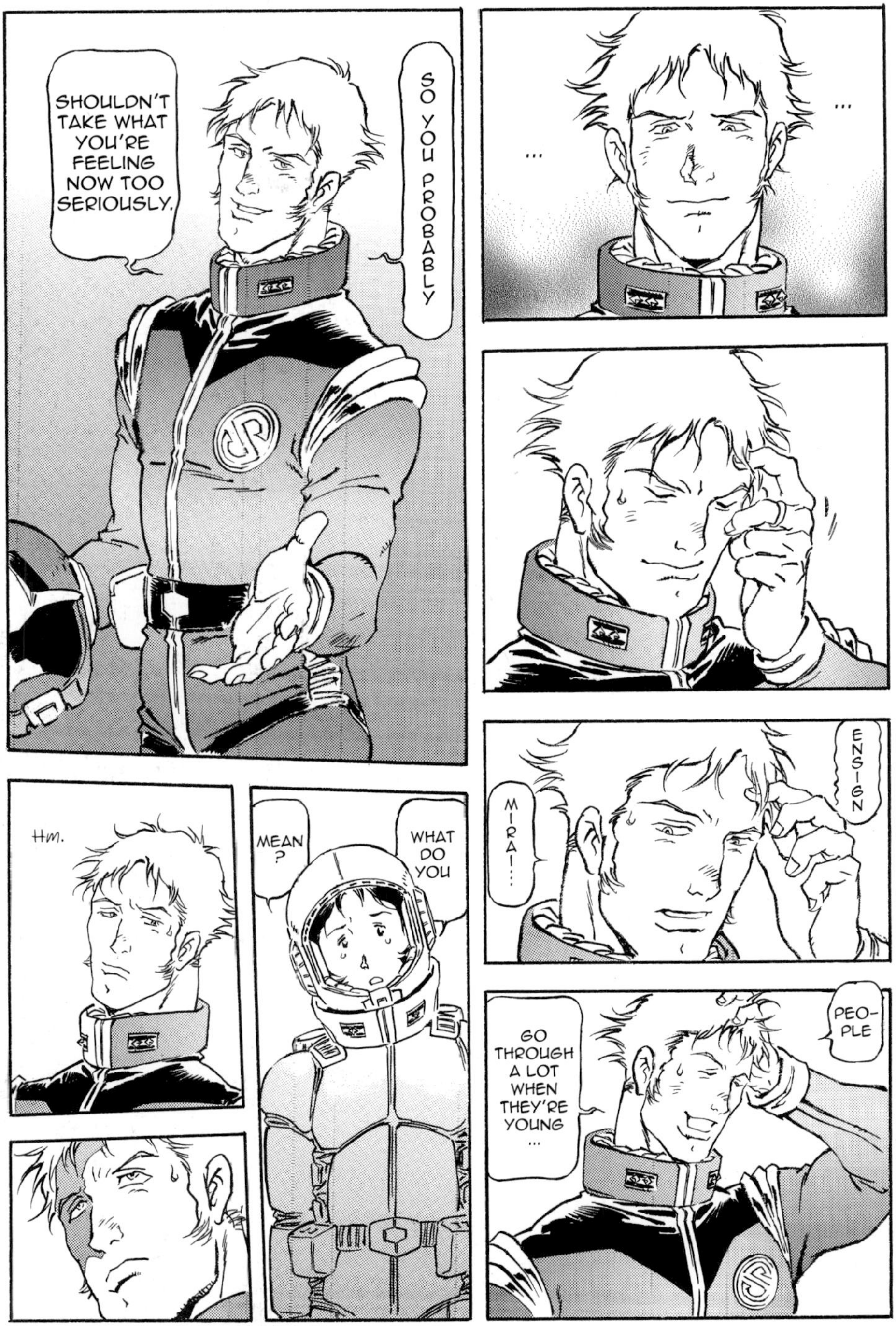
...
...
SO YOU PROBABLY
SHOULDN'T TAKE WHAT YOU'RE FEELING NOW TOO SERIOUSLY.
ENSIGN
MIRA!...
PEO-PLE
GO THROUGH A LOT WHEN THEY'RE YOUNG ...
WHAT DO YOU
MEAN?
Hm.

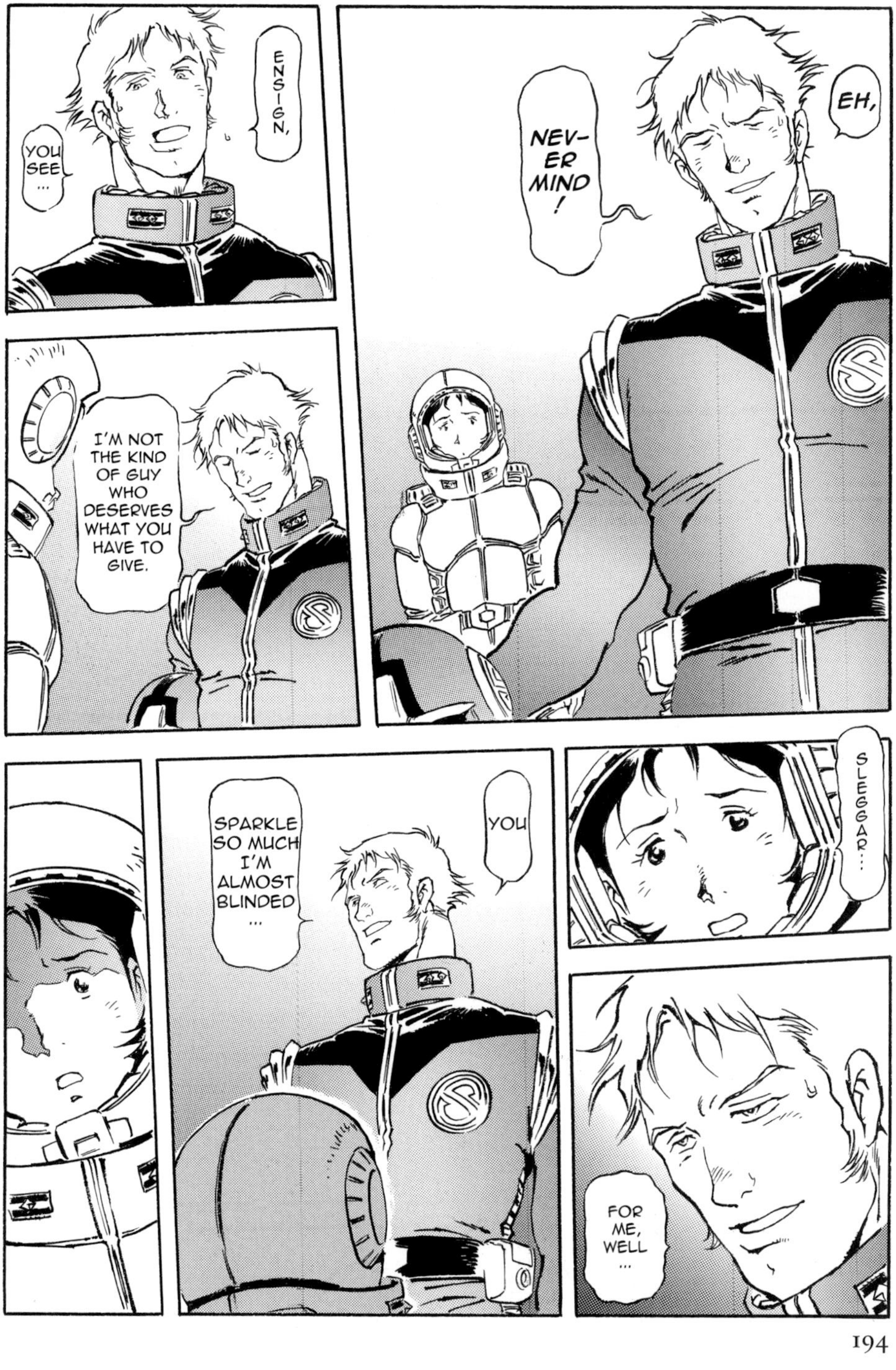
EH,
NEVER MIND!
ENSIGN,
YOU SEE...
I'M NOT THE KIND OF GUY WHO DESERVES WHAT YOU HAVE TO GIVE.
SLEGGAR...
FOR ME, WELL...
YOU
SPARKLE SO MUCH I'M ALMOST BLINDED...

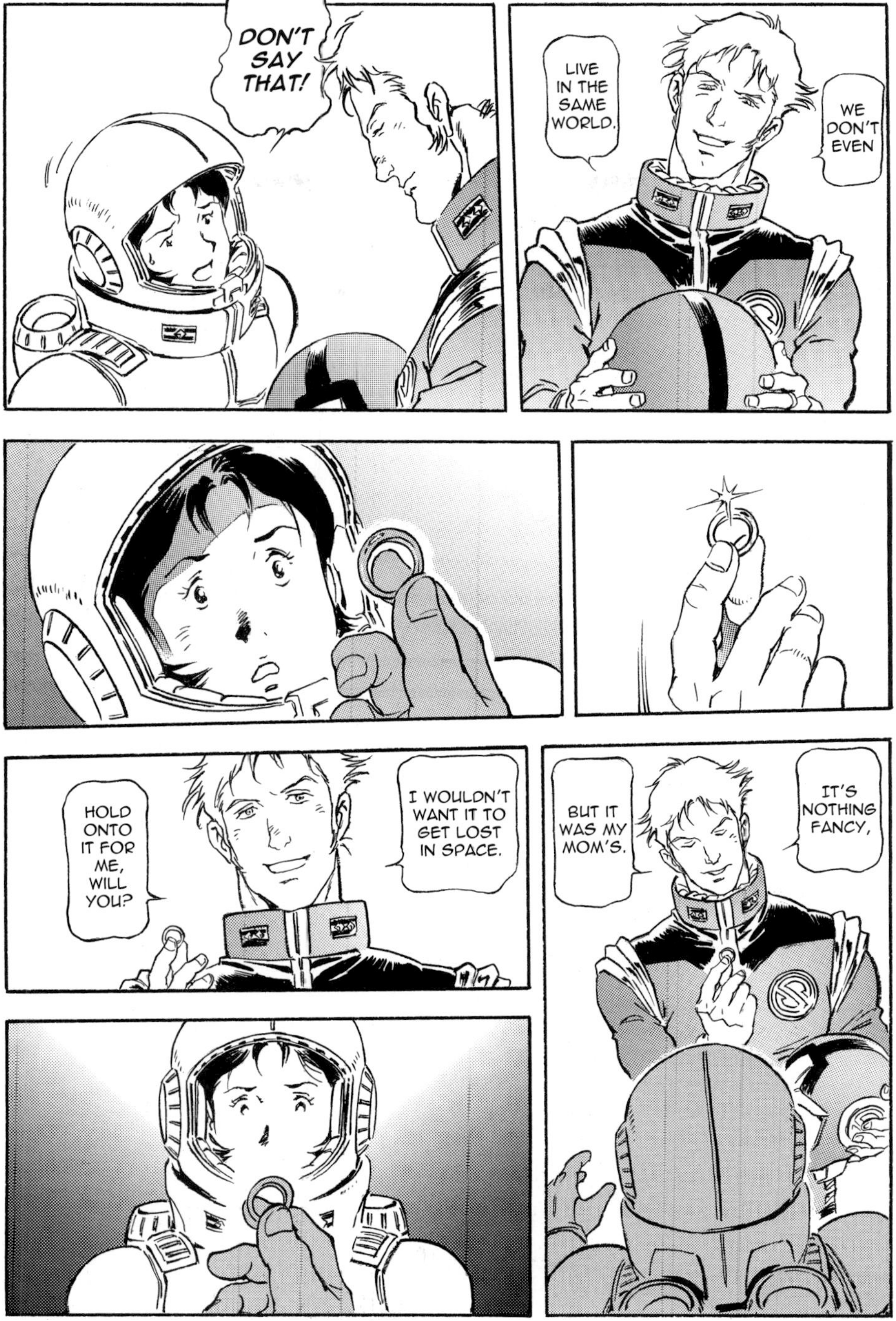
WE DON'T EVEN
LIVE IN THE SAME WORLD.
DON'T SAY THAT!
IT'S NOTHING FANCY,
BUT IT WAS MY MOM'S.
I WOULDN'T WANT IT TO GET LOST IN SPACE.
HOLD ONTO IT FOR ME, WILL YOU?

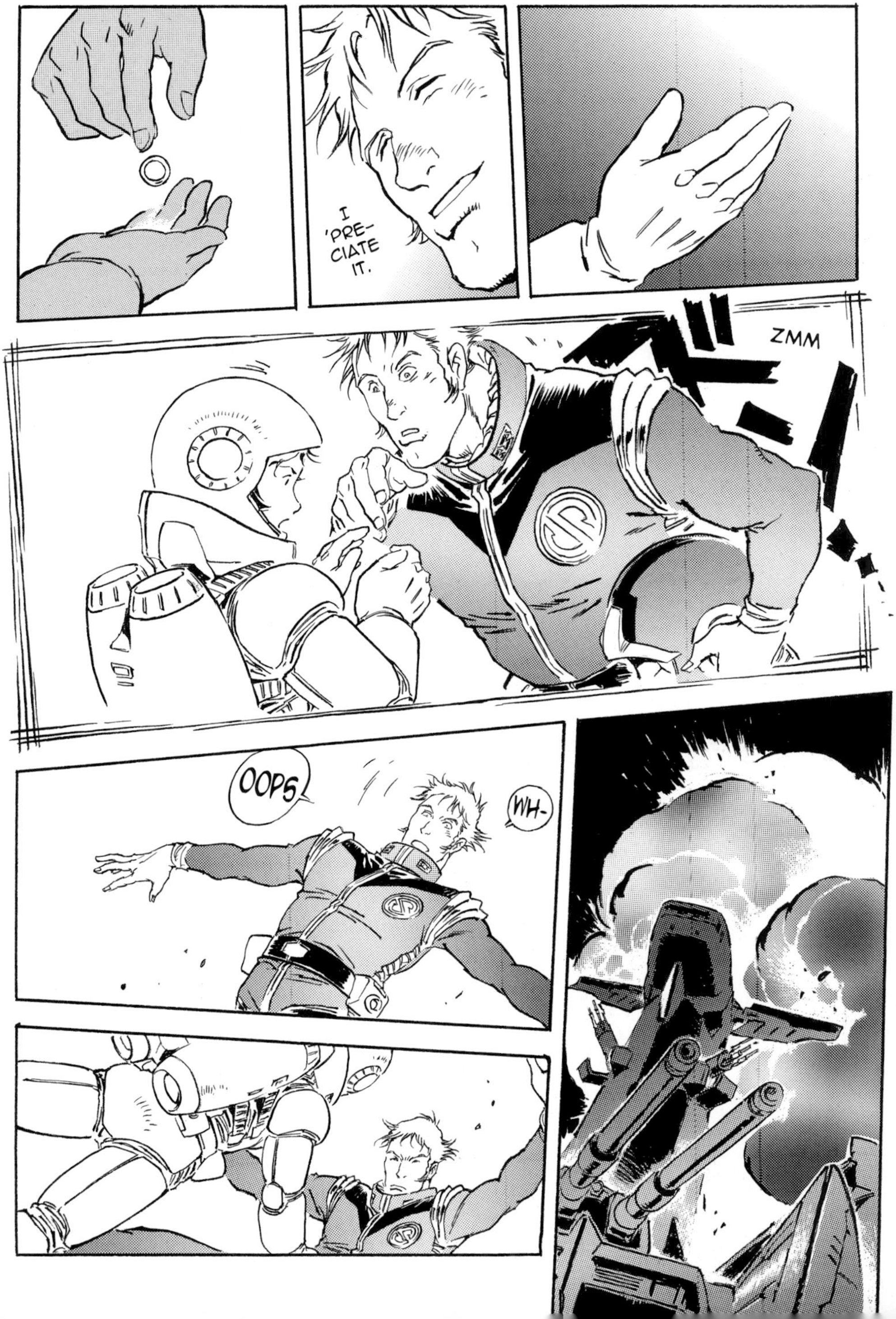
I 'PRECIATE IT.
ZMM
WH-
OOPS

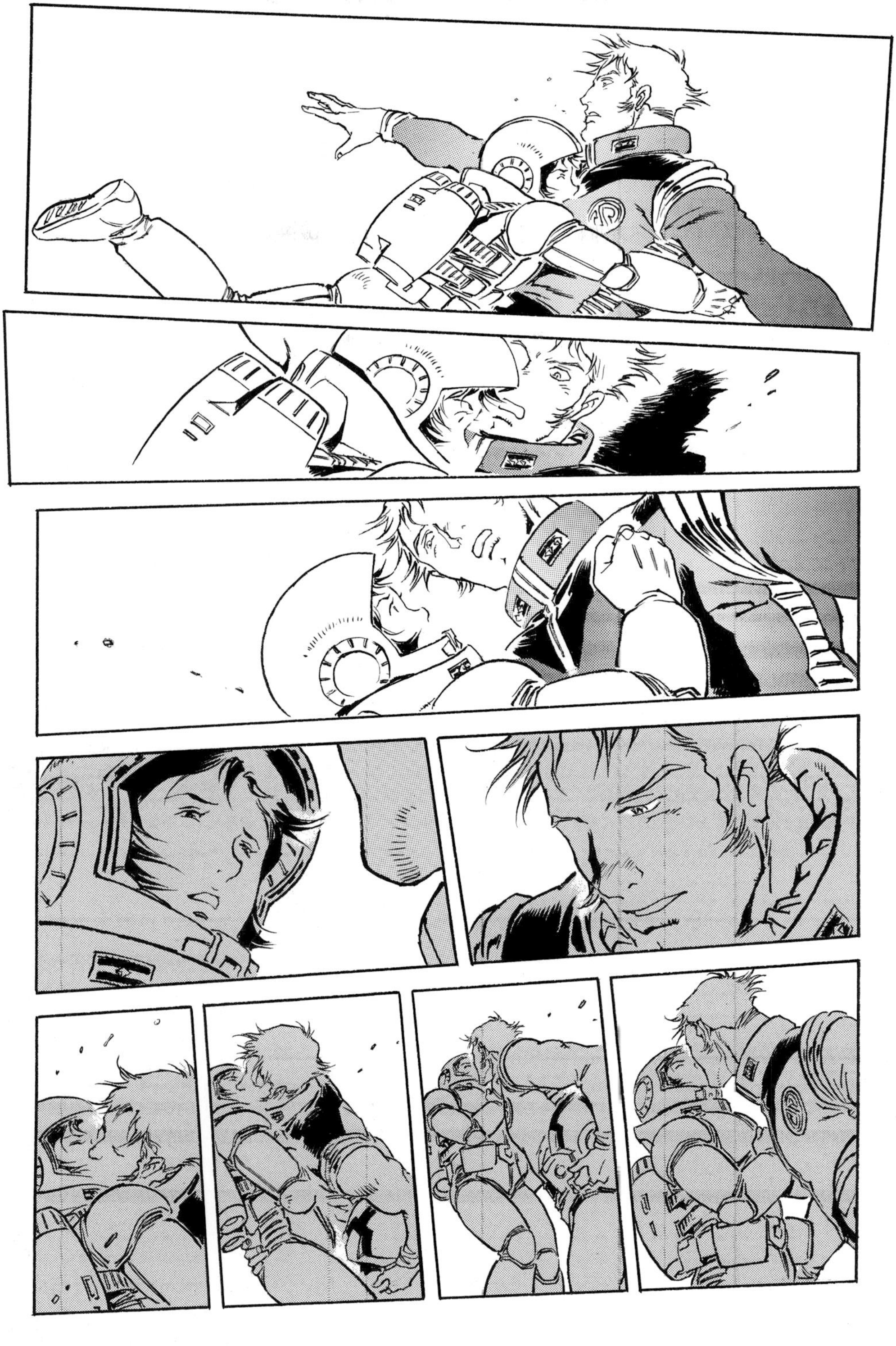

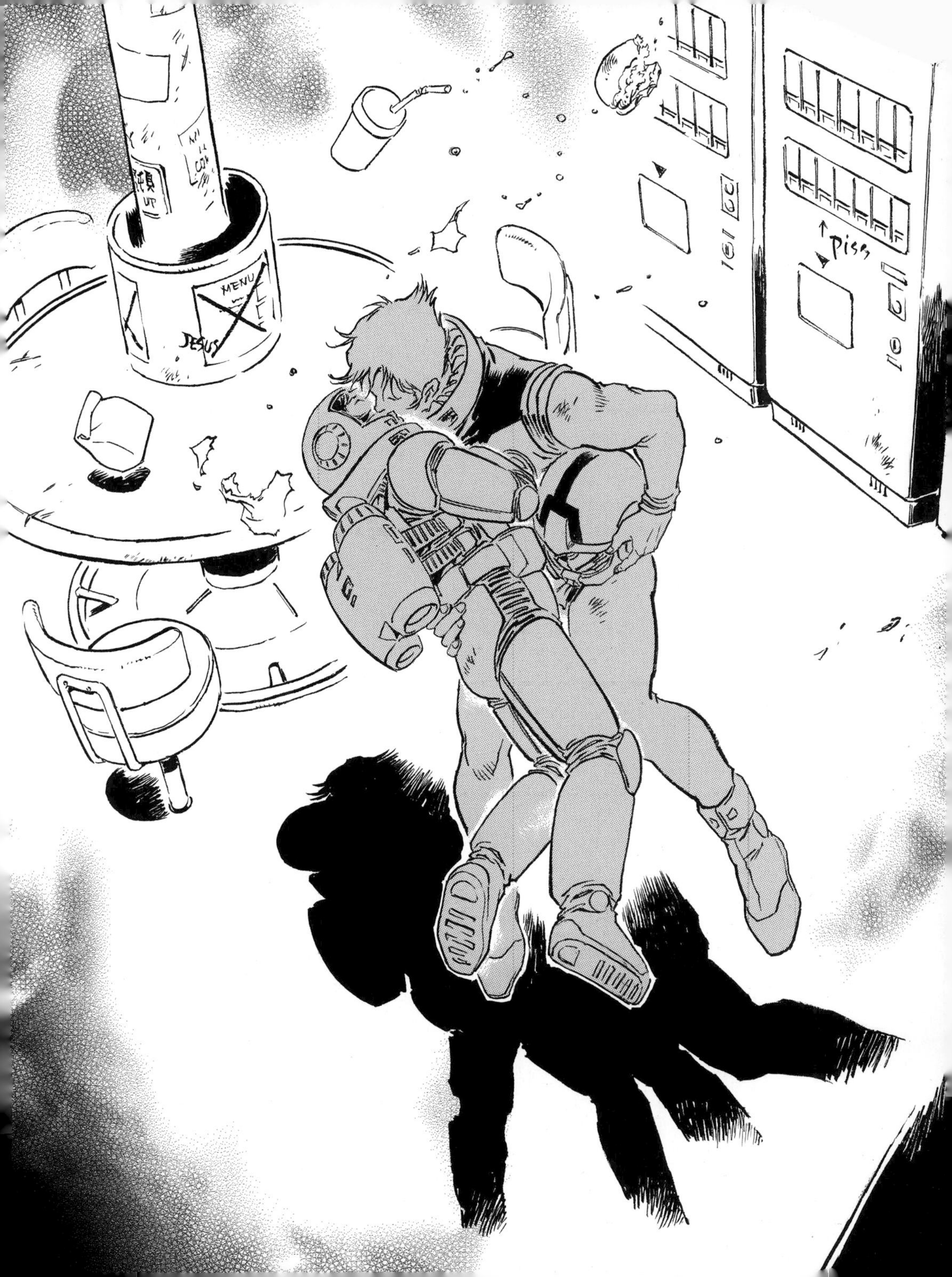
MENU
JESUS

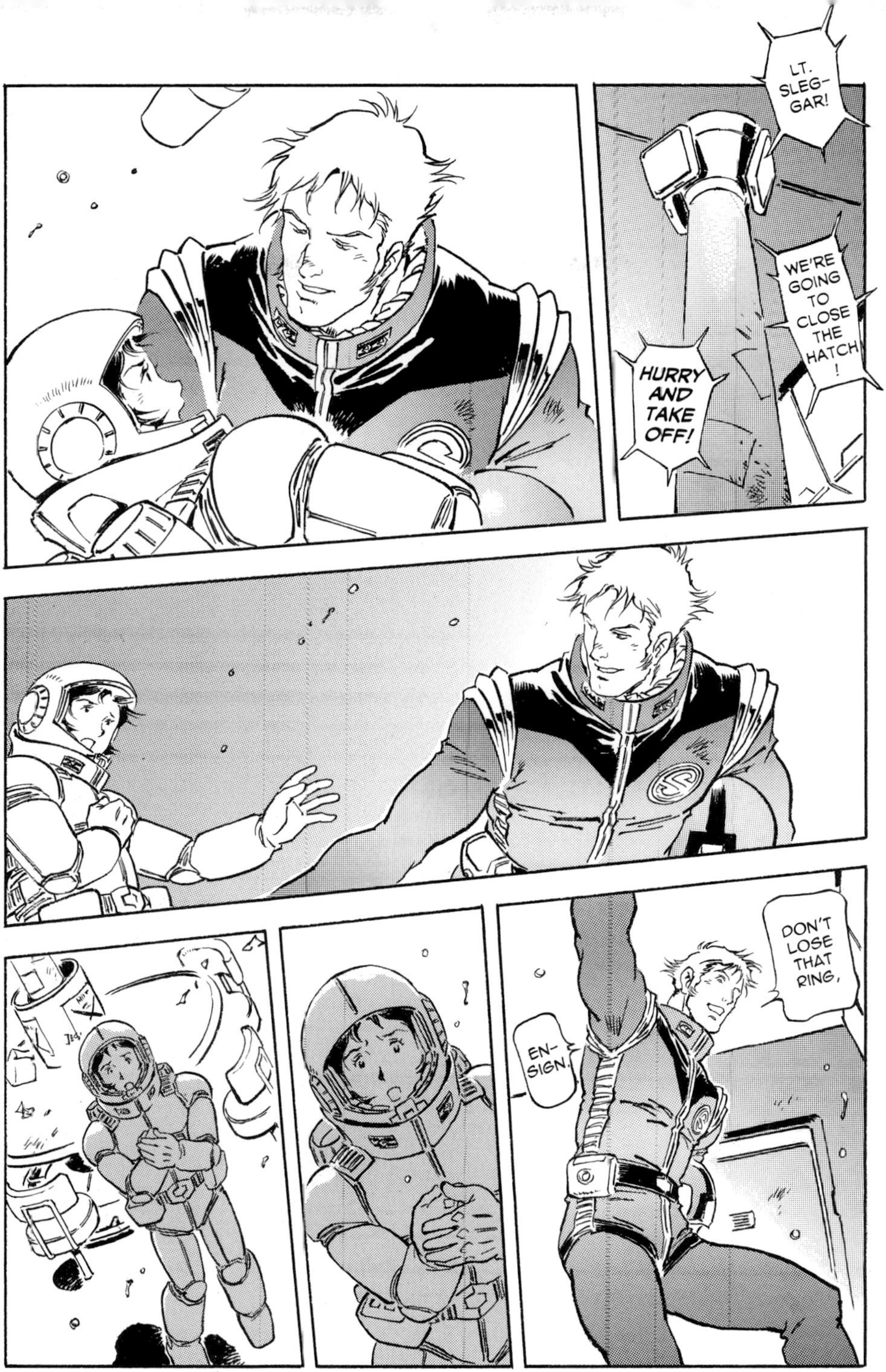
LT. SLEG-GAR!
WE'RE GOING TO CLOSE THE HATCH!
HURRY AND TAKE OFF!
DON'T LOSE THAT RING,
EN-SIGN.

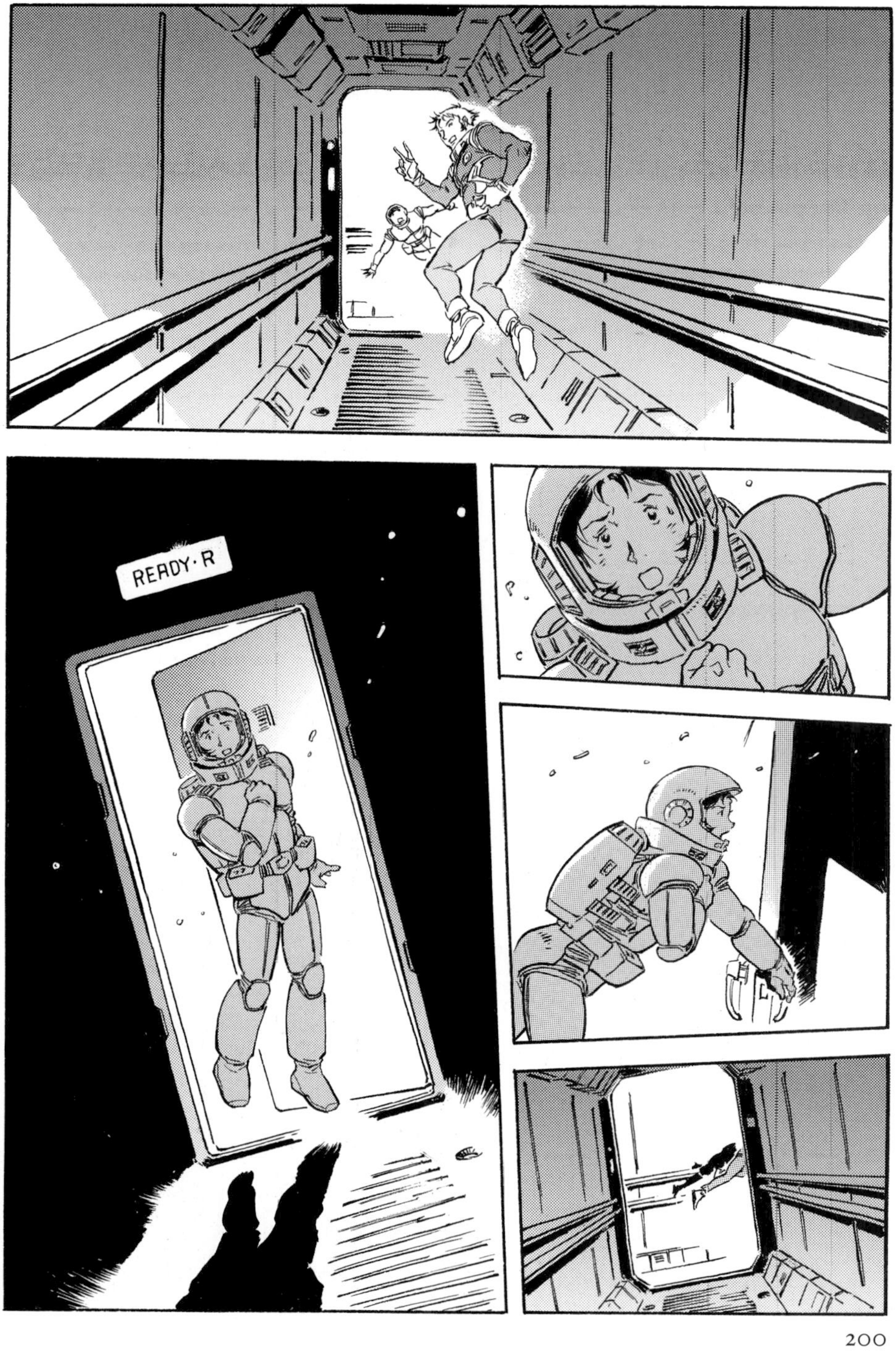
READY·R

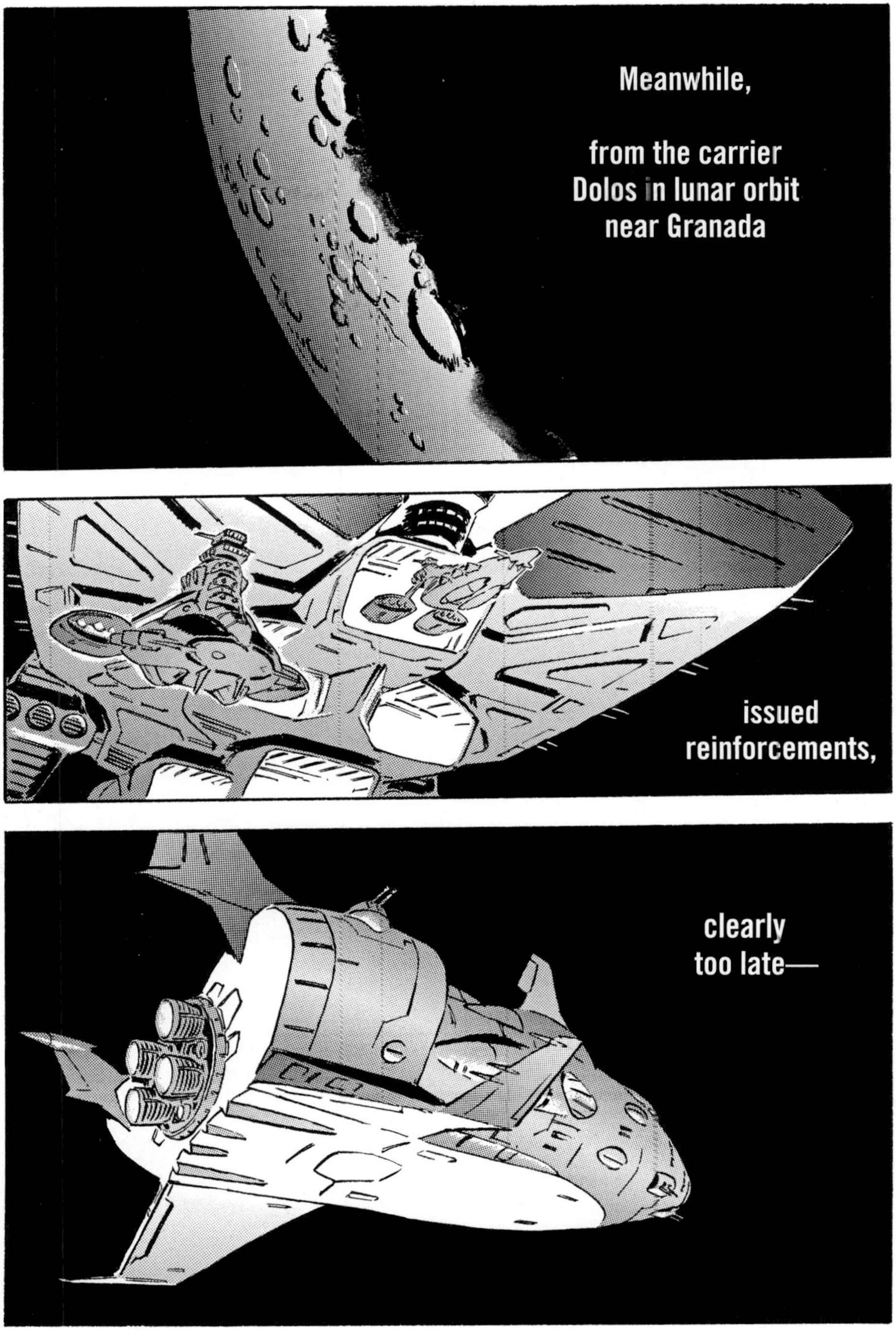
Meanwhile,
from the carrier Dolos in lunar orbit near Granada
issued reinforcements,
clearly too late—

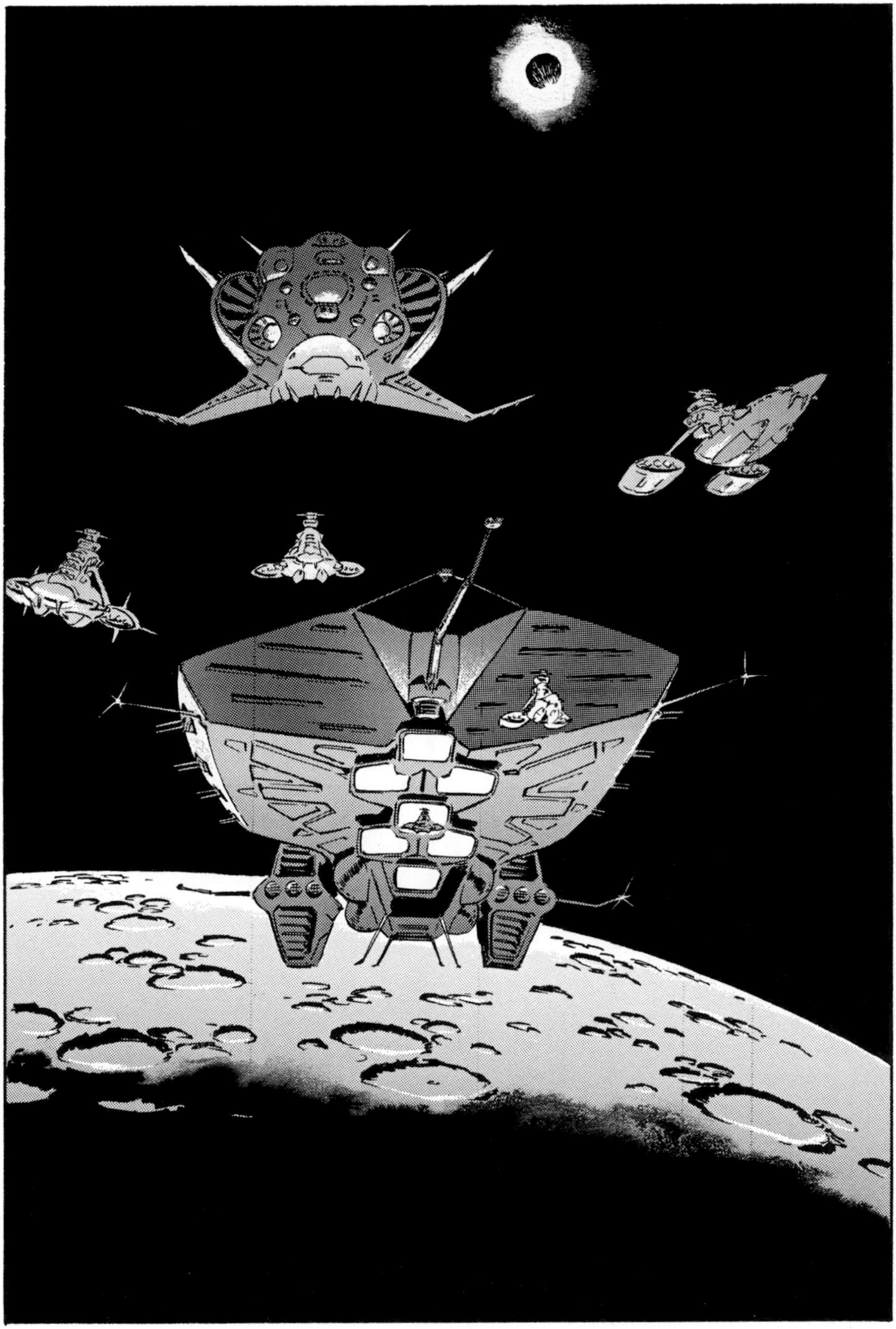

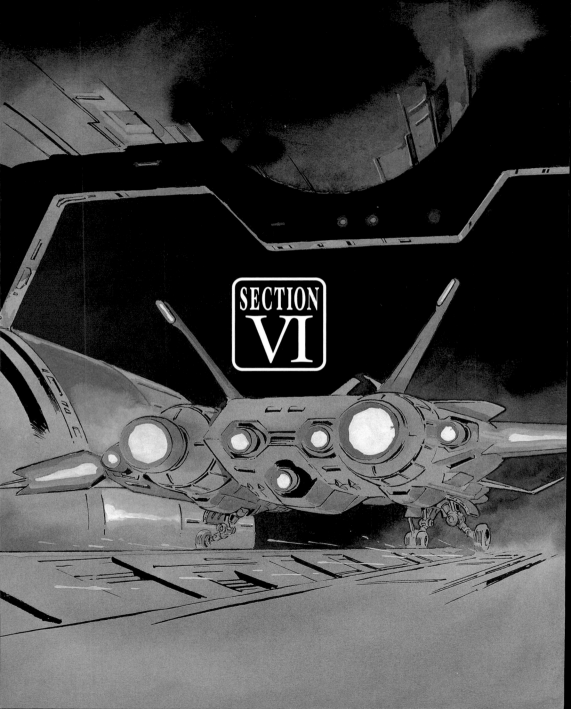

SECTION
VI

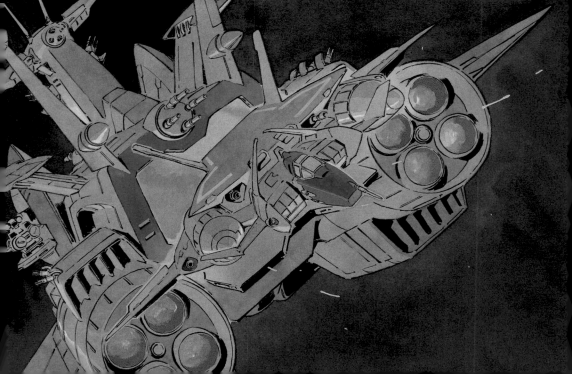

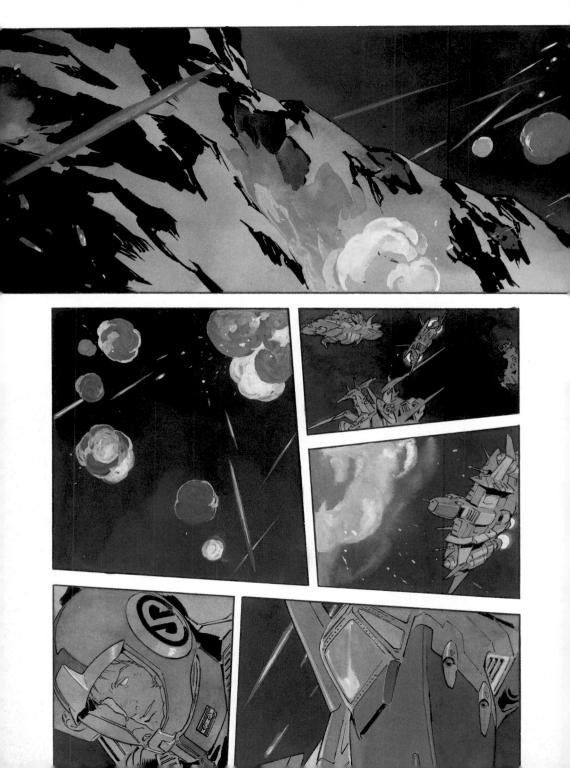

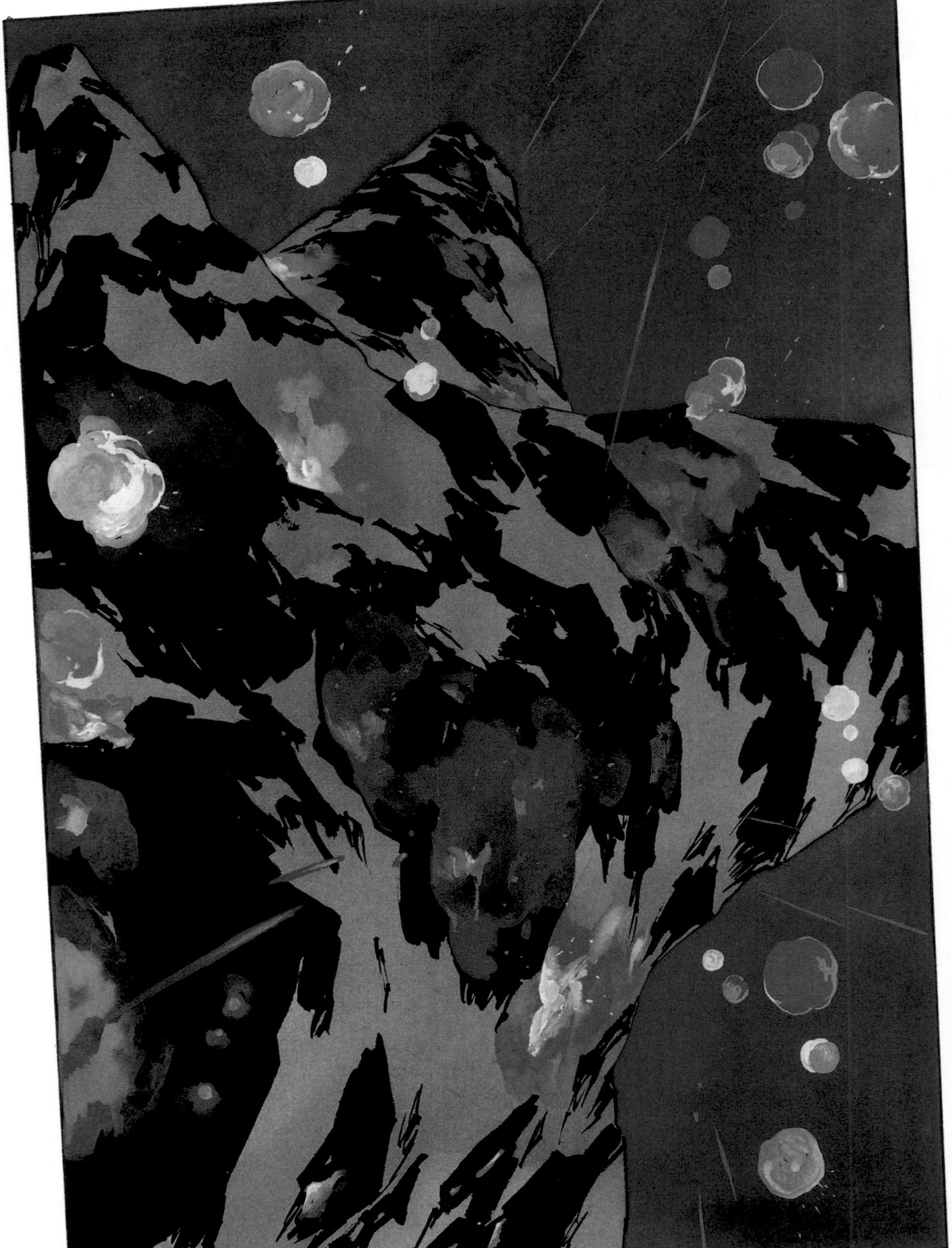

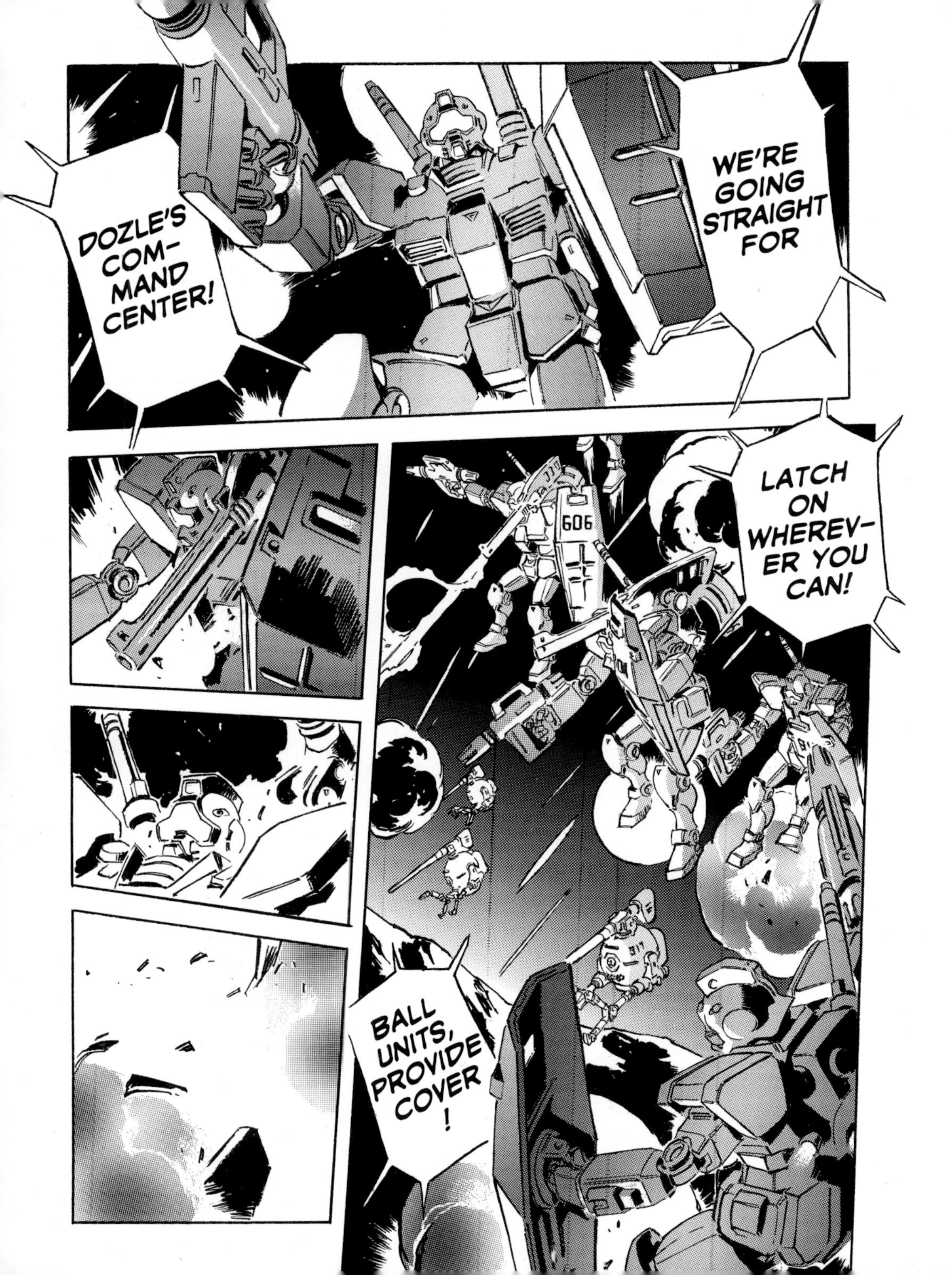
WE'RE GOING STRAIGHT FOR
DOZLE'S COM-MAND CENTER!
LATCH ON WHEREV-ER YOU CAN!
606
BALL UNITS, PROVIDE COVER!

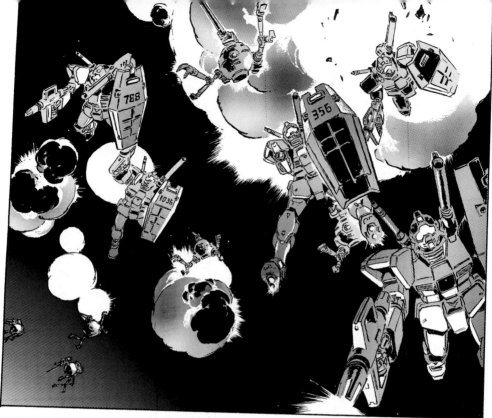

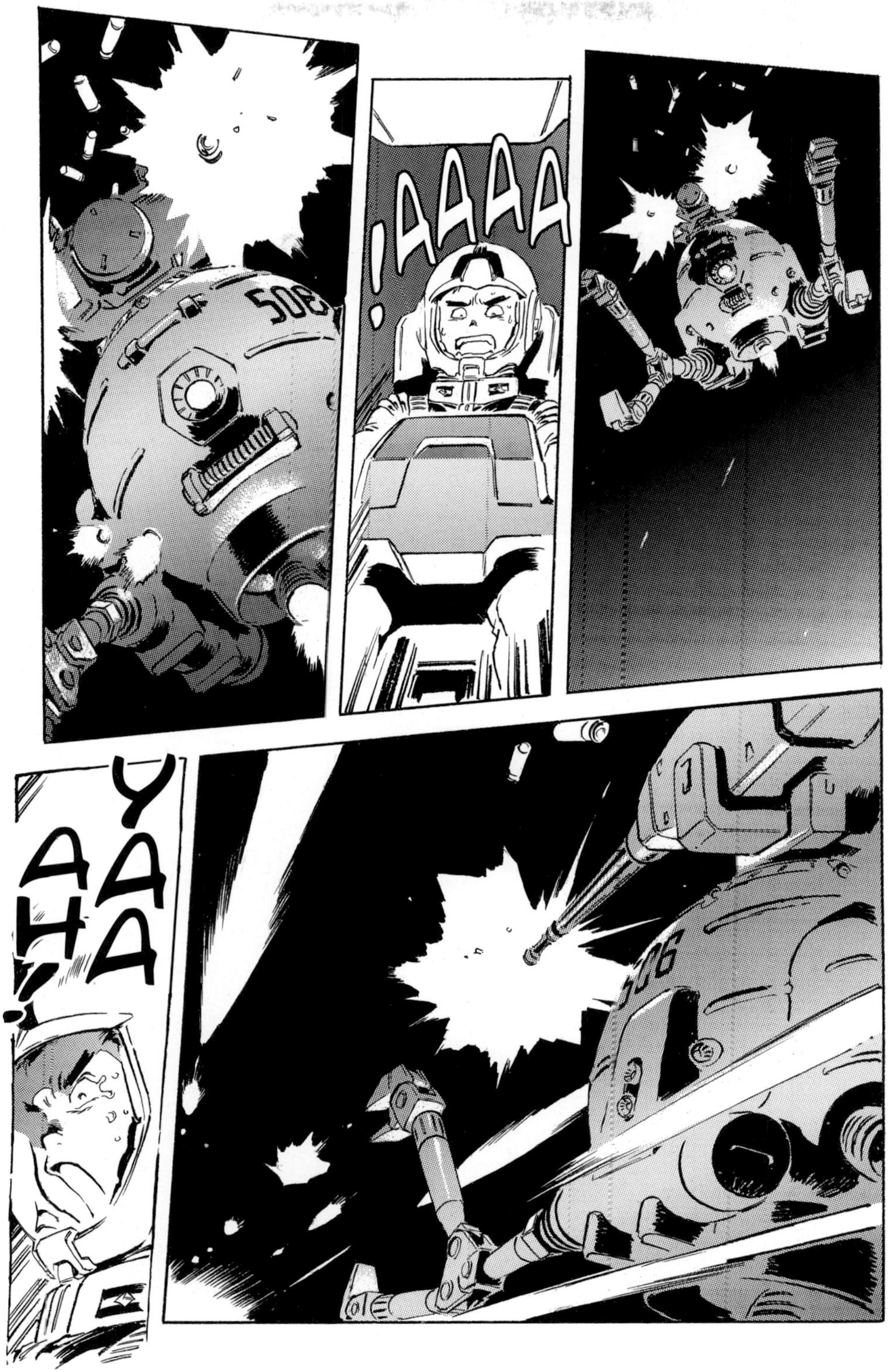
AAAA!
YAAAH!

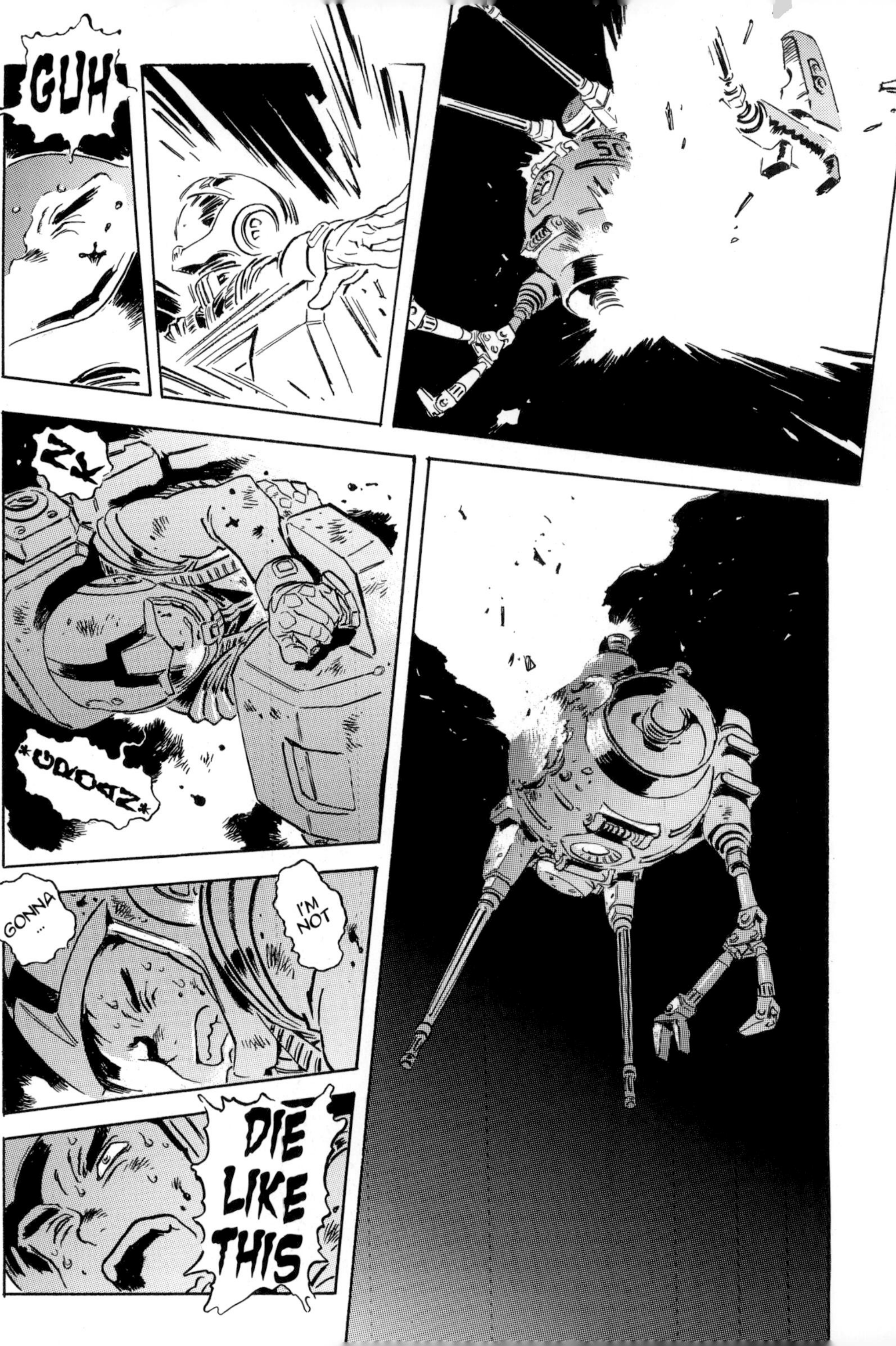
GUH
ZK
GROAZ
I'M NOT
GONNA ...
DIE LIKE THIS

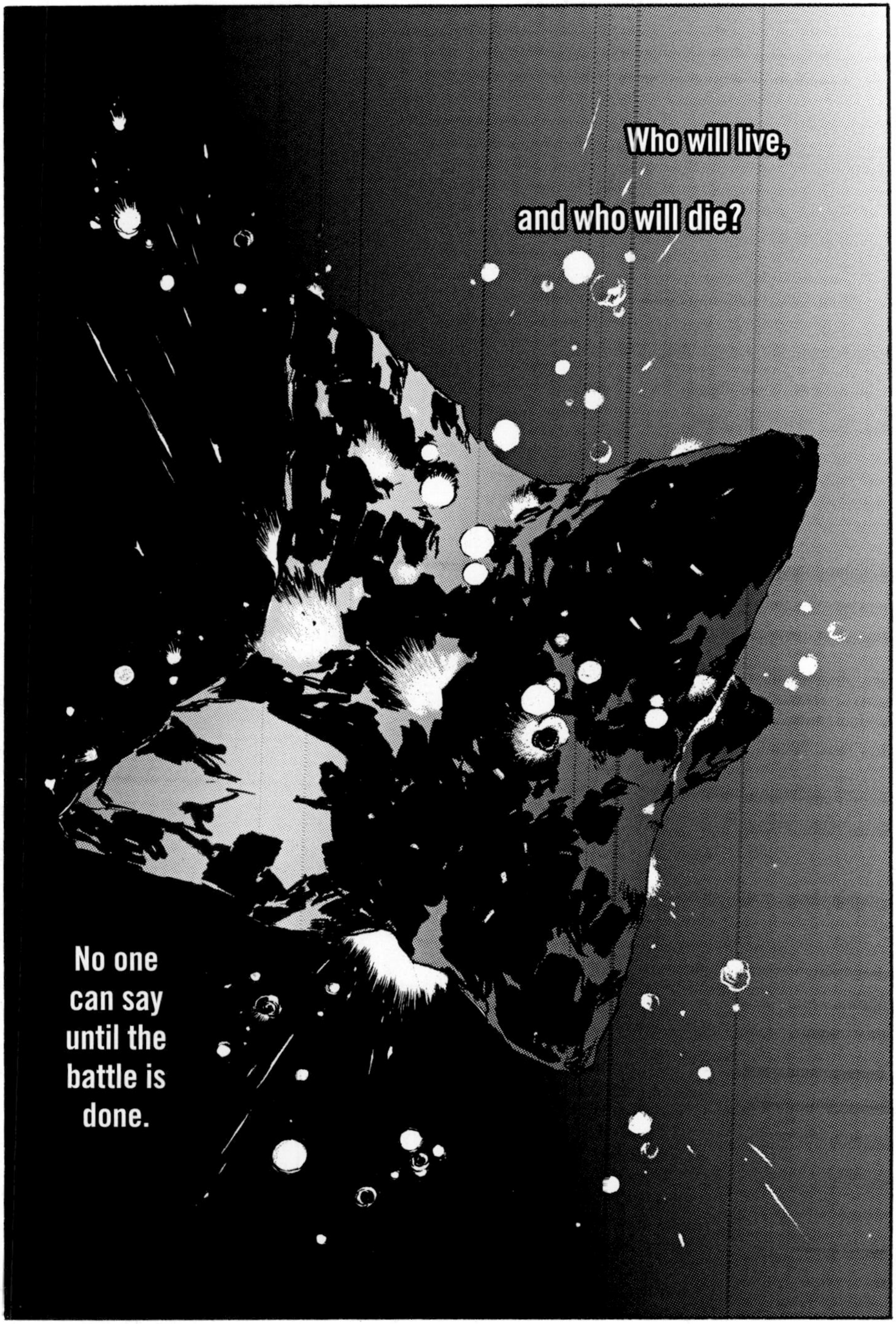
Who will live,
and who will die?
No one can say until the battle is done.

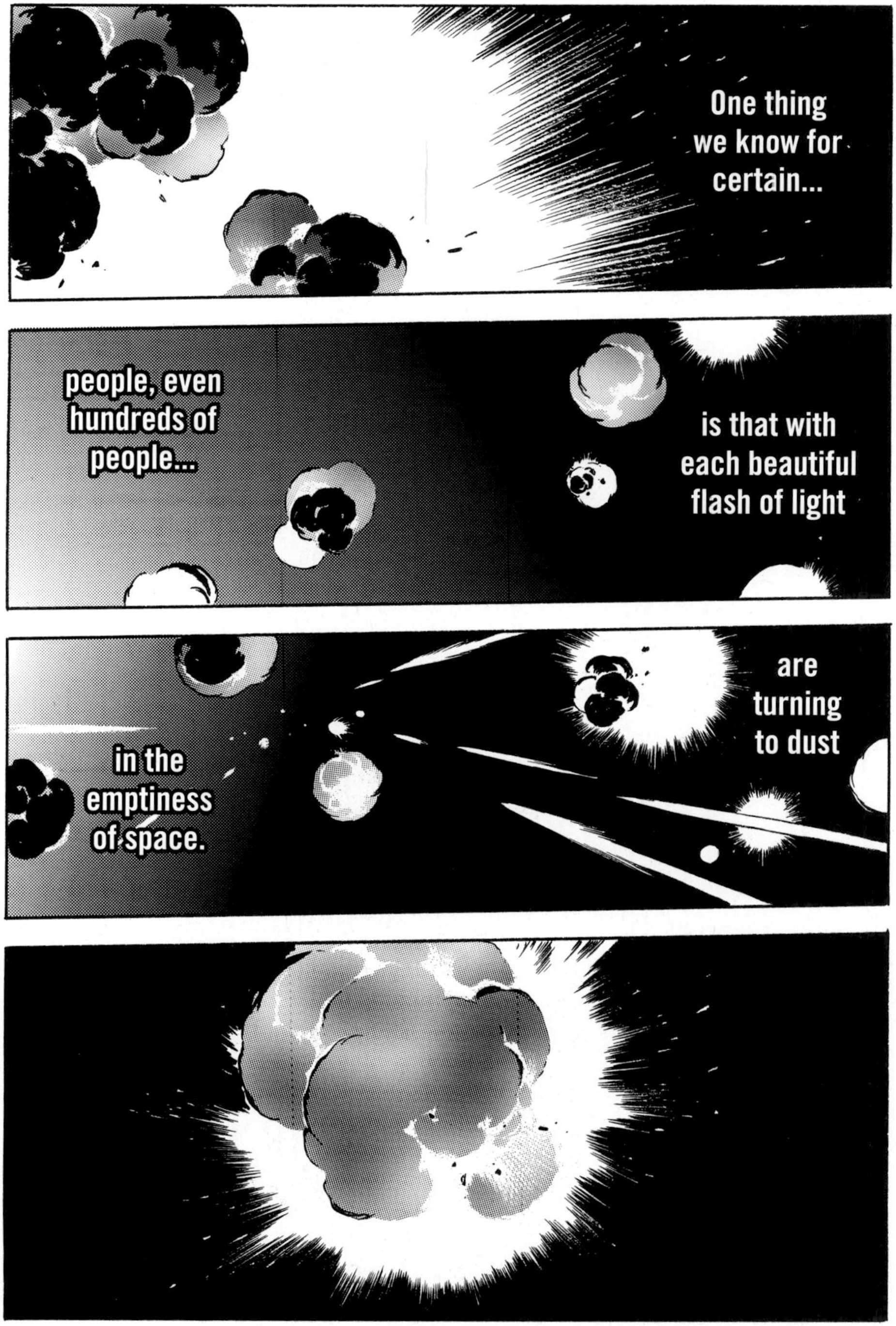
One thing we know for certain...
is that with each beautiful flash of light
people, even hundreds of people...
are turning to dust
in the emptiness of space.

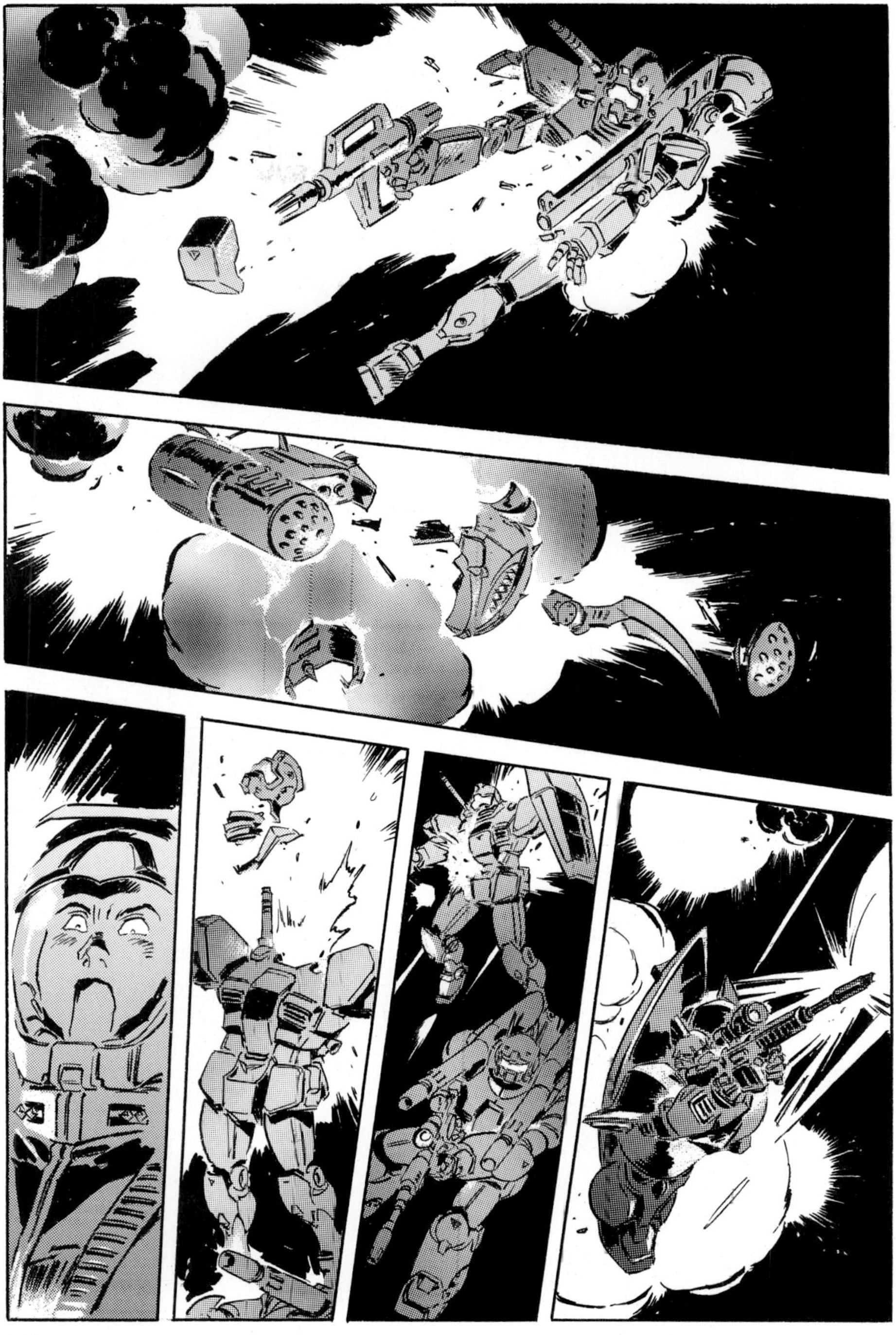

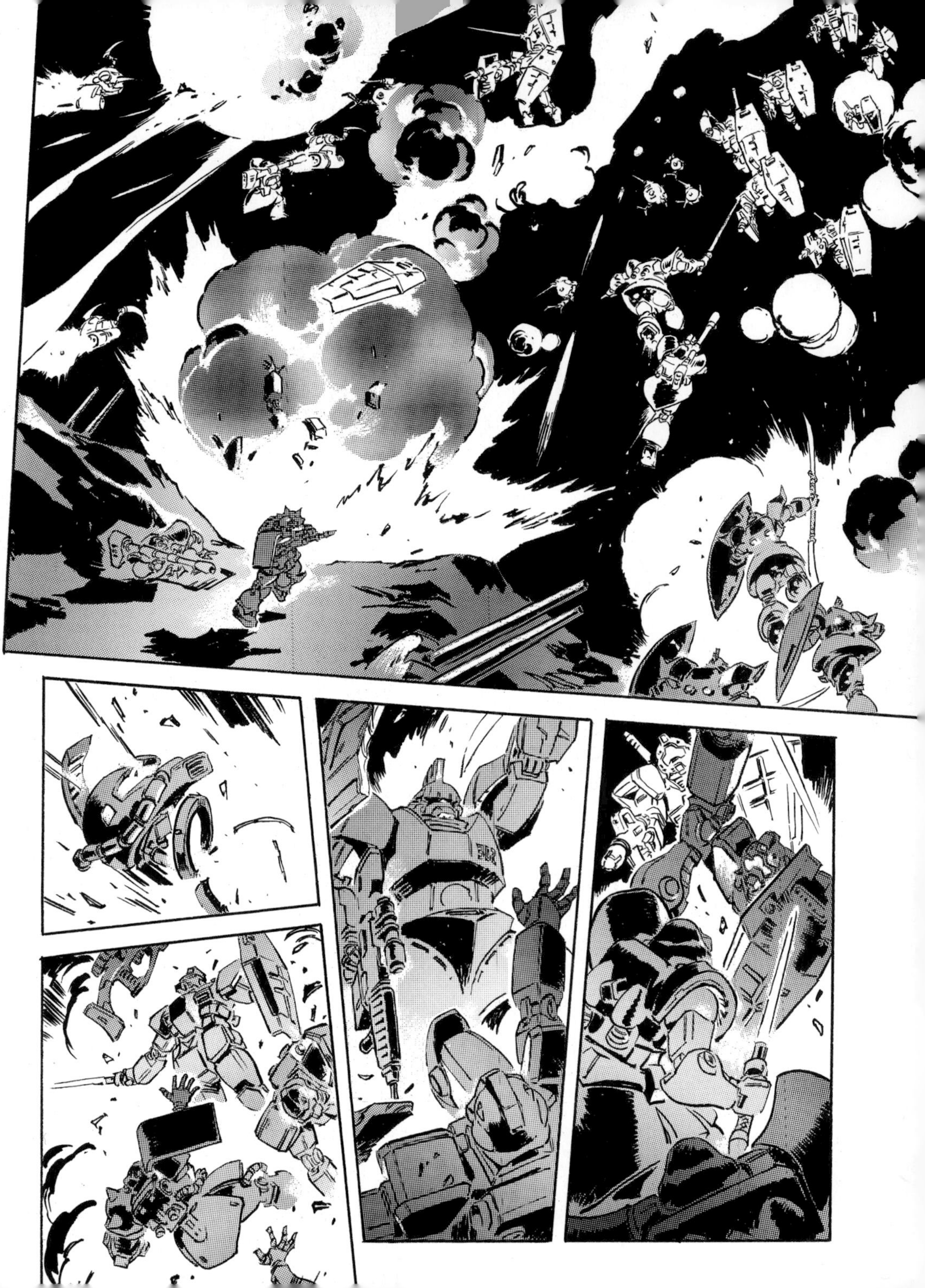

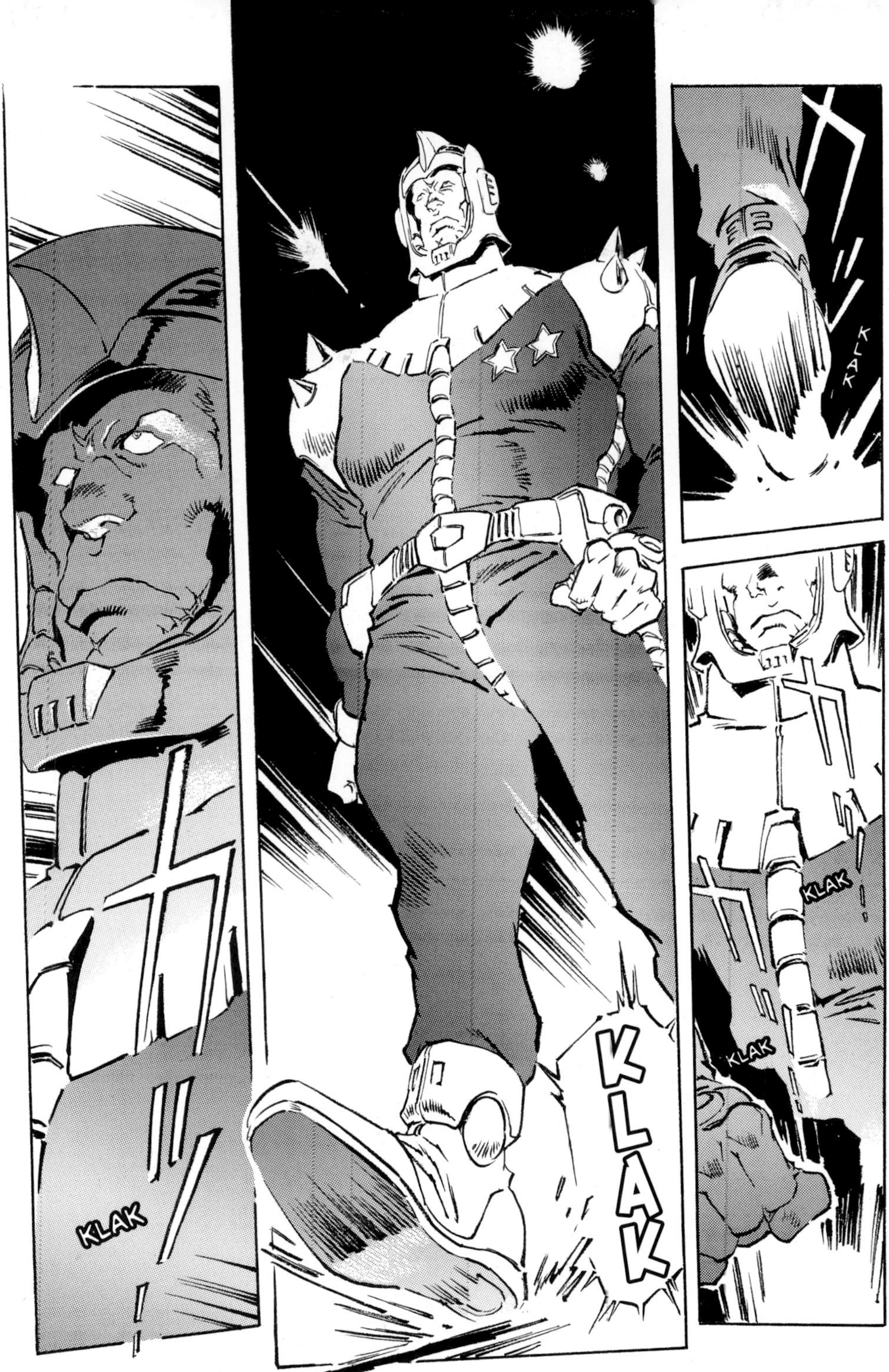
KLAK
KLAK
KLAK
KLLAK
KLAK

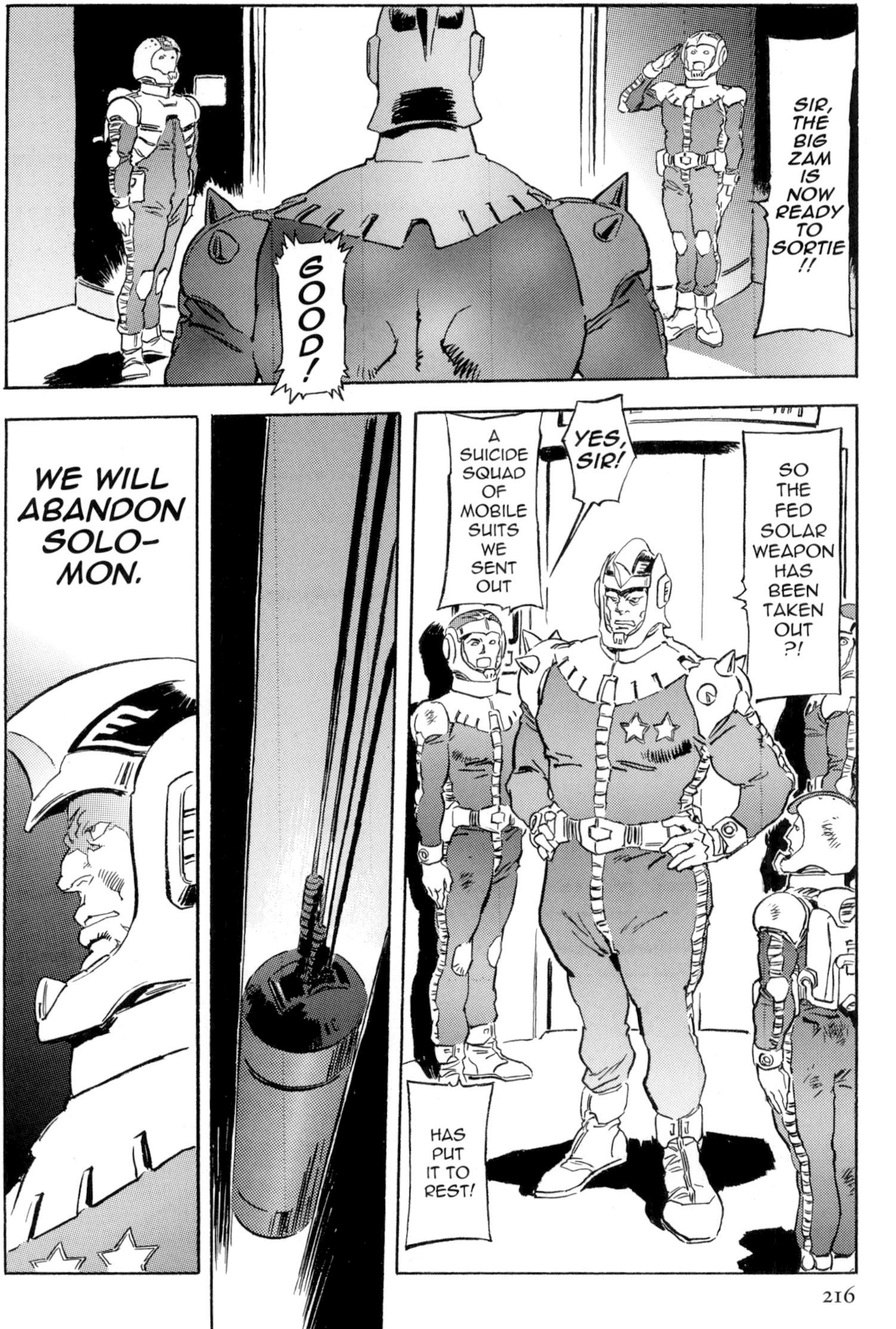
SIR, THE BIG ZAM IS NOW READY TO SORTIE!!
GOOD!
SO THE FED SOLAR WEAPON HAS BEEN TAKEN OUT?!
YES, SIR!
A SUICIDE SQUAD OF MOBILE SUITS WE SENT OUT
HAS PUT IT TO REST!
WE WILL ABANDON SOLO-MON.

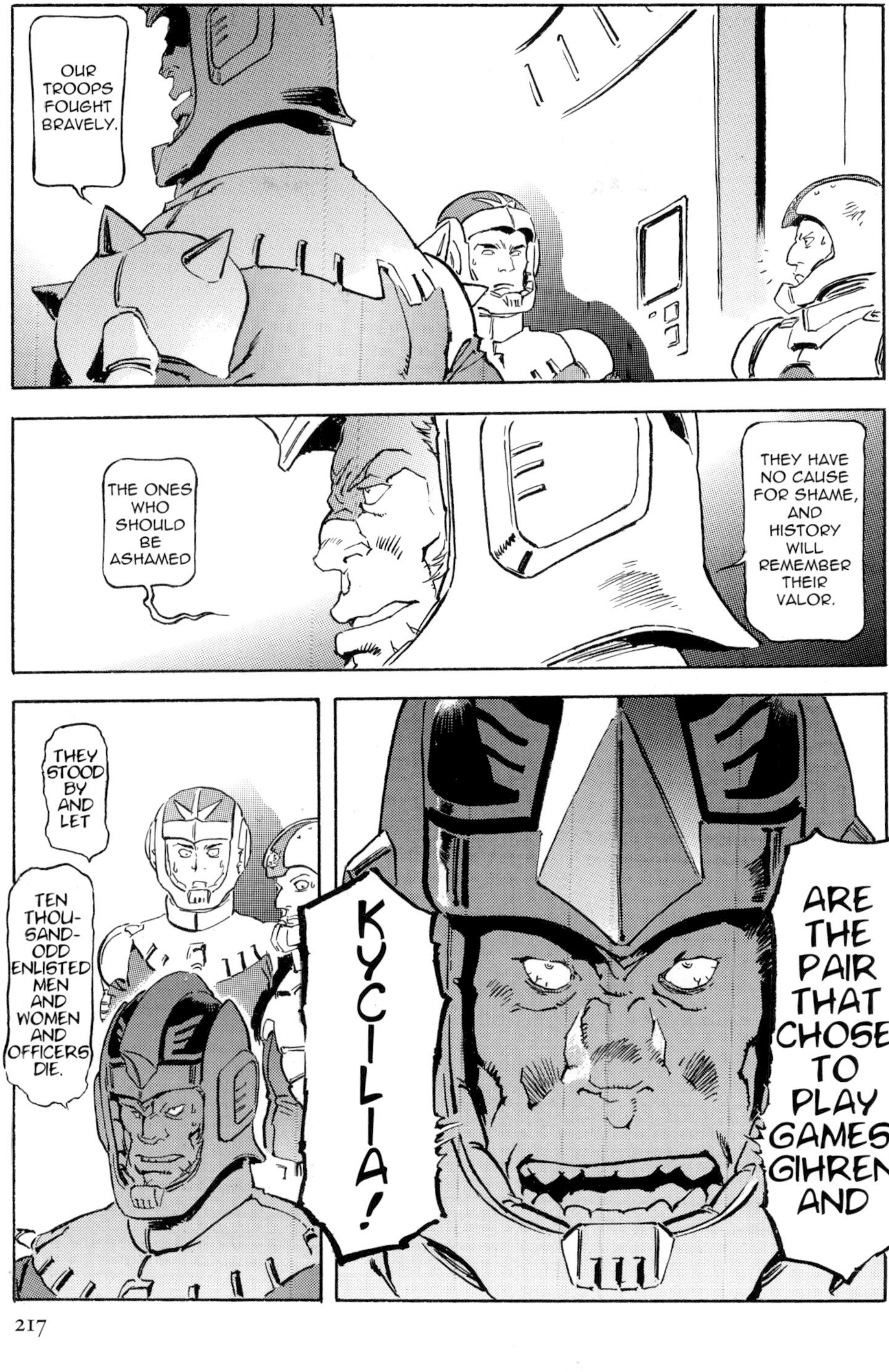
OUR TROOPS FOUGHT BRAVELY.
THEY HAVE NO CAUSE FOR SHAME, AND HISTORY WILL REMEMBER THEIR VALOR.
THE ONES WHO SHOULD BE ASHAMED
ARE THE PAIR THAT CHOSE TO PLAY GAMES, GIHREN AND
KYCILIA!
THEY STOOD BY AND LET
TEN THOUSAND-ODD ENLISTED MEN AND WOMEN AND OFFICERS DIE.

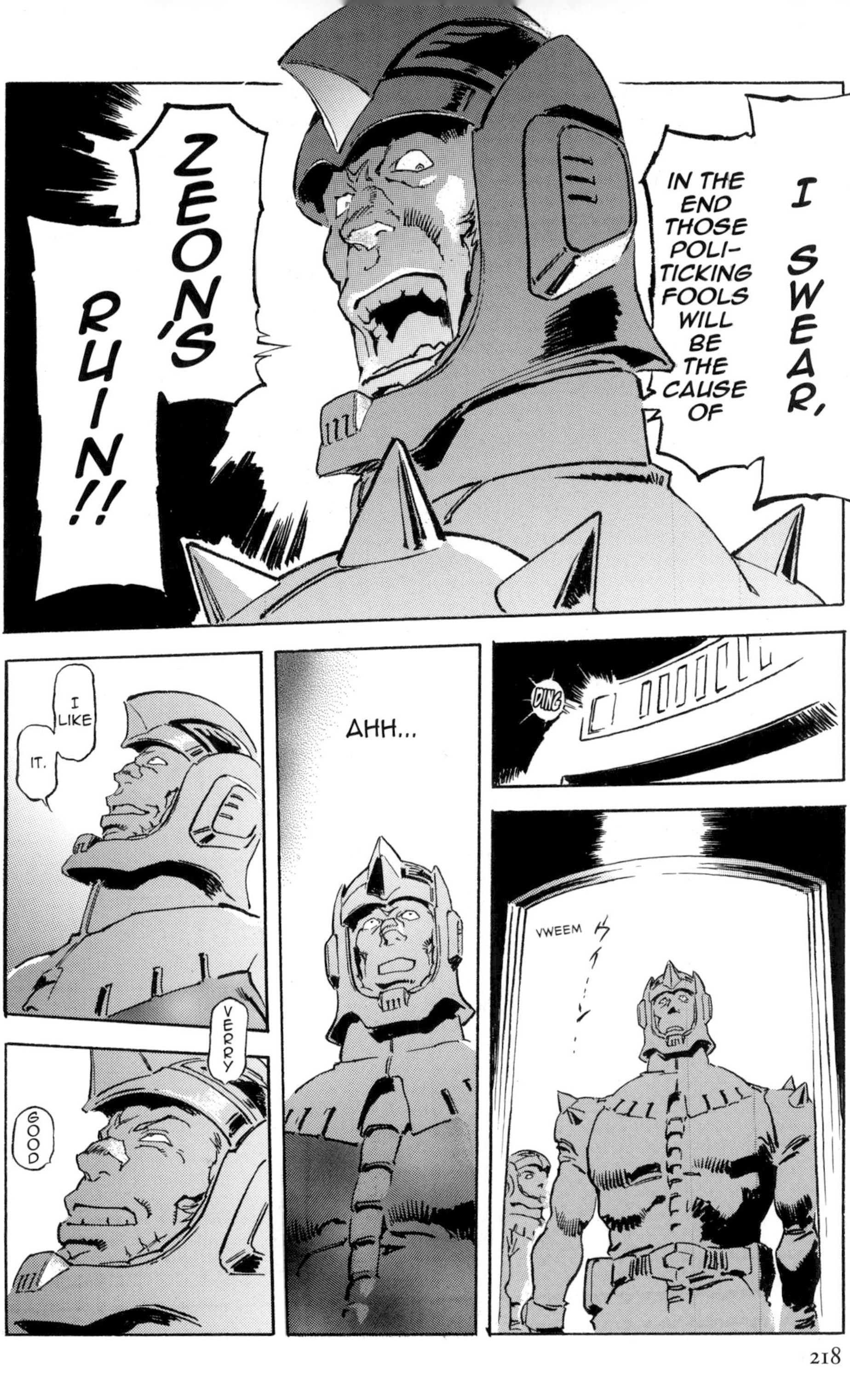
I SWEAR,
IN THE END THOSE POLI-TICKING FOOLS WILL BE THE CAUSE OF
ZEON'S RUIN!!
DING
VWEEM
AHH...
I LIKE IT.
VERRY GOOD

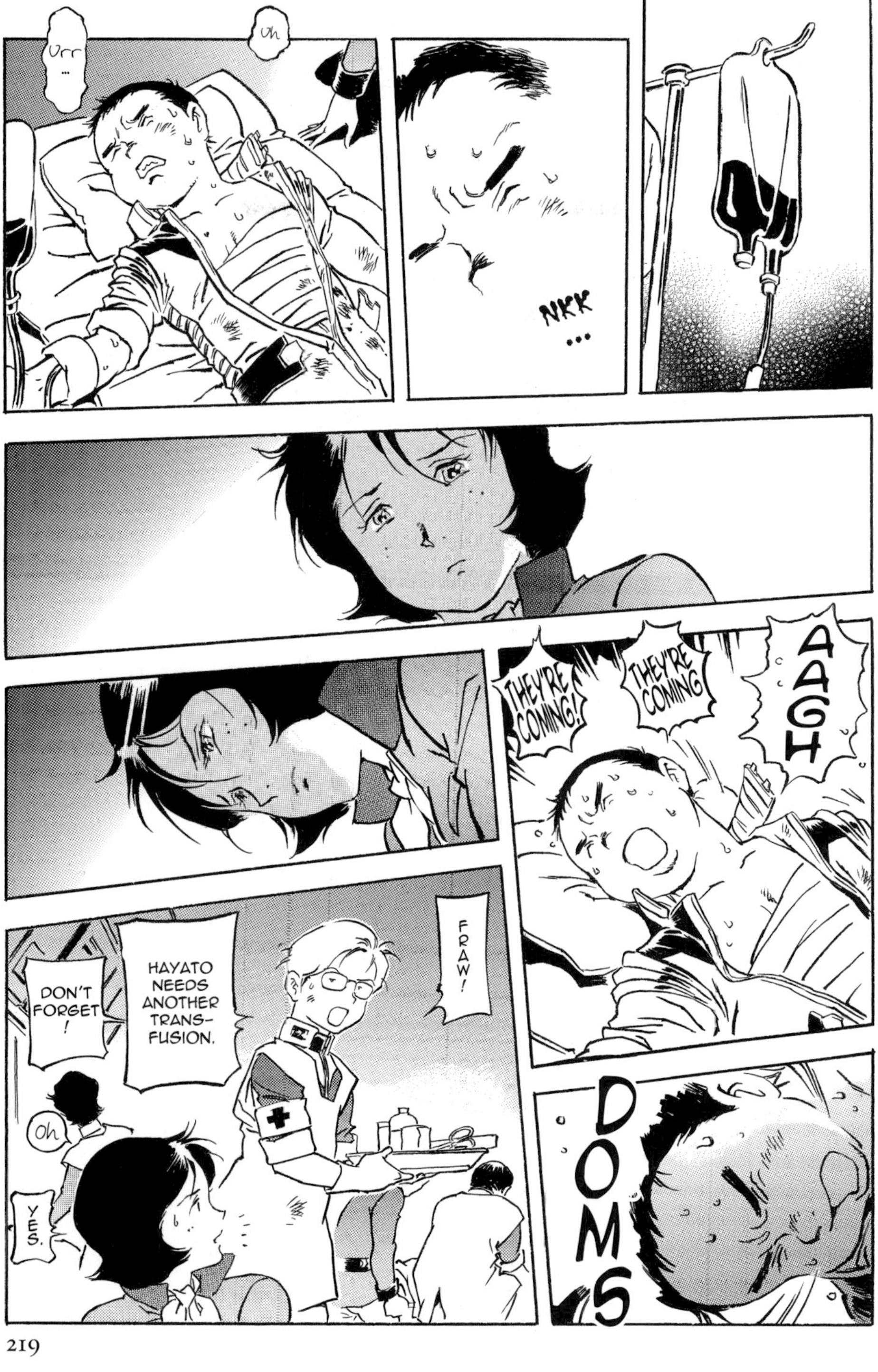
Oh
Urr ...
NKK ...
AAGH
THEY'RE COMING
THEY'RE COMING!
DOMS
FRAW!
HAYATO NEEDS ANOTHER TRANS-FUSION.
DON'T FORGET!
Oh
YES.

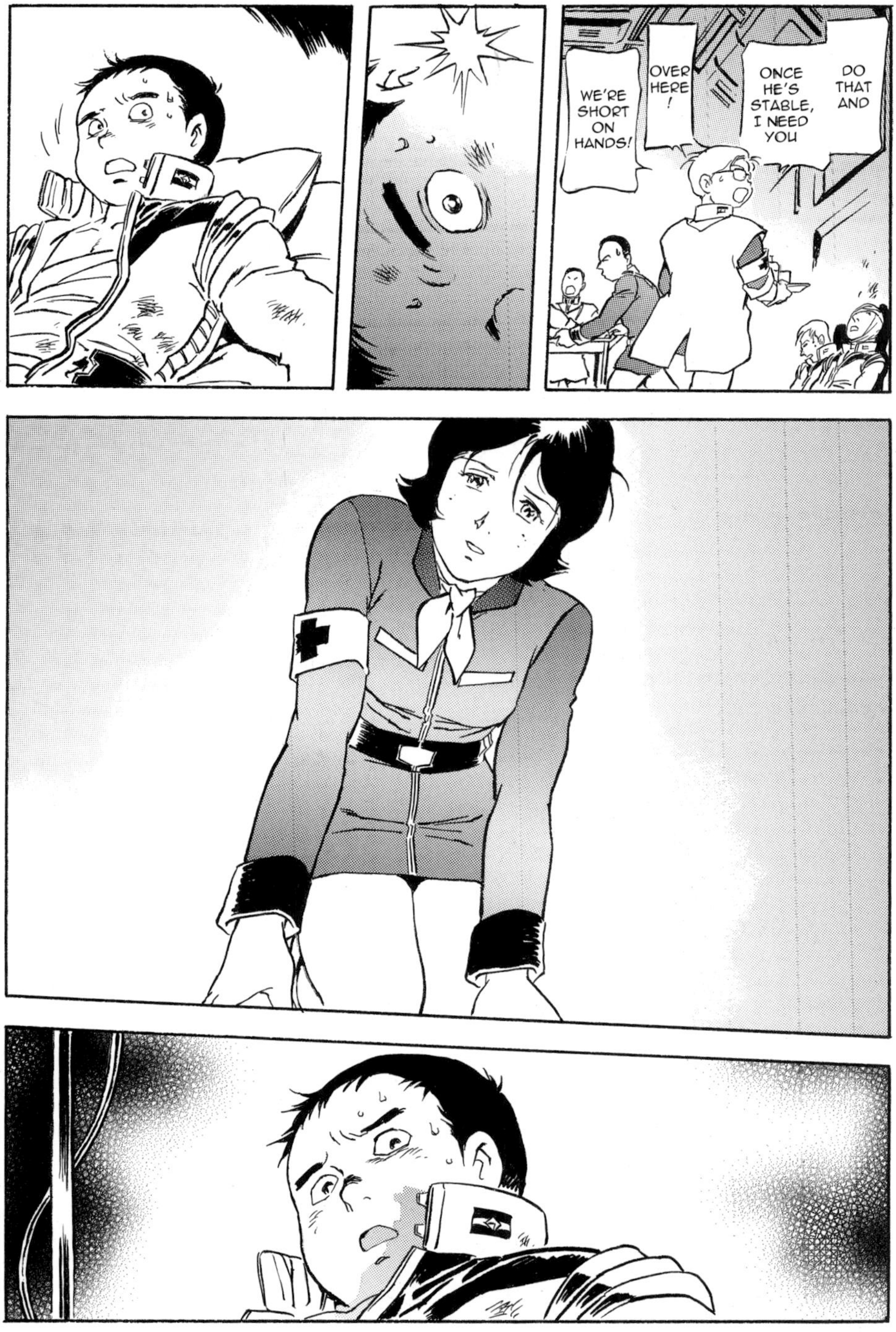
DO THAT AND
ONCE HE'S STABLE, I NEED YOU
OVER HERE!
WE'RE SHORT ON HANDS!

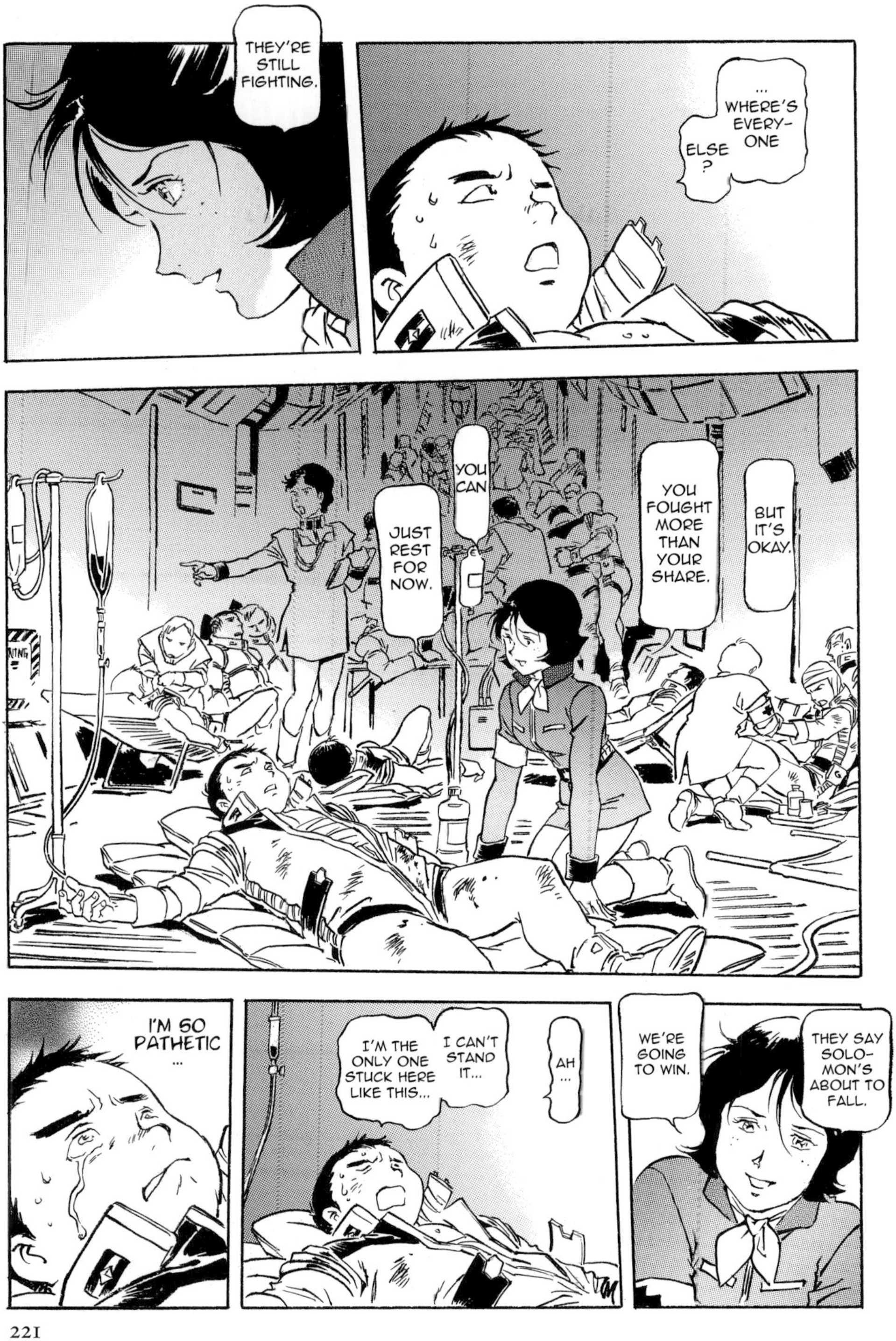
... WHERE'S EVERYONE ELSE ?
THEY'RE STILL FIGHTING.
BUT IT'S OKAY.
YOU FOUGHT MORE THAN YOUR SHARE.
YOU CAN
JUST REST FOR NOW.
THEY SAY SOLOMON'S ABOUT TO FALL.
WE'RE GOING TO WIN.
AH ...
I CAN'T STAND IT...
I'M THE ONLY ONE STUCK HERE LIKE THIS...
I'M SO PATHETIC ...

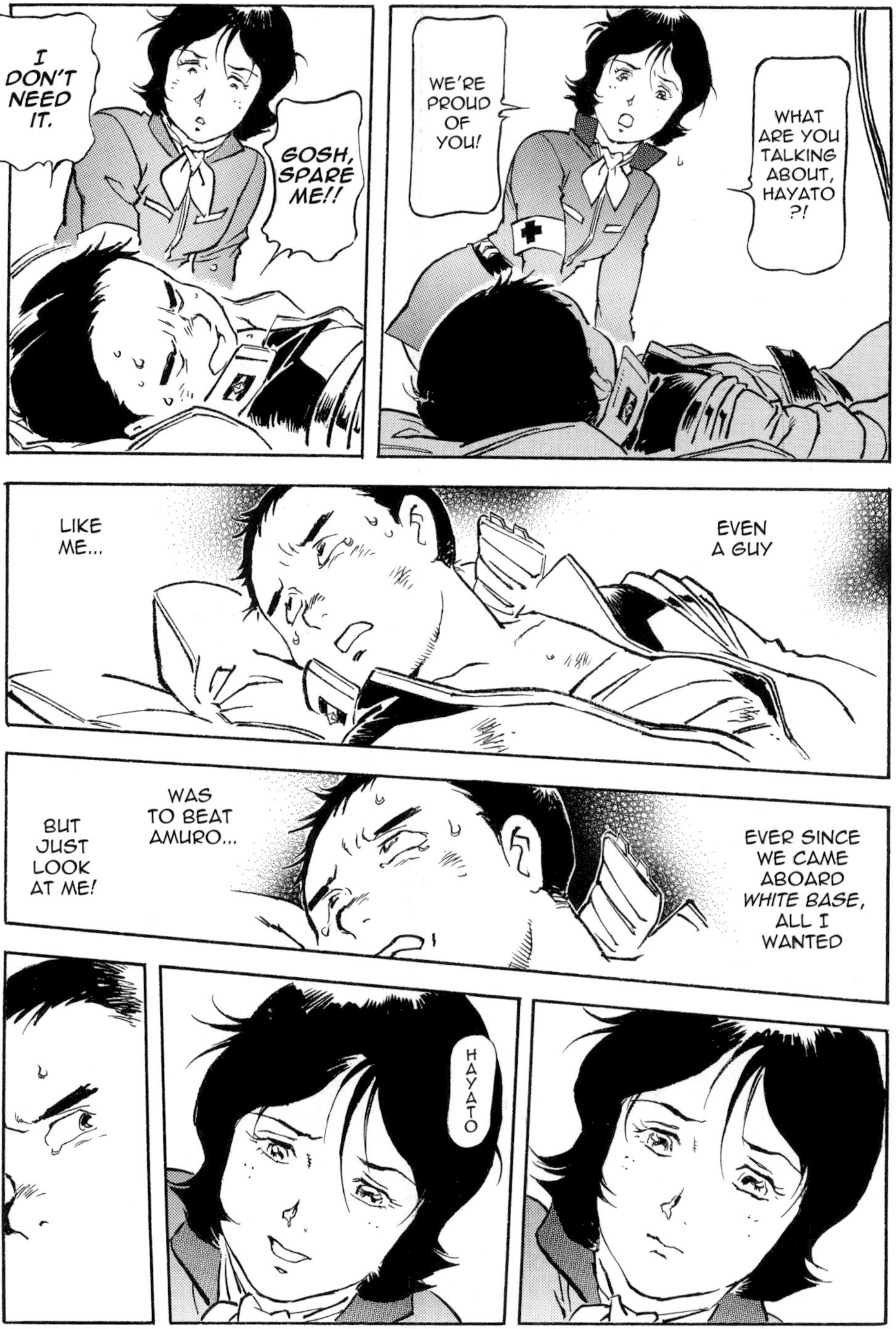
WHAT ARE YOU TALKING ABOUT, HAYATO?!
WE'RE PROUD OF YOU!
GOSH, SPARE ME!!
I DON'T NEED IT.
EVEN A GUY
LIKE ME...
EVER SINCE WE CAME ABOARD WHITE BASE, ALL I WANTED
WAS TO BEAT AMURO...
BUT JUST LOOK AT ME!
HAYATO

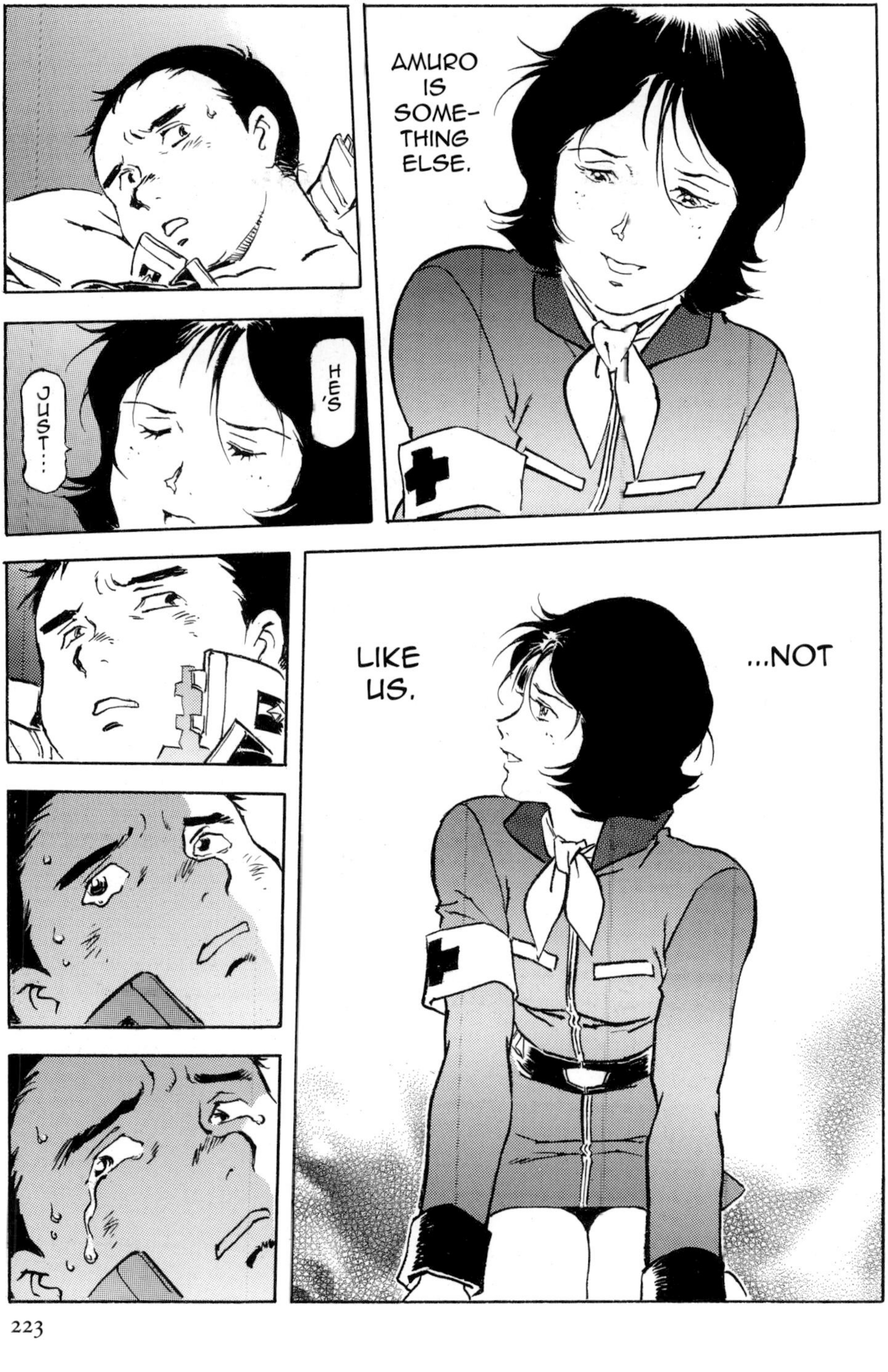
AMURO IS SOME-THING ELSE.
HE'S
JUST...
...NOT
LIKE US.

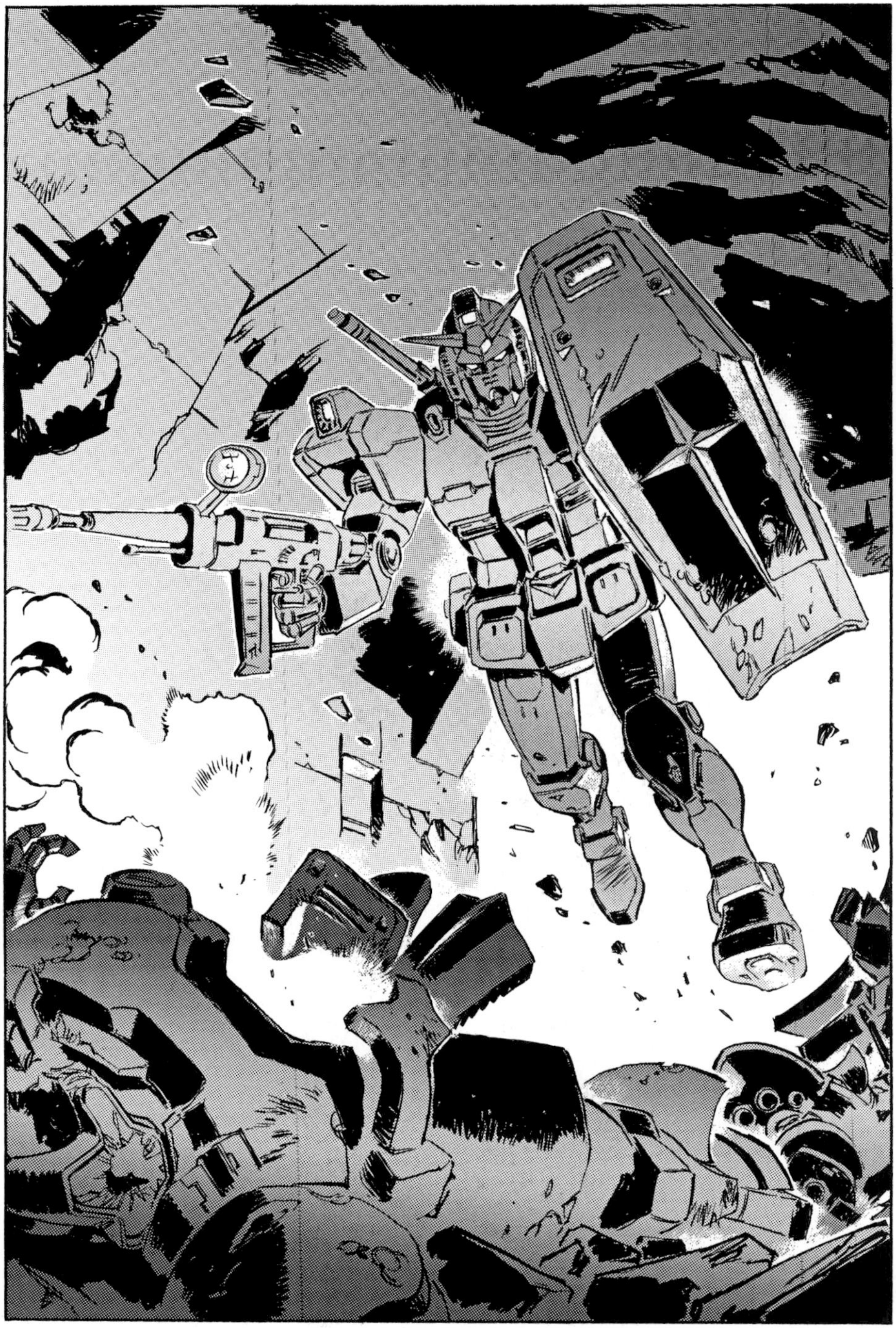

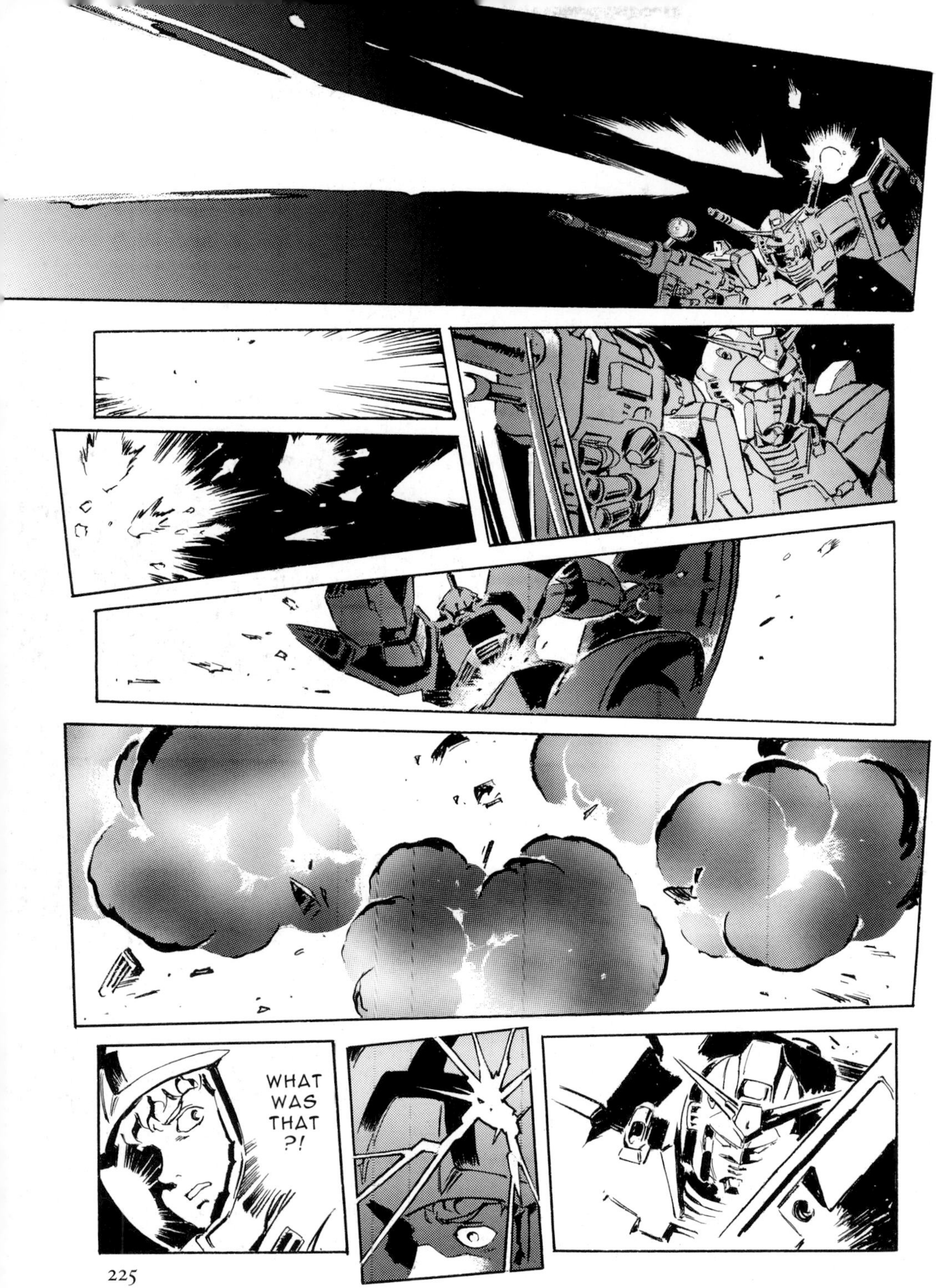
WHAT WAS THAT ?!

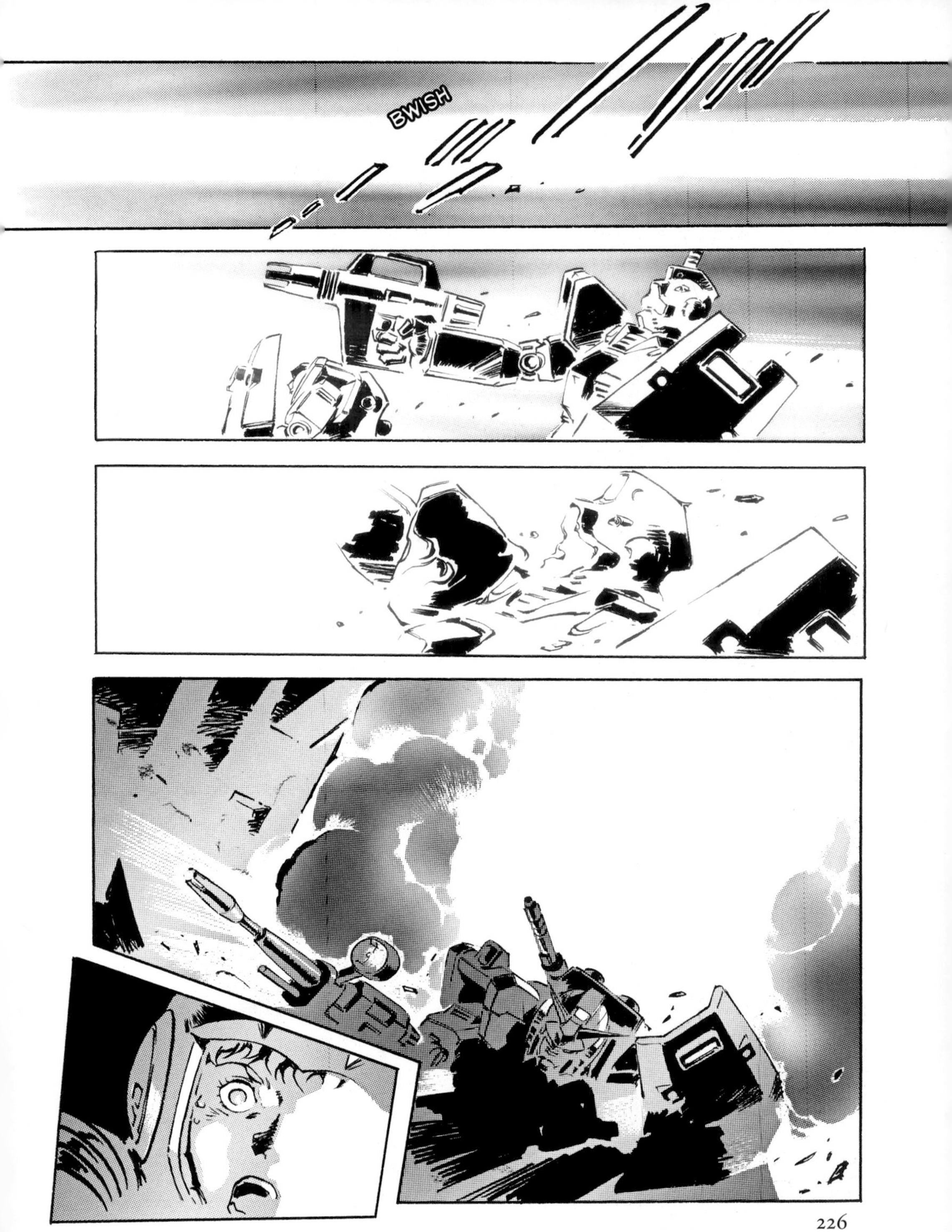
BWISH

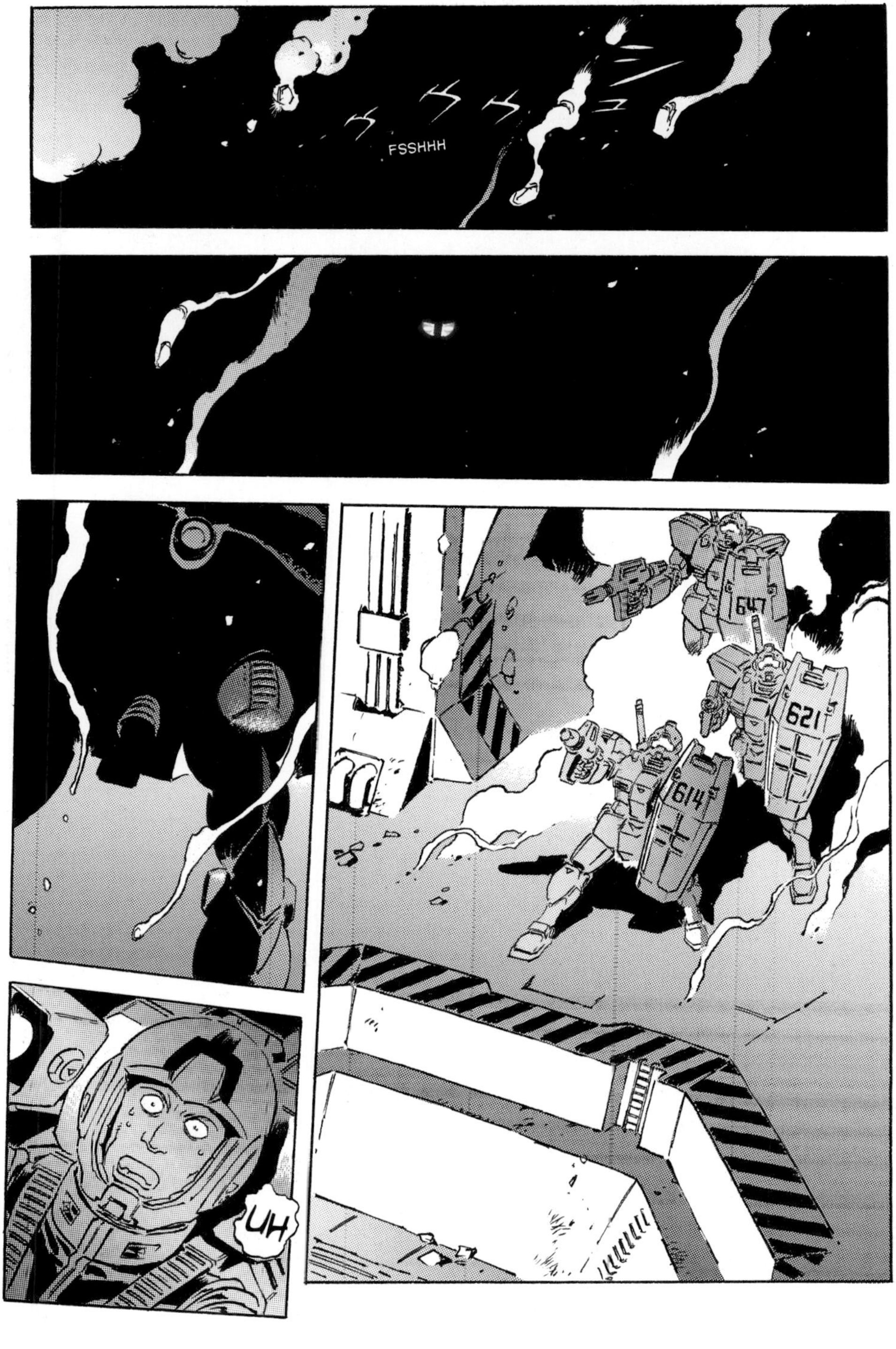
FSSHHH
647
621
614
UH

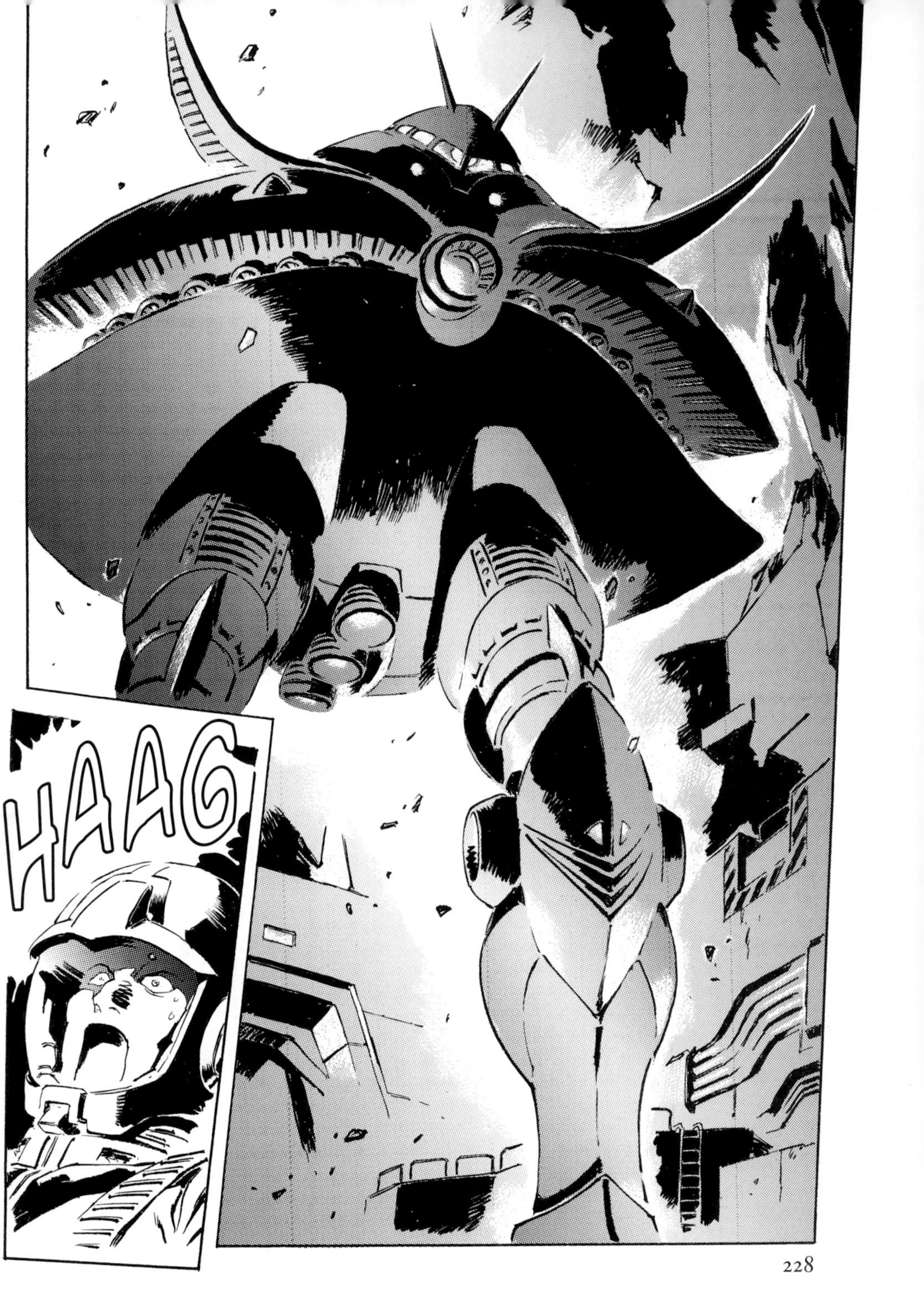
HAAG

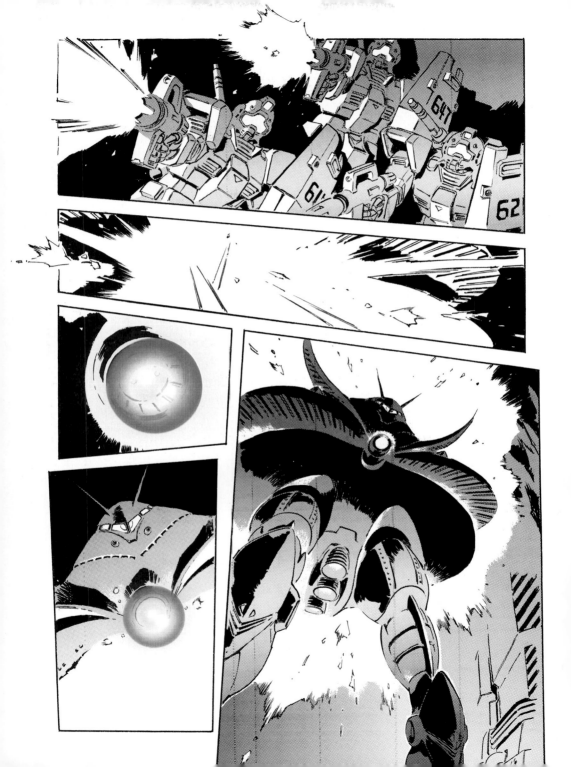

Ah

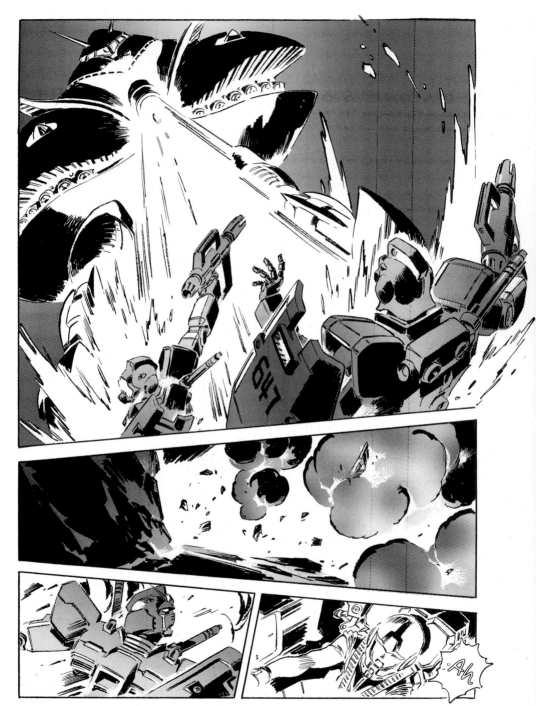

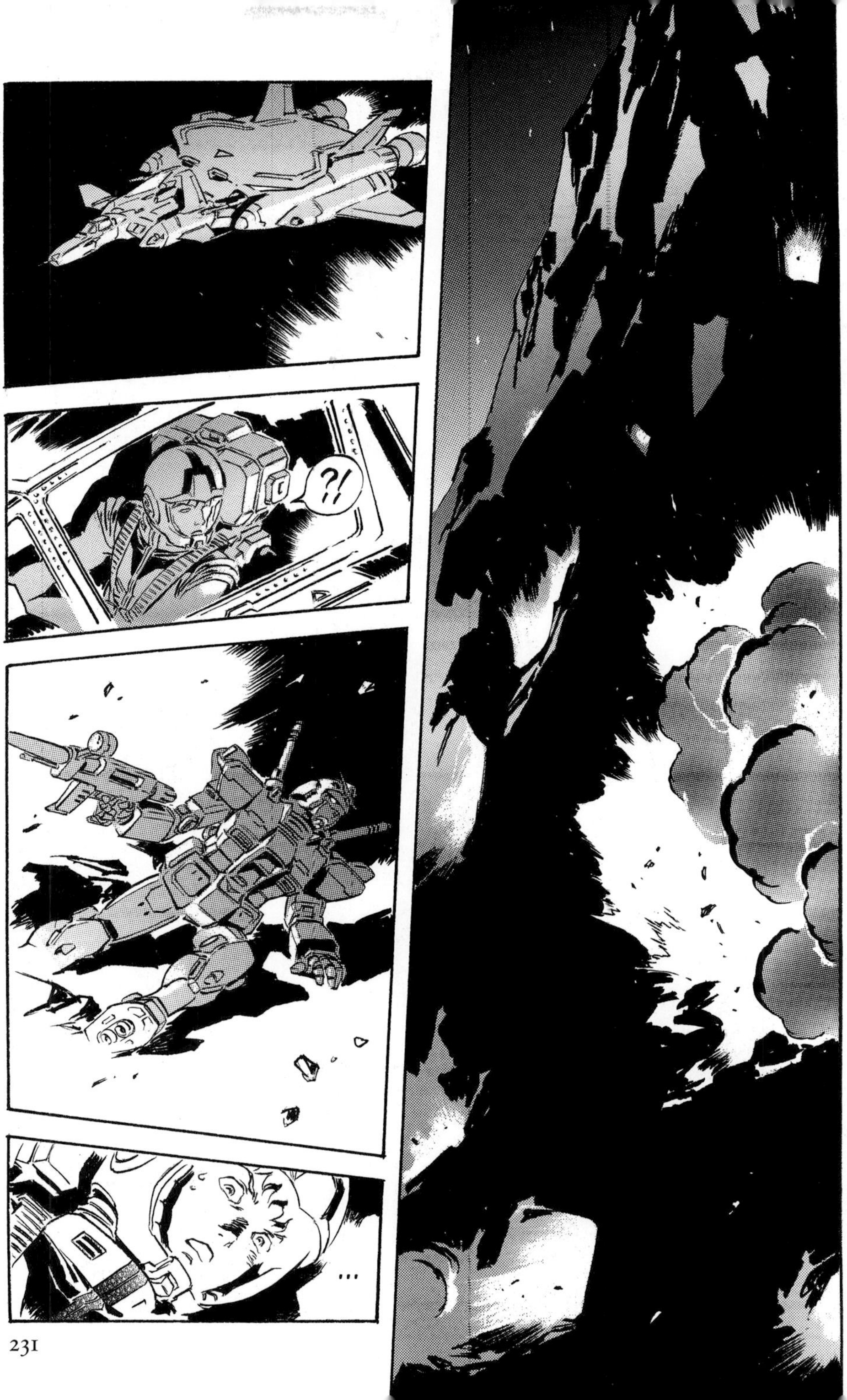
?!
...

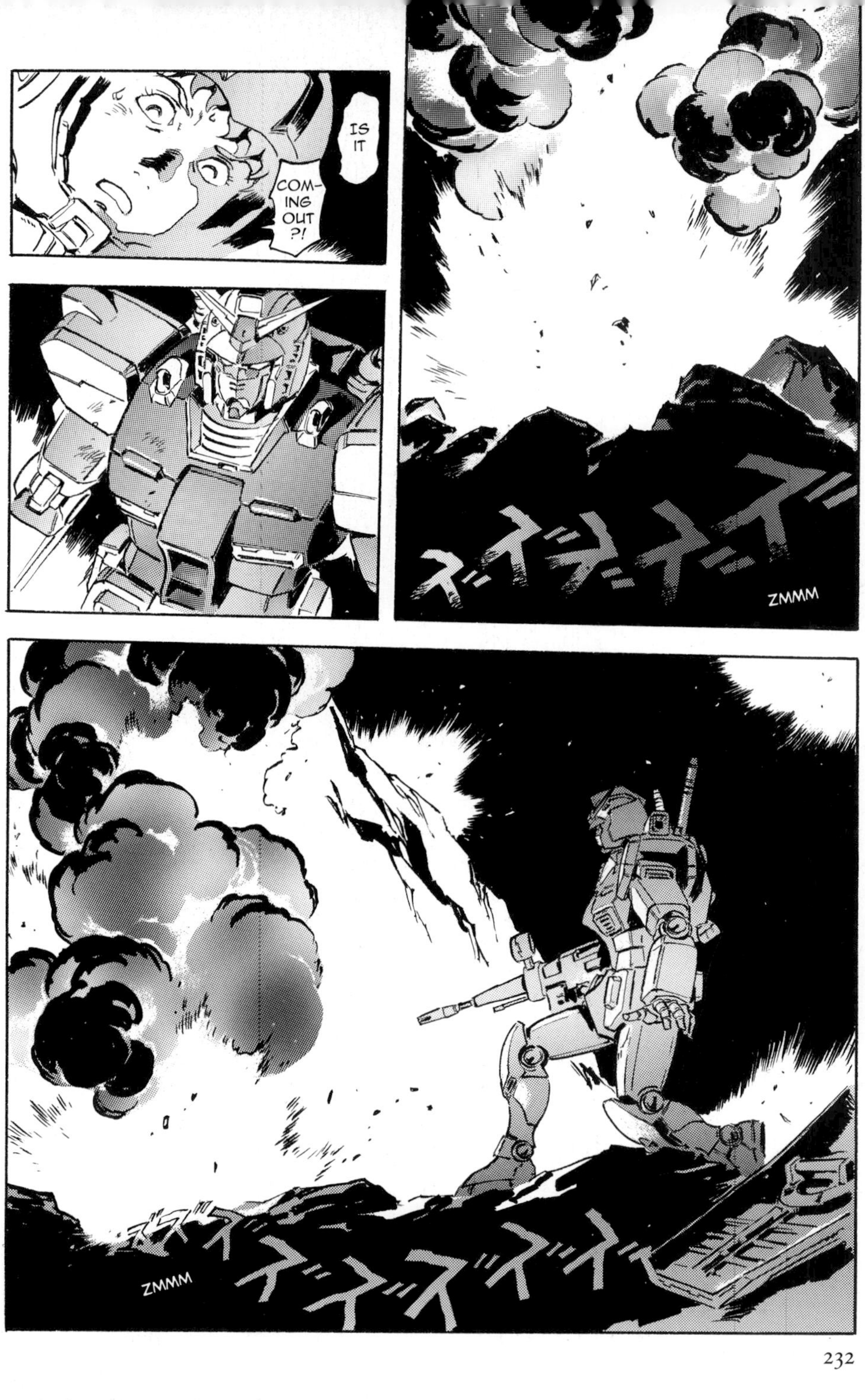
ZMMM
IS IT COMING OUT?!
ZMMM

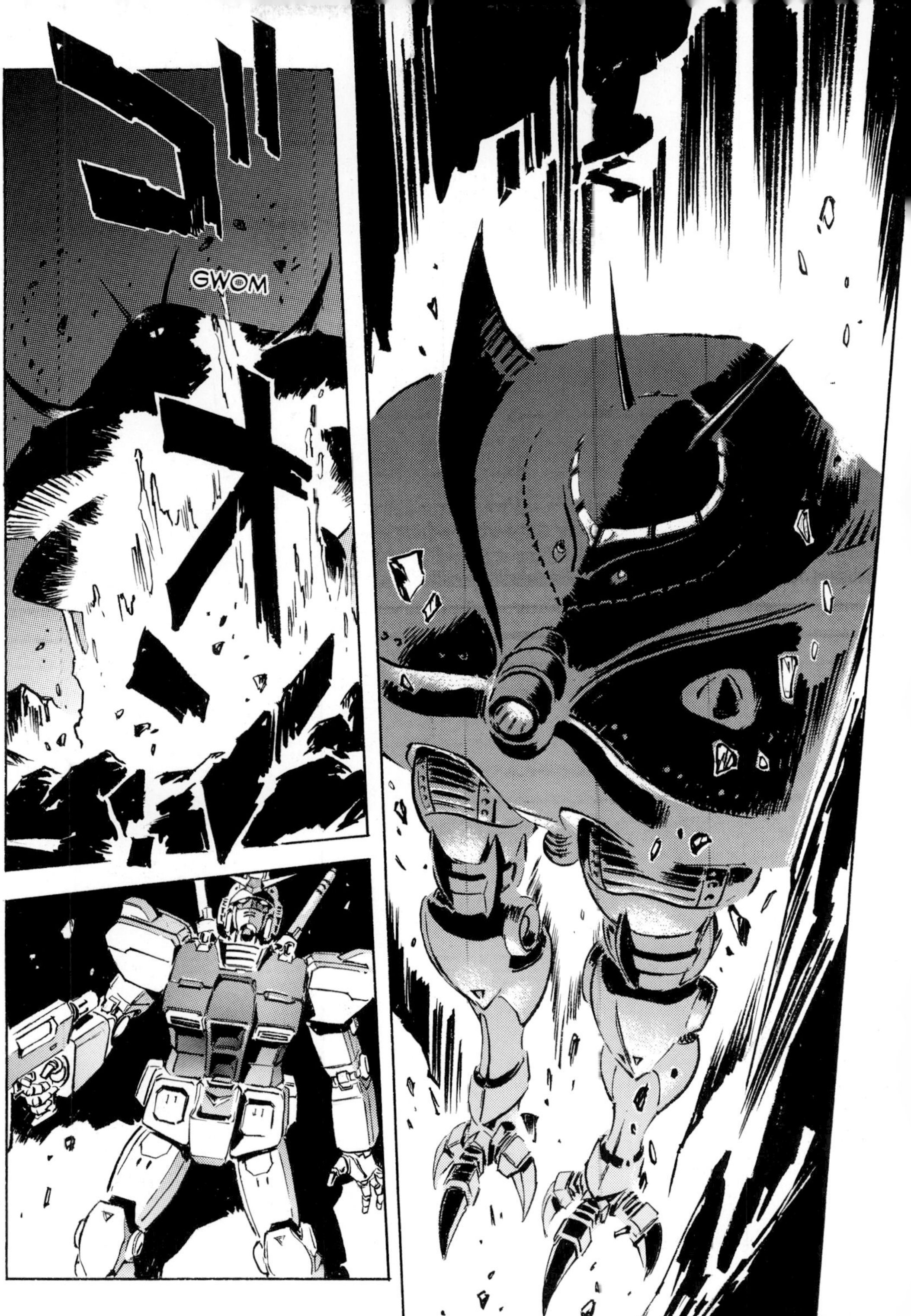
GWOM

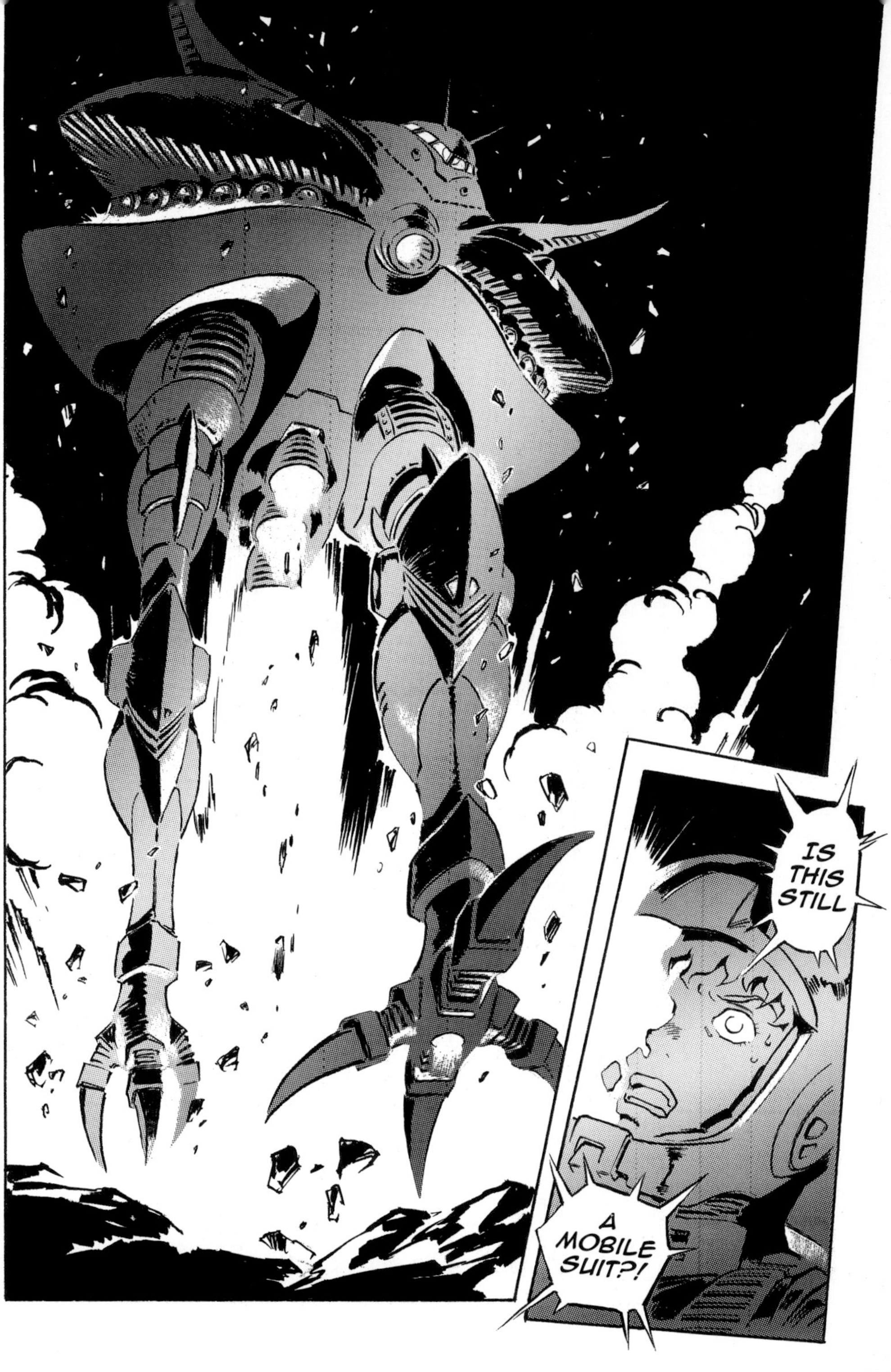
IS THIS STILL
A MOBILE SUIT?!

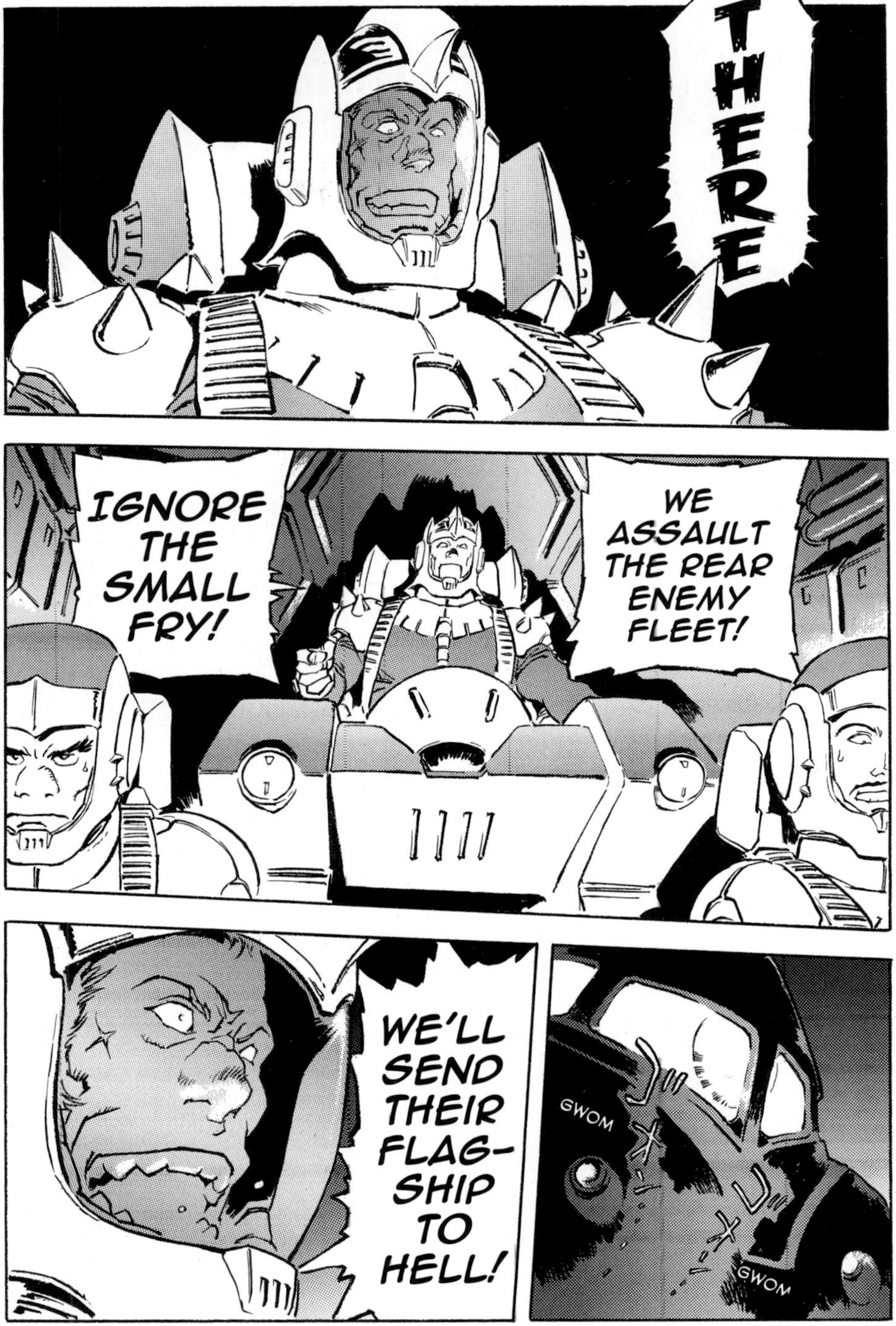
THERE
WE ASSAULT THE REAR ENEMY FLEET!
IGNORE THE SMALL FRY!
GWOM
GWOM
WE'LL SEND THEIR FLAG-SHIP TO HELL!

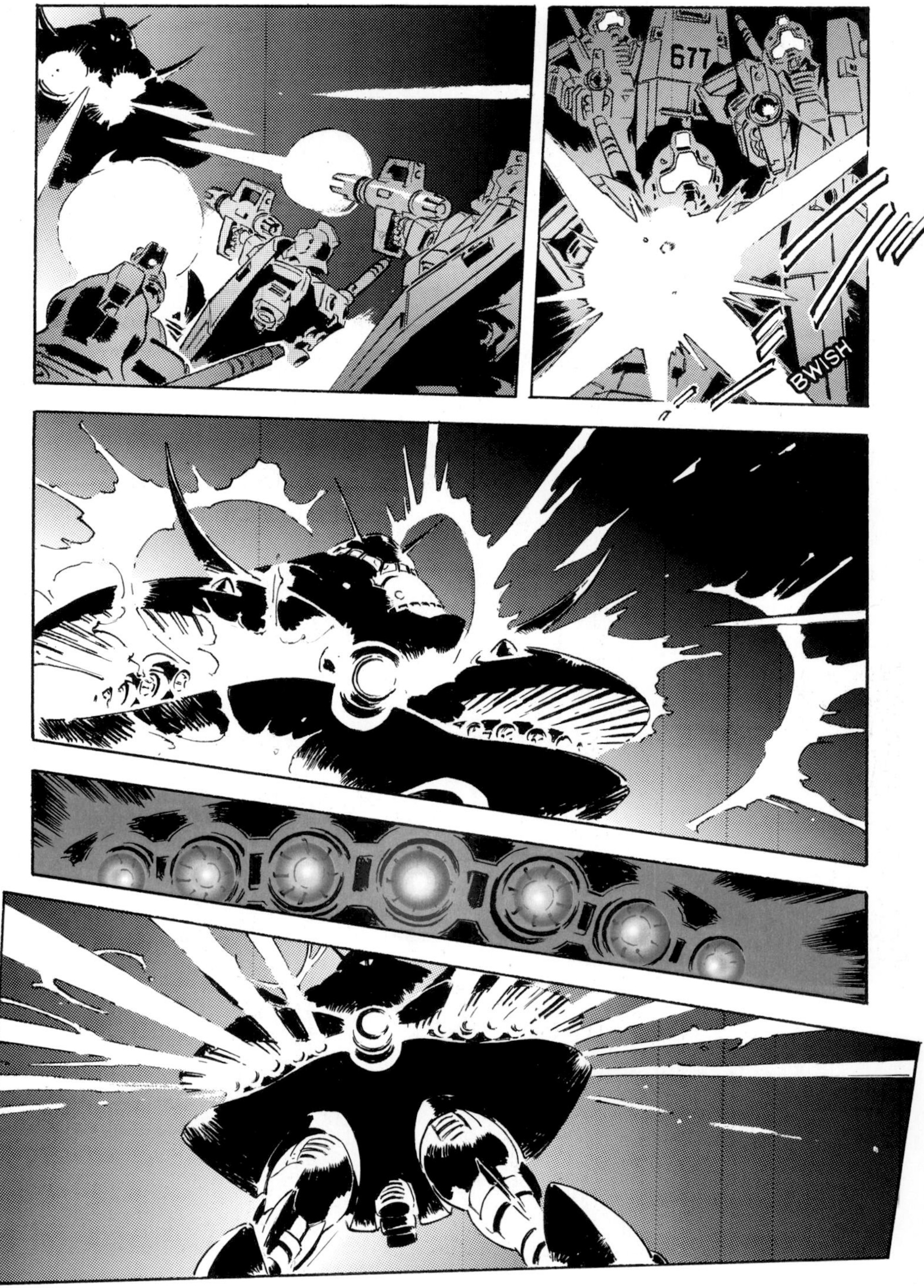
677
BWISH

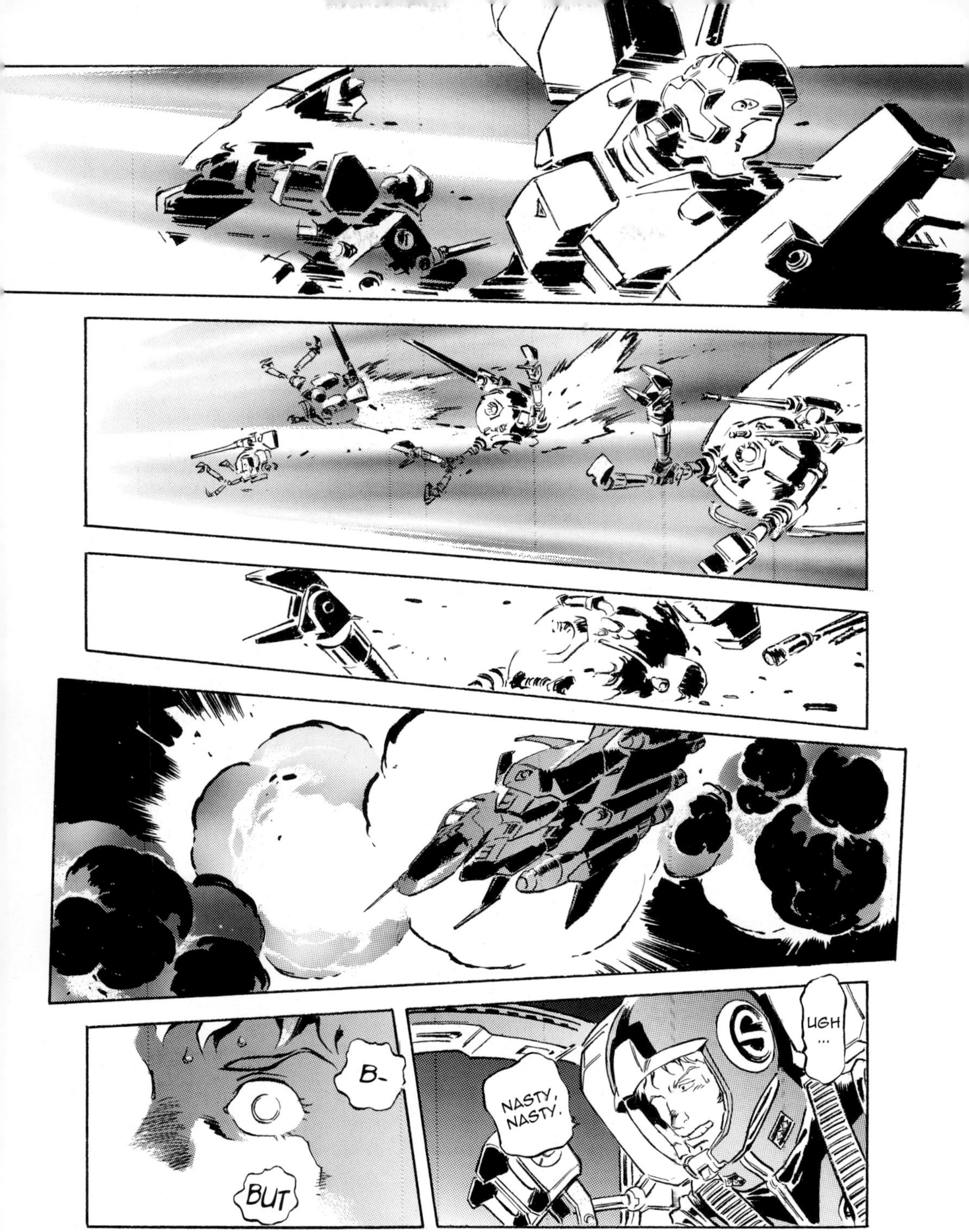
UGH ...
NASTY, NASTY.
B-
BUT

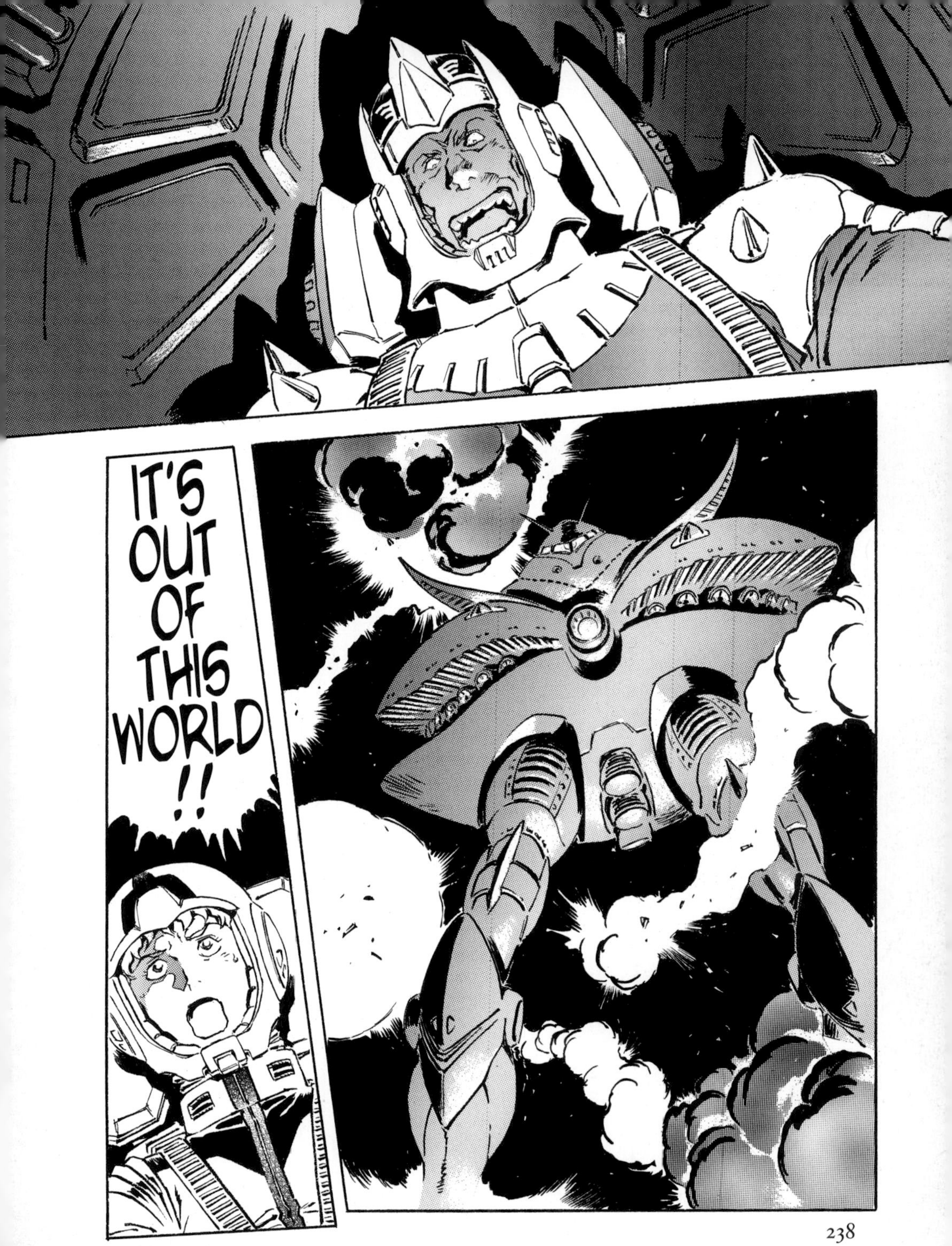
IT'S OUT OF THIS WORLD!!

SECTION VII

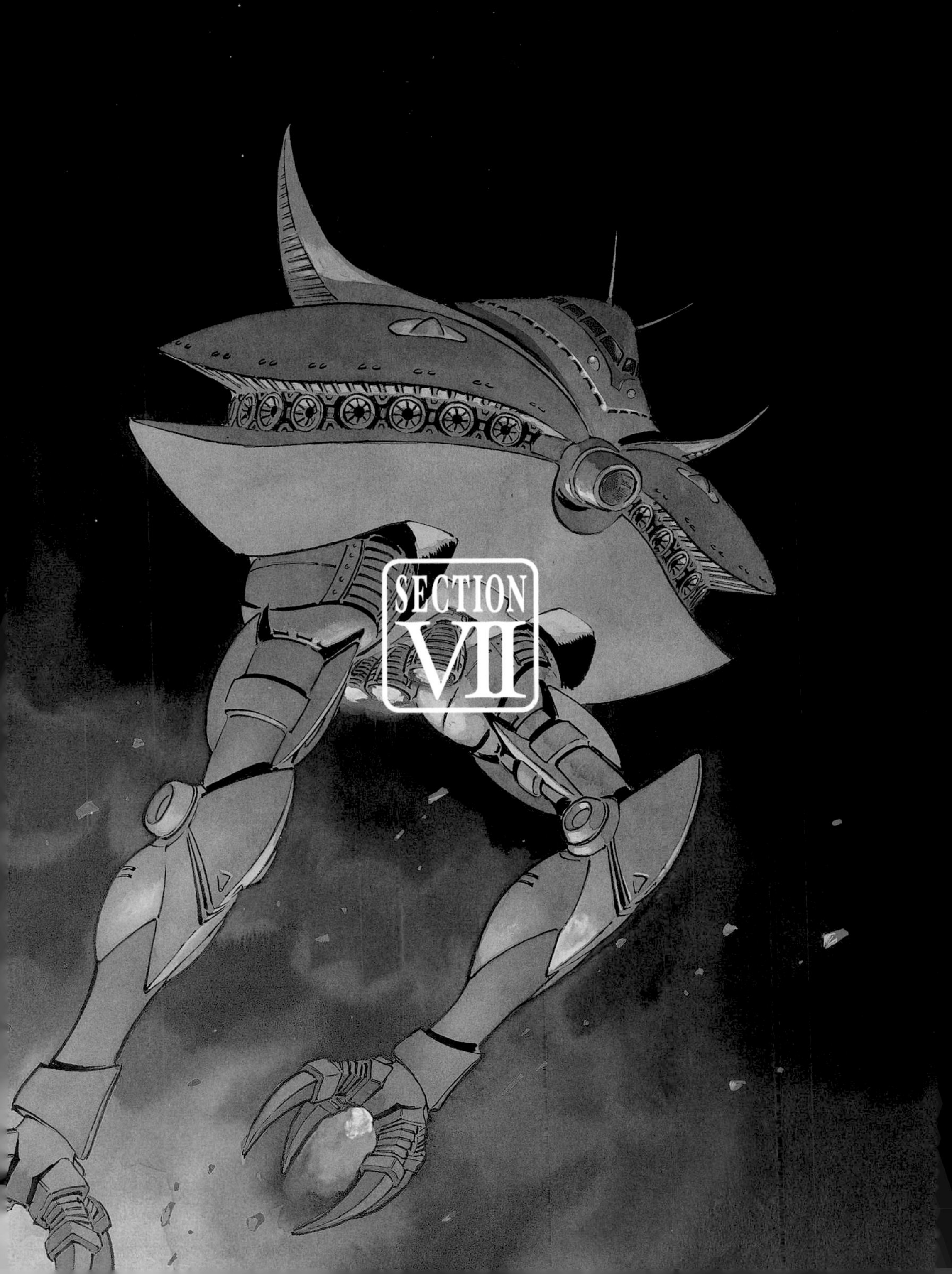

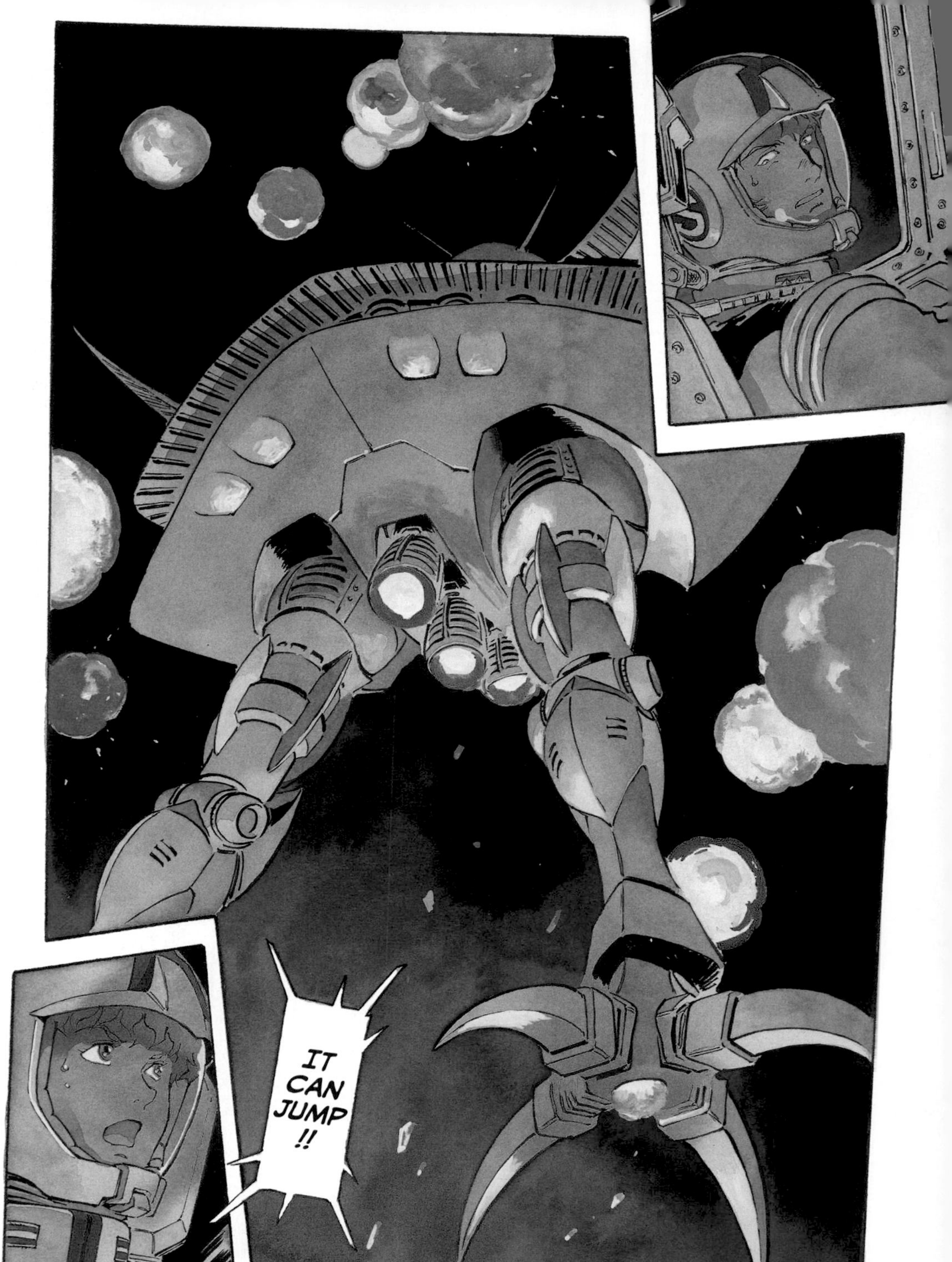
IT CAN JUMP !!

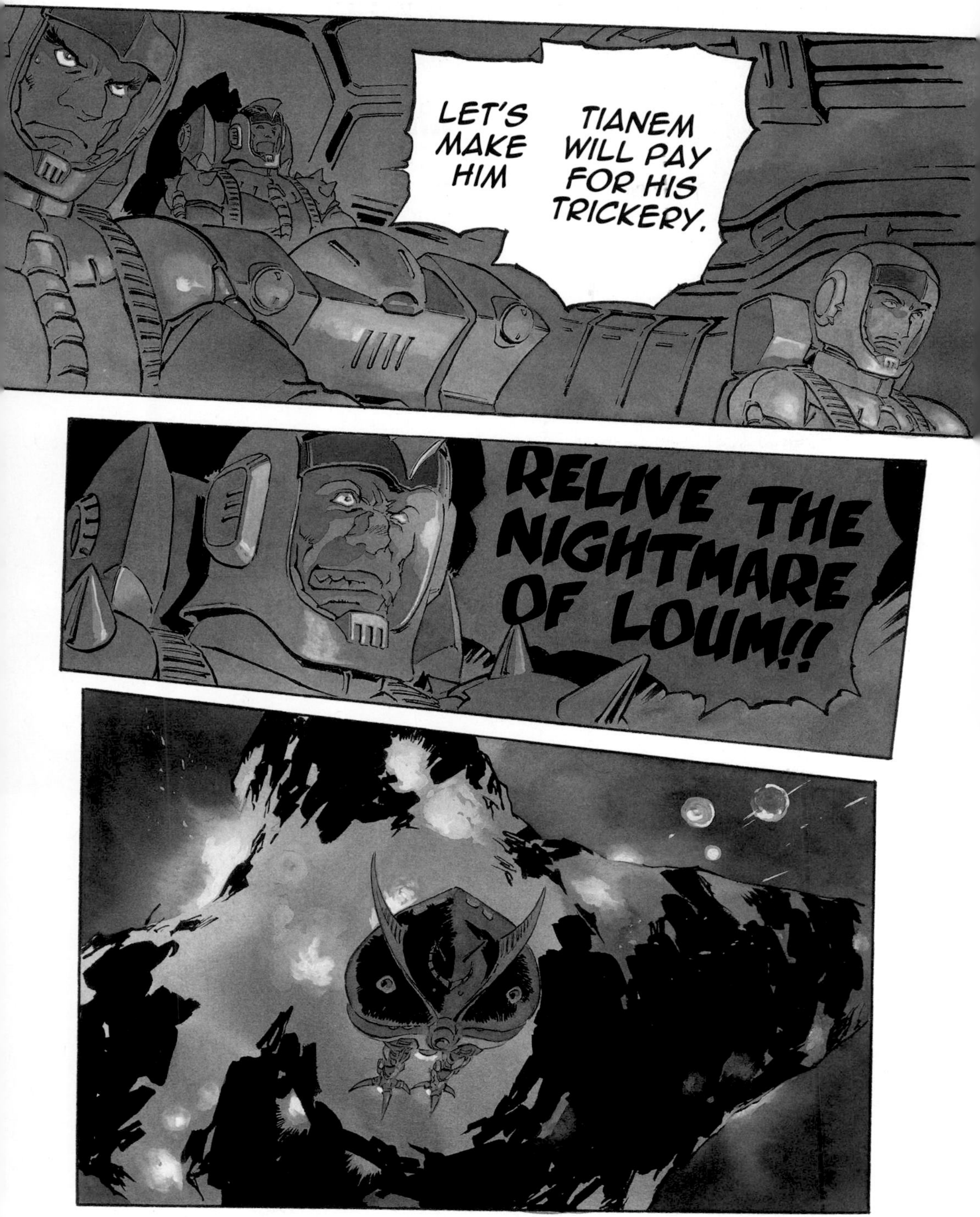
TIANEM WILL PAY FOR HIS TRICKERY.
LET'S MAKE HIM
RELIVE THE NIGHTMARE OF LOUM!!

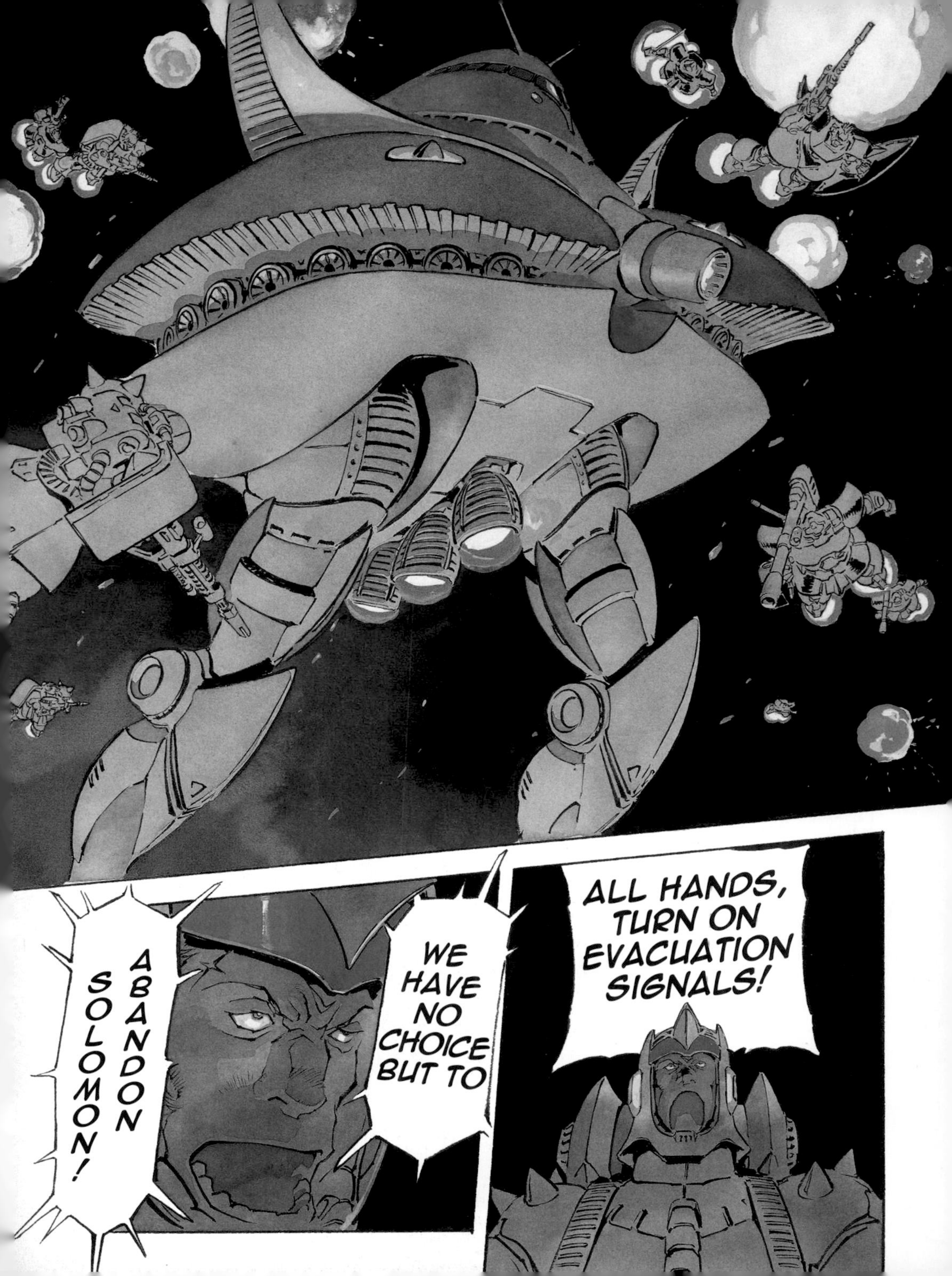
ALL HANDS, TURN ON EVACUATION SIGNALS!
WE HAVE NO CHOICE BUT TO
ABANDON SOLOMON!

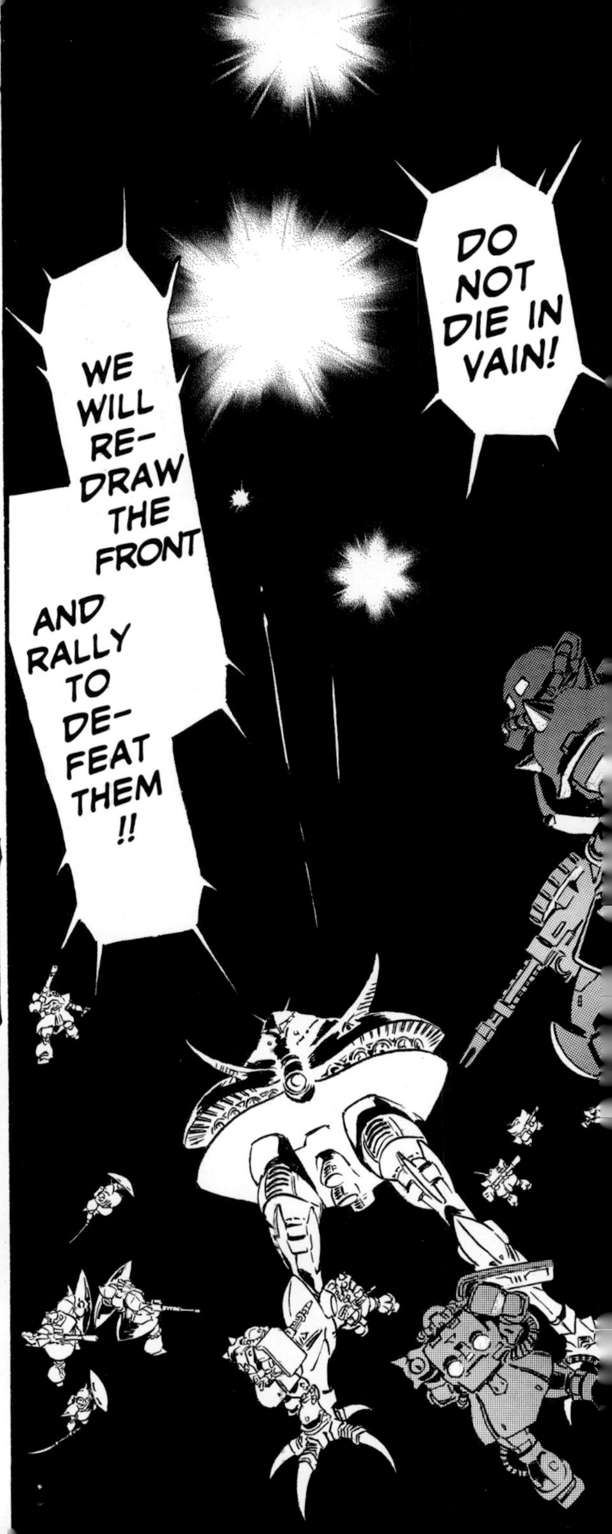
DO NOT DIE IN VAIN!
WE WILL RE-DRAW THE FRONT
AND RALLY TO DE-FEAT THEM!!

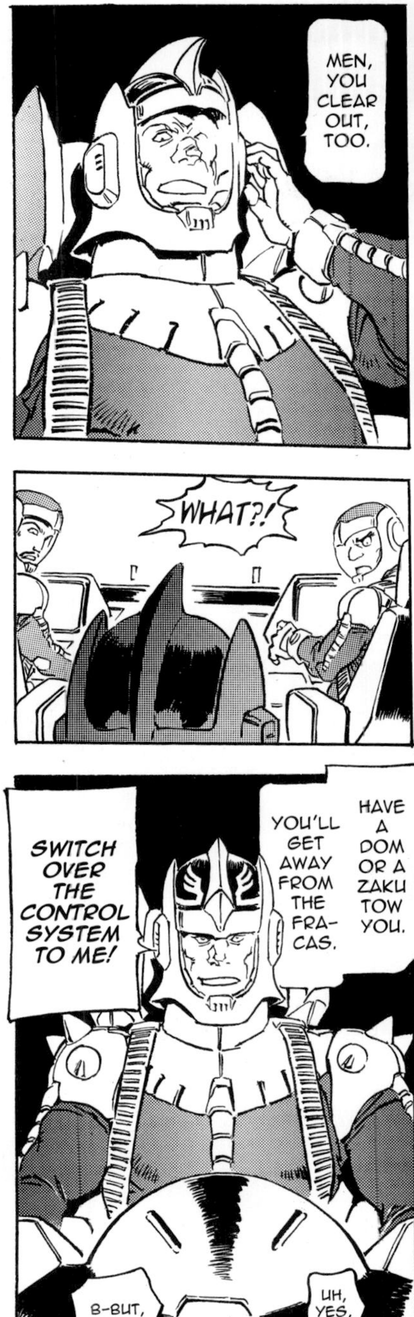
MEN, YOU CLEAR OUT, TOO.
WHAT?!
HAVE A DOM OR A ZAKU TOW YOU.
YOU'LL GET AWAY FROM THE FRA-CAS.
SWITCH OVER THE CONTROL SYSTEM TO ME!
UH, YES, SIR...
B-BUT, YOUR EXCEL-LENCY!

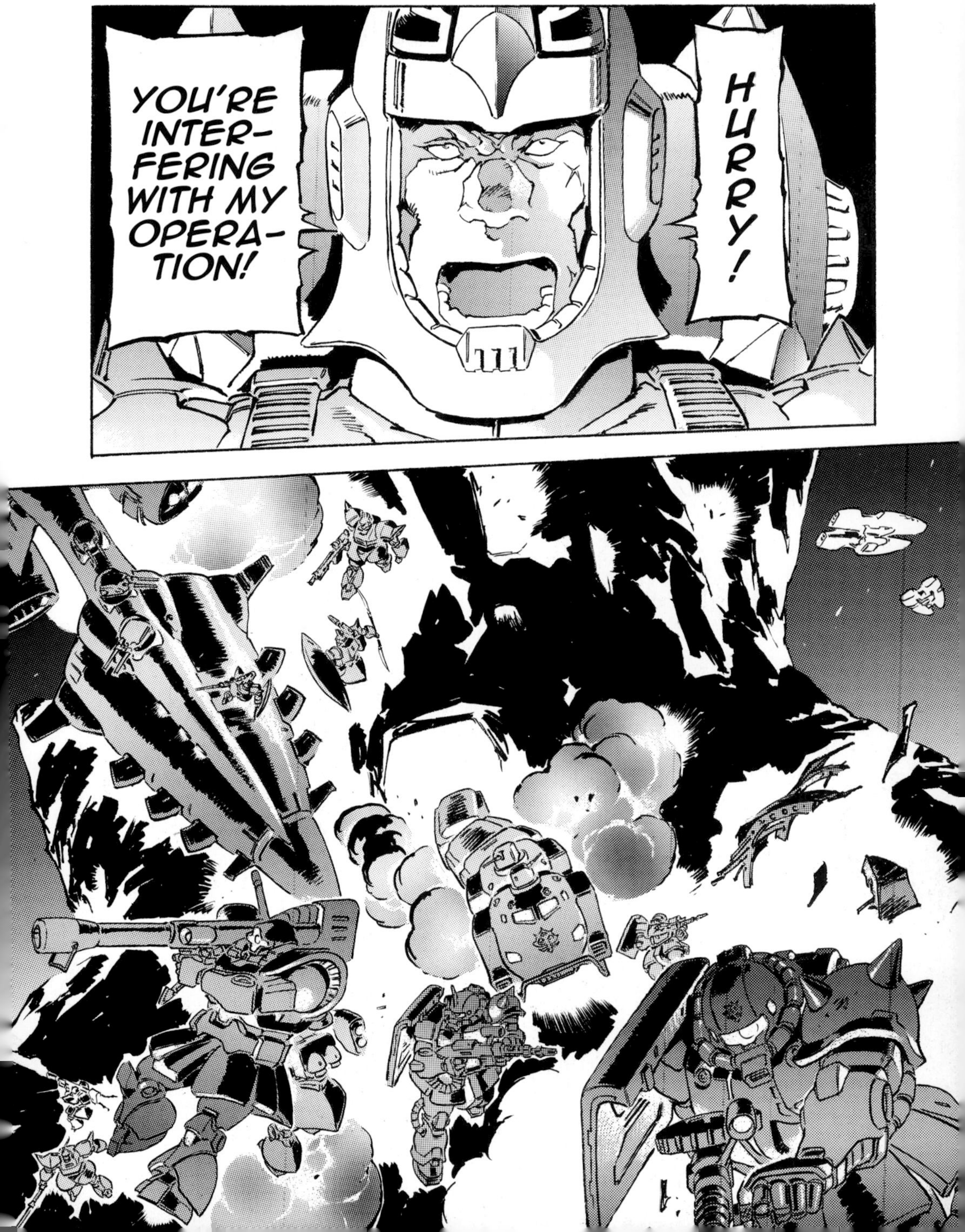
HURRY!
YOU'RE INTERFERING WITH MY OPERATION!

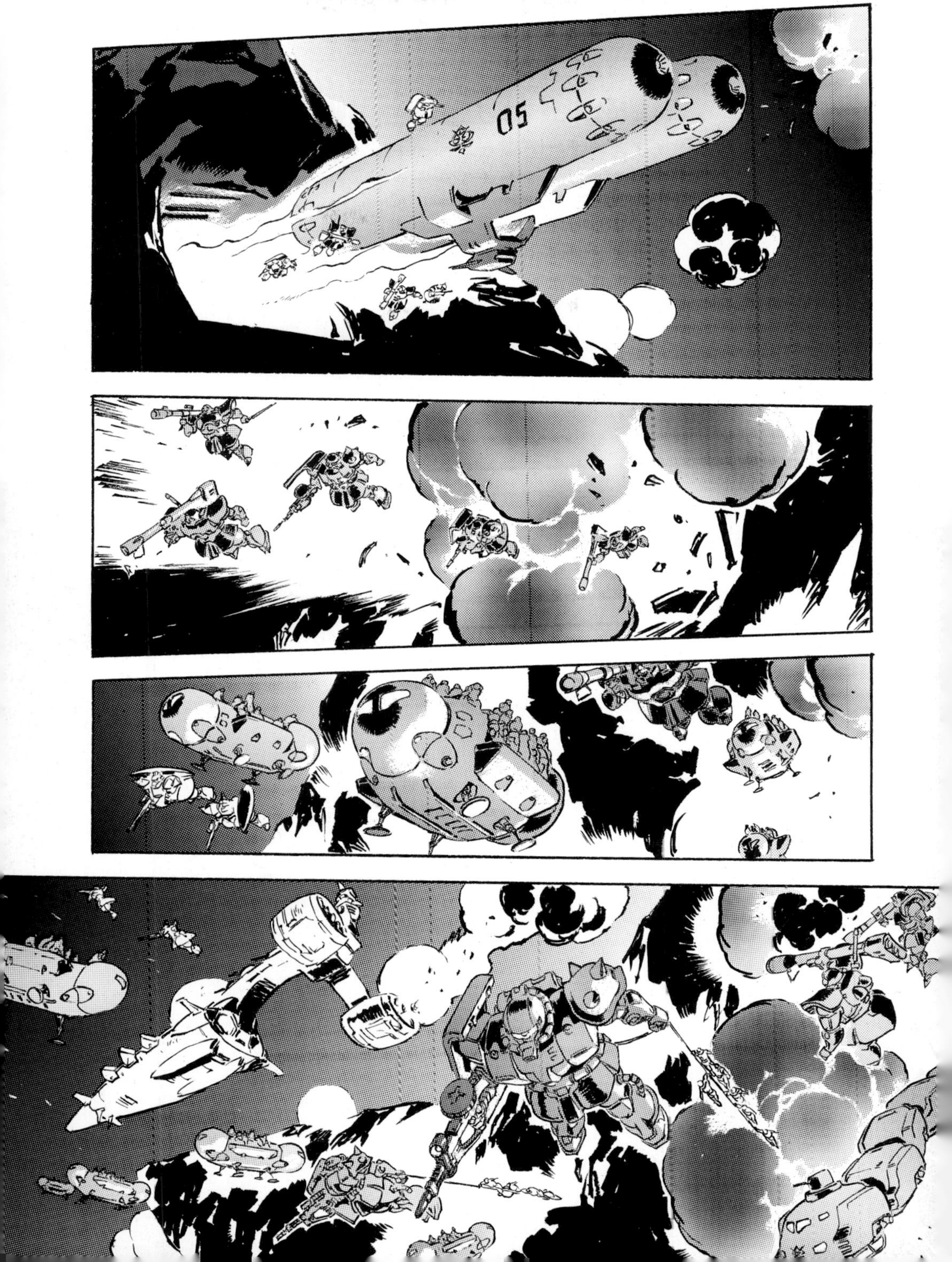

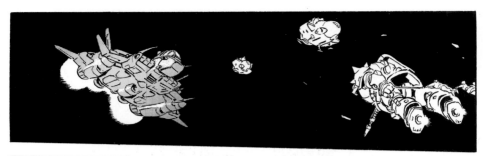

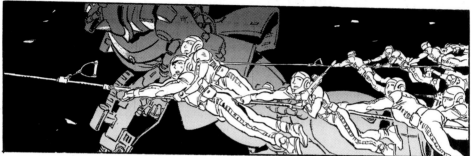

MY STYLE...

HEY, GOING AFTER YOU ISN'T QUITE

!!

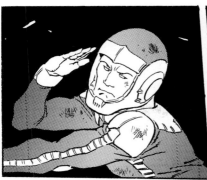
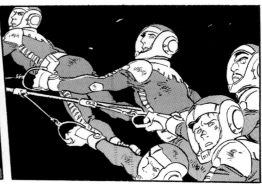

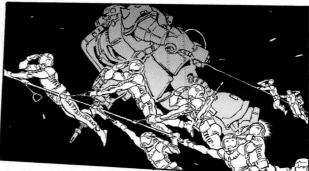
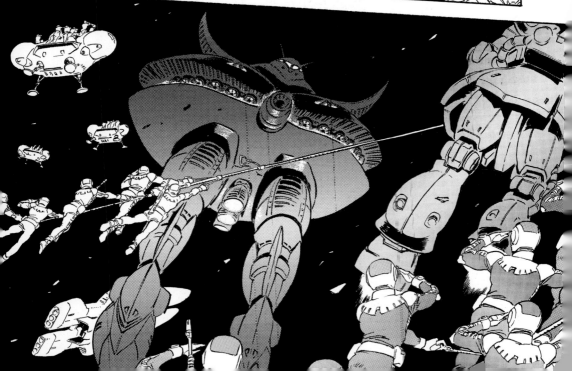

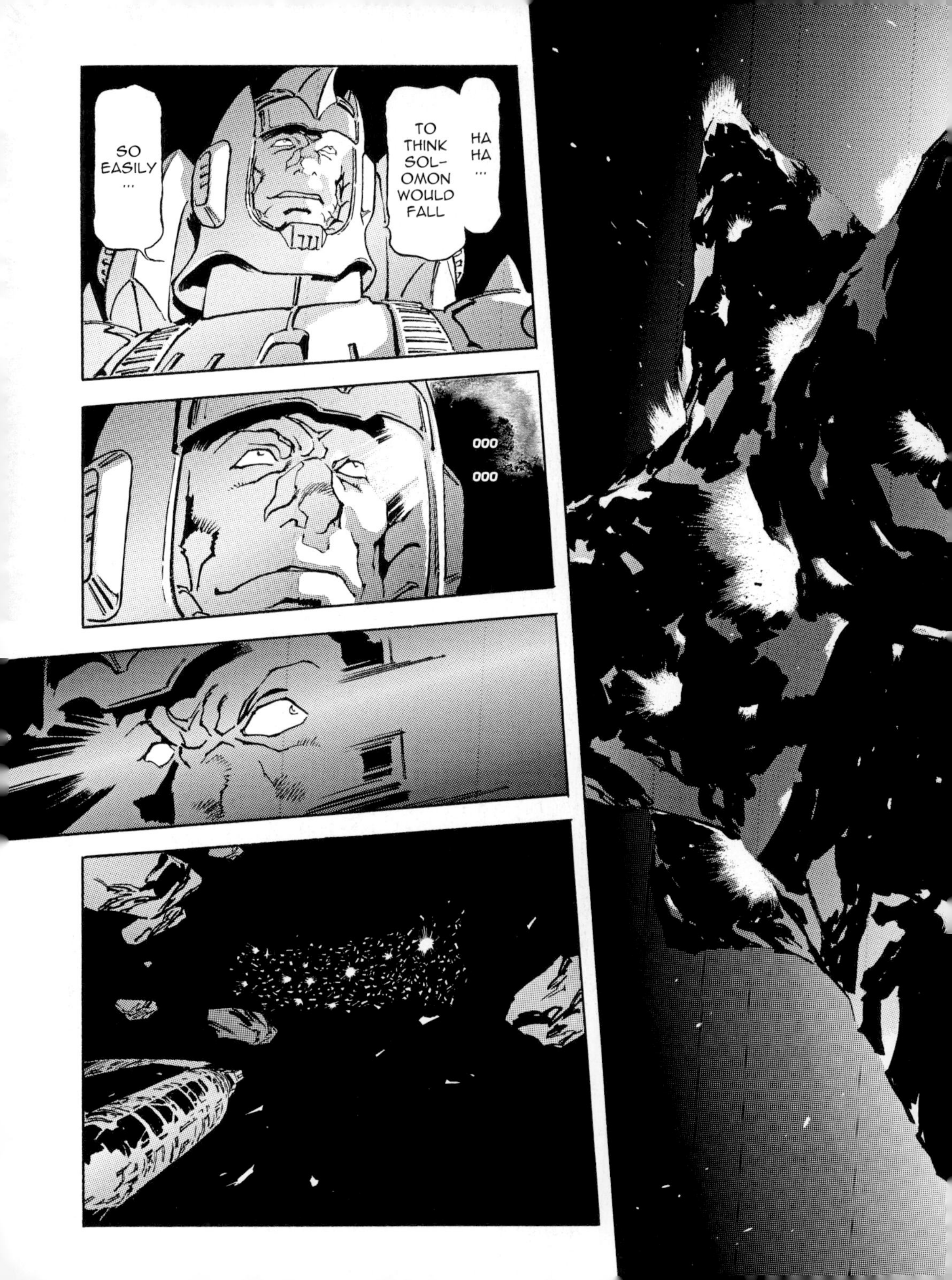
HA HA ...
TO THINK SOL-OMON WOULD FALL
SO EASILY ...
OOO
OOO

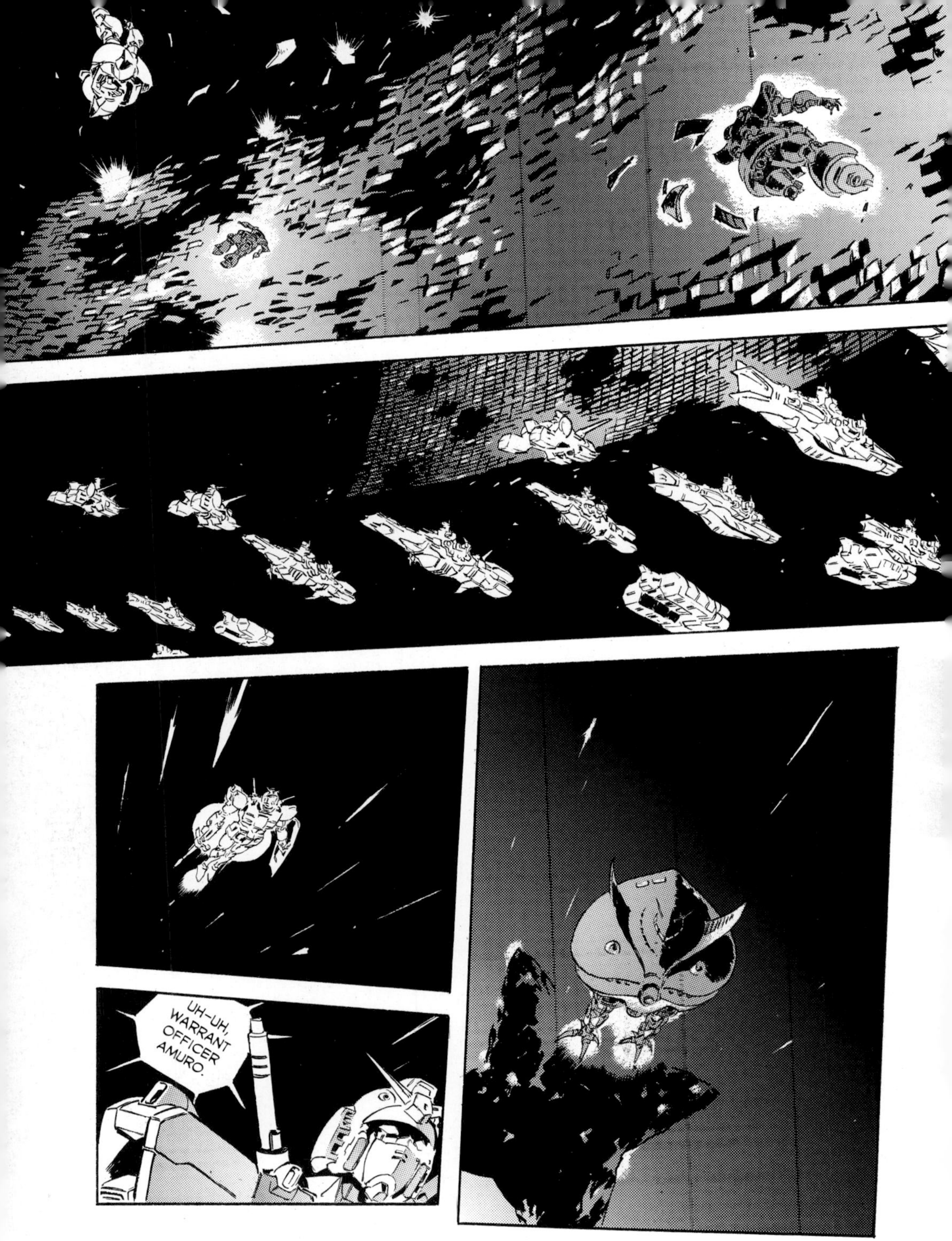
UH-UH, WARRANT OFFICER AMURO.

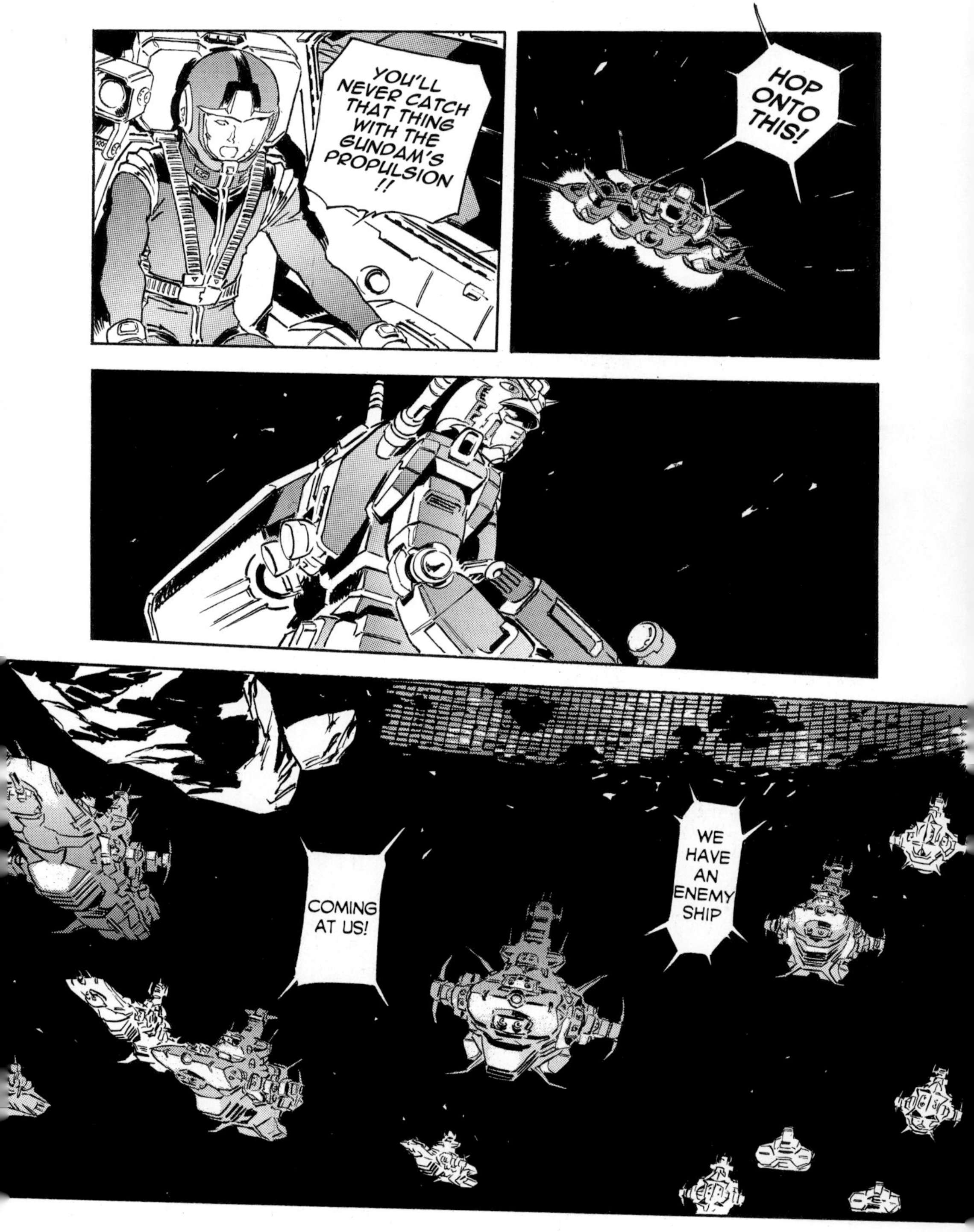
HOP ONTO THIS!
YOU'LL NEVER CATCH THAT THING WITH THE GUNDAM'S PROPULSION!!
WE HAVE AN ENEMY SHIP
COMING AT US!

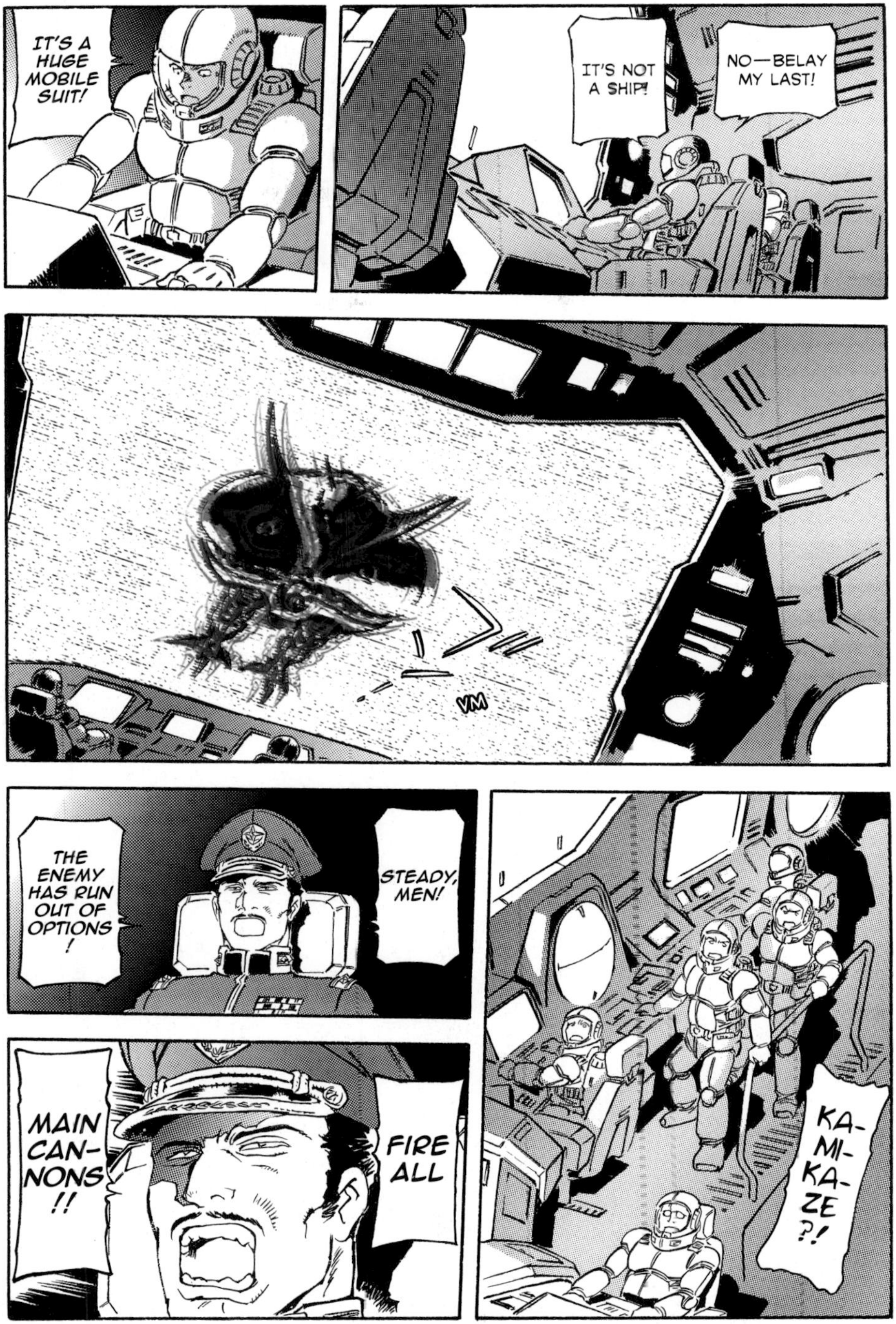
NO—BELAY MY LAST!
IT'S NOT A SHIP!
IT'S A HUGE MOBILE SUIT!
VM
KA-MI-KA-ZE?!
STEADY, MEN!
THE ENEMY HAS RUN OUT OF OPTIONS!
FIRE ALL
MAIN CAN-NONS!!

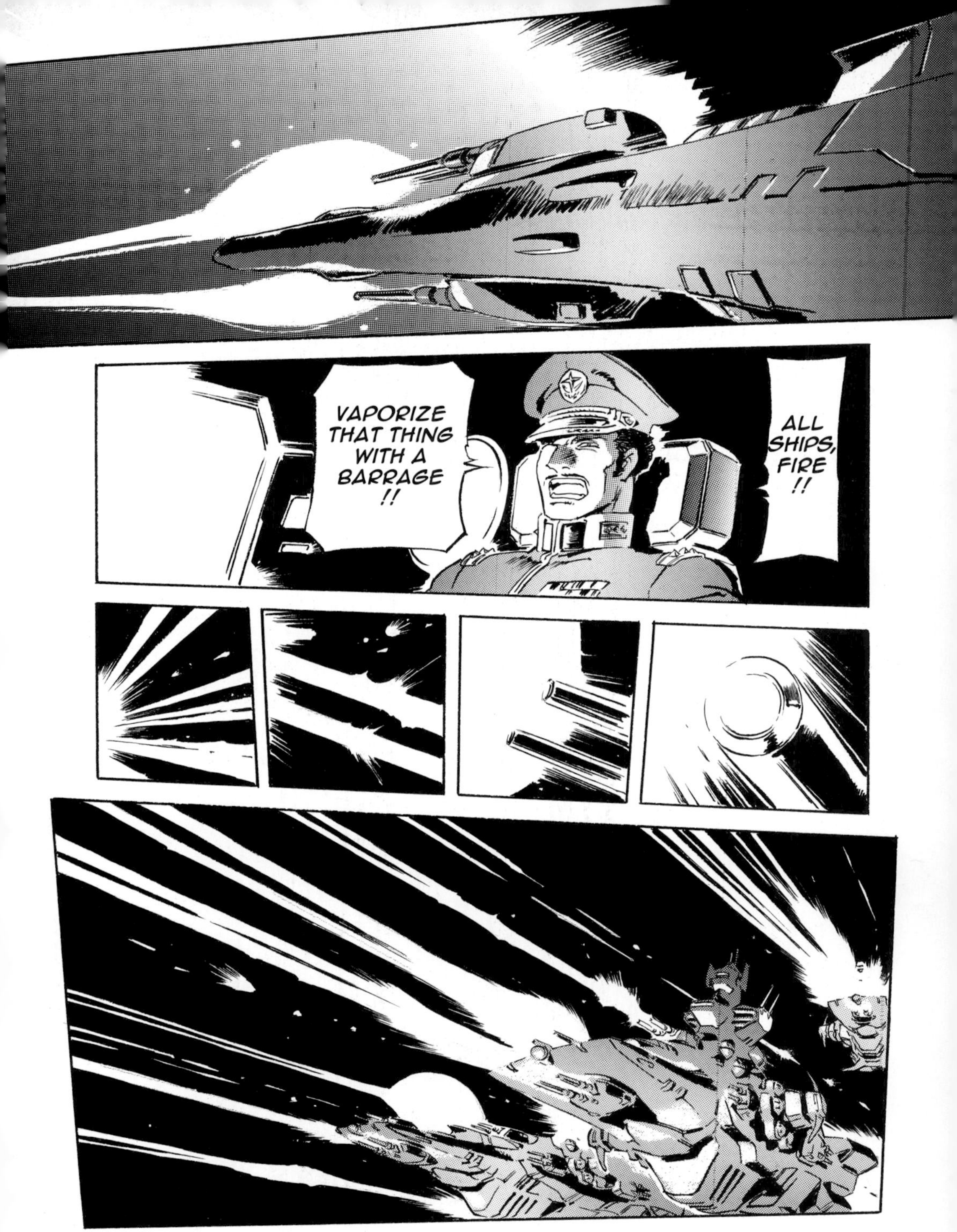
ALL SHIPS, FIRE !!
VAPORIZE THAT THING WITH A BARRAGE !!

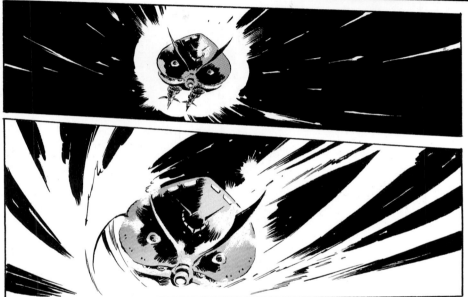

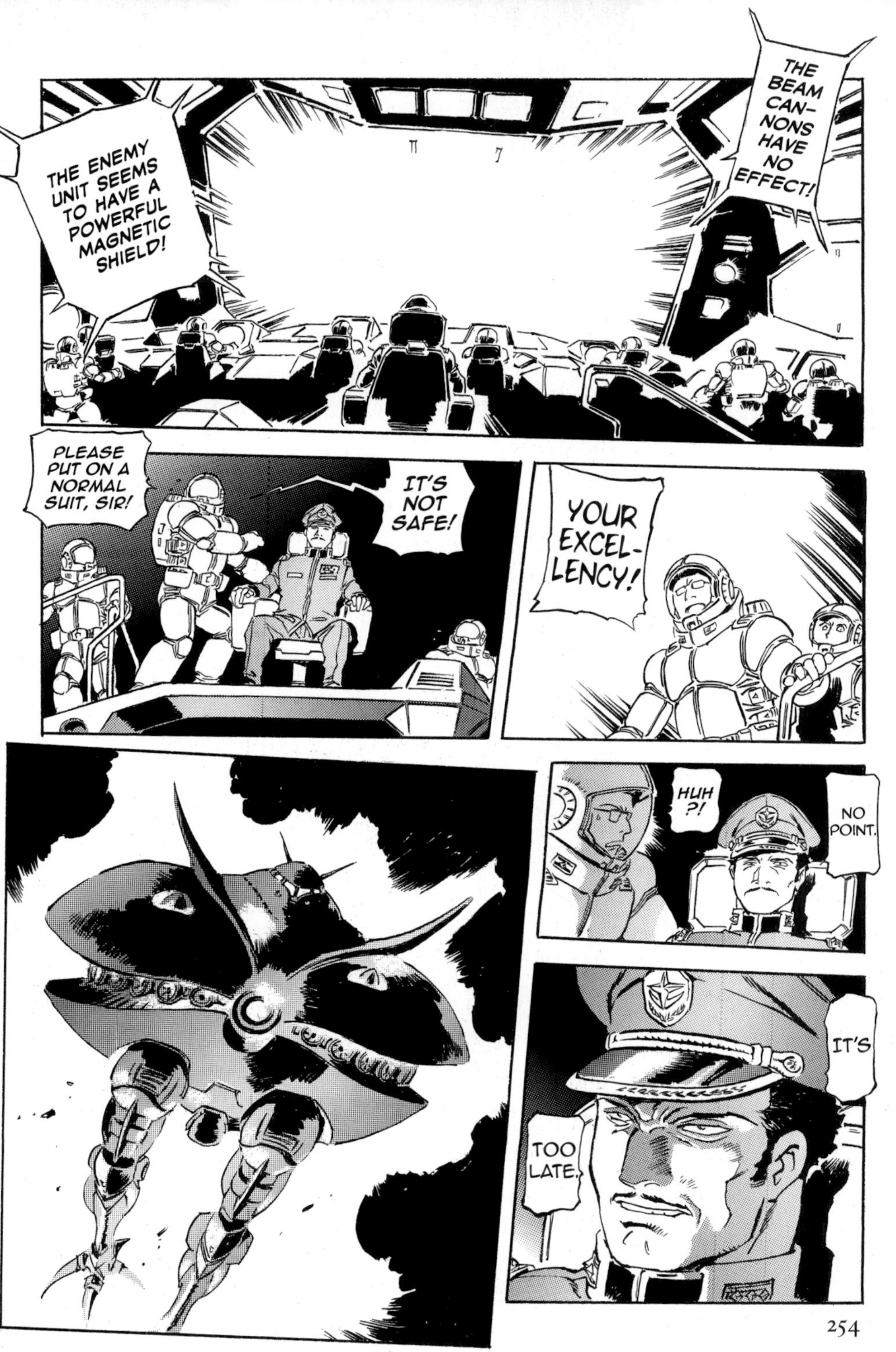
THE BEAM CAN-NONS HAVE NO EFFECT!
THE ENEMY UNIT SEEMS TO HAVE A POWERFUL MAGNETIC SHIELD!
YOUR EXCEL-LENCY!
IT'S NOT SAFE!
PLEASE PUT ON A NORMAL SUIT, SIR!
HUH ?!
NO POINT.
IT'S
TOO LATE.

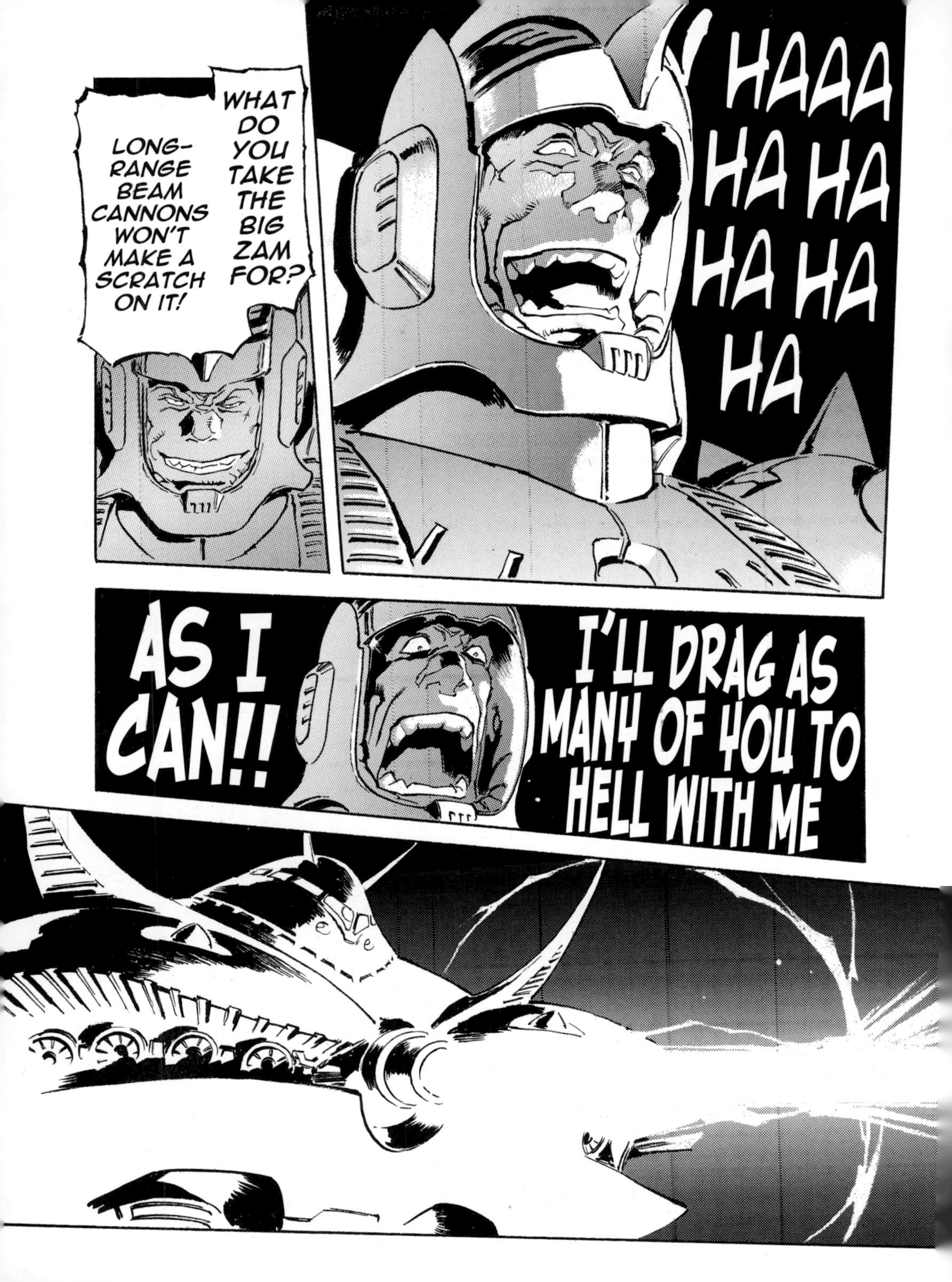
HAAA HA HA HA HA HA
WHAT DO YOU TAKE THE BIG ZAM FOR?
LONG-RANGE BEAM CANNONS WON'T MAKE A SCRATCH ON IT!
I'LL DRAG AS MANY OF YOU TO HELL WITH ME
AS I CAN!!

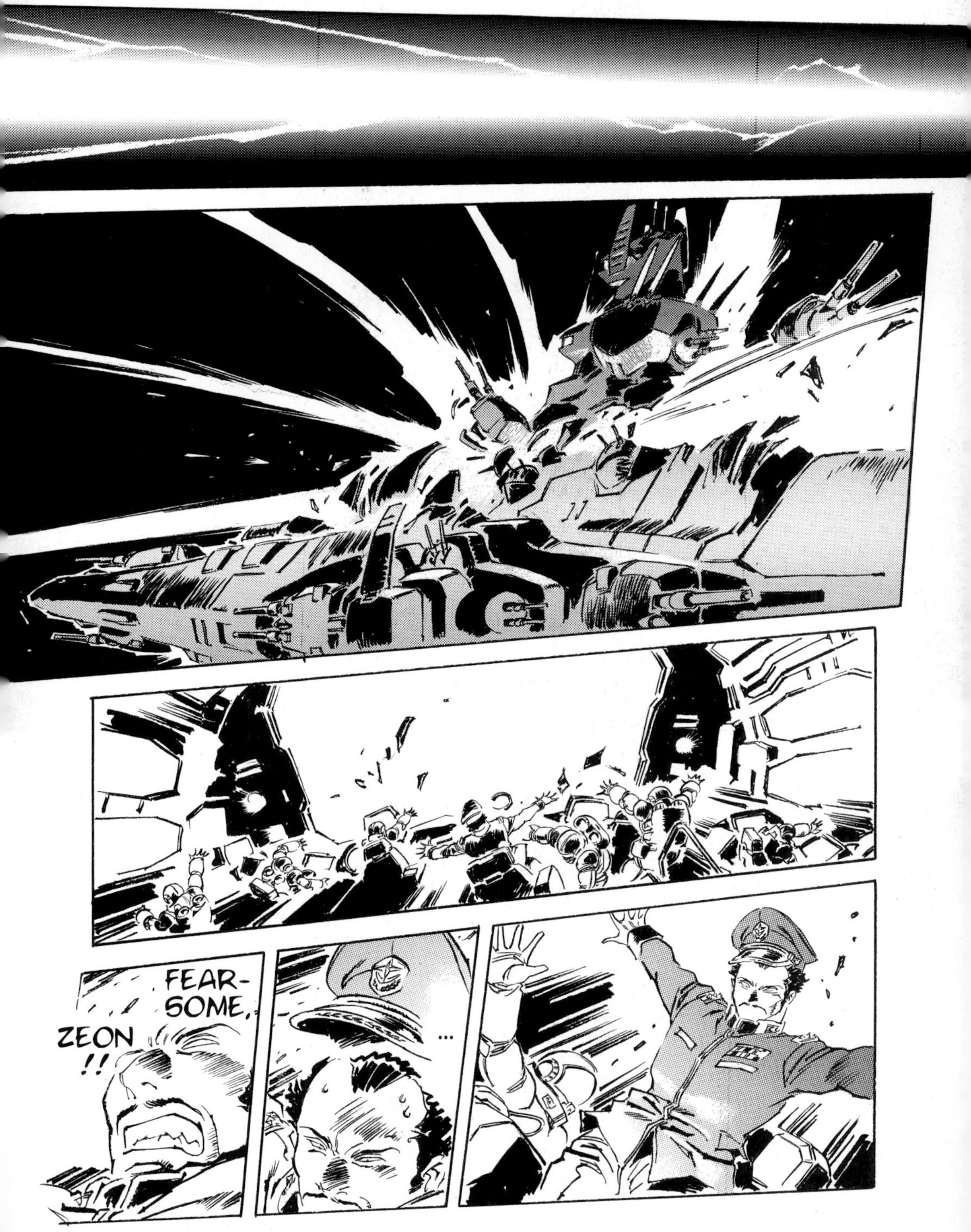
...
FEAR-
SOME,
ZEON
!!

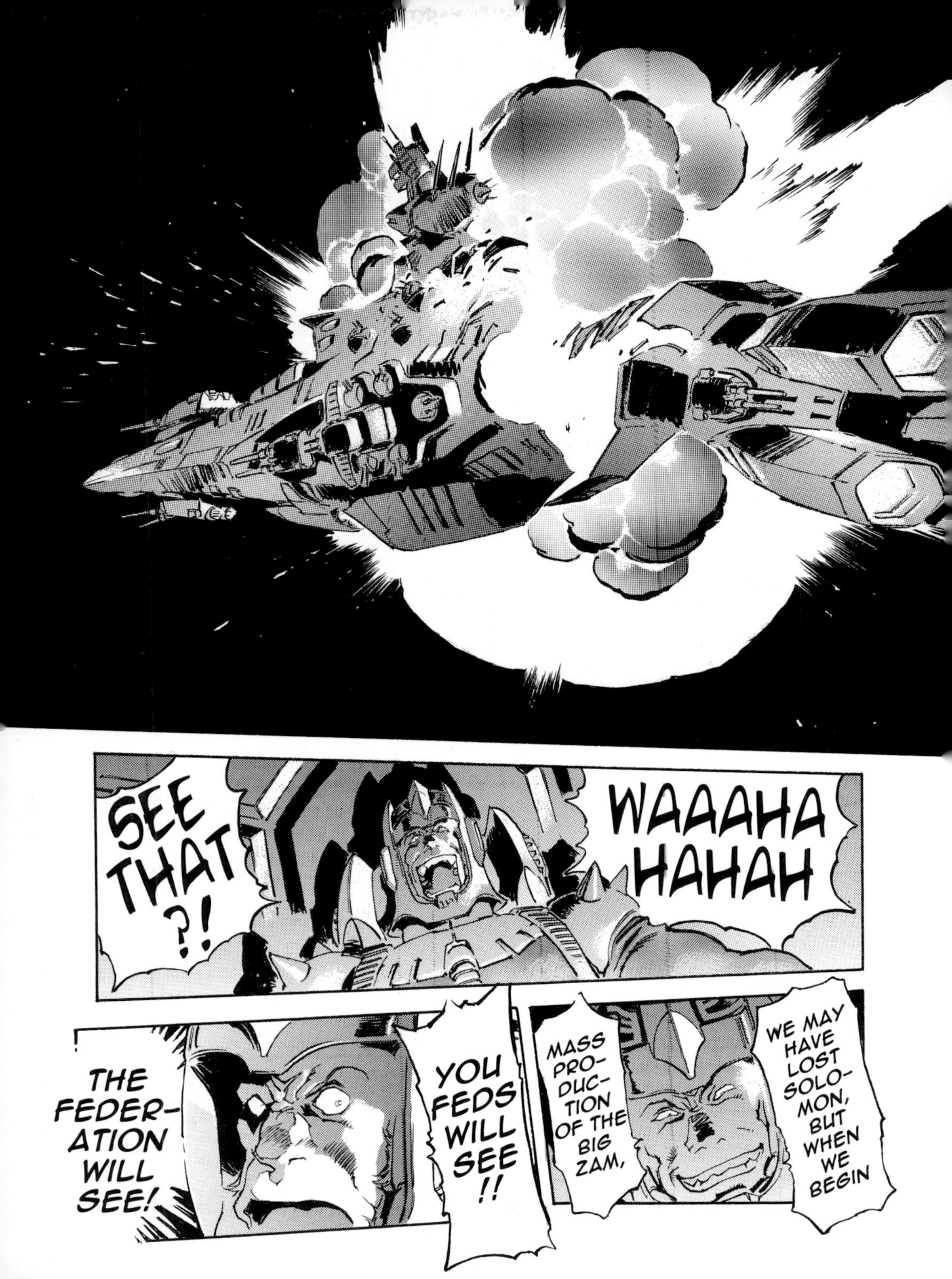
WAAAHA HAHAH
SEE THAT ?!
WE MAY HAVE LOST SOLOMON, BUT WHEN WE BEGIN
MASS PRODUCTION OF THE BIG ZAM,
YOU FEDS WILL SEE !!
THE FEDERATION WILL SEE!

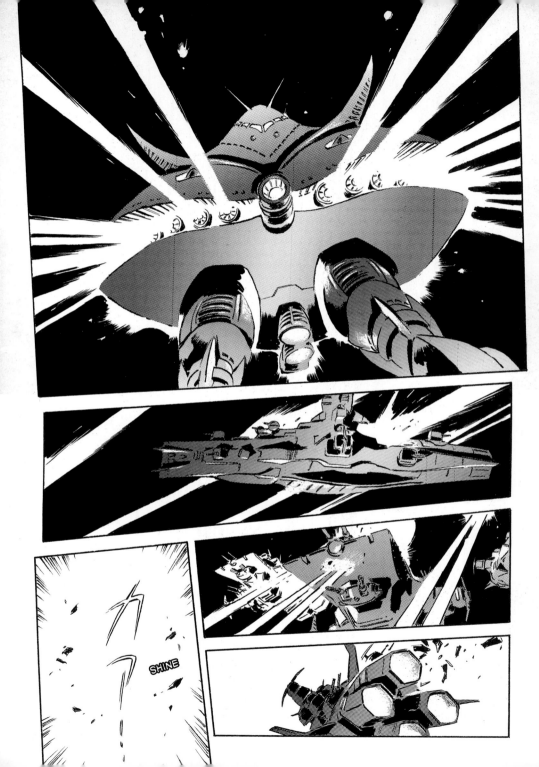

SHINE

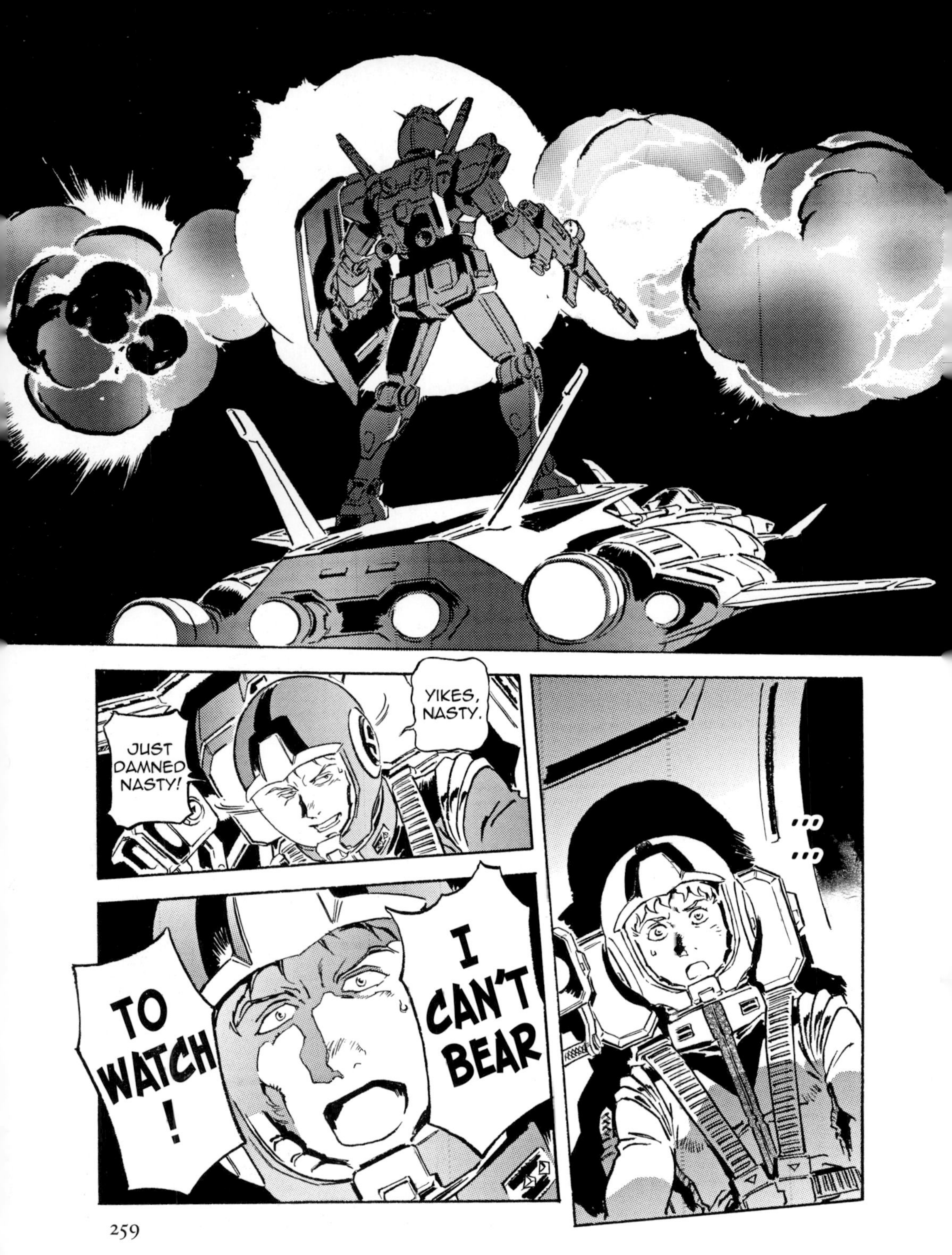

...
...
YIKES, NASTY.
JUST DAMNED NASTY!
I CAN'T BEAR TO WATCH!

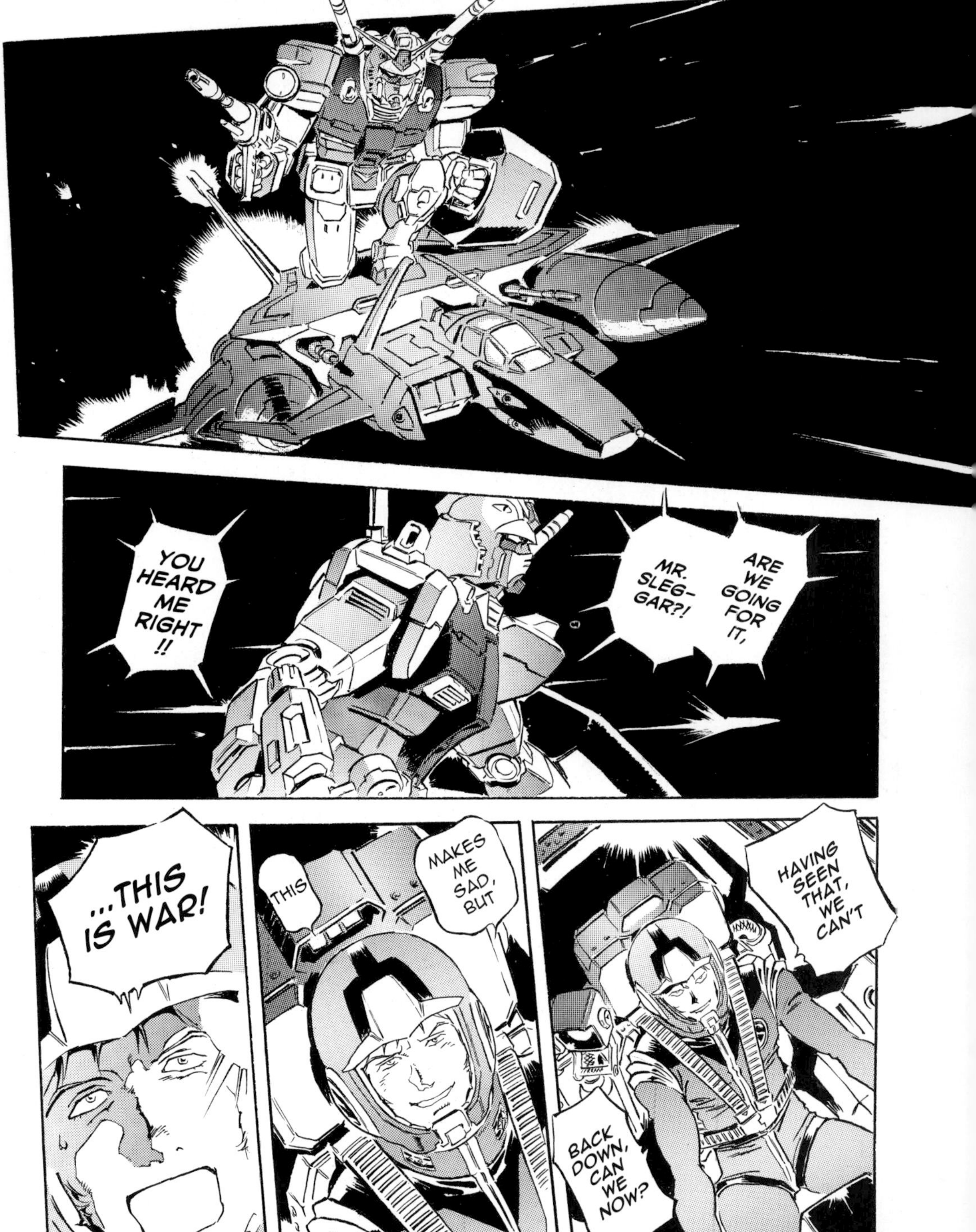
ARE WE GOING FOR IT,
MR. SLEG-GAR?!
YOU HEARD ME RIGHT!!
HAVING SEEN THAT, WE CAN'T
BACK DOWN, CAN WE NOW?
MAKES ME SAD, BUT
THIS
...THIS IS WAR!

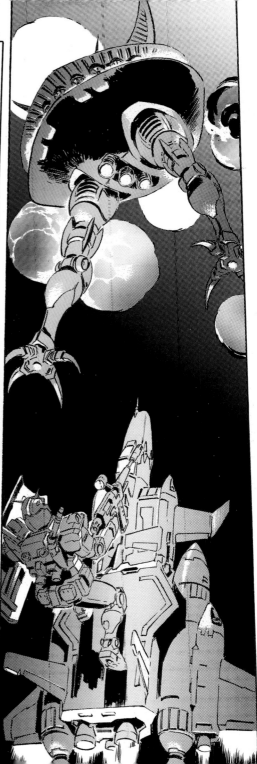

HEY, GUN-DAM!

YOU TAKE CARE

OF THE REST !!

IF THAT THING HAS A BEAM BARRIER...

OH, RIGHT!

WE CAN ATTACK ITS BLIND SPOT!

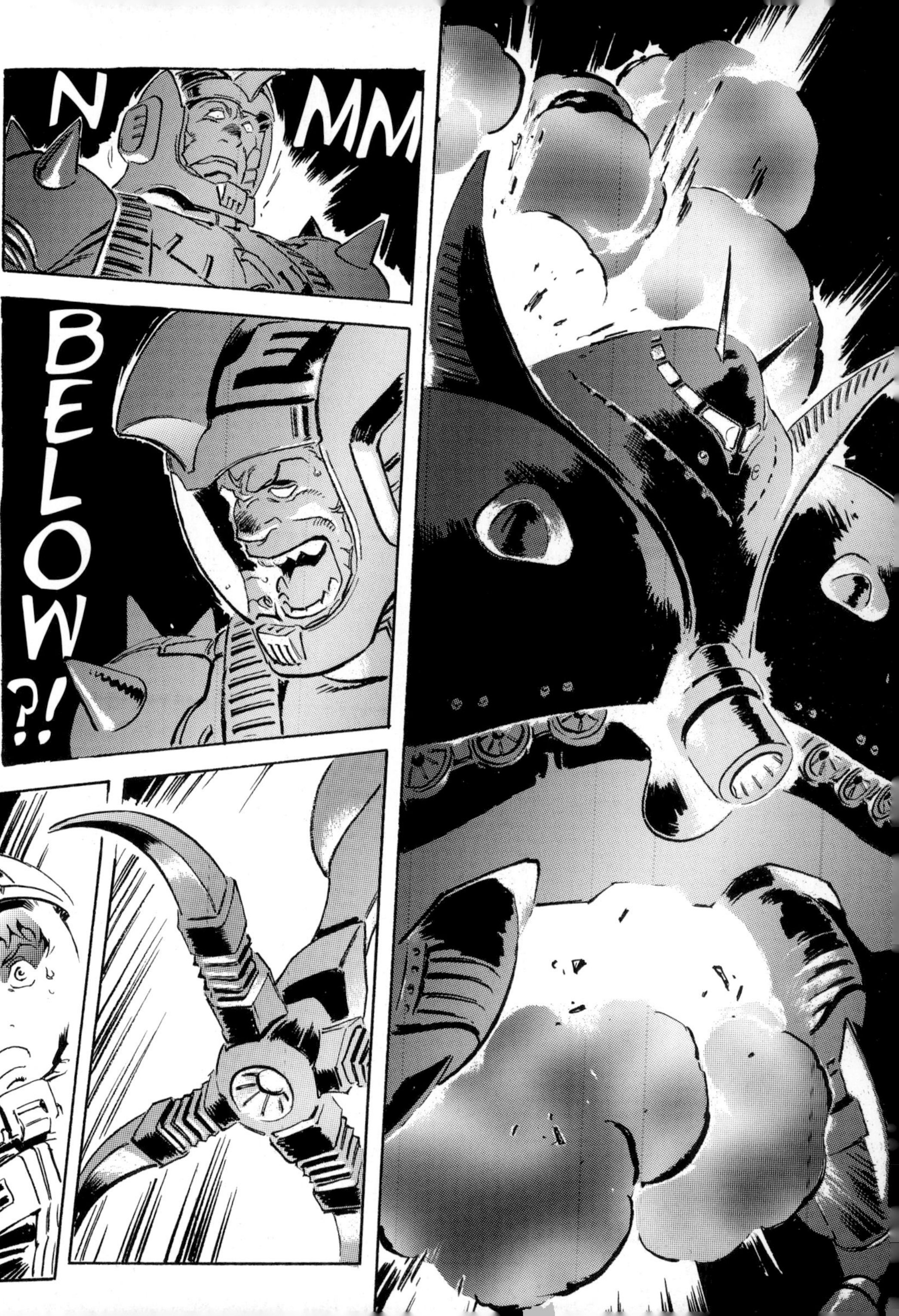
N MM
BELOW?!

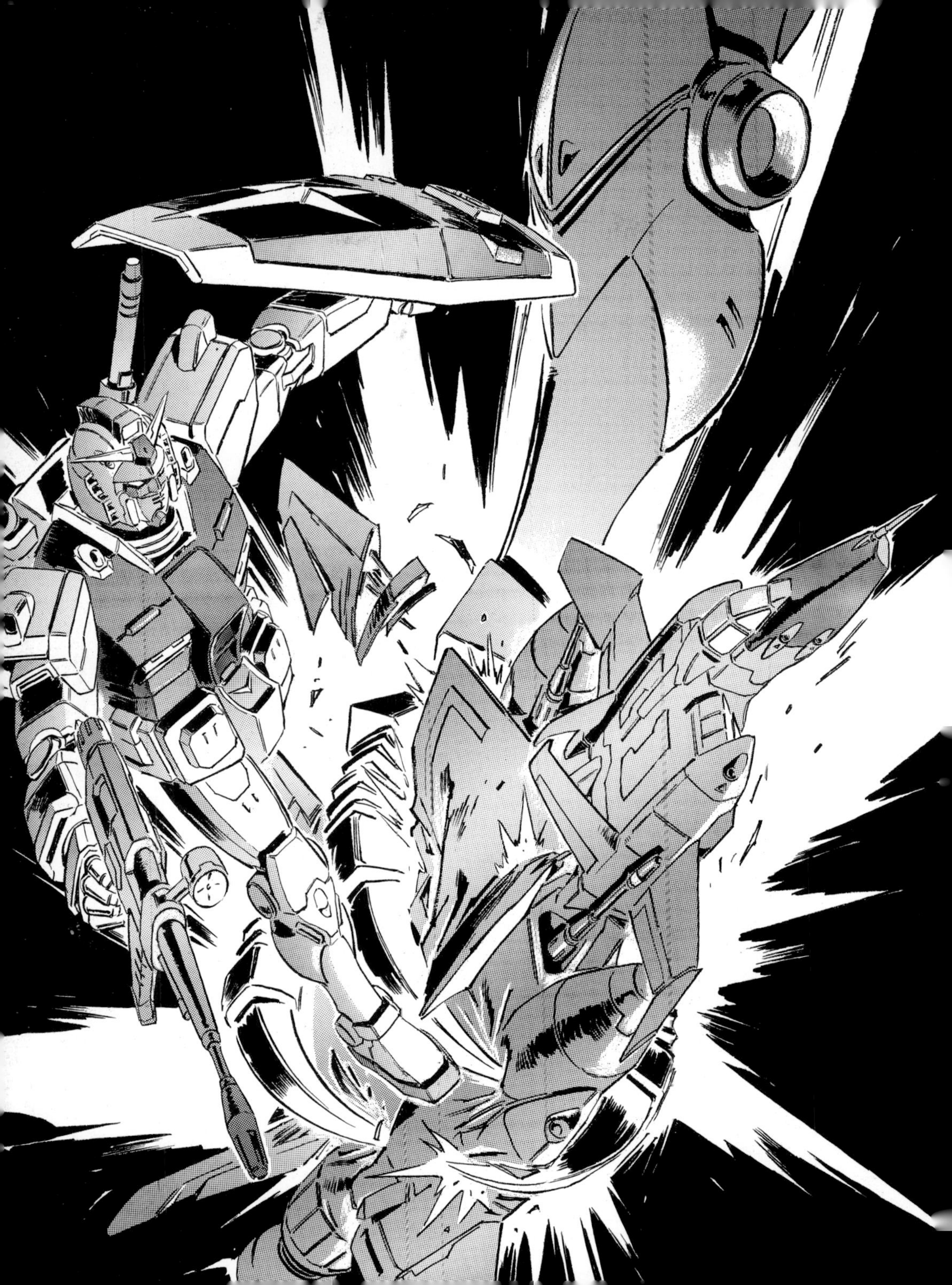

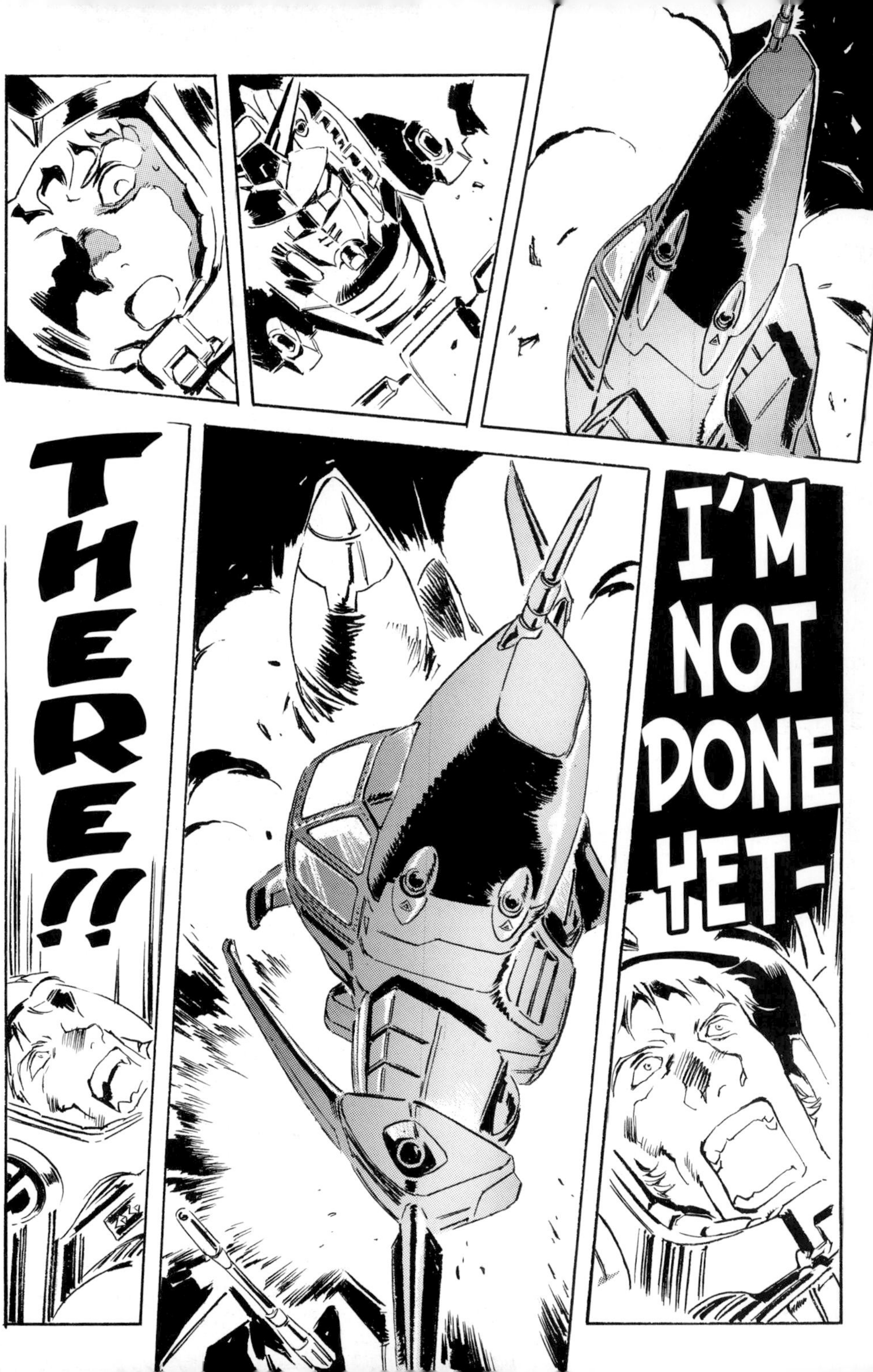
I'M NOT DONE YET-
THERE!!

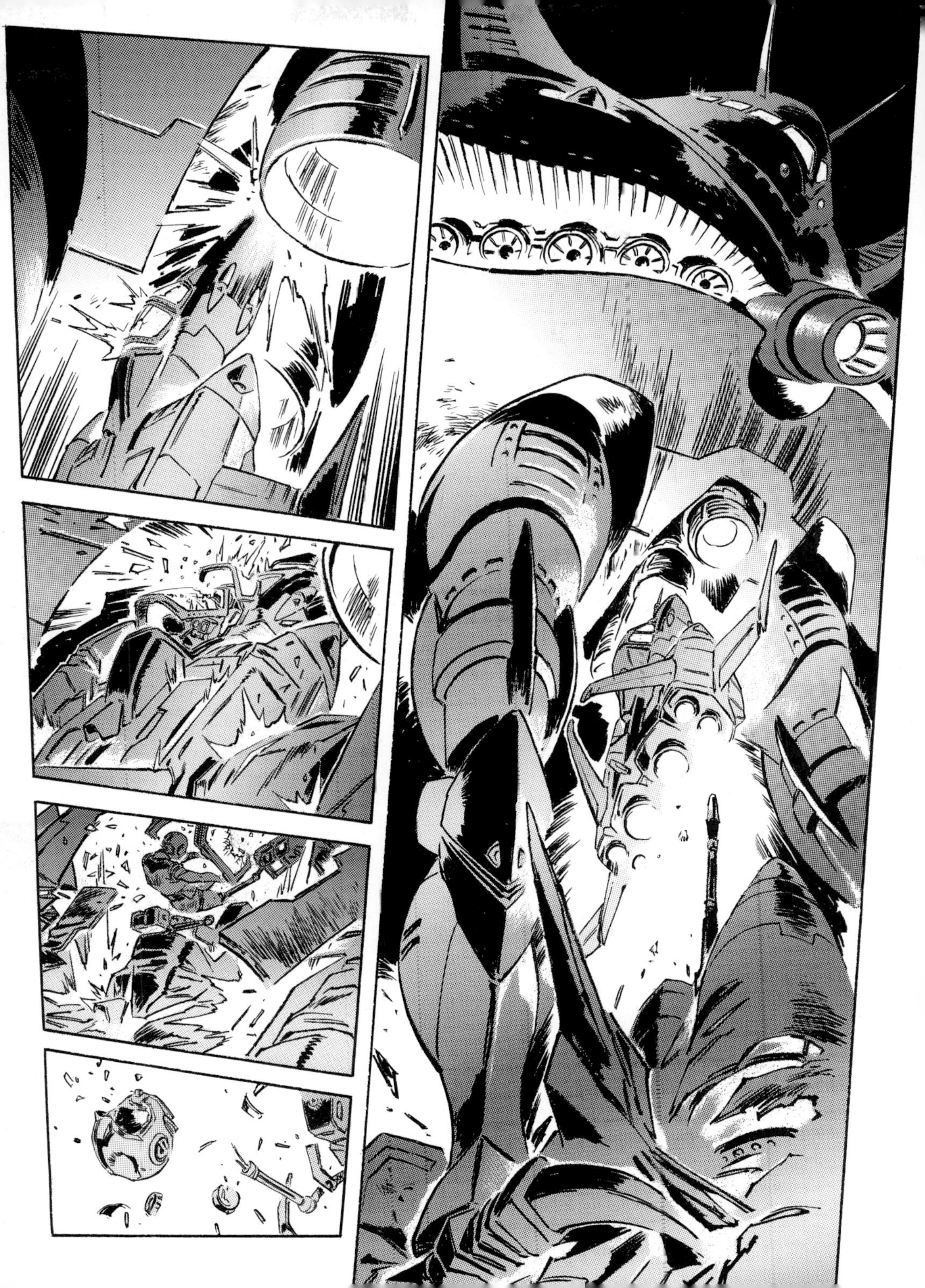

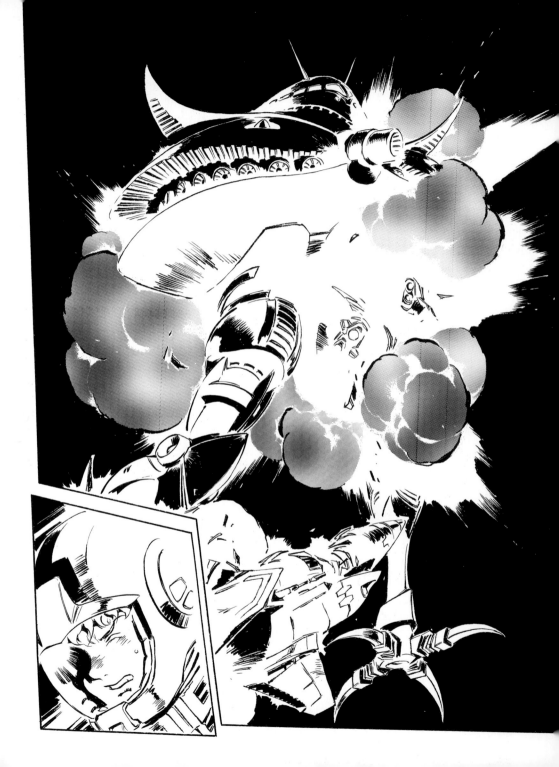

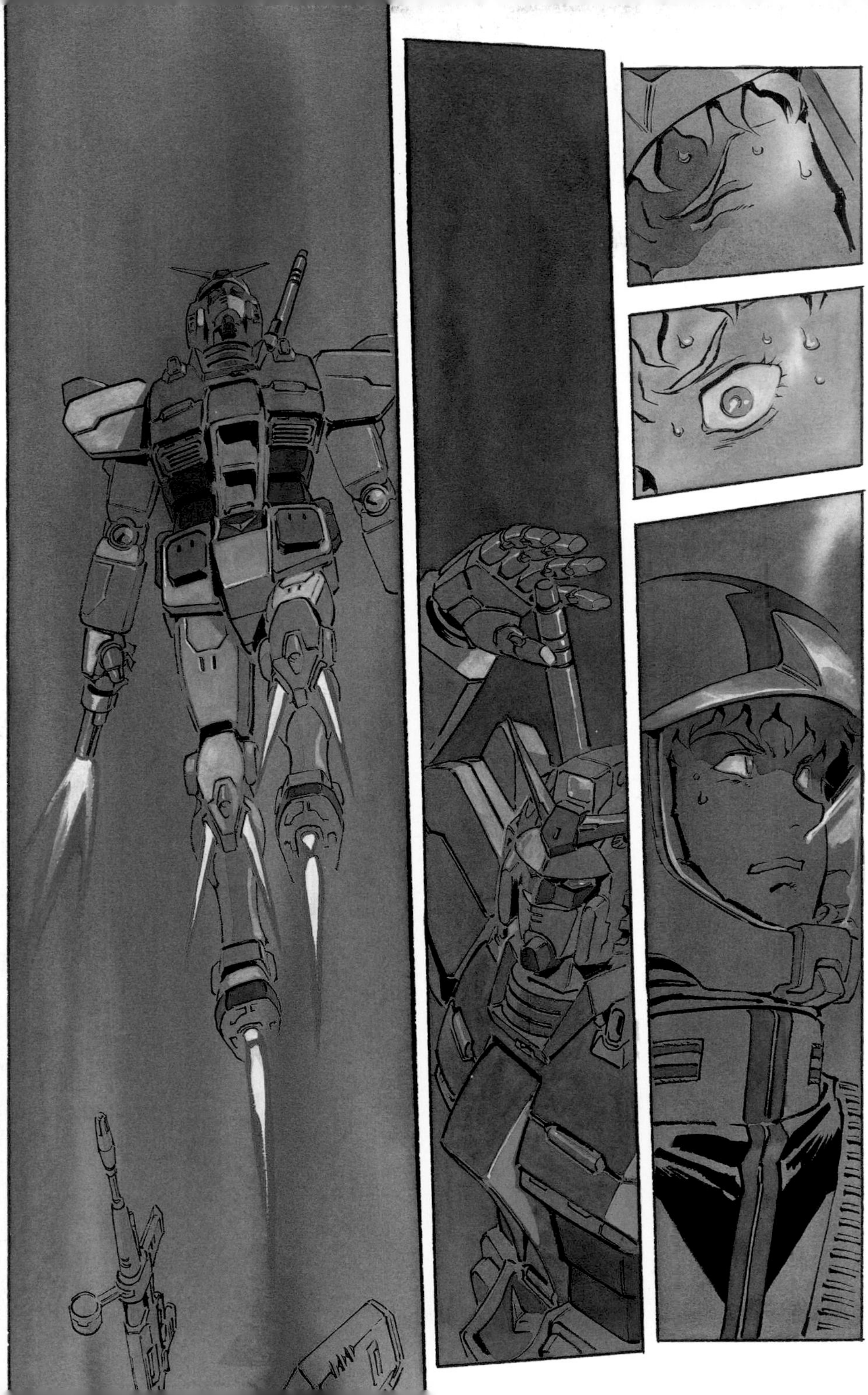

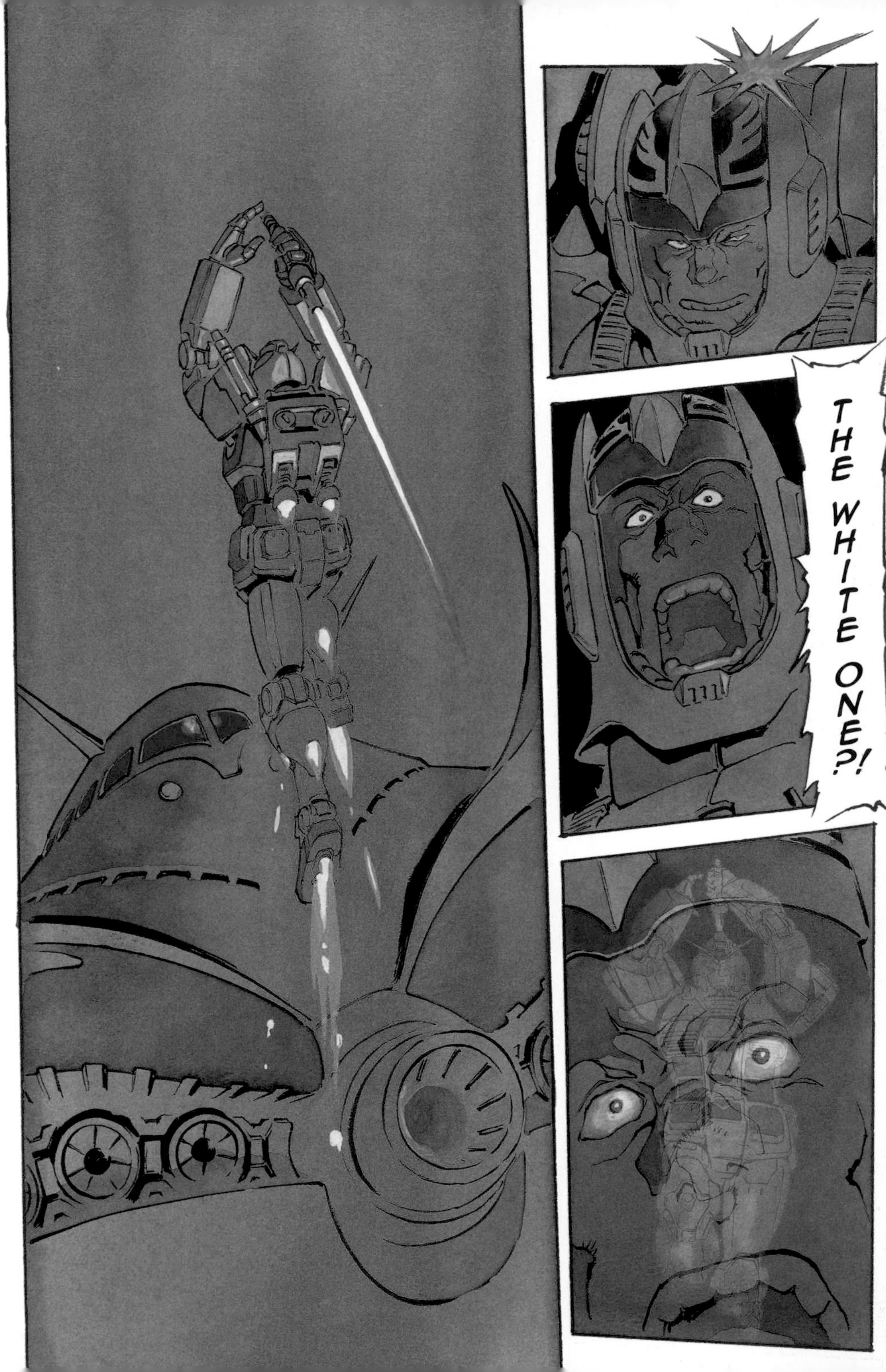
THE WHITE ONE?!

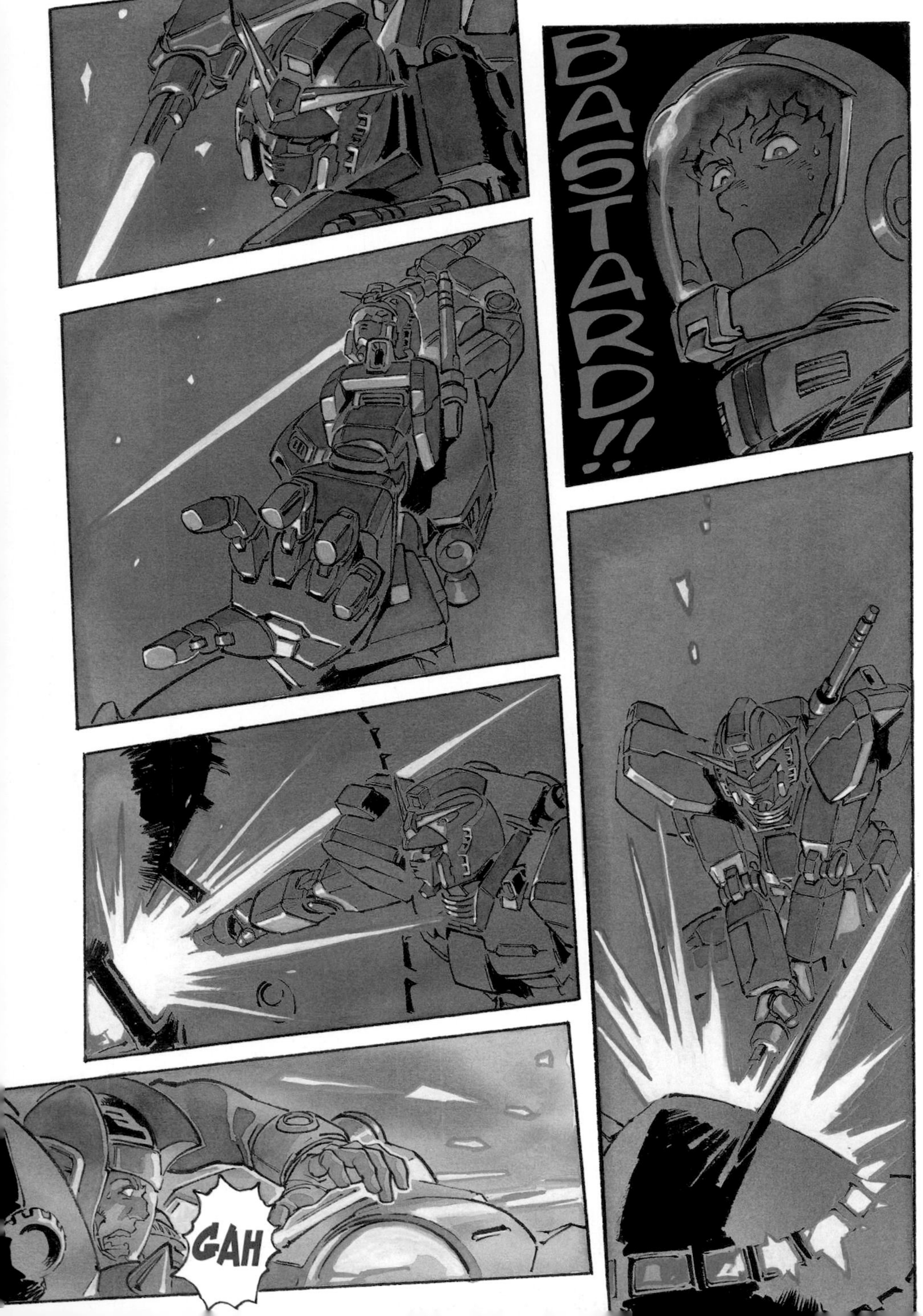
BASTARD!!
GAH

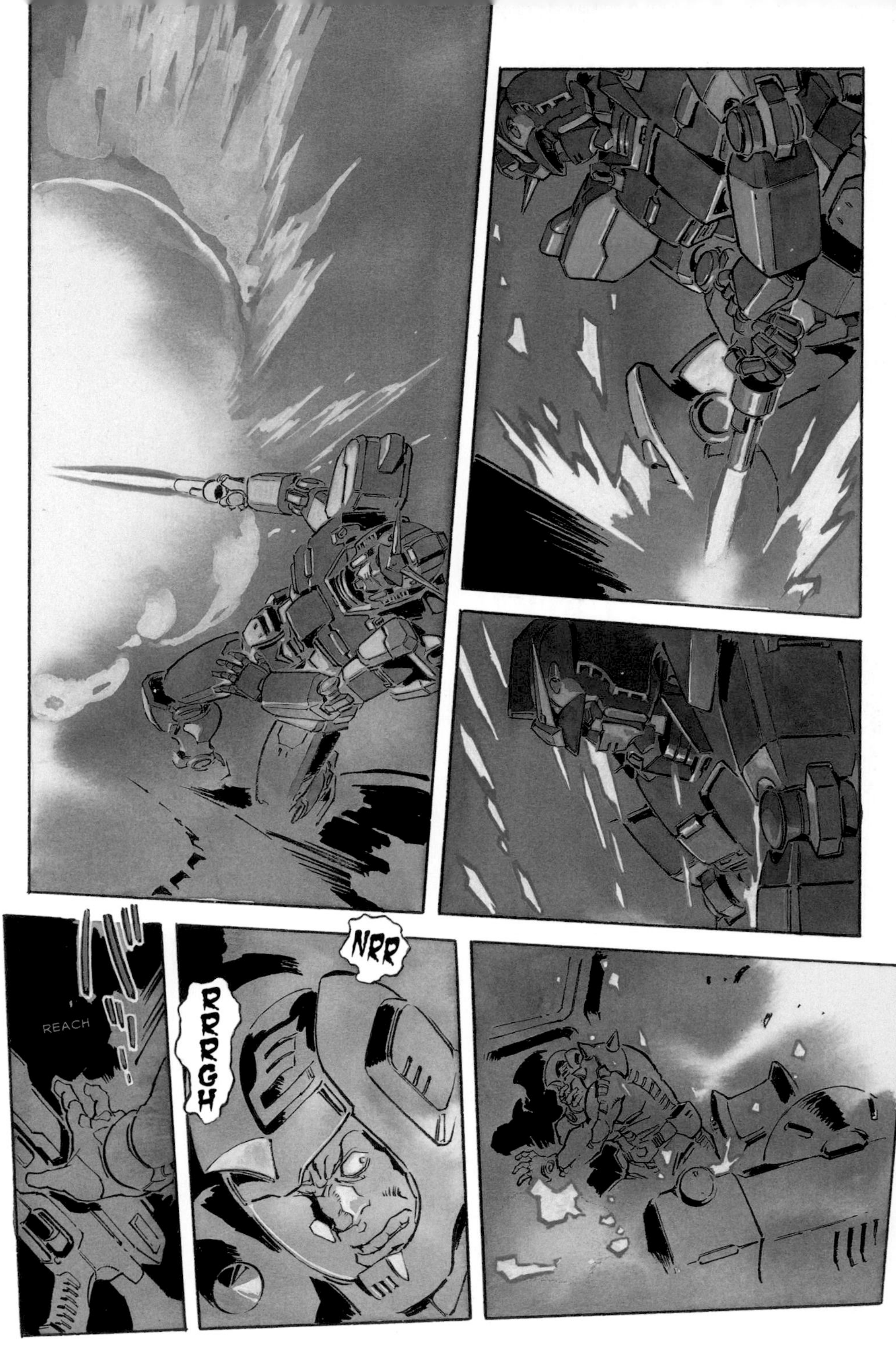
NRR
RRRGH
REACH

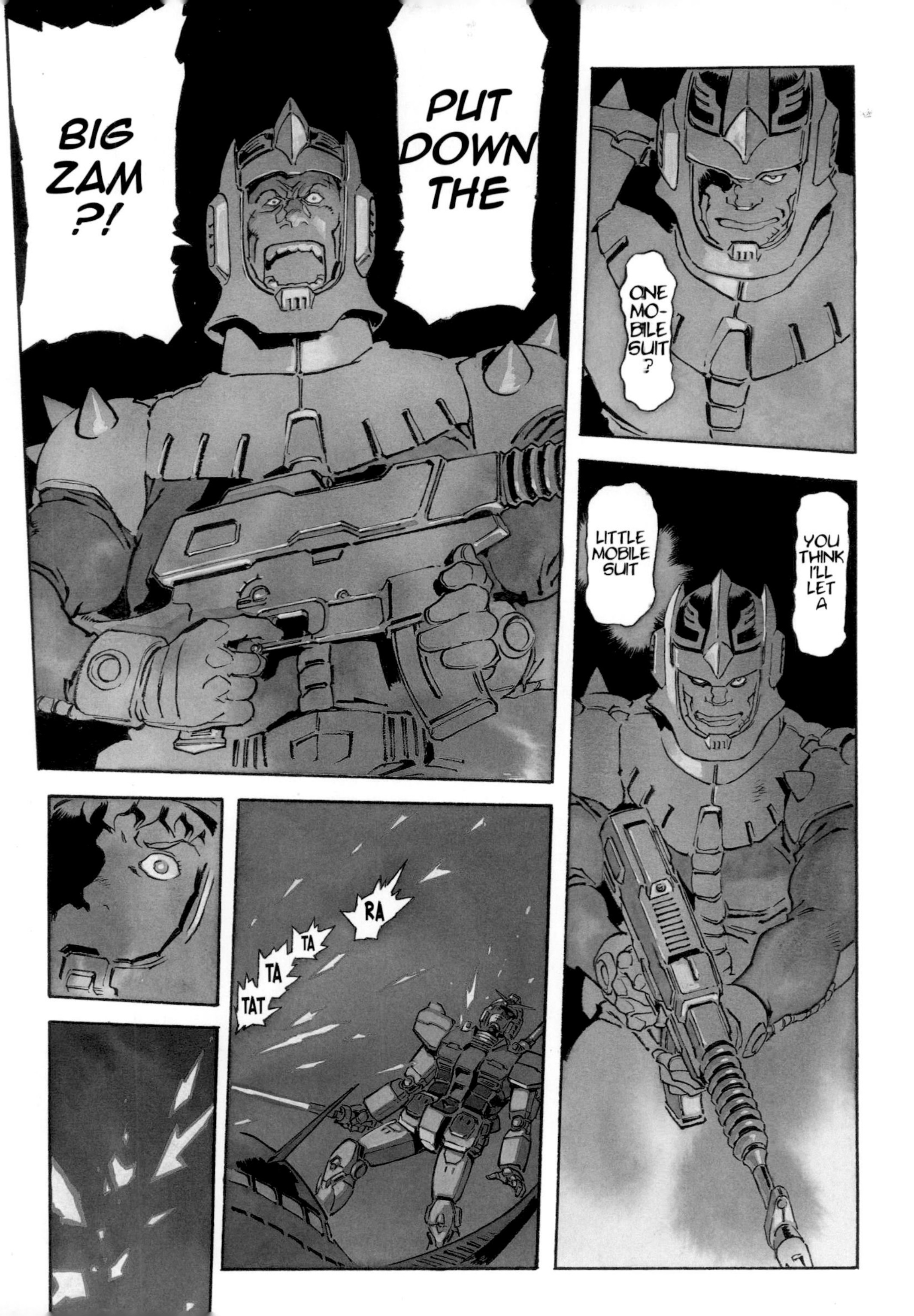
ONE MOBILE SUIT?
PUT DOWN THE
BIG ZAM?!
YOU THINK I'LL LET A
LITTLE MOBILE SUIT
RA
TA
TA
TAT

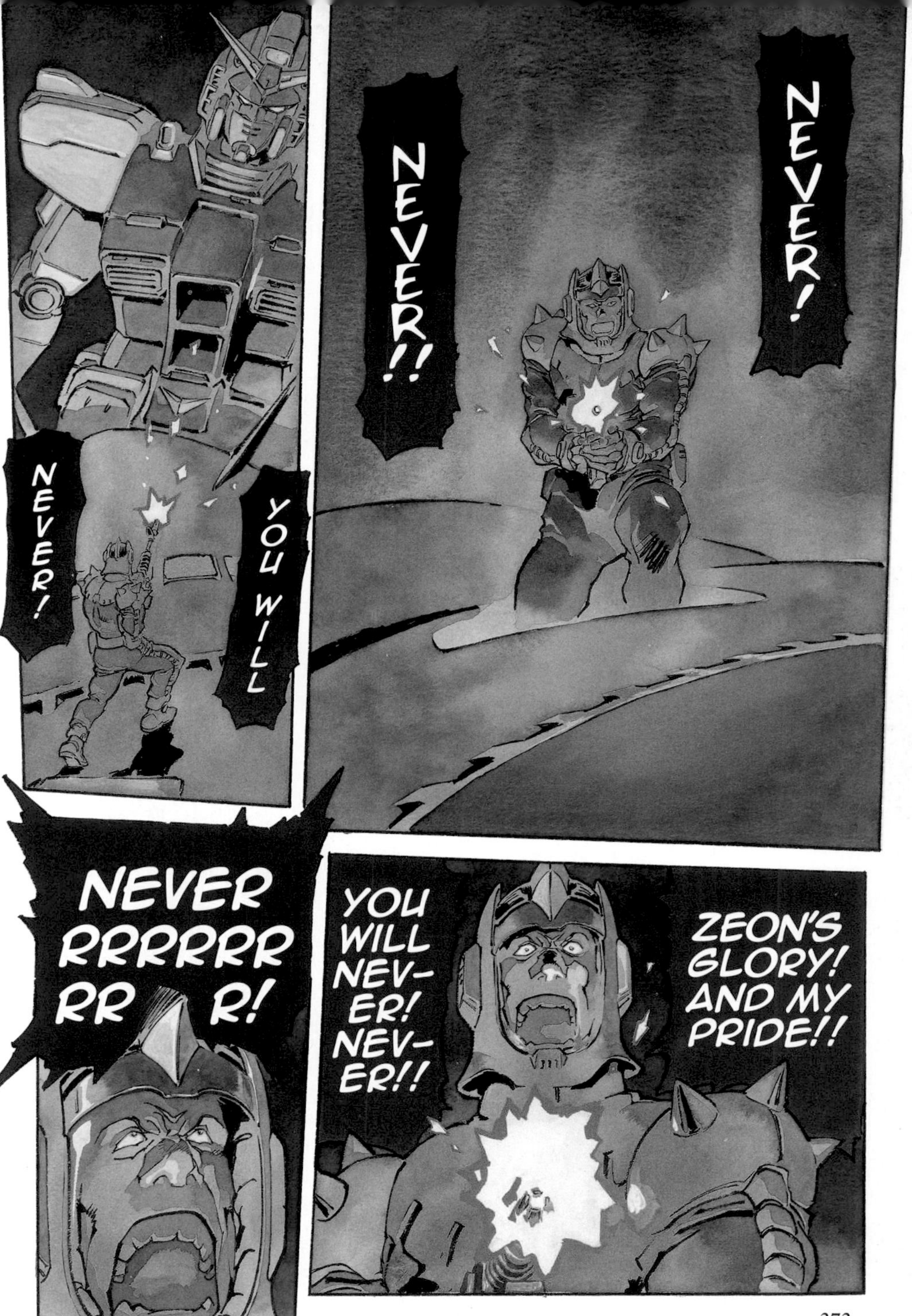
NEVER!
NEVER!!
YOU WILL
NEVER!
ZEON'S GLORY! AND MY PRIDE!!
YOU WILL NEV-ER! NEV-ER!!
NEVER RRRRRR RR R!

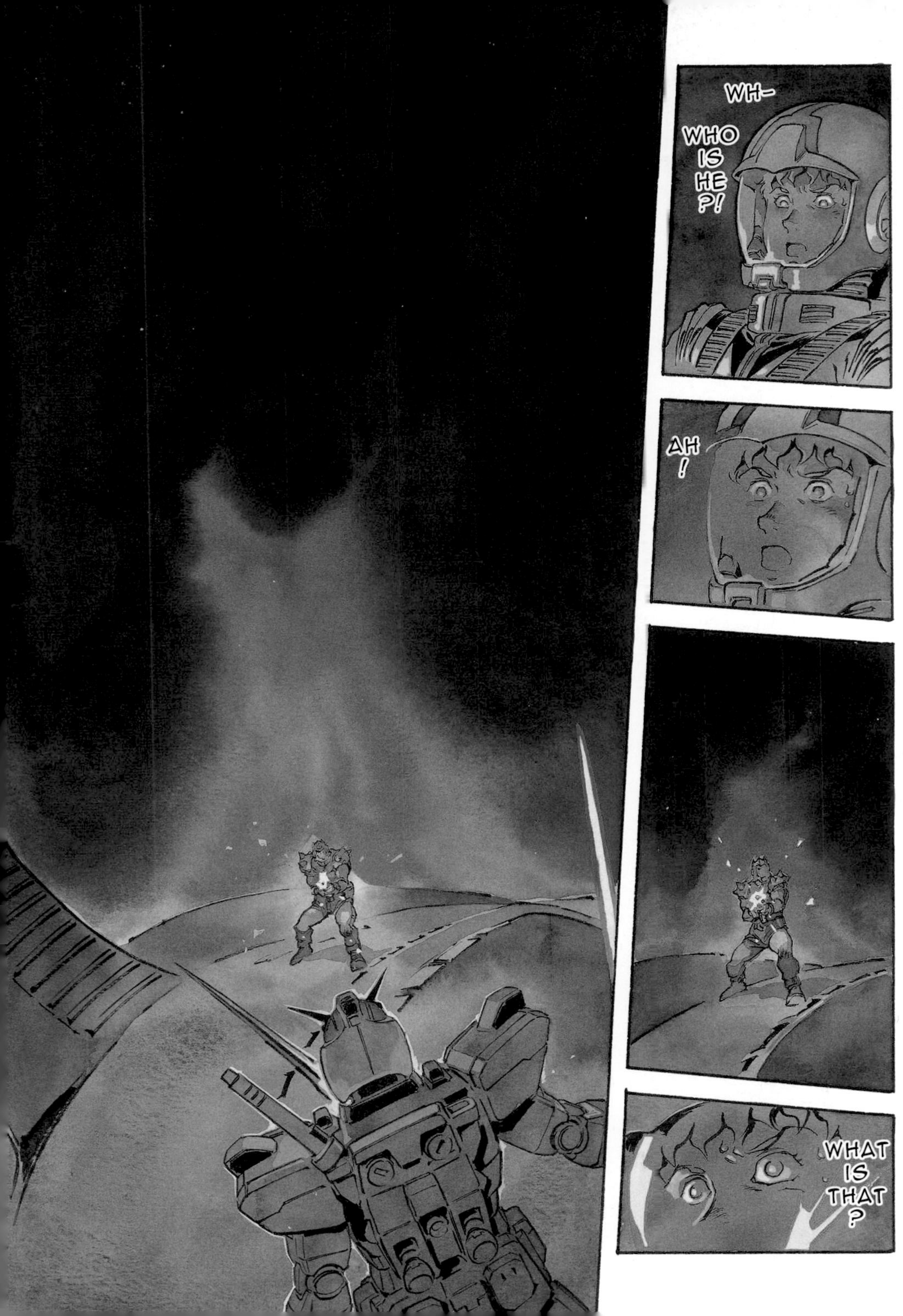
WH-
WHO IS HE?!
AH!
WHAT IS THAT?

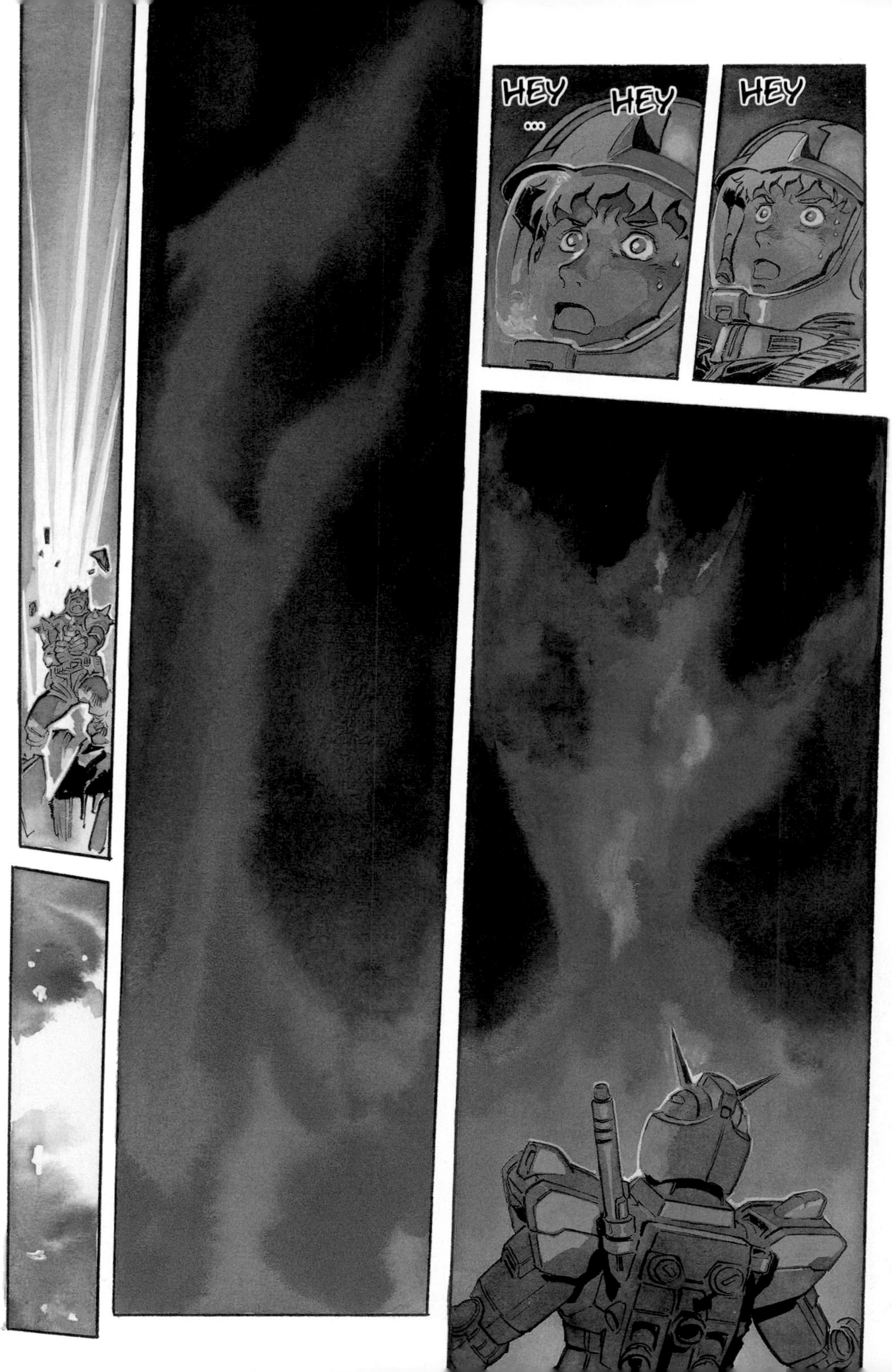
HEY
HEY
HEY
...

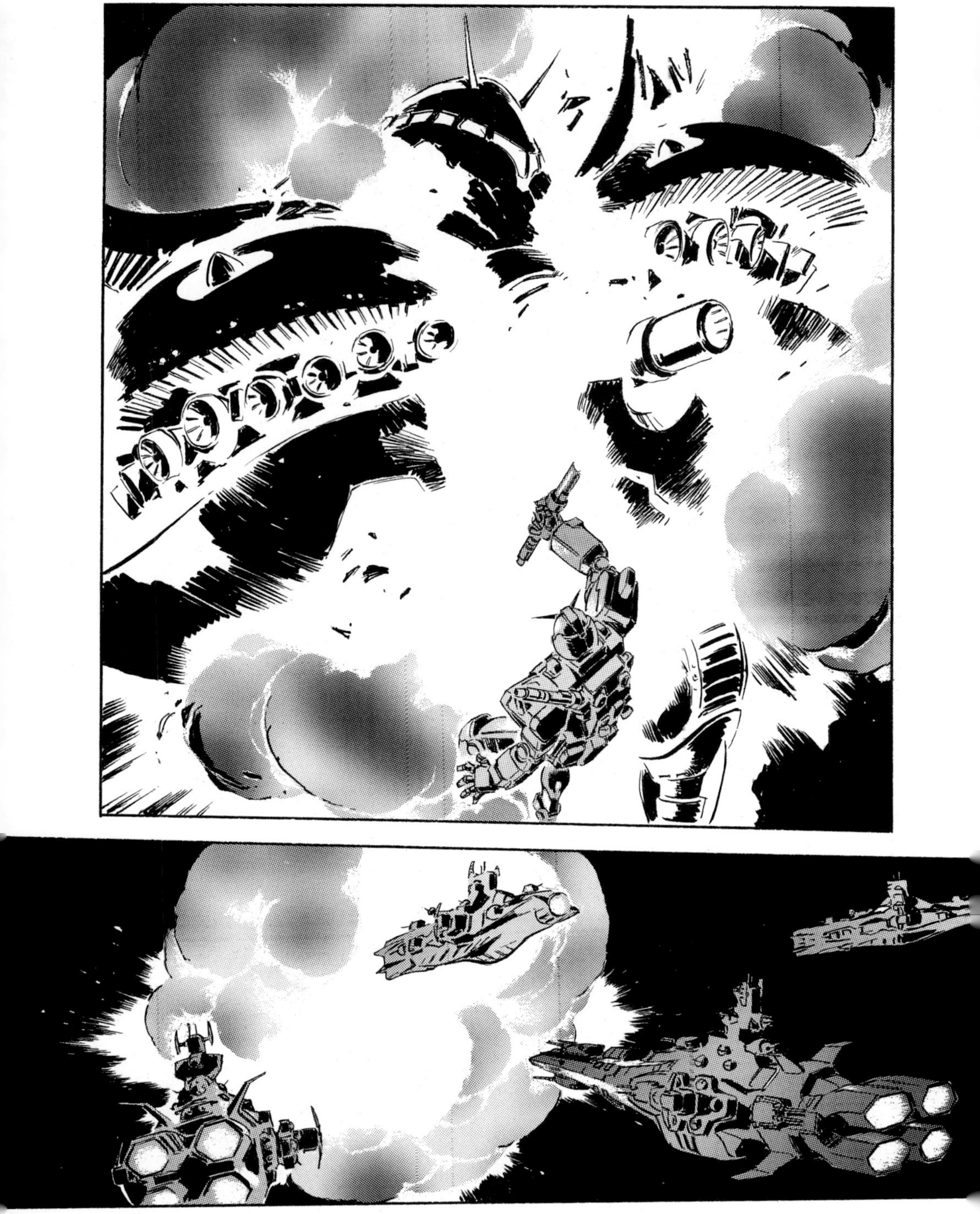

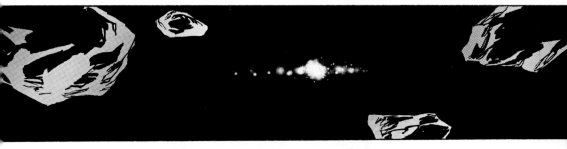

OHH...

SOLO-MON...

IS FALLEN.

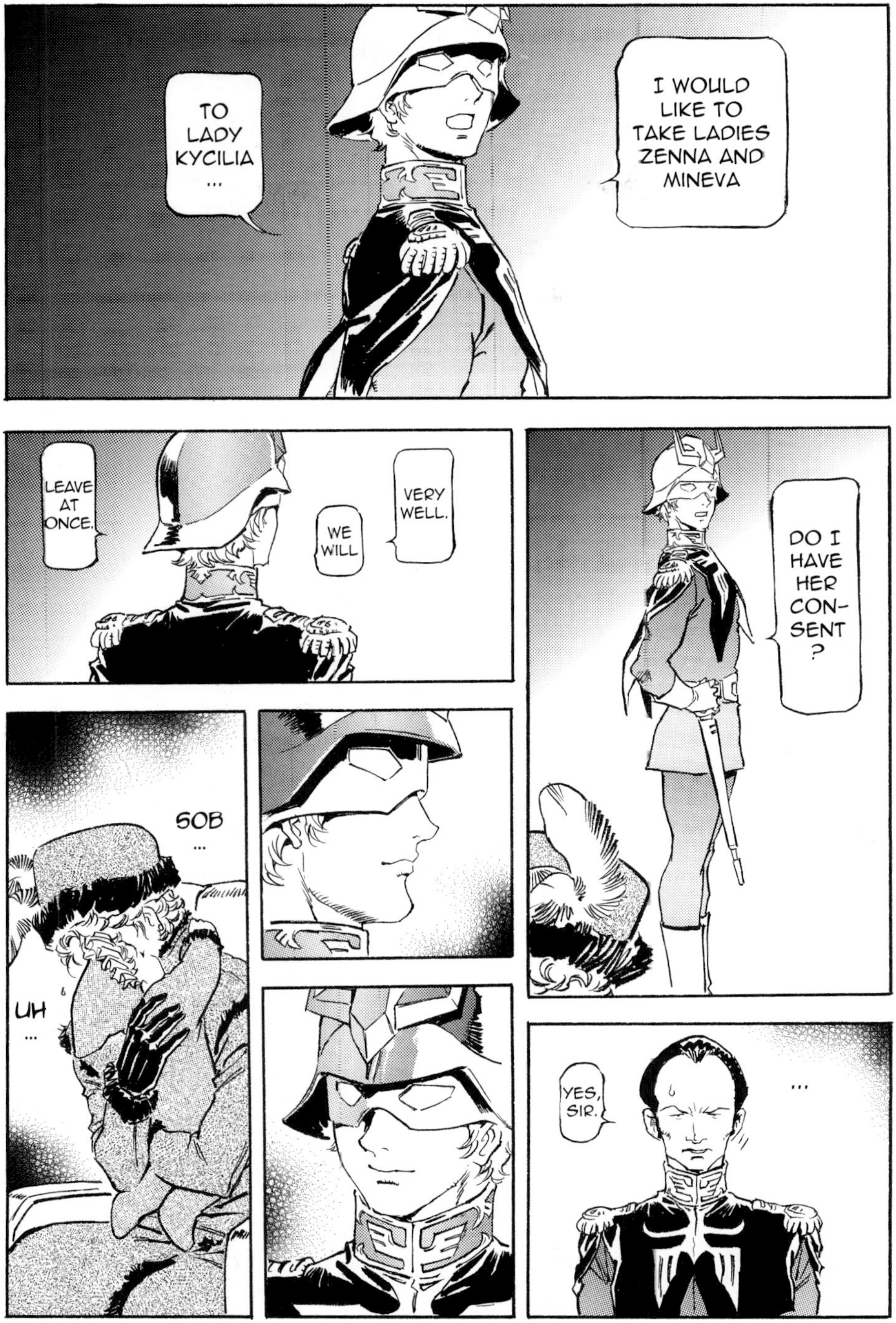
I WOULD LIKE TO TAKE LADIES ZENNA AND MINEVA
TO LADY KYCILIA ...
DO I HAVE HER CON-SENT?
VERY WELL.
WE WILL
LEAVE AT ONCE.
YES, SIR.
...
SOB ...
UH ...

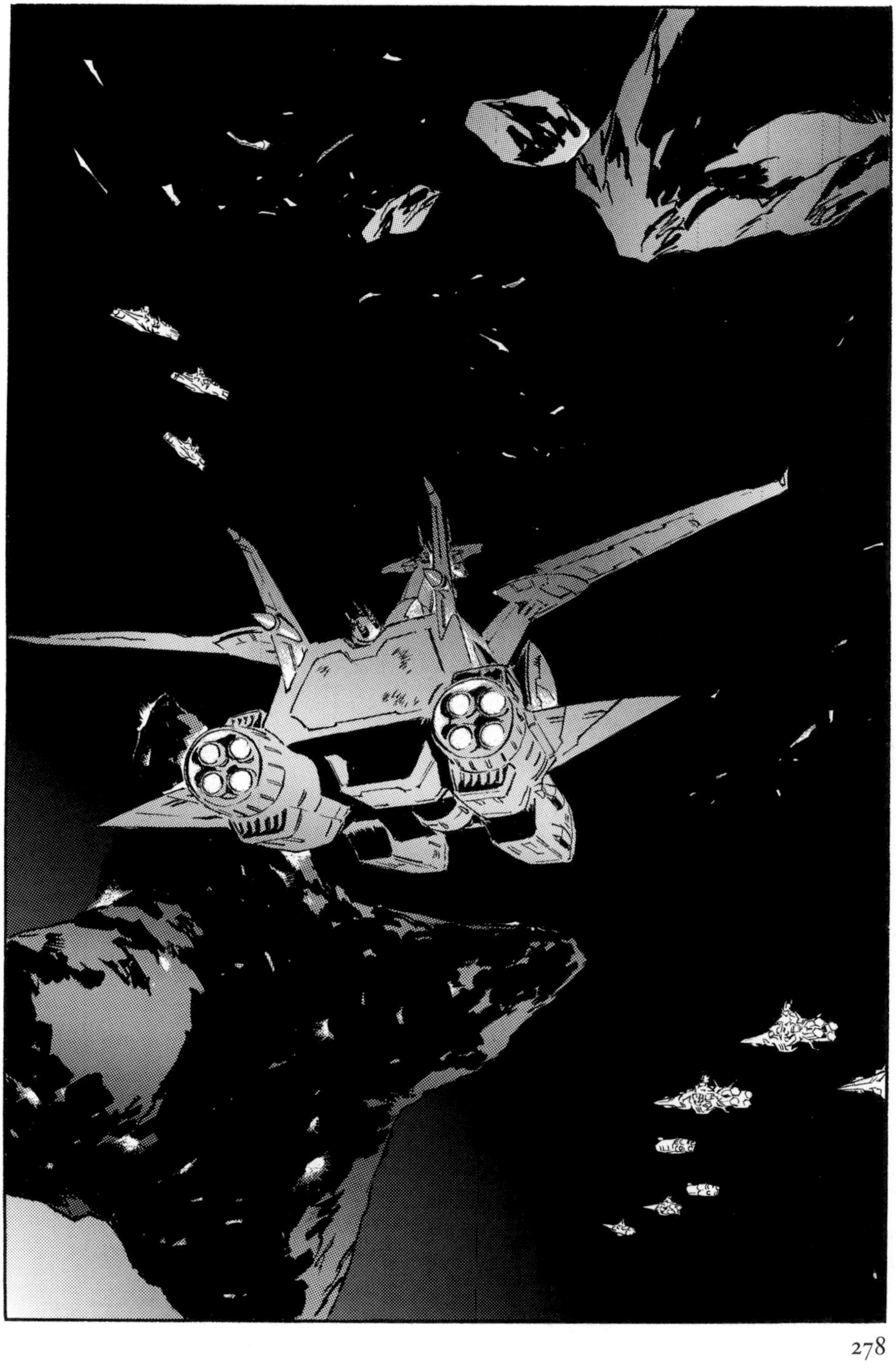

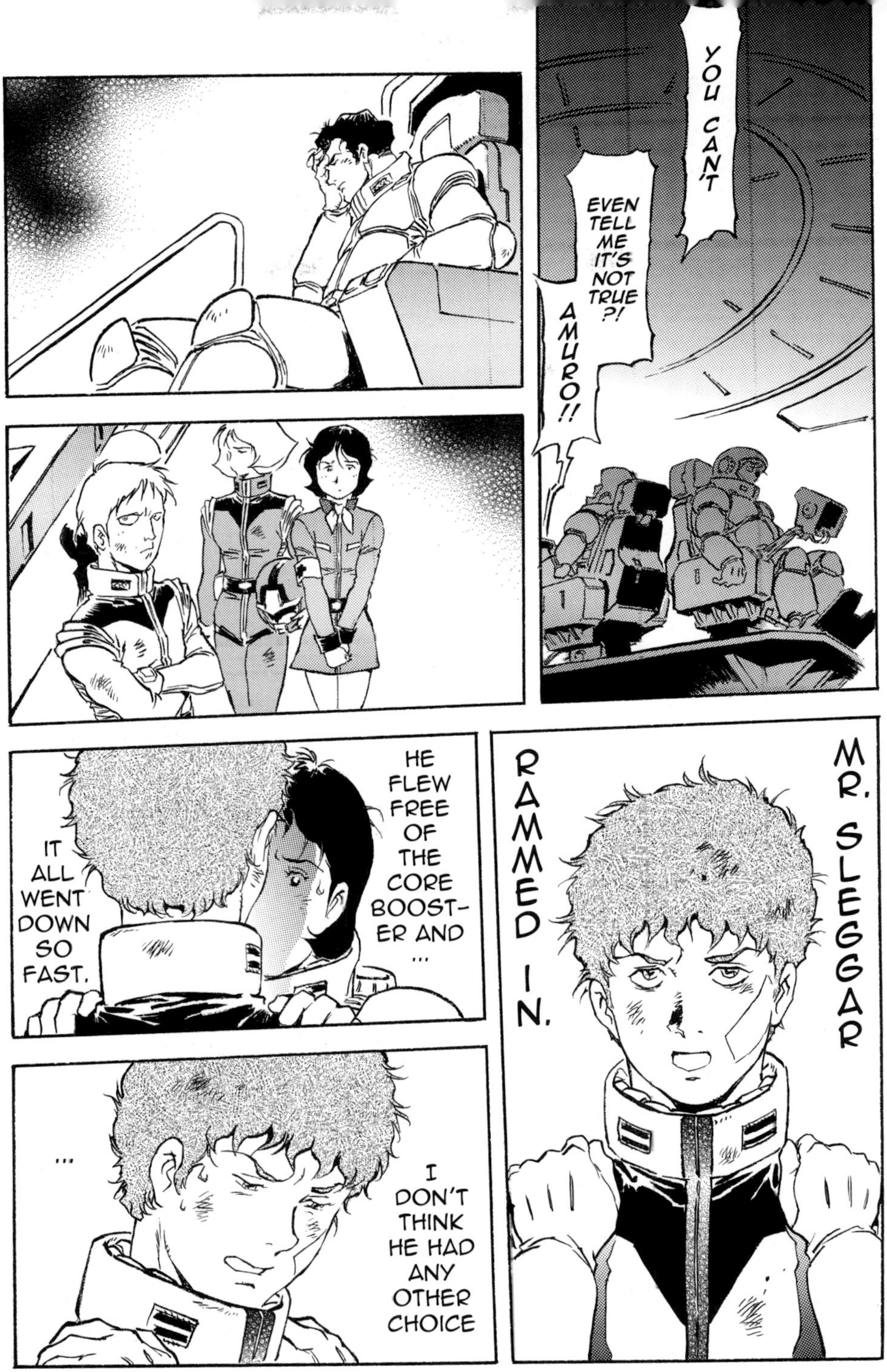
YOU CAN'T
EVEN TELL ME IT'S NOT TRUE ?!
AMURO!!
MR. SLEGGAR RAMMED IN.
HE FLEW FREE OF THE CORE BOOSTER AND ...
IT ALL WENT DOWN SO FAST.
...
I DON'T THINK HE HAD ANY OTHER CHOICE

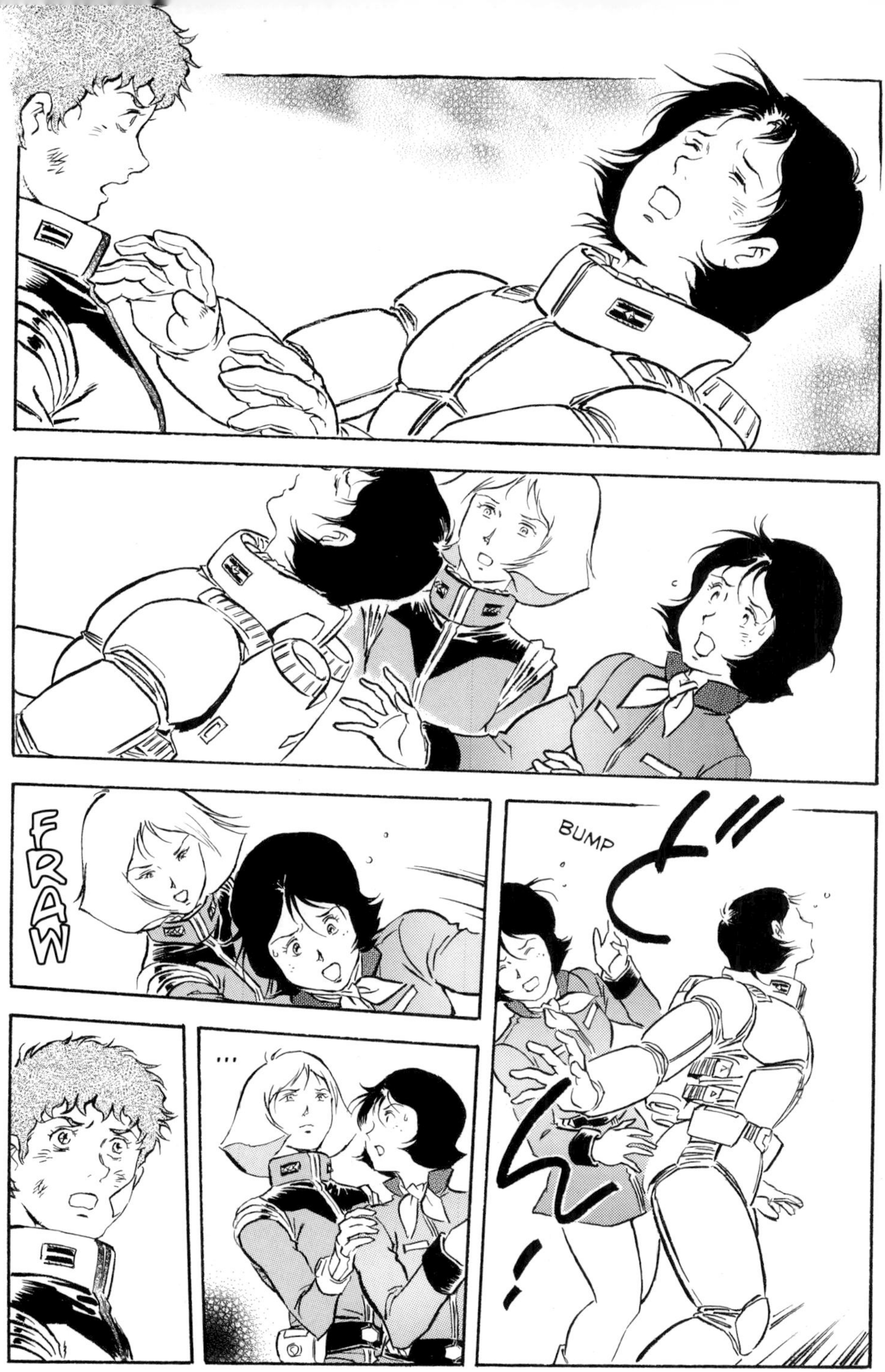
BUMP
FRAW
...

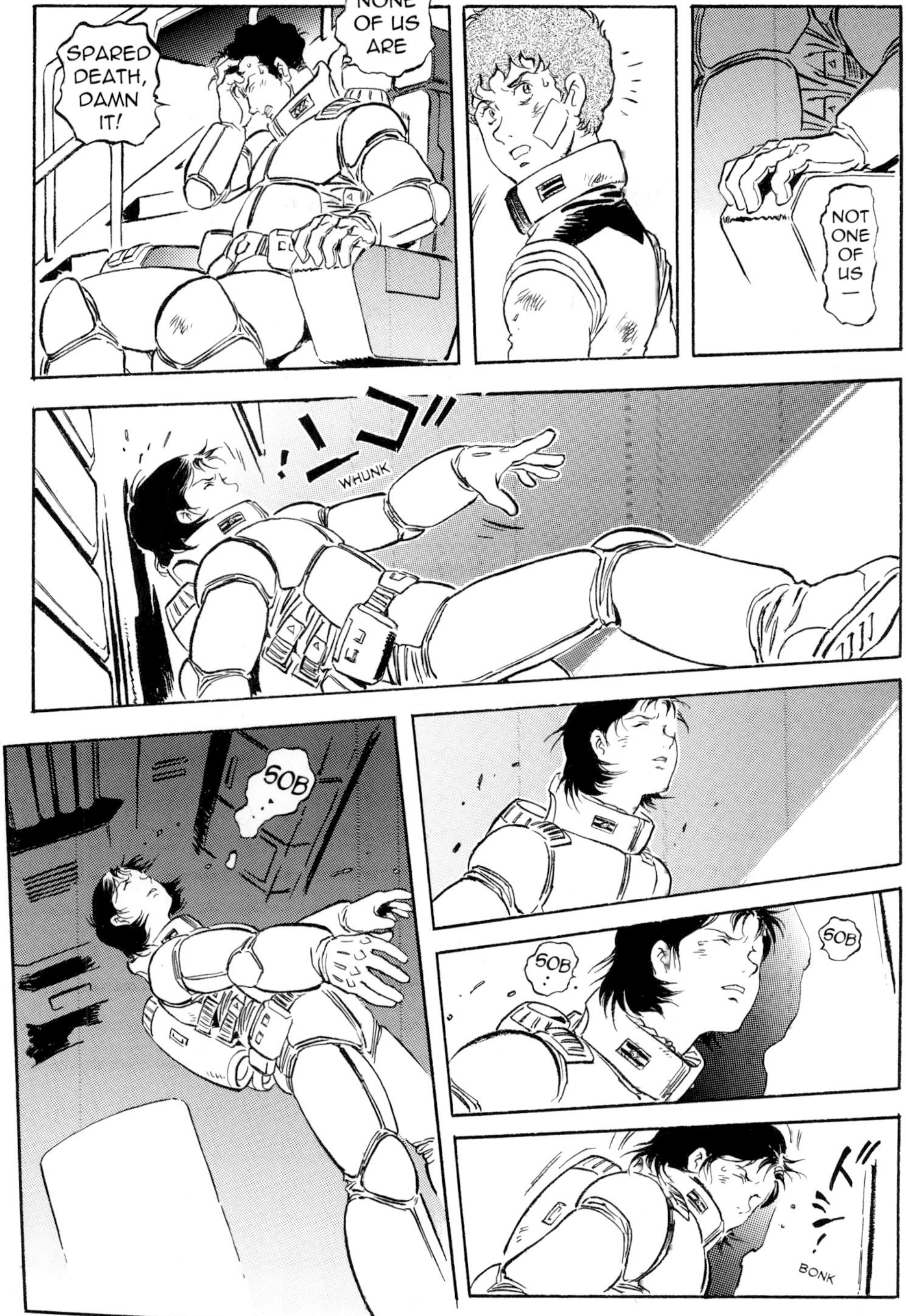
NOT ONE OF US —
NONE OF US ARE
SPARED DEATH, DAMN IT!
WHUNK
SOB
SOB
BONK
SOB

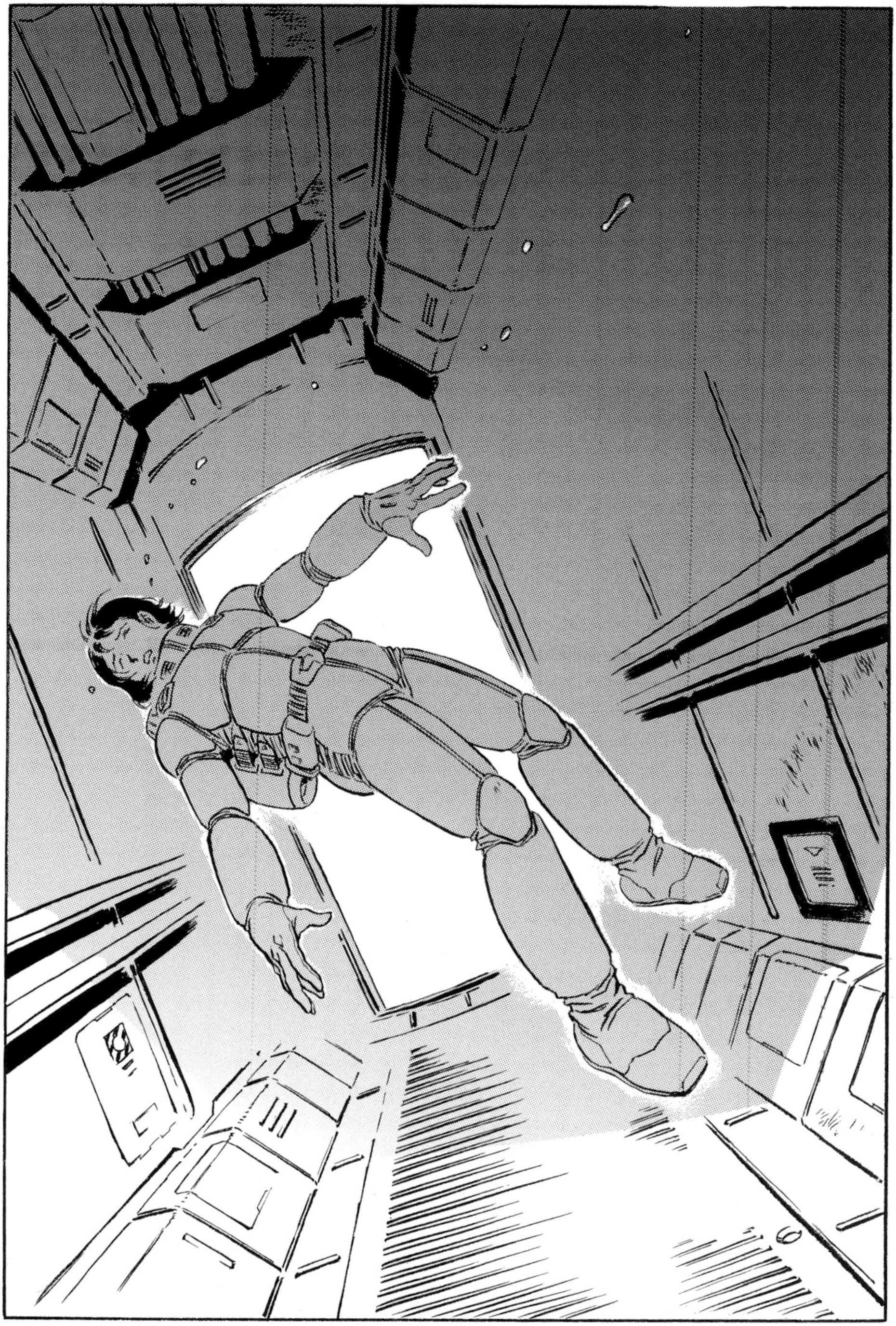

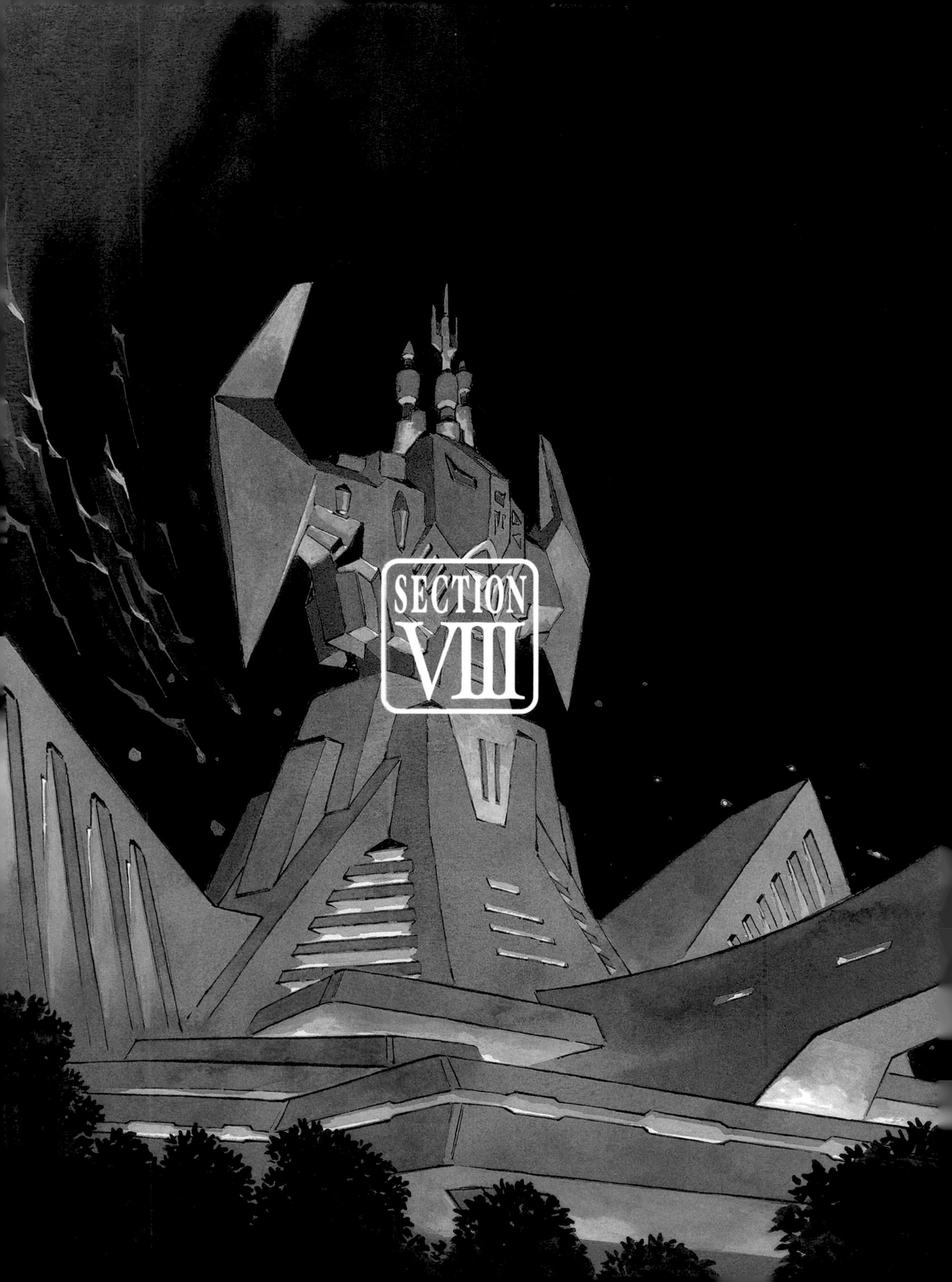

SECTION VIII

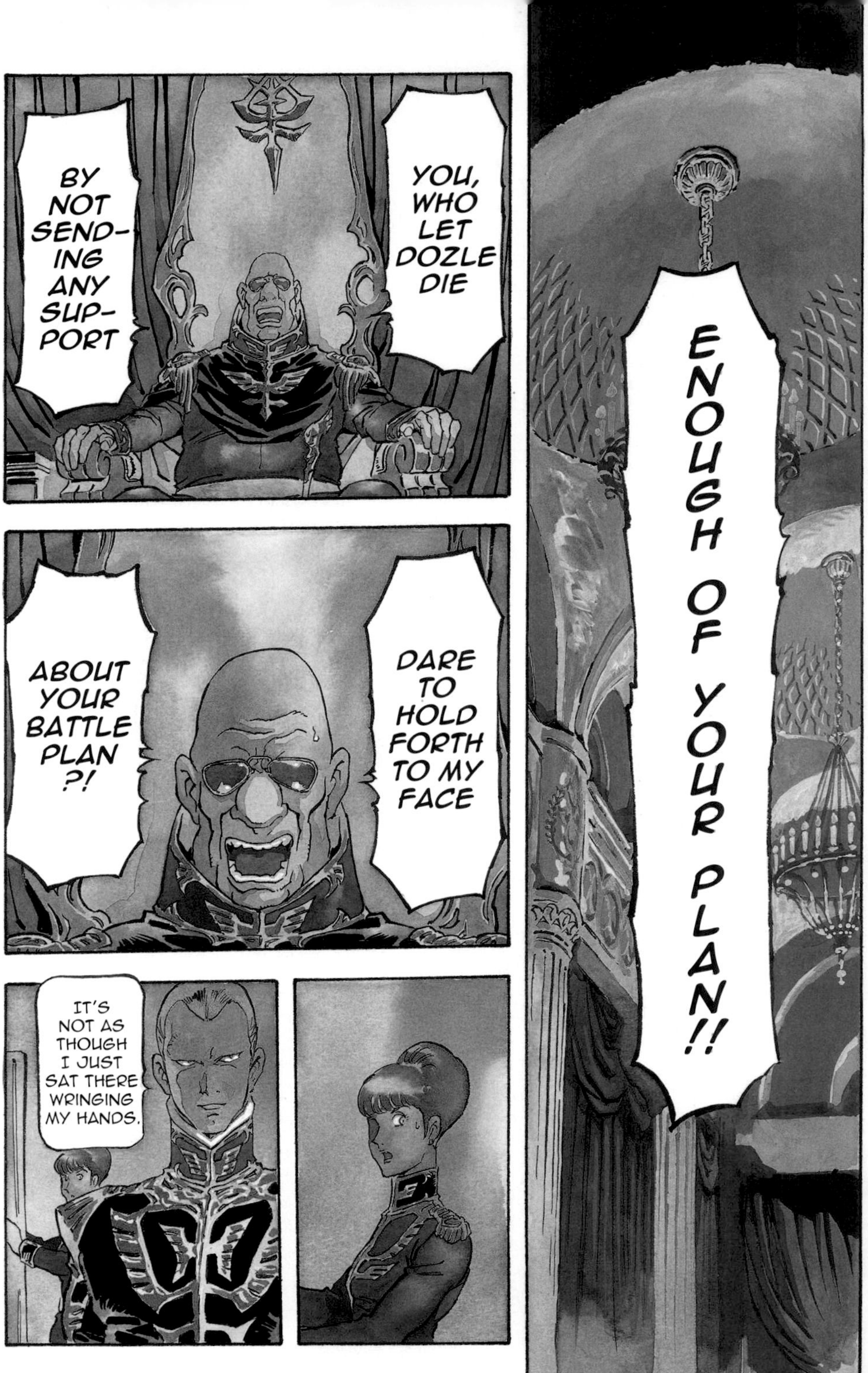
ENOUGH OF YOUR PLAN!!
YOU, WHO LET DOZLE DIE
BY NOT SENDING ANY SUPPORT
DARE TO HOLD FORTH TO MY FACE
ABOUT YOUR BATTLE PLAN?!
IT'S NOT AS THOUGH I JUST SAT THERE WRINGING MY HANDS.

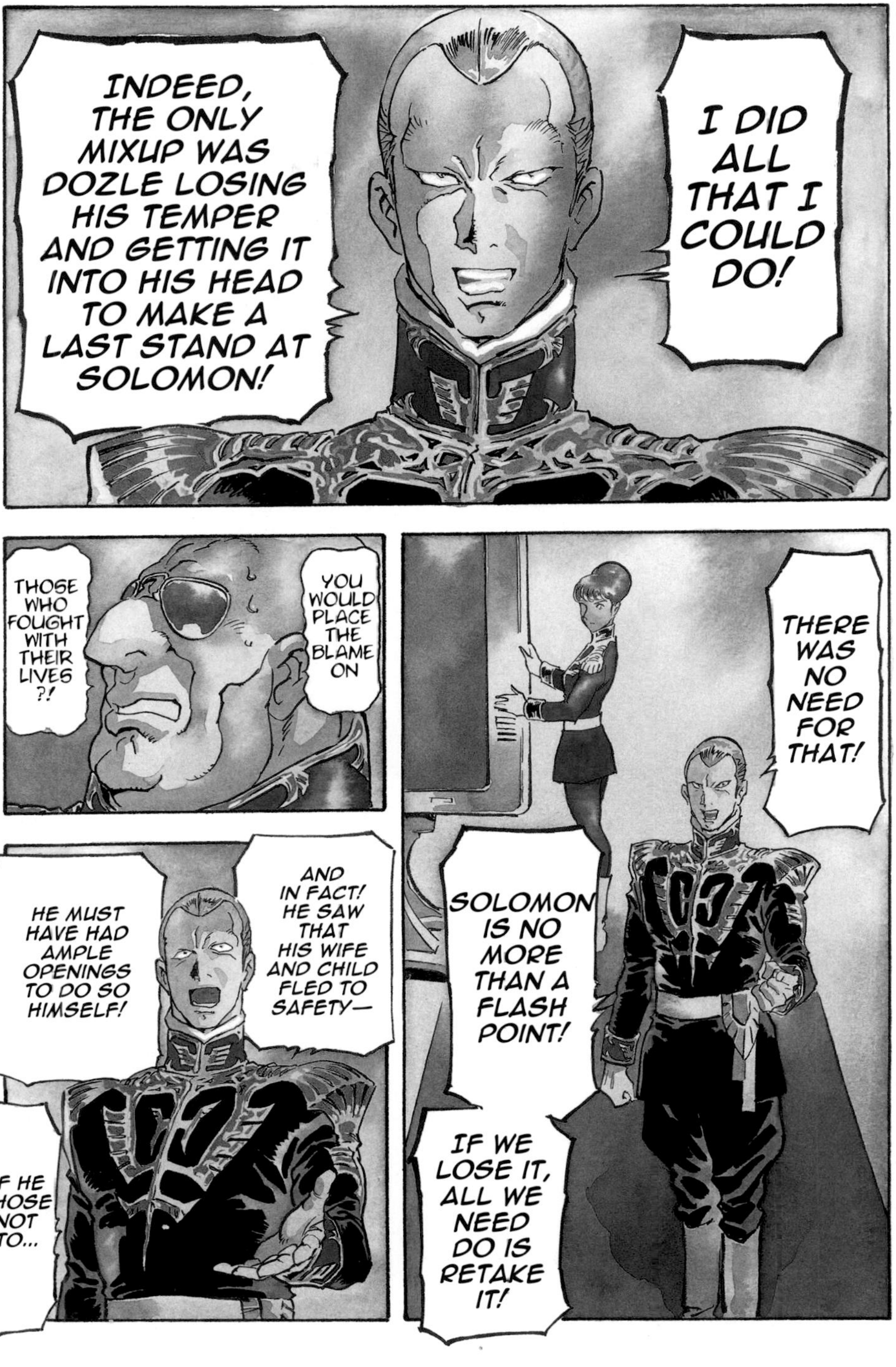

I DID ALL THAT I COULD DO!
INDEED, THE ONLY MIXUP WAS DOZLE LOSING HIS TEMPER AND GETTING IT INTO HIS HEAD TO MAKE A LAST STAND AT SOLOMON!
THERE WAS NO NEED FOR THAT!
SOLOMON IS NO MORE THAN A FLASH POINT!
IF WE LOSE IT, ALL WE NEED DO IS RETAKE IT!
YOU WOULD PLACE THE BLAME ON
THOSE WHO FOUGHT WITH THEIR LIVES?!
AND IN FACT! HE SAW THAT HIS WIFE AND CHILD FLED TO SAFETY—
HE MUST HAVE HAD AMPLE OPENINGS TO DO SO HIMSELF!
IF HE CHOSE NOT TO...

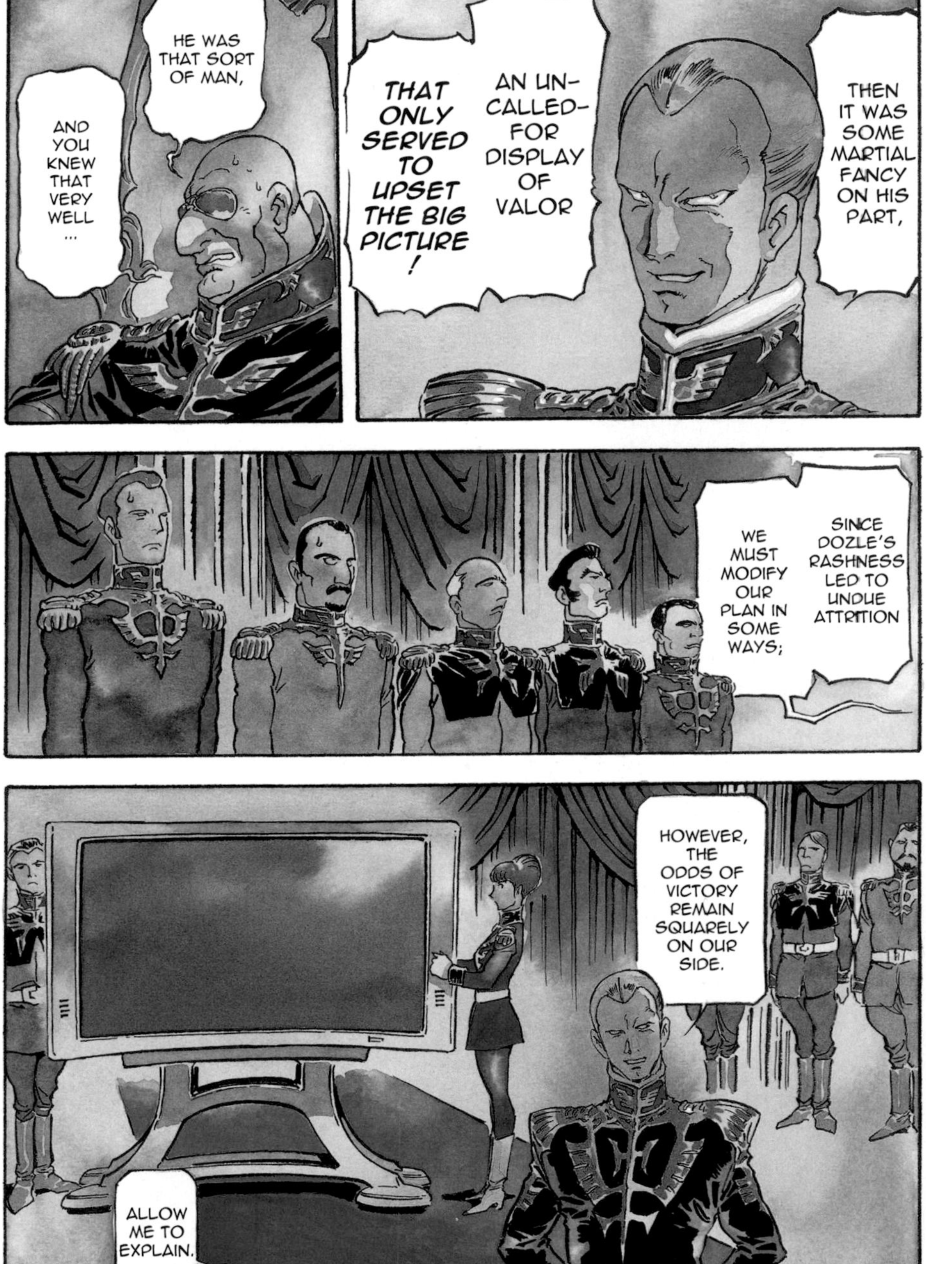
THEN IT WAS SOME MARTIAL FANCY ON HIS PART,
AN UN-CALLED-FOR DISPLAY OF VALOR
THAT ONLY SERVED TO UPSET THE BIG PICTURE!
HE WAS THAT SORT OF MAN,
AND YOU KNEW THAT VERY WELL...
SINCE DOZLE'S RASHNESS LED TO UNDUE ATTRITION
WE MUST MODIFY OUR PLAN IN SOME WAYS;
HOWEVER, THE ODDS OF VICTORY REMAIN SQUARELY ON OUR SIDE.
ALLOW ME TO EXPLAIN.

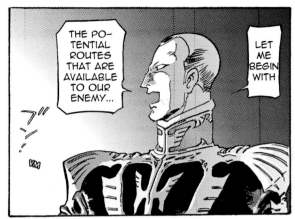

...
...
LET ME BEGIN WITH
THE PO-TENTIAL ROUTES THAT ARE AVAILABLE TO OUR ENEMY...
VM
WHERE CAN WE EXPECT THE ENEMY TO ATTACK NOW THAT THEY MAY STRIKE OUT OF SOLOMON?!
TWO TARGETS COME READILY TO MIND.
IF WE COUNT OUT GRANADA, WHICH THEY EFFECTIVELY TOOK OFF THE TABLE WHEN THEY WENT AFTER SOLOMON,
WE'RE LEFT WITH ZEON ITSELF, AND A BAOA QU.
THE CHOICE WILL BE REVIL'S AS HE HEADS THEM,

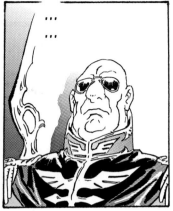

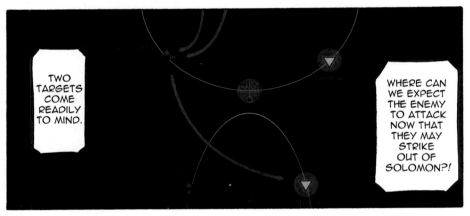

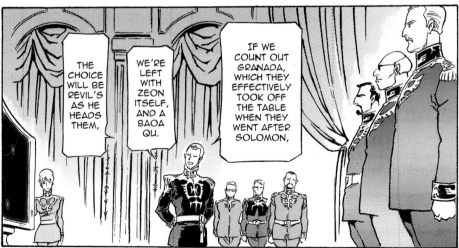

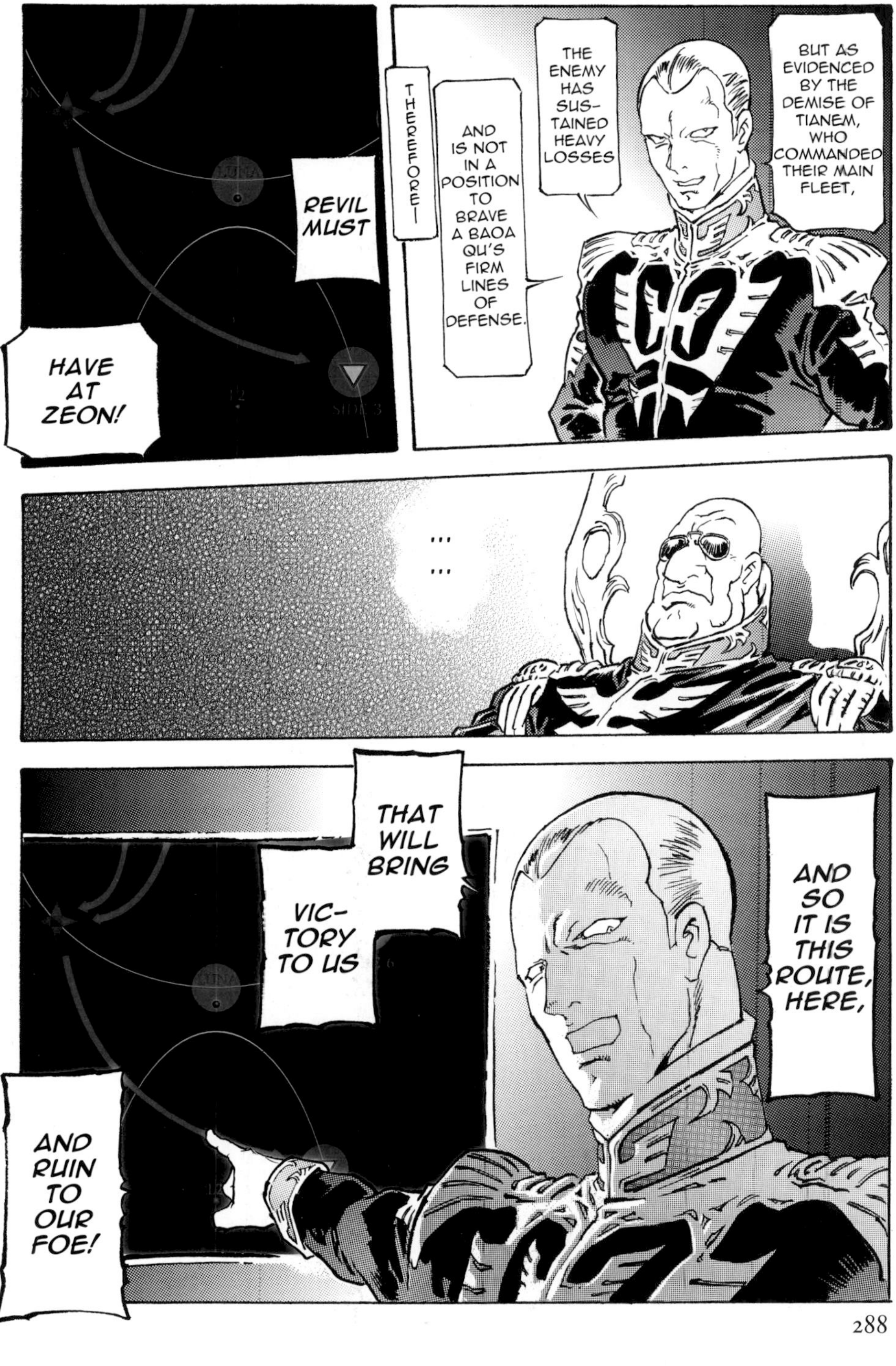

BUT AS EVIDENCED BY THE DEMISE OF TIANEM, WHO COMMANDED THEIR MAIN FLEET,
THE ENEMY HAS SUS-TAINED HEAVY LOSSES
AND IS NOT IN A POSITION TO BRAVE A BAOA QU'S FIRM LINES OF DEFENSE.
THEREFORE—
REVIL MUST
HAVE AT ZEON!
... ...
AND SO IT IS THIS ROUTE, HERE,
THAT WILL BRING
VIC-TORY TO US
AND RUIN TO OUR FOE!

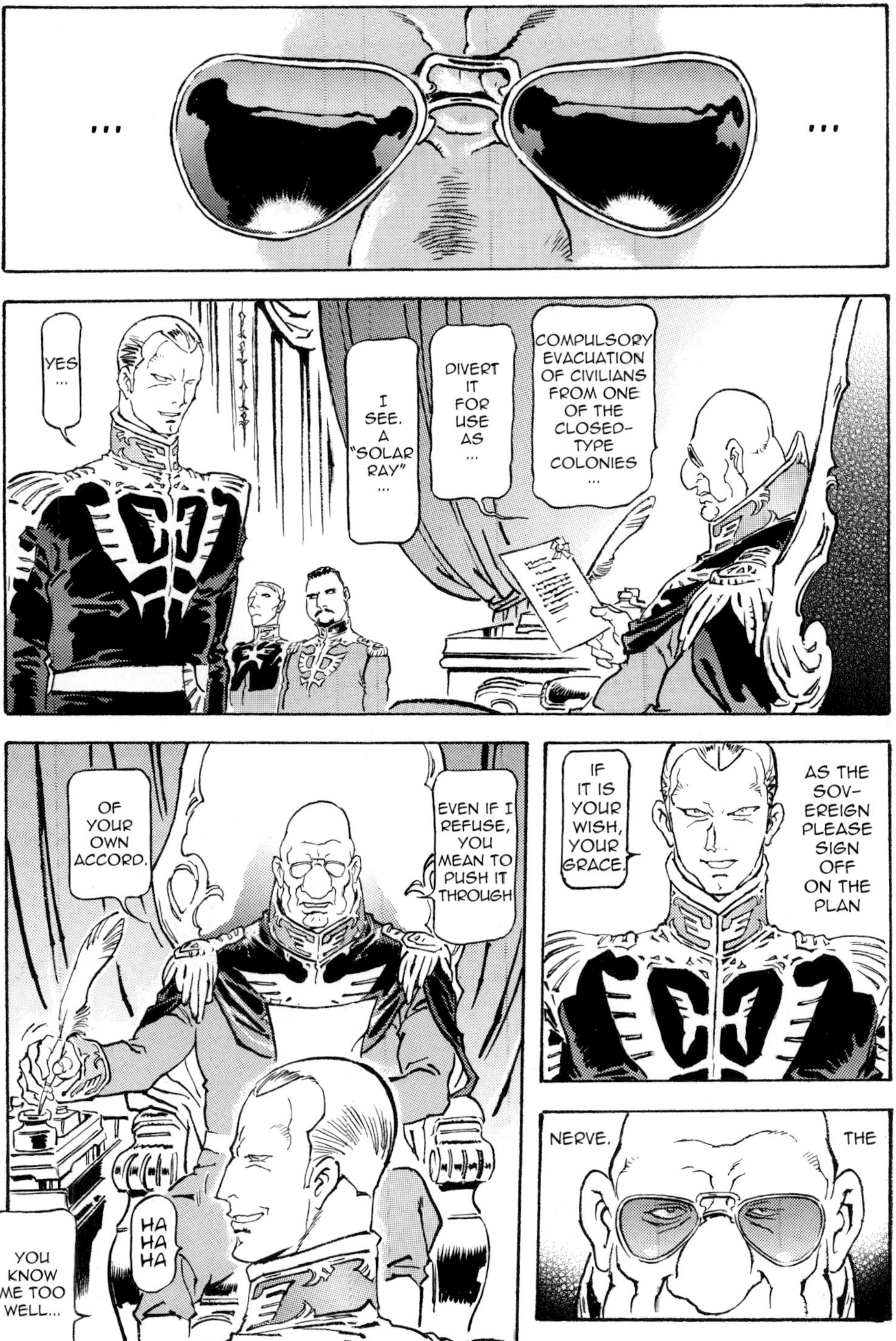
...
...
COMPULSORY EVACUATION OF CIVILIANS FROM ONE OF THE CLOSED-TYPE COLONIES ...
DIVERT IT FOR USE AS ...
I SEE. A "SOLAR RAY" ...
YES ...
AS THE SOVEREIGN PLEASE SIGN OFF ON THE PLAN
IF IT IS YOUR WISH, YOUR GRACE.
THE
NERVE.
EVEN IF I REFUSE, YOU MEAN TO PUSH IT THROUGH
OF YOUR OWN ACCORD.
HA HA HA
YOU KNOW ME TOO WELL...

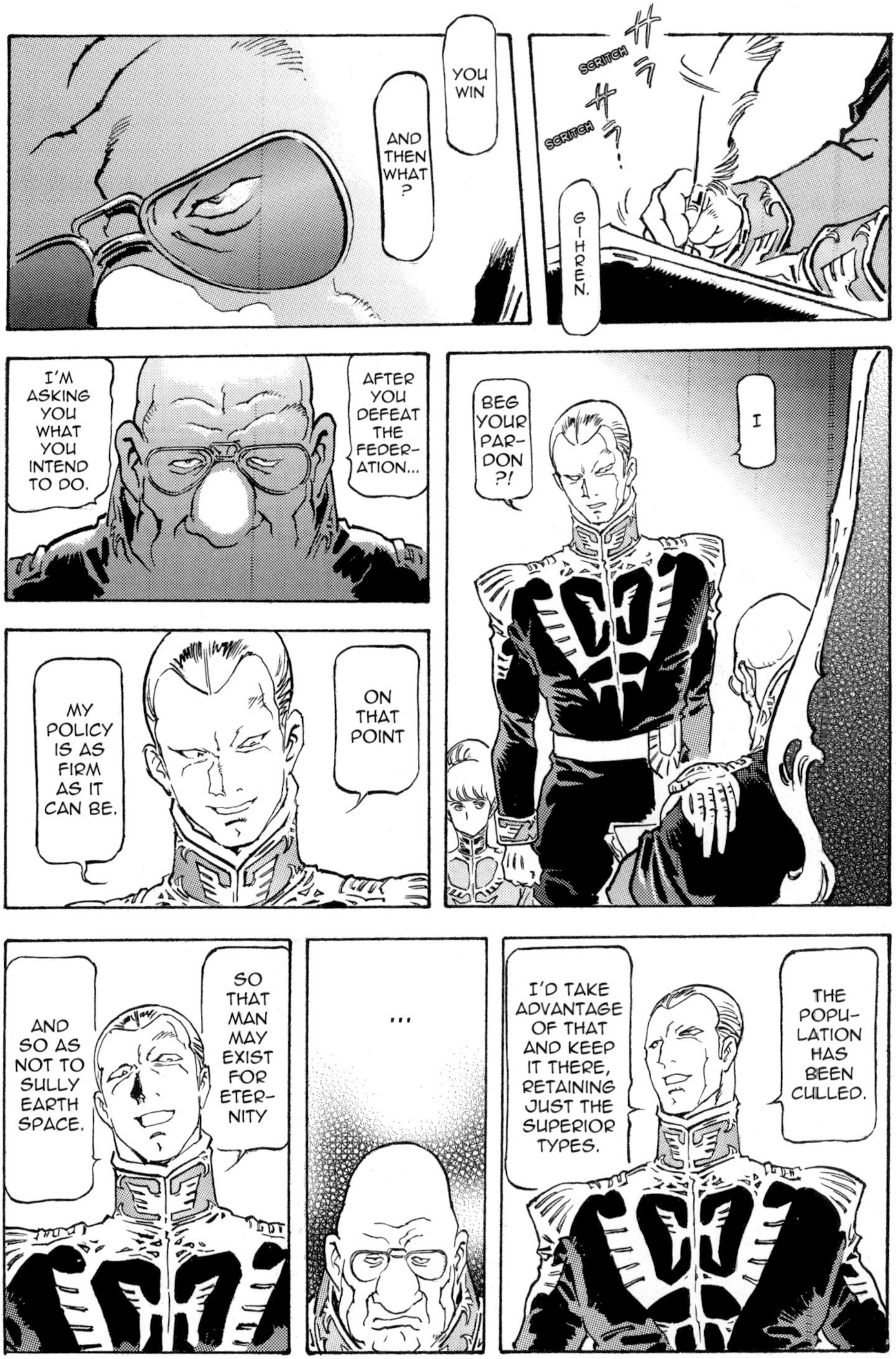
SCRITCH
SCRITCH
GIHREN.
YOU WIN
AND THEN WHAT?
I
BEG YOUR PARDON?!
AFTER YOU DEFEAT THE FEDERATION...
I'M ASKING YOU WHAT YOU INTEND TO DO.
ON THAT POINT
MY POLICY IS AS FIRM AS IT CAN BE.
THE POPULATION HAS BEEN CULLED.
I'D TAKE ADVANTAGE OF THAT AND KEEP IT THERE, RETAINING JUST THE SUPERIOR TYPES.
...
SO THAT MAN MAY EXIST FOR ETERNITY
AND SO AS NOT TO SULLY EARTH SPACE.

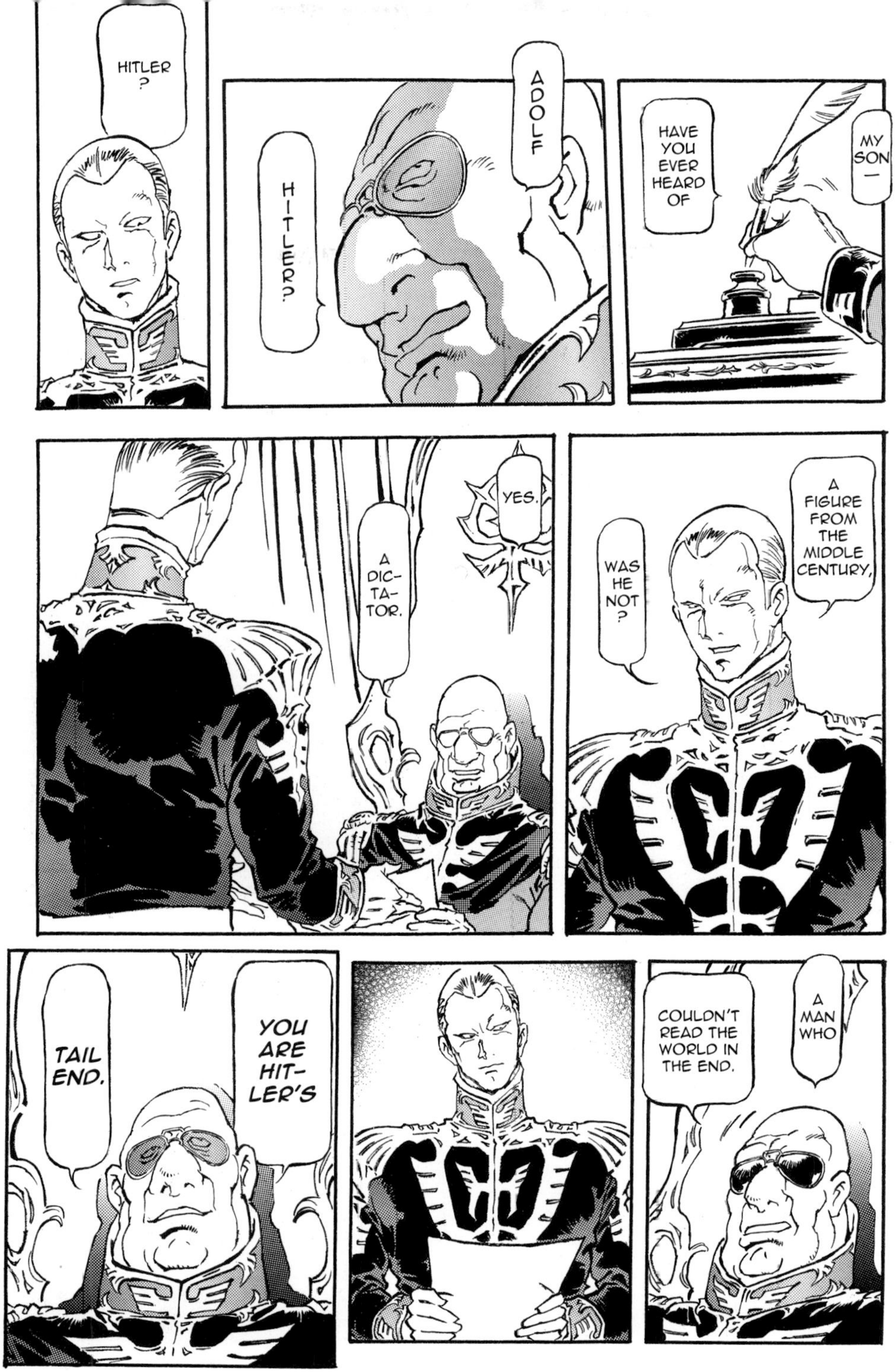
MY SON—
HAVE YOU EVER HEARD OF
ADOLF
HITLER?
HITLER?
A FIGURE FROM THE MIDDLE CENTURY,
WAS HE NOT?
YES.
A DICTATOR.
A MAN WHO
COULDN'T READ THE WORLD IN THE END.
YOU ARE HITLER'S
TAIL END.

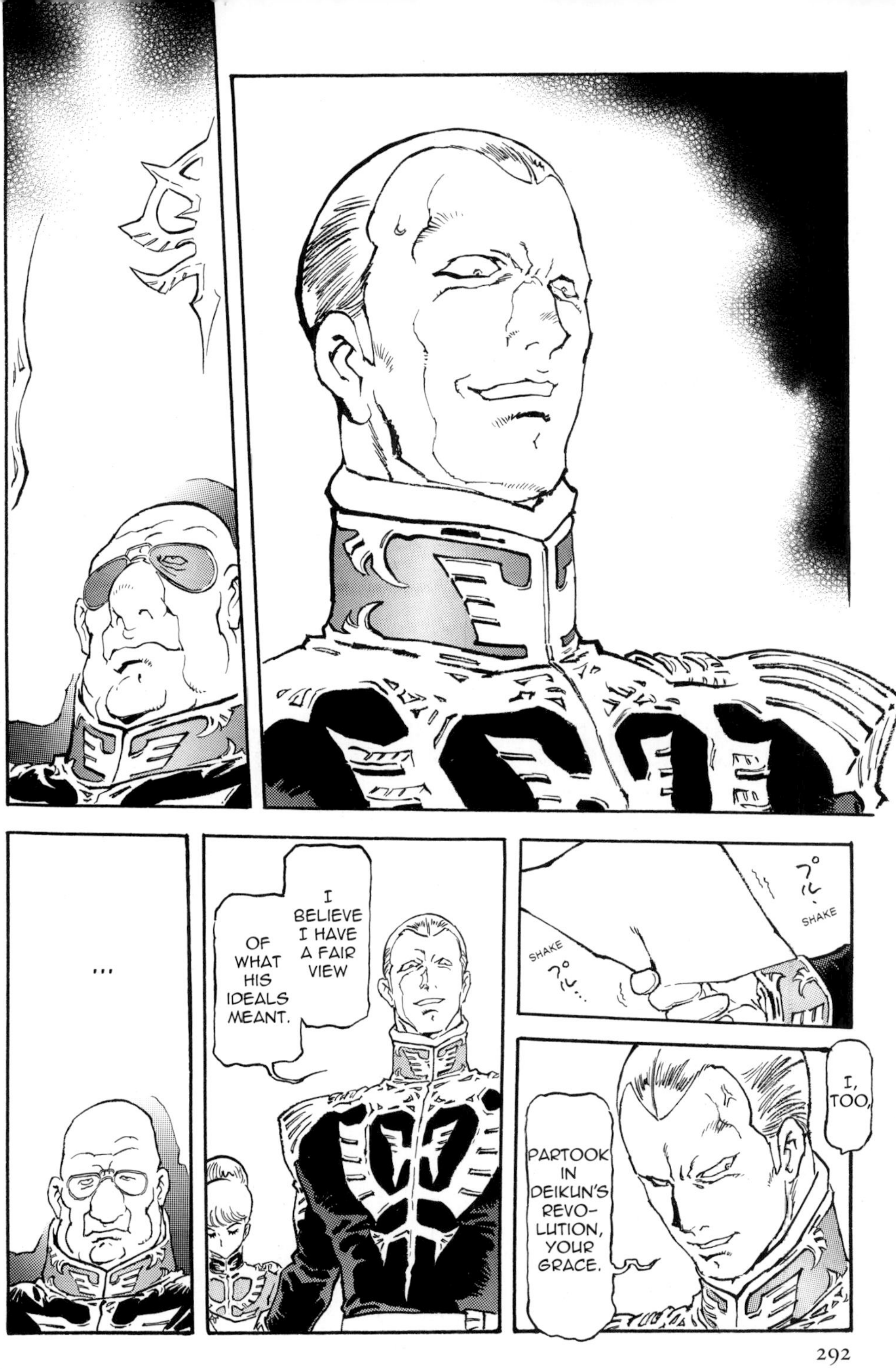
プル
SHAKE
SHAKE
プル…
I, TOO,
PARTOOK IN DEIKUN'S REVOLUTION, YOUR GRACE.
I BELIEVE I HAVE A FAIR VIEW
OF WHAT HIS IDEALS MEANT.
...

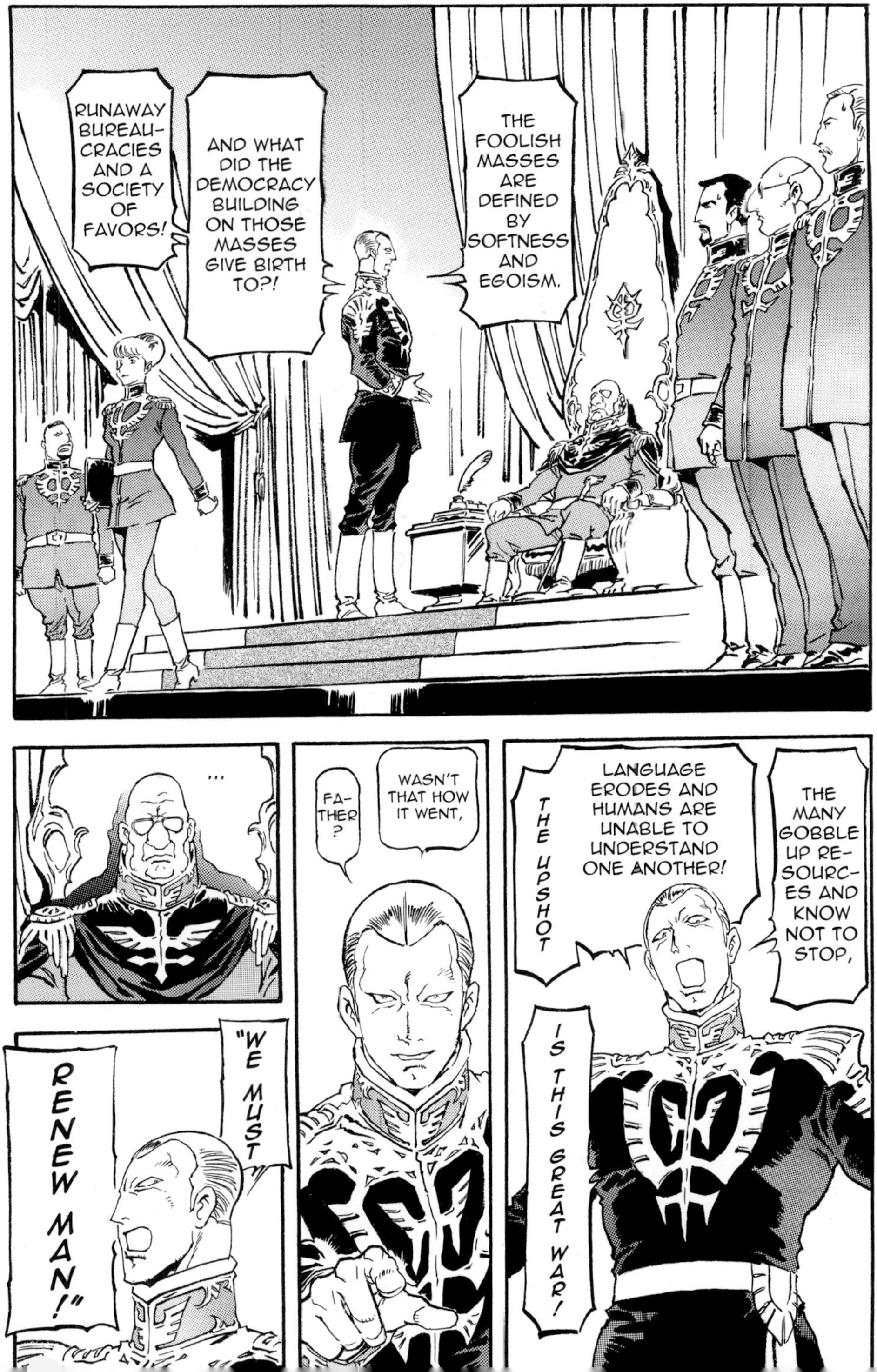
THE FOOLISH MASSES ARE DEFINED BY SOFTNESS AND EGOISM.
AND WHAT DID THE DEMOCRACY BUILDING ON THOSE MASSES GIVE BIRTH TO?!
RUNAWAY BUREAU-CRACIES AND A SOCIETY OF FAVORS!
THE MANY GOBBLE UP RE-SOURC-ES AND KNOW NOT TO STOP,
LANGUAGE ERODES AND HUMANS ARE UNABLE TO UNDERSTAND ONE ANOTHER!
THE UPSHOT
IS THIS GREAT WAR!
WASN'T THAT HOW IT WENT,
FA-THER?
...
"WE MUST
RENEW MAN!"

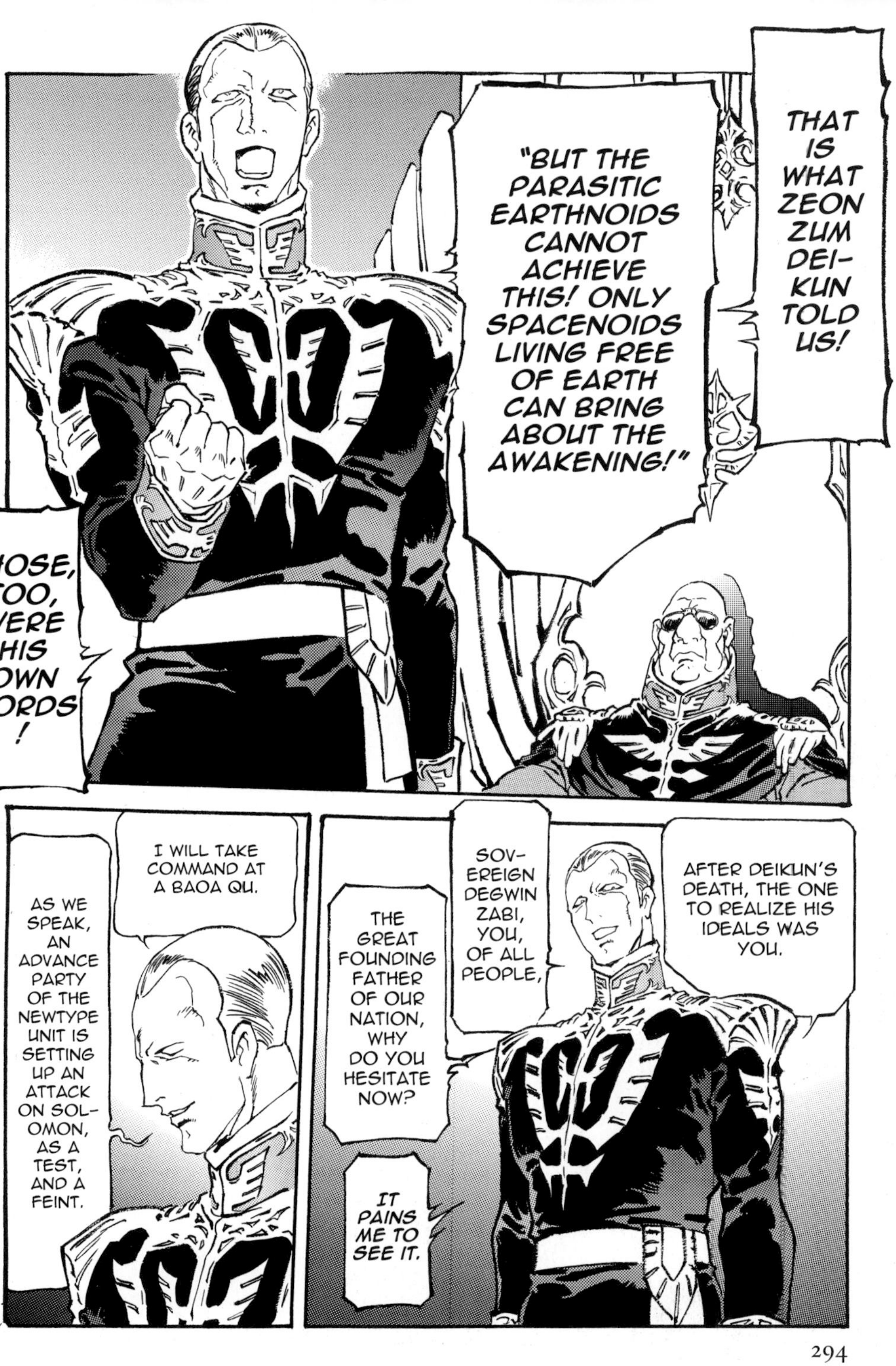
THAT IS WHAT ZEON ZUM DEIKUN TOLD US!
"BUT THE PARASITIC EARTHNOIDS CANNOT ACHIEVE THIS! ONLY SPACENOIDS LIVING FREE OF EARTH CAN BRING ABOUT THE AWAKENING!"
THOSE, TOO, WERE HIS OWN WORDS!
AFTER DEIKUN'S DEATH, THE ONE TO REALIZE HIS IDEALS WAS YOU.
SOVEREIGN DEGWIN ZABI, YOU, OF ALL PEOPLE,
THE GREAT FOUNDING FATHER OF OUR NATION, WHY DO YOU HESITATE NOW?
IT PAINS ME TO SEE IT.
I WILL TAKE COMMAND AT A BAOA QU.
AS WE SPEAK, AN ADVANCE PARTY OF THE NEWTYPE UNIT IS SETTING UP AN ATTACK ON SOLOMON, AS A TEST, AND A FEINT.

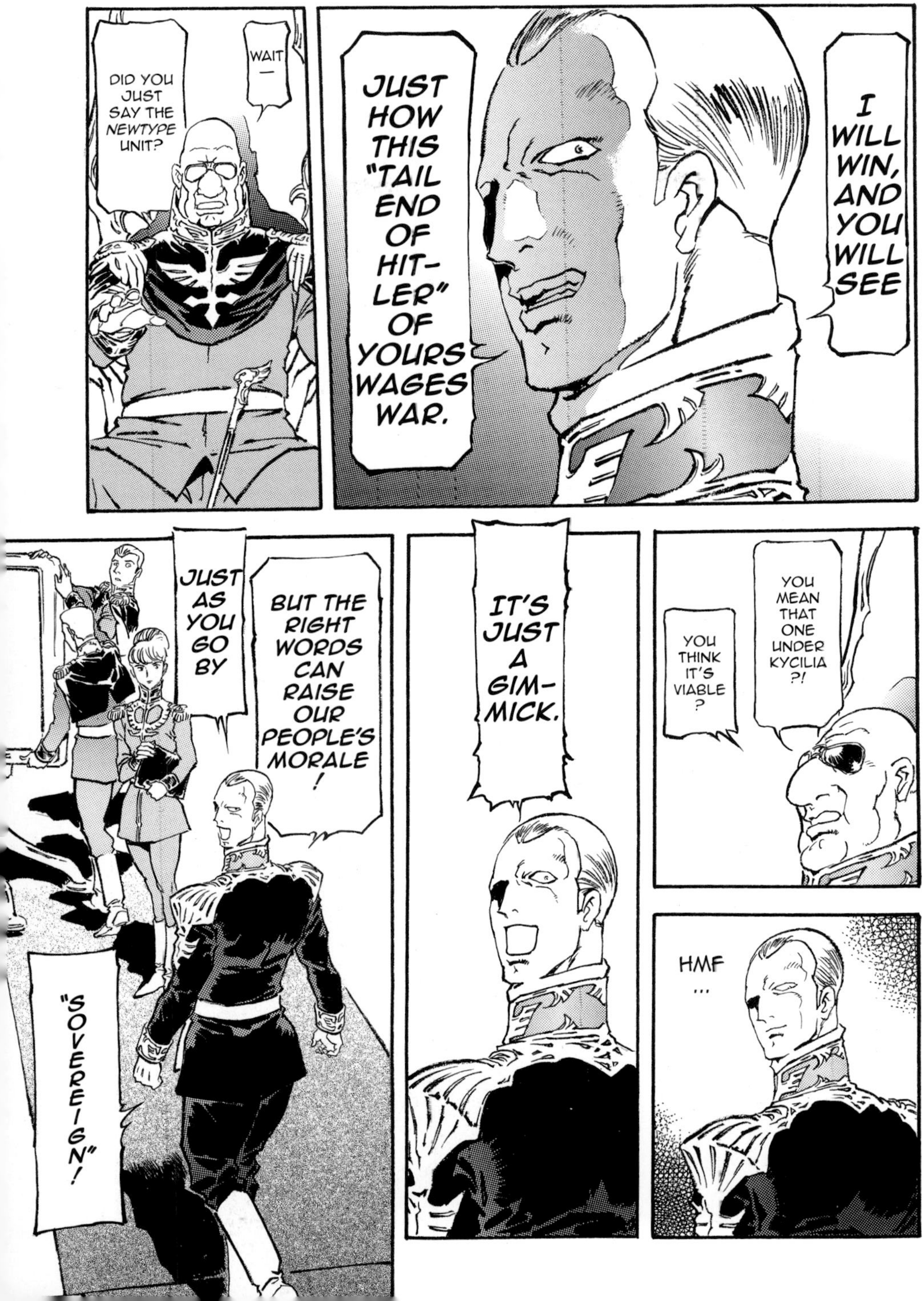
I WILL WIN, AND YOU WILL SEE
JUST HOW THIS "TAIL END OF HITLER" OF YOURS WAGES WAR.
WAIT—
DID YOU JUST SAY THE NEWTYPE UNIT?
YOU MEAN THAT ONE UNDER KYCILIA ?!
YOU THINK IT'S VIABLE ?
HMF ...
IT'S JUST A GIMMICK.
BUT THE RIGHT WORDS CAN RAISE OUR PEOPLE'S MORALE !
JUST AS YOU GO BY
"SOVEREIGN"!

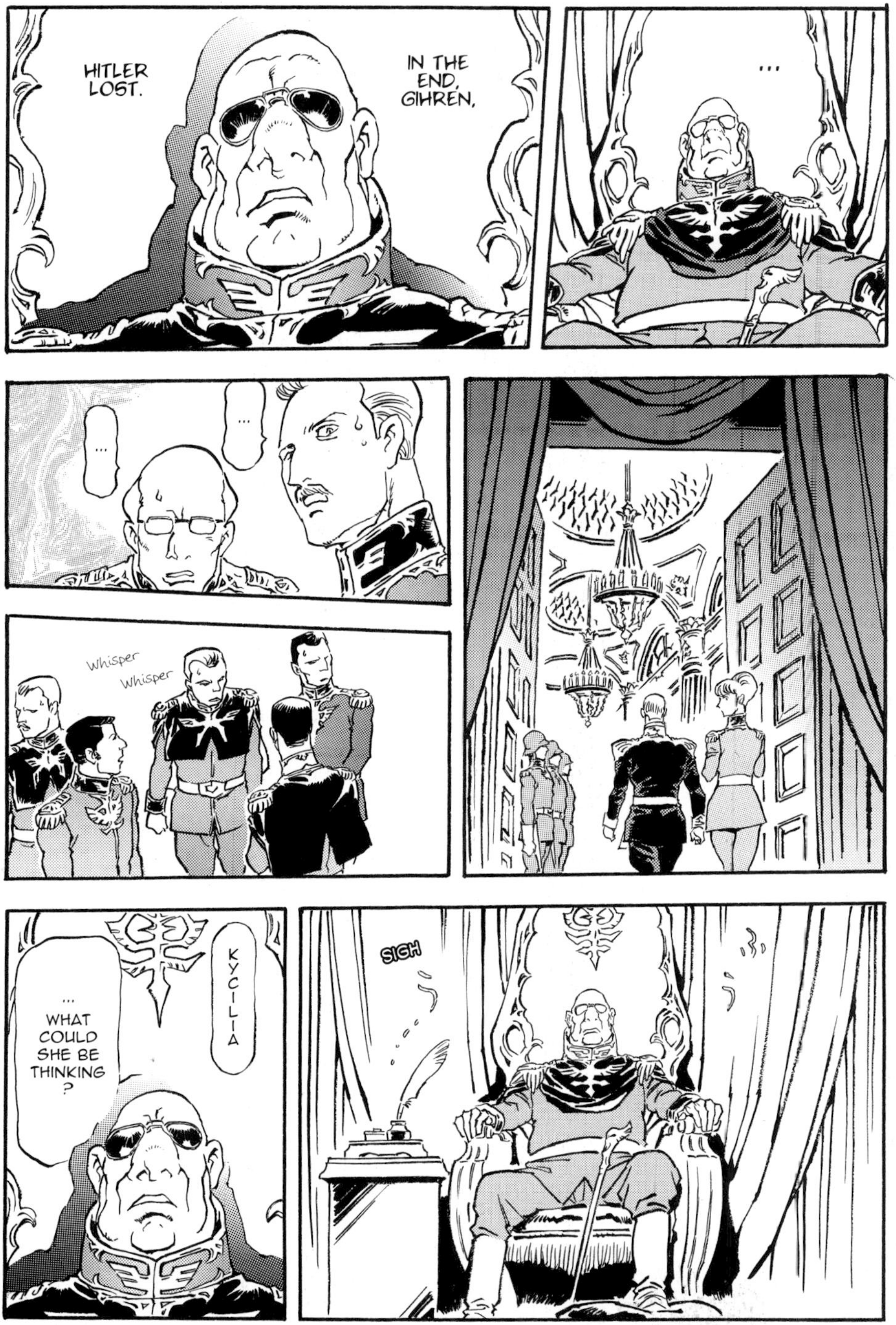
...
IN THE END, GIHREN,
HITLER LOST.
...
...
Whisper
Whisper
SIGH
KYCILIA
... WHAT COULD SHE BE THINKING?

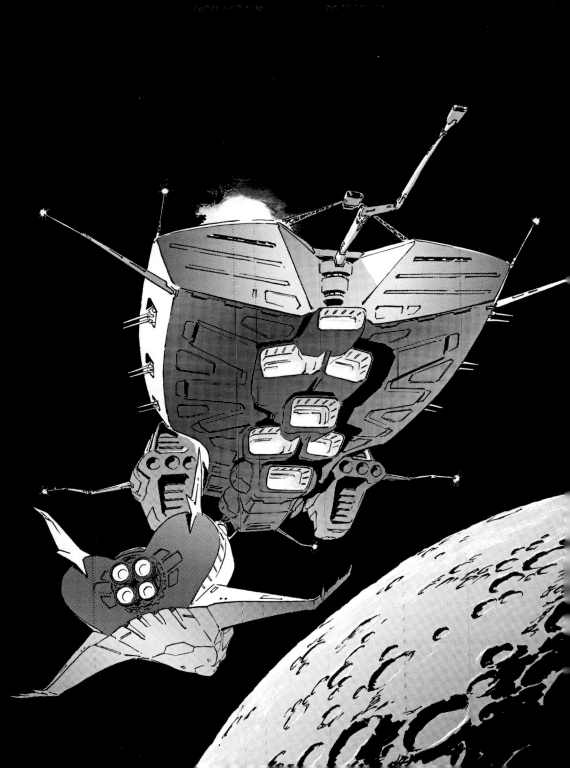

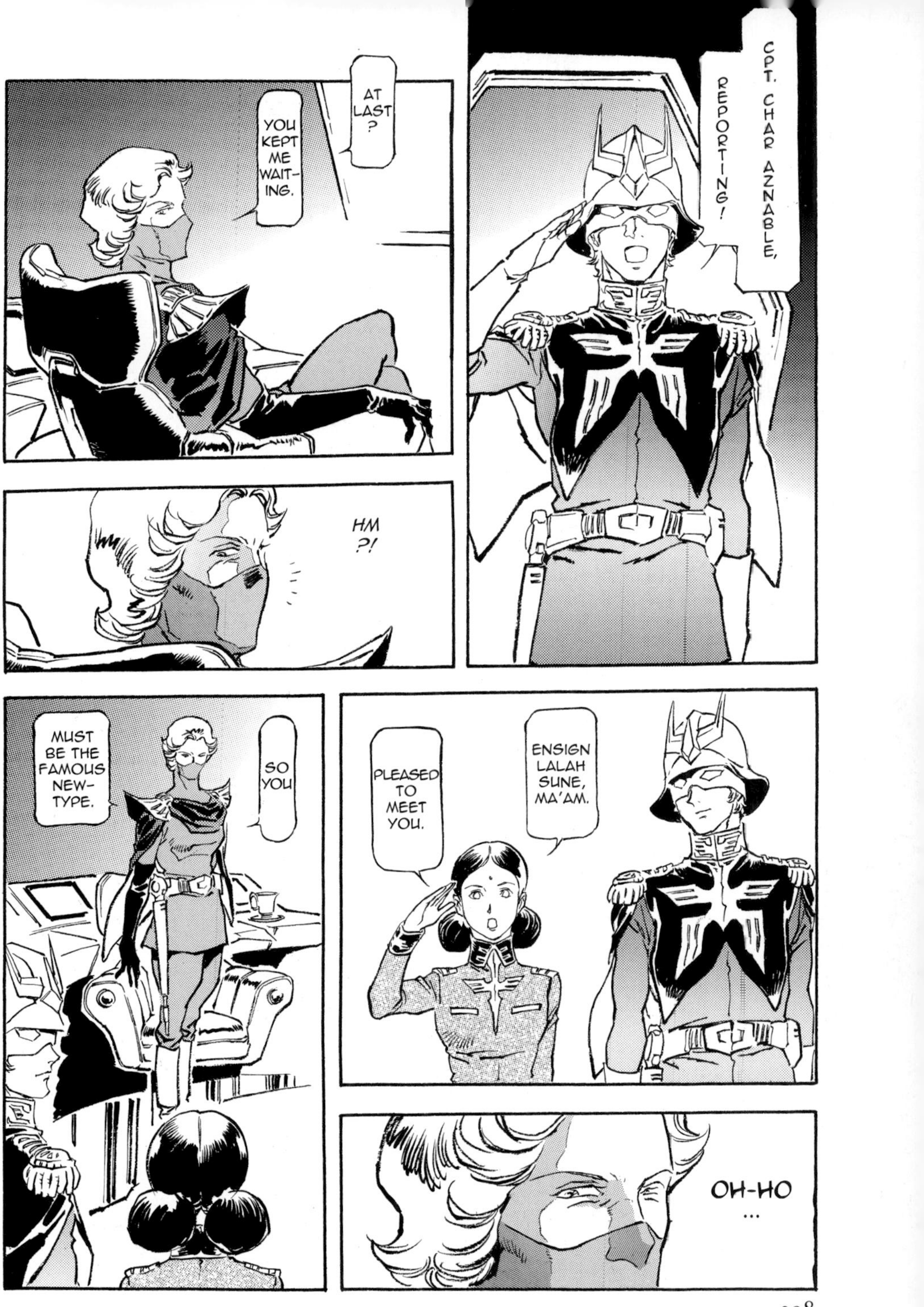
CPT. CHAR AZNABLE, REPORTING!
AT LAST?
YOU KEPT ME WAITING.
HM ?!
ENSIGN LALAH SUNE, MA'AM.
PLEASED TO MEET YOU.
OH-HO ...
SO YOU
MUST BE THE FAMOUS NEW-TYPE.

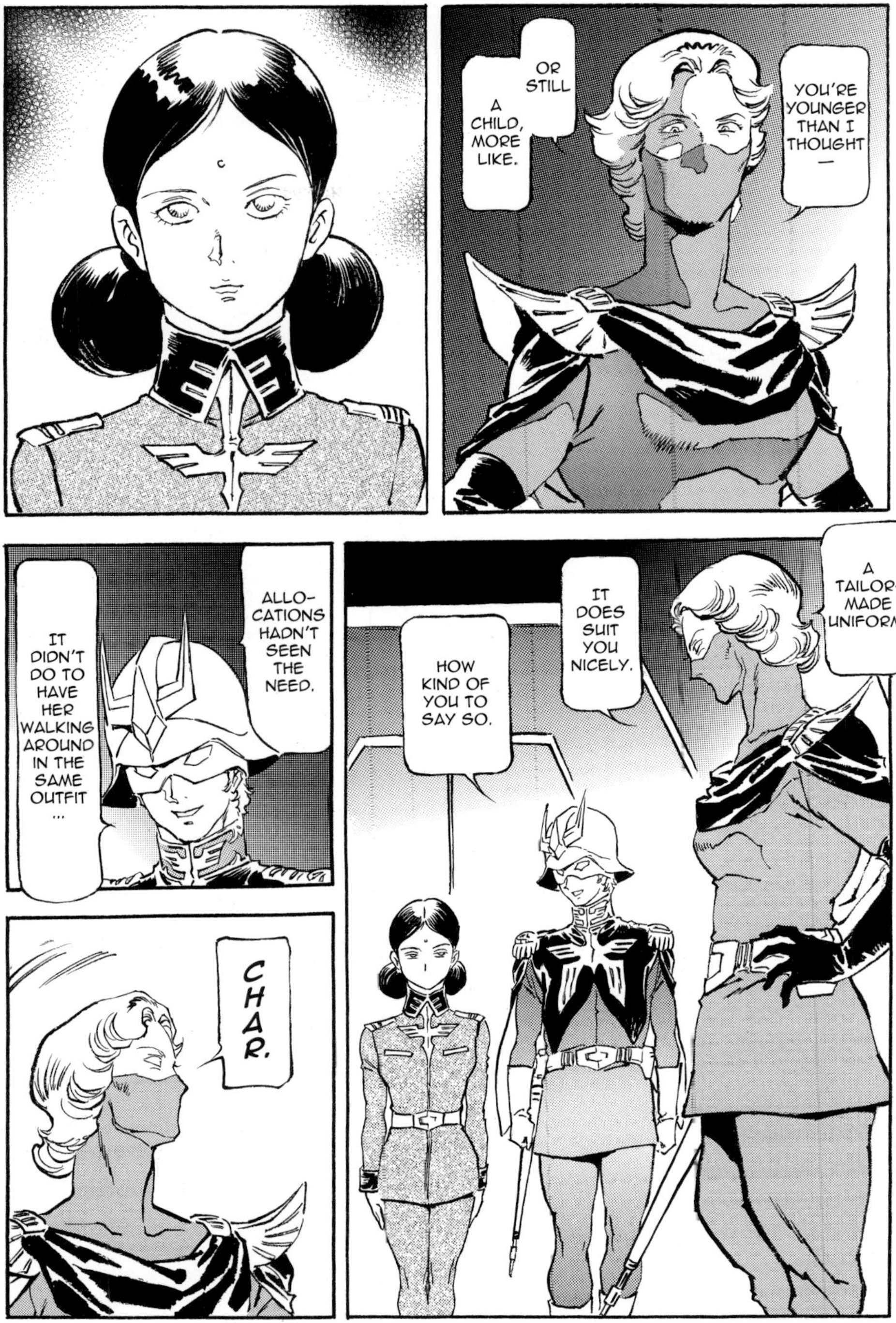
YOU'RE YOUNGER THAN I THOUGHT —
OR STILL A CHILD, MORE LIKE.
A TAILOR-MADE UNIFORM.
IT DOES SUIT YOU NICELY.
HOW KIND OF YOU TO SAY SO.
ALLO-CATIONS HADN'T SEEN THE NEED.
IT DIDN'T DO TO HAVE HER WALKING AROUND IN THE SAME OUTFIT ...
CHAR.

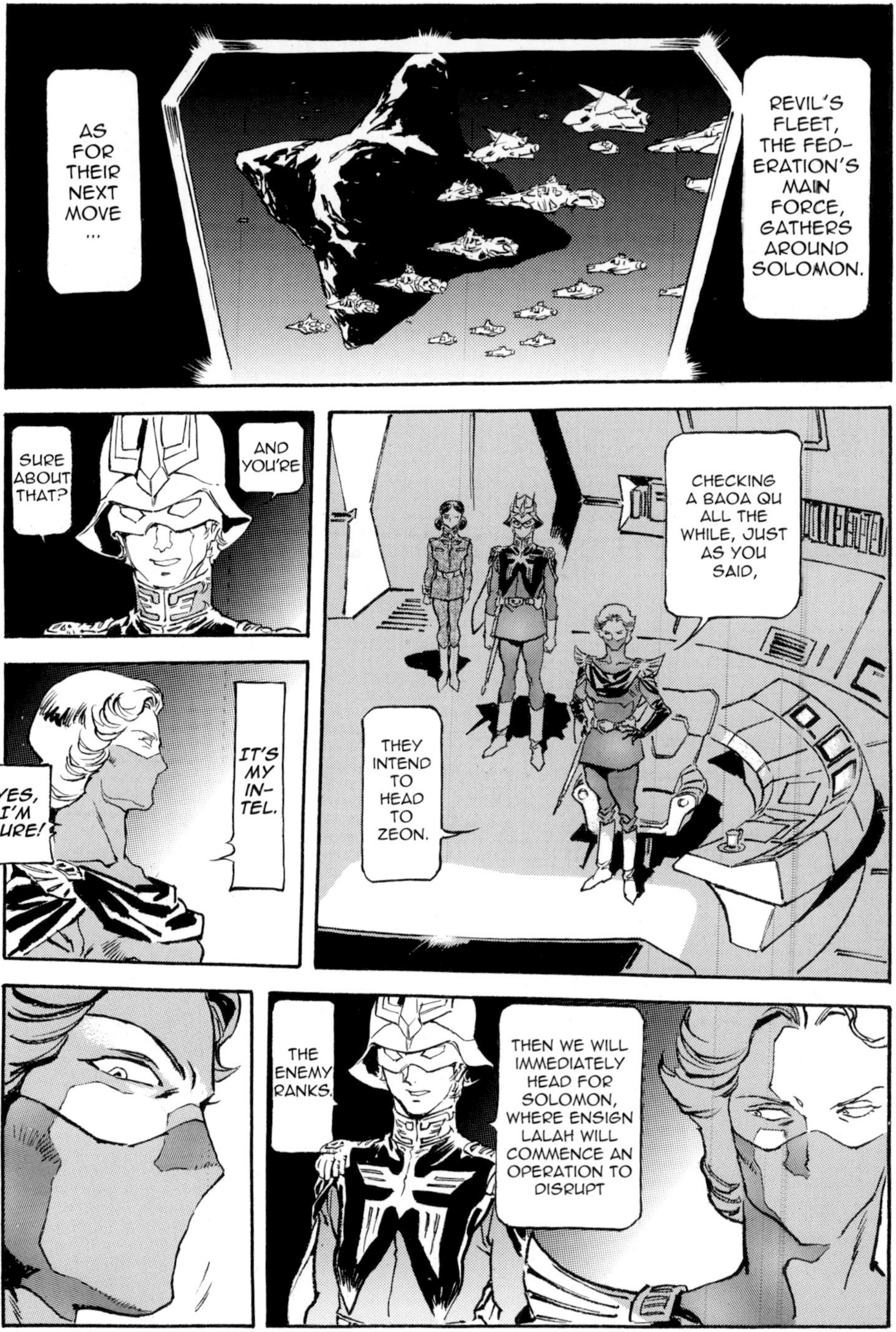
REVIL'S FLEET, THE FED-ERATION'S MAIN FORCE, GATHERS AROUND SOLOMON.
AS FOR THEIR NEXT MOVE ...
CHECKING A BAOA QU ALL THE WHILE, JUST AS YOU SAID,
THEY INTEND TO HEAD TO ZEON.
AND YOU'RE
SURE ABOUT THAT?
IT'S MY IN-TEL.
YES, I'M SURE!
THEN WE WILL IMMEDIATELY HEAD FOR SOLOMON, WHERE ENSIGN LALAH WILL COMMENCE AN OPERATION TO DISRUPT
THE ENEMY RANKS.

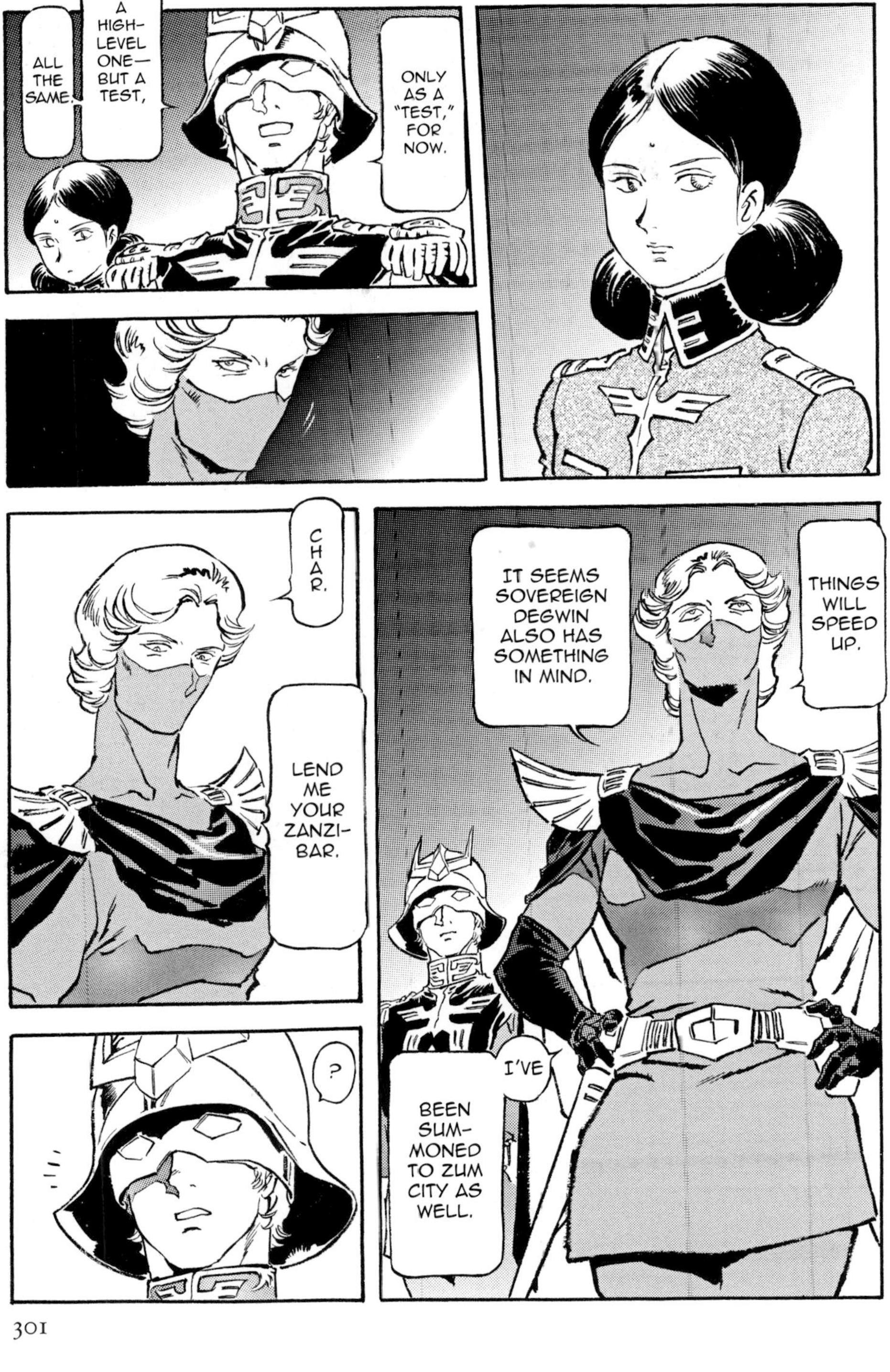
ONLY AS A "TEST," FOR NOW.
A HIGH-LEVEL ONE— BUT A TEST,
ALL THE SAME.
THINGS WILL SPEED UP.
IT SEEMS SOVEREIGN DEGWIN ALSO HAS SOMETHING IN MIND.
I'VE BEEN SUMMONED TO ZUM CITY AS WELL.
CHAR.
LEND ME YOUR ZANZIBAR.
?

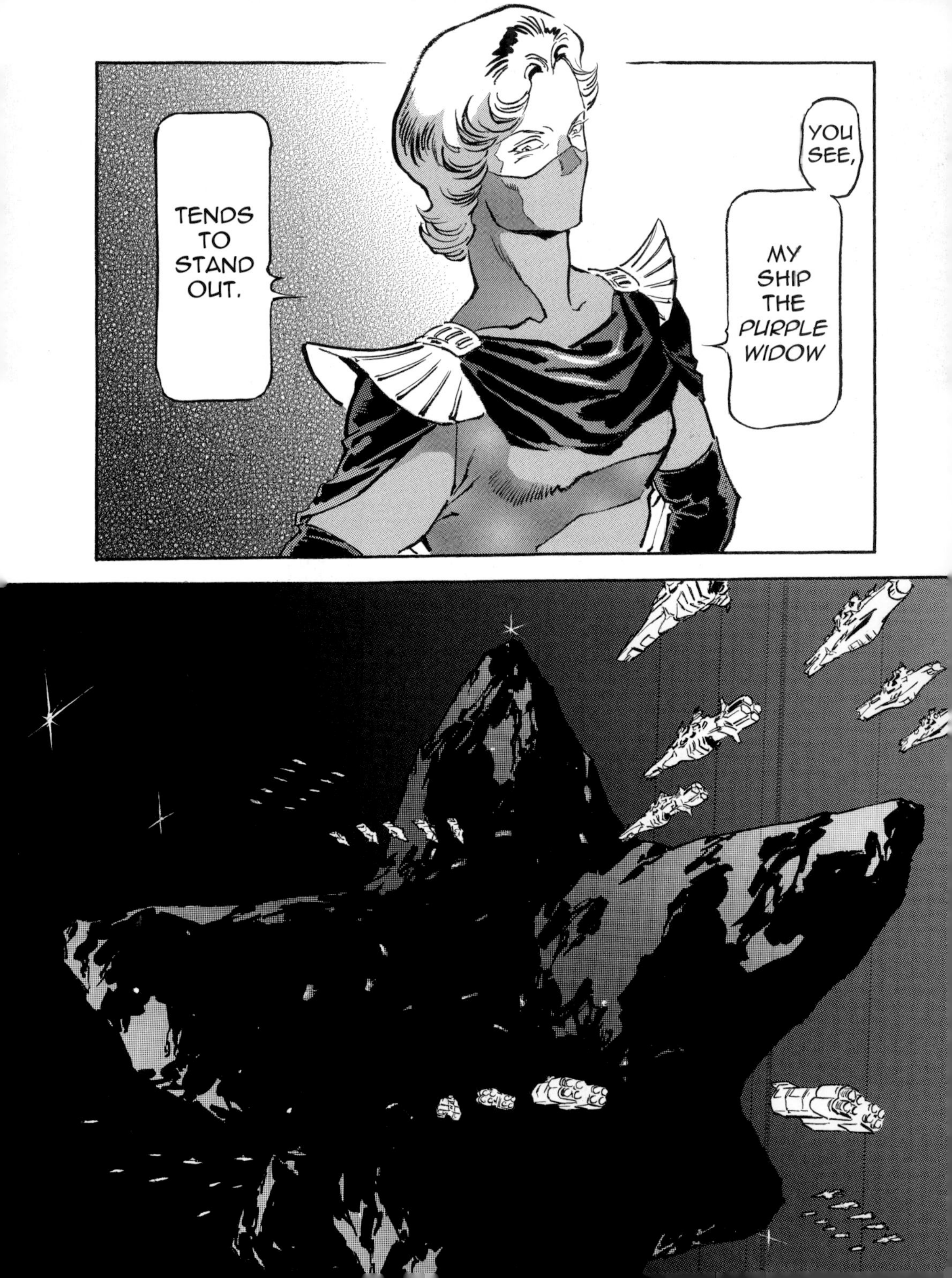
YOU SEE,
MY SHIP THE *PURPLE WIDOW*
TENDS TO STAND OUT.

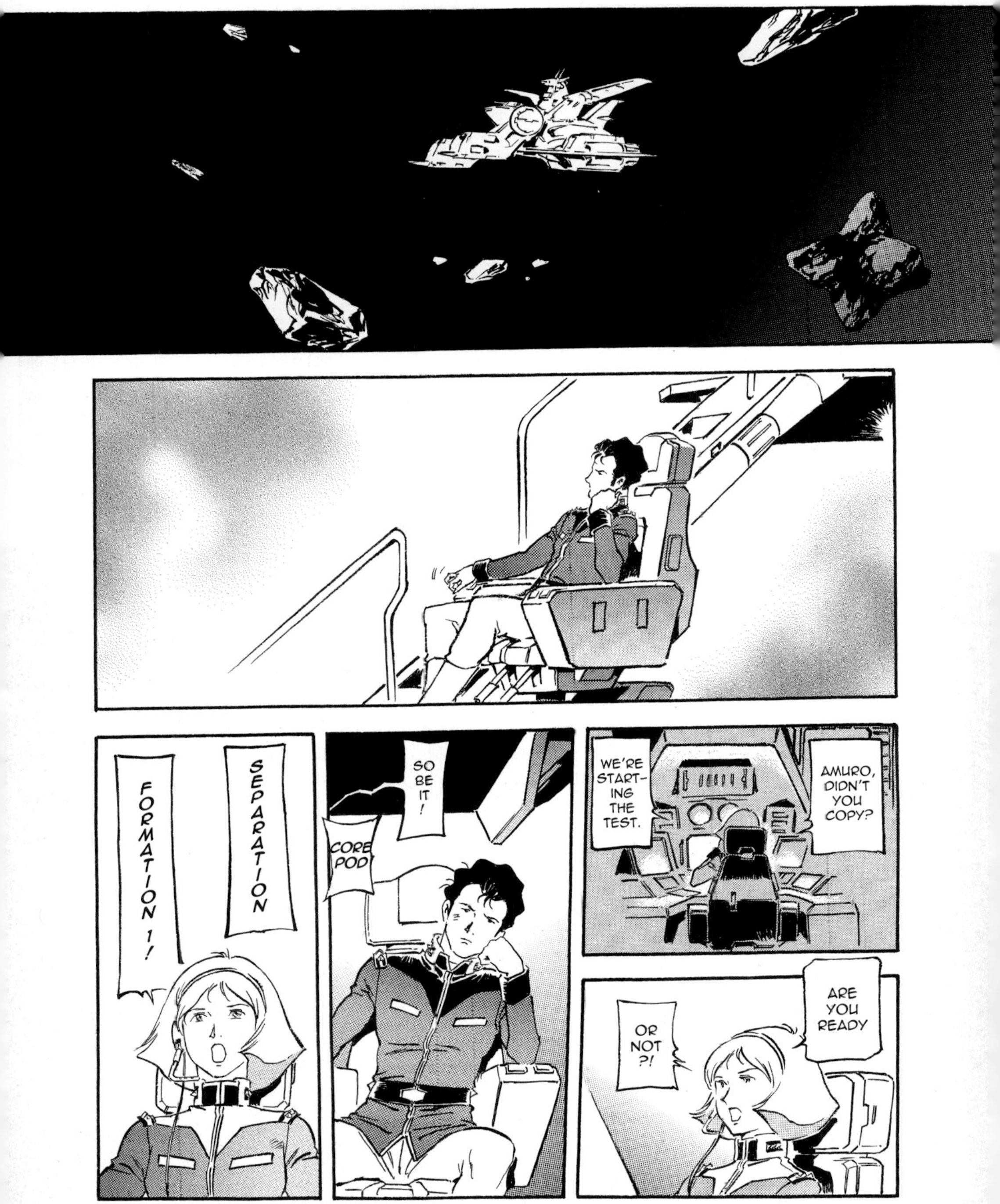
AMURO, DIDN'T YOU COPY?
WE'RE STARTING THE TEST.
ARE YOU READY
OR NOT ?!
SO BE IT!
CORE POD
SEPARATION
FORMATION 1!

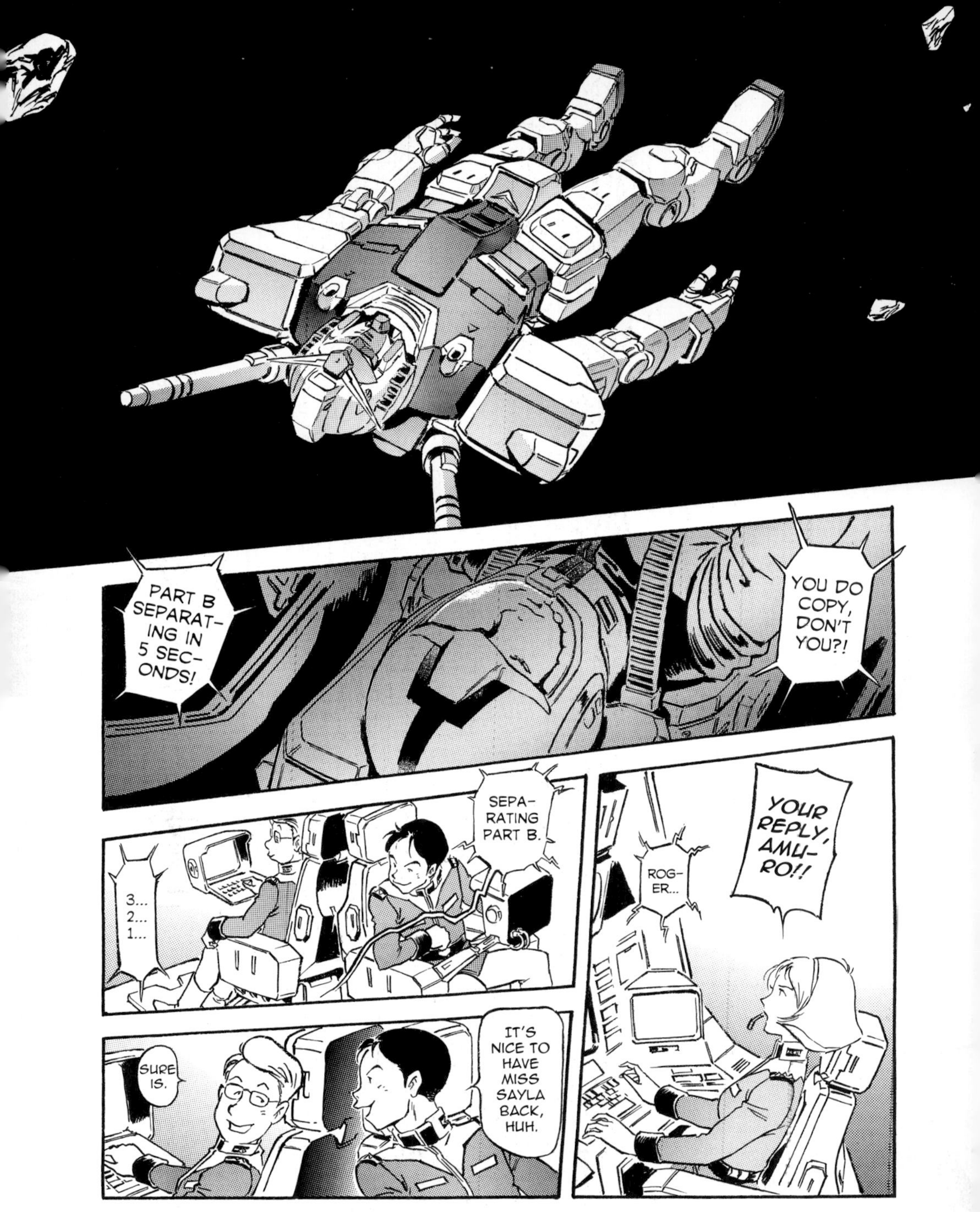
YOU DO COPY, DON'T YOU?!
PART B SEPARATING IN 5 SECONDS!
YOUR REPLY, AMURO!!
ROGER...
SEPARATING PART B.
3... 2... 1...
IT'S NICE TO HAVE MISS SAYLA BACK, HUH.
SURE IS.

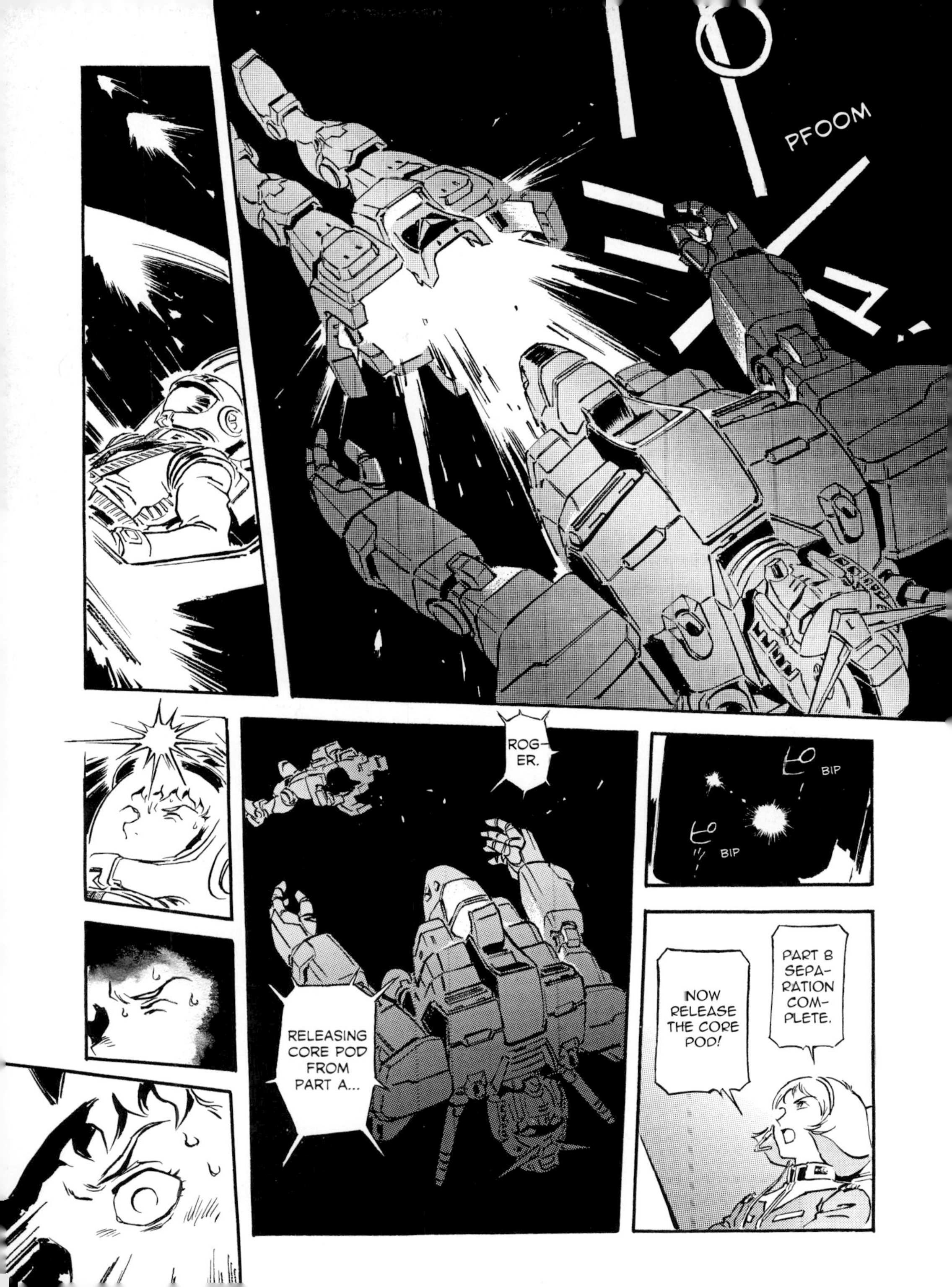
PFOOM
ピ
BIP
ピ
BIP
PART B SEPA-RATION COM-PLETE.
NOW RELEASE THE CORE POD!
ROG-ER.
RELEASING CORE POD FROM PART A...

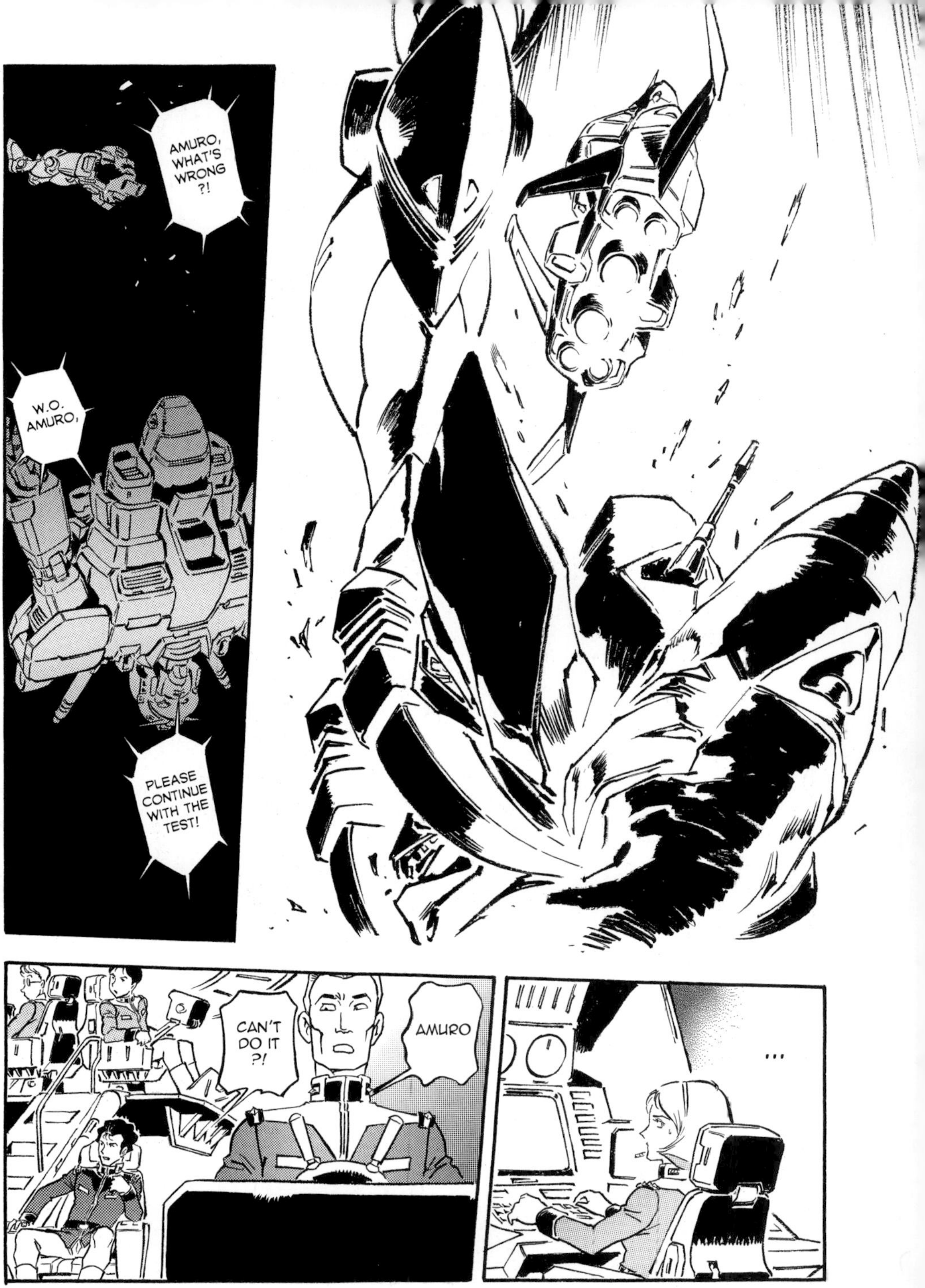
AMURO, WHAT'S WRONG ?!
W.O. AMURO,
PLEASE CONTINUE WITH THE TEST!
...
AMURO
CAN'T DO IT ?!

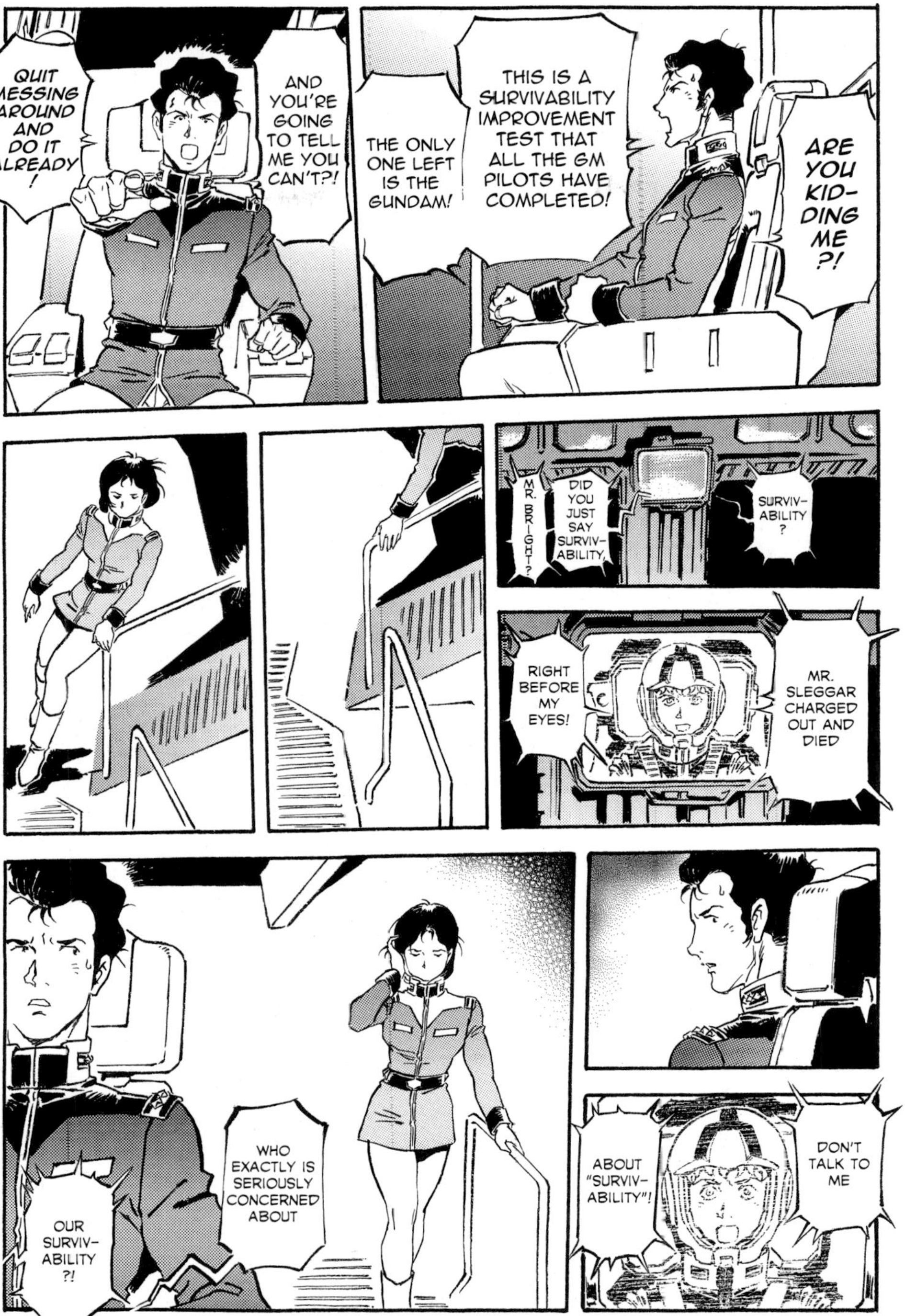
ARE YOU KIDDING ME?!
THIS IS A SURVIVABILITY IMPROVEMENT TEST THAT ALL THE GM PILOTS HAVE COMPLETED!
THE ONLY ONE LEFT IS THE GUNDAM!
AND YOU'RE GOING TO TELL ME YOU CAN'T?!
QUIT MESSING AROUND AND DO IT ALREADY!
SURVIVABILITY?
DID YOU JUST SAY SURVIVABILITY,
MR. BRIGHT?
MR. SLEGGAR CHARGED OUT AND DIED
RIGHT BEFORE MY EYES!
DON'T TALK TO ME
ABOUT "SURVIVABILITY"!
WHO EXACTLY IS SERIOUSLY CONCERNED ABOUT
OUR SURVIVABILITY?!

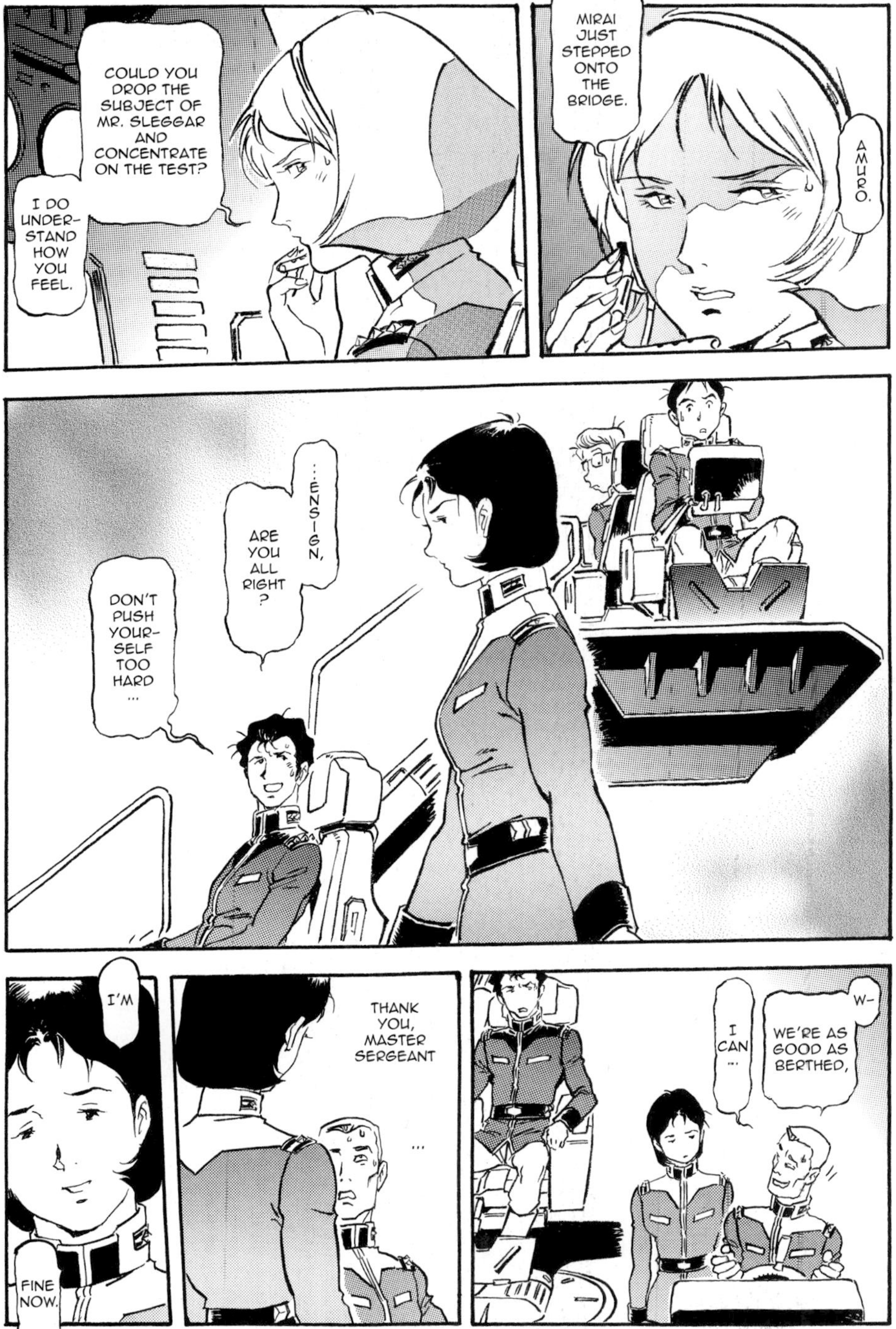
AMURO.
MIRAI JUST STEPPED ONTO THE BRIDGE.
COULD YOU DROP THE SUBJECT OF MR. SLEGGAR AND CONCENTRATE ON THE TEST?
I DO UNDER-STAND HOW YOU FEEL.
...ENSIGN,
ARE YOU ALL RIGHT?
DON'T PUSH YOUR-SELF TOO HARD ...
W-
WE'RE AS GOOD AS BERTHED,
I CAN ...
THANK YOU, MASTER SERGEANT
...
I'M
FINE NOW.

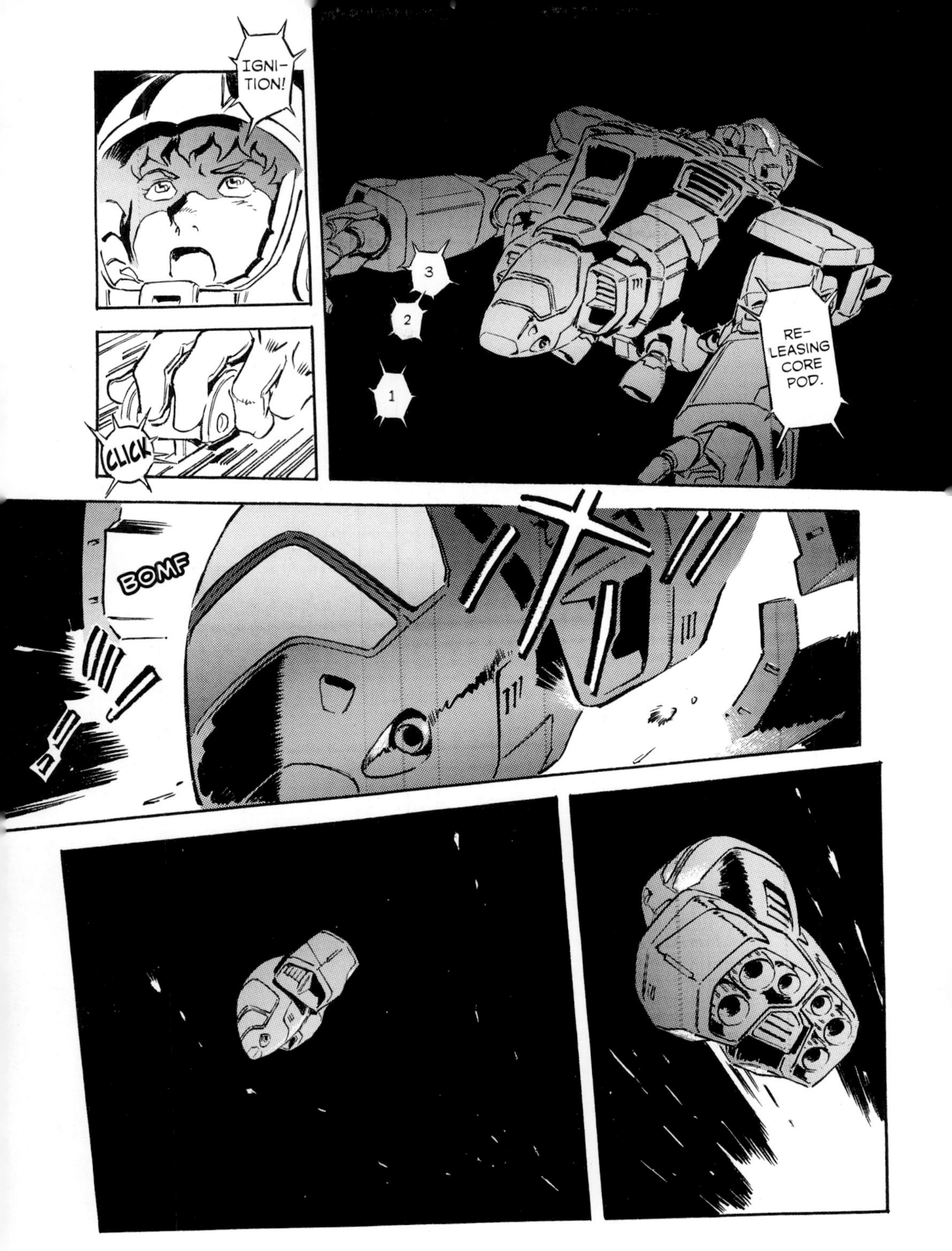
RE-LEASING CORE POD.
3
2
1
IGNI-TION!
CLICK
BOMF

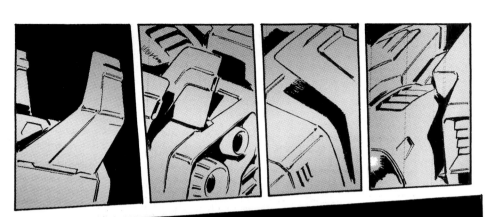

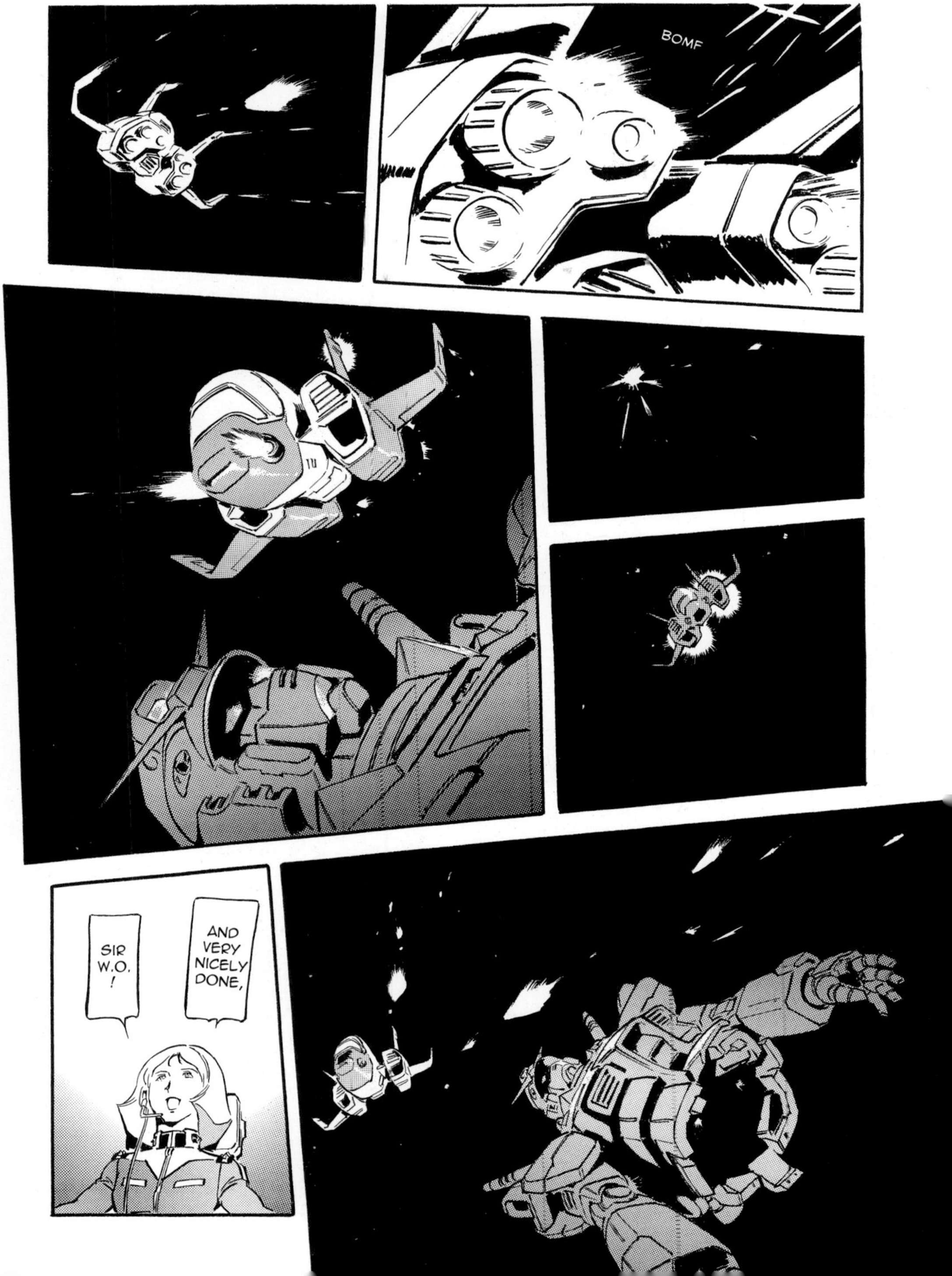
BOMF
AND VERY NICELY DONE,
SIR W.O.!

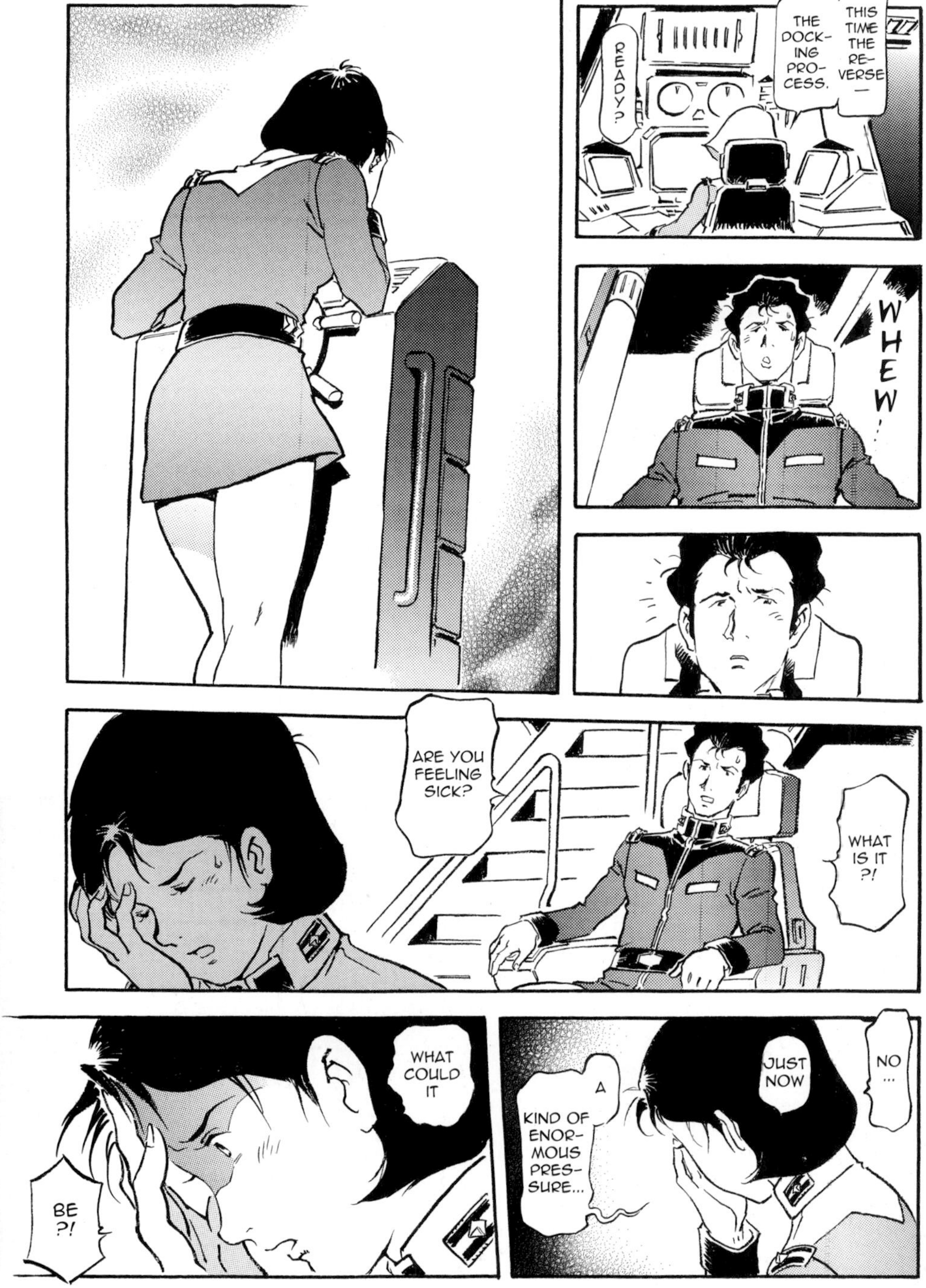
THIS TIME THE REVERSE—
THE DOCKING PROCESS.
READY?
WHEW...
WHAT IS IT?!
ARE YOU FEELING SICK?
NO...
JUST NOW
A KIND OF ENORMOUS PRESSURE...
WHAT COULD IT BE?!

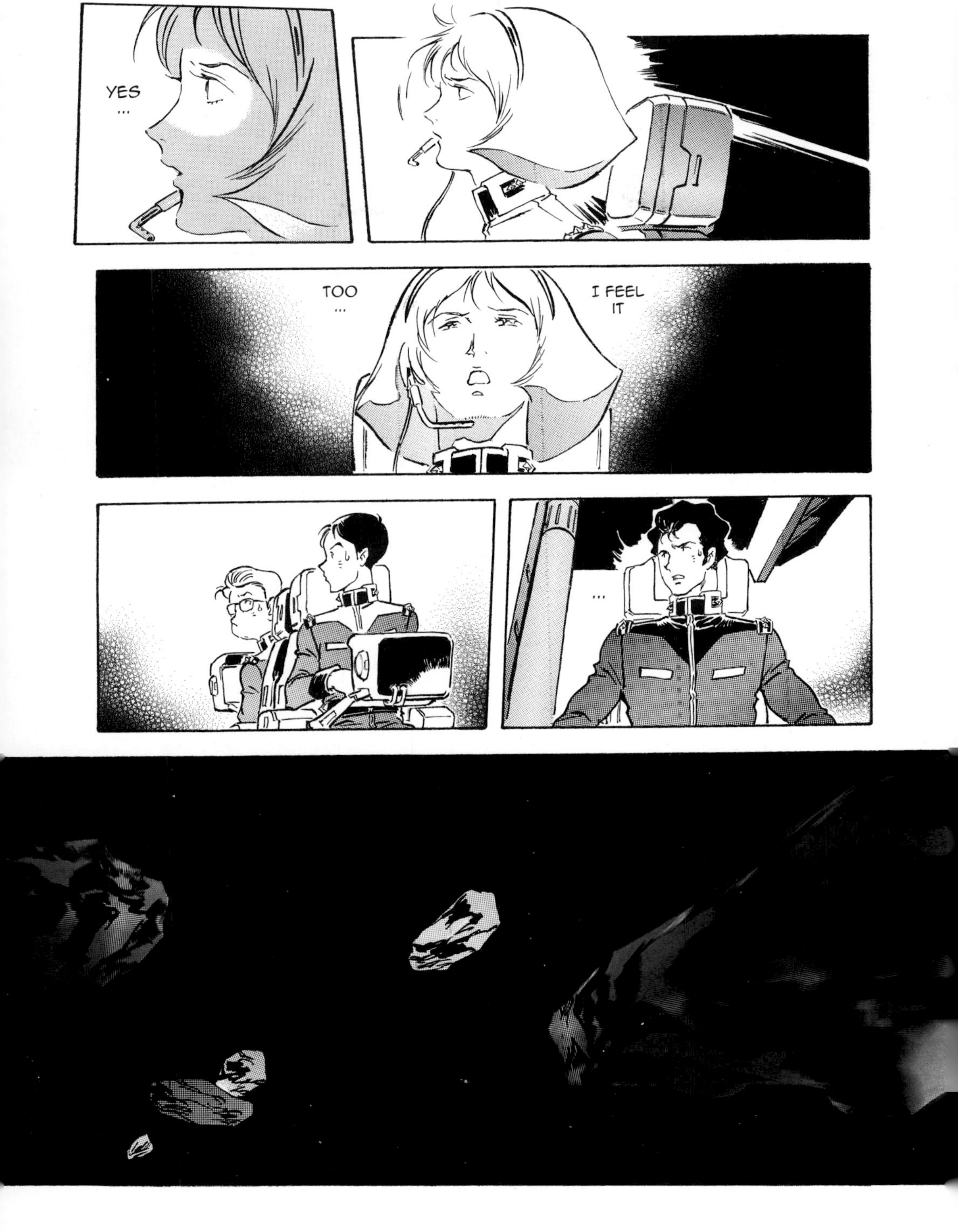
YES ...
I FEEL IT
TOO ...
...

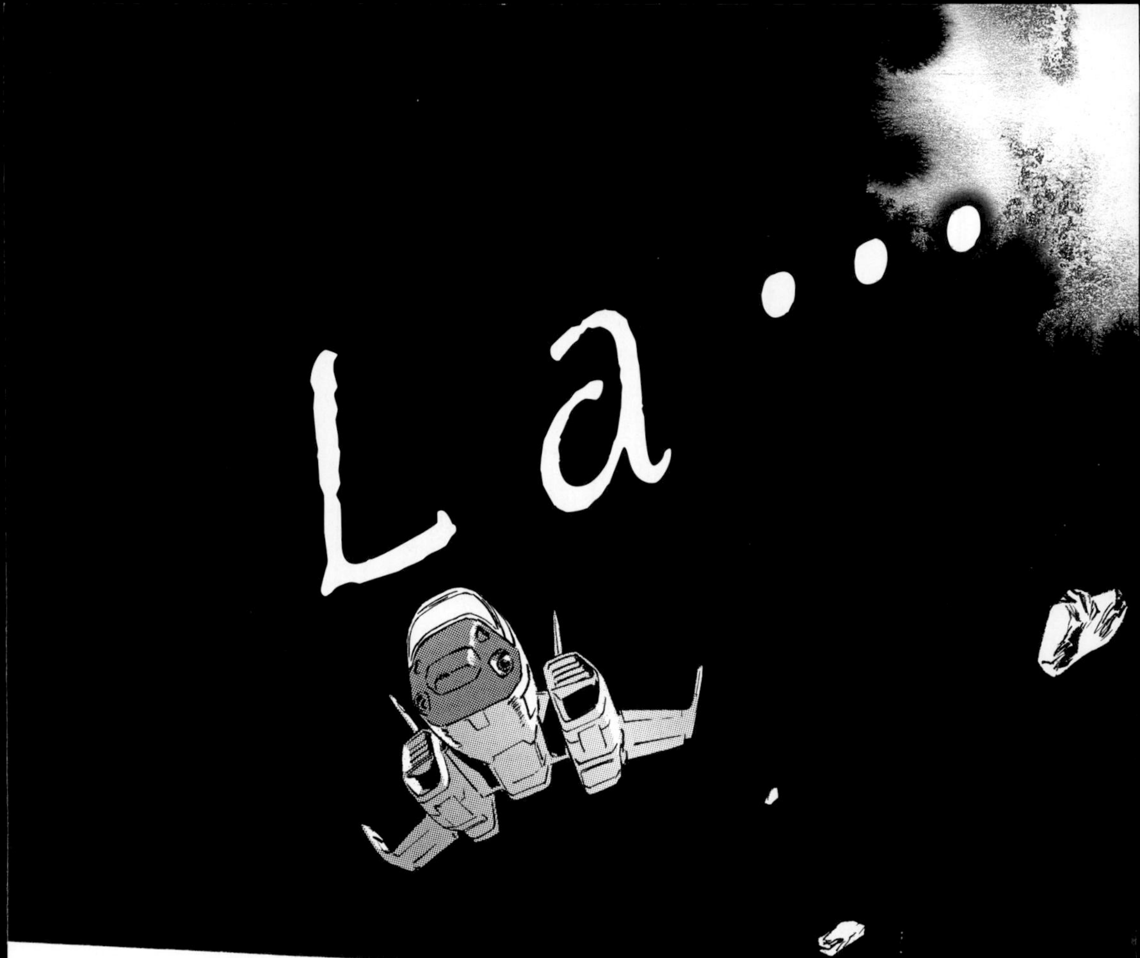
La...
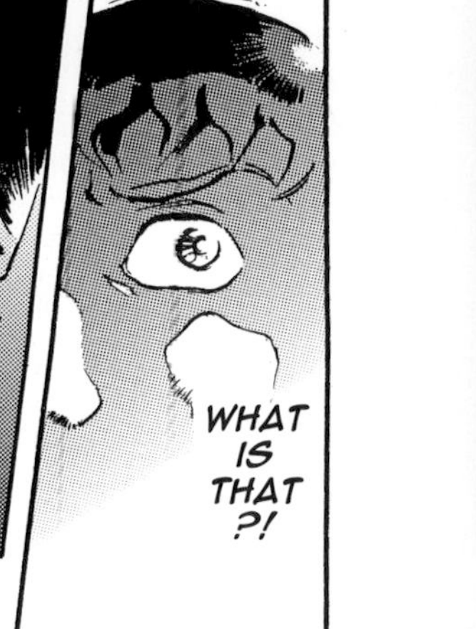
WHAT IS THAT ?!
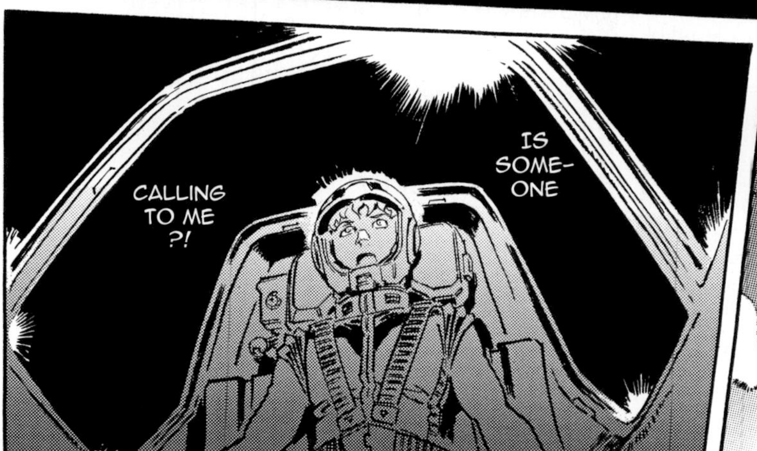
IS SOME- ONE
CALLING TO ME ?!

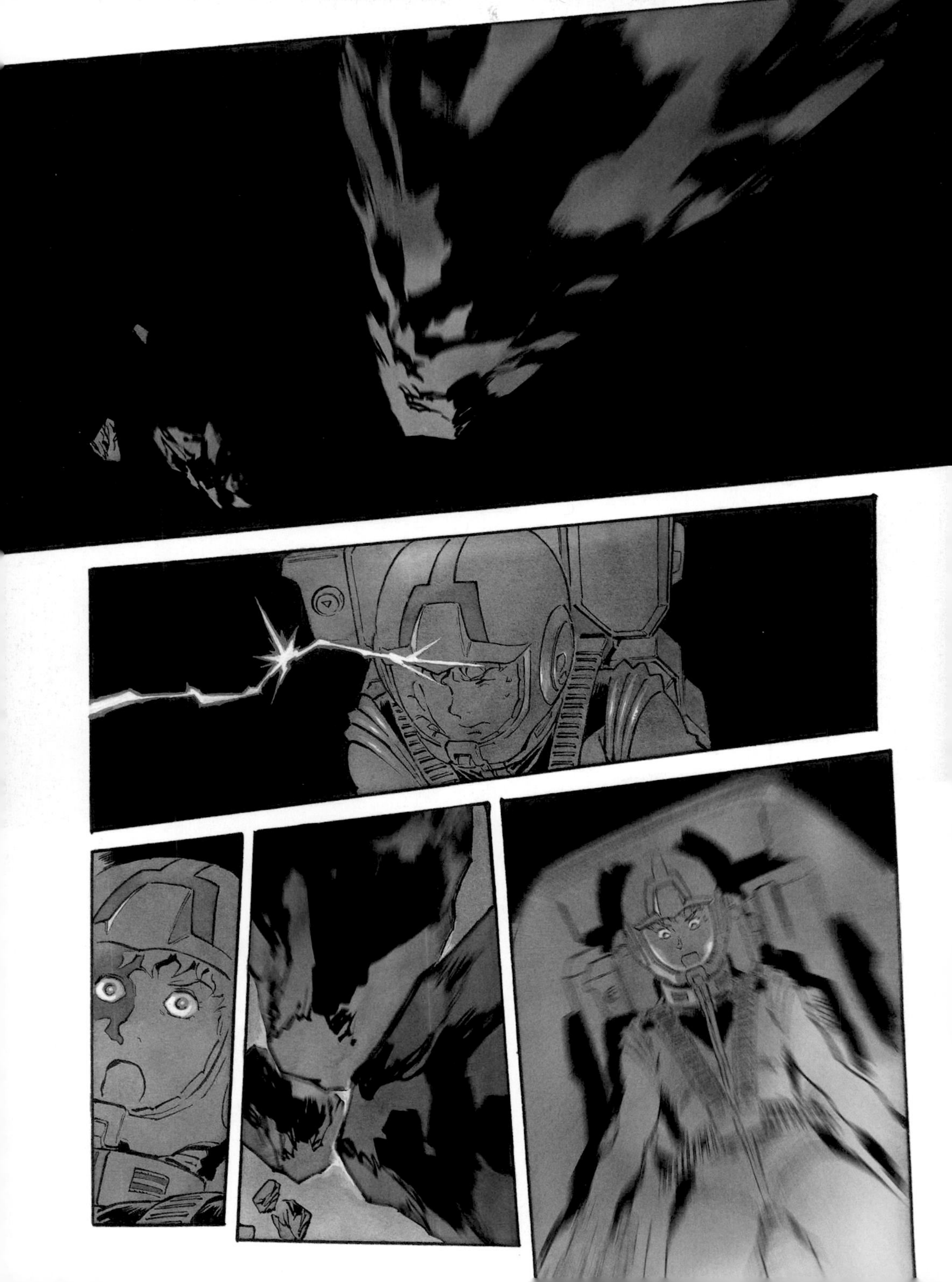

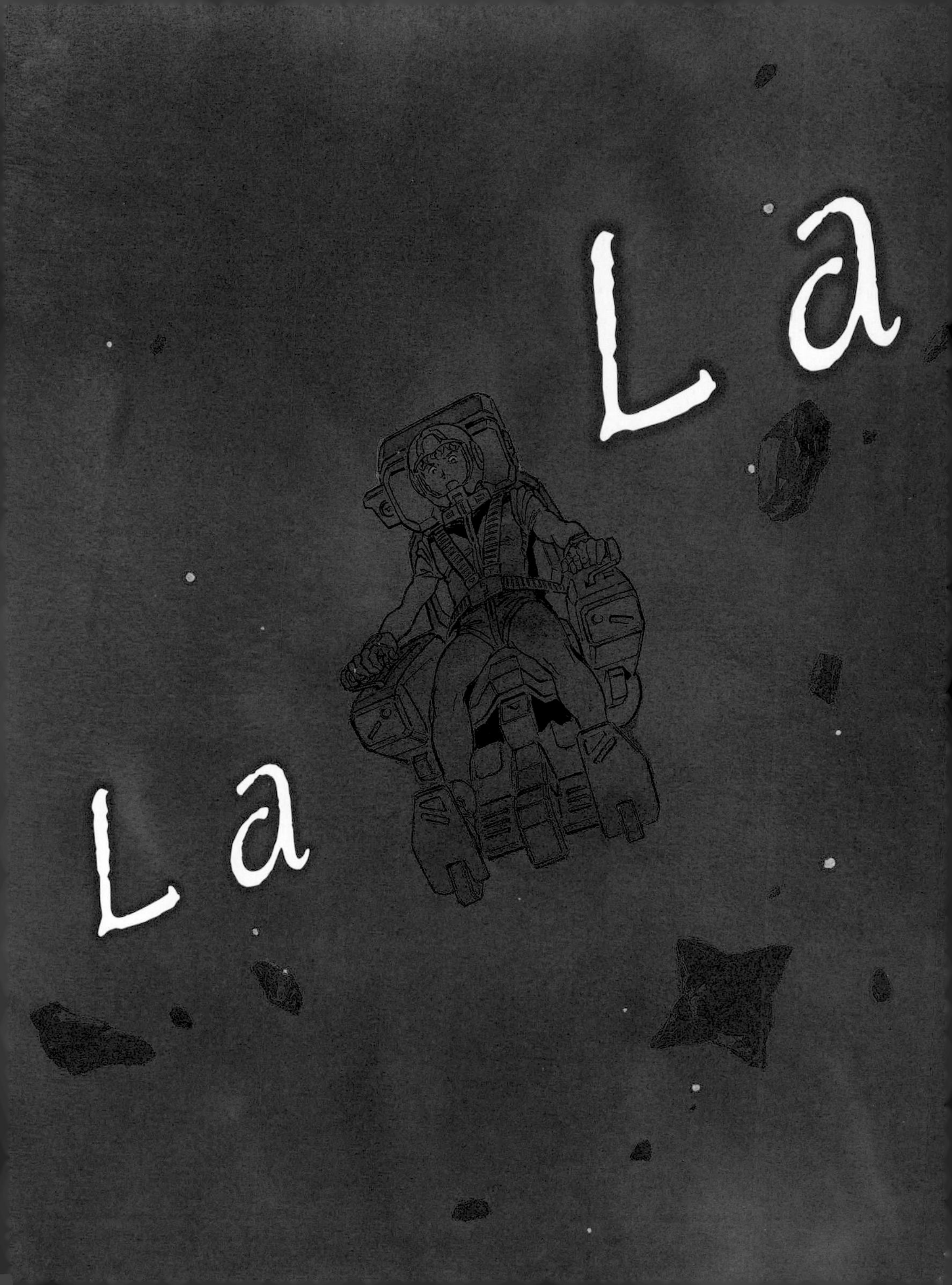
La
La

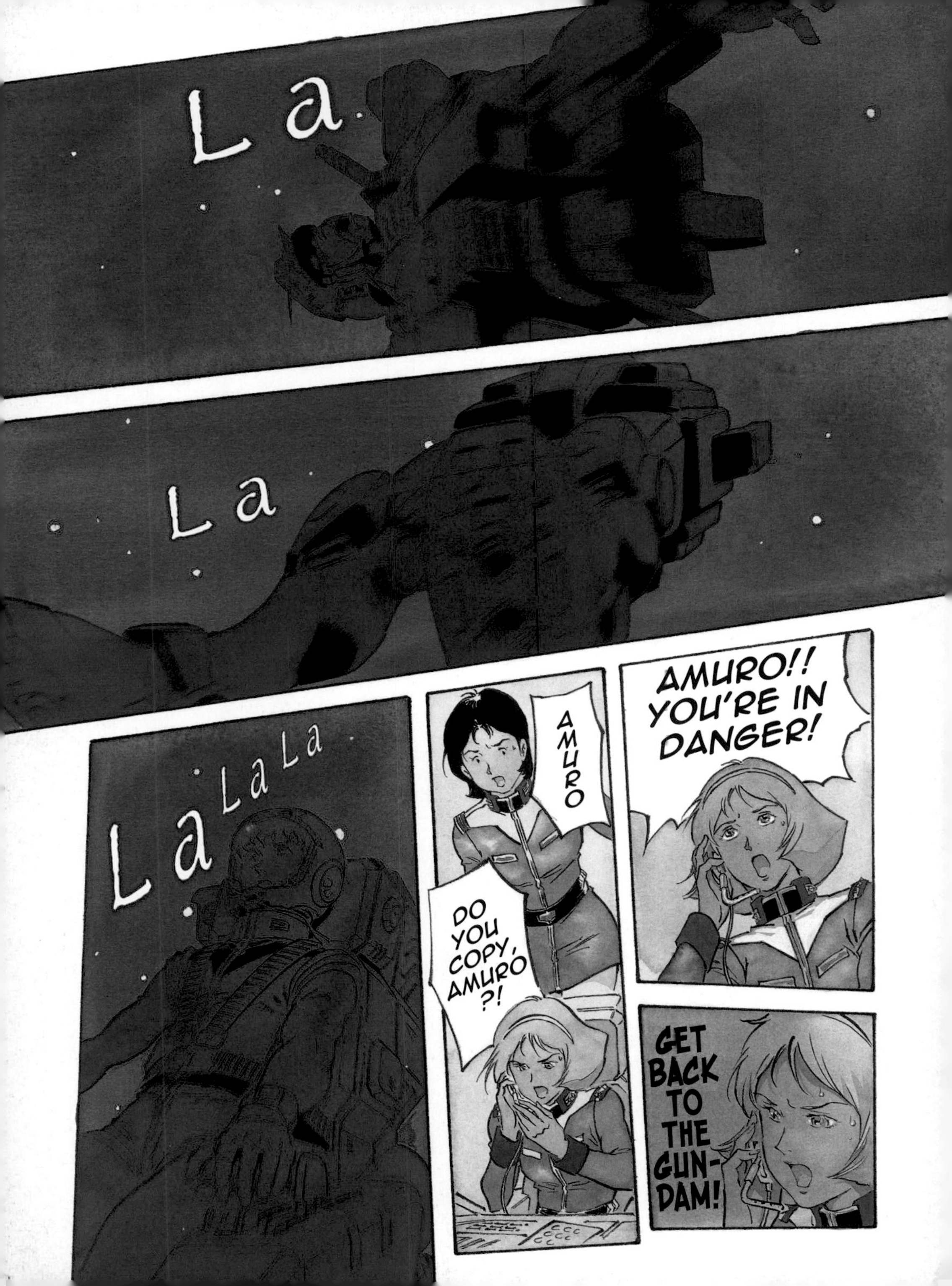
La
La
AMURO!! YOU'RE IN DANGER!
GET BACK TO THE GUN-DAM!
AMURO
DO YOU COPY, AMURO?!
La La La La

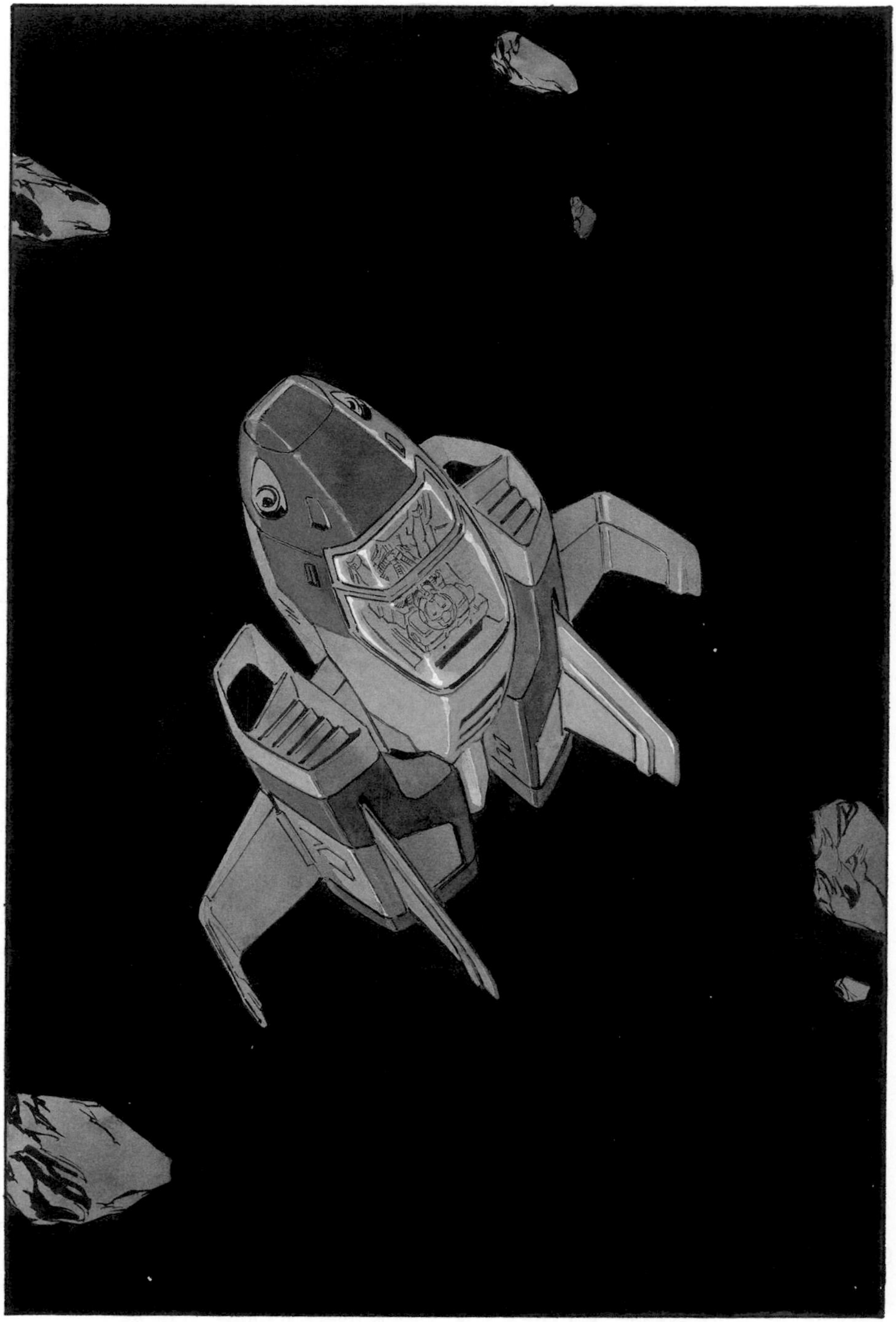

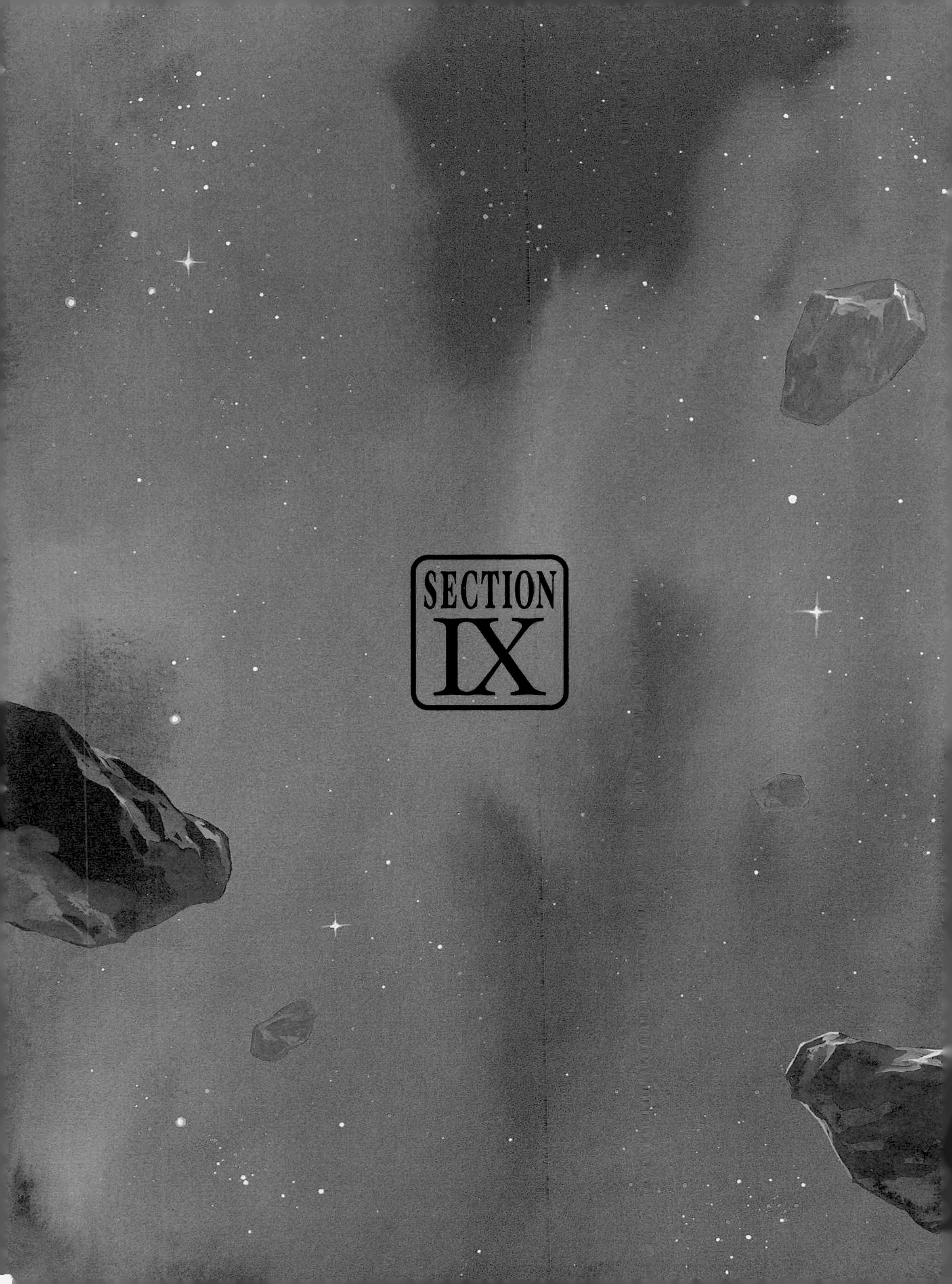
SECTION
IX

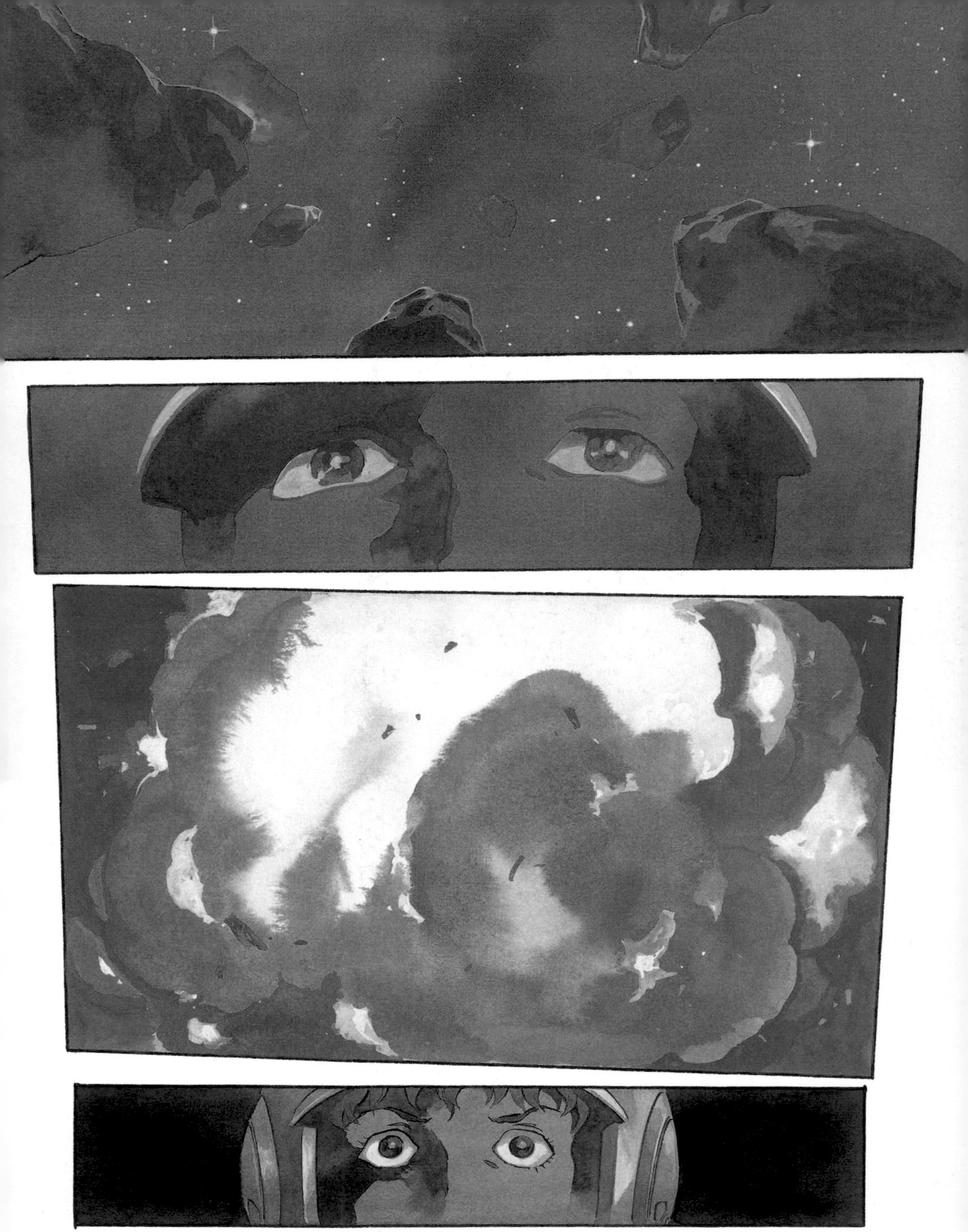

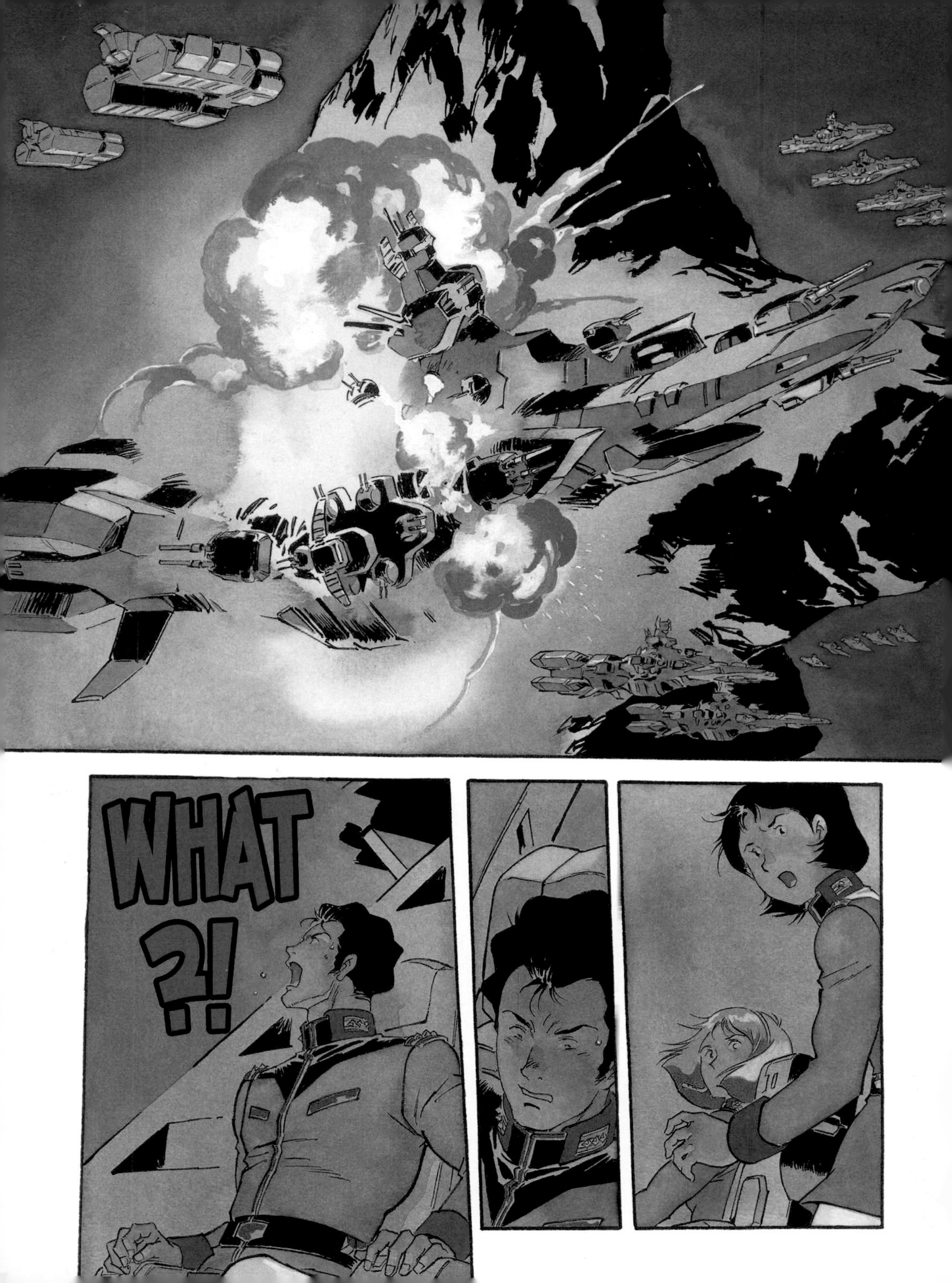
WHAT ?!

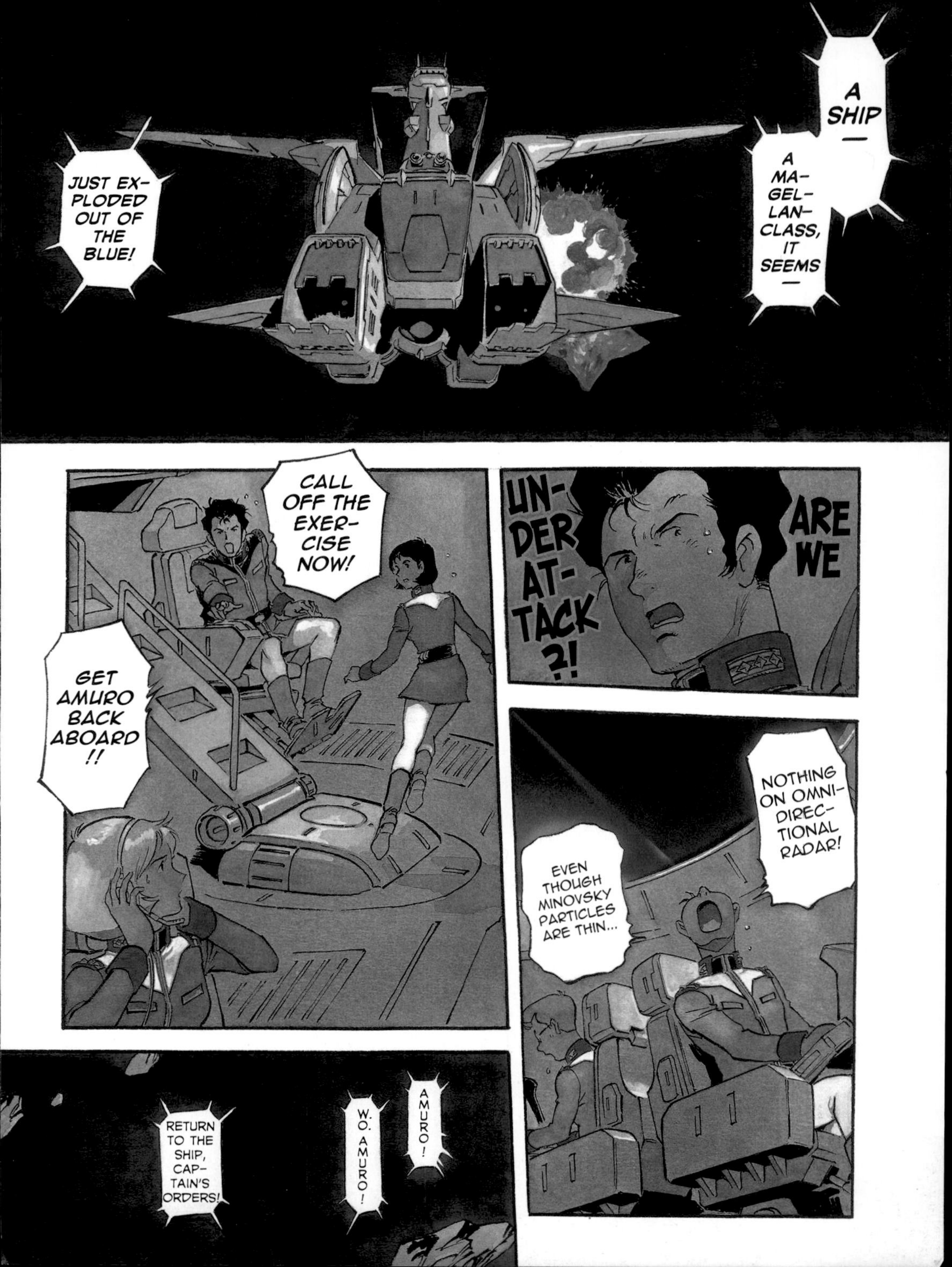
A SHIP — A MAGELLAN-CLASS, IT SEEMS —
JUST EXPLODED OUT OF THE BLUE!
ARE WE UNDER ATTACK?!
NOTHING ON OMNIDIRECTIONAL RADAR!
EVEN THOUGH MINOVSKY PARTICLES ARE THIN...
CALL OFF THE EXERCISE NOW!
GET AMURO BACK ABOARD!!
AMURO!
W.O. AMURO!
RETURN TO THE SHIP, CAPTAIN'S ORDERS!

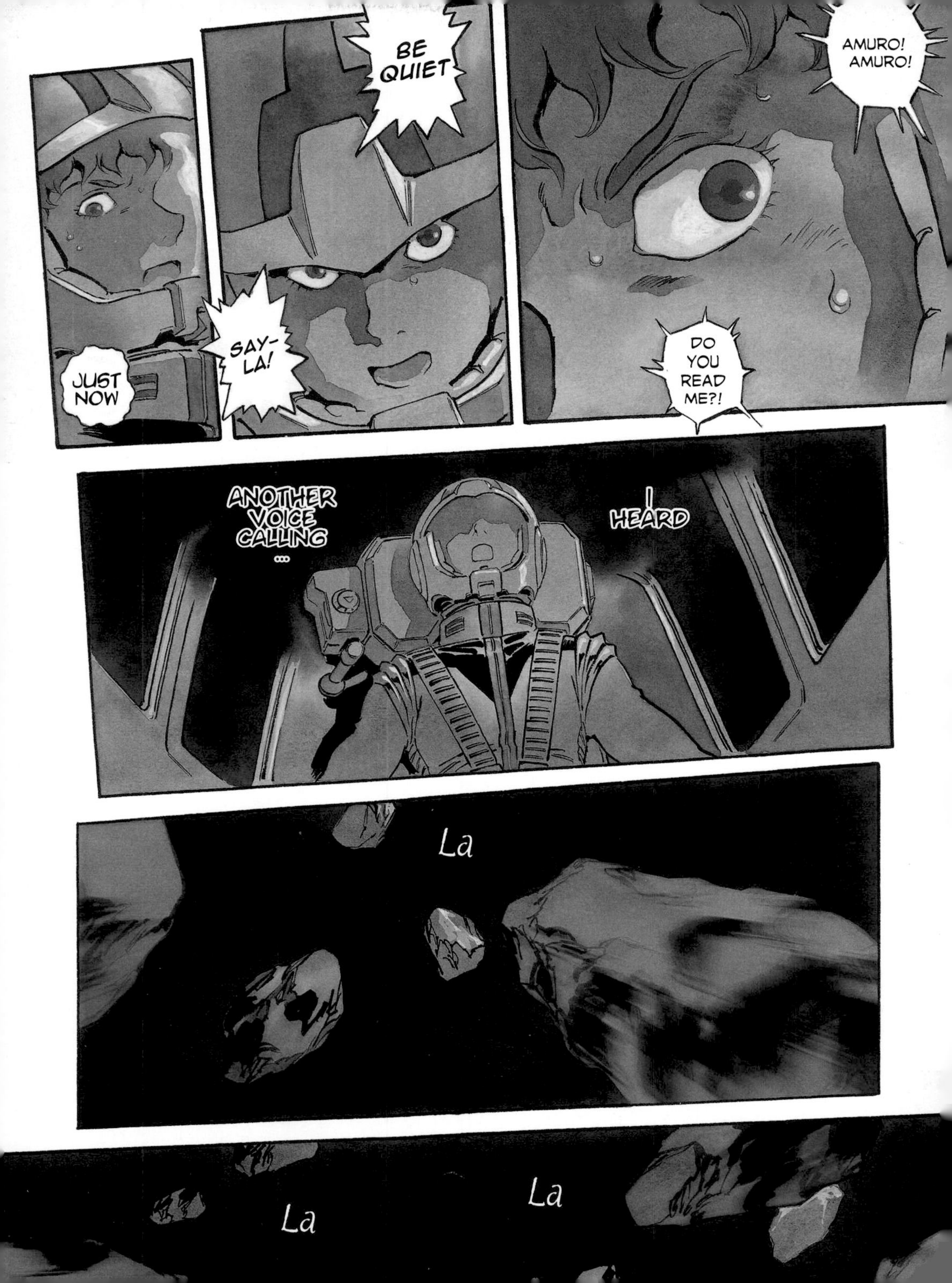
AMURO! AMURO!
DO YOU READ ME?!
BE QUIET
SAY-LA!
JUST NOW
I HEARD
ANOTHER VOICE CALLING ...
La
La
La

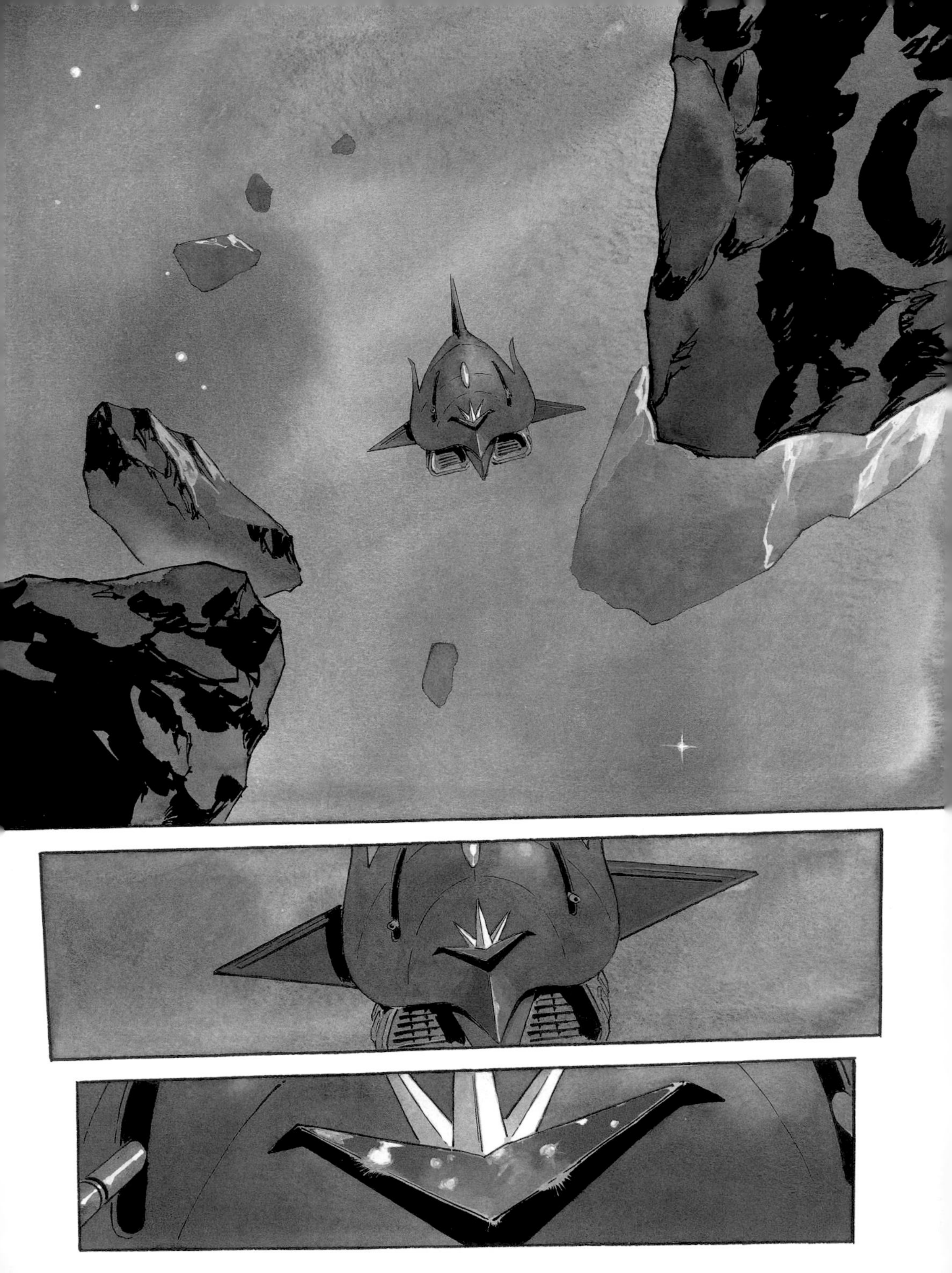

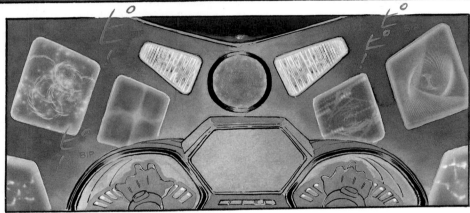

LALAH
?

ARE YOU
GETTING
TIRED,

YES,

CAP-
TAIN.

NO,
NOT
YET.

I
CAN
KEEP
GO-
ING.

DON'T
OVERDO
IT, THIS
IS

YOUR
FIRST
TRY.

TAKE
A
REST.

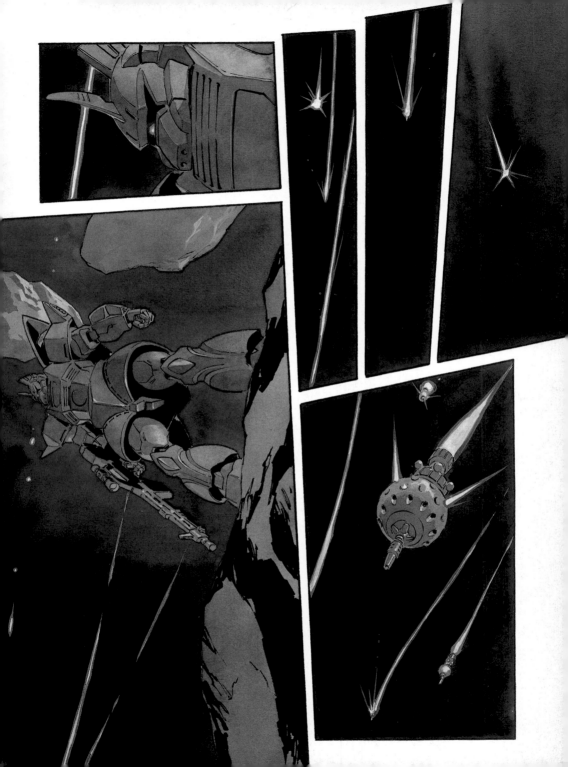

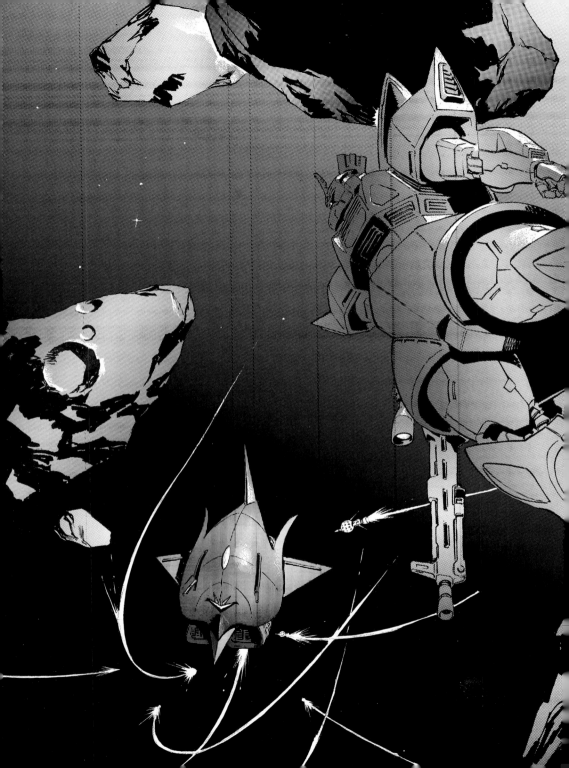

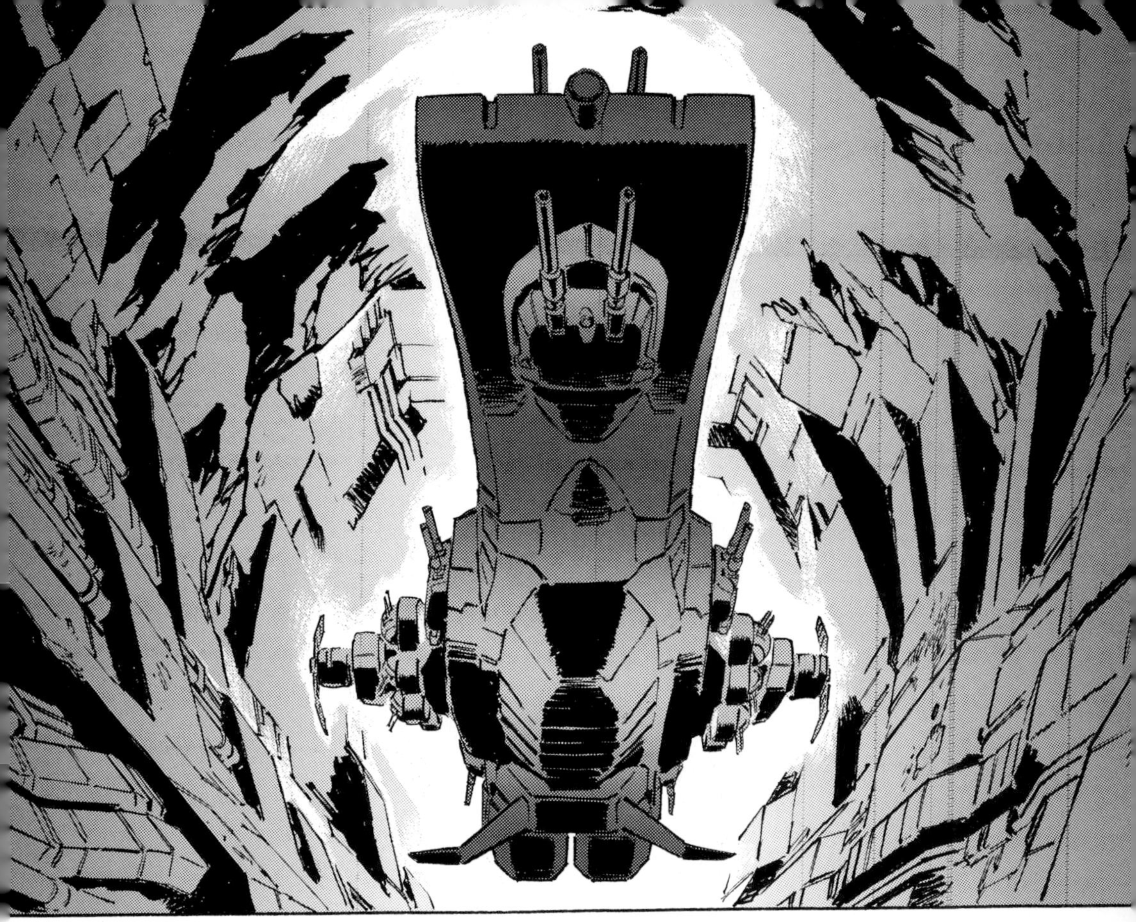

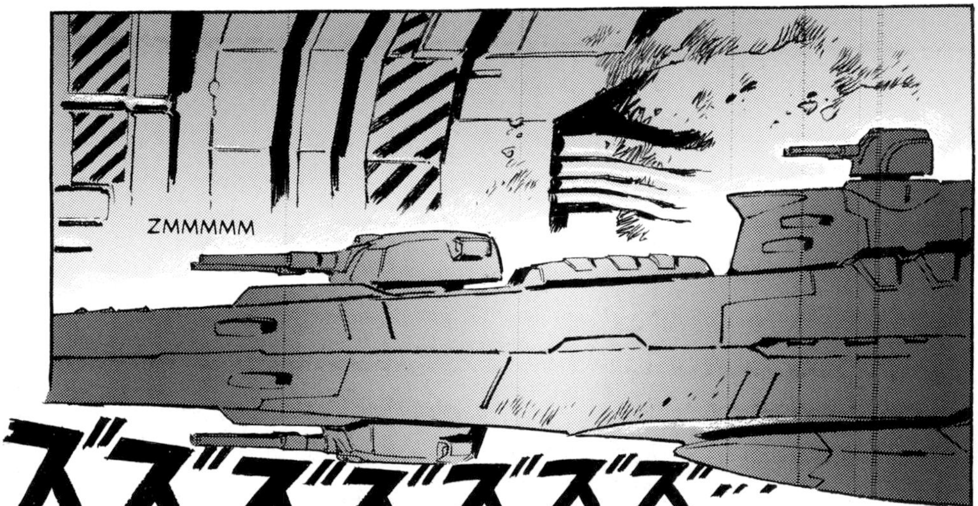
ZMMMMM
ズズズズズズ・・

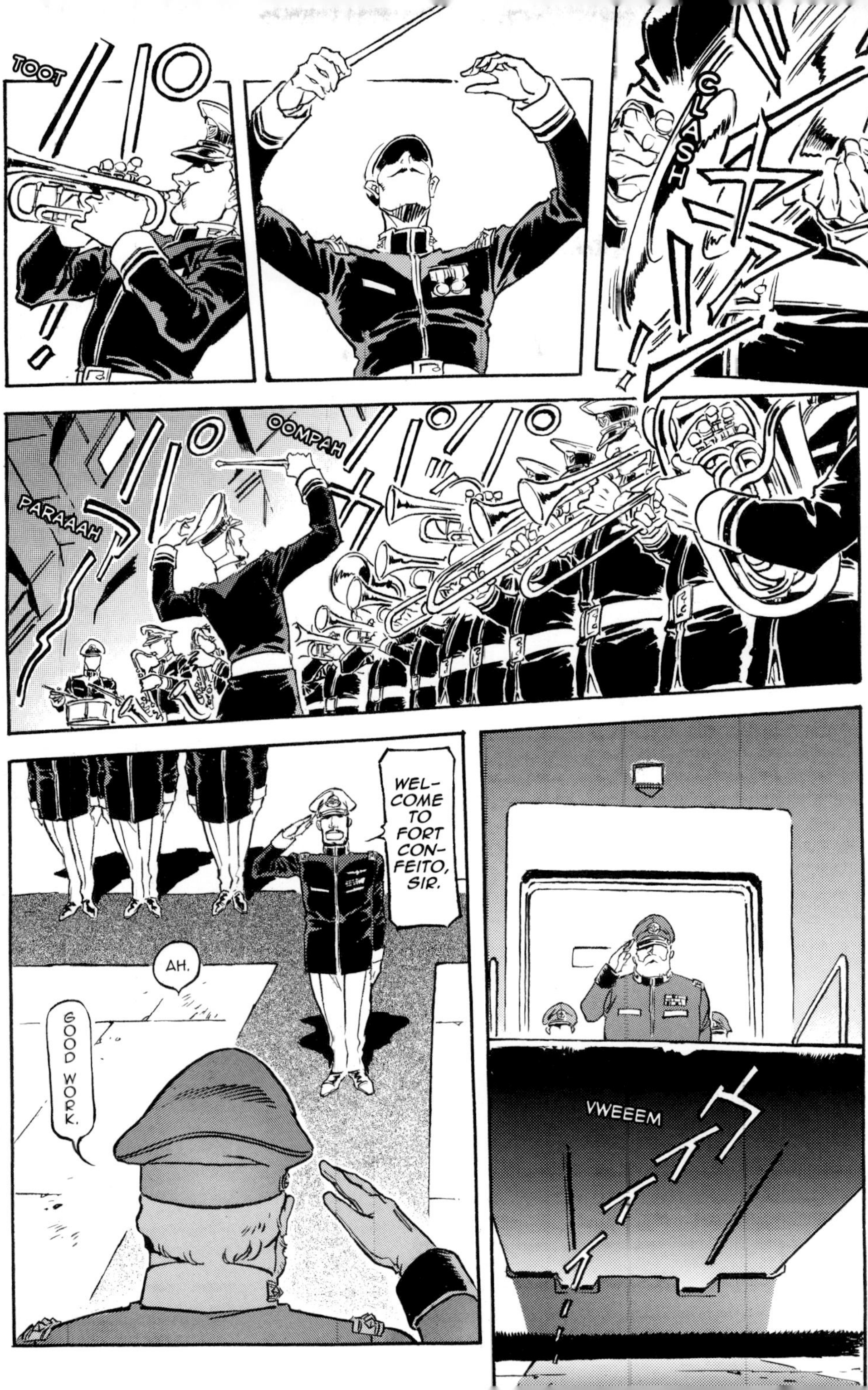
CLASH
TOOT
OOMPAH
PARAAAH
VWEEEM
WELCOME TO FORT CONFEITO, SIR.
AH.
GOOD WORK.

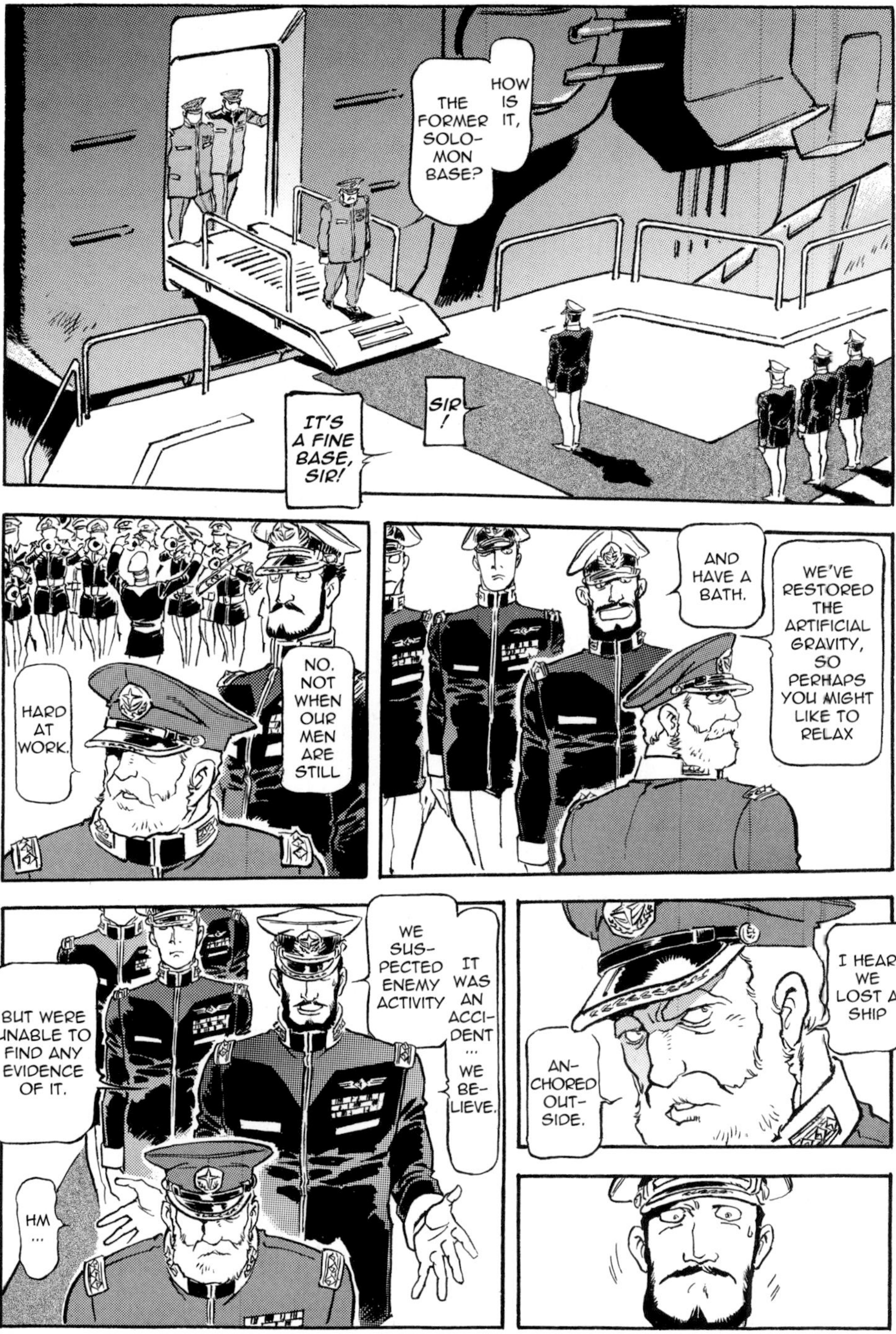
HOW IS IT, THE FORMER SOLOMON BASE?
SIR!
IT'S A FINE BASE, SIR!
WE'VE RESTORED THE ARTIFICIAL GRAVITY, SO PERHAPS YOU MIGHT LIKE TO RELAX
AND HAVE A BATH.
NO. NOT WHEN OUR MEN ARE STILL
HARD AT WORK.
I HEAR WE LOST A SHIP
ANCHORED OUTSIDE.
IT WAS AN ACCIDENT... WE BELIEVE.
WE SUSPECTED ENEMY ACTIVITY
BUT WERE UNABLE TO FIND ANY EVIDENCE OF IT.
HM...

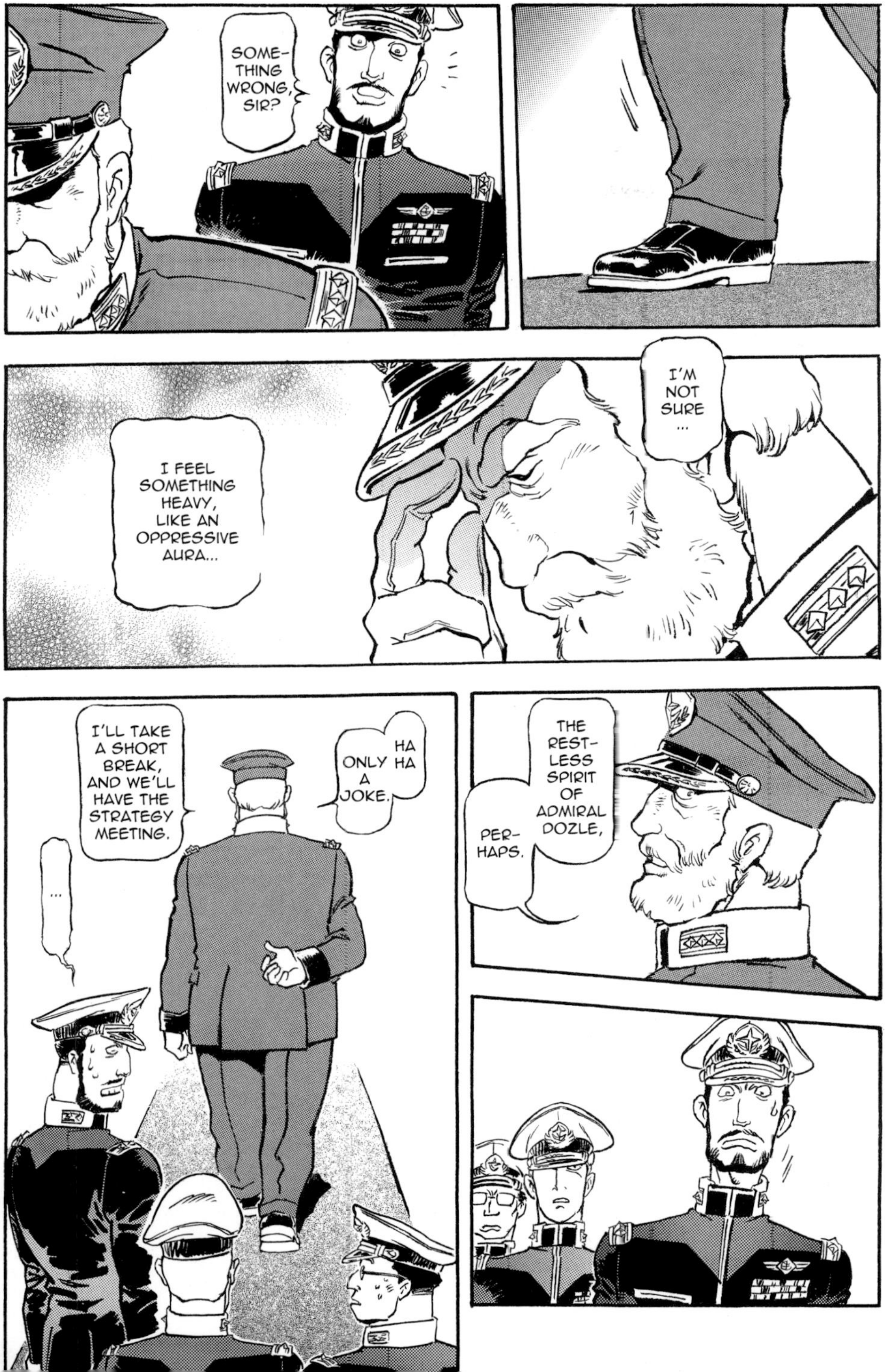
SOME-THING WRONG, SIR?
I'M NOT SURE ...
I FEEL SOMETHING HEAVY, LIKE AN OPPRESSIVE AURA...
THE REST-LESS SPIRIT OF ADMIRAL DOZLE,
PER-HAPS.
HA HA ONLY A JOKE.
I'LL TAKE A SHORT BREAK, AND WE'LL HAVE THE STRATEGY MEETING.
...

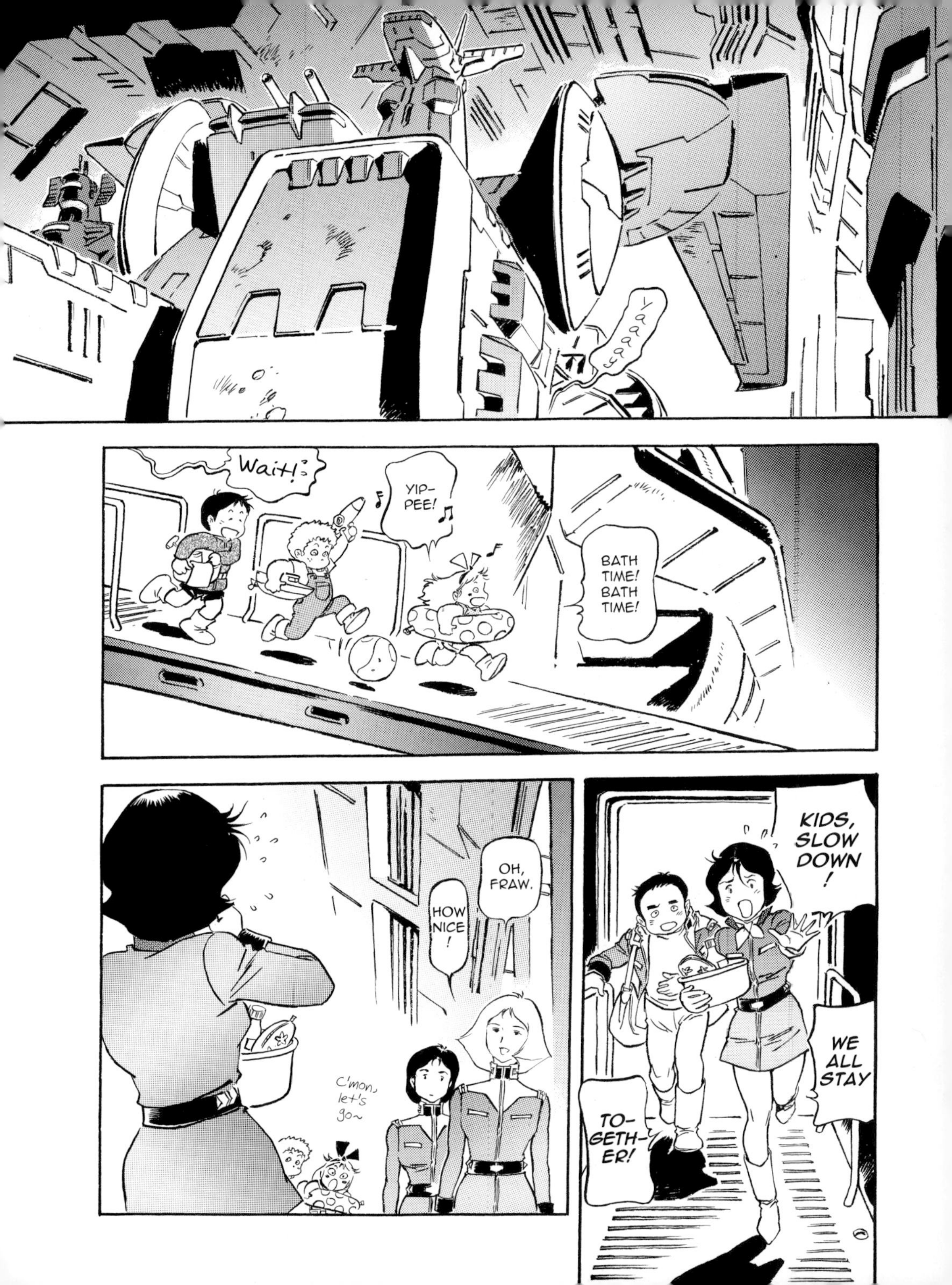
Yaaaay
BATH TIME! BATH TIME!
YIP-PEE!
Wait!
KIDS, SLOW DOWN!
WE ALL STAY
TO-GETH-ER!
OH, FRAW.
HOW NICE!
C'mon, let's go~

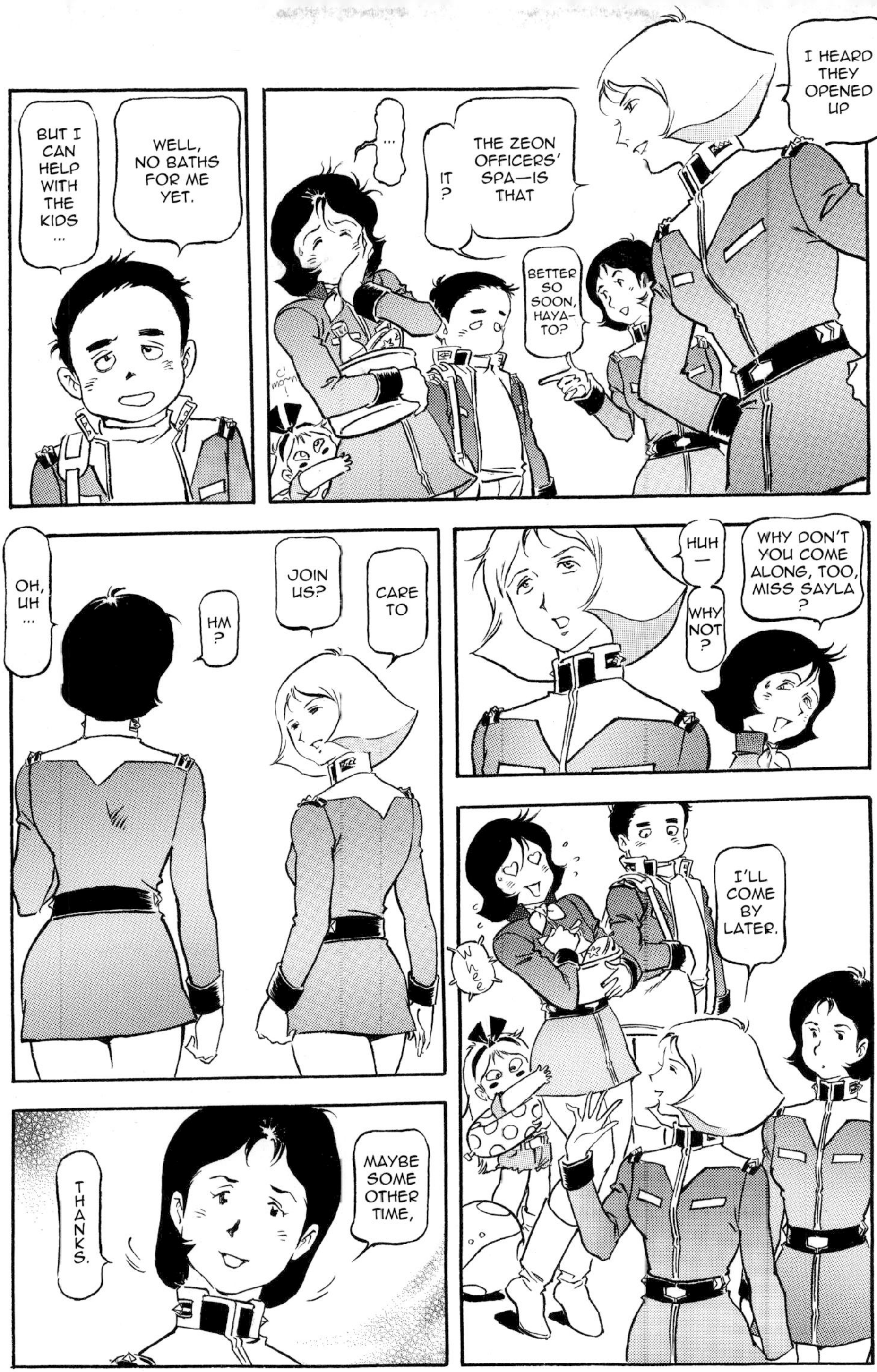
I HEARD THEY OPENED UP
THE ZEON OFFICERS' SPA—IS THAT IT?
...
BETTER SO SOON, HAYATO?
C'MON!
WELL, NO BATHS FOR ME YET.
BUT I CAN HELP WITH THE KIDS...
WHY DON'T YOU COME ALONG, TOO, MISS SAYLA?
HUH— WHY NOT?
CARE TO JOIN US?
HM?
OH, UH...
I'LL COME BY LATER.
Whee
MAYBE SOME OTHER TIME,
THANKS.

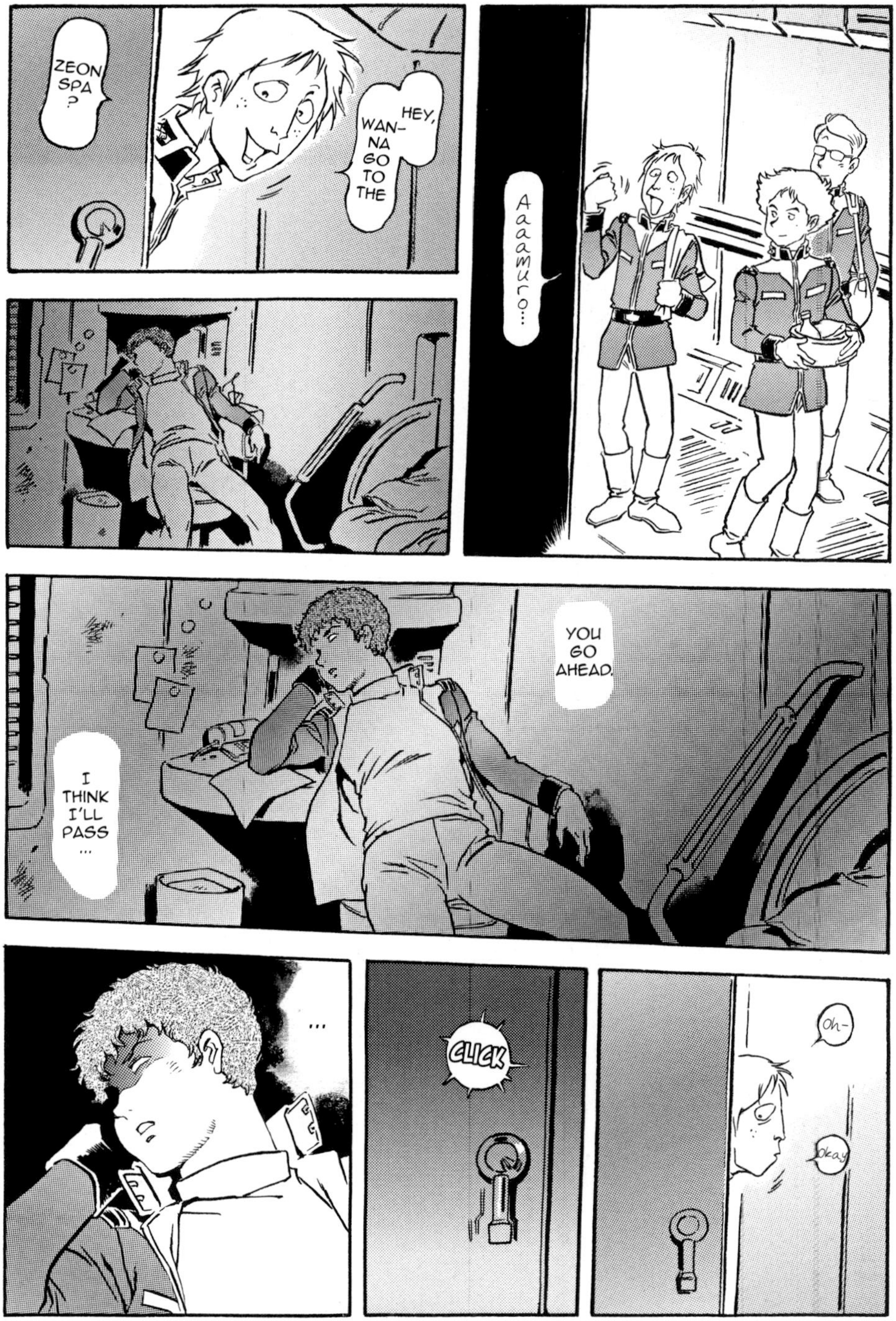
Aaaamuro...
HEY, WAN-NA GO TO THE
ZEON SPA ?
YOU GO AHEAD.
I THINK I'LL PASS ...
Oh-
okay
CLICK
...

...

AGAIN!

La

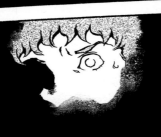

La

La

LA...LA...

...

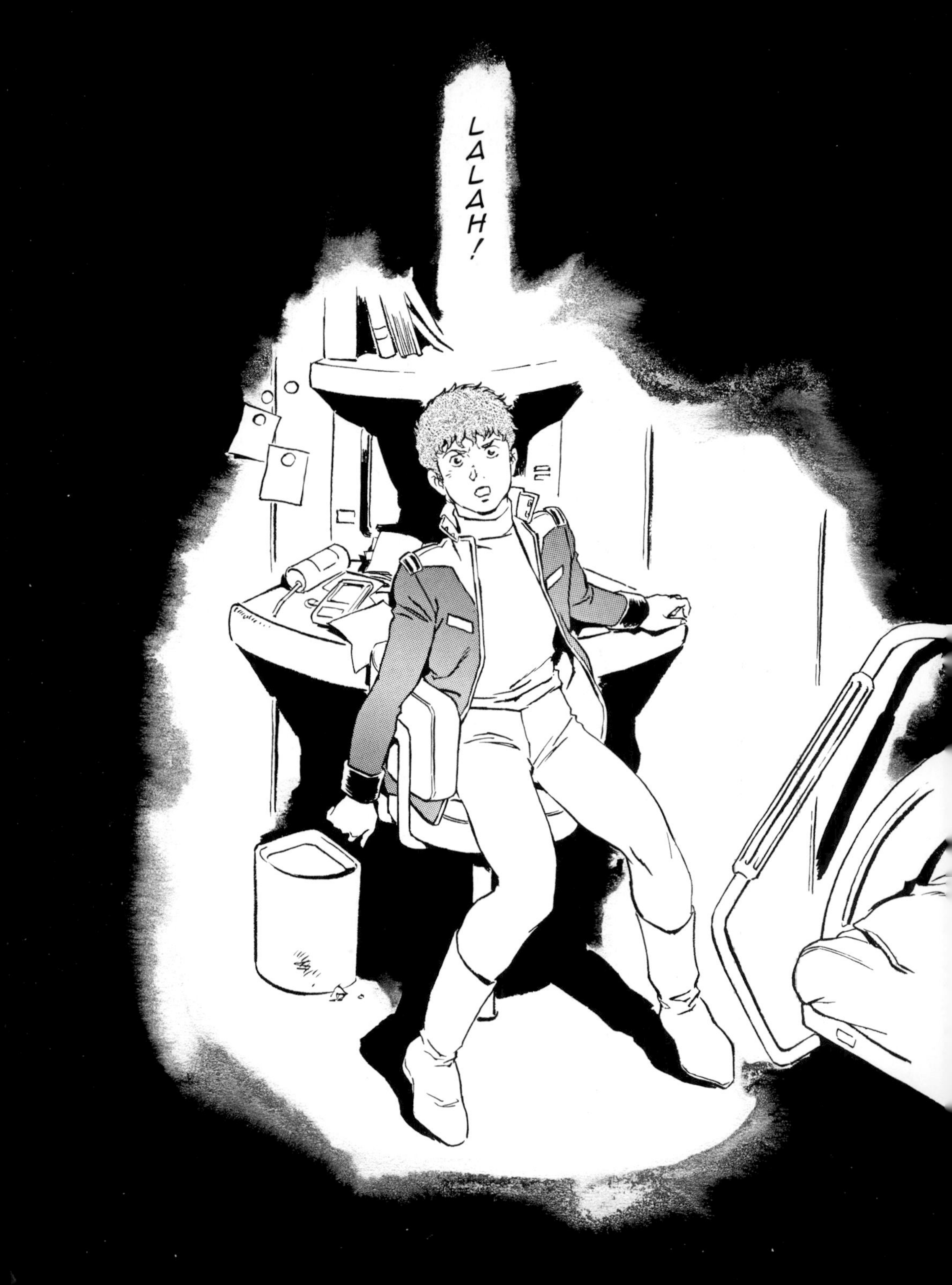
LALAH!

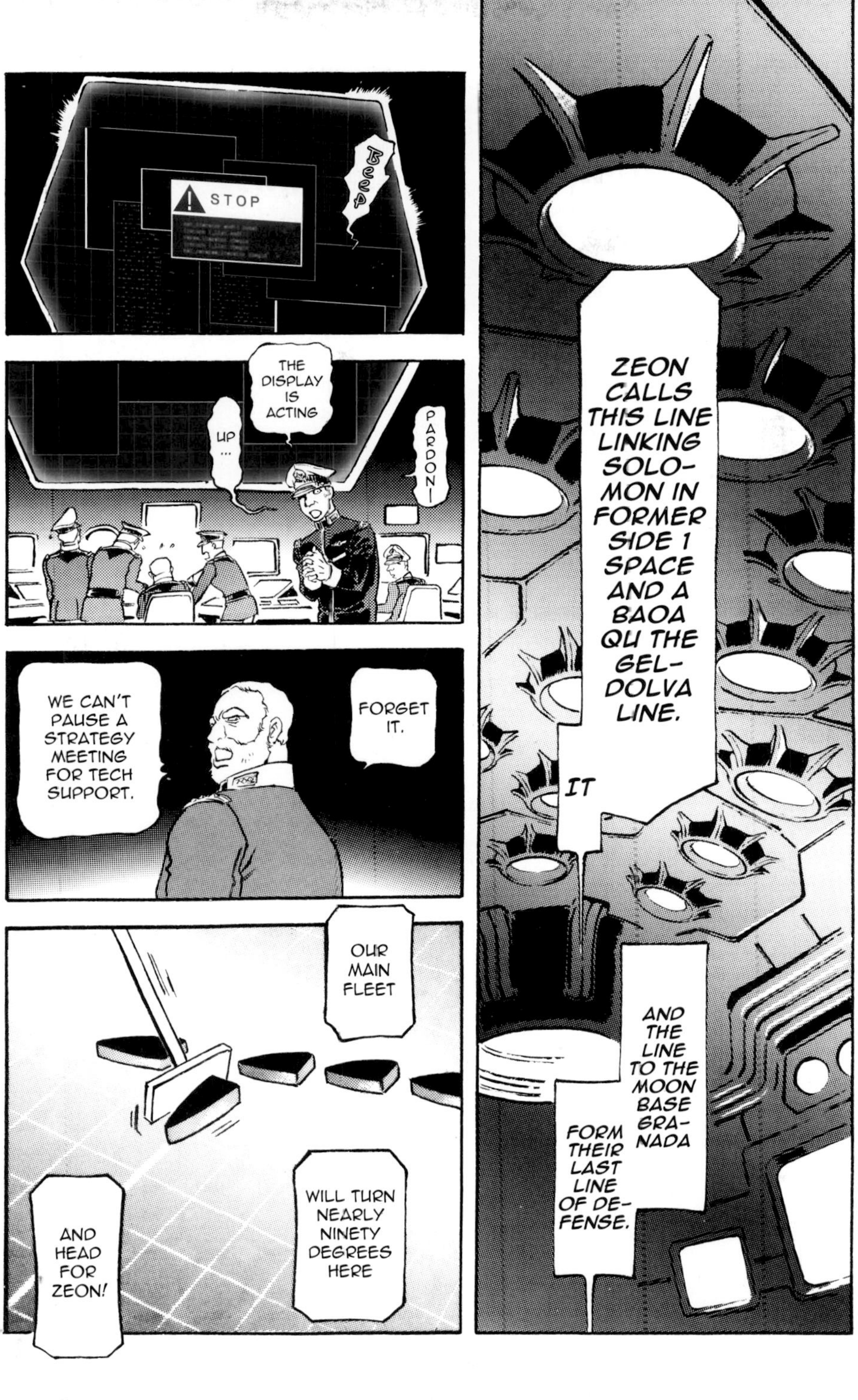
ZEON CALLS THIS LINE LINKING SOLOMON IN FORMER SIDE 1 SPACE AND A BAOA QU THE GELDOLVA LINE.
IT
AND THE LINE TO THE MOON BASE GRANADA
FORM THEIR LAST LINE OF DEFENSE.
Beep
STOP
PARDON!
THE DISPLAY IS ACTING
UP...
FORGET IT.
WE CAN'T PAUSE A STRATEGY MEETING FOR TECH SUPPORT.
OUR MAIN FLEET
WILL TURN NEARLY NINETY DEGREES HERE
AND HEAD FOR ZEON!

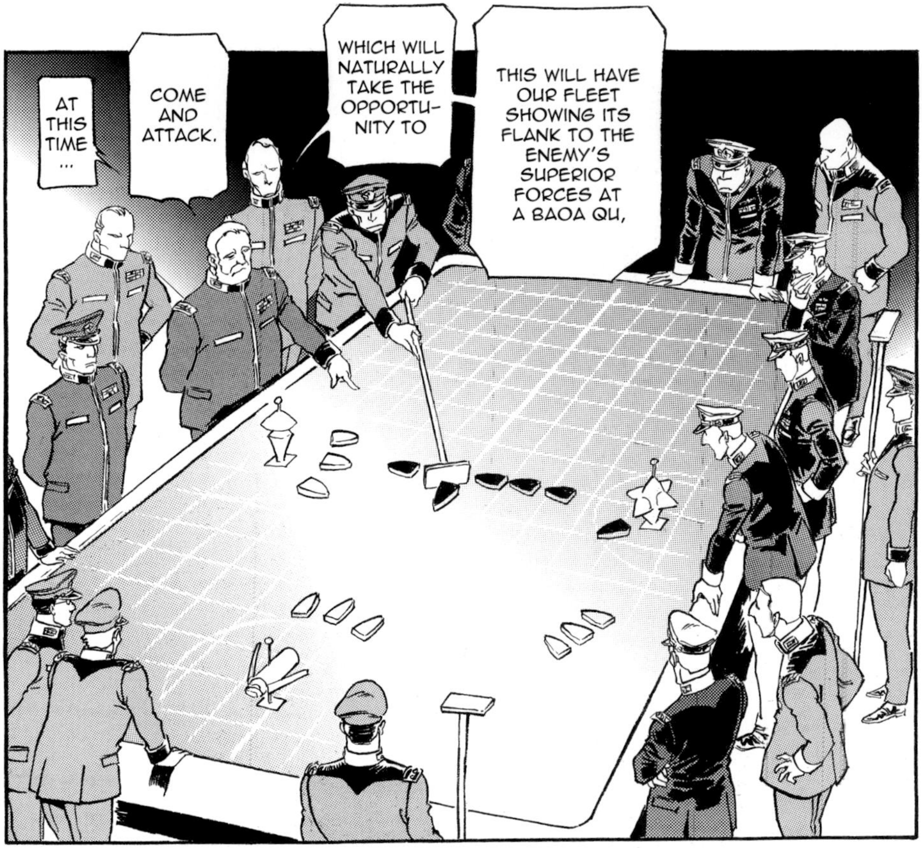
THIS WILL HAVE OUR FLEET SHOWING ITS FLANK TO THE ENEMY'S SUPERIOR FORCES AT A BAOA QU,
WHICH WILL NATURALLY TAKE THE OPPORTUNITY TO
COME AND ATTACK.
AT THIS TIME ...

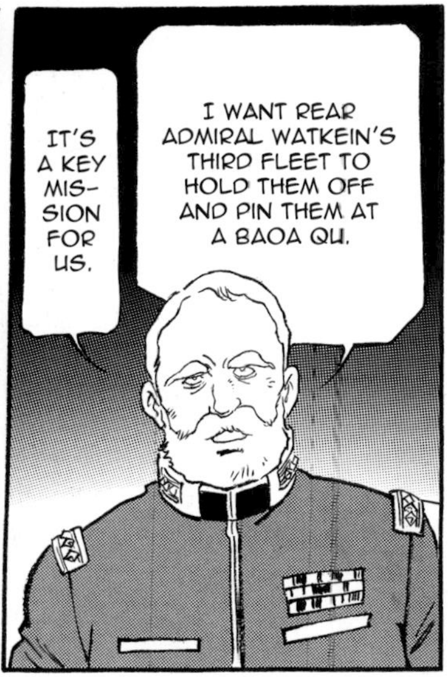
I WANT REAR ADMIRAL WATKEIN'S THIRD FLEET TO HOLD THEM OFF AND PIN THEM AT A BAOA QU.
IT'S A KEY MISSION FOR US.

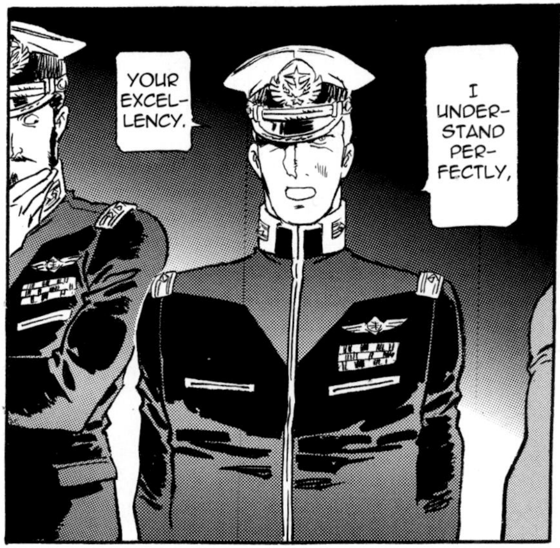
I UNDERSTAND PERFECTLY,
YOUR EXCELLENCY.

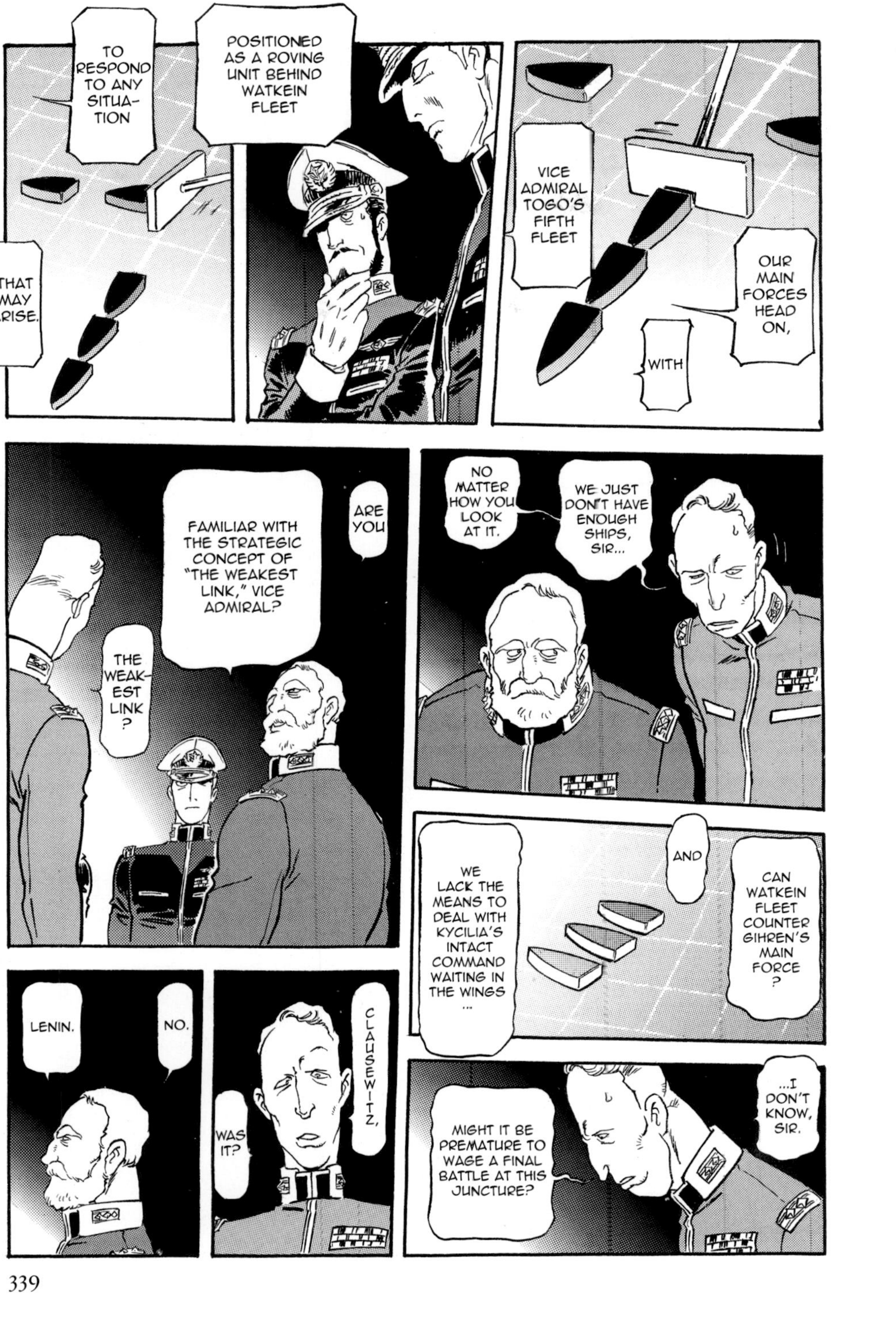
OUR MAIN FORCES HEAD ON,
WITH
VICE ADMIRAL TOGO'S FIFTH FLEET
POSITIONED AS A ROVING UNIT BEHIND WATKEIN FLEET
TO RESPOND TO ANY SITUATION
THAT MAY ARISE.
WE JUST DON'T HAVE ENOUGH SHIPS, SIR...
NO MATTER HOW YOU LOOK AT IT.
CAN WATKEIN FLEET COUNTER GIHREN'S MAIN FORCE?
AND
WE LACK THE MEANS TO DEAL WITH KYCILIA'S INTACT COMMAND WAITING IN THE WINGS...
ARE YOU
FAMILIAR WITH THE STRATEGIC CONCEPT OF "THE WEAKEST LINK," VICE ADMIRAL?
THE WEAKEST LINK?
...I DON'T KNOW, SIR.
MIGHT IT BE PREMATURE TO WAGE A FINAL BATTLE AT THIS JUNCTURE?
CLAUSEWITZ,
WAS IT?
NO.
LENIN.

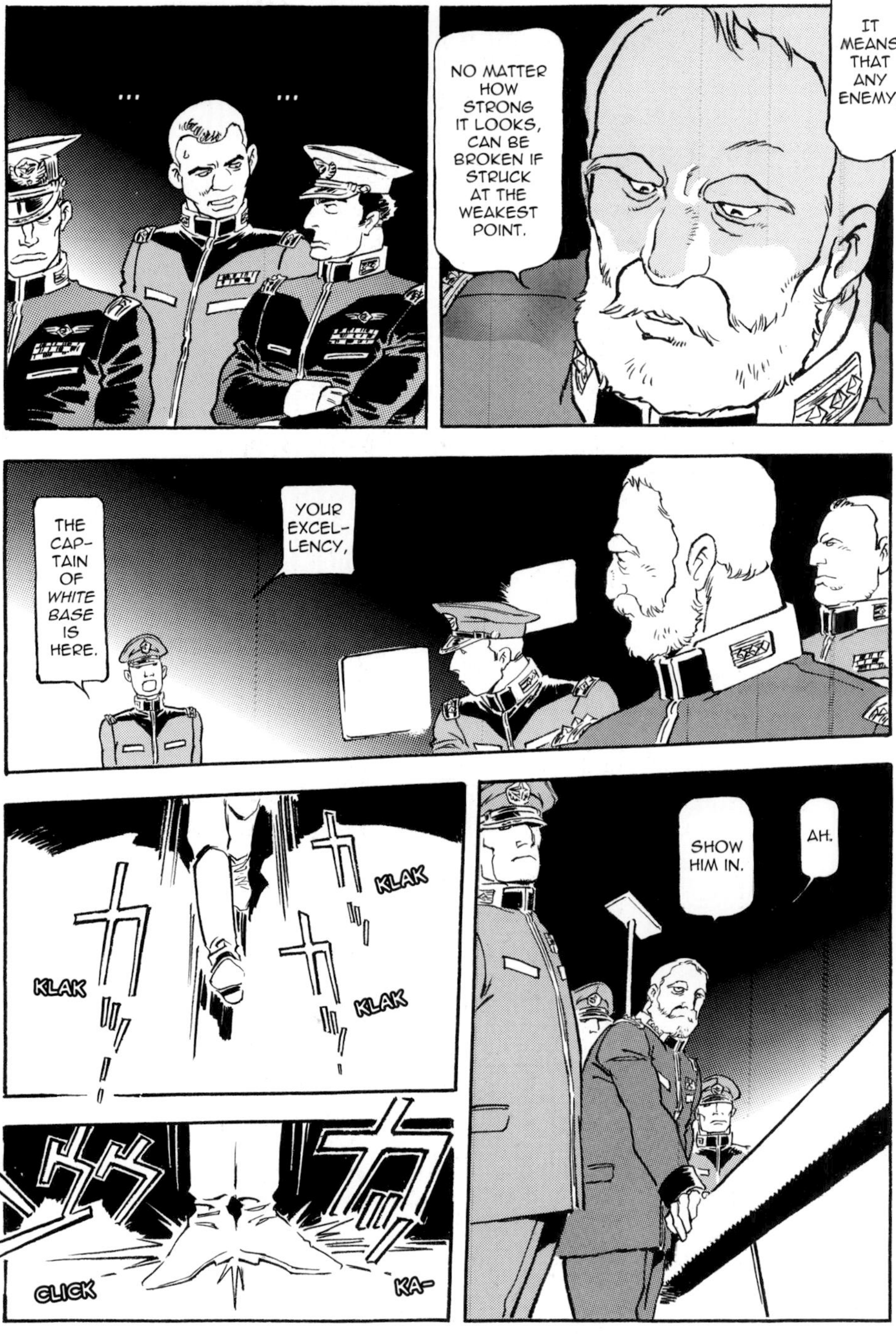
IT MEANS THAT ANY ENEMY,
NO MATTER HOW STRONG IT LOOKS, CAN BE BROKEN IF STRUCK AT THE WEAKEST POINT.
...
...
YOUR EXCELLENCY,
THE CAPTAIN OF WHITE BASE IS HERE.
AH.
SHOW HIM IN.
KLAK
KLAK
KLAK
KA-
CLICK

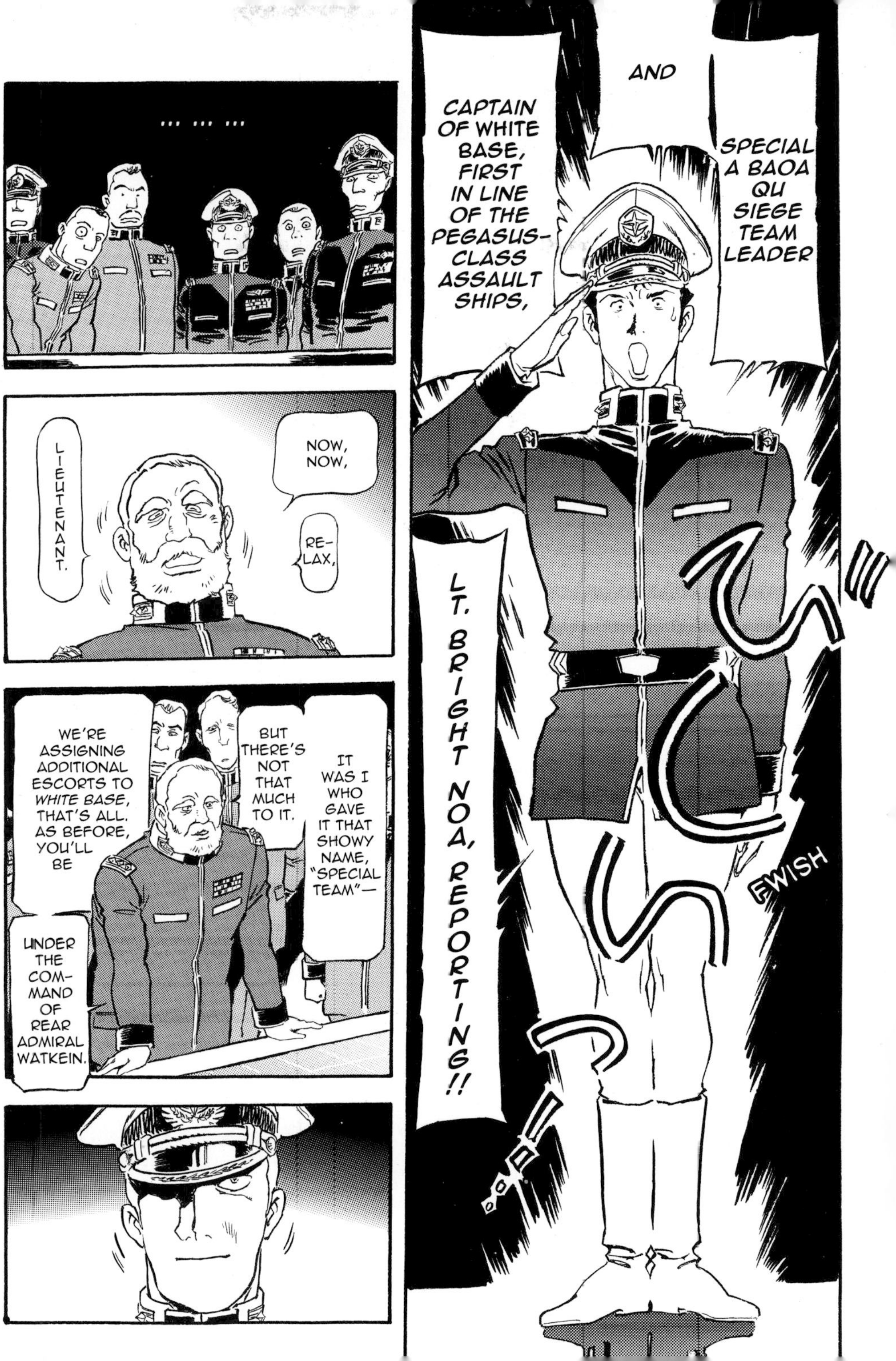
CAPTAIN OF WHITE BASE, FIRST IN LINE OF THE PEGASUS-CLASS ASSAULT SHIPS,
AND
SPECIAL A BAOA QU SIEGE TEAM LEADER
LT. BRIGHT NOA, REPORTING!!
FWISH
... ...
NOW, NOW,
RE-LAX,
LIEUTENANT.
IT WAS I WHO GAVE IT THAT SHOWY NAME, "SPECIAL TEAM"—
BUT THERE'S NOT THAT MUCH TO IT.
WE'RE ASSIGNING ADDITIONAL ESCORTS TO *WHITE BASE*, THAT'S ALL. AS BEFORE, YOU'LL BE
UNDER THE COMMAND OF REAR ADMIRAL WATKEIN.

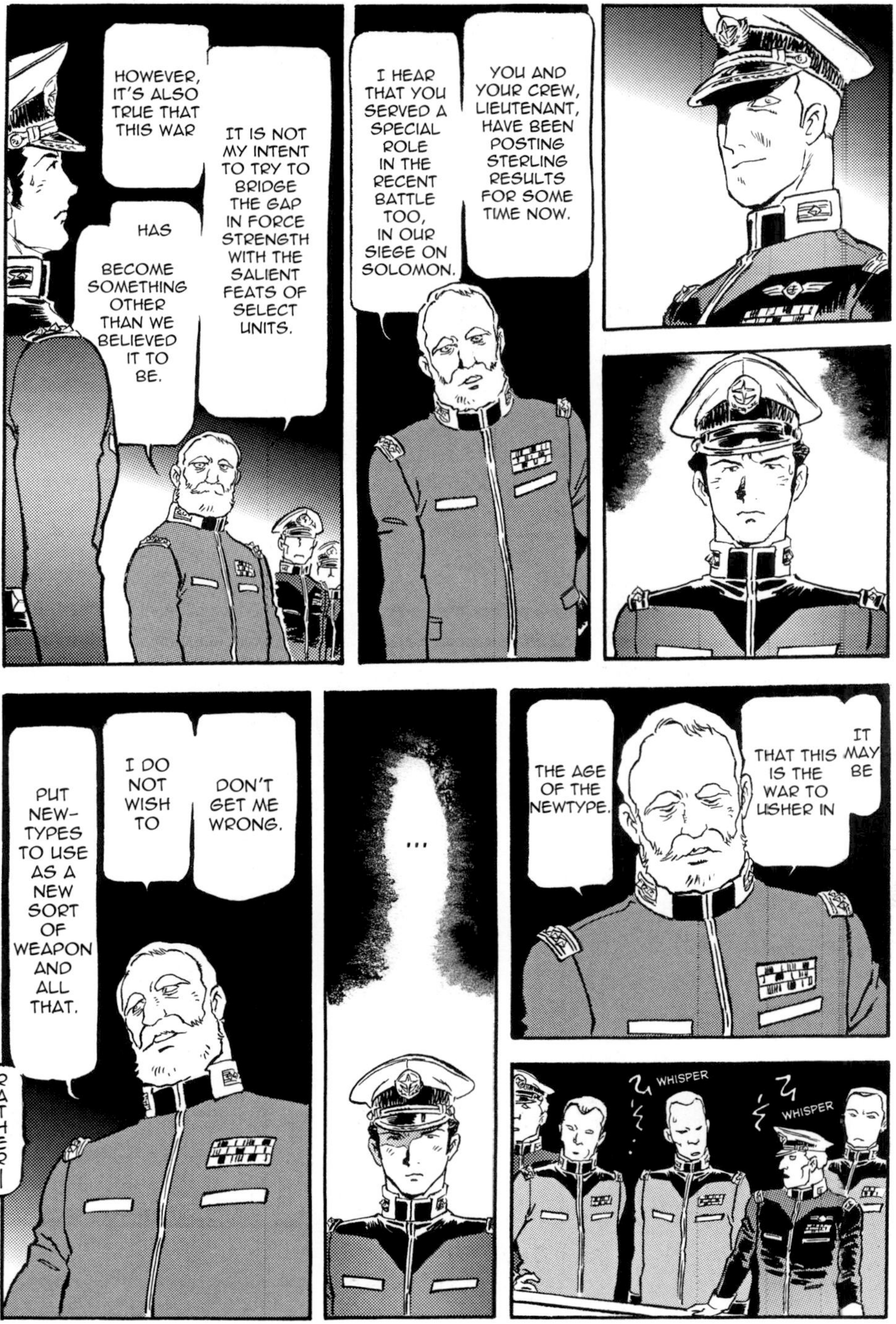
YOU AND YOUR CREW, LIEUTENANT, HAVE BEEN POSTING STERLING RESULTS FOR SOME TIME NOW.
I HEAR THAT YOU SERVED A SPECIAL ROLE IN THE RECENT BATTLE TOO, IN OUR SIEGE ON SOLOMON.
IT IS NOT MY INTENT TO TRY TO BRIDGE THE GAP IN FORCE STRENGTH WITH THE SALIENT FEATS OF SELECT UNITS.
HOWEVER, IT'S ALSO TRUE THAT THIS WAR
HAS
BECOME SOMETHING OTHER THAN WE BELIEVED IT TO BE.
IT MAY BE
THAT THIS IS THE WAR TO USHER IN
THE AGE OF THE NEWTYPE.
WHISPER
WHISPER
...
DON'T GET ME WRONG.
I DO NOT WISH TO
PUT NEW-TYPES TO USE AS A NEW SORT OF WEAPON AND ALL THAT.
RATHER—

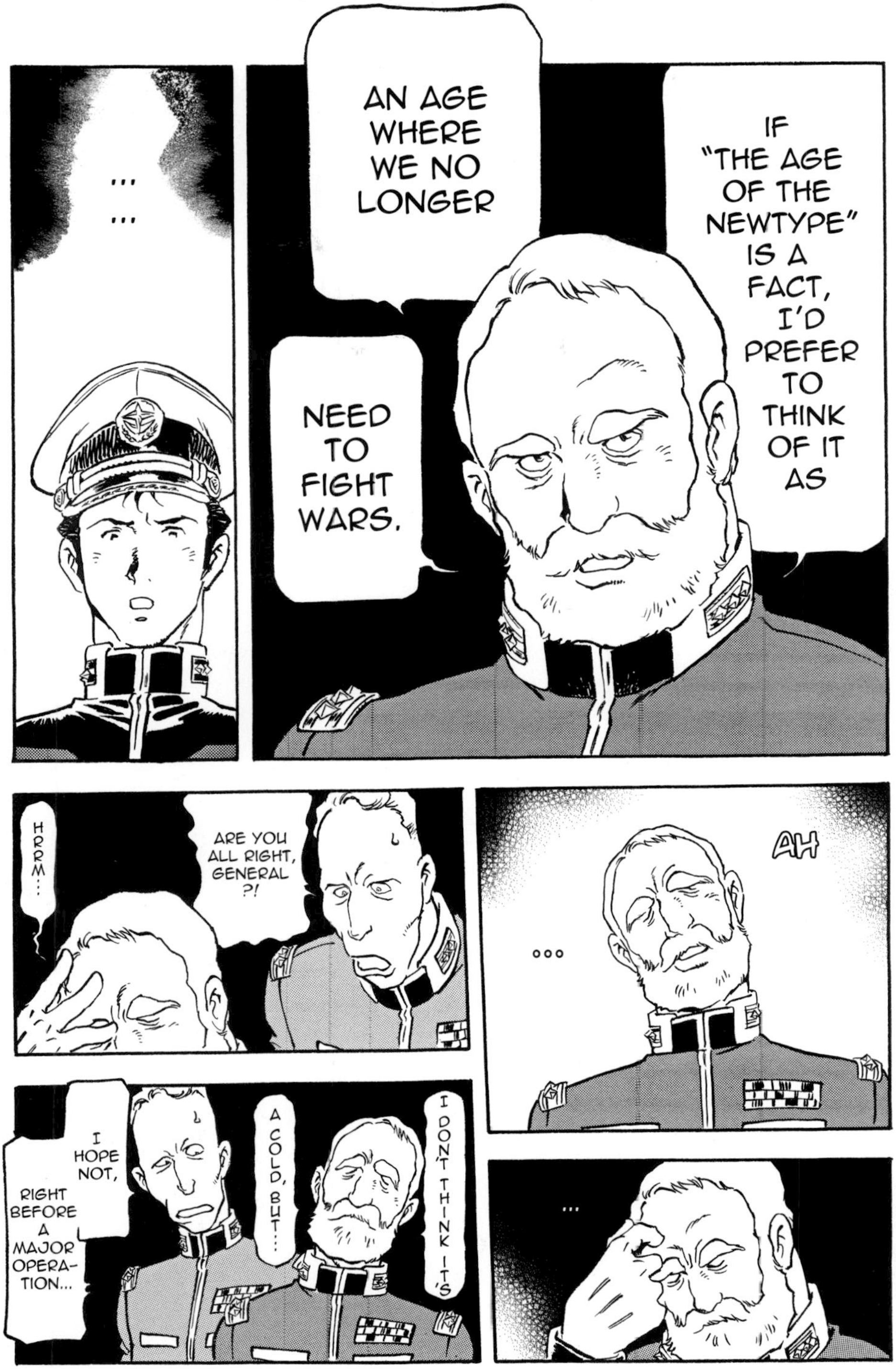
IF "THE AGE OF THE NEWTYPE" IS A FACT, I'D PREFER TO THINK OF IT AS
AN AGE WHERE WE NO LONGER
NEED TO FIGHT WARS.
... ...
AH
...
ARE YOU ALL RIGHT, GENERAL?!
HRRM...
...
I DON'T THINK IT'S
A COLD, BUT...
I HOPE NOT, RIGHT BEFORE A MAJOR OPERA-TION...

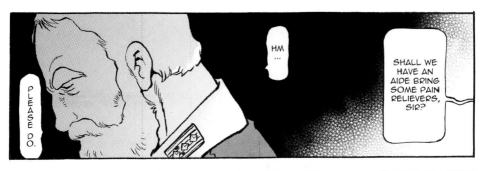

HM
...

SHALL WE HAVE AN AIDE BRING SOME PAIN RELIEVERS, SIR?

PLEASE DO.

I NAME IT...

THIS OPERATION MAY WELL BRING AN END TO THE GREAT WAR OF OUR TIME.

GEN-TLE-MEN.

NOW THEN,

"OPERATION STAR ONE."

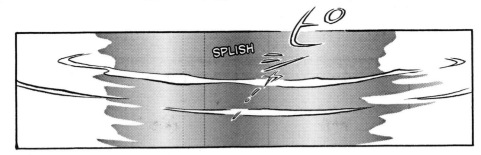

SPLISH

. . . !

... AGAIN

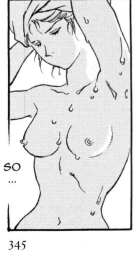

SO
...

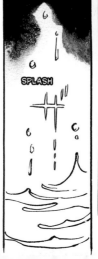

SPLASH

IT CALLS!

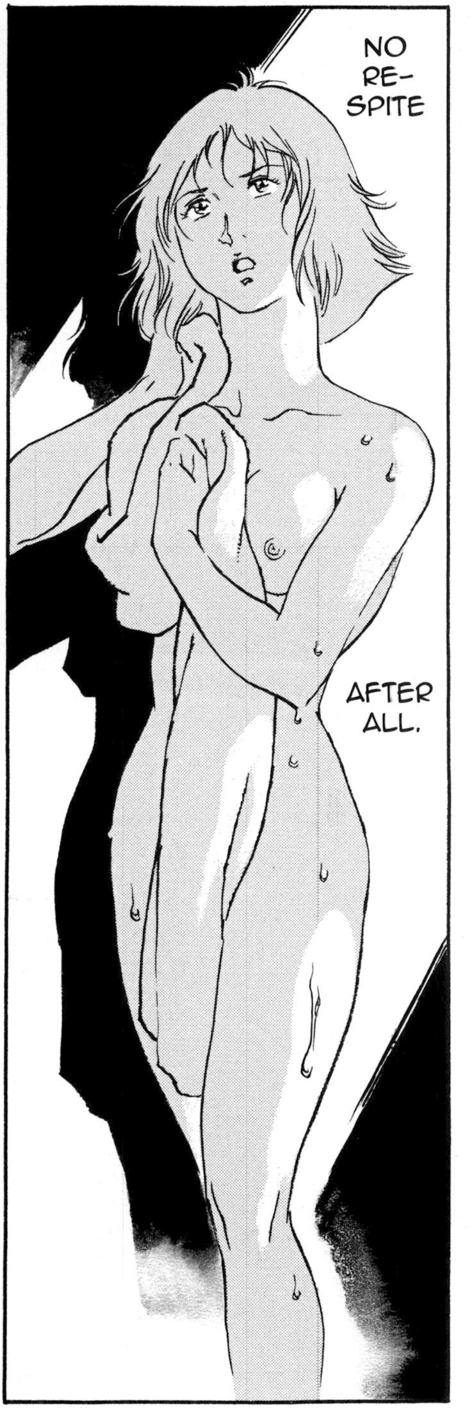
NO RE-SPITE
AFTER ALL.
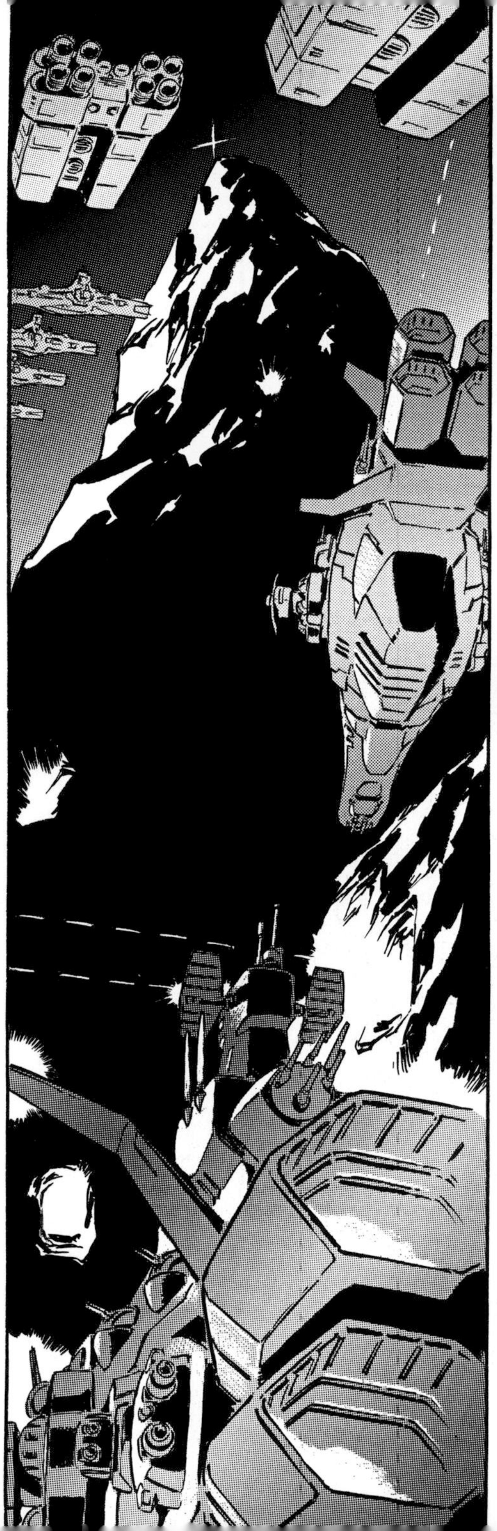

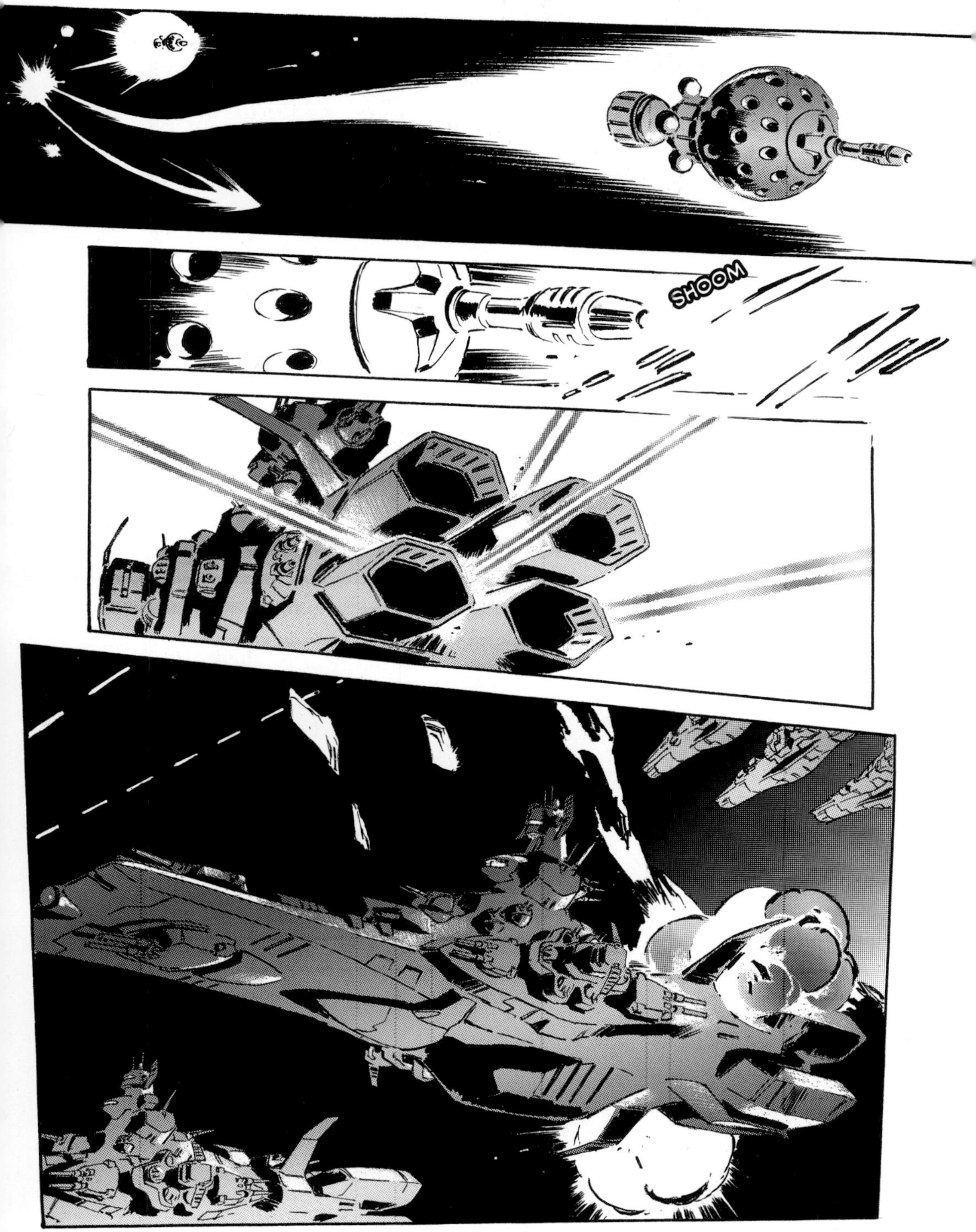
SHOOM

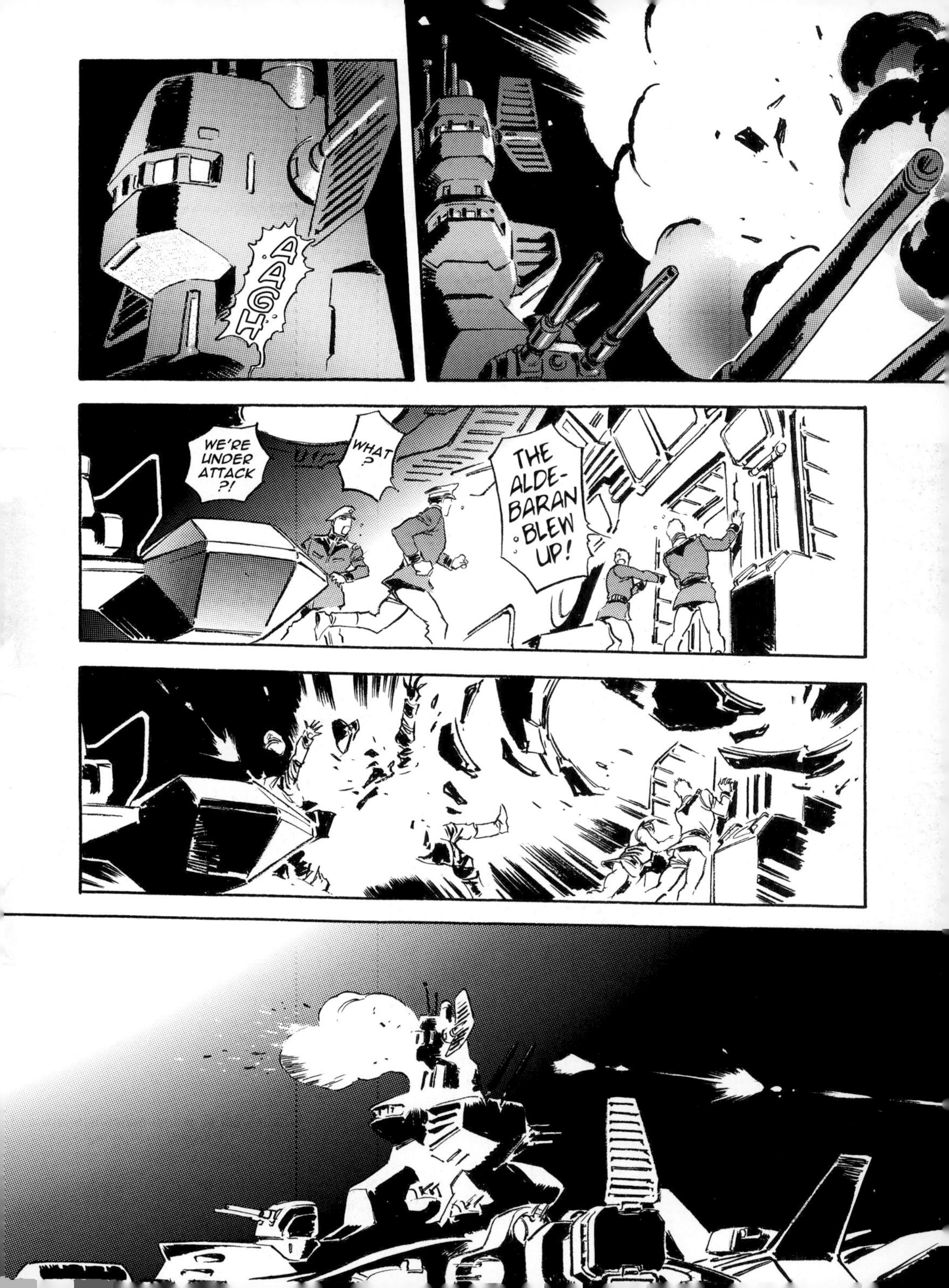
AAGH
THE ALDE-BARAN BLEW UP!
WHAT?
WE'RE UNDER ATTACK?!

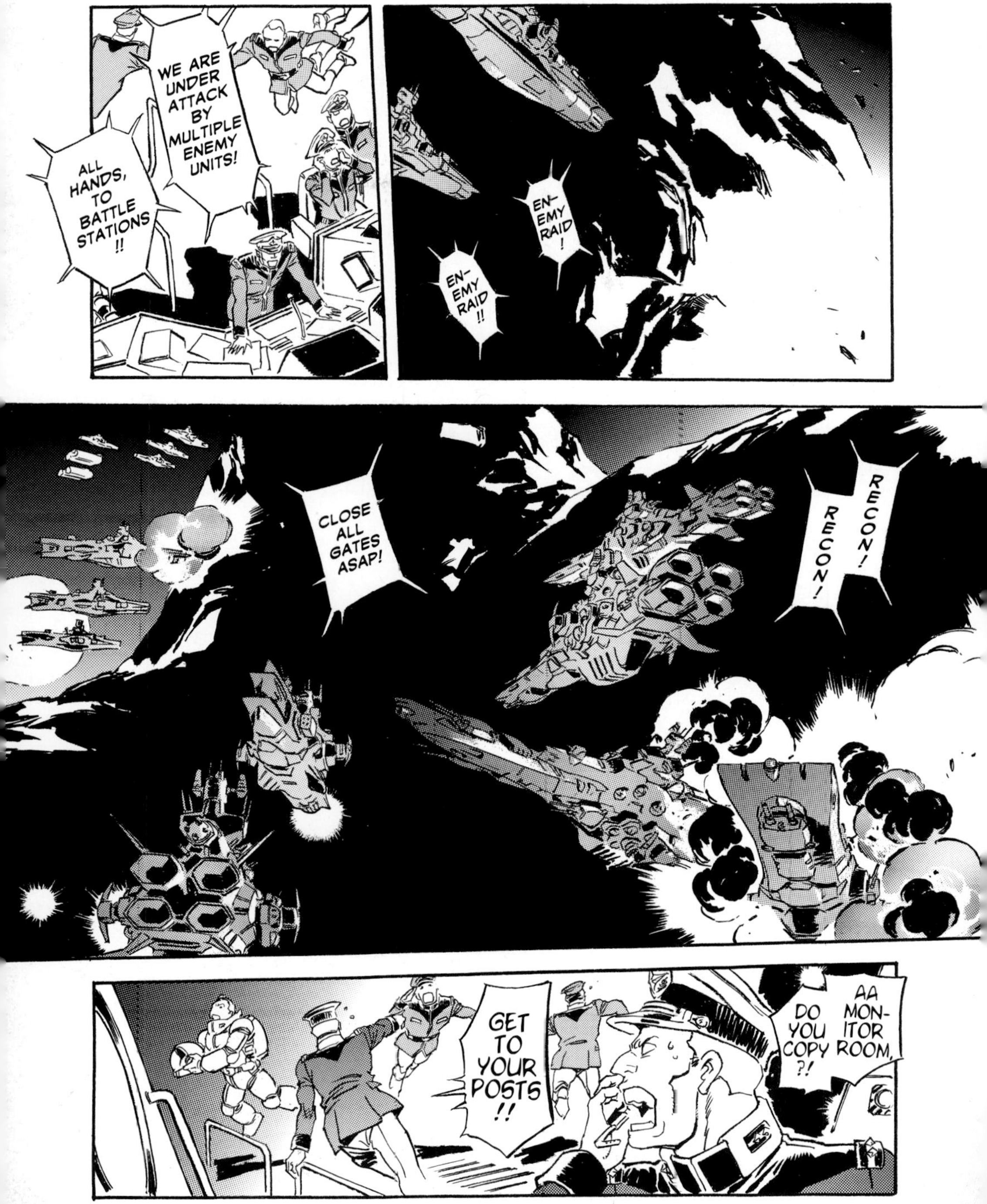
ENEMY RAID!
ENEMY RAID!!
WE ARE UNDER ATTACK BY MULTIPLE ENEMY UNITS!
ALL HANDS, TO BATTLE STATIONS!!
RECON!
RECON!
CLOSE ALL GATES ASAP!
AA MONITOR ROOM, DO YOU COPY?!
GET TO YOUR POSTS!!

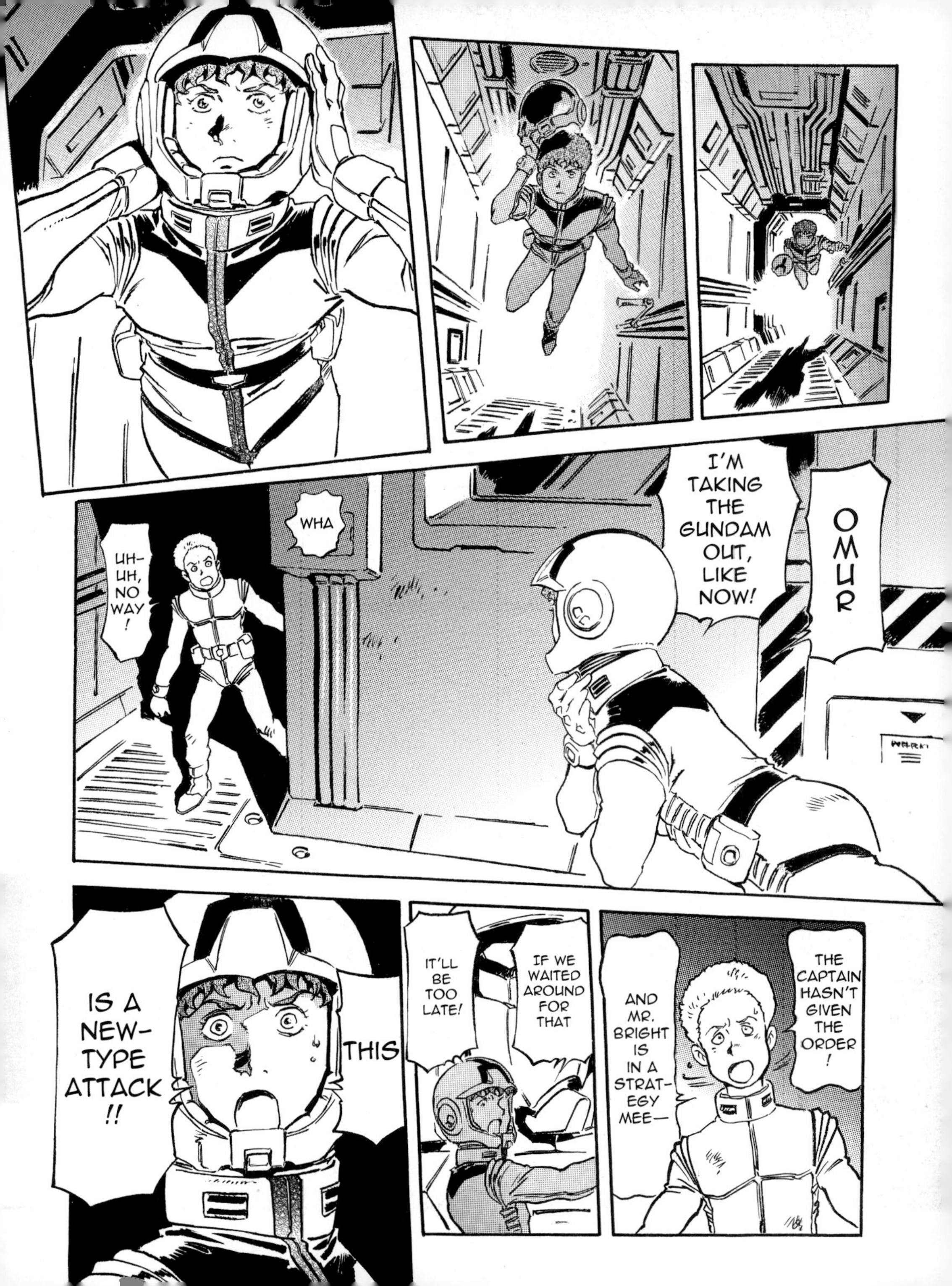
OMUR
I'M TAKING THE GUNDAM OUT, LIKE NOW!
WHA
UH-UH, NO WAY!
THE CAPTAIN HASN'T GIVEN THE ORDER!
AND MR. BRIGHT IS IN A STRATEGY MEE—
IF WE WAITED AROUND FOR THAT
IT'LL BE TOO LATE!
THIS
IS A NEW-TYPE ATTACK!!

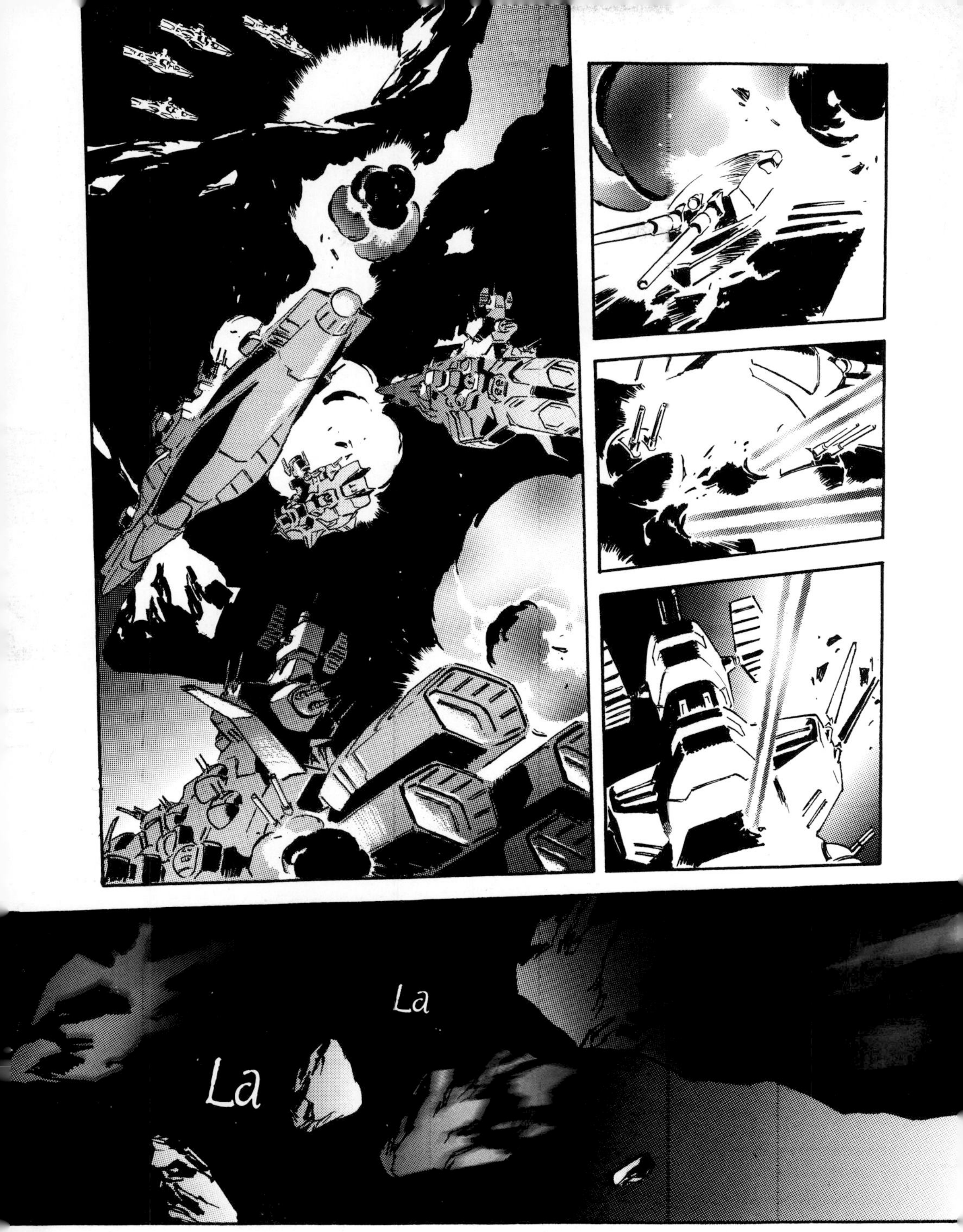
La
La

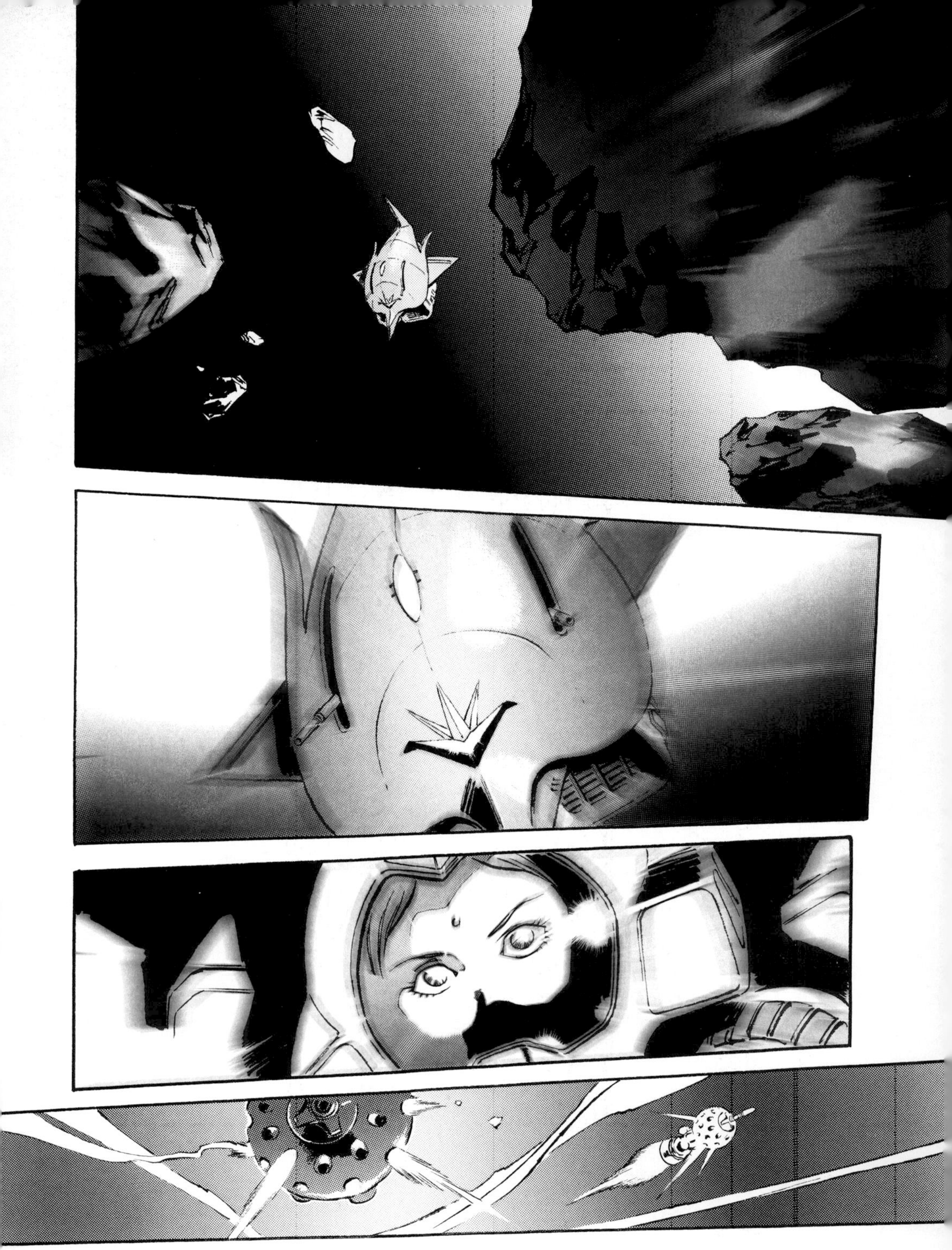

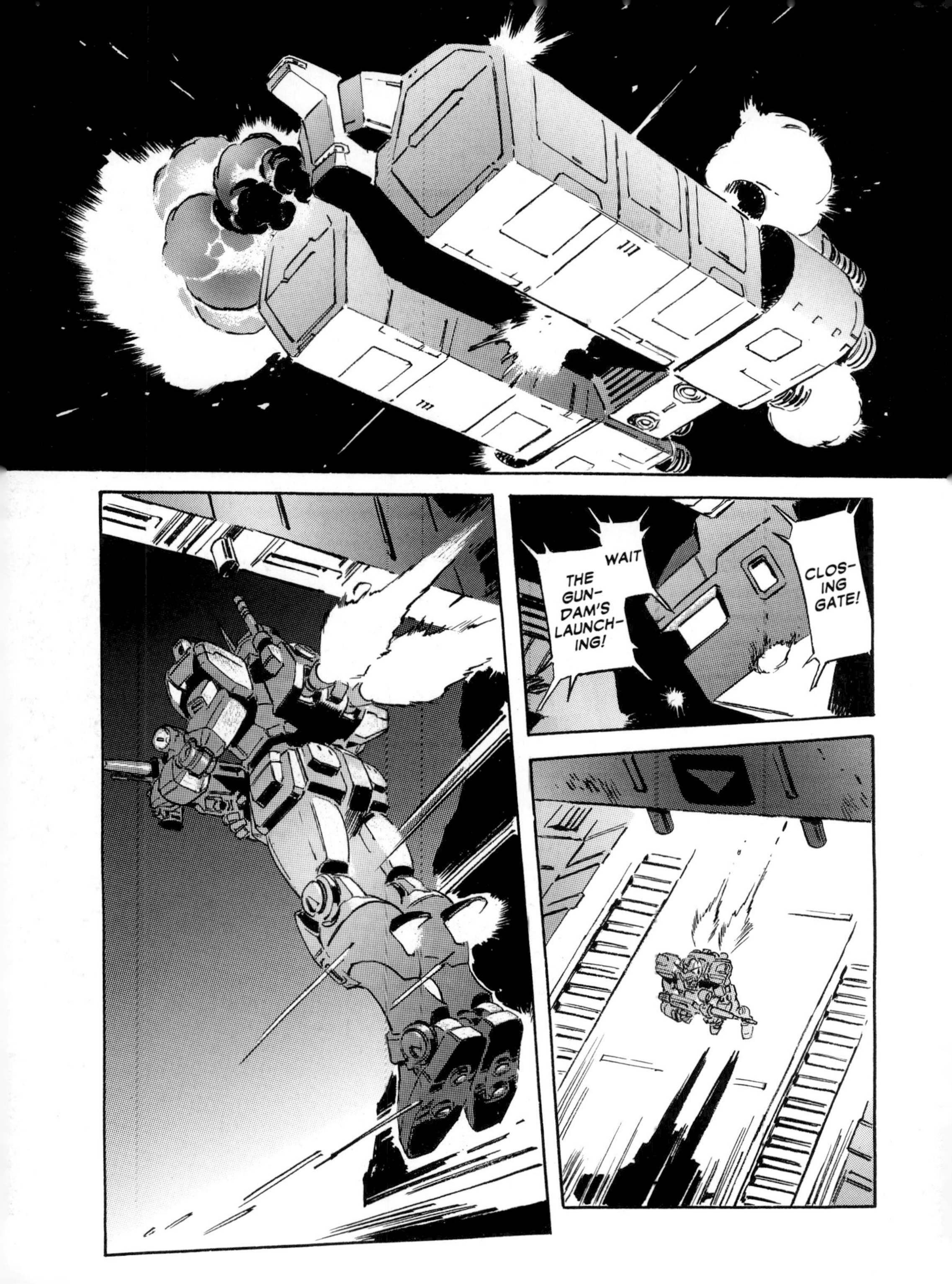
CLOSING GATE!
WAIT THE GUNDAM'S LAUNCHING!

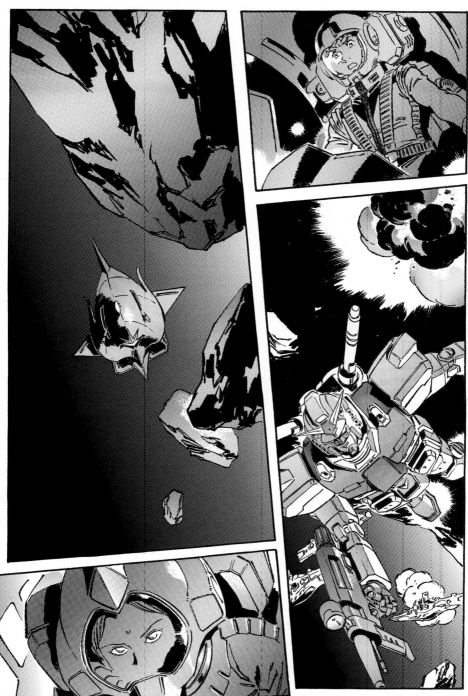

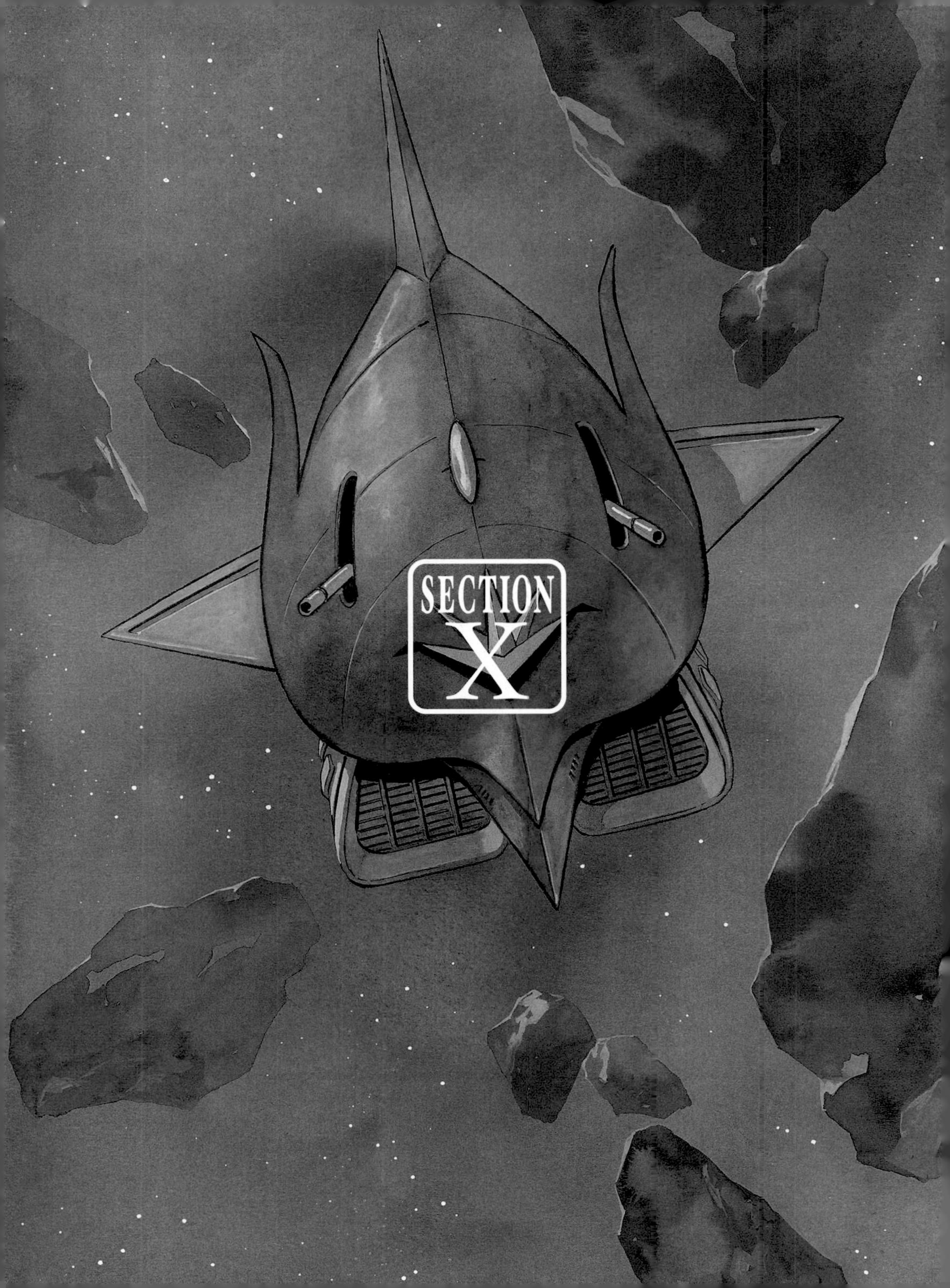
SECTION
X

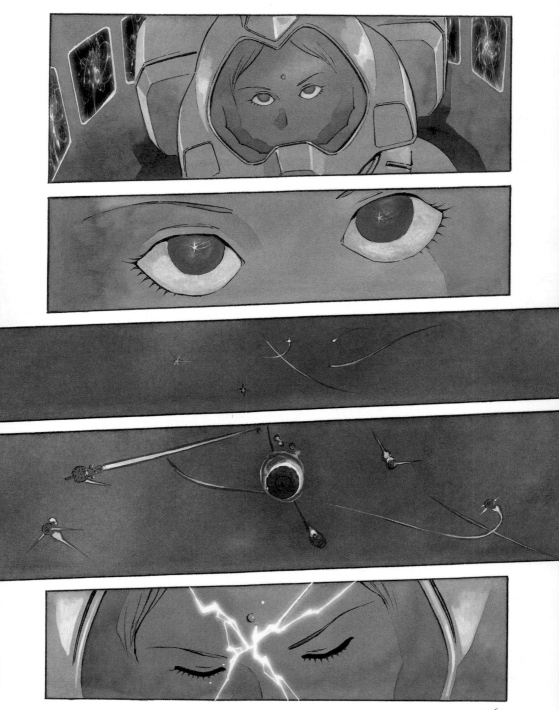

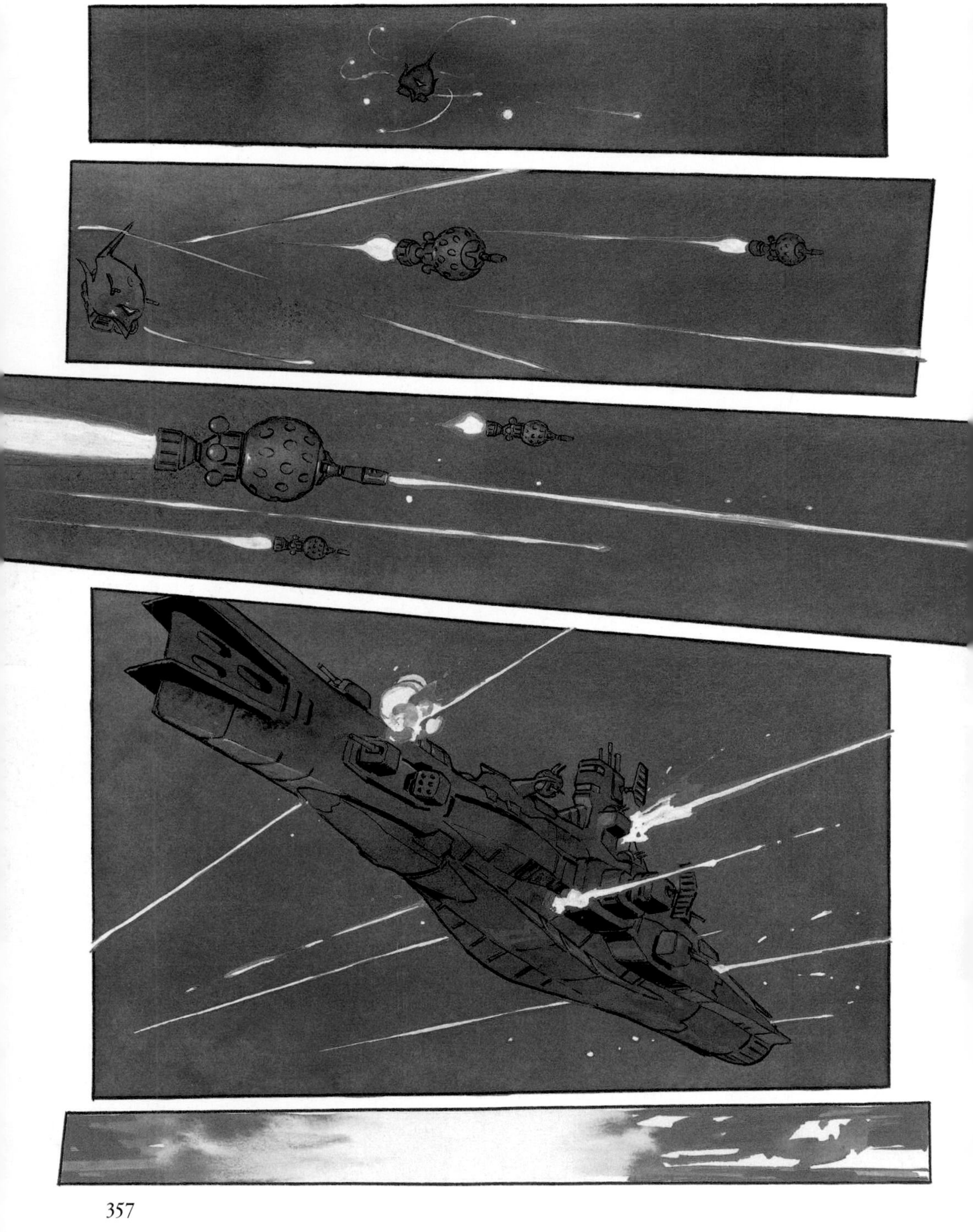

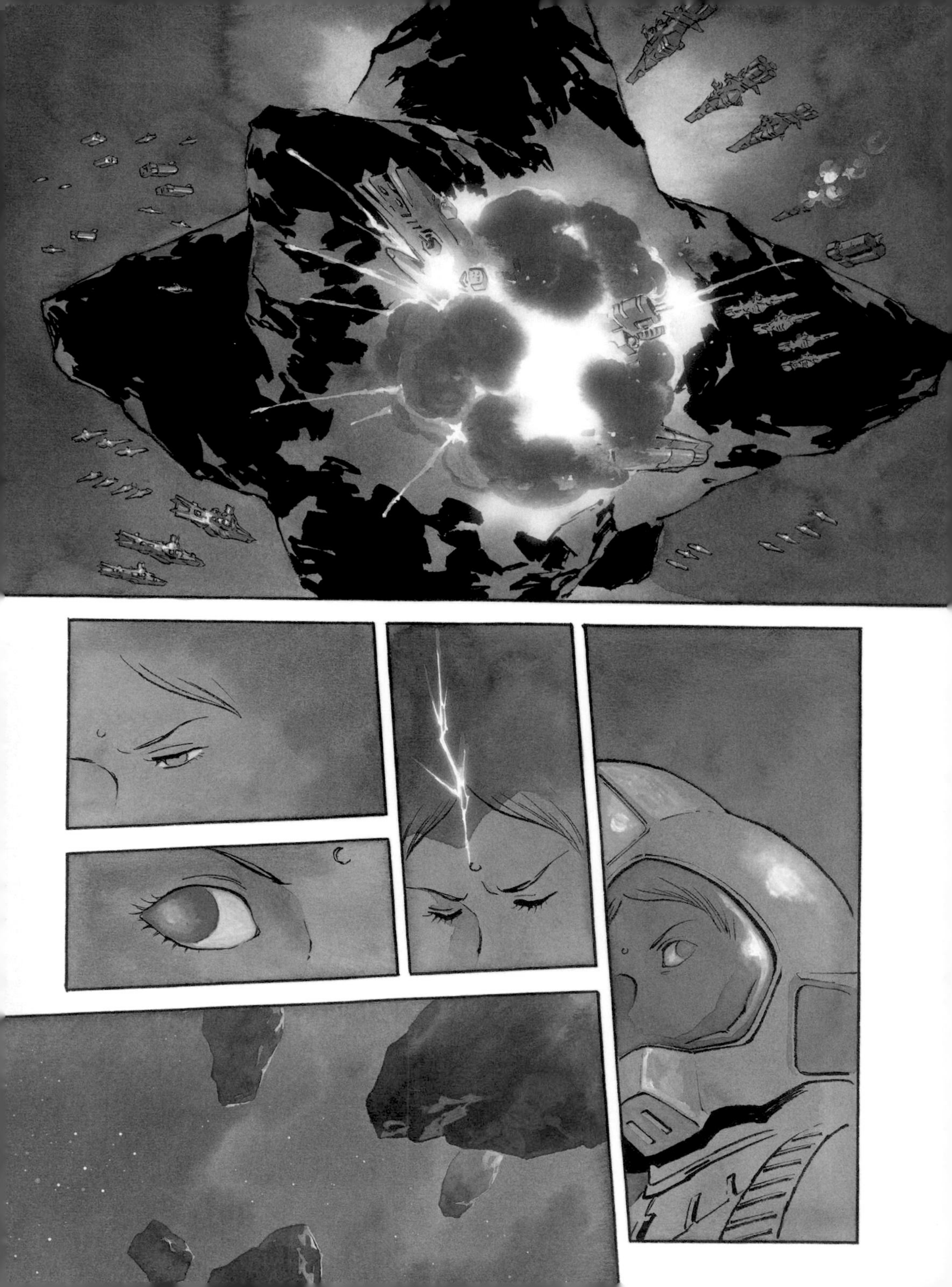

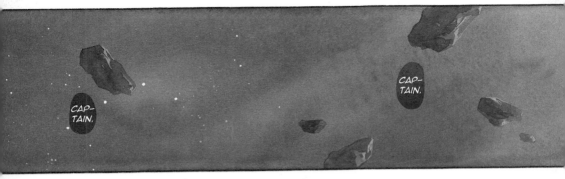

CAP-
TAIN.

CAP-
TAIN.

TO
GO,
LALAH.

WAY

WHAT
IS IT?

HM
?

?

CAP-
TAIN.

THAT'S
NOT
IT,

SOME-ONE OTHER THAN YOU
IS
WITH ME...
IN TOUCH
WITH ME ...

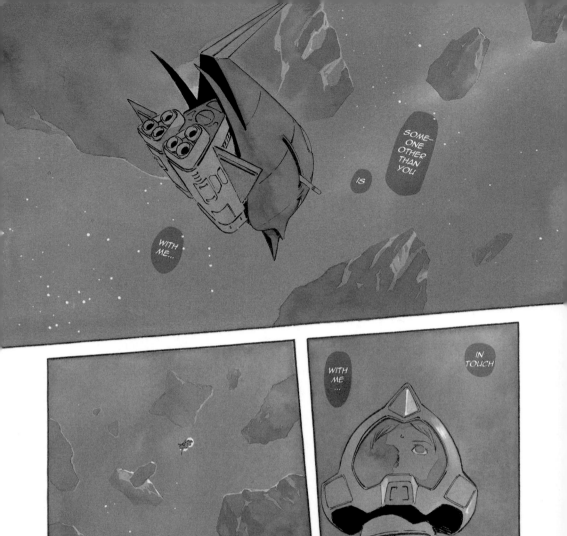

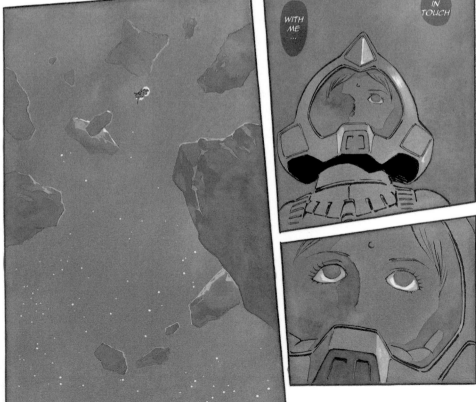

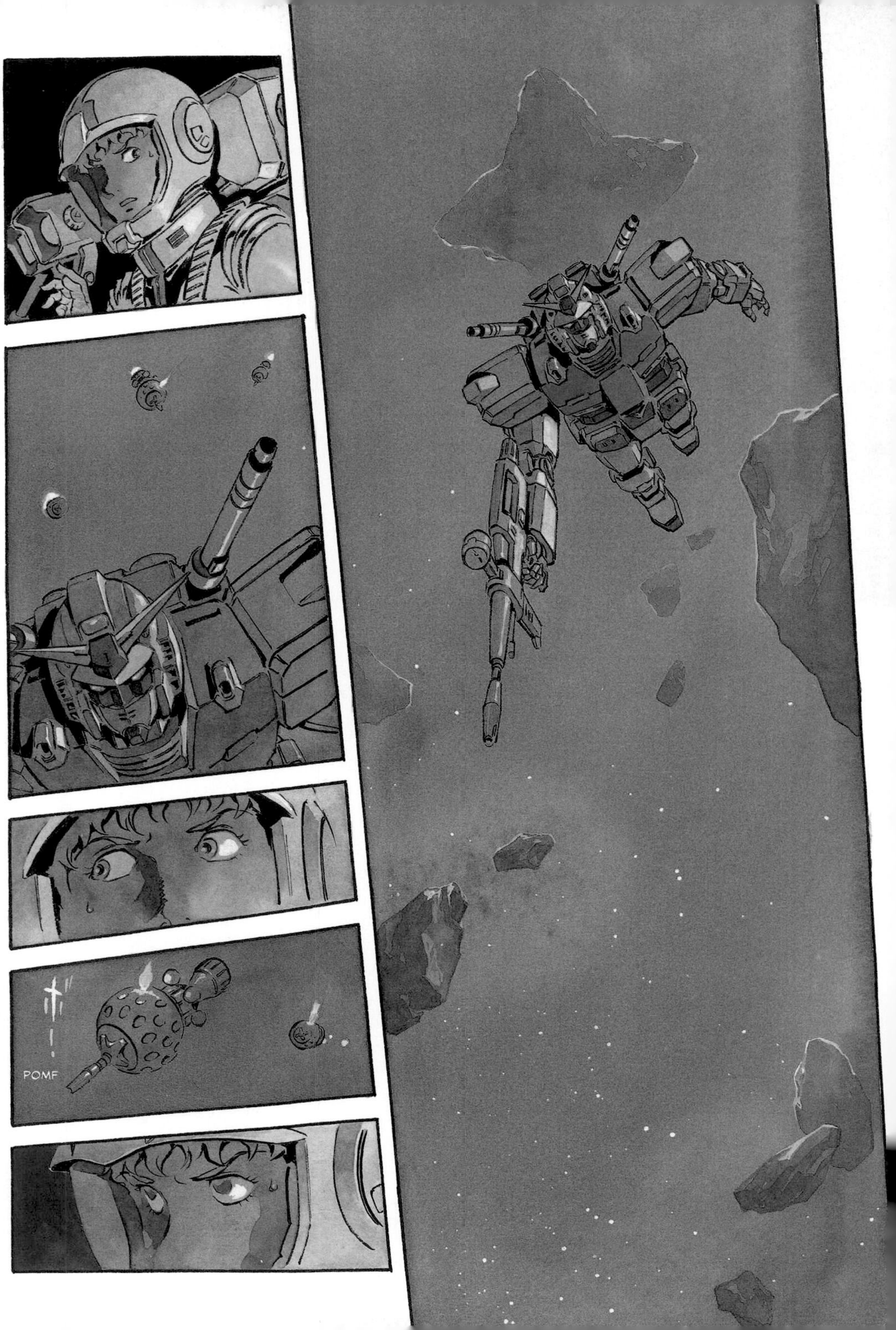
POMF

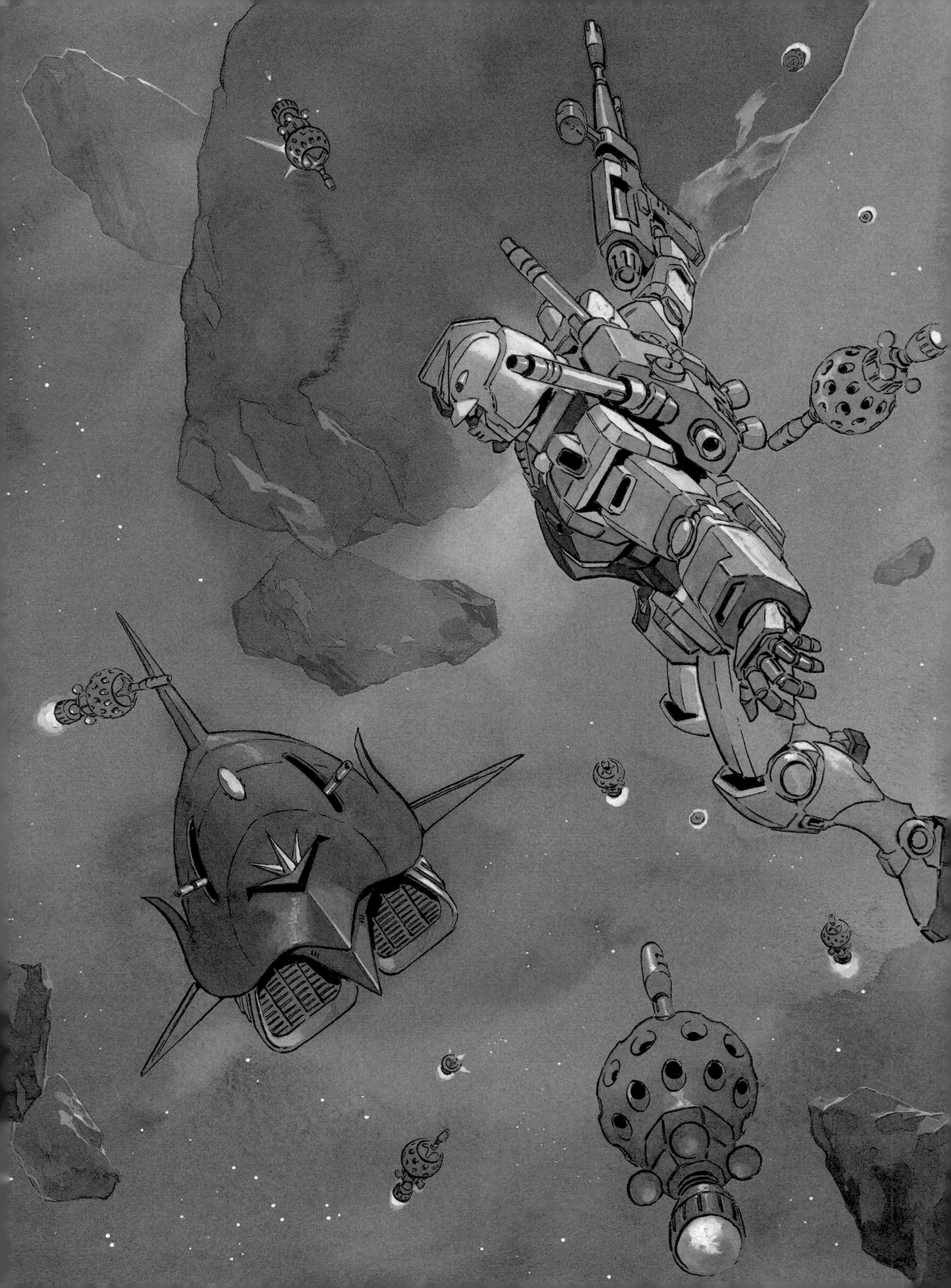

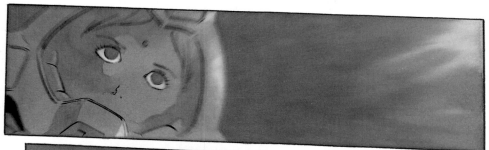

I FELT THAT IT WAS YOU, AMURO.

IT REALLY

WAS YOU, LALAH.

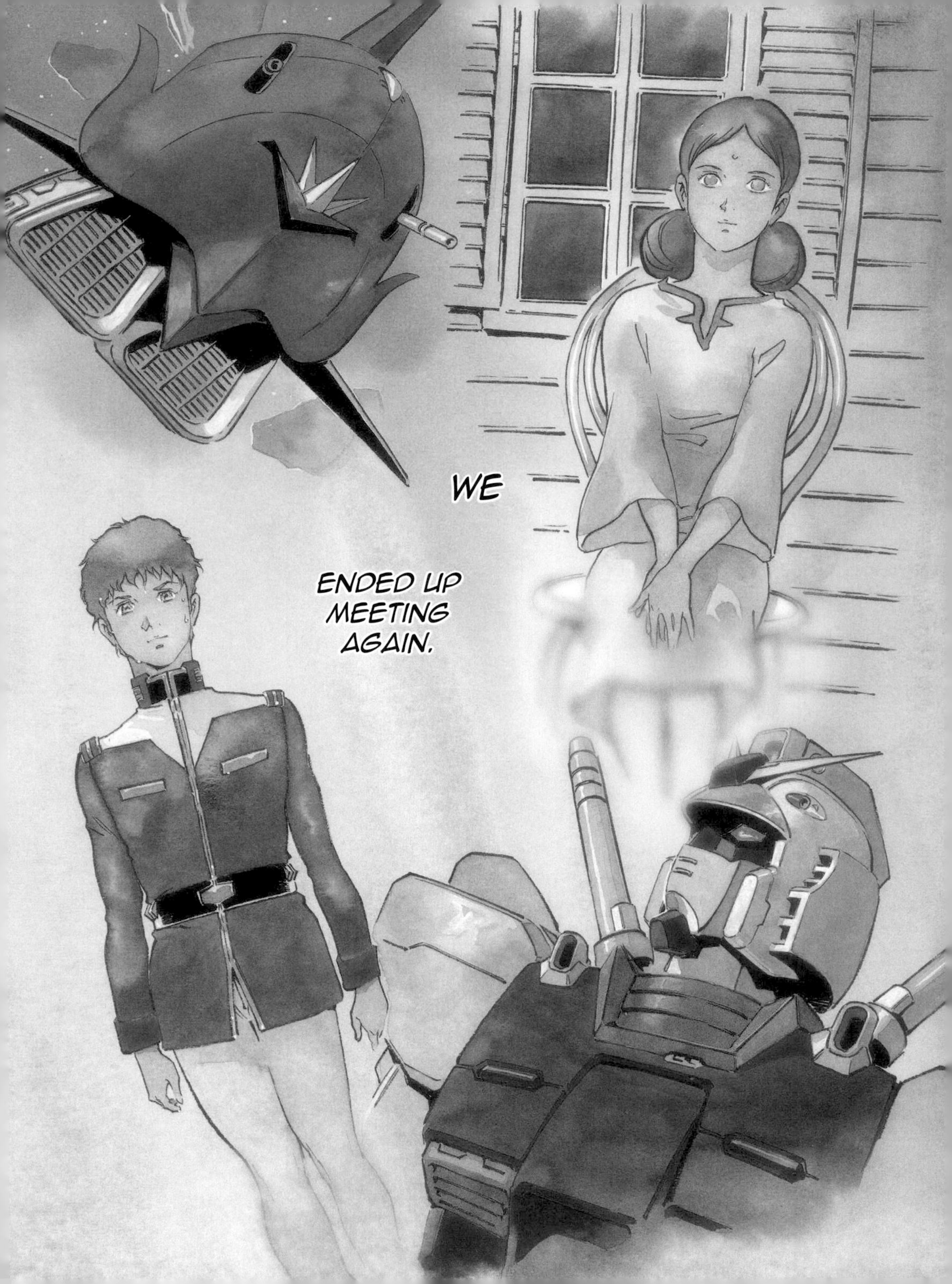
WE
ENDED UP MEETING AGAIN.

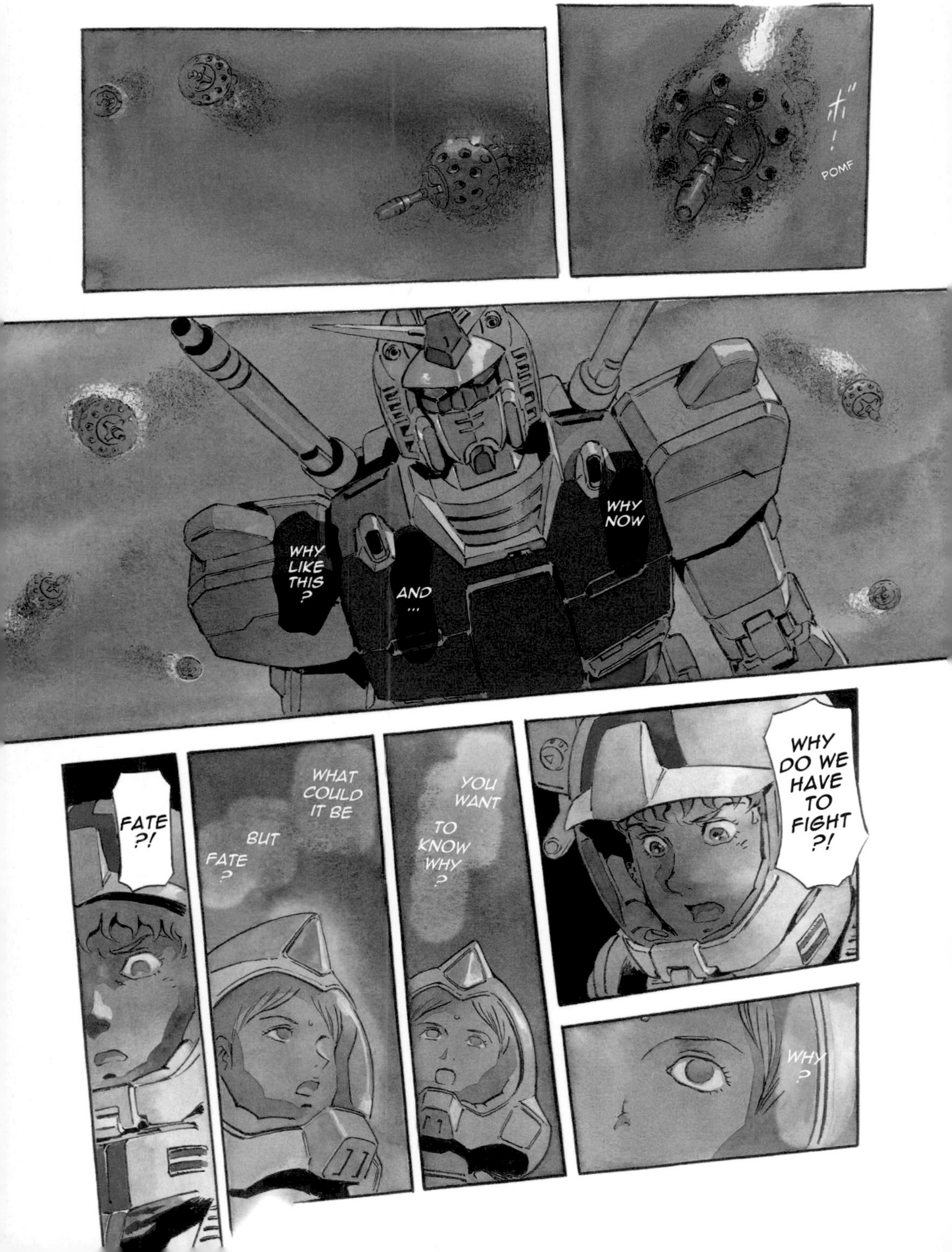
ボ!
POMF
WHY NOW
AND ...
WHY LIKE THIS ?
WHY DO WE HAVE TO FIGHT ?!
WHY ?
YOU WANT TO KNOW WHY ?
WHAT COULD IT BE BUT FATE ?
FATE ?!

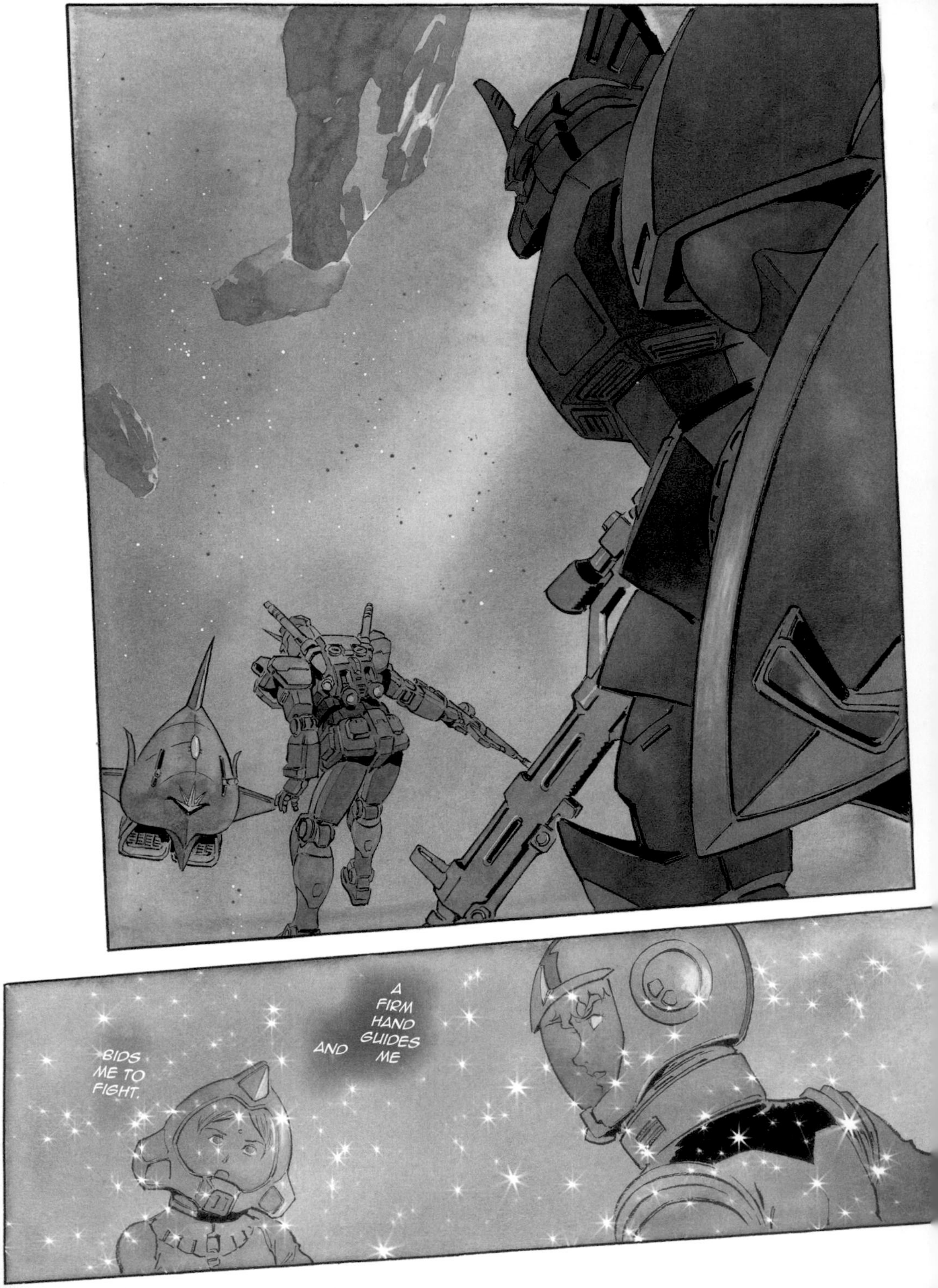
A FIRM HAND GUIDES ME
AND
BIDS ME TO FIGHT.

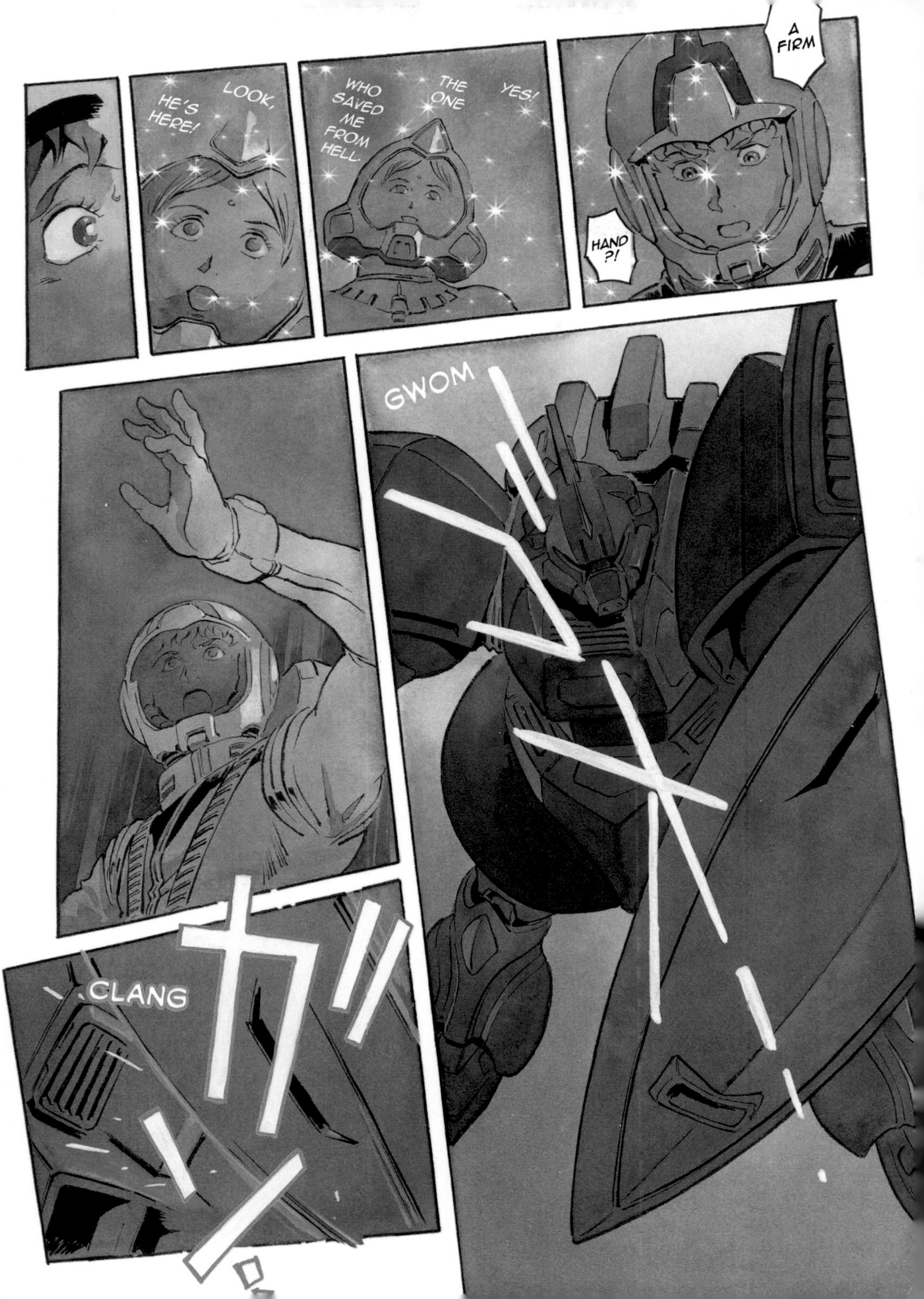
A FIRM
HAND ?!
YES!
THE ONE
WHO SAVED ME FROM HELL.
LOOK,
HE'S HERE!
GWOM
CLANG

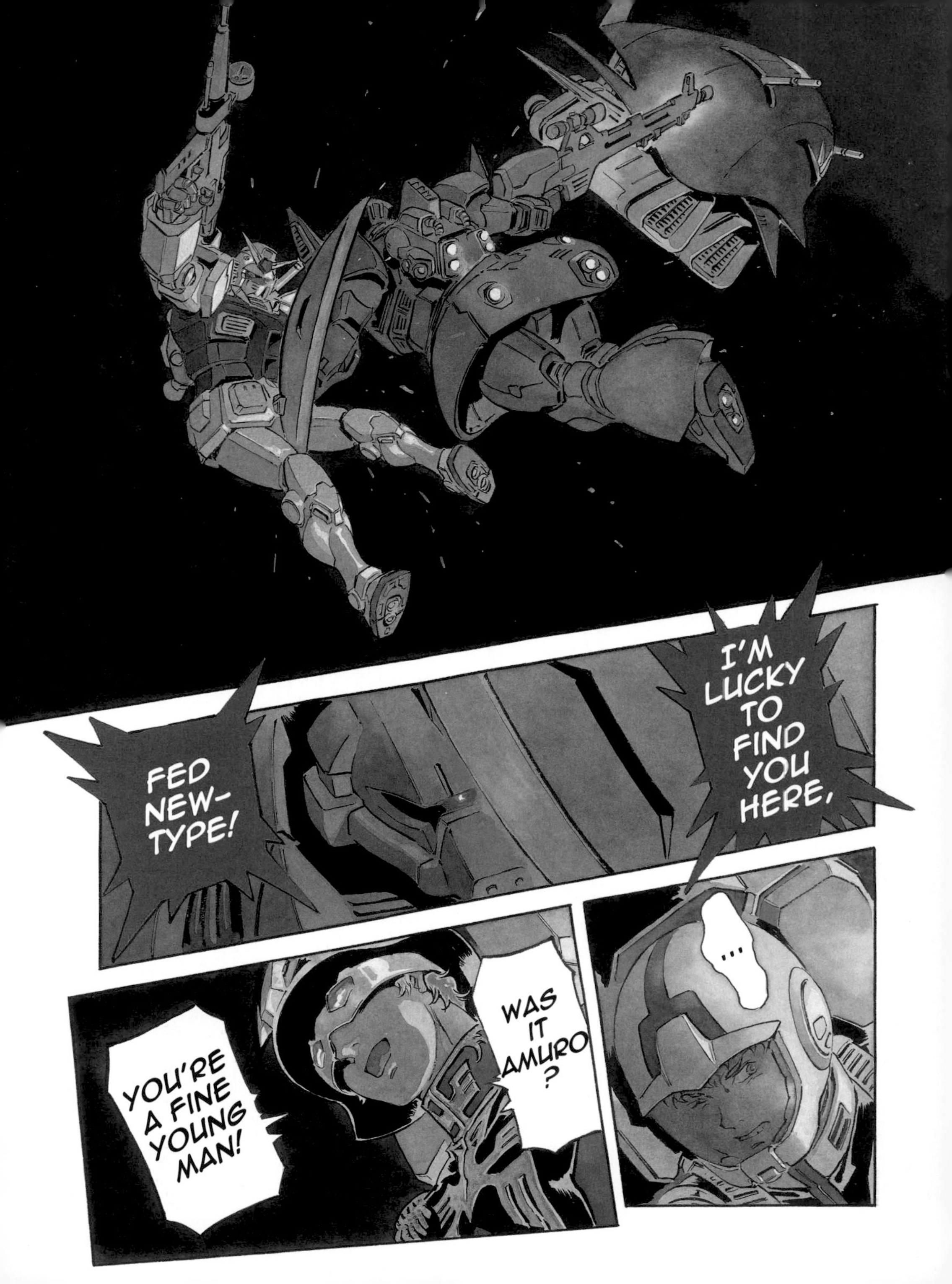
I'M LUCKY TO FIND YOU HERE,
FED NEW-TYPE!
...
WAS IT AMURO?
YOU'RE A FINE YOUNG MAN!

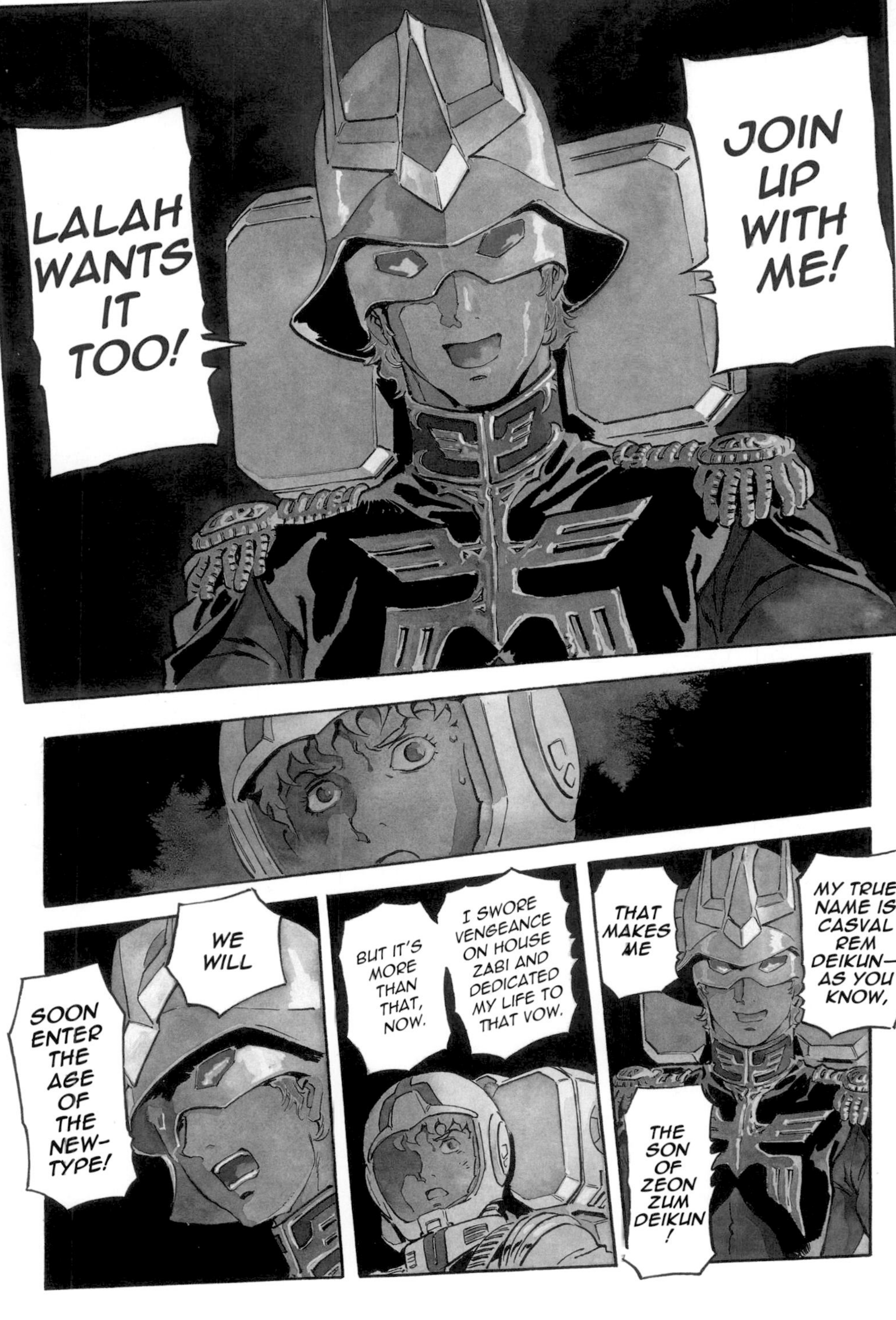
JOIN UP WITH ME!
LALAH WANTS IT TOO!
MY TRUE NAME IS CASVAL REM DEIKUN—AS YOU KNOW,
THAT MAKES ME
THE SON OF ZEON ZUM DEIKUN!
I SWORE VENGEANCE ON HOUSE ZABI AND DEDICATED MY LIFE TO THAT VOW.
BUT IT'S MORE THAN THAT, NOW.
WE WILL
SOON ENTER THE AGE OF THE NEW-TYPE!

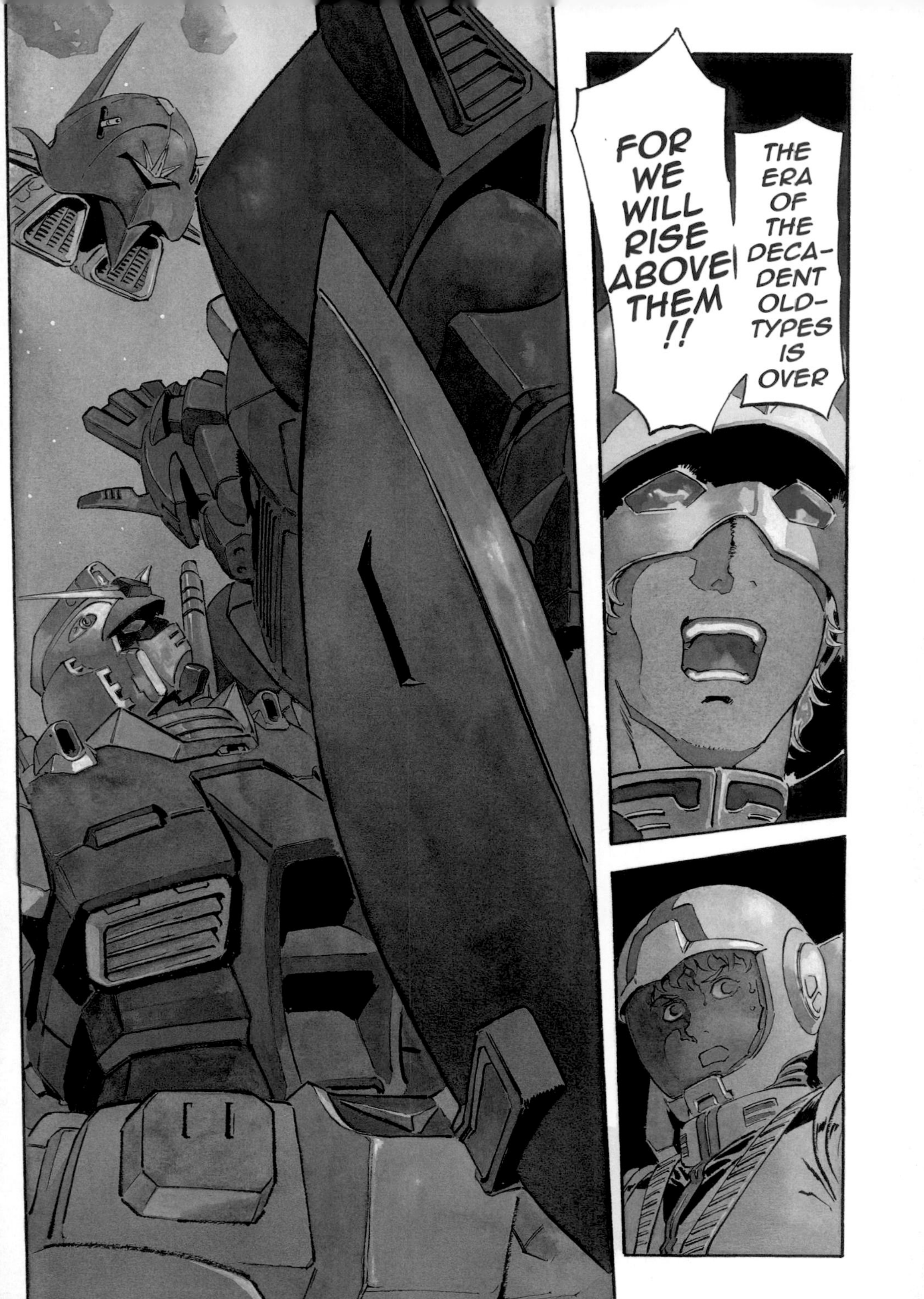
THE ERA OF THE DECADENT OLD-TYPES IS OVER
FOR WE WILL RISE ABOVE THEM!!

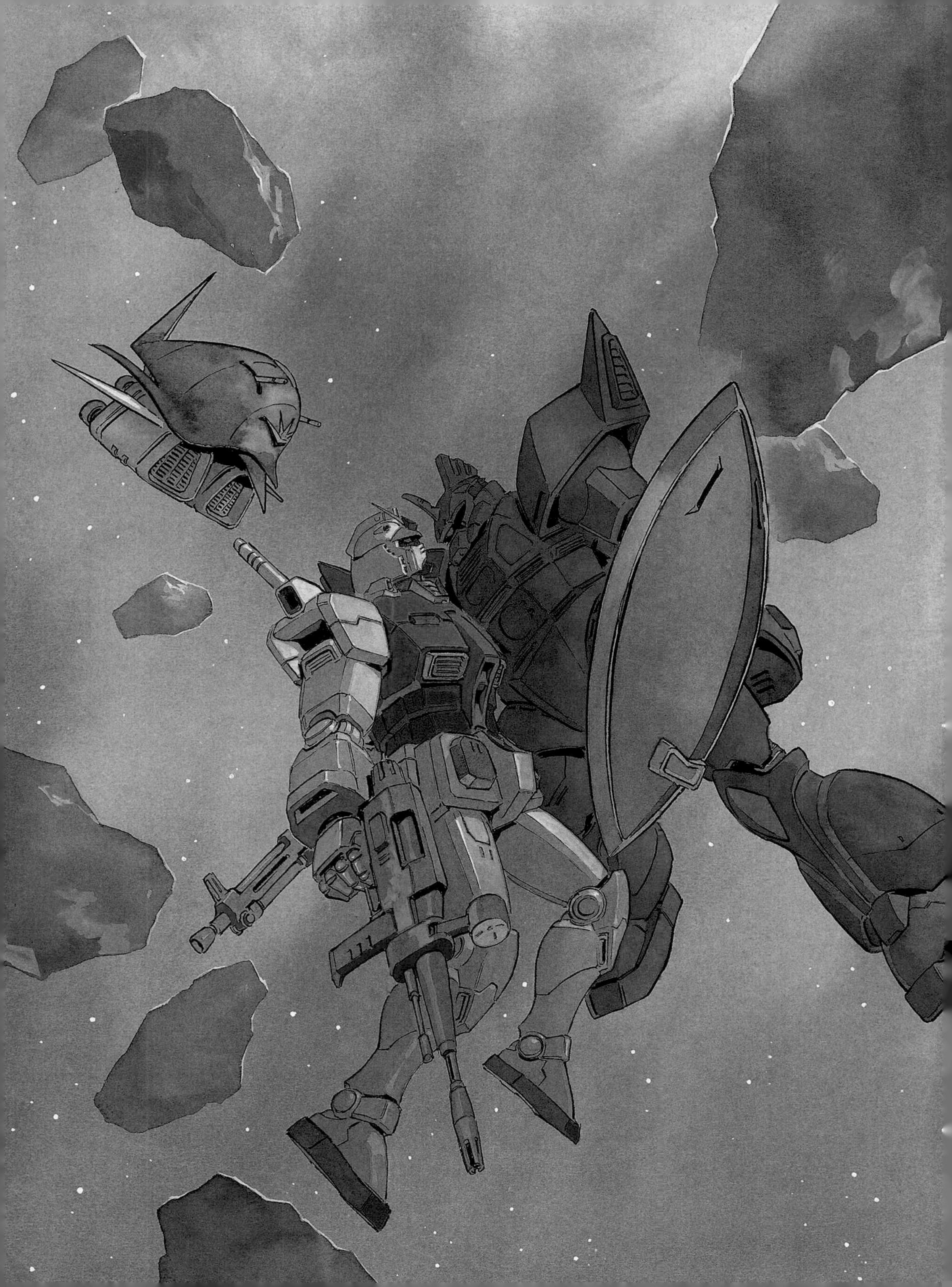

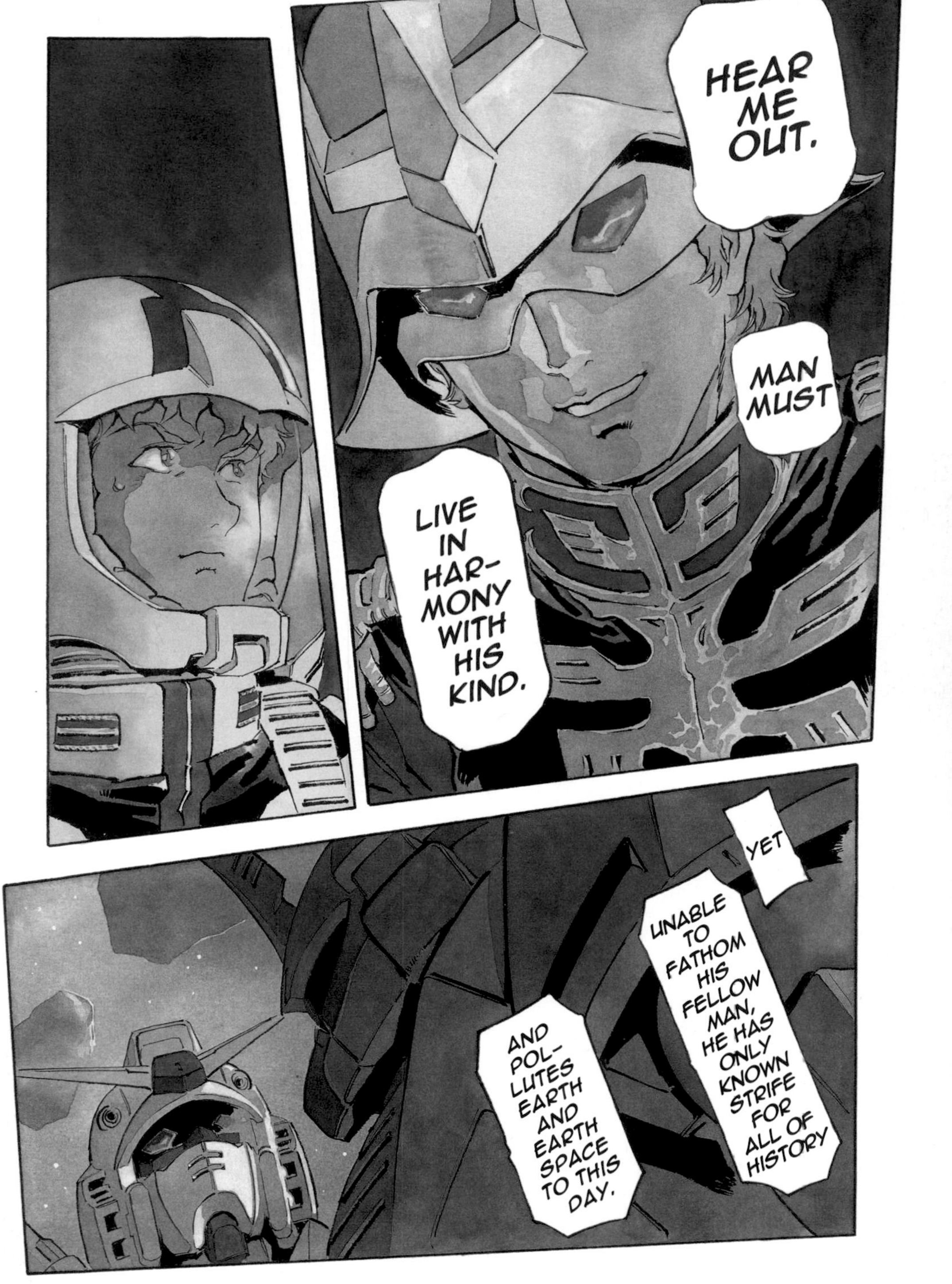
HEAR ME OUT.
MAN MUST
LIVE IN HAR-MONY WITH HIS KIND.
YET
UNABLE TO FATHOM HIS FELLOW MAN, HE HAS ONLY KNOWN STRIFE FOR ALL OF HISTORY
AND POL-LUTES EARTH AND EARTH SPACE TO THIS DAY.

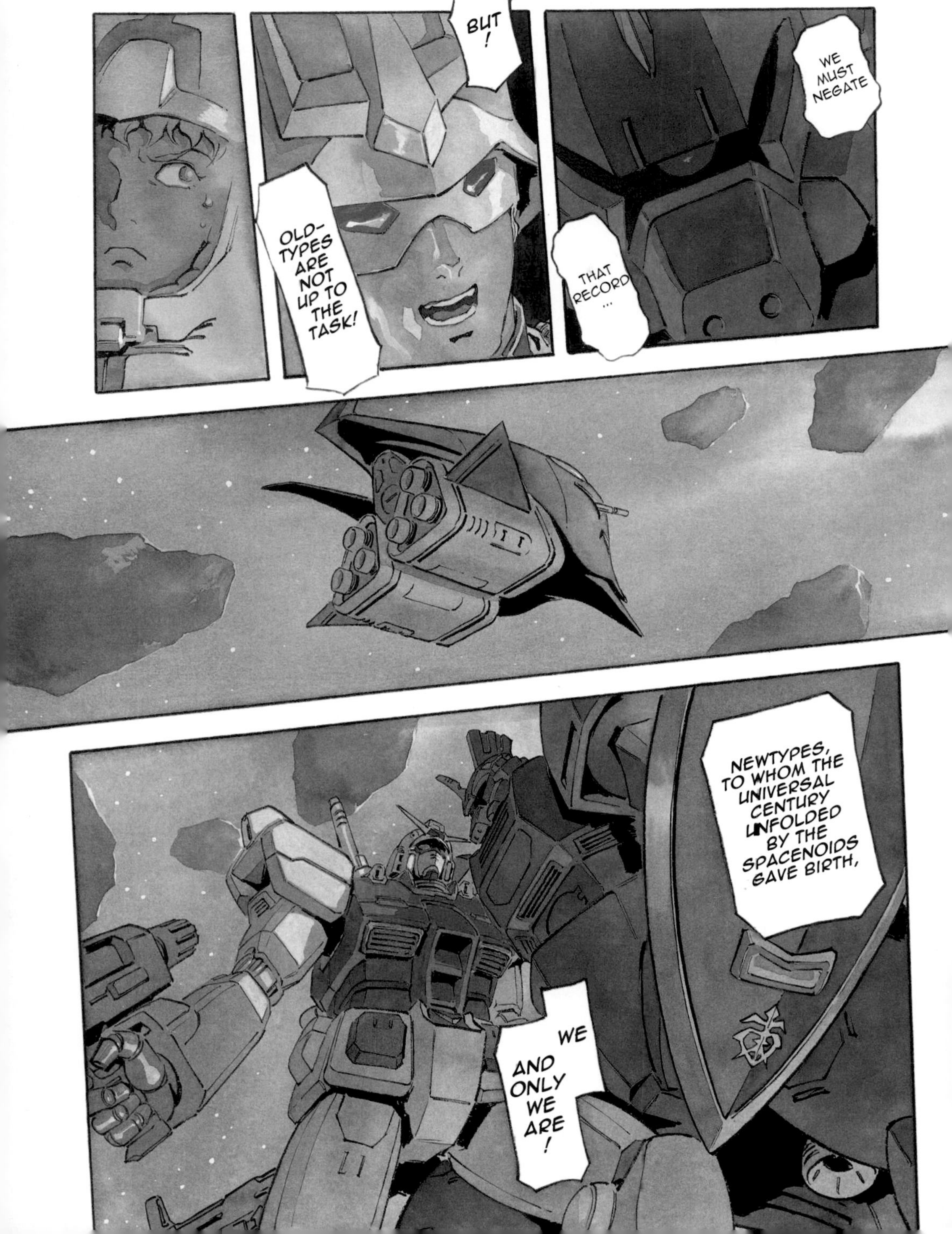
WE MUST NEGATE
THAT RECORD ...
BUT!
OLD-TYPES ARE NOT UP TO THE TASK!
NEWTYPES, TO WHOM THE UNIVERSAL CENTURY UNFOLDED BY THE SPACENOIDS GAVE BIRTH,
WE AND ONLY WE ARE!

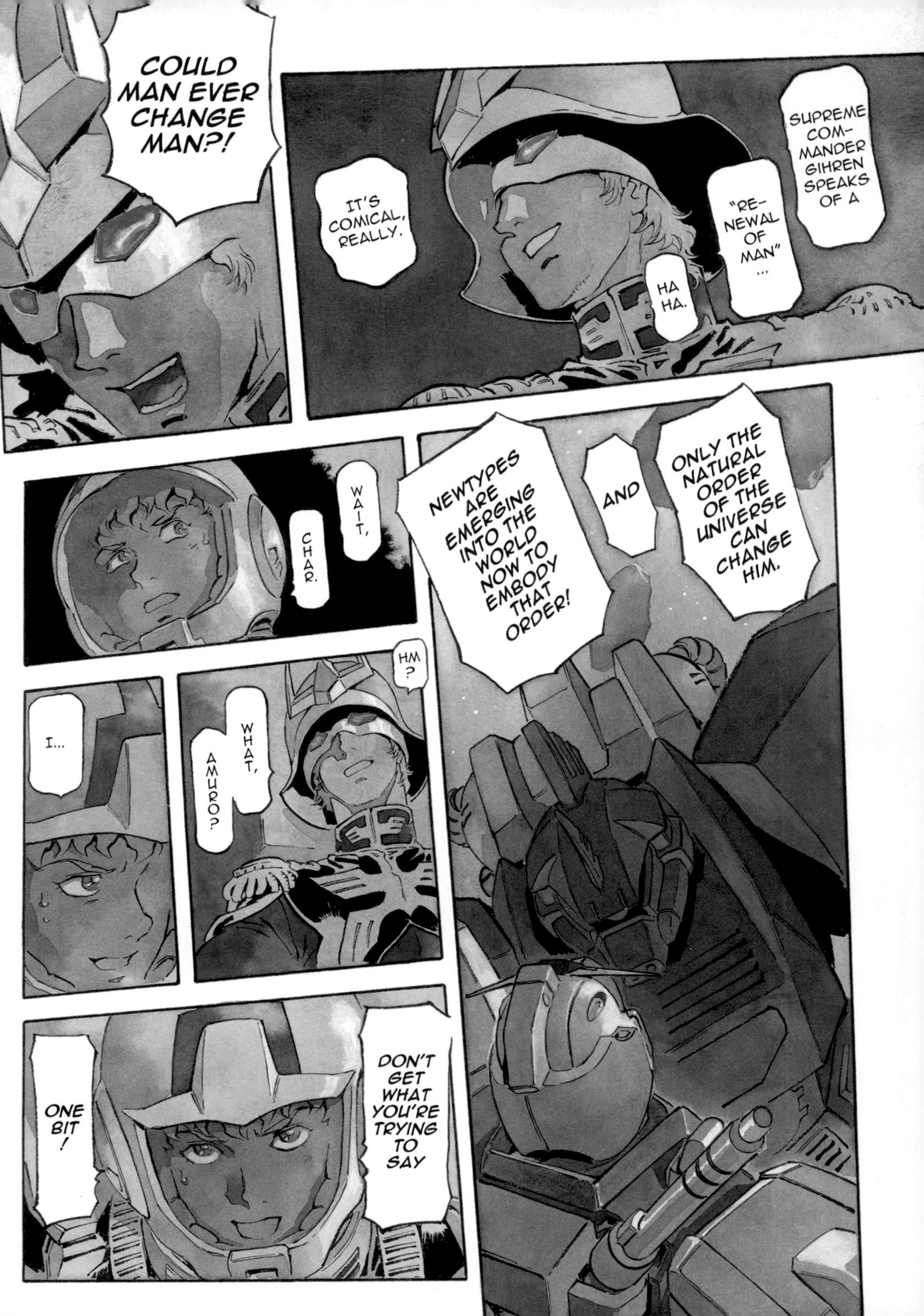
SUPREME COM-MANDER GIHREN SPEAKS OF A
"RE-NEWAL OF MAN"...
HA HA.
IT'S COMICAL, REALLY.
COULD MAN EVER CHANGE MAN?!
ONLY THE NATURAL ORDER OF THE UNIVERSE CAN CHANGE HIM.
AND
NEWTYPES ARE EMERGING INTO THE WORLD NOW TO EMBODY THAT ORDER!
WAIT,
CHAR.
HM?
WHAT,
AMURO?
I...
DON'T GET WHAT YOU'RE TRYING TO SAY
ONE BIT!

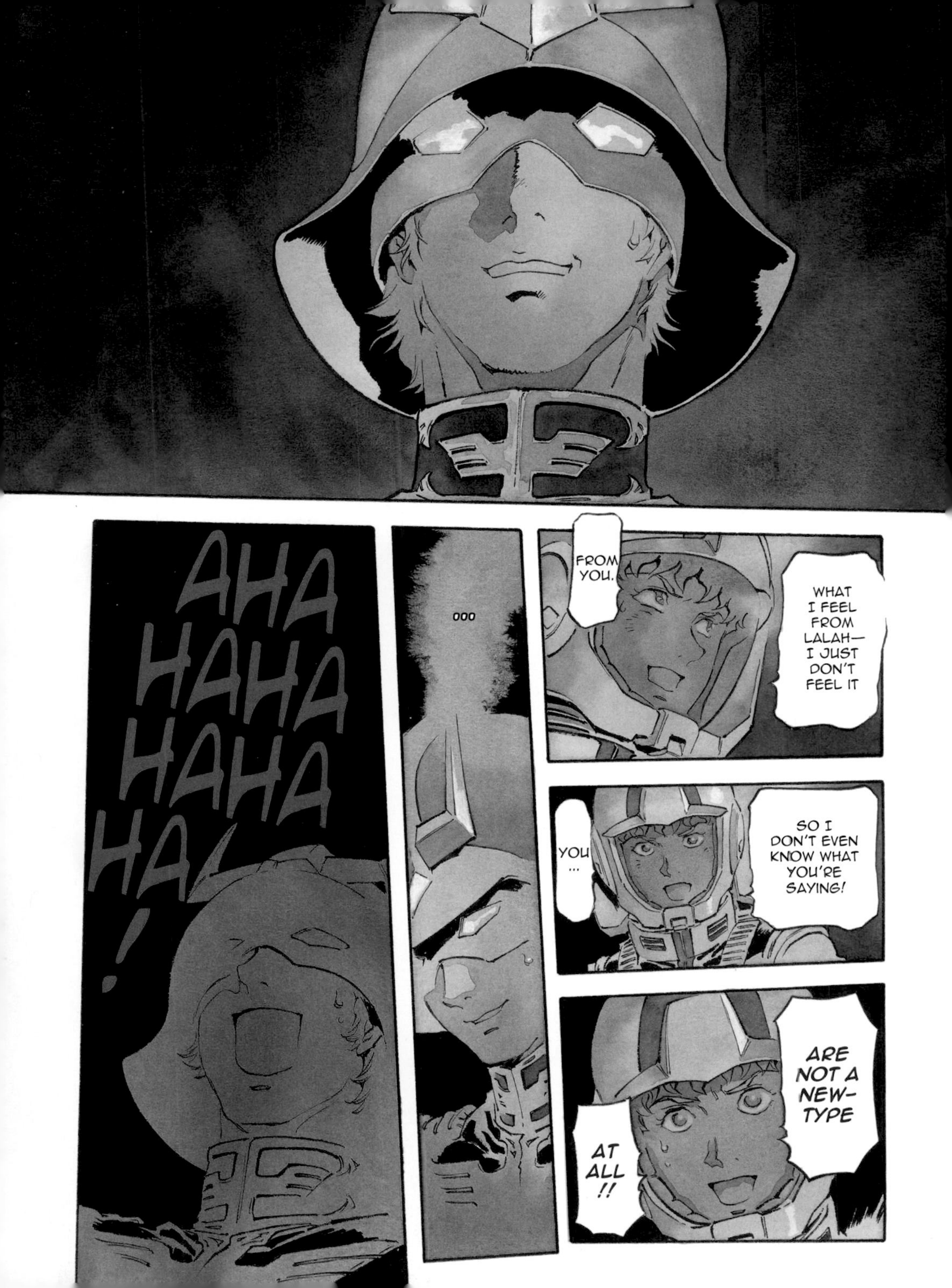
WHAT I FEEL FROM LALAH— I JUST DON'T FEEL IT
FROM YOU.
SO I DON'T EVEN KNOW WHAT YOU'RE SAYING!
YOU ...
ARE NOT A NEW-TYPE
AT ALL !!
AHA HAHA HAHA HA!

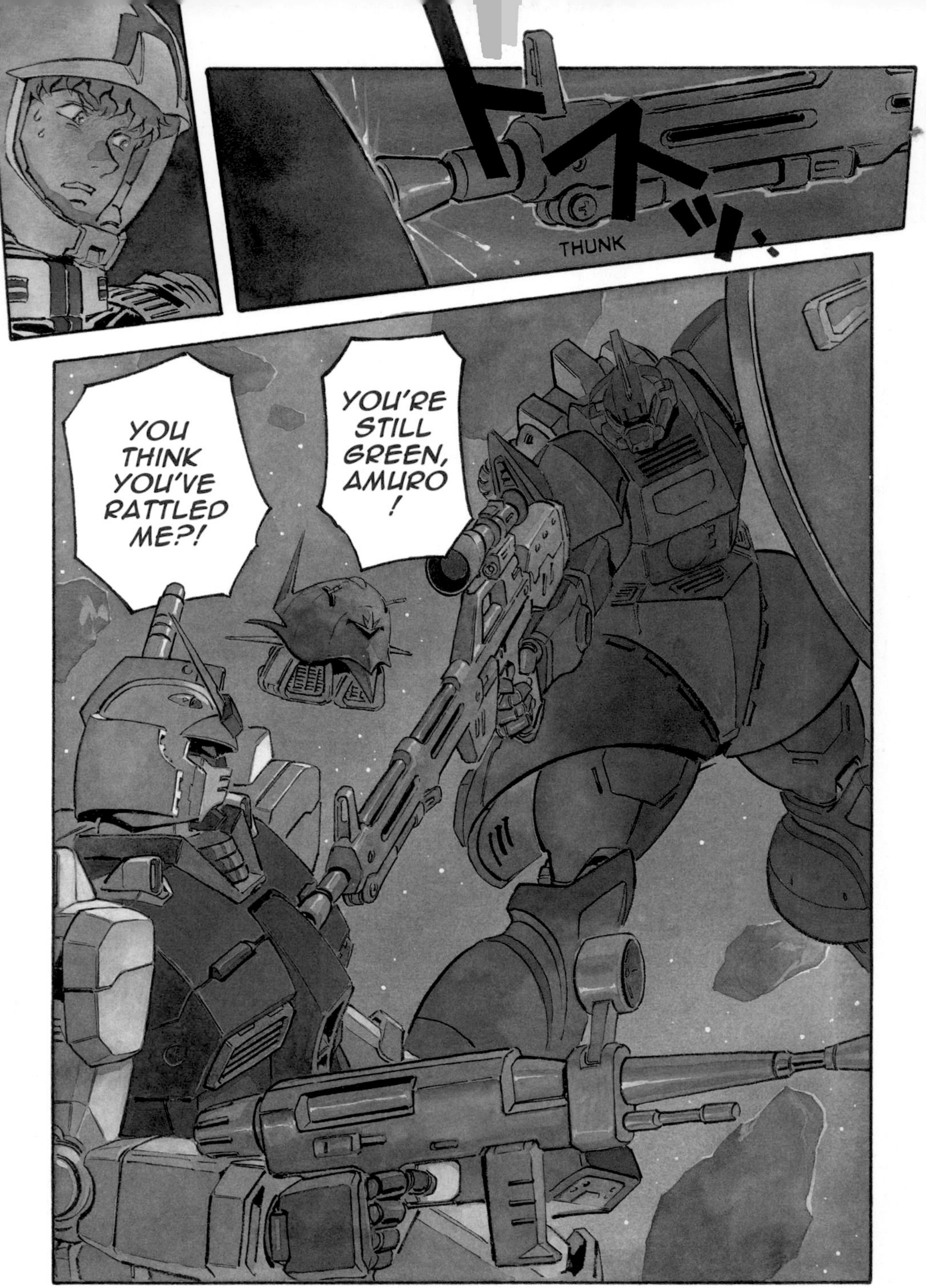
THUNK
YOU'RE STILL GREEN, AMURO!
YOU THINK YOU'VE RATTLED ME?!

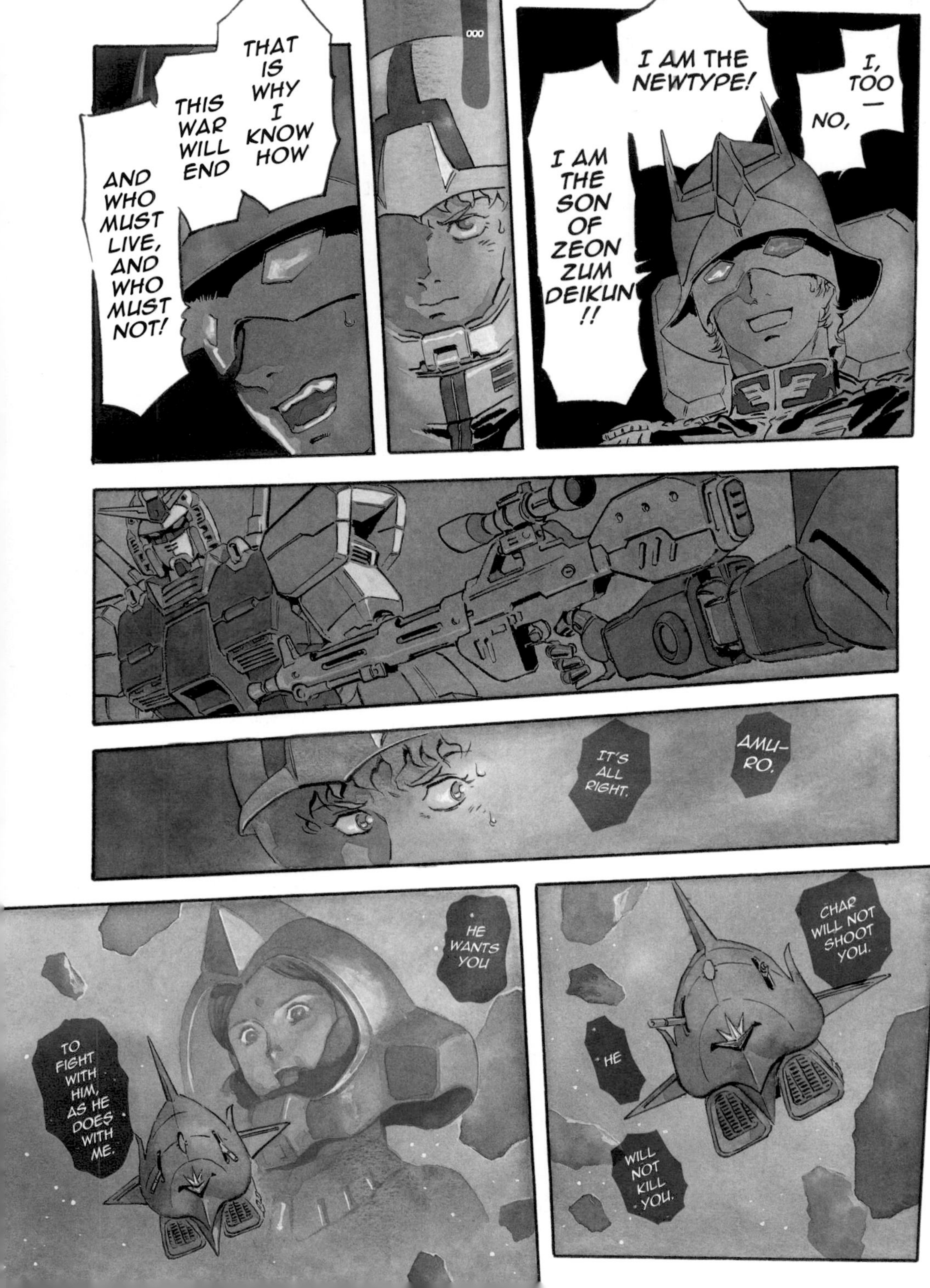
I, TOO— NO,
I AM THE NEWTYPE!
I AM THE SON OF ZEON ZUM DEIKUN!!
...
THAT IS WHY I KNOW HOW THIS WAR WILL END
AND WHO MUST LIVE, AND WHO MUST NOT!
AMU-RO.
IT'S ALL RIGHT.
CHAR WILL NOT SHOOT YOU.
HE
WILL NOT KILL YOU.
HE WANTS YOU
TO FIGHT WITH HIM, AS HE DOES WITH ME.

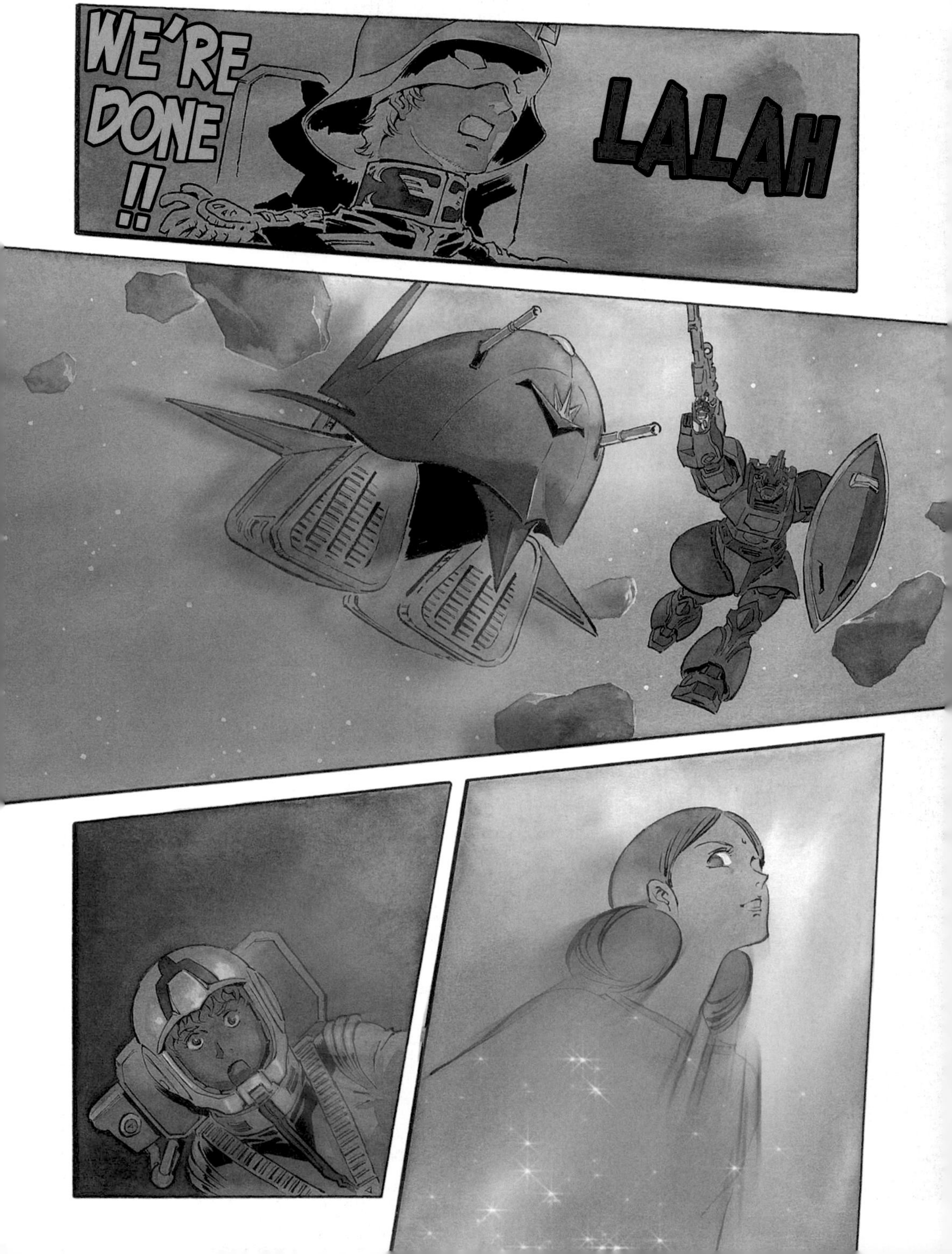
LALAH
WE'RE DONE !!

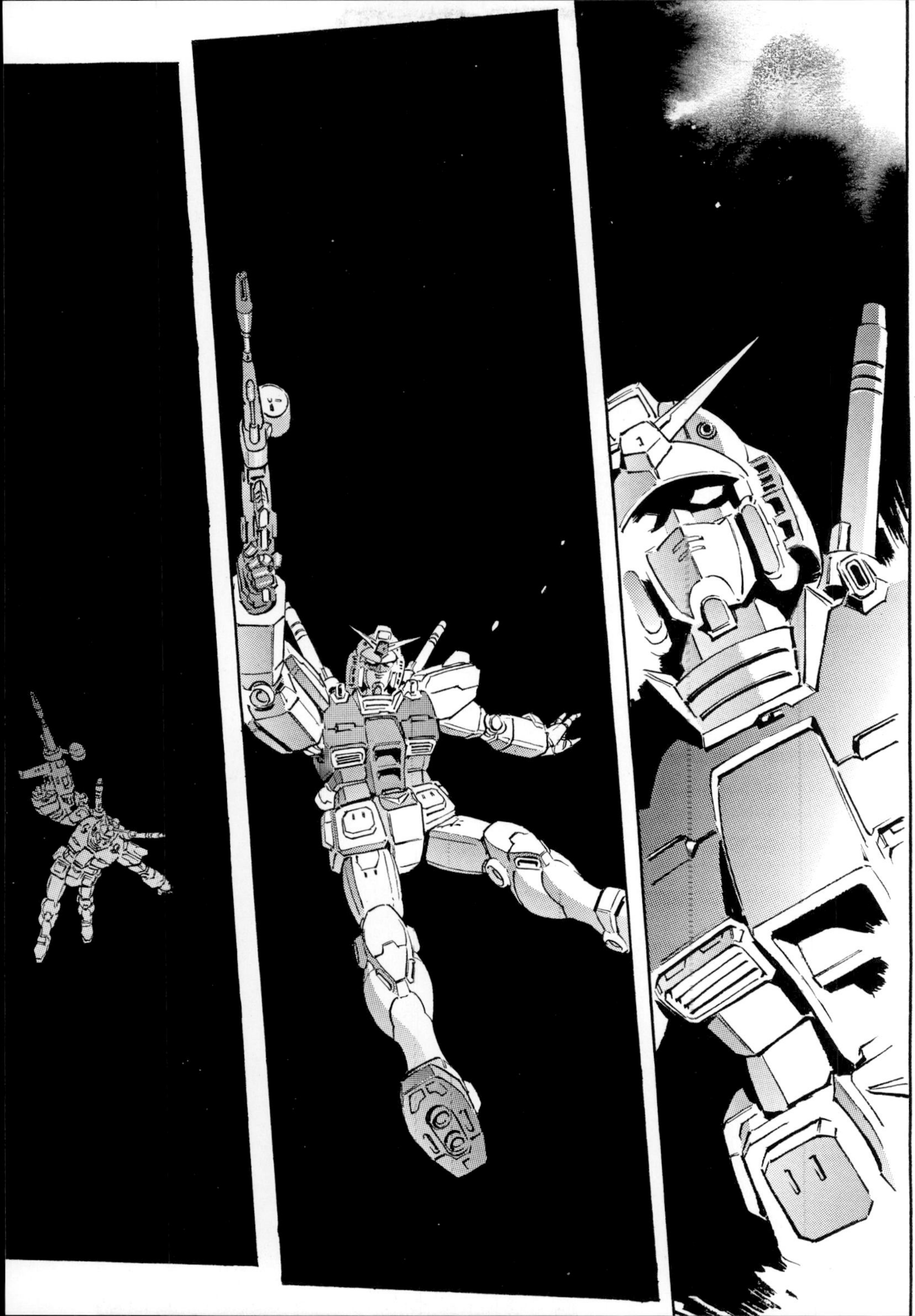

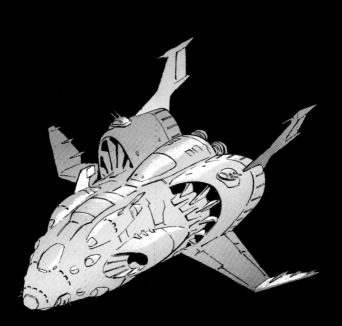

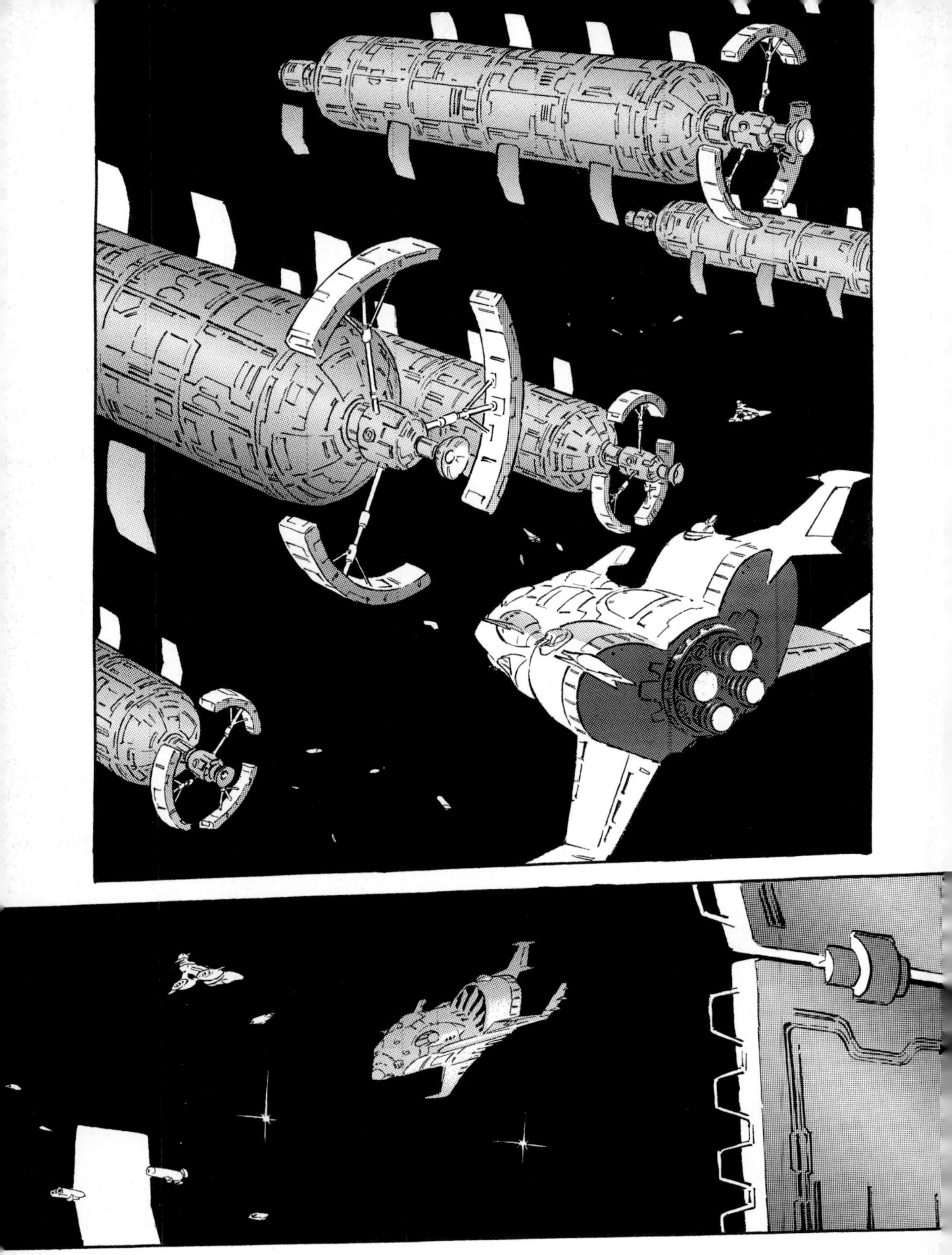

IT SEEMS TO HAVE BEGUN.

THE THIRD BUNCH, MAHAL...

IT WASN'T SUCH A BAD COLONY.

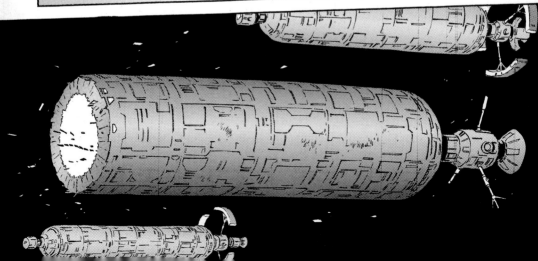

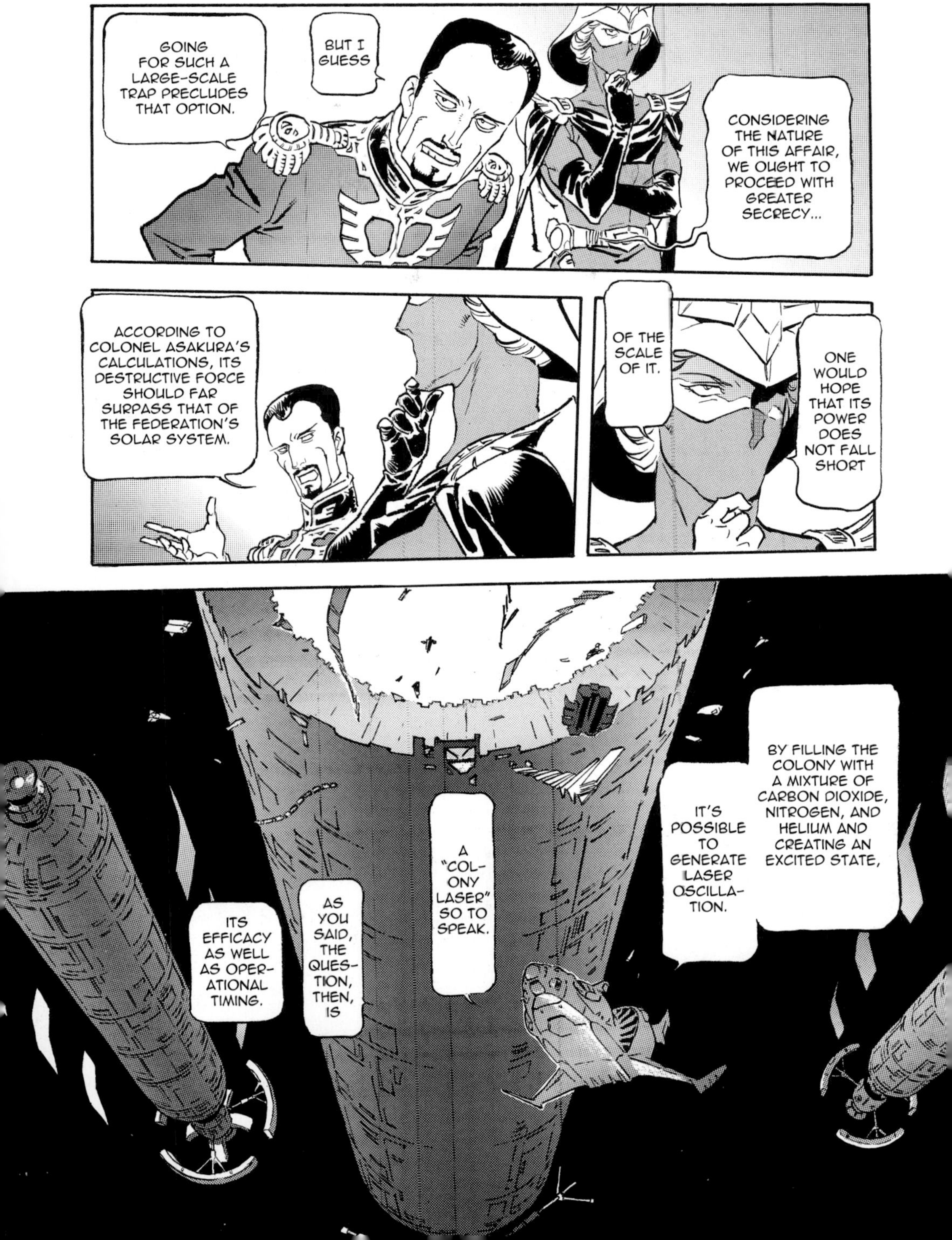
CONSIDERING THE NATURE OF THIS AFFAIR, WE OUGHT TO PROCEED WITH GREATER SECRECY...
BUT I GUESS
GOING FOR SUCH A LARGE-SCALE TRAP PRECLUDES THAT OPTION.
ONE WOULD HOPE THAT ITS POWER DOES NOT FALL SHORT
OF THE SCALE OF IT.
ACCORDING TO COLONEL ASAKURA'S CALCULATIONS, ITS DESTRUCTIVE FORCE SHOULD FAR SURPASS THAT OF THE FEDERATION'S SOLAR SYSTEM.
BY FILLING THE COLONY WITH A MIXTURE OF CARBON DIOXIDE, NITROGEN, AND HELIUM AND CREATING AN EXCITED STATE,
IT'S POSSIBLE TO GENERATE LASER OSCILLA-TION.
A "COL-ONY LASER" SO TO SPEAK.
AS YOU SAID, THE QUES-TION, THEN, IS
ITS EFFICACY AS WELL AS OPER-ATIONAL TIMING.

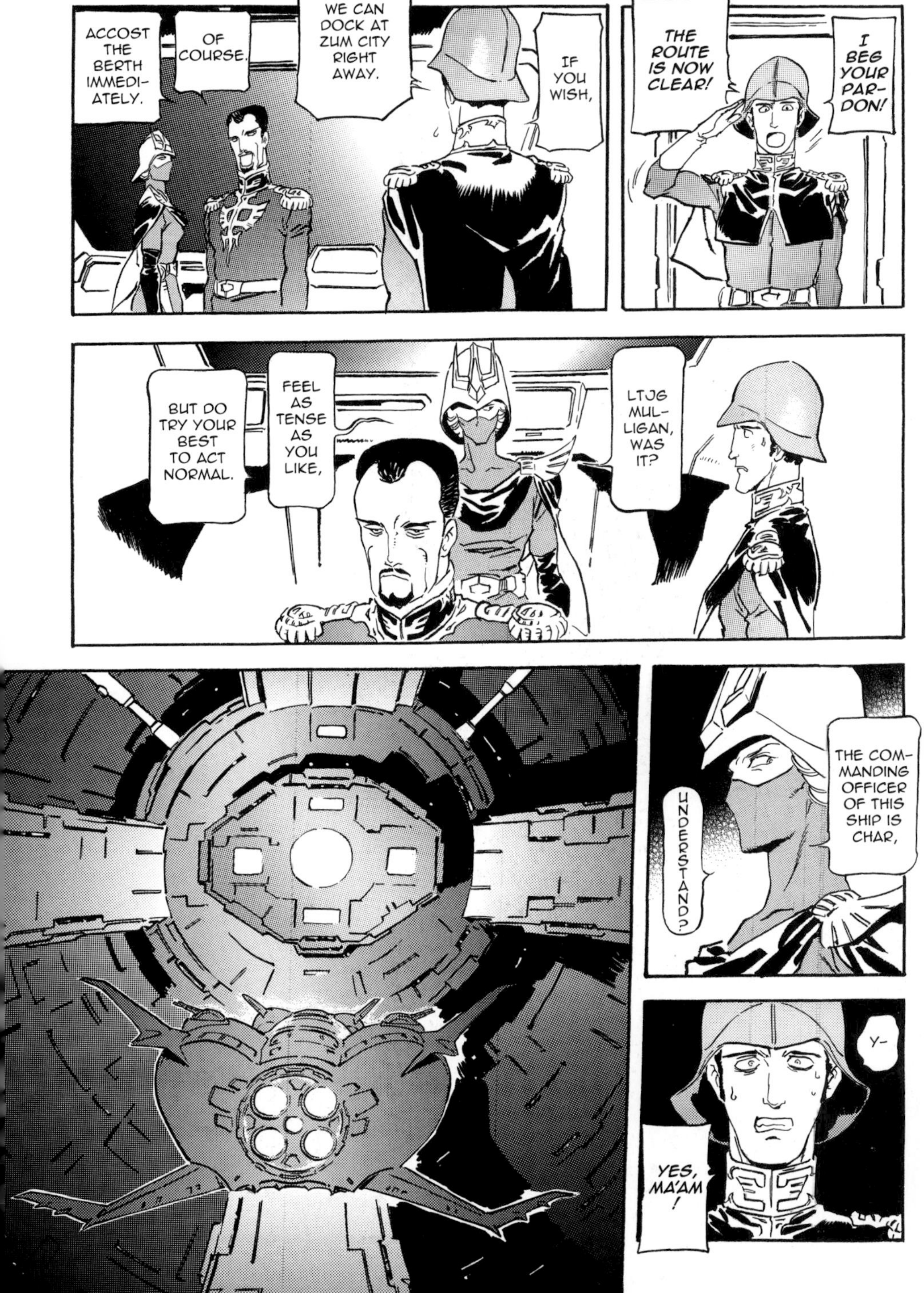
I BEG YOUR PARDON!
THE ROUTE IS NOW CLEAR!
IF YOU WISH,
WE CAN DOCK AT ZUM CITY RIGHT AWAY.
OF COURSE.
ACCOST THE BERTH IMMEDIATELY.
LTJG MULLIGAN, WAS IT?
FEEL AS TENSE AS YOU LIKE,
BUT DO TRY YOUR BEST TO ACT NORMAL.
THE COMMANDING OFFICER OF THIS SHIP IS CHAR,
UNDERSTAND?
Y-
YES, MA'AM!

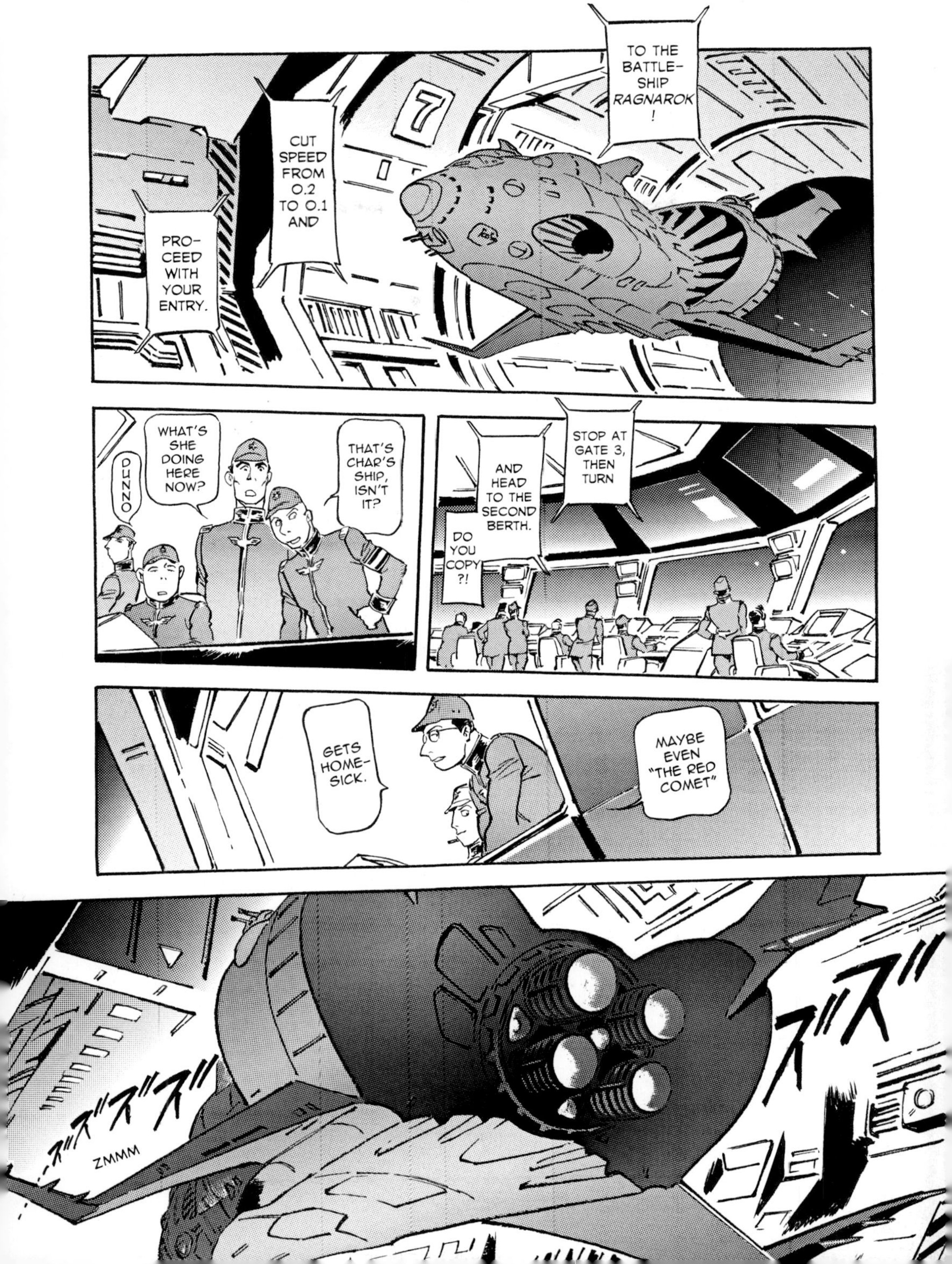

TO THE BATTLE-SHIP RAGNAROK!
CUT SPEED FROM 0.2 TO 0.1 AND
PRO-CEED WITH YOUR ENTRY.
STOP AT GATE 3, THEN TURN
AND HEAD TO THE SECOND BERTH.
DO YOU COPY?!
THAT'S CHAR'S SHIP, ISN'T IT?
WHAT'S SHE DOING HERE NOW?
DUNNO
MAYBE EVEN "THE RED COMET"
GETS HOME-SICK.
ズズ
ズズズズ
ZMMM

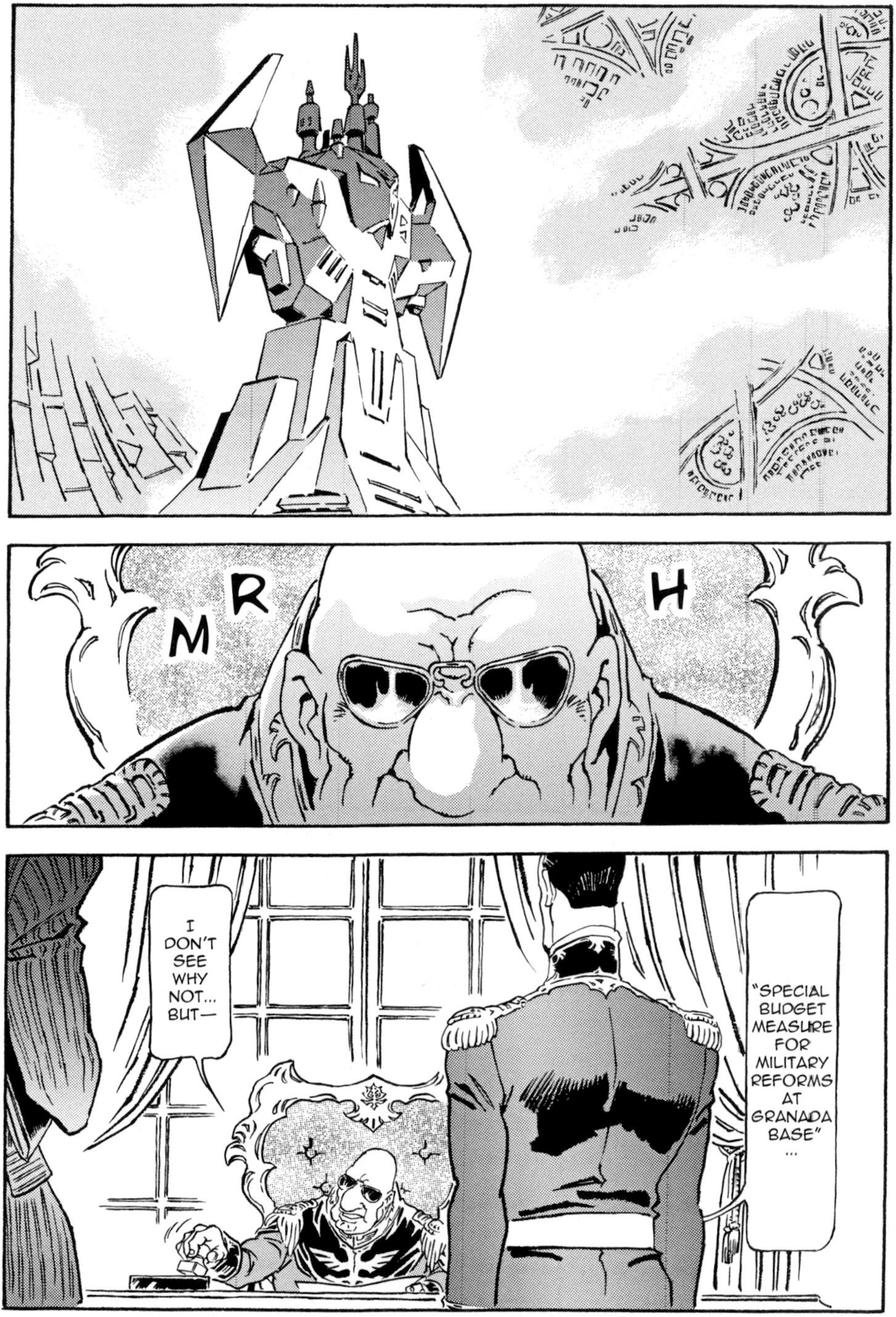
MRH
"SPECIAL BUDGET MEASURE FOR MILITARY REFORMS AT GRANADA BASE"...
I DON'T SEE WHY NOT... BUT—

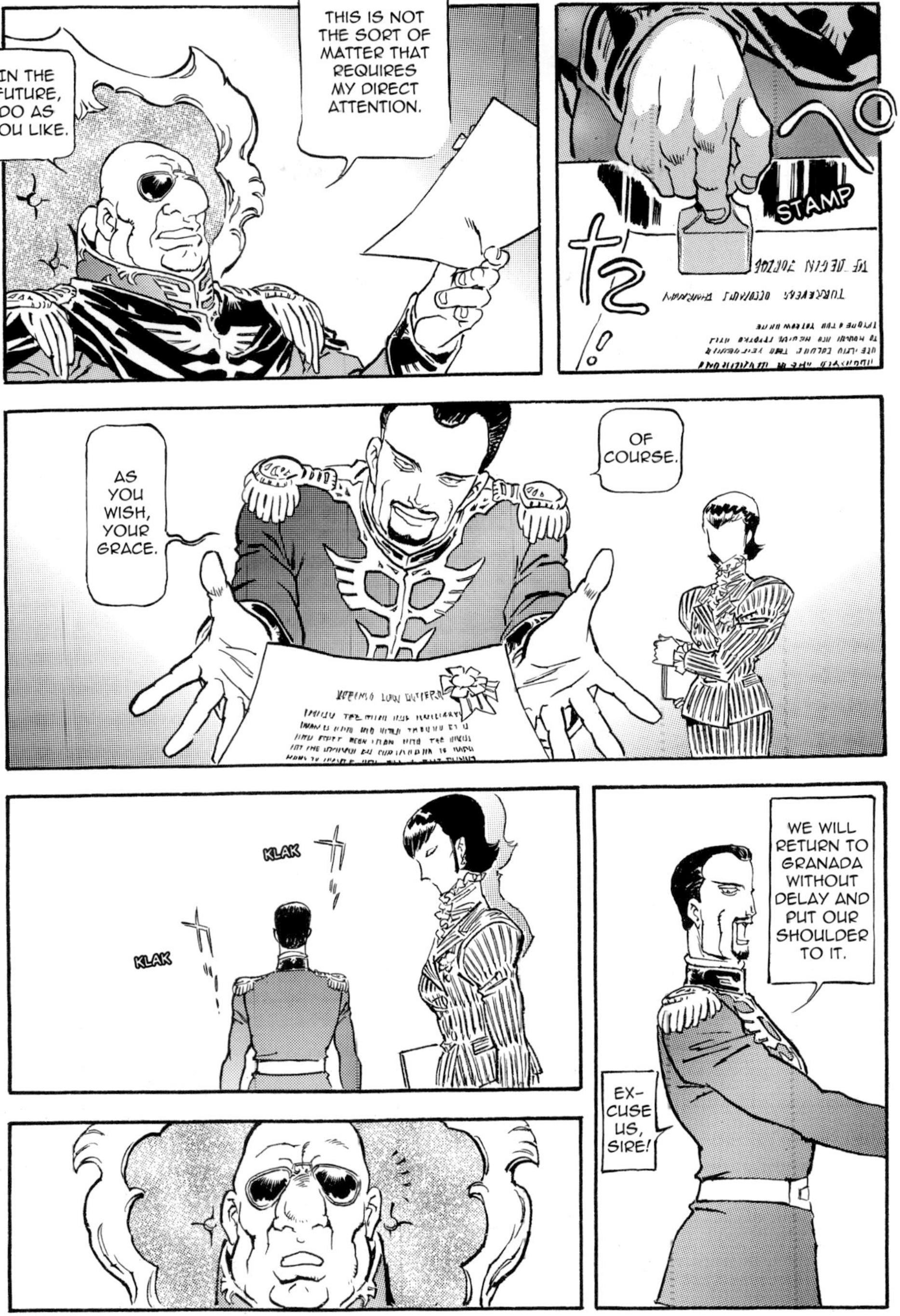
STAMP
THIS IS NOT THE SORT OF MATTER THAT REQUIRES MY DIRECT ATTENTION.
IN THE FUTURE, DO AS YOU LIKE.
OF COURSE.
AS YOU WISH, YOUR GRACE.
WE WILL RETURN TO GRANADA WITHOUT DELAY AND PUT OUR SHOULDER TO IT.
EX-CUSE US, SIRE!
KLAK
KLAK

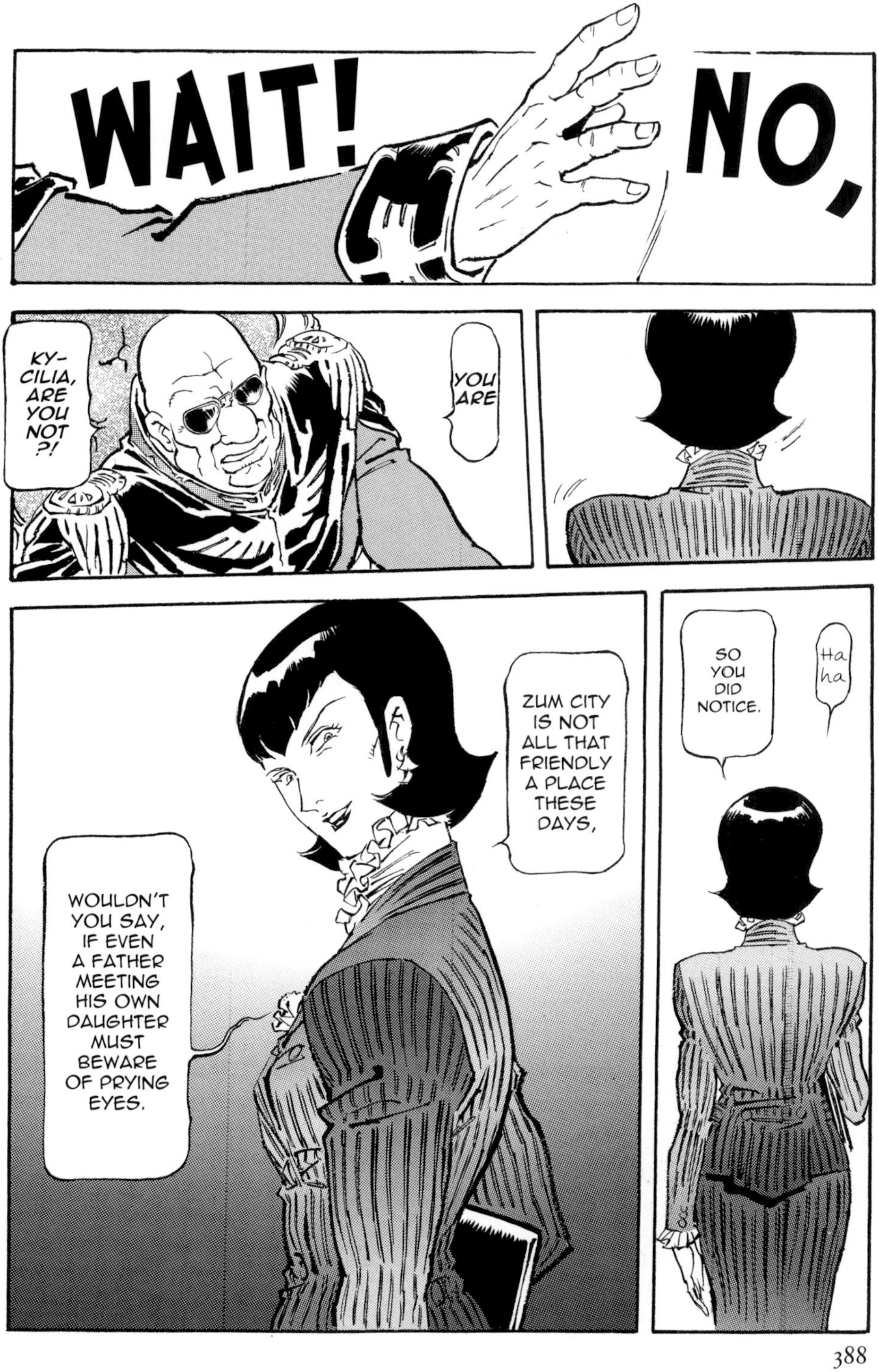
WAIT!
NO,
YOU ARE
KY-CILIA, ARE YOU NOT?!
Ha ha
SO YOU DID NOTICE.
ZUM CITY IS NOT ALL THAT FRIENDLY A PLACE THESE DAYS,
WOULDN'T YOU SAY, IF EVEN A FATHER MEETING HIS OWN DAUGHTER MUST BEWARE OF PRYING EYES.

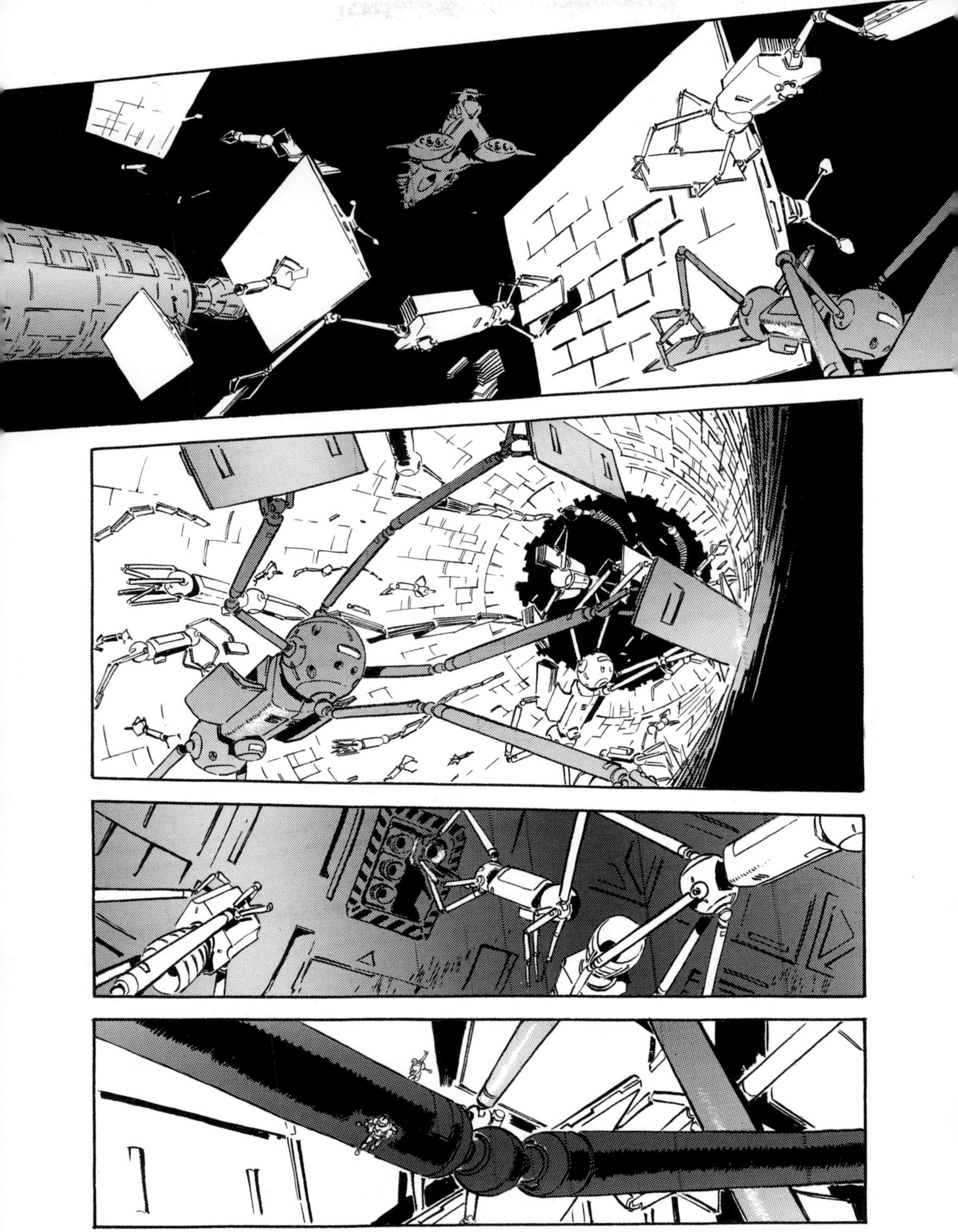

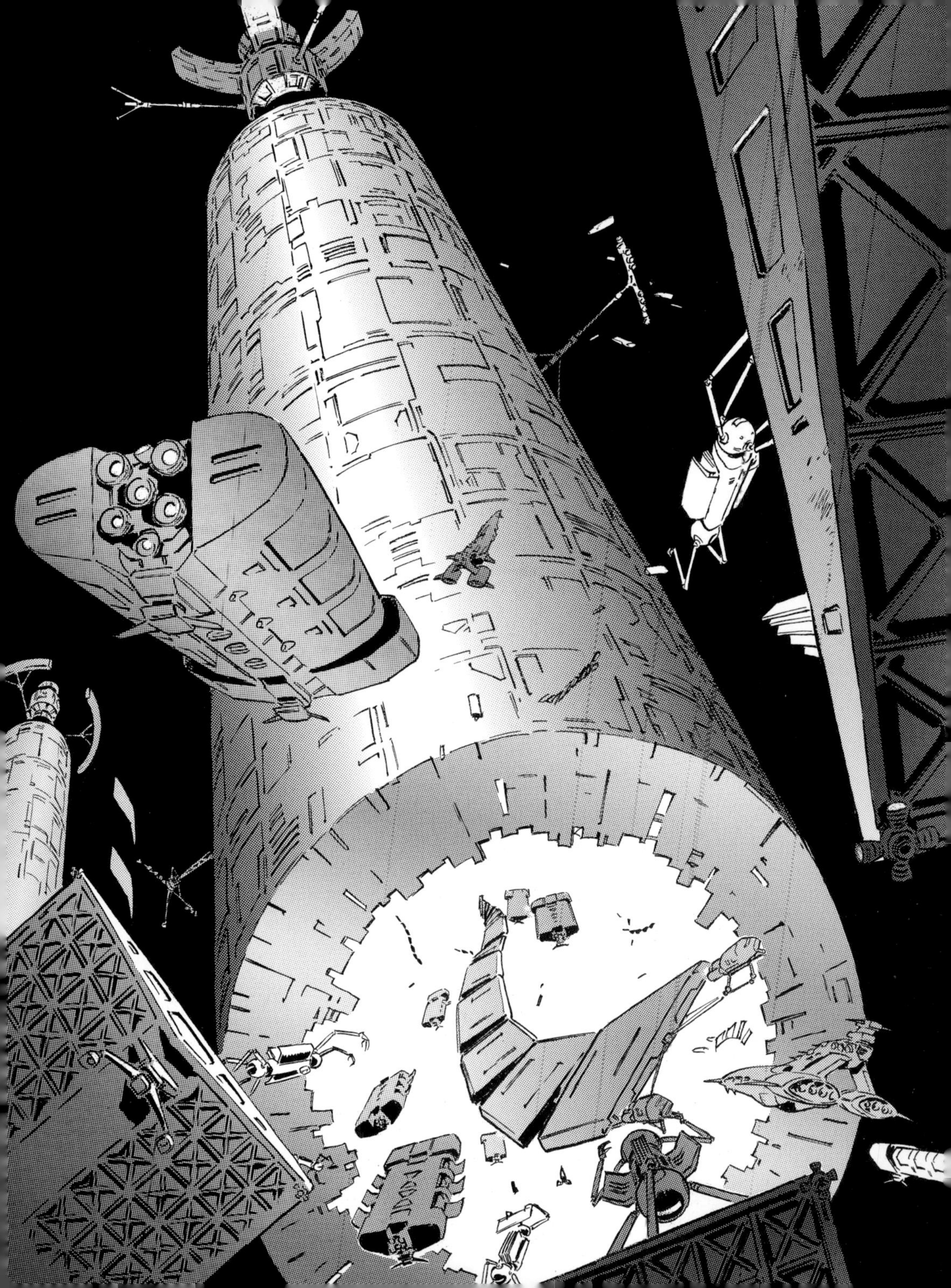

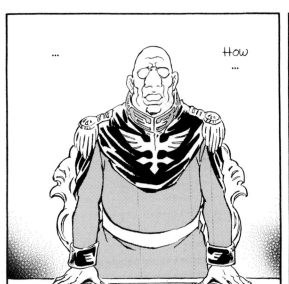

... HOW ...

YOU ... good OF

SIIIGH

SLUMP

I HEARD YOU WISHED TO SPEAK TO ME ABOUT SOMETHING.

AND I'M HAPPY TO SEE YOU ARE WELL.

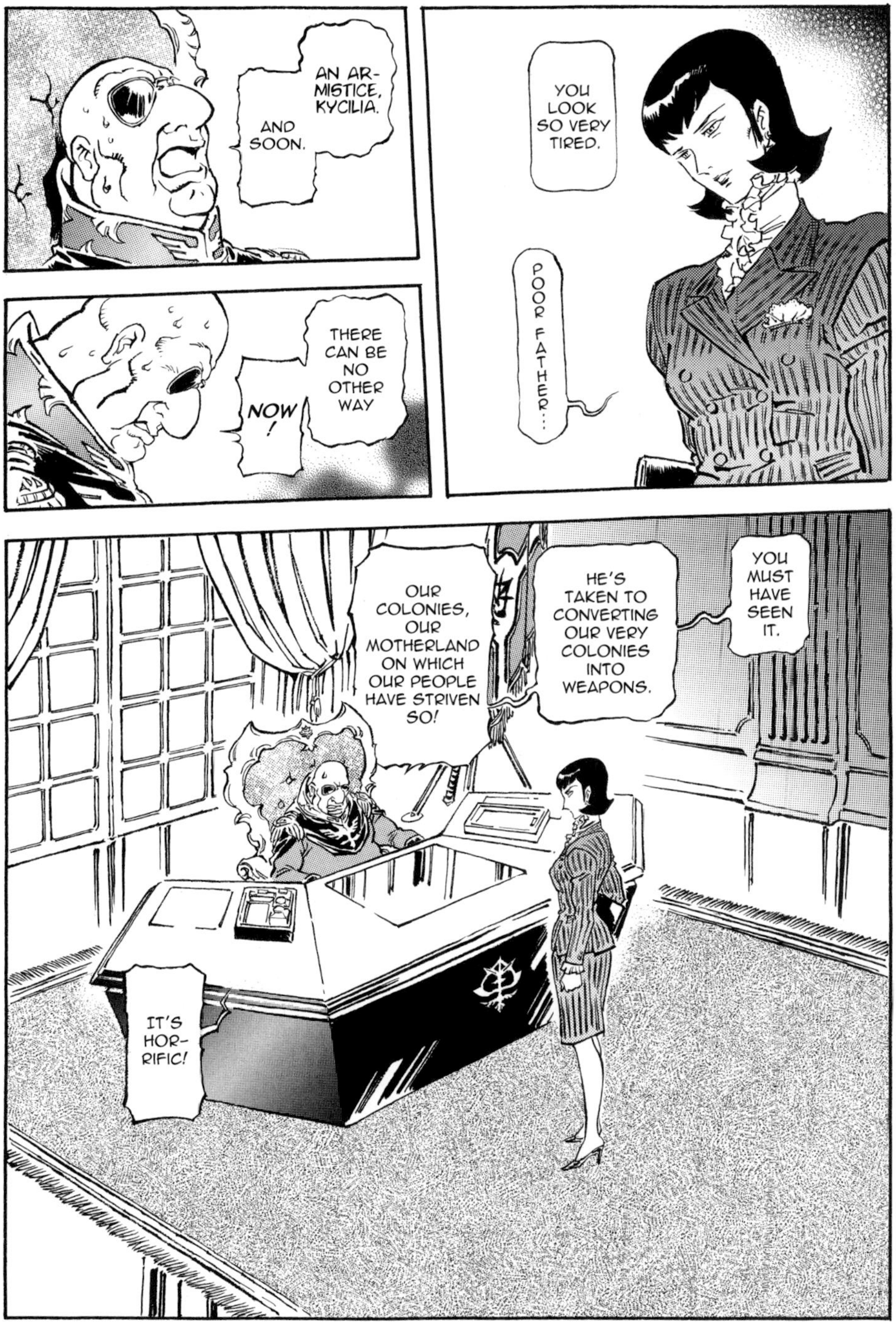
YOU LOOK SO VERY TIRED.
POOR FATHER...
AN ARMISTICE, KYCILIA.
AND SOON.
THERE CAN BE NO OTHER WAY
NOW!
YOU MUST HAVE SEEN IT.
HE'S TAKEN TO CONVERTING OUR VERY COLONIES INTO WEAPONS.
OUR COLONIES, OUR MOTHERLAND ON WHICH OUR PEOPLE HAVE STRIVEN SO!
IT'S HORRIFIC!

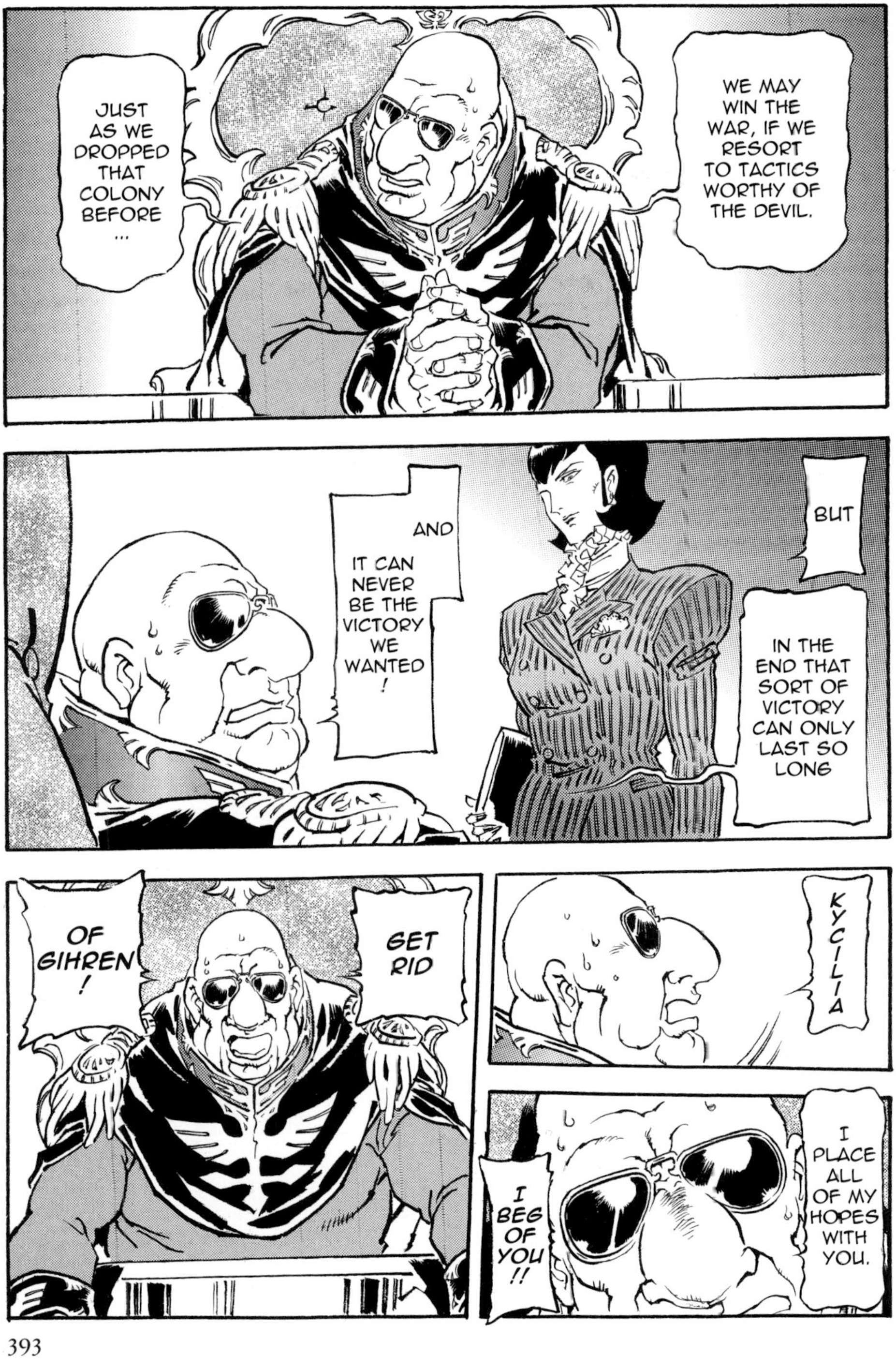

WE MAY WIN THE WAR, IF WE RESORT TO TACTICS WORTHY OF THE DEVIL.
JUST AS WE DROPPED THAT COLONY BEFORE ...
BUT
IN THE END THAT SORT OF VICTORY CAN ONLY LAST SO LONG
AND
IT CAN NEVER BE THE VICTORY WE WANTED !
KYCILIA
I PLACE ALL OF MY HOPES WITH YOU.
I BEG OF YOU !!
GET RID
OF GIHREN !

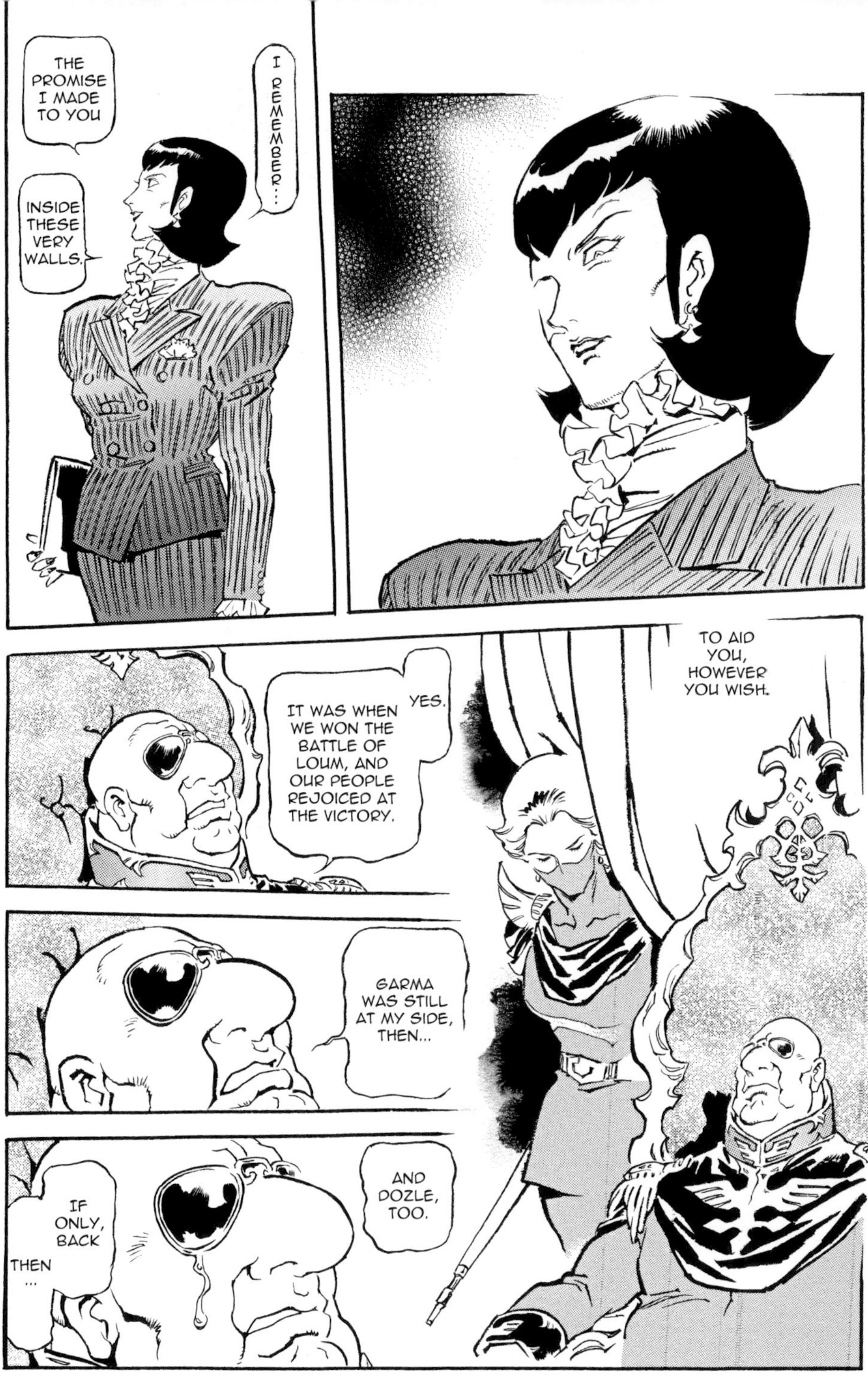
I REMEMBER...
THE PROMISE I MADE TO YOU
INSIDE THESE VERY WALLS.
TO AID YOU, HOWEVER YOU WISH.
YES.
IT WAS WHEN WE WON THE BATTLE OF LOUM, AND OUR PEOPLE REJOICED AT THE VICTORY.
GARMA WAS STILL AT MY SIDE, THEN...
AND DOZLE, TOO.
IF ONLY, BACK THEN ...

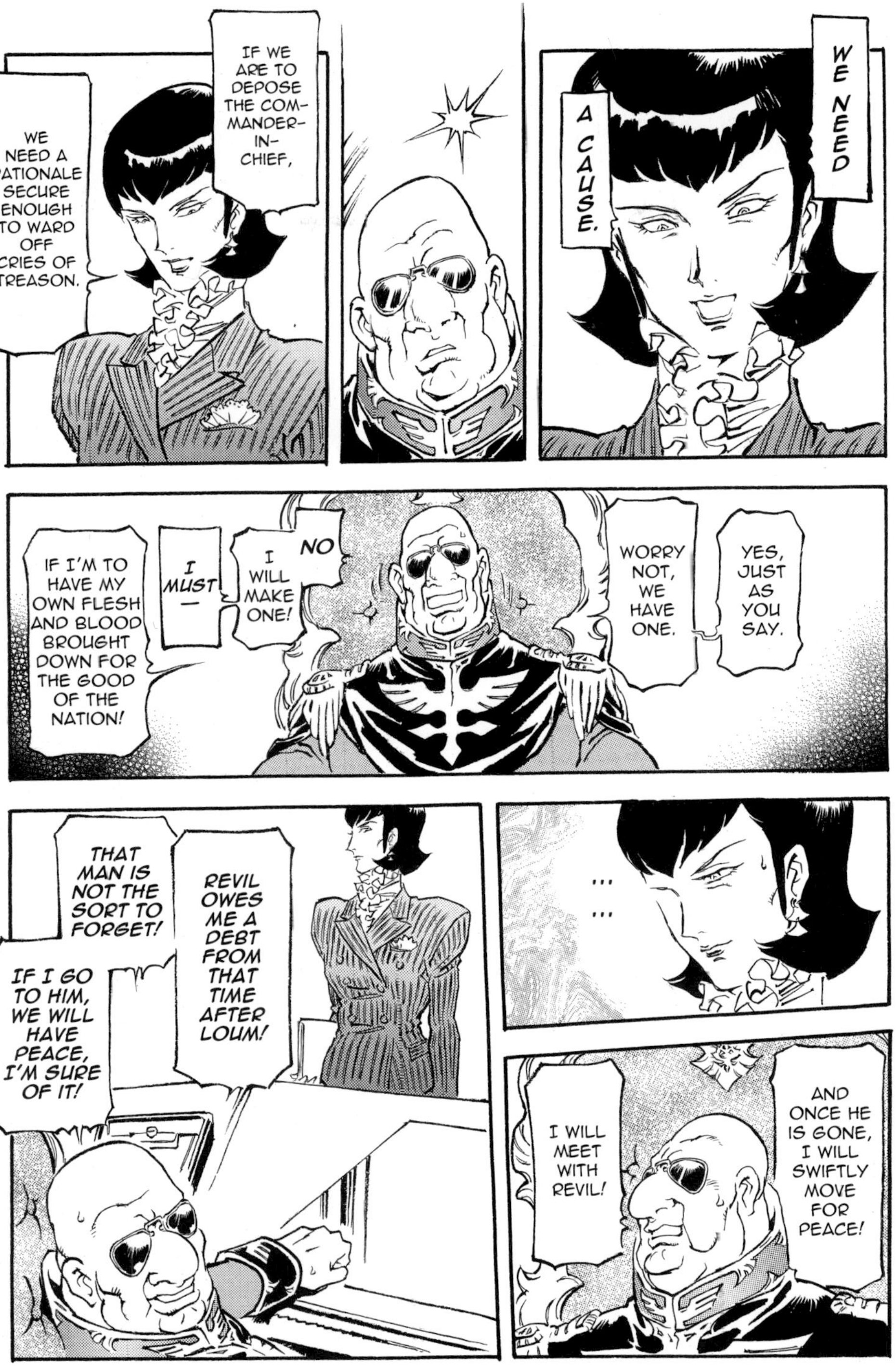
WE NEED
A CAUSE.
IF WE ARE TO DEPOSE THE COMMANDER-IN-CHIEF,
WE NEED A RATIONALE SECURE ENOUGH TO WARD OFF CRIES OF TREASON.
YES, JUST AS YOU SAY.
WORRY NOT, WE HAVE ONE.
NO
I WILL MAKE ONE!
I MUST—
IF I'M TO HAVE MY OWN FLESH AND BLOOD BROUGHT DOWN FOR THE GOOD OF THE NATION!
... ...
AND ONCE HE IS GONE, I WILL SWIFTLY MOVE FOR PEACE!
I WILL MEET WITH REVIL!
REVIL OWES ME A DEBT FROM THAT TIME AFTER LOUM!
THAT MAN IS NOT THE SORT TO FORGET!
IF I GO TO HIM, WE WILL HAVE PEACE, I'M SURE OF IT!

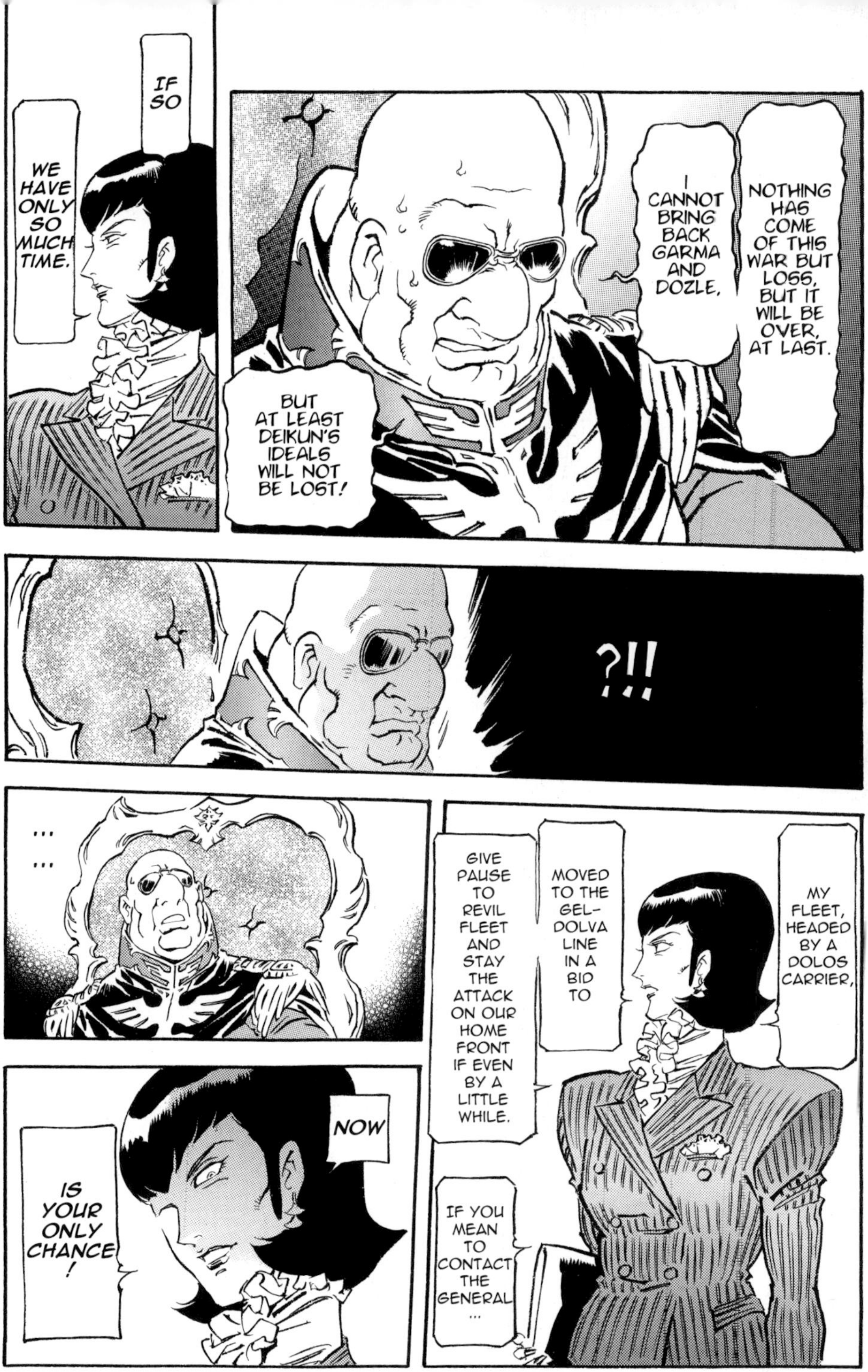
NOTHING HAS COME OF THIS WAR BUT LOSS, BUT IT WILL BE OVER, AT LAST.
I CANNOT BRING BACK GARMA AND DOZLE,
BUT AT LEAST DEIKUN'S IDEALS WILL NOT BE LOST!
IF SO
WE HAVE ONLY SO MUCH TIME.
?!!
MY FLEET, HEADED BY A DOLOS CARRIER,
MOVED TO THE GEL-DOLVA LINE IN A BID TO
GIVE PAUSE TO REVIL FLEET AND STAY THE ATTACK ON OUR HOME FRONT IF EVEN BY A LITTLE WHILE.
IF YOU MEAN TO CONTACT THE GENERAL ...
... ...
NOW
IS YOUR ONLY CHANCE!

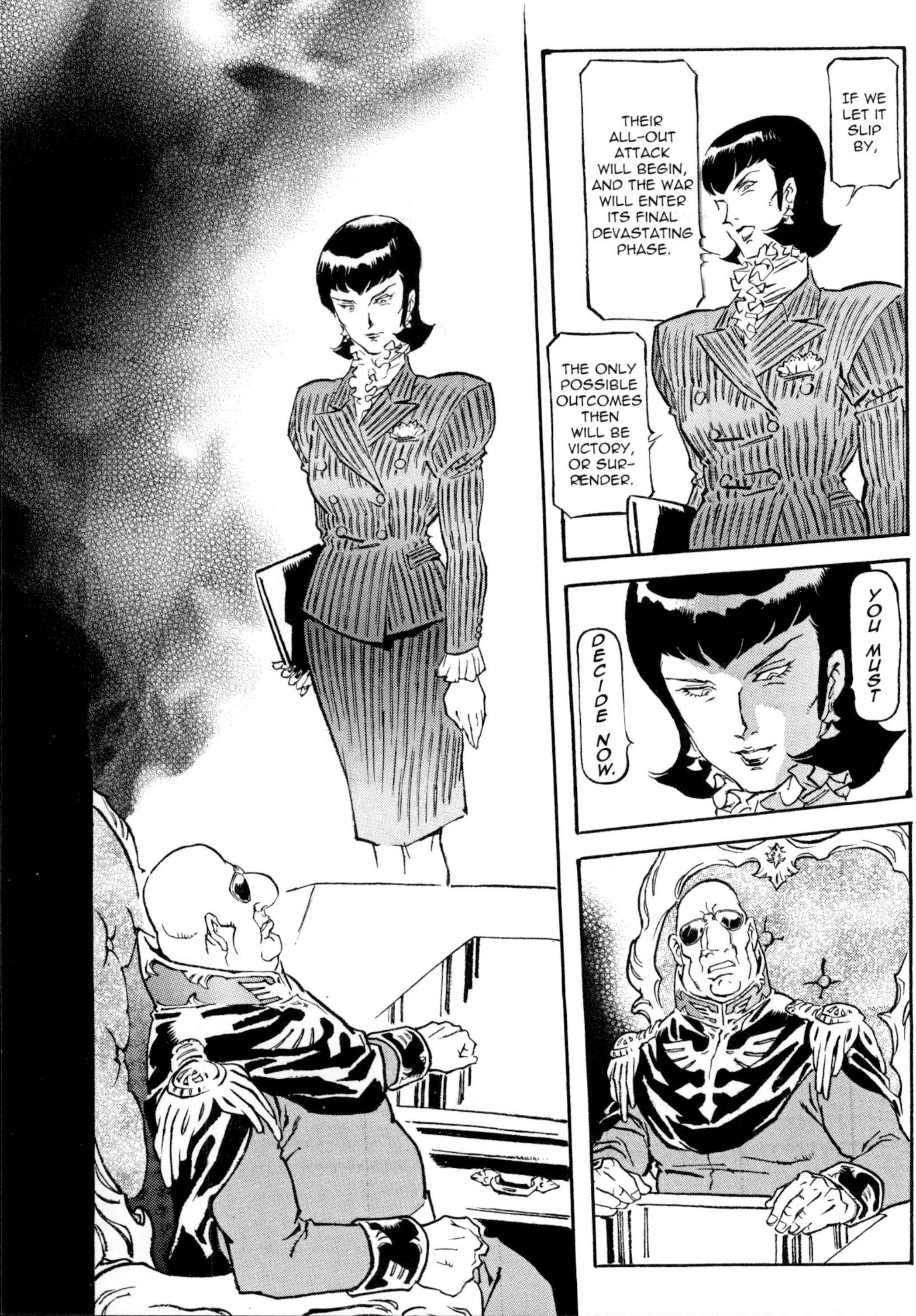
IF WE LET IT SLIP BY,
THEIR ALL-OUT ATTACK WILL BEGIN, AND THE WAR WILL ENTER ITS FINAL DEVASTATING PHASE.
THE ONLY POSSIBLE OUTCOMES THEN WILL BE VICTORY, OR SUR-RENDER.
YOU MUST
DECIDE NOW.

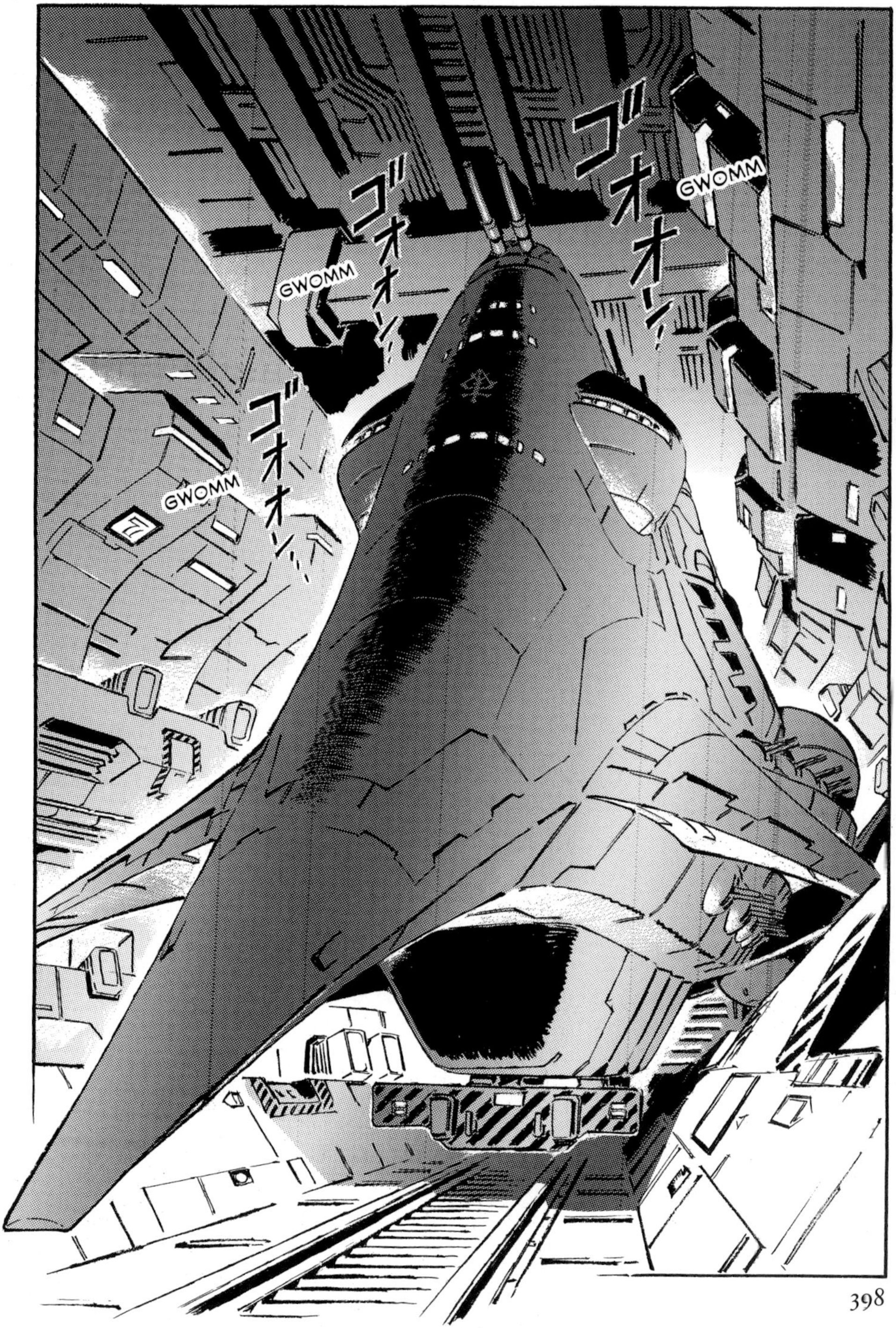
ゴオオン!!
GWOMM
ゴオオン!!
GWOMM
ゴオオン!!
GWOMM

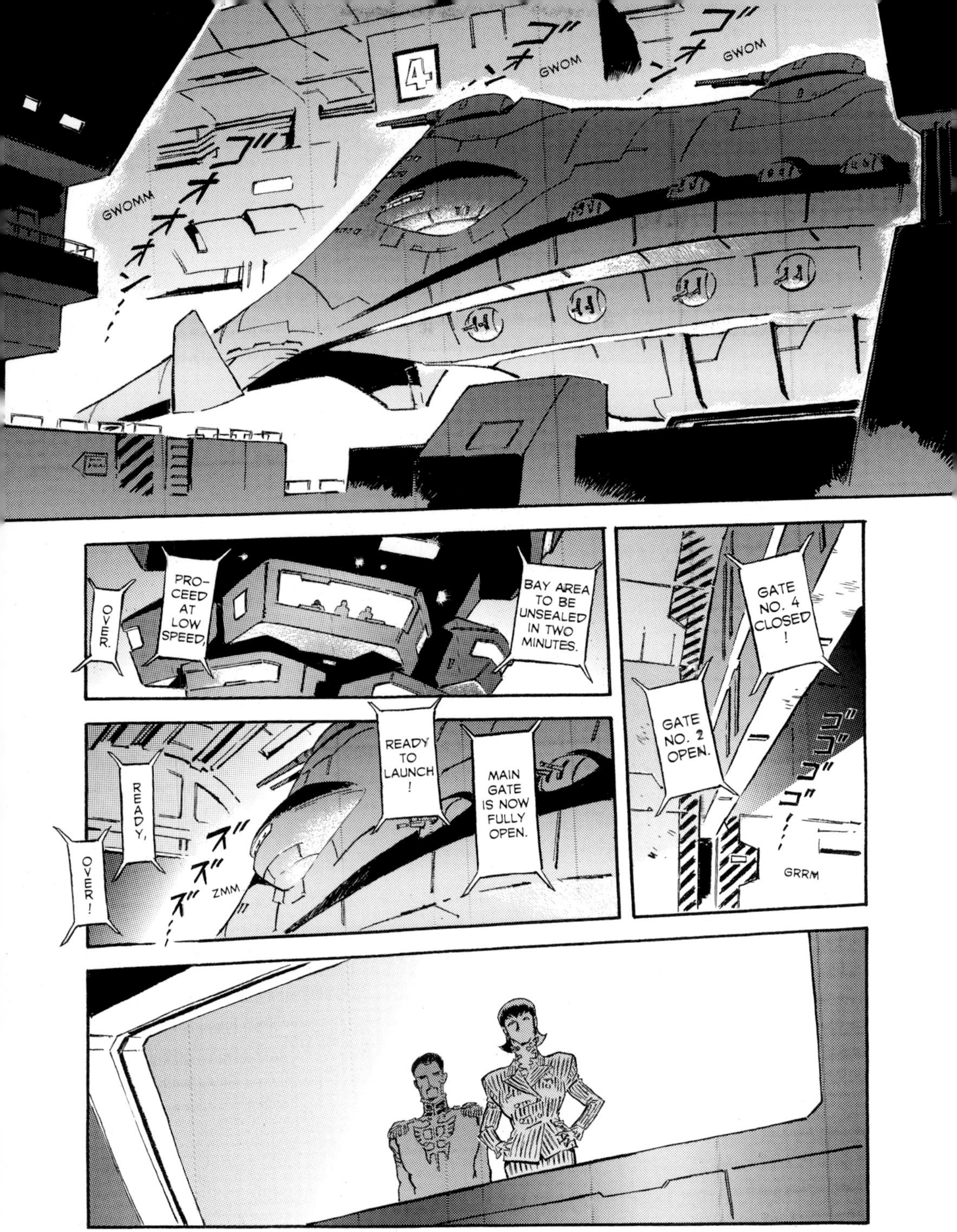
GWOM
GWOM
GWOMM
GATE NO. 4 CLOSED!
GATE NO. 2 OPEN.
GRRM
BAY AREA TO BE UNSEALED IN TWO MINUTES.
PROCEED AT LOW SPEED,
OVER.
MAIN GATE IS NOW FULLY OPEN.
READY TO LAUNCH!
READY,
OVER!
ZMM

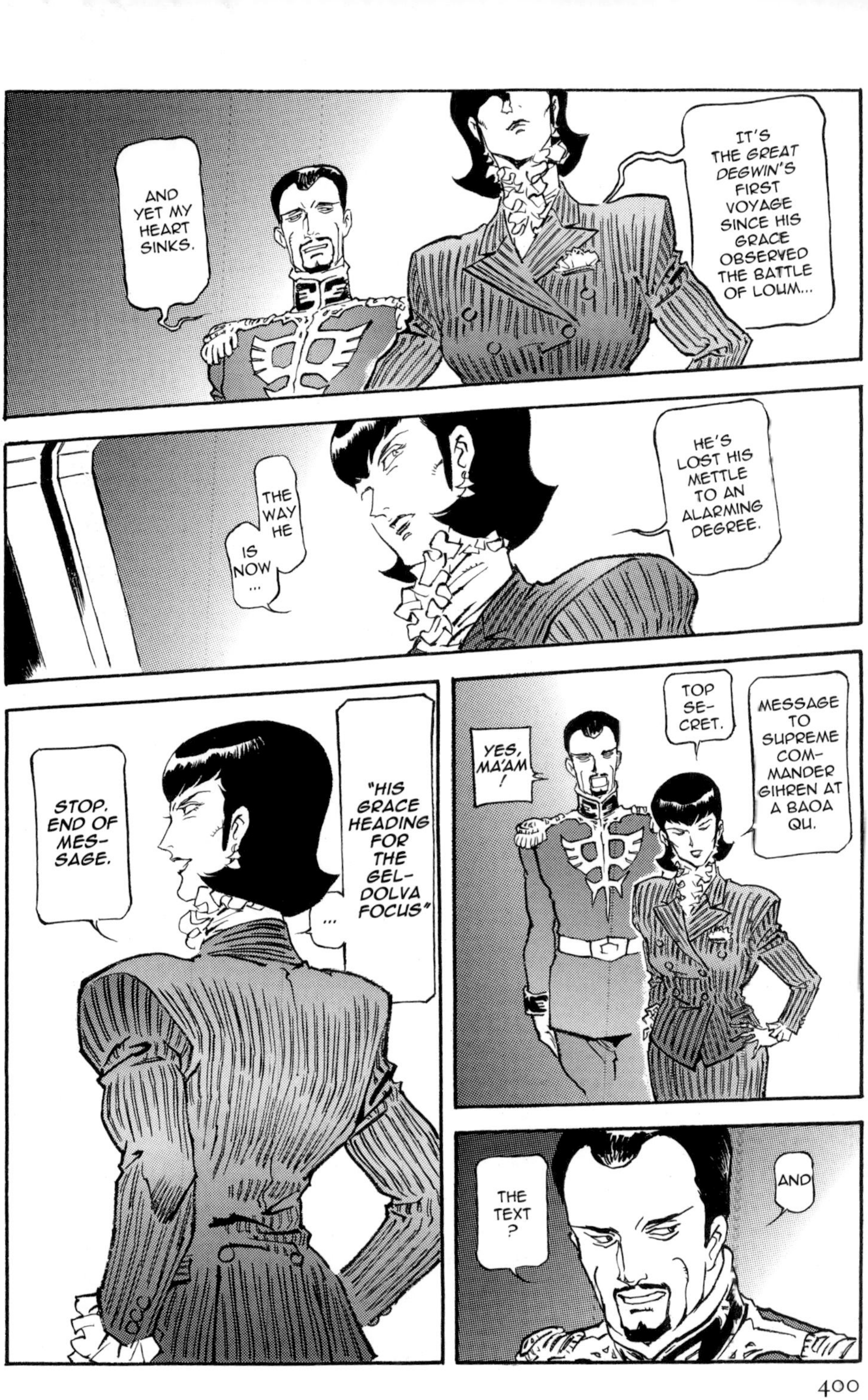
IT'S THE GREAT DEGWIN'S FIRST VOYAGE SINCE HIS GRACE OBSERVED THE BATTLE OF LOUM...
AND YET MY HEART SINKS.
HE'S LOST HIS METTLE TO AN ALARMING DEGREE.
THE WAY HE IS NOW ...
MESSAGE TO SUPREME COMMANDER GIHREN AT A BAOA QU.
TOP SECRET.
YES, MA'AM!
AND
THE TEXT?
"HIS GRACE HEADING FOR THE GELDOLVA FOCUS"
...
STOP. END OF MESSAGE.

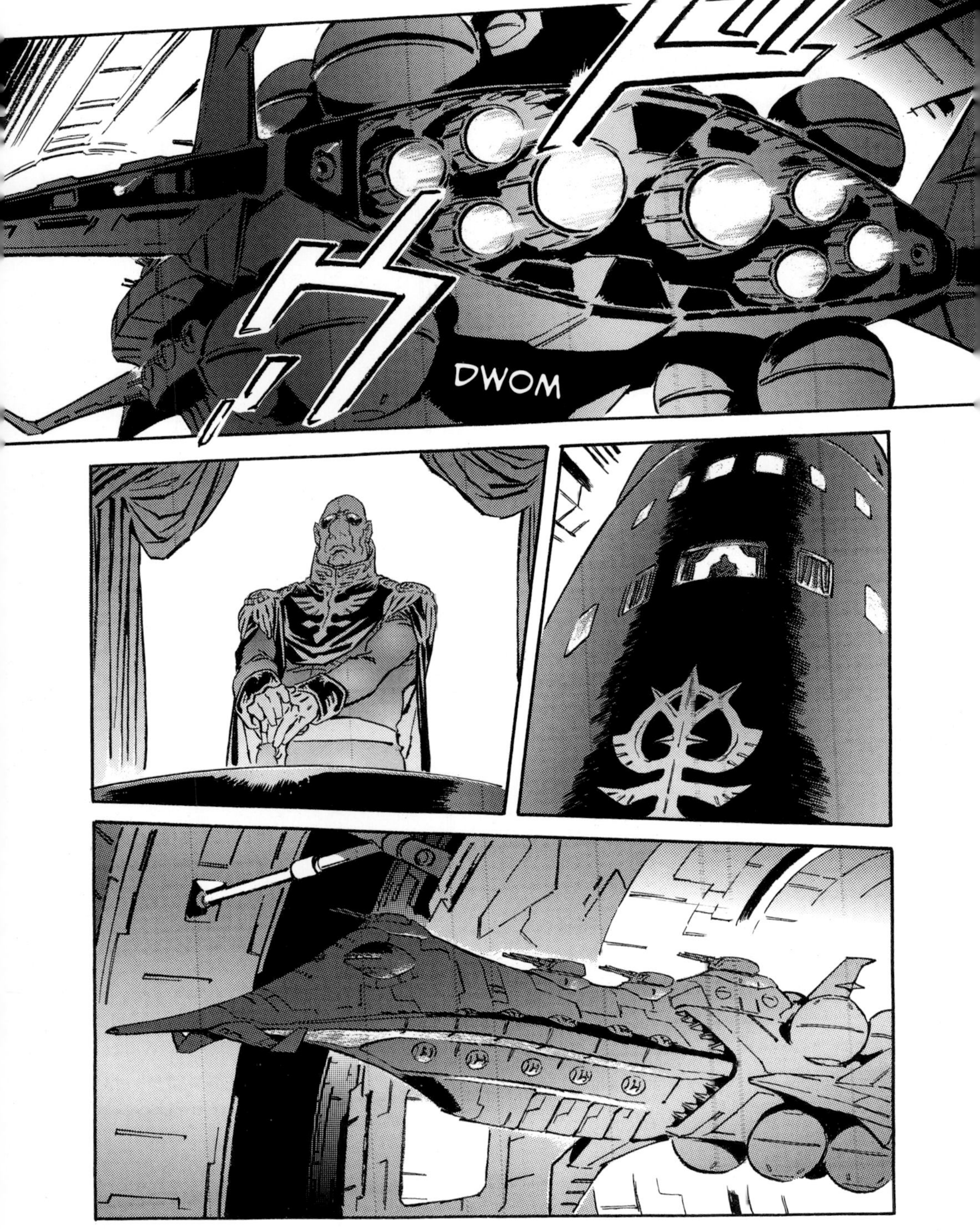
DWOM

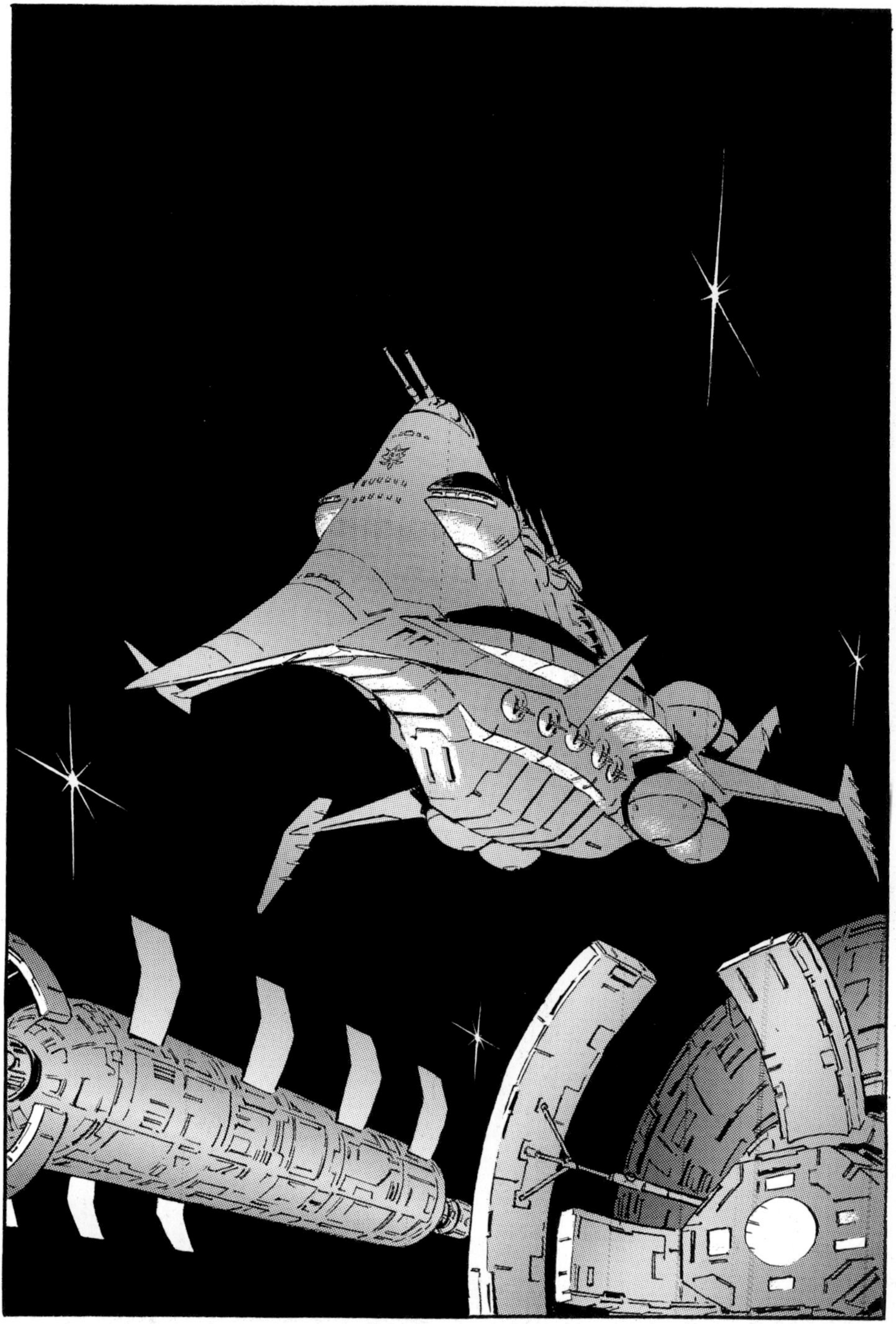

to be continued...

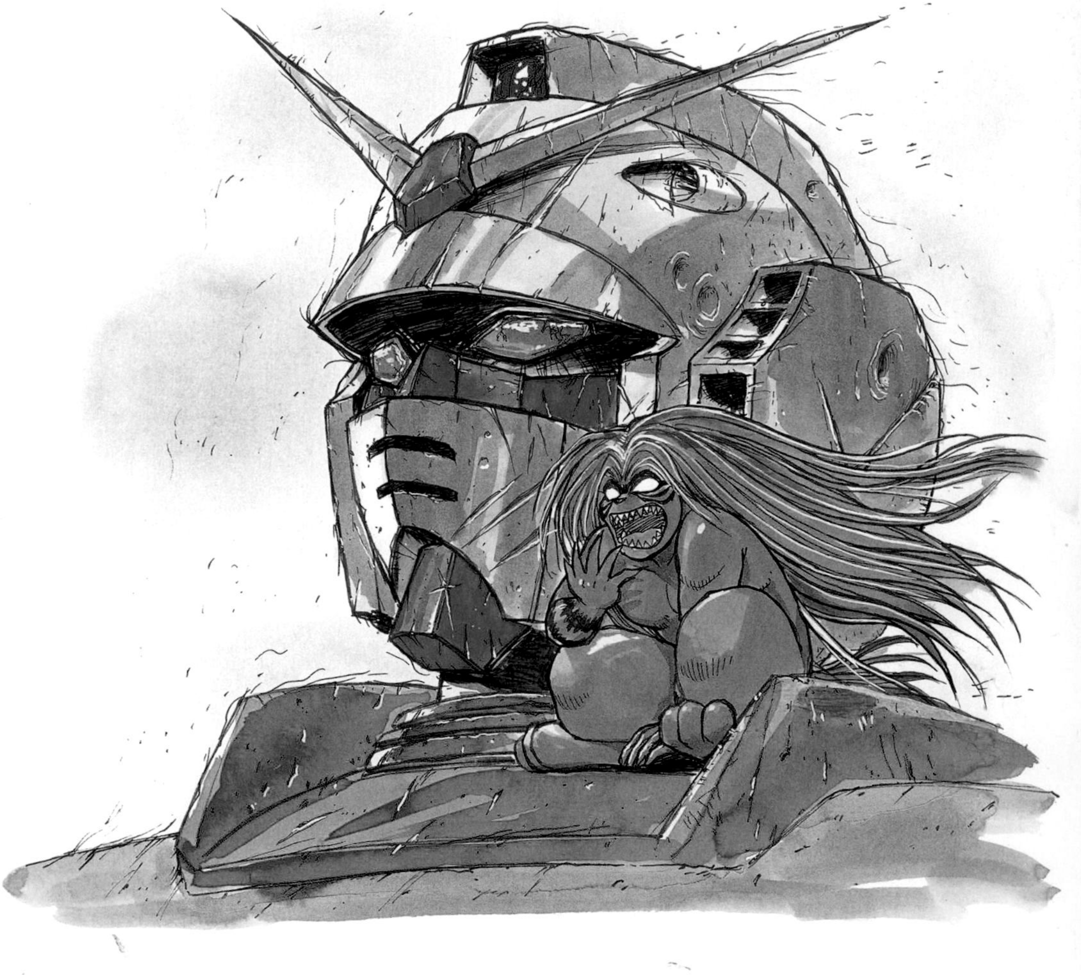

Kazuhiro Fujita

Born May 24, 1964, in Hokkaido. A manga artist, he made his debut with *Renrakusen Kitan* (Ferryboat Tales) in 1988. The next year, his work *Ushio to Tora* (Ushio and Tora) took the second Shonen Sunday Comics Grand Prix and was then serialized. In 1991 he won the 37th Shogakukan Manga Award in the boys' manga category. He is most famous for *Karakuri Circus* (Clockwork Circus). Since 2008, he has been working on *Gekko Jorei* (Moonlight Act), an ambitious manga based on fairy tales. He remains one of the foremost names in the boys' manga genre.

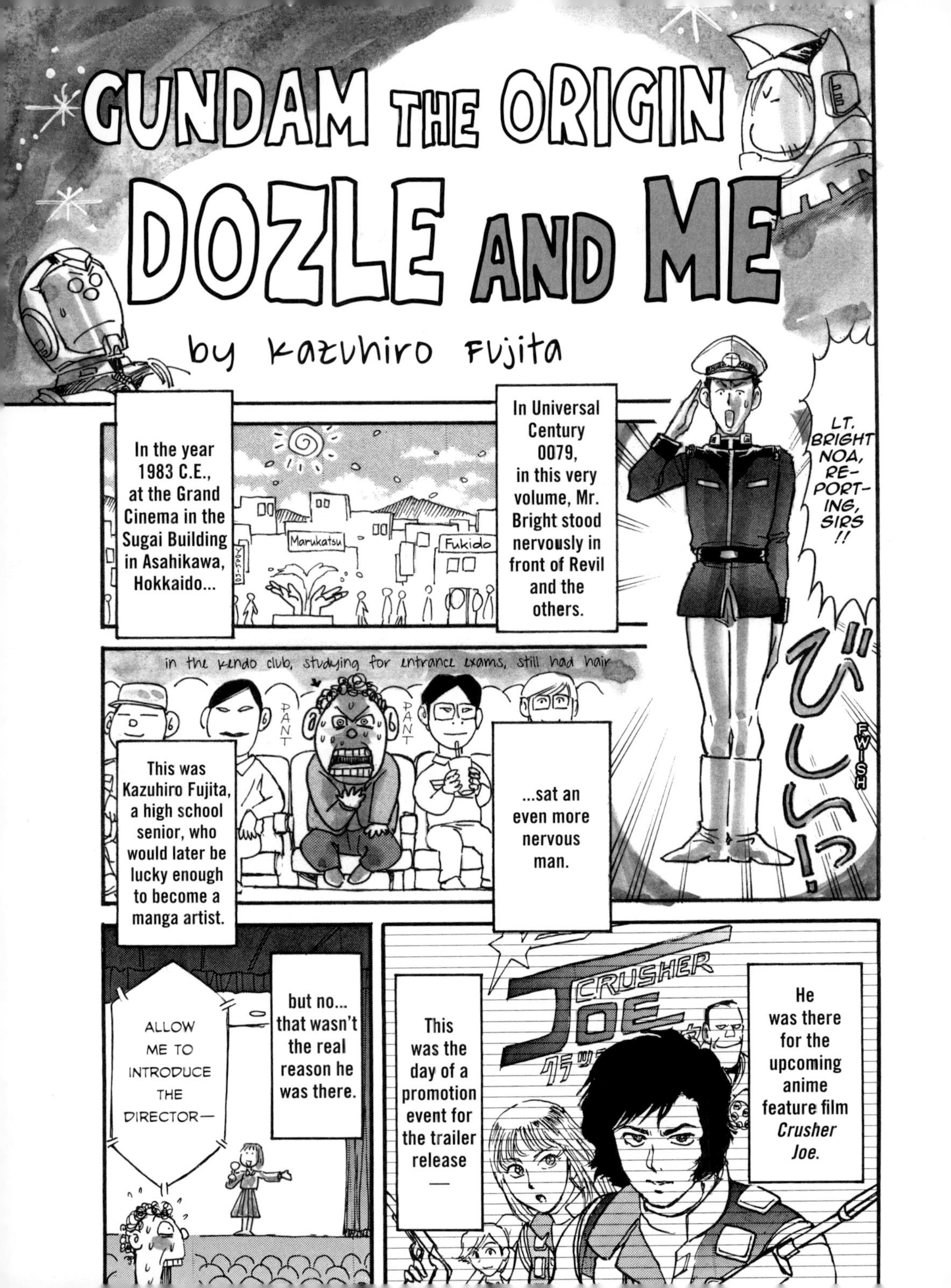
GUNDAM THE ORIGIN
DOZLE AND ME
by Kazuhiro Fujita
In Universal Century 0079, in this very volume, Mr. Bright stood nervously in front of Revil and the others.
LT. BRIGHT NOA, REPORTING, SIRS!!
びしっ!
FWISH
In the year 1983 C.E., at the Grand Cinema in the Sugai Building in Asahikawa, Hokkaido...
Fukido
Marukatsu
in the kendo club, studying for entrance exams, still had hair
...sat an even more nervous man.
PANT
PANT
This was Kazuhiro Fujita, a high school senior, who would later be lucky enough to become a manga artist.
He was there for the upcoming anime feature film *Crusher Joe*.
CRUSHER JOE
This was the day of a promotion event for the trailer release —
but no... that wasn't the real reason he was there.
ALLOW ME TO INTRODUCE THE DIRECTOR—

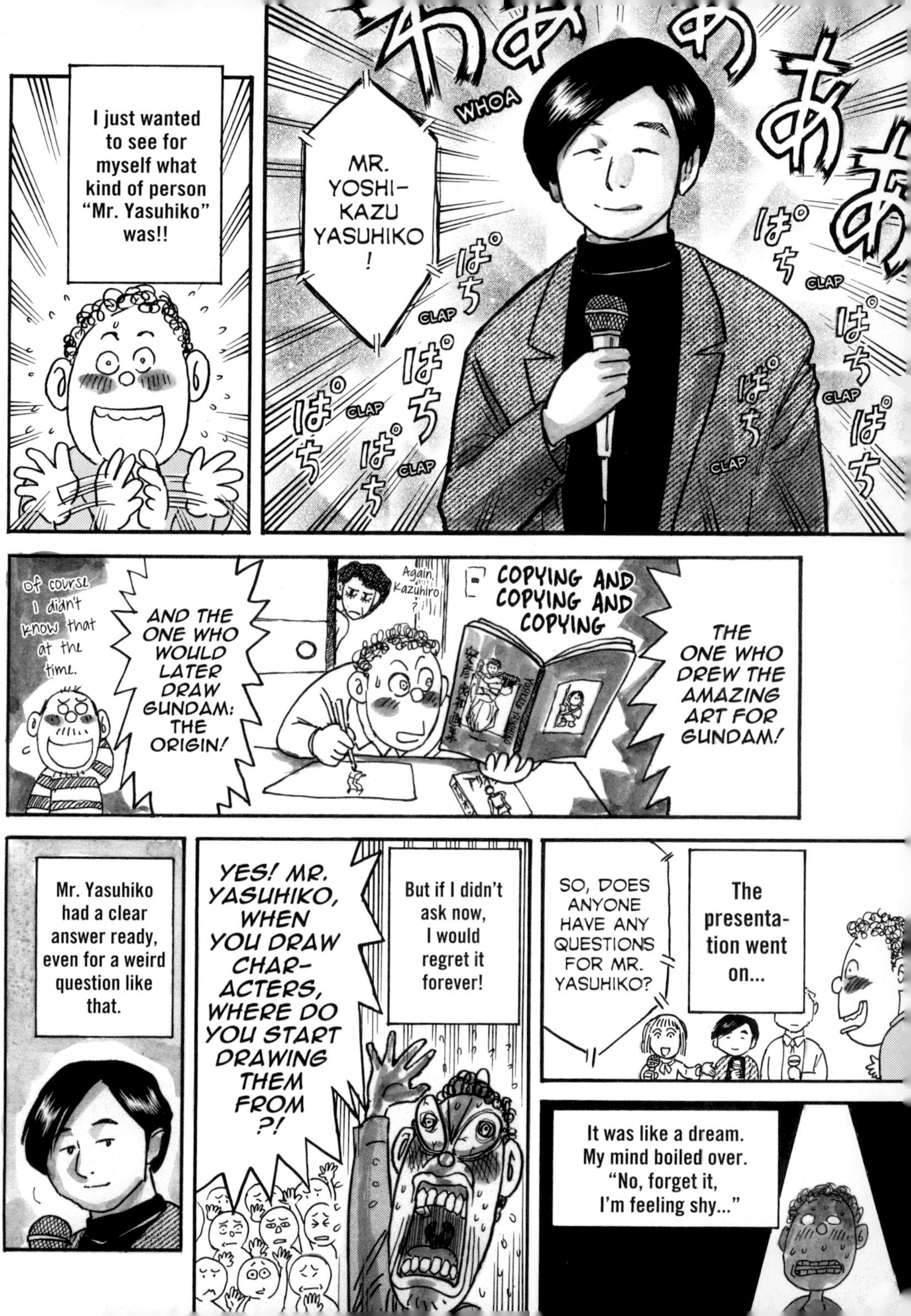

わああああ
WHOA
MR. YOSHI-KAZU YASUHIKO!
ぱち CLAP
ぱち CLAP
ぱち CLAP
ぱち CLAP
I just wanted to see for myself what kind of person "Mr. Yasuhiko" was!!
THE ONE WHO DREW THE AMAZING ART FOR GUNDAM!
COPYING AND COPYING AND COPYING
Again, Kazuhiro?
AND THE ONE WHO WOULD LATER DRAW GUNDAM: THE ORIGIN!
Of course I didn't know that at the time.
The presenta-tion went on...
SO, DOES ANYONE HAVE ANY QUESTIONS FOR MR. YASUHIKO?
It was like a dream. My mind boiled over. "No, forget it, I'm feeling shy..."
But if I didn't ask now, I would regret it forever!
YES! MR. YASUHIKO, WHEN YOU DRAW CHAR-ACTERS, WHERE DO YOU START DRAWING THEM FROM?!
Mr. Yasuhiko had a clear answer ready, even for a weird question like that.

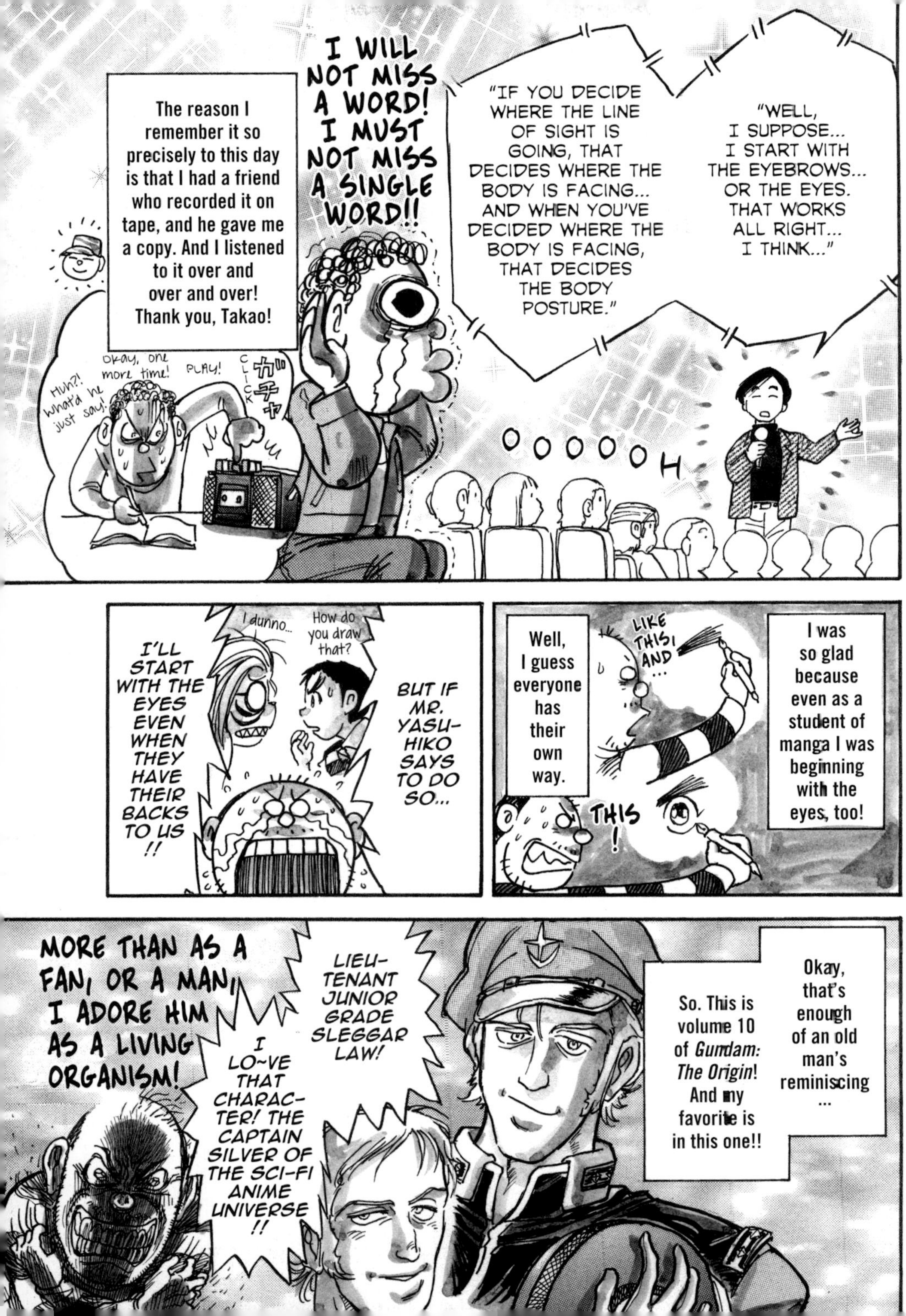
"WELL, I SUPPOSE... I START WITH THE EYEBROWS... OR THE EYES. THAT WORKS ALL RIGHT... I THINK..."
"IF YOU DECIDE WHERE THE LINE OF SIGHT IS GOING, THAT DECIDES WHERE THE BODY IS FACING... AND WHEN YOU'VE DECIDED WHERE THE BODY IS FACING, THAT DECIDES THE BODY POSTURE."
OOOOOH
I WILL NOT MISS A WORD! I MUST NOT MISS A SINGLE WORD!!
The reason I remember it so precisely to this day is that I had a friend who recorded it on tape, and he gave me a copy. And I listened to it over and over and over! Thank you, Takao!
CLICK カチャ
PLAY!
Okay, one more time!
Huh?! What'd he just say!
I was so glad because even as a student of manga I was beginning with the eyes, too!
LIKE THIS, AND...
THIS!
Well, I guess everyone has their own way.
BUT IF MR. YASUHIKO SAYS TO DO SO...
How do you draw that?
I dunno...
I'LL START WITH THE EYES EVEN WHEN THEY HAVE THEIR BACKS TO US!!
Okay, that's enough of an old man's reminiscing...
So. This is volume 10 of *Gundam: The Origin*! And my favorite is in this one!!
LIEUTENANT JUNIOR GRADE SLEGGAR LAW!
I LO~VE THAT CHARACTER! THE CAPTAIN SILVER OF THE SCI-FI ANIME UNIVERSE!!
MORE THAN AS A FAN, OR A MAN, I ADORE HIM AS A LIVING ORGANISM!

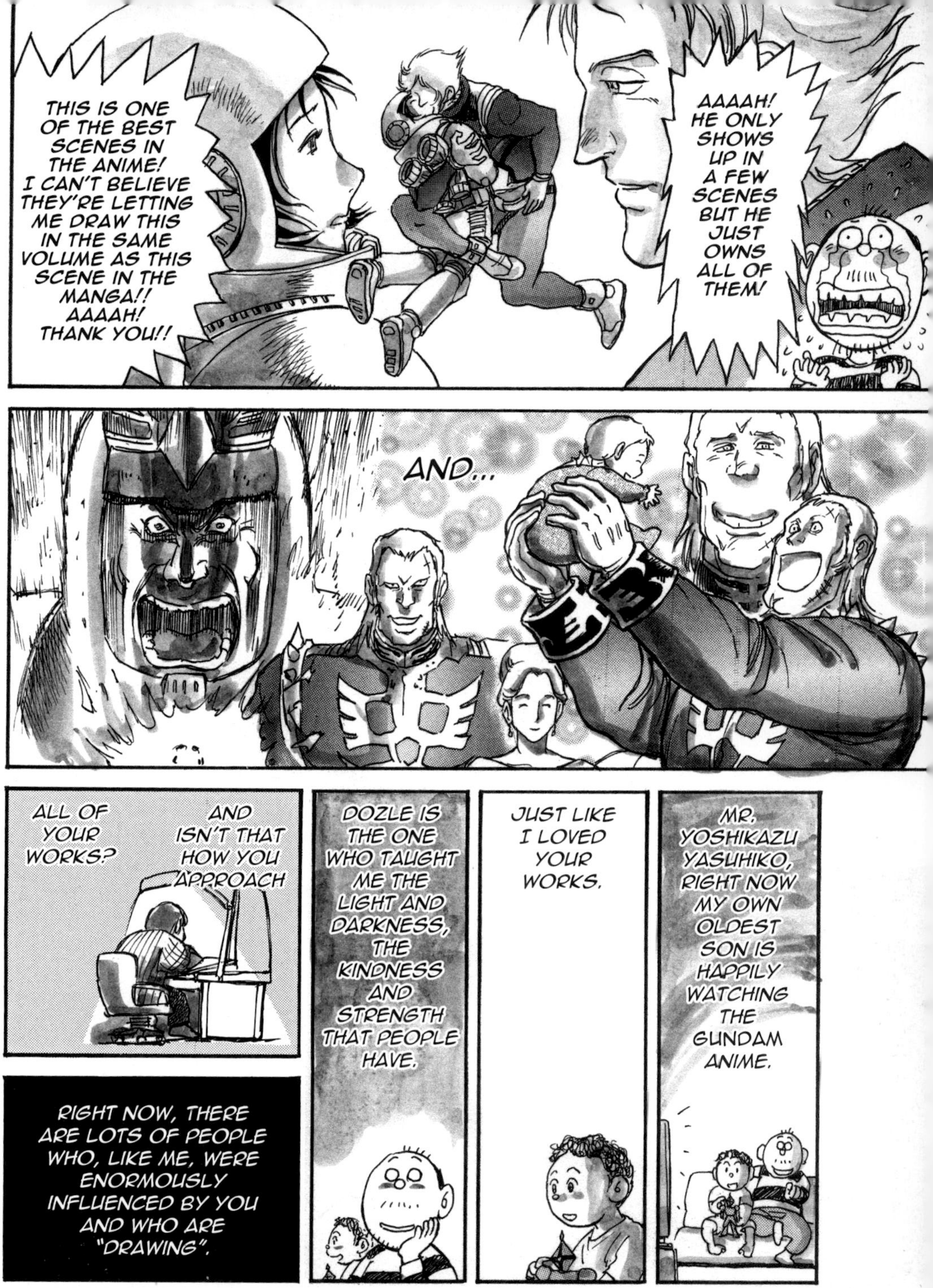
AAAAH! HE ONLY SHOWS UP IN A FEW SCENES BUT HE JUST OWNS ALL OF THEM!
THIS IS ONE OF THE BEST SCENES IN THE ANIME! I CAN'T BELIEVE THEY'RE LETTING ME DRAW THIS IN THE SAME VOLUME AS THIS SCENE IN THE MANGA!! AAAAH! THANK YOU!!
AND...
MR. YOSHIKAZU YASUHIKO, RIGHT NOW MY OWN OLDEST SON IS HAPPILY WATCHING THE GUNDAM ANIME.
JUST LIKE I LOVED YOUR WORKS.
DOZLE IS THE ONE WHO TAUGHT ME THE LIGHT AND DARKNESS, THE KINDNESS AND STRENGTH THAT PEOPLE HAVE.
AND ISN'T THAT HOW YOU APPROACH
ALL OF YOUR WORKS?
RIGHT NOW, THERE ARE LOTS OF PEOPLE WHO, LIKE ME, WERE ENORMOUSLY INFLUENCED BY YOU AND WHO ARE "DRAWING".

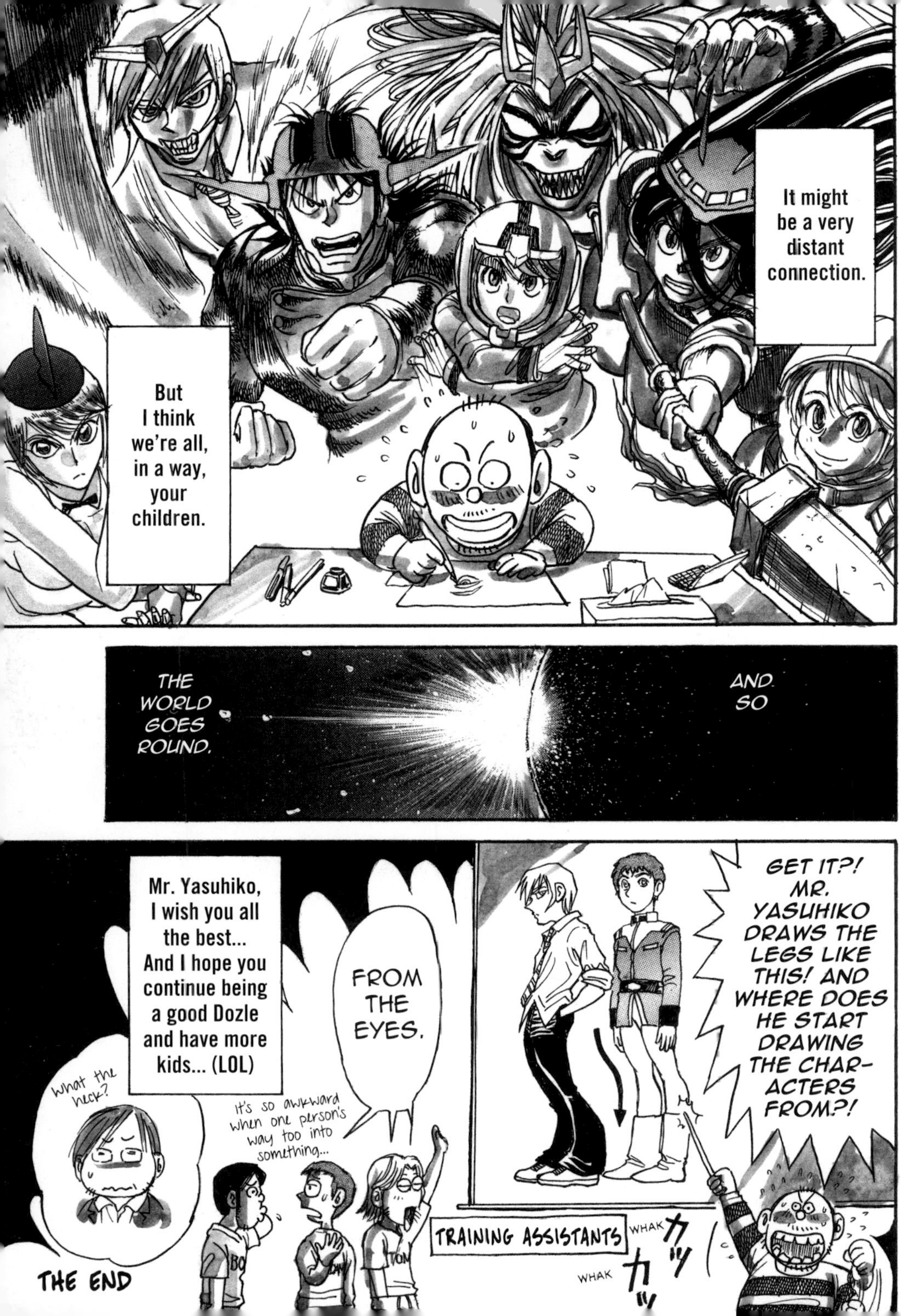
It might be a very distant connection.
But I think we're all, in a way, your children.
AND SO
THE WORLD GOES ROUND.
GET IT?! MR. YASUHIKO DRAWS THE LEGS LIKE THIS! AND WHERE DOES HE START DRAWING THE CHARACTERS FROM?!
TRAINING ASSISTANTS
WHAK
WHAK
FROM THE EYES.
Mr. Yasuhiko, I wish you all the best... And I hope you continue being a good Dozle and have more kids... (LOL)
It's so awkward when one person's way too into something...
what the heck?
THE END

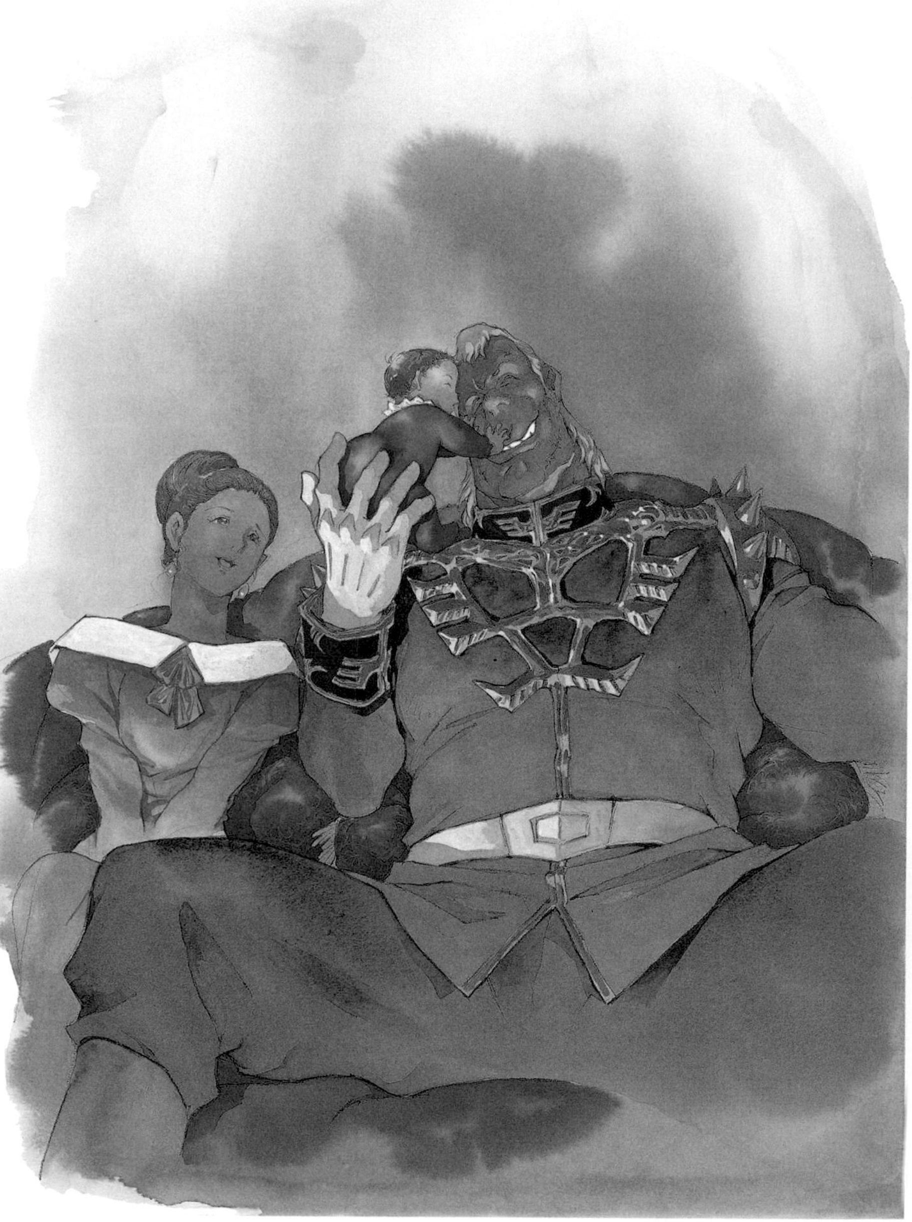

• Pencil and watercolor on B4 board / 2008

Dozle and Family

Now, now, Mineva, Daddy's face isn't a toy. But, anyway, it's a good thing you didn't inherit your father's looks...

—Yasuhiko

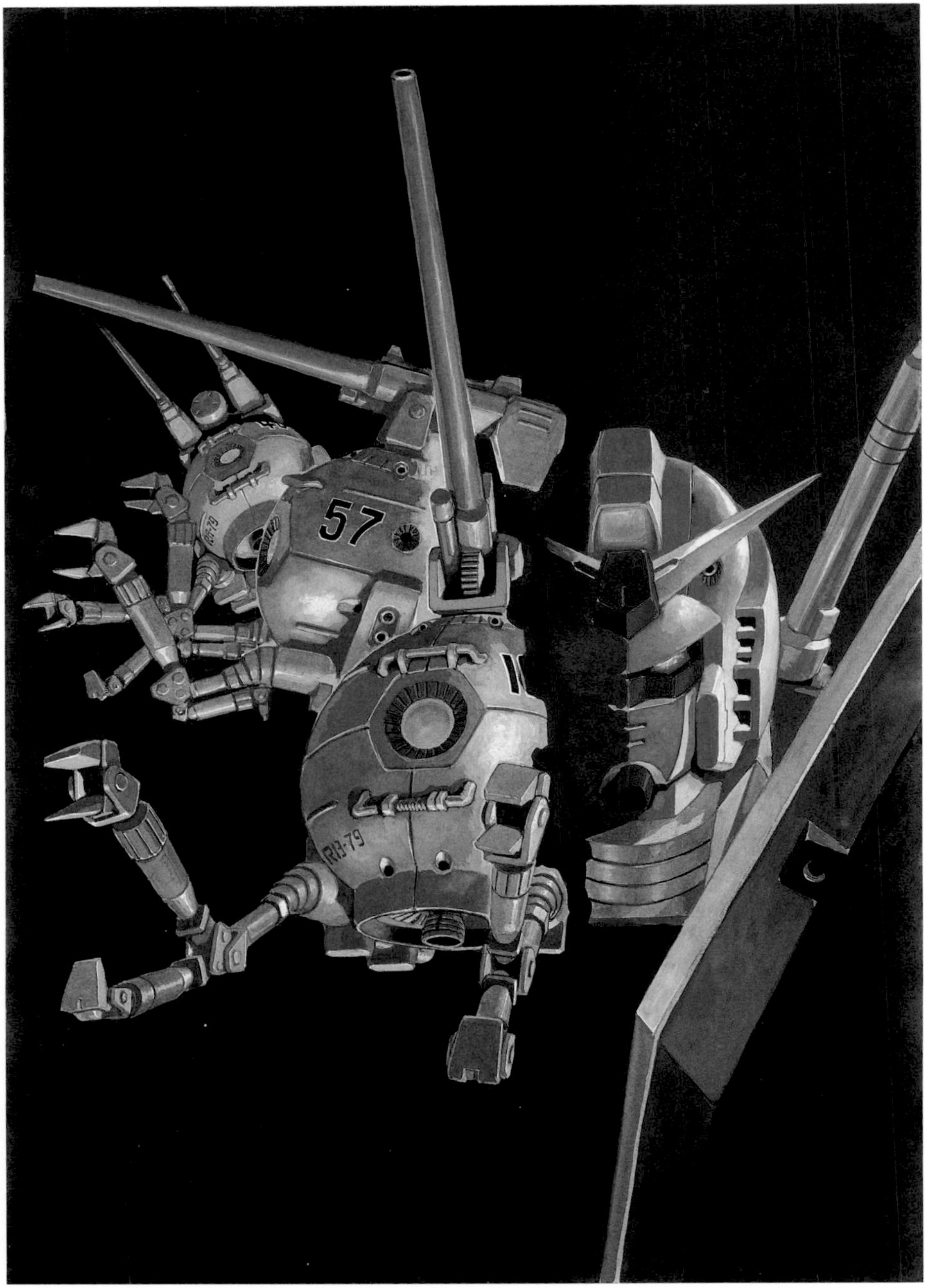
57
RB-79

The Ball • Gouache on B4 board / 2009

Lovable, pathetic Ball. What can those little hands possibly be for? It will forever remain a mystery...

—Yasuhiko

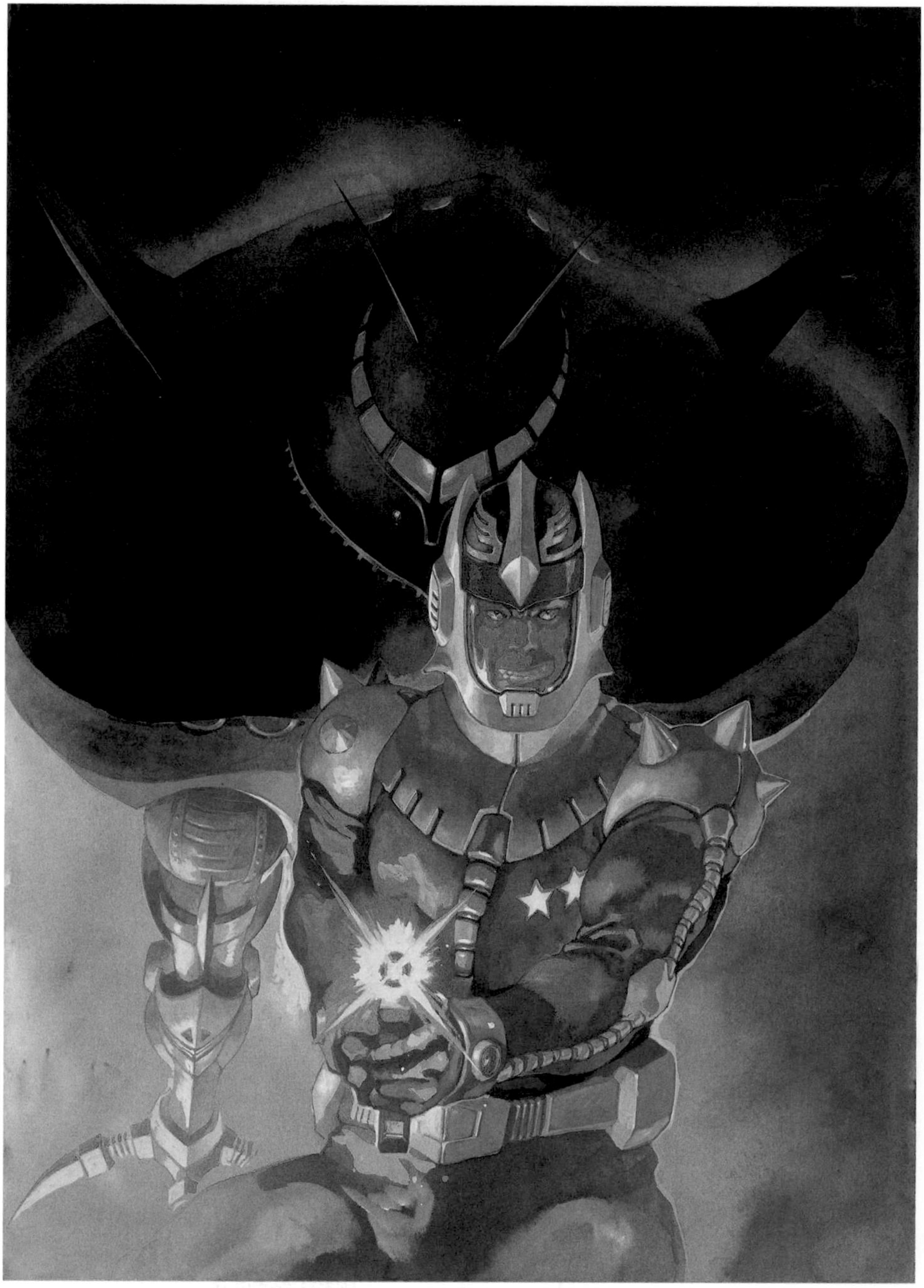

• Gouache on B4 board / 2009

Vice Admiral Dozle in Close-Range Combat

I couldn't let Dozle die wearing a standard-issue helmet. So I fussed over the design of this helmet quite a bit. Maybe I fussed too much…

—Yasuhiko

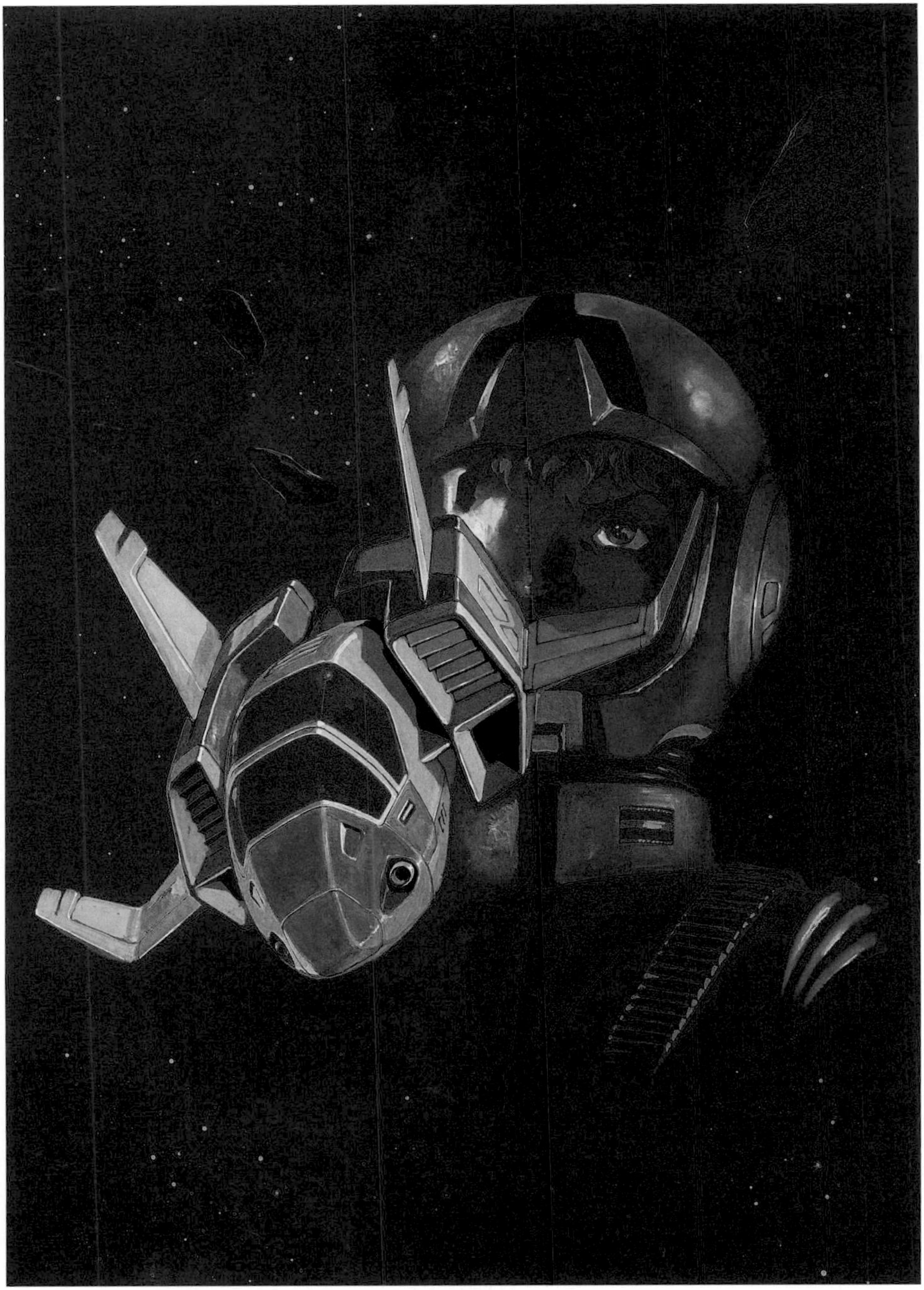

The Core Pod

• Gouache on B4 board / 2009

The Core Fighter thing had bothered me for ages, and Mr. Okawara redesigned it to our satisfaction. All you Gundam fans, I hope you can get used to seeing it this way. —Yasuhiko

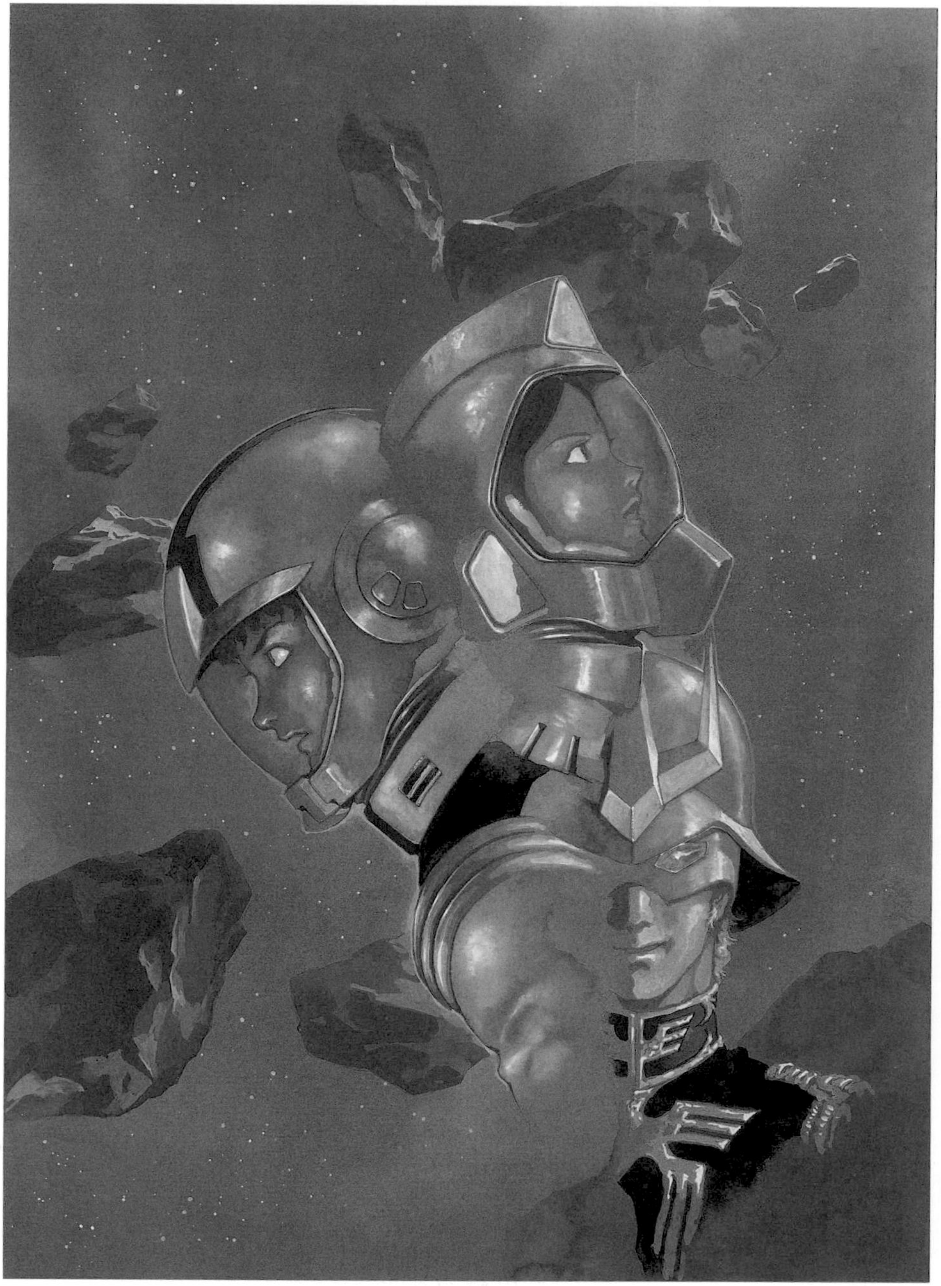

• Gouache on B4 board / 2009

Resonance

Their eyes don't meet but their thoughts are synced up... The color for this image had to be *green*. The original had Sayla, too... But no. However you look at it, we don't need her here.

—Yasuhiko

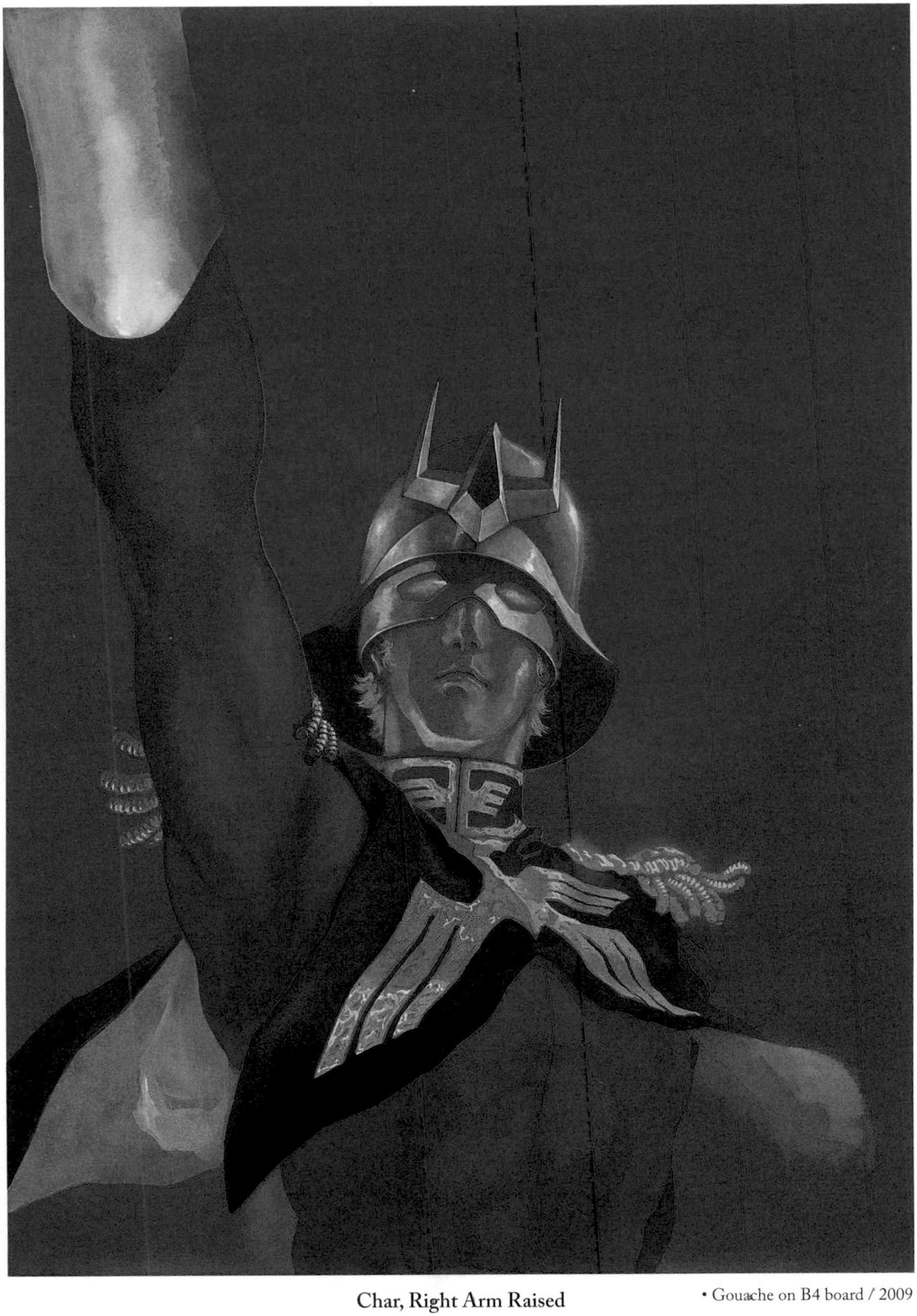

Char, Right Arm Raised

• Gouache on B4 board / 2009

Editorial told me, "This issue has a Char focus, so Char please." I've drawn him a whole lot, Char. And I bet I will from now on, too. My pleasure, Char.

—Yasuhiko

AIZOUBAN MOBILE SUIT GUNDAM THE ORIGIN vol. 10

Translation: Melissa Tanaka

Production: Grace Lu
Hiroko Mizuno
Anthony Quintessenza

© Yoshikazu YASUHIKO 2012

© SOTSU • SUNRISE

Edited by KADOKAWA SHOTEN
First published in Japan in 2012 by KADOKAWA CORPORATION, Tokyo

English translation rights arranged with KADOKAWA CORPORATION,
through Tuttle-Mori Agency, Inc., Tokyo

Translation copyright © 2015 Vertical, Inc.

Published by Vertical, Inc., New York

Originally published in Japanese as *Kidou Senshi Gundam THE ORIGIN*
volumes 19 and 20 in 2009, 2010 and re-issued in hardcover as *Aizouban Kidou Senshi Gundam
THE ORIGIN X -Soromon-* in 2012, by Kadokawa Shoten, Co., Ltd.

Kidou Senshi Gundam THE ORIGIN first serialized in *Gundam Ace,*
Kadokawa Shoten, Co., Ltd., 2001-2011

ISBN: 978-1-941220-16-0

Manufactured in the United States of America

First Edition

Vertical, Inc.
451 Park Avenue South
7th Floor
New York, NY 10016
www.vertical-inc.com